THE JAPANESE INFORMAL EMPIRE IN CHINA, 1895–1937

This book is based on a conference sponsored
by the Joint Committee on Japanese Studies and
the Joint Committee on Chinese Studies
of the American Council of Learned Societies
and the Social Science Research Council.

THE JAPANESE INFORMAL EMPIRE IN CHINA, 1895–1937

Edited by
Peter Duus, Ramon H. Myers,
and Mark R. Peattie

CONTRIBUTORS

Banno Junji
Barbara J. Brooks
Alvin D. Coox
Peter Duus
Albert Feuerwerker
Nakagane Katsuji
Kitaoka Shin'ichi

Sophia Lee
Ramon H. Myers
Mark R. Peattie
Douglas R. Reynolds
Mizoguchi Toshiyuki
William D. Wray

Princeton University Press / Princeton, New Jersey

Library of Congress Cataloging-in-Publication Data

The Japanese informal empire in China, 1895–1937 / edited by Peter Duus,
Ramon H. Myers, and Mark R. Peattie.
p.   cm.
Includes index.
ISBN 0–691–05561–0 (alk. paper)
1. Japan—Foreign relations—China—Congresses. 2. China—Foreign relations—Japan—
Congresses. 3. Japan—Foreign economic relations—China—Congresses. 4. China—
Foreign economic relations—Japan—Congresses. 5. Japan—Foreign relations—1868–
1912—Congresses. 6. Japan—Foreign relations—1912–1945—Congresses. 7. China—
Foreign relations—1912–1949—Congresses. I. Duus, Peter, 1933–   .
II. Myers, Ramon Hawley, 1929–   .   III. Peattie, Mark R., 1930–   .
DS849.C6J33 1989
327.52051—dc19   88–28311
                                                                              CIP

Publication of this volume has been assisted by a grant
from the Japan Foundation

*This volume is dedicated to Marius B. Jansen
whose distinguished and pioneering scholarship
on Sino-Japanese relations has provided departure points
for much of what has been written in these pages.*

Contents

Preface   ix

Introduction / Japan's Informal Empire in China, 1895–1937: An
Overview.   *Peter Duus*   xi

PART I: Trade and Investment   1

Chapter 1 / The Changing Pattern of Sino-Japanese Trade, 1884–
1937.   *Mizoguchi Toshiyuki*   10

Chapter 2 / Japan's Big-Three Service Enterprises in China, 1896–
1936.   *William D. Wray*   31

Chapter 3 / Zaikabō: Japanese Cotton Mills in China, 1895–
1937.   *Peter Duus*   65

Chapter 4 / Japanese Imperialism in Manchuria: The South
Manchuria Railway Company, 1906–1933.   *Ramon H. Myers*   101

Chapter 5 / Manchukuo and Economic Development.
Nakagane Katsuji   133

PART II: Culture and Community   159

Chapter 6 / Japanese Treaty Port Settlements in China, 1895–
1937.   *Mark R. Peattie*   166

Chapter 7 / Training Young China Hands: Tōa Dōbun Shoin and
Its Precursors, 1886–1945.   *Douglas R. Reynolds*   210

Chapter 8 / The Foreign Ministry's Cultural Agenda for China:
The Boxer Indemnity.   *Sophia Lee*   272

PART III: Experts and Subimperialists   307

Chapter 9 / Japanese Industrialists and Merchants and the Anti-
Japanese Boycotts in China, 1919–1928.   *Banno Junji*   314

Chapter 10 / China Experts in the Army.   *Kitaoka Shin'ichi*   330

Chapter 11 / China Experts in the Gaimushō, 1895–1937.
Barbara J. Brooks   369

Chapter 12 / The Kwantung Army Dimension.   *Alvin D. Coox*   395

PART IV: Commentary   429

Chapter 13 / Japanese Imperialism in China: A Commentary.
    Albert Feuerwerker   431

Contributors   439
Index   443

Preface

By the summer of 1937, when the Marco Polo Bridge Incident erupted into the Second Sino-Japanese War, the Japanese flag could be found flying over a vast expanse in East Asia and the western Pacific: the colonies of Taiwan, Korea, and Sakhalin; the island mandates in the Pacific; the satellite regime of Manchukuo in Northeast China; and a network of treaty port settlements in China. This mix of formal and informal empire had been created rapidly, in the space of a generation, beginning with the First Sino-Japanese War of 1894–1895.

This volume, a companion to *The Japanese Colonial Empire, 1895–1945* (published in 1984), focuses on the evolution of Japan's informal empire in China between the two Sino-Japanese wars. As editors, we have addressed several broad themes: How well did the Japanese exploit their treaty rights in China? Why were the Japanese able to overtake the other foreign powers so rapidly? What was the nature of the Japanese community in China? How did Japan's expanding informal empire in China influence decision making in business and politics and the management of affairs of state in Japan?

The contributors to this volume were asked to address these issues. The resulting studies were presented at a conference held in August 1985 at the Hoover Institution on War, Revolution and Peace, Stanford University, sponsored by the Joint Committee on Japanese Studies and the Joint Committee on Chinese Studies of the American Council of Learned Societies and the Social Science Research Council, with funds provided by the Ford Foundation, the National Endowment for the Humanities, and the Japan Society for the Promotion of Science. These institutions provided funds to help us prepare this volume for publication, and we are grateful for their generous support.

Douglas Reynolds wishes to acknowledge his great debt to Professors Etō Shinkichi, president of Asia University of Tokyo, and Hirano Ken'ichirō, University of Tokyo, for their generous guidance and assistance during his years of research and teaching in Tokyo, 1976–1980. He is also indebted to the efficient staff of Gaikō Shiryōkan in Tokyo; to the staff of Waseda University Library, which houses a rich collection of China-related published works; and to Kurai Ryōzō, president of Tōa Gakuin and senior board member of Kazankai in Tokyo, "successor" organizations to Tōa Dōbunkai. He also wishes to thank Frank Drago, cartographer of the Department of Geography, Georgia State University, for his fine maps.

Sophia Lee wishes to thank Professors Abe Hiroshi, Etō Shinkichi, and Hirano Kenichiro for their help and encouragement. In addition to participants at the conference, Professors Noriko Kamachi, Ernest P. Young, Steven Ericson, and Robert Borgen provided valuable comments on her chapter.

Ted Bestor of the Joint Committee on Japanese Studies of the Social Science Research Council was very helpful in the planning of the conference. Maxine Douglas, secretary of the East Asian Collection of the Hoover Institution, helped to plan and manage the conference, as well as to handle the voluminous correspondence between the editors, participants, and other relevant parties. Margaret Case, the East Asian editor of Princeton University Press, provided generous assistance with arranging publication. We are grateful for the assistance of all the above and particularly to Princeton University Press for publishing this volume, which we hope will stimulate more research on the complex issues raised in this study.

We gratefully acknowledge the permission by Kadokawa Shoten and Uchio Shobō to display photographs contained in their publications showing the Japanese presence in China before World War II. We also thank Cambridge University Press for its permission to use four maps from the *Cambridge History of China, Vol. 12, Part 1, Republican China 1912-1949*, edited by John K. Fairbank.

Introduction

Japan's Informal Empire in China, 1895–1937: An Overview

Peter Duus

What so often obfuscates the study of modern imperialism is the fact that not every imperialistic relationship is necessarily a colonial one. Since the onset of the industrial revolution, the ability of one country to dominate another is often a function of greater economic development rather than sheer military strength, and the boundaries of empire do not always align themselves with where the map is painted red. Imperialist expansion can, and often does, take less visible and less direct forms than territorial conquest. As Ronald Robinson and John Gallagher pointed out in a classic essay, any attempt to understand nineteenth-century British imperialism simply by looking at the "formal empire" (i.e., the colonial possessions) is "rather like judging the size and character of an iceberg solely from the parts above the waterline."[1] Empires, like icebergs, usually bulk larger below the waterline, and that is what keeps them afloat. Without looking at the submerged portions of an empire, one cannot fully grasp its extent.

Certainly this was true of Japanese imperialism in the early twentieth century. No one would deny the importance of Japan's formal colonial empire in shaping its relations with the outside world, its image of itself, and even the trajectory of its economic growth. But it is arguable that this empire had a less profound impact on the course of modern Japanese history than did the Japanese presence in China, where direct political control was limited in extent and duration. Until the Manchurian incident, Japanese imperialism in China was not "formal" so much as "informal," defined by its participation in the unequal treaty system. The Japanese had to accommodate themselves to the fact of Chinese sovereignty, however fragile or tenuous that might be, and they had to be mindful of the interests of the other treaty powers. Despite the limited run of their writ, or perhaps because of it, Japanese foreign policy was constantly hostage to

---

[1] John Gallagher and Ronald Robinson, "The Imperialism of Free Trade," *Economic History Review*, ser. 2, vol. 6 (1953), pp. 1–15.

events in China. Since their presence in China was less secure or stable than it was in the colonial empire, the Japanese came to regard China as a "problem," the resolution of which carried the temptation to further expansion.

To remove the "China problem" from the domestic political history of Japan during this period is to render it incomprehensible. Just as the debate over the "Korean problem" cast a long shadow over Japan's political development in the early Meiji period, so too the "China problem" became the catalyst of crisis and contention during the early twentieth century. Debate on what to do in China created new political coalitions and dissolved old ones; a perceived failure in China policy could bring a government down and a perceived success could shield it from attacks on other grounds; decisions on China policy could reshape national financial priorities and deflect the allocation of national resources; and above all, the outcome of decisions in the debate on the "China problem" could literally become a matter of life and death for thousands of young men called on to carry them out on the battleground. The outbreak of World War II, the most cataclysmic event in twentieth-century Japanese history, was triggered by a desperate attempt to bring about a final solution to the "China problem," not by any concern over the formal empire.

The political importance of China in domestic politics was obviously a consequence of its strategic significance to Japan. With the securing of a leasehold on the Liaotung Peninsula and the annexation of Korea after the Russo-Japanese War, the Japanese for the first time in their history shared a common border with China, and the protection of that border became an axiom of Japanese foreign policy. Political fires in China burned on a shore no longer distant, and the temptation to extinguish them was strong, particularly after the Revolution of 1911 destroyed what fragile political stability there was in China. By contrast, the formal colonies provided little cause for strategic concern once they came under Japanese control. Although anti-Japanese movements might occur in the colonies, they were easily crushed. Military buildup in the colonies in the 1910s and 1920s focused mainly on the China problem. The demand of the army to increase the Japanese garrison in Korea by two divisions in 1911–1912, for example, was less a response to concern over internal events in Korea than to the possible impact of the Chinese revolution on the peninsula.

But it should not be forgotten that the salience of China as a "problem" was a matter of economic as well as strategic concern. In fact, it was a desire for trade, not security, that initially sparked Japan's post-Restoration interest in China. Until the 1930s, the Japanese presence in China was far more important to the home country in economic terms than its control over the formal colonies. In 1910, the total volume of commodity trade with China (including the Kwantung territory) was about five times that with Korea and Taiwan combined. While that disparity declined as the Japanese pursued active programs of colonial economic development, the China market loomed an El Dorado in the eyes of Japanese trading, industrial, and shipping interests. The colonies produced important food crops for Japan, but it was China that supplied important industrial raw materials—raw cotton, iron ore, and coal—and it was China that possessed a vast population of potential consumers of Japanese manufactures. Disruptions in colonial trade were few, for the Japanese enjoyed de facto monopoly, but disruptions in the China trade were frequent and often precipitated sectoral dislocations in the domestic economy. Similarly, private investment felt a far stronger pull from China than from either of the major colonies. It was in the treaty ports and concessions in China, rather than in Taiwan and Korea, that Japan's first multinational manufacturing firms got their start.

Because of its importance to them, the Japanese created myths about China far more potent and complex than any myths they created about Taiwan or Korea. In the colonies, it was simple enough to proclaim a policy of assimilation on the ground that the local populations were eager to benefit from Japanese tutelage or that the traditional ruling classes through corruption or incompetence had forfeited any claims to an independent national existence. But China was different. Not only did it remain an independent nation, it also boasted a venerable cultural tradition, one to which the origins of Japanese civilization could be traced. The reaction of the Japanese to China, as reflected in literary, journalistic, and political comment, was multilayered and complex, mingling contempt for China's present with respect for its past. Yearnings for solidarity with China were often confounded by a sense of Japanese superiority. Many Japanese felt their country empowered, even obliged, by their successful modernization to help the Chinese climb the path to national wealth and strength. Few Chinese shared that perspective, and what the Japanese regarded as political intransigence or backwardness, the Chinese saw as patriotic resistance. Over time, this gap in perception led to mounting frustration in Japan, and a conviction that the uplift of China had to be achieved by unilateral Japanese action, rather than Sino-Japanese cooperation.

It is perhaps because of China's significance to modern Japan (and vice versa) that so much has been written by Western and Asian historians about the relationship between the two countries in the early twentieth century. Yet much of this work has focused on the intersection between the two national histories, and it has implicitly or explicitly been shaped by a search for the origins of conflict between them. Given the frequency and intensity of such conflict, to say nothing of its disastrous outcome, such an interpretative orientation is easy to understand.

But it is also possible to approach the Japanese experience in China as terrain for explorations in the comparative history of imperialism. While the Japanese imperialist presence in China was legitimized by the same kind of treaty arrangements enjoyed by the British, the French, the Americans, and other Westerners, the Japanese interaction with Chinese society, polity, and economy was often quite different. Why was the Japanese presence in China similar, yet so very different from that of the other foreigners? What was distinctive about the way the Japanese behaved and organized themselves in China? How did the impact of Japan on the Chinese economy and society differ from that of the other foreigners? What was the impact of the Japanese presence in China on the Japanese metropolis? And why was it that in the end the Japanese attempted to expand their sphere of power in China, just as other foreign powers began to retreat from theirs? The essays in this volume cannot provide the answers to all these questions, but they attempt to answer some and perhaps suggest lines of future historical exploration as well.

THE UNEQUAL TREATY SYSTEM AS INFORMAL IMPERIALISM

Modern Sino-Japanese relations developed within the context of the "unequal treaty system," an institutional structure established by the British, the inventors of "informal imperialism." During the mid-nineteenth century, Great Britain not only expanded its formal colonial holdings, but also built a formidable "empire without colonies." In many parts of the world, the British eschewed territorial acquisition for practical reasons. Crumbling, older empires like Ottoman Turkey and Ch'ing China were too weak to resist British demands for trade, but strong enough or large enough to make conquest unthinkable. More important, territorial acquisition was not necessarily the object of British policy. Rather, the British sought privileged access to overseas markets that could be integrated with their own expanding metropolitan economy through the export of British goods and capital and the import of raw materials and agricultural goods. As Gallagher and Robinson observed, "Perhaps the most common political technique of British expansion was the treaty of free trade and friendship made with or imposed on a weaker state. . . . The treaties with Persia in 1836 and 1837, the Turkish treaties of 1838 and 1861, the Japanese treaty of 1858, the favours extracted from Zanzibar, Siam and Morocco, the hundreds of anti-slavery treaties signed with crosses by African chiefs—all these treaties enabled the British government to carry forward trade with these regions."[2] Such, too, was the goal of the mid-century treaties with China—the Treaty of Nanking (1842), the Treaty of Tientsin (1858), the Peking Convention (1860), and the Chefoo Convention (1876)—all of which pried its market open ever wider. Under the cloak of free-trade ideology, the British attempted to advance their economic advantage over poorer and weaker peoples without incurring the costs of governing them. The essence of British policy, as Gallagher and Robinson observed, was "trade with informal control if possible; trade with rule when necessary."

The concept of informal imperialism has frequently been called into question on both empirical and theoretical grounds. It has been argued, for example, that in a region like South America, where the British were alleged to have established an informal empire, the British government was never prepared to exercise informal control, and in any case, never as much as British businessmen, merchants, and financiers demanded. The "dominant characteristics of British commercial and financial diplomacy," D.C.M. Platt has written, "were non-intervention and *laissez-faire*, and imperialism, informal or formal, was the last thing to be expected from *laissez-faire*."[3]

More important, the concept of "informal imperialism" has been criticized for inflating the definition of imperialism out of shape. What was "informal control," after all, and where did informal empire end and non-imperialistic trading relationships begin? Why were British trade and investment in China or Latin America to be regarded as "informal imperialism," whereas British trade and investment in Belgium or the United States were not? The concept of "informal empire" seemed to provide no clear theoretical boundaries and merely substituted one set of conceptual difficulties for the old ones. Only recently has there been an attempt to formulate a formal model in a systematic way, although that model, which is based largely on the case of China, may be excessively precise for historians.[4]

---

[2] Ibid.

[3] D. C. M. Platt, *Trade and Politics in British Foreign Policy* (London: Oxford University Press, 1968), p. 397.

[4] The model is to be found in Jurgen Osterhammel, "Semi-Colonialism and Informal Empire in Twentieth Century China: Toward a Framework of Analysis," in Wolfgange J. Mommsen and Jurgen Osterhammel, eds., *Imperialism and After: Continuities and Discontinuities* (London: Allen and Unwin, 1986), pp. 290–314. Osterhammel suggests that the features of an "ideal type" of informal empire are the following: "(1) A power differential exists between two countries and is exploited by the stronger country (henceforth S) in pursuit of its own real or perceived interests in the weaker country (henceforth W). (2) S avoids direct rule over W, but possesses effective veto power over its domestic policy-making, intervening against any attempt to infringe upon its real or perceived interests in that particular country. (3) S has the capability to impose basic guidelines for foreign-policy orientation on

In customary parlance, imperialism implies an asymmetrical power relationship between two societies, the metropolitan society exercising some degree of political dominance over the peripheral one. What distinguishes informal imperialism from nonimperialistic trading relationships, therefore, is the use of coercive methods. Normal trading relationships between modern societies presumably rest on mutual consent and a shared sense of advantage. The will of one party is bent to the other not by force or threat of force but by persuasion. The Belgians welcomed British trade in the nineteenth century, but the Ch'ing government did not. Hence, although it would be difficult to call British trade with a poorer and weaker Belgium imperialistic, it seems entirely appropriate to apply that term to the trading relationship established under the Treaty of Nanking or any of the other "unequal treaties." This was a trading relationship forced on the Chinese as a result of British naval and military power, and it was maintained by the implicit or explicit presence of British gunboats on the Chinese coast and in the treaty ports. As Rutherford Alcock observed, "all diplomacy in these regions which does not rest on a solid substratum of force, or an element of strength, to be laid bare when gentler processes fail, rests on false premises, and must of necessity fail in its object."[5] It was quite clear to all at the time that China's post-Opium War trading relationship would not have come into being except for the willingness of the British to use coercion and the inability of the Chinese to resist effectively. What was involved was not dependency or hegemony but what Robinson in a recent essay has called an "unequal contract" signed under duress.[6]

W, ideally including it in assymetrical alliances which are controlled by the hegemonial state. (4) S maintains some sort of military establishment in W and/or is in a position to bring influence to bear on W's armed forces (through military aid, advisers, and so on). (5) Nationals of S maintain a substantial economic establishment in W, consisting of various types of businesses ranging from agency houses to subsidiaries of multinational corporations. (6) Foreign actors are monopolistically or quasi-monopolistically entrenched in those sectors of W's economy that show above average rates of growth; the basic economic decisions concerning the allocation of resources in these sectors are taken by foreigners. (7) Public finance in W is, to a significant extent, controlled by foreign private and/or government banks; this control may be used to enforce political compliance. (8) W is a net recipient of capital (business and portfolio investment). (9) S's hold over the inferior nation is supported by the collaboration of indigenous rulers and comprador groups; 'big brother' reserves the right to intervene in struggles for power, supporting contenders of his choice. (10) Indigenous collaborators partly or completely share a common 'cosmology' with the political and economic elites of the superior nation." As Osterhammel himself admits, this is a "fairly restrictive" definition of informal empire, and certainly one that requires a bit of stretching to fit the Chinese case, but it is nonetheless a suggestive working definition.

[5] Quoted in W. G. Beasley, *Japanese Imperialism 1894–1945* (Oxford: Clarendon Press, 1987), p. 20. This useful survey of Japanese imperialism is perhaps the first published work to apply the term "informal empire" to Japanese activities in China in a sustained way.

[6] Ronald Robinson, "The Eccentric Idea of Imperialism, With or Without Empire," in Mommsen and Osterhammel, eds., *Imperialism and After*, pp. 267–289. This article repre-

The imperialist techniques that the British invented spread to other industrially developing societies in much the same way, though not necessarily to the same extent that the steam locomotive and the power loom did. While the dramatic territorial and colonial expansion of the late nineteenth century, particularly the partition of Africa, has attracted the attention of students of imperialism, equally striking was the widespread application of the techniques of "informal imperialism." Throughout the globe, the industrially advanced European nations extended their control over poorer and weaker agricultural societies by the establishment of protectorates, the creation of spheres of influence, the acquisition of privileged trade enclaves, or the signing of unequal treaties. The vast and largely uninhabited expanses of sub-Saharan Africa could be subdivided and annexed at relatively low cost, but such was not the case with more densely populated and complexly organized societies in other parts of the world, particularly in East Asia.

The techniques of "informal empire" were most appropriate where the paramount motive behind European (and later Japanese) expansion was economic penetration rather than strategic concern. As Grover Clark has observed, "Where economic advantage could be secured without actual annexation of territory, it was felt perhaps as well to avoid the complications and responsibilities which went with political control."[7] If an expanding metropolitan power could secure privileged access to a peripheral economy without having to bear the costs of administering the local state or controlling the local population, so much the better. If the Chinese markets could be made safe for British calicoes by unequal treaties, then there was no need to displace the Ch'ing government or to detach more than a small piece of territory like Hong Kong as a base for British trade. Throughout the nineteenth century, the British and other treaty powers eschewed the temptation to assume any form of political control outside Hong Kong and the treaty ports, and they continued to let the Chinese handle their own political and administrative affairs.

On the other hand, as Ronald Robinson has pointed out, the techniques of "informal empire require the presence of a collaborative structure in the peripheral societies." Even in the formal colonial empires, an imperialist metropole rarely relied on main force alone to achieve its goals; it also had to find allies in the society it sought to control. "Collaboration" is an ambiguous term, of course. It can imply either enthusiastic cooperation or grudging acquiescence to a superior force. Robinson has used the term broadly to include not only indigenous collaborators such as ruling elites, merchants, and landlords, but also "subimperialists," settlers or

sents Robinson's latest formulation. It argues more strongly than his previous work for the necessity of looking at conditions on the periphery that facilitated the expansion of the metropolitan core.

[7] Grover Clark, *A Place in the Sun* (New York: Macmillan, 1936), p. 28.

traders from the metropole who paved the way for economic and political penetration. However the term might be parsed or construed, the main point is that imperialism, and especially informal imperialism, requires the willingness of indigenous collaborators, for reasons of interest, advantage, fear, or vulnerability, to accept a degree of subordination to the metropolitan power. "Without the voluntary or enforced cooperation of their ruling elites," observes Robinson, "economic resources could not be transferred, strategic interests protected or xenophobic reaction and traditional resistance to change contained."[8]

In the case of Ch'ing China, collaboration was visible at many levels. In the treaty ports, it was most visible in the emergence of the compradors, shroffs, and other middlemen involved in the foreign trade; it was visible as well in the willingness of the Chinese to rely on foreign mercenaries like Frederick Townshend Ward to help suppress the T'ai-ping rebels; and it was visible in the emergence of a Chinese Imperial Customs Service manned by both foreigners and Chinese. All these collaborative arrangements, as John Fairbank has pointed out, were made possible by a Chinese tradition of attempting to subdue "barbarians" by co-opting them. The grudging concession of treaty rights by the Ch'ing government was a means of "barbarian management," converting the seaborne Westerners from "outside barbarians" into "inside barbarians," at least pacifying them, if not turning them into vassals. From the Ch'ing government's point of view, collaboration with the foreigners was a means of resisting or averting deeper foreign political penetration. Only in the 1890s did a younger generation of Chinese elite begin to see collaboration as a form of national betrayal.

The development of "informal imperialism" in China took a rather different form from informal empire elsewhere. It was a collective or cooperative enterprise.[9] From the outset, China was never an exclusive preserve for British trade. The inclusion of the most favored nation clause in the Treaty of Nanking by the Chinese, who probably saw it as a way of playing the barbarians off against one another, and the subsequent willingness of the Ch'ing to sign unequal treaties with other powers, did much to prevent China from becoming the object of inter-European competition, as the Ottoman Empire was at the time, and sub-Saharan Africa was to become. All the major powers had a stake in maintaining the treaty structure, and the gains by any one were automatically shared by all. In this sense, none of the foreign powers enjoyed strictly bilateral relations with China; such relations were always embedded in the multi-

[8] Edward Roger John Owen, *Studies in the Theory of Imperialism* (London: Longmans, 1973), p. 121.

[9] For a more extended discussion of the "cooperative" character of the Western penetration of China, see Osterhammel, "Semi-Colonialism."

lateral treaty structure. With the possible exception of the British, it was difficult for any power to act as an autonomous free agent in dealing with the Chinese government, at least with respect to treaty rights, since such dealings invariably had implications for other treaty powers as well. In contrast to Britain's informal empire in other parts of the world, informal empire in China rested on a balance-of-power base.

To be sure, European competition for territory in Asia did become intense in the late nineteenth century—in Central Asia, Tibet, Indochina, and Korea. In these areas, strategic advantage was at stake, not economic advantage. This competition was prompted in part by the emergence of Russia and Japan as regional powers, but its impact on China proper was limited. While the "partition of China" seemed imminent to some during the "race for concessions" in the late 1890s, it was quickly halted by the reluctance of the treaty powers to upset the advantages of shared or collective imperialism. The rules of collective informal empire were reformulated in the doctrine of the Open Door. The treaty powers realized that maintaining a balance-of-power equilibrium in China was less costly than risking conflict through competition, and they reaffirmed the basic rules of the game under the same free-trade ideology that had justified the establishment of the treaty system in the first place.

What competition existed under the unequal treaty system during the nineteenth century was largely economic. This competition, however, was rather one-sided. Since Britain possessed the largest and most productive economy among the foreign powers, and the largest navy, it was the principal beneficiary of the system. There were other guests at the table, but the British enjoyed the lion's share. British goods dominated the foreign import market, British ships dominated foreign trade, and British merchants constituted the elite within the treaty ports. Other foreigners might grumble about British supremacy, but none was prepared to challenge it except under the free-trade rules of informal empire. Until the appearance of the Japanese on the scene, these rules assumed that the foreign powers would not infringe on the core of Chinese territory.

JAPAN IN THE UNEQUAL TREATY SYSTEM

The Japanese did not become full participants in the unequal treaty system until 1895, but they had been trying to acquire treaty power status since the Meiji Restoration. In 1870, the new government in Tokyo dispatched a mission to China with a request for a trade treaty of the kind enjoyed by the Western powers, including a most favored nation clause and the right to travel and trade in the interior. If the treaty were drawn up any differently, the Japanese emissaries argued disingenuously, the Western powers might worry about the formation of an anti-Western league between China and Japan. The reaction of Li Hung-chang to the Japanese request was blunt—and predictable: "We cannot do anything about the Western nations, but we should not allow any such treatment from Japan. The Japanese are poor, greedy and untrustworthy. Because the proximity of the two countries facilitates intercourse, and because both peoples are of the same stock and use the same script, it would be very much more disadvantageous for us to grant the Japanese permission to go into China's interior than it was to give such rights to the Westerners."[10] The Japanese negotiators had to return home in 1871 with a treaty and a set of trade regulations that put the two countries on a more or less equal footing. The Japanese were permitted to trade, purchase land, set up consulates, and exercise consular jurisdiction in all the open ports in China, and the Chinese were extended the same rights in the open ports of Japan. The home government in Tokyo, angered by the ineptness of its diplomats, tried to revise those terms but met with angry rebuffs from Li Hung-chang. The agreements were finally ratified on April 30, 1873.

No doubt one of the motives behind the Japanese demand for treaty privileges was its quest for international recognition. As Itō Hirobumi noted in 1899, the main element that had promoted progress and development following the Meiji Restoration was "the hope of competing with the Powers for leadership."[11] This competitive drive undoubtedly lay behind the attempt to secure an unequal treaty with the Chinese in the 1870s. Having committed themselves in 1868 to an all-out program of building national "wealth and power" through the introduction of institutions and technology from the "civilized" nations of the West, the Japanese leadership felt entitled to an equality of status with the West. Indeed, while trying to negotiate an unequal treaty with China, the Japanese were also trying to revise their own unequal treaties with the West. But claims to "civilized" status rang hollow in the 1870s, and the Iwakura mission had as little success as the mission to China. It was only in the 1890s that the Meiji leaders were able to demonstrate their country's "enlightenment" in contrast to the "barbarism" of China. Indeed, Japanese propaganda emphasized that the Sino-Japanese War was not a struggle over power or territory, but a conflict between a backward-looking China seeking to keep an equally backward-looking Korea under its control and a progressive, forward-looking Japan determined to bring the benefits of "civilization" to the peninsula. When the Japanese won the war, they naturally claimed the prerogatives of the other "civilized" nations in China.

---

[10] Chow Jen Hwa, *China and Japan: The History of Chinese Diplomatic Missions in Japan, 1877–1911* (Singapore: Chopmen Enterprises, 1975), p. 41.

[11] Momatsu Midori, *Itō-Kō chokuwa* (Tokyo: Chikura Shobō, 1936), p. 332.

Beyond the search for recognition as a power, however, lay other, more tangible motives. In the 1890s, a majority of the Japanese population remained agrarian, but new mechanized factories powered by steam were moving into production every year, and light industry began to take off. Two decades earlier, the Japanese had sought to build industries capable of competing with the influx of foreign manufactured goods, a defensive industrialization centering on import substitution, but by the 1890s many had begun to think of Japan as an exporter of manufactured goods. Indeed, the promotion of exports was seen as essential to the expansion of an economy dependent on the outside for industrial raw materials. The slogan of "building Japan as an industrial and commercial power" (*shō-kōrikkoku*) supplanted the older slogan of "building national wealth and power" (*fukoku kyōhei*). The Japanese leadership was well aware that Japan could not hope to compete with Western manufacturers in Western markets, but they did perceive comparative advantage for Japanese manufacturers in Asian regional markets. If the Japanese were able to play under the same rules as the Westerners in China, they were likely to do very well. Shipping costs were lower for Japanese manufacturers than for goods shipped from the West, and Japanese labor costs were lower even than those in British-owned mills in India. The economic provisions of the Treaty of Shimonoseki were thus intended to facilitate Japanese commercial penetration of China, just as earlier unequal treaties had facilitated penetration by the British and other Western nations. As Komura Jutarō observed in March 1895, China was likely to become the chief market for Japanese manufactured goods and marine products. "It goes without saying," he wrote, "that in the commercial treaty which is to be newly concluded, we must add the most favored nation clause and secure the same interests as possessed by other nations."[12]

It is interesting to note, however, that the Japanese also expanded the scope of the treaty system in significant ways in 1895. The Treaty of Shimonoseki included new rights not yet enjoyed by the other powers—the opening of new ports (Shashi, Chungking, Soochow, and Hangchow), steam navigation rights on the Yangtze River from Ichang to Chungking and on the Woosung River from Shanghai to Soochow and Hangchow, and manufacturing rights in the treaty ports that exempted goods produced from tariff duties. Since all these rights were automatically extended to powers with most favored nation status, it seems clear that the Japanese intended to win support for the peace settlement with China by promoting the interests of the Westerners as well as their own. The commercial provisions of the treaty, Nathan Pelcovits has remarked, "read

---

[12] Gaimushō, ed., *Komura gaikō shi*, vol. 1 (Tokyo: Hara Shobō, 1966), p. 61.

like something out of a British Chamber of Commerce memorial."[13] It was well known that the British wanted manufacturing rights in the treaty ports but had met resistance from officials like Li Hung-chang who wanted to protect modern native industry. While there is no evidence that the British pressured the Japanese to include manufacturing rights in the settlement with China, they were clearly pleased. When the Russian ambassador approached the British about asking the Japanese to give up the Liaotung Peninsula, Lord Kimberley replied that he was hesitant to interfere, since "the commercial clauses of the Japanese peace terms were so full of promise for all the powers which enjoyed the advantage of the most-favored nation agreement."[14]

Although the Japanese took advantage of China's weakness in 1895 to advance their economic interests, one should not forget that the Japanese leadership had territorial ambitions on the continent as well. The war had begun because of Sino-Japanese rivalry in Korea. While the Treaty of Shimonoseki established the basis of informal empire in China, it also brought Taiwan and the Pescadores under direct Japanese colonial control. Many Japanese at the time called for direct territorial concessions in China proper, too. The Japanese army wanted the cession of the Liaotung Peninsula, and some party politicians in the Diet demanded the annexation of territory in Shantung, Kiangsu, Fukien, and Kwangtung. These demands were quite unrealistic. In 1895 Japan was militarily strong enough to force the Ch'ing government to the bargaining table, but not strong enough to pursue a policy of territorial aggrandizement against the wishes of the other powers. The Triple Intervention forced the Japanese leadership to abide by the rules of "informal imperialism" that assumed Chinese territory would not be subject to annexation or partition.

As we have already pointed out, these rules were breached during the race for concessions in the late 1890s, and this opened the way for divisions among the Japanese elite about how to deal with China. As W. G. Beasley has suggested, there emerged an "army" orientation toward China policy and a "foreign ministry" orientation. During the late 1890s powerful figures within the Japanese army like Yamagata Aritomo and Katsura Tarō were convinced that the partition of China was inevitable. If the Germans, the Russians, the French, and the British were all acquiring leaseholds and exclusive economic rights in violation of the rules of informal empire, then the Japanese should join in, too. This view was played out in the abortive attempt of the army leadership to seize control of Amoy in 1900. But many civilian leaders, less inclined to adventurism,

[13] Nathan A. Pelcovits, *Old China Hands and the Foreign Office* (New York: Institute of Pacific Relations, 1948), p. 175.

[14] William L. Langer, *The Diplomacy of Imperialism, 1890–1902*, 2d ed. (New York: Alfred A. Knopf, 1951), p. 179.

were confident that China would remain intact. They were imperialists, but cautious imperialists, who had a keen sense of how the game of informal empire was played in China. As Katō Takaaki, the minister to England, noted in 1899, "If the foreign powers partitioned China and acquired their own territory there, they would be merely increasing their expenditures to no real end, for their advantage [*rieki*] would be no different than at present. For that reason, nearly all the foreign powers are agreed that the status quo in China should be maintained, that no country should violate it, that China's independence should be maintained, and that the [powers'] own interests should be maintained through the expansion of commercial rights in China's interior."[15] The success of Open Door Note diplomacy confirmed this observation.

The tension between these two points of view within the Japanese leadership was resolved in the short term by the acquisition of rights in Manchuria after the Russo-Japanese War. Thereafter, the military was able to secure the foothold on the continent it had been seeking since the Sino-Japanese War. Not only was Korea turned into a protectorate, then formally annexed, but the Japanese acquired control over the Russian leasehold and concession in southern Manchuria. Because of its strategic importance, the Liaotung Peninsula became the army's political and administrative bailiwick on the continent. But the acquisition of a Manchurian sphere of influence in no sense violated the framework of the unequal treaty system. It merely involved a shift in the balance among the powers, with the Japanese supplanting the Russians in the Northeast. Nor was Chinese sovereignty seriously violated in a formal sense. The Japanese, after all, were in Manchuria on the basis of a treaty negotiated with the Chinese, and the leasehold was for a fixed term of years. And as Itō Hirobumi made clear in high-level debate over China policy in 1906, "Manchuria is not Japanese territory. It is part of China. . . . The responsibility for governing Manchuria rests with China."[16] Whatever the long-term hopes of the military establishment, top civilian leaders intended to keep the door open there, as it was in the rest of China. They knew that the British and the Americans would not tolerate any attempt to create a zone of Japanese privilege, and they did not want to jeopardize the larger economic interest Japan enjoyed in China under the treaty system.

During the two decades following the Russo-Japanese War, the Japanese did in fact prosper in the collective informal empire. From the turn of the century, Japanese began pouring into China in large numbers, just as they were pouring into Korea and Taiwan. While the Westerners tended to confine themselves to the treaty port enclaves or to a few pock-

---

[15] Speech to the Nihon Keizaikai reported in *Chūgai shōgyō shimbun*, December 20, 1899.

[16] Inoue Kiyoshi, *Nihon teikokushugi no keisei* (Tokyo: Iwanami Shoten, 1975), p. 300.

ets of missionary enterprise in the interior, the Japanese were everywhere, penetrating the back country with their goods, sitting in the councils of local warlords, reconnoitering the plains of Manchuria and Mongolia, worshipping in the great Buddhist temples and monasteries, and crowding into their settlements in Shanghai and Hankow. By 1930, the Japanese in China outnumbered all the British, Americans, and other Westerners put together. And they also had proven themselves better able to exploit the economic opportunities provided by the unequal treaty system. On the eve of the Manchurian incident, by almost every quantifiable indicator Japan had displaced Great Britain as the paramount foreign economic power in China. The investment of men and money, human and financial capital in China had proven as profitable as any futile attempt to seize territory there might have. The Japanese once again demonstrated their ability to take a foreign invention, in this case the unequal treaty system, and turn it to their advantage in ways the foreign inventor was unable to.

JAPAN AND THE COLLAPSE OF THE UNEQUAL TREATY SYSTEM

Ironically, however, just when Japan appeared to be emerging as the paramount foreign economic power in China within the framework of the treaty system, it embarked on a new policy of establishing more direct political control over Manchuria, setting in motion a process that ended in the collapse of that system. In effect, Japan seceded from the collective informal empire precisely at the moment when it was poised to take fullest advantage of it. How can one account for this paradoxical behavior?

The answer, of course, is that the treaty structure was already under attack by indigenous Chinese forces. The collaborative structure sustaining the foreigners' collective informal empire began to weaken in the wake of the 1911 Revolution. This political upheaval was precipitated in large measure by the willingness of the Ch'ing to tolerate foreign economic penetration. By the 1920s, the institutions of informal empire became the target of powerful new nationalist movements in China. Boycotts, demonstrations, and strikes against foreign merchants and mill owners directly assaulted the most tangible and visible manifestations of foreign economic interests in China, and the partial reunification of China under the Kuomintang brought to power a government committed in principle to ending the unequal treaty system itself. What emerged was a systemic crisis of informal imperialism in China.

The reaction of imperialist metropoles to the breakdown of collaborative structures has historically followed two patterns. In the nineteenth century, the rise of indigenous resistance movements often prompted a shift from informal empire to full political annexation. The revolt of Arabi Pasha, for example, prompted the British takeover of Egypt in the early 1880s when it became clear that British interests could not be protected without British occupation and British control of the administrative structure. In the twentieth century, particularly after World War I, imperialist metropoles have often withdrawn in the face of anticolonial national resistance movements. The ultimate response of the British to the rise of a powerful Indian nationalist movement in the 1920s and 1930s was withdrawal and the restoration of political control to indigenous authority after World War II. In the case of China, where the imperialist presence was a collective one, the response to the rise of anti-imperialist nationalism was fragmented. Although the other treaty powers seemed willing to opt for a loosening of the system, if not total withdrawal, the Japanese reacted by attempting a deeper political penetration of China.

The British, for example, were at first deeply ambivalent toward the rise of Chinese nationalism, particularly during the anti-British outbursts in 1925–1927. At the time of the May 30th incident in 1925, the British government dispatched military forces to Shanghai and attempted to persuade the other powers, including Japan, to do so as well. But by late 1926 it indicated a willingness to negotiate a revision of the treaties and tried to take the lead in supporting the new Kuomintang government. The British made no compromise on the question of extraterritoriality, nor were they willing to give up their main territorial concessions, but they did make tactical concessions to Chinese demands for "rights recovery." To maintain British trade in China, they tried to avoid a direct clash with nationalist forces. In December 1928, the British government hurried to concede tariff autonomy before the Americans did; in 1929, it ended its embargo on arms shipments to China; in 1930, it restored Weihaiwei to Chinese control, surrendered concessions at Amoy and two other ports, and invested Boxer indemnity money in a fund to support cultural, educational, and other philanthropic work in China; and in 1931, it agreed to turn the Salt Administration over to Chinese control. The Colonel Blimps at club bars in Shanghai doubtless grumbled about this shift in policy, but the British Foreign Office took a balanced view. As Lord Cadogan put it in 1935, British trade with China was important, but "not so important as to warrant incurring vital risks for its protection," nor was it "an imperial issue that would justify the taking of vital risks."[17]

If the British showed a willingness to accept the slow demise of the collective informal empire in the face of Chinese nationalism, the reaction of the Japanese was more complex. Their imperialist priorities were quite different. The Japanese had a great deal more to lose than the British if the treaty system unraveled, and a broader range of interests to be pro-

[17] Stephen Lyon Endicott, *Diplomacy and Enterprise: British China Policy, 1933–1937* (Manchester: Manchester University Press, 1975), p. 55.

tected. Precisely because Japan had prospered under the system, its leaders were more intensely concerned over its possible demise. The Japanese public, politicians, and decision makers became passionate over events in China, just as the British were about the growth of nationalist forces in India, Egypt, and other parts of their formal empire. A widespread consensus about the "special" character of the relationship between Japan and China made the fate of the treaty structure "an imperial issue" for the Japanese in a way that it was not for British officials. For Japan, the China problem was one that would justify "the taking of vital risks."

The Japanese accepted the rules of the unequal treaty system when they signed the Treaty of Shimonoseki, but they were never quite at ease with the other treaty powers. From the outset, many Japanese argued that Japan's relationship with China was qualitatively different from that of the Western powers. After all, as men as diverse as Okakura Tenshin and Yamagata Aritomo often pointed out, the two peoples shared a "common culture and common race" (dōbun dōshu), and it was natural for Japanese to think that they had a special sympathy for China or a depth of understanding that Westerners did not. The Chinese and the Japanese, moreover, shared a recent historical experience in common. Both had been the objects of Western gunboat diplomacy, and in the Bakumatsu period some Japanese even had proposed that Japan make common cause with China in resisting the Western encroachment. But in the 1890s, when the failure of China to modernize and its defeat in the Sino-Japanese War precluded any notion of common alliance or common cause, there emerged the notion—embodied in the "Ōkuma doctrine," or the idea of "the yellow man's burden"—that the Japanese, in repayment of their cultural debt to China, should take an active role in pulling China up the steep path toward "civilization."

By the 1920s, the emergence of Japan as a major industrial and military power in Asia moved the idea of a special relationship a step beyond ties of sentiment and history. Japanese economic interests in China were as important, in absolute terms, as the economic interests of the Westerners, and more important in relative terms. As the Japanese manufacturing sector grew, and particularly as more and more of its production depended on export markets in the 1920s, China loomed larger and larger in economic significance. In an uncertain world economy, the market and resources of China came to be linked inextricably in many minds with Japan's well-being. As business pressure groups frequently reminded the public, a disruption of trade or threats to Japanese assets in China were likely to have damaging ripple effects on the Japanese economy.

Equally important, China was of greater strategic importance to Japan than it was to the other foreign powers. As Ishii Kikujirō told the American secretary of state in 1917, "A civil war or collapse in China may not have any direct effect on other nations, but to Japan it will be a matter of life and death. A civil war in China will immediately be reflected in Japan, and the downfall of China means the downfall of Japan."[18] The onset of internal disorder in China in the wake of the 1911 Revolution tempted Japanese military leaders on more than one occasion to try carving out new strategic footholds in China proper; they were beset by anxieties over the threat internal instability in China posed to Japanese security. Much of this anxiety focused on the Northeast, where Japanese economic interests were concentrated and where Japan already maintained a wedge of "formal empire" on the Liaotung Peninsula. In strategic, as well as economic thinking, the notion of a special relationship with China fed a sense of vulnerability and insecurity.

Consensus on the existence of a special relationship did not assure a consensus on China policy. There was a range of opinion on how to respond to the breakdown of Chinese collaboration with the treaty structure. Not everyone in Japan was willing to take "vital risks" in quite the same way. Among those most concerned with the economic and trading interests protected by the unequal treaties, there were many, such as Foreign Minister Shidehara, who were willing to accept a slow phasing-out of the treaty structure, albeit with a greater degree of reluctance than shown by the British. On the other hand, the business firms represented by the Shanghai Chamber of Commerce saw erosion of the treaty structure as a threat and wanted the government to use force to maintain the empire in the name of "protecting Japanese nationals and property." Officials in the South Manchuria Railway Company feared the impact of Chinese nationalism on their enterprise but wanted Japan to expand its interests north of the Great Wall through peaceful economic development. The Manchurian Youth League called for a "spontaneous" independence movement in the Northeast, and staff officers in the Kwantung Army wanted to detach Manchuria from the rest of the informal empire and turn it into a political dependency completely under the control of Japan. It was difficult at the time to make sense out of this cacophony of domestic political voices, but it is clear that after the assassination of Chang Tso-lin in 1928 a new political coalition of forces advocating a "strong" China policy was taking shape, urging the governments in power to take the "vital risks" that Great Britain and the other foreign powers eschewed.

Yet no Japanese cabinet before 1931 showed any disposition to do so. While the Tanaka cabinet was willing to use Japanese military force to protect the interests of its Manchurian client, Chang Tso-lin, it refused

---

[18] Kamikawa Hikomatsu, ed., *Japanese-American Diplomatic Relations in the Meiji-Taisho Era* (Tokyo: Pan-Pacific Press, 1958), p. 345.

to use his assassination as an excuse to expand Japan's territorial control in the Northeast. Its successor, the Hamaguchi cabinet, returned to the moderate policies of Shidehara, who made grudging concessions to the Kuomintang government in order to protect Japanese trade with China. All the protests, blandishments, and harangues of treaty port and domestic pressure groups advocating a more aggressive policy in China were not enough to overcome the fundamental caution of the Tokyo government.

But it was impossible for the home government to resist the kind of pressure applied by the Kwantung Army—the military fait accompli. The Kwantung staff officers, including a number of younger and bolder China experts like Kōmoto Daisaku, realized that the only way to move the government on the China issue was by following the principle of "act first whenever possible." The institutional independence of the army high command, where the Kwantung staff officers found many sympathizers, enabled the Kwantung Army in 1931 to force on the home government a commitment it could not gracefully repudiate without risking humiliation abroad or military insurrection at home. The evidence suggests that the Kwantung Army officers were not particularly interested in the impact of their actions on the treaty structure, which they saw as under threat already. Rather, they were anxious to prevent the spread of Chinese anti-imperialism north of the Great Wall. Their concern was not to maintain the informal empire but to consolidate Japanese assets and protect Japanese strategic interests in the Northeast as a hedge against a collapse of the collaborative structure in China proper.

To achieve this, they created Manchukuo, an invention of their own. Neither a formal colony nor a sphere of influence protected by the rules that governed the informal empire to the south, Manchukuo was a separate state under Chinese leaders who took their orders from Japanese army officers and civilian officials. It most closely resembled the satellite states that Soviet imperialism created in Eastern Europe after World War II. Just why the Japanese chose this particular form of domination is not clear. Perhaps it was a natural extension of the idea of a special relationship, just as the postwar East European satellites were a natural outgrowth of pre-Soviet pan-Slavism. Or perhaps the myth of Manchurian independence was ultimately a concession to the larger currents of anti-imperialism gathering force in the rest of the world and often echoed in Japan's own self-assessments of its continental policy after 1931. Whatever the motives, this experiment with a new form of imperialist control proved unsuccessful. It was extremely costly, involving the huge transfer of financial resources and human capital to Manchuria without any commensurate payoff. The Japanese had been far better served by participation through the techniques of informal empire, which had allowed such profitable enterprises as the Japanese-owned cotton mills and the South Manchuria Railway to flourish.

Needless to say, the push into Manchuria led eventually to a wider war whose costs in lives and capital were immeasurable. One of the lesser costs was the end of the unequal treaty system. In hopes of winning Chinese support and convincing other Asian leaders of the sincerity of its "anti-imperialist" crusade, Japan promised in 1943 to abandon the institution of informal imperialism.[19] At almost the same time that the Americans and the British announced their willingness to give up extraterritorial rights in China, the Tōjō government set forth a new set of guidelines on China policy that envisaged relinquishing Japanese concessions and settlements, renouncing its special administrative rights in the legation quarter, and phasing out its right of extraterritoriality. The practical effect of this new policy was slight, but its symbolic significance was enormous. It was an implicit admission that Japanese China policy had gone off track in 1931. How much wiser it would have been to have adopted such a policy a decade and a half before!

Hindsight, of course, confers perfect vision. The simple fact is that making concessions to Chinese nationalism in the late 1920s and early 1930s was very difficult when domestic political emotions were running so high in Japan. The tragedy was that by abandoning the policy line advocated by moderate imperialists like Itō Hirobumi, Katō Takaaki, Shidehara Kijurō, and others after the Russo-Japanese War, Japan assumed a set of obligations, responsibilities, and commitments in China that far exceeded its capacities to maintain when they were challenged by Chinese nationalism. Direct control over the Northeast, and later in the occupied zones south of the Great Wall, became a millstone around Japan's neck. It distorted domestic economic growth and deflected domestic political development. For China, the consequences were even more drastic. Far from achieving an end to the unequal treaty system and its institutions, Chinese nationalism brought down on itself a holocaust that destroyed the lives of millions and altered the course of China's modern history. Although the treaty system symbolized national humiliation, it had provided China with a more peaceful and stable framework for its initial relationship with the developed world than did the policy of partition the Japanese pursued. In this sense, one can argue that informal imperialism may have been a lesser evil for the dominated as well as for the dominators.

[19] Akira Iriye, *Power and Culture: The Japanese-American War, 1941–1945* (Cambridge: Harvard University Press, 1981), pp. 98–108.

PART I

Trade and Investment

The rapid expansion of the Japanese economic presence in the informal empire in China during the first three decades of the twentieth century was nothing short of extraordinary. Whether one measures that expansion by value of foreign assets, direct investment, total trade, number of firms, size of resident population, or shipping tonnage, it is clear that Japan had caught up with or surpassed Great Britain by 1930 (table I.1). In China south of the Great Wall, British investments, estimated as balance sheet values, still exceeded Japan's by a 2:1 ratio.[1] But if the values

Table I.1
Comparison of British and Japanese Interests in China, 1899–1931

	1899	1914	1931
Direct trade with China (HK taels, millions)			
Great Britain	53.9	113.3	170.9
Japan	53.1	184.9	543.7
Population in China			
Great Britain	5,562	8,966	13,015
Japan	2,440	80,219	255,686
Number of firms in China			
Great Britain	401	590	1,027
Japan	195	1,269	4,633
Shipping capacity in China (tons)			
Great Britain	23.3	61.2	52.2
Japan	2.8	23.4	45.6
Investment in China (U.S.$ million)			
Great Britain	260.3	607.5	1,189.2
Japan	1.0	219.6	1,136.9

Source: C. F. Remer, Foreign Investment in China, passim.

[1] Fujiwara Sadao, "Kindai Chūgoku ni okeru gaikoki toshi zandara no suikei," Tōa keizai kenkyū 45, 4 (November 1976): 51. According to Fujiwara, in 1936 England's total direct investment in finance, communications, manufacturing, and utilities for China proper (excluding Manchuria and railway enterprises) amounted to $569 million, compared with $242 million for Japan, $186 million for the United States, and $57 million for France. In 1931, Japan's total investment in Manchuria alone came to around $850 million. See chapter 4, note 79.

of foreign assets in all of China are compared, those of Japan exceeded all the other foreign powers' combined. The Japanese predominance owed much to their control of the South Manchuria Railway Company, which in 1931 controlled assets worth over 570 million dollars.

Undoubtedly Japan's proximity to China accounted for its ability to overtake the other foreign powers so quickly. British trade and investment came to China via the Suez Canal and the Indian Ocean, but Japan's had only to make a short hop across the Straits of Tsushima or the Yellow Sea. But one should not forget that Japanese economic interests in China expanded rapidly because Japan's domestic economy was expanding so rapidly. The economy of Great Britain, the leading imperial power in China at the turn of the century, had long since matured, and its initial growth spurt was over. While the average annual growth of real GNP in Japan between 1913 and 1935 was 2.6 percent, that of Great Britain was only 0.7 percent. As Japan's domestic economic activities expanded, so did its external. Its burgeoning manufacturing sector was hungry for markets and raw materials, and China was a convenient source of both. Had Japan's economic performance been sluggish, it is unlikely that its economic presence in China would have grown so fast.

If Japanese economic expansion in China was more rapid than that of the other powers, its economic dependence on China became more substantial. For the other foreign powers, including the British, China remained a relatively minor market and supplier of raw materials. The British, for example, were far more dependent on colonial markets than on the China market. For every pound of cotton yarn Great Britain sold to China in 1930, it sold seventy in India. But for Japan the informal empire in China was far more important economically than its formal colonies were. Even in 1930, after three decades of development in Taiwan and Korea, Japan's trade with China was still nearly three times as large as its colonial trade. During the early twentieth century, Japan's exports to China accounted for about one-fifth of its total exports, and its imports came to around 12 to 15 percent. Not surprisingly, over time Japanese trade tended to increase in areas where it had more substantial assets. As Professor Mizoguchi's chapter suggests, Japan became more and more dependent on trade with the northeastern provinces in Manchuria than on trade with Central China.

Japanese investment in the informal empire in China also rivaled investment in the formal colonial empire. According to the estimates of Kaneko Fumio, in the late 1920s Japanese corporate investment in Manchuria alone, for example, amounted to 966 million yen, more than the amount invested in Korea and Taiwan combined (434 million yen in Korea and 408 million yen in Taiwan).[2] In 1930, the total paid-up capital of

[2] Kaneko Fumio, "Prewar Japanese Investments in Colonized Taiwan, Korea and Man-

joint stock companies operating in Manchuria exceeded that in the two colonies. The semigovernmental South Manchuria Railway Company and its congeries of affiliated enterprises accounted for much of this imbalance, but it should not be forgotten that large-scale private manufacturing capital found China more attractive as a place for investment than the formal colonies. As Professor Duus's chapter shows, there were dozens of privately owned Japanese cotton mills in the Chinese treaty ports by 1930, but hardly any in Korea or Taiwan. Except for the Taiwan sugar industry, colonial investment was of relatively marginal interest to Japanese industrial capitalists before the 1930s. By contrast, it seems unlikely that Britain's trade and investment in its informal empire (however defined) ever surpassed its trade and investments in its colonies.

The expanding Japanese economic presence in China was accomplished by that peculiar combination of private initiative and government encouragement that characterized Japanese expansion into the world market after the 1890s. While the British and American penetration of the China market in the nineteenth century was largely the work of private adventurers and entrepreneurs, the Meiji government was an active promoter of trade. The economic importance of China to Japan—and the promise of its future—was an article of faith at the highest level of decision making. As Itō Hirobumi observed in a speech after returning from a trip to China in 1898, "Among the other countries confronting our own, there is none that surpasses us in proximity to China, in close access to all its ports, and in convenience of navigation. It must be said that our country occupies the best position with respect to the China trade. If we take good advantage of that position to carry on trade, it will not be at all difficult to make our country the central source of supply of goods for all ports both in the north and south of China."[3]

From the 1890s onward, the Japanese government made a concerted effort to promote the growth of the China trade as part of a larger policy of expanding Japanese exports in world markets. The Yokohama Specie Bank extended its network of branch offices in China to provide credit to Japanese traders and facilitate foreign exchange transactions; the Foreign Ministry dispatched commercial attachés to its new consulates in the treaty ports to provide a flow of information and reports on local markets; the Diet passed legislation giving subsidies to shipping lines in the China trade; government banks extended long-term, low-interest credit to traders involved in key export industries such as cotton yarn or made loans to Chinese mines that supplied the burgeoning state steel industry with coal; and in 1906 the quasi-governmental South Manchuria Railway

---

churia: A Quantitative Analysis," *Annals of the Institute of Social Sciences* (Tokyo University), no. 23 (1982): 82.

[3] Itō Hirobumi, "Tai-Shin shosaku," *Jitsogyō no Nihon* 1, 19: 9.

Company took over all the assets formerly controlled by the Russians in South Manchuria. The Japanese government was much more active in promoting the China trade for its nationals than Western governments were. (On the other hand, as William Wray points out in his essay, specific government policies, such as its position on the 1934 Chinese tariff schedules, sometimes ran counter to business interests.)

The pattern of Japanese enterprise in China therefore differed from the Western pattern. Western trading companies, banks, and mining or manufacturing firms operating in China were by and large private firms, organized by private initiative and relying on private sources of capital. Key Western trading firms like Jardine, Matheson or Carlowitz & Co. had been the creation of "subimperialists" who got to China during the early days of the treaty system. By the turn of the century, multinationals such as Standard Oil, the British-American Tobacco Company, and the Singer Sewing Machine Company also made their appearance in China, and metropolitan capital began to flow into banking, mining, and other non-trade enterprises. But with the possible exception of Russian ventures like the Russo-Asiatic Bank and some German companies, the role of the government in promoting these enterprises was minimal. The British Foreign Office felt bound to secure access to foreign markets "unfairly" closed to trade, but once these markets were open, British traders and investors were expected to make their own way in competition with others. For example, the Foreign Office deliberately refused to guarantee railway loans in China in the 1890s and insisted that private firms should take the initiative in the matter.

As several chapters in this section make clear, Japanese enterprise in China often involved direct government support. An enterprise like the South Manchuria Railway Company, discussed by Myers and Nakagane, found no counterpart among Western enterprises. Not only was half its capital put up by the Japanese government, but the selection of its management was largely in the hands of the government. While operated as a profit-making enterprise, the company was conceived as an instrument to promote "cultural forms for military preparedness" (*bunsoteki bubi*), as envisaged by Gotō Shimpei, to guarantee Japan a strategic presence in northeastern China. The company's operations reinforced that presence with a complex network of economic ties to the metropolis, paving the way for Japanese settlement in the region. Before the 1930s, there were several other important government or quasi-governmental firms at work in China, such as the Oriental Development Company, the Bank of Taiwan, and the Bank of Chosen, all of which were primarily involved in financing trade or other enterprises.

To be sure, there were also purely private firms like the Japanese-owned cotton mills described by Duus. These were entirely the creation of private capitalists looking at new opportunities for profit, and they were operated solely with profit in mind. Neither did they enjoy significant government support other than the customary sort marshalled on behalf of the lives and property of Japanese nationals abroad. But there were also private firms that operated with direct or indirect government assistance (and sometimes assisted the government in pursuing its goals). As Wray shows, shipping firms like NYK, OSK, and Nisshin Kaisen enjoyed government subsidies, and trading firms like Mitsui and Okura served as conduits for government loans to the Ta-yeh mines. All of this, of course, reflected patterns of government-enterprise relations that obtained in the metropolis.

Most Western enterprises, with the exception of the Russian, tended to focus their activities on the southern and central parts of China. Commercially, these were the richest regions of China, and it was here that the earliest treaty ports were established. Certainly the Japanese, even though late entrants into the informal empire, were well aware that the wealth of China was concentrated there. As Wray's paper shows, those service firms most important in the China trade (Mitsui Bussan, the Yokohama Specie Bank, and NYK Lines) first became active in the lower Yangtze, around Hankow in particular, trying to create a niche where they could avoid the more intense Western competition in Shanghai, Canton, and Hong Kong. Japanese coal exports went mainly to Shanghai and Hong Kong, where they accounted for about half of the coal imported there. But it was in the north that Japan most easily established its economic preponderance.

After the Russo-Japanese War, Japan's economic center of gravity in China shifted north. Even before the Russo-Japanese War, its exports of cotton yarn to ports in North China (including Manchuria) exceeded those to Shanghai and Hankow, and after the war exports of Japanese cotton cloth drove British and American goods out of the Manchurian market. The Japanese not only enjoyed a special political position in the North, but their metropolitan economy came to depend greatly on that region's raw and semiprocessed materials. The trade statistics compiled by Mizoguchi suggest that while the share of Japanese exports going to "mainland China" remained at 75–100 percent before 1930, Japanese imports from the Kwantung Leased Territory increased to nearly half of the total import trade from China over the same period. Although Japanese exports sought out the populous markets of mainland China for the products of textile and other light industries, the economic modernization of the Northeast under the impact of Japanese investment in transportation and resource development created a flow of agricultural and mineral exports to Japan.

As for direct investment, the importance of North China, especially

Manchuria, was large from the outset. According to Remer's estimates, 68.9 percent of all Japanese direct investment was in Manchuria in 1914, and 62.9 percent in 1930. Here were to be found not only the extensive facilities and assets of the SMR and its affiliated companies but also the preponderance of Japanese investment in public utilities (gas and electricity), mining ventures, blast furnaces and ironworks, oil production plants, sawmills, and woodworking plants. Obviously this concentration of direct investment in the Northeast was related to the policy of economic modernization and resource development pursued by the government, and the pattern of resource exports to the metropolis. The other major cluster of Japanese direct investment—the cotton spinning and weaving mills in Shanghai and Tsingtao—was, in effect, a Japanese-owned import-substitution industry designed to protect the Japanese share in the China market.

Whether the Japanese employed an economic or business style in China different from Western enterprises is a fascinating subject but one not thoroughly explored by the papers in this volume. We know that Japanese enterprises operating abroad in the late twentieth century bring a particular management style with them (viz., the personnel policies of Japanese-owned manufacturing facilities in the United States, such as the Sony television plant in San Diego or the Nissan automobile factory in Tennessee). Whether this was equally true of Japanese enterprise in early twentieth-century China is less clear. Nevertheless, there are scattered hints that the Japanese approached the China market or China investment with some distinctive tactics. For example, some Japanese enterprises dispensed with the services of compradors. Mitsui Bussan abolished that system in its Shanghai branch in 1899, its Tientsin branch in 1900, and its Hong Kong branch in 1902; between 1917 and 1924, the Yokohama Specie Bank abandoned its compradors, although it eventually reinstated them; and the Japanese-owned cotton mills tried to bypass Chinese labor contractors by employing workers directly. While more research on the subject is required, Japanese enterprises in China might have been less dependent on Chinese mediators and agents than other foreign firms.

We presume that the Japanese had less need to rely on Chinese intermediaries—and perhaps less inclination to do so. For one thing, the language barrier was less formidable, and for another it was much easier for a Japanese to blend into the Chinese environment than for a big-nosed Westerner. Indeed, as Wray indicates, Mitsui Bussan encouraged its employees to learn the Chinese language, wear Chinese clothes, familiarize themselves with local Chinese commercial customs and practices, and even acquire Chinese wives. Institutions like the Tōa Dōbunkai (discussed by Douglas Reynolds in chapter 7), for which no Western counterpart existed, created a manpower pool of young Japanese trained in the

Chinese language and familiar with Chinese society who could be recruited into Japanese enterprises and could deal directly with Chinese customers, clients, and staff. It may well be that this greater familiarity with Chinese culture, and greater access to information about it, gave advantages to Japanese enterprises that the Western firms did not enjoy.

Finally, Japan's economic interests in Manchuria changed dramatically after 1932, when part of Japan's informal empire joined its formal empire. The Japanese military's takeover of Manchuria paved the way for the creation of a puppet state, Manchukuo, to be directly managed by the Kwantung Army. The industrialization of Manchuria, as described by Nakagane in chapter 5, heavily depended on the tremendous transfer of financial, physical, and human resources from Japan to Manchuria with little benefit to Japan. Manchukuo marked the end of Japan's informal empire in China.

CHAPTER 1

The Changing Pattern of Sino-Japanese Trade, 1884–1937

Mizoguchi Toshiyuki

Japan underwent a remarkable economic development between the Meiji Restoration and World War II. The rapid growth of foreign trade was a key factor in this development. Because Japan had few raw materials to sustain rapid industrial growth, foreign sources of supply like China had to be found and developed. Modern technology, too, was acquired by importing machinery and equipment from the West. To earn the foreign exchange to buy these goods, Japan had to produce what foreigners wanted badly enough to buy. Trade, therefore, was an important two-way traffic.

CHANGES IN JAPAN'S FOREIGN TRADE OVER TIME

Yet the role of foreign trade in Japan's economic development should not be exaggerated, as some scholars have done.[1] Minami Ryoshin has pointed out that the share of Japan's foreign trade of gross domestic product (GDP) was fairly low—in fact, lower than the ratios for Western countries.[2] Japan's foreign trade amounted to 14.4 percent of GDP in 1885–1890, 20.2 percent in 1891–1900, 24.4 percent in 1901–1911, 35.9 percent in 1911–1920, 34.5 percent in 1921–1930, and 39.1 percent in 1931–1940. These values are lower than the highest prewar figures for the United Kingdom (43.5 percent) and France (53.7 percent).[3] These comparisons suggest that while trade played an important role in Japan's prewar economic development, one should not overemphasize Japan's dependence on trade.

But what role did the China trade play in Japan's overall trade in the

---

[1] Shinohara Miyohei and Tuvia Blumenthal, *Nihon keizai no seichō yōin* (Factors in Japan's economic growth) (Tokyo: Tōyō Keizai Shimpōsha, 1971).

[2] Minami Ryoshin, *Nihon no keizai hatten* (Economic development of Japan) (Tokyo: Tōyō Keizai Shimpōsha, 1981).

[3] See Simon Kuznets, "Quantitative Aspects of Economic Growth of Nations," *Economic Development and Cultural Changes* 15, 2 (1967).

pre-World War II period? Changes over time in Japan's foreign trade with seven different regions may be identified: (1) Taiwan and Korea, (2) China, including the Kwantung Leased Territory and "Manchuria," (3) Hong Kong, (4) the rest of Asia, (5) North America, (6) Europe, and (7) other areas.[4] Although governed by Japan, the Kwantung Leased Territory served as an important conduit for Japan's trade with China. Hong Kong served as an entrepot in the trade between China and other countries and deserves to be treated separately.

From the outset, China's markets were important to Japan. They accounted for about 20 percent of Japan's exports and 12 percent or more of its imports for over sixty years (table 1.1). Although Japan's share of trade with China remained quite constant over time, Japan's trade with its colonies and with the rest of Asia increased as a proportion of the country's total trade.

Before Japan began its march toward industrialization, its major exports were primary goods like raw copper and raw silk (table 1.2).[5] After Japan's textile industry began to develop in the mid-1880s, the country began importing raw textile materials, and textile products began to occupy a large share of Japan's exports. These exports were essential to Japan's industrialization, because they paid for the imports of machinery and equipment from the developed countries. Exports of such light industry products as processed foods and sundry goods also became significant in the 1880s and 1890s.

Since the beginning of the twentieth century, Japan's heavy manufacturing industry had been promoted through policies of the government. As it had done for light industry, the government used public monies to establish factories, then transferred them to the private sector. Although Japan was still poor, with little capital and surplus labor, the leaders were dedicated to making Japan wealthy and militarily strong. Economic development at this time owed far more to political and military decisions and events than to any other factors. Japan's first heavy manufacturing

---

[4] Data for tracing these changes in trade were obtained from Ippei Yamazawa and Yūzo Yamamoto, *Bōeki to kokusai shūshi* (Foreign trade and balance of payments) (Tokyo: Tōyō Keizai Shimpōsha, 1979). *Japan Foreign Trade Statistics*, published by Japan's Ministry of Finance, covers the foreign trade of Japan proper (Japan and South Sakhalin). Data for trade with Japan's two major colonies, Taiwan and Korea, can be found in *Taiwan Foreign Trade Statistics*, published by the Governor-General of Taiwan, and in *Korea Foreign Trade Statistics*, published by the Governor-General of Korea. The Kwantung Leased Territory is included, but as a foreign country, in the Japanese Ministry of Finance data. Henceforth, all authors of this volume will refer to the Kwantung region of southern Manchuria as the Kwantung Leased Territory. For further discussion of this term, see chapter 4, note 34.

[5] Raw silk is usually classified as a textile product. Raw silk should be treated as a separate commodity in Japan's foreign trade, because little value is added by the manufacturing industry.

TABLE 1.1
Changes over Time in Japan's Foreign Trade, by Area (percent)

	Korea & Taiwan	China	Hong Kong	Other Asia	North America	Europe	Other
			EXPORTS				
1877–1886	1.2[a]	20.6[b]	—	1.1	37.2	37.5	3.5
1887–1896	1.9[a]	9.6[c]	16.0	3.3	37.2	29.9	2.1
1897–1906	8.1	20.1	11.3	5.9	30.0	21.4	3.2
1907–1916	11.0	22.2	4.3	11.5	28.9	18.8	3.3
1917–1926	12.7	22.0	3.1	14.4	34.3	8.6	4.9
1927–1936	20.8	19.0	1.8	17.8	24.3	7.2	9.1
1930–1939	25.5	22.1	1.2	17.1	17.2	7.2	9.7
			IMPORTS				
1877–1886	1.3[a]	19.4[b]	—	7.0	8.6	63.4	0.3
1887–1896	3.0[a]	14.5[c]	7.8	14.6	8.8	50.8	0.5
1897–1906	4.7	12.5	2.1	25.9	17.2	36.8	0.8
1907–1916	11.0	14.4	0.2	26.8	28.2	12.2	7.2
1917–1926	15.9	15.4	0.1	21.5	27.2	13.6	5.8
1927–1936	22.4	14.0	0.1	16.6	25.8	12.0	9.1
1930–1939	25.2	12.2	0.1	15.4	26.8	10.3	10.0

Source: Yamazawa and Yamamoto, Bóeki to Kokusai Shūshi, pp. 206–13.
[a] Korea only.
[b] Includes Taiwan and Hong Kong.
[c] Includes Taiwan.

industries still could not compete in world markets because their unit costs were too high. These new enterprises had to market their products at home and in Japan's colonies. Consequently, of all industries that could compete abroad, those producing textile products came to play a crucial role in obtaining the foreign exchange needed for economic development.

These imperatives of early industrialization, therefore, greatly determined the composition of Japan's imports (see table 1.2). Before the mid-1880s, Japan's major imports had been manufactured consumer goods. As light industry developed, however, import substitution expanded dramatically. On the other hand, imports of raw materials for the manufacturing industries (such as textile raw materials) and capital goods also increased significantly. Such capital goods included machinery and equipment for Japan's industry, which in turn meant that the advanced technologies of the developed world were being transferred to Japan. In addition, imports of food items like rice eventually accounted for an increasing share of Japan's trade. These imports satisfied the rising demand of the cities for food, which was not being met by the slow expansion of food supply from the farming sector. This large importation of food pre-

TABLE 1.2

Changes over Time in Japan's Foreign Trade, by Commodity Group (percent)

| | EXPORTS | | | | |
	Primary goods	Raw silk	Textile goods	CMM products	Other manu-facturing products
1877–1886	42.6	36.8	6.1	6.7	7.8
1887–1896	31.4	34.1	14.8	8.3	11.4
1897–1906	21.5	26.2	27.4	9.0	15.9
1907–1916	17.2	24.6	28.9	12.5	16.5
1917–1926	8.1	28.4	35.2	14.3	14.0
1927–1936	6.7	20.5	36.3	19.7	16.8
1930–1939	6.8	13.1	35.0	26.5	18.6
	IMPORTS				
	Crude food	Textile raw matls.	Other raw matls.	CMM products	Other manu-facturing products
1877–1886	0.8	1.6	7.9	21.3	68.4
1887–1896	7.1	14.8	6.3	29.0	42.8
1897–1906	13.8	22.9	6.4	32.8	24.1
1907–1916	10.3	32.6	7.1	34.4	15.6
1917–1926	16.1	29.5	8.7	30.8	14.9
1927–1936	19.0	28.6	13.4	25.2	13.8
1930–1939	17.5	25.1	15.4	29.7	12.3

Source: Yamazawa and Yamamoto, Bōeki to kokusai shūshi, pp. 176–99.

Note: CMM products include chemicals, metals, metal products, and machinery.

vented a rise in real wages in the manufacturing sector, and as wages lagged behind price increases, enterprises were able to reinvest more capital accumulation for earnings.

Shionoya Yuichi's estimates of Japan's imports, classified into consumer goods, capital goods, and unfinished goods, provide further evidence to validate this line of reasoning.[6] According to Shionoya, Japan's capital goods share went from 10 to 20 percent during the early stages of industrialization, remaining nearly constant afterward, while the share of consumer goods declined from 50 to 10 percent between 1870 and 1930.

THE TREND OF SINO-JAPANESE TRADE

Although China took a relatively stable share of Japan's total trade, one should not conclude that Sino-Japanese trade grew at a slow rate, because

[6] Shionoya Yuichi, "Patterns of Industrial Development," in Lawrence R. Klein and Kazushi Ohkawa, eds., Economic Growth: The Japanese Experience Since the Meiji Era (Homewood, Ill.: Richard D. Irwin, 1968).

Japanese foreign trade as a whole rapidly increased during this period.[7] For example, Japanese exports in real terms increased thirtyfold between the 1890s and 1930s, and imports increased tenfold, leaving a large trade surplus on Japan's side after 1900 (table 1.3). This surplus became one of the major sources of Japan's direct investment in China. The Kwantung Leased Territory and the puppet state of Manchukuo increasingly played an important role in Sino-Japanese trade after 1931. From figure 1.1 one can observe the share of trade from the Kwantung Leased Territory, Manchuria, and all other Chinese provinces (denoted by "Mainland China," excluding Taiwan after 1897, the Kwantung Leased Territory after 1907, and Manchukuo after 1932). Mainland China maintained a 75 to 80 percent share of Japan's exports before 1930, but that share greatly declined during the 1930s. If one assumes that the figures for the Kwantung Leased Territory for 1930 should have covered Japan's trade with Northeast China before 1932, it can then be concluded that Central and South China's shares of the Japan trade sharply declined.

As for the changing composition of Sino-Japanese trade, except in 1887–1896, when marine products took the lead, textiles were Japan's most important export to China, and their share rose continuously until the mid-1920s (table 1.4). As textile production and exports constituted a major engine of Japan's economic development, China became an important market for Japan's textiles. Fluctuations in textile sales to the China market greatly influenced the Japanese textile industries and the domestic economy as well, but these linkages are still little understood. By the 1930s, products of heavy manufacturing industries began to take an increasing share of overall Japanese exports to China. This new trade development was closely related to Japan's direct investments in Northeast China, which are described in greater detail in chapter 5.

Japan's major imports from China were agricultural products and chemicals, including medicines and natural fertilizers like bean cake. When agricultural products are reclassified into two subcategories, cereals and textile raw materials, it is clear that cereal imports from Northeast China greatly increased in the 1930s, contributing to that region's larger share of trade, as shown in figure 1.1.

TRADE WITHIN THE FORMAL AND INFORMAL EMPIRES

Japan maintained trade relations throughout the world, and its partners can be classified by type of trade relationship. The first category comprised the two main colonies of the formal Japanese empire, Taiwan and

---

[7] Estimates of Sino-Japanese trade are derived from the Japanese Ministry of Finance's *Annual Report of Foreign Trade Statistics* and from Hsiao Liang-lin, *China's Foreign Trade Statistics, 1864–1949* (Cambridge: Harvard University Press, 1974).

TABLE 1.3
Changes in Sino-Japanese Trade over Time

	1887–1896	1897–1906	1907–1916	1917–1926	1927–1936	1930–1939
Nominal exports (¥1,000)	8,460	56,190	139,790	453,360	438,950	671,340
Nominal imports (¥1,000)	13,060	39,670	87,600	364,300	318,120	374,670
Real exports (¥1,000)	20,104	74,001	159,660	254,062	405,331	627,196
Real imports (¥1,000)	37,321	84,384	141,931	279,090	344,080	407,641
Export-import ratio (%)	64.8	141.6	159.6	124.4	137.9	159.2
Terms of trade (%)	120.2	148.6	141.9	136.7	117.1	116.5

Source: Calculated from data from Japanese Ministry of Finance.
Note: Real terms are defined in 1934–1936 average prices.

FIGURE 1.1   Sino-Japanese trade according to Chinese regions

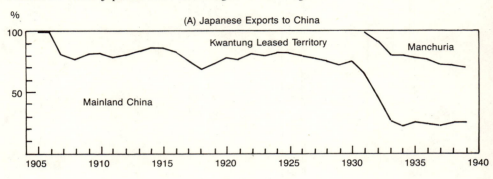

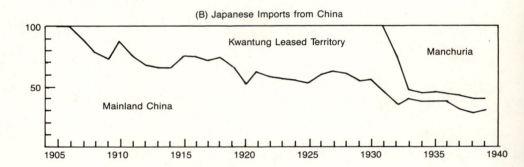

Korea.[8] These preferential partners made it possible for Japan to raise import taxes and create various barriers to discourage trade with other countries as well as to develop those goods it wanted to import, such as rice. Japanese merchants also received many privileges to trade in these colonies.

The next category of markets consisted of the Western developed countries and areas of Asia occupied by European powers, like India. Japan had to compete for a share of these markets, so its exports were limited to a few commodities like textiles and sundry goods. Japan was

[8] Because trade with Northeast China is included in the figures reported in *Foreign Trade of China* for 1932, it is impossible to make the adjustment for that year. In addition to Taiwan and Korea, Japan's other colonies were South Sakhalin, Micronesia, and the Kwantung Leased Territory. The Kwantung Leased Territory has been included in the discussion of China; Japanese trade with South Sakhalin and Micronesia was relatively small. For trade statistics regarding these colonies, see T. Mizoguchi and M. Umemara, eds., *Kyū-Nihon shokuminchi keizai tōkei* (Economic statistics of the colonies of the Japanese Empire) (Tokyo: Tōyō Keizai Shimpōsha, 1988).

reluctant to import from these areas and preferred to develop its import-competing industries.

Japan's informal empire made up the final group of markets. Before 1932, Japan had acquired economic privileges in Northeast China, including the Kwantung Leased Territory and the area ceded to the South Manchuria Railway Company. Mainland China may be considered as belonging to the third category, the informal empire.

To compare Japan's trade with these markets, a simple ratio, called the Regional Concentration Ratio (RCR), is used for both exports and imports. The RCR of country A trading (exporting or importing) with country B is defined as:

$$\text{RCR} = \frac{\text{Share of particular group of commodities in A's trade with B}}{\text{Corresponding share in A's total trade}}$$

The RCR will equal 1 when country A's markets are homogenous. An RCR value significantly higher than 1 indicates that country A depends heavily on country B for a particular commodity group. Although the ratio is simple to calculate, it tends to fluctuate irregularly when the denominator is small. Thus, it is necessary to adopt a broader classification system than used in table 1.4. By considering only the imports and exports of major groups of commodities, table 1.5 is constructed to show how Japan's trade differed between its formal and informal empire partners.

Japan's Exports

Did Japanese textile exports to China grow over time? According to table 1.5, the RCRs for Japanese textile exports to China, Taiwan, and Korea were very low. Japanese textile products flowed into other markets, indicating that Japan competed very successfully in the world textile market. Therefore, the regional textile shares for these three world trading areas were low, as table 1.6 shows. Textiles here include crude silk, which, as one of Japan's major exports before World War II, was a small component of Japan's exports to China, Taiwan, and Korea. If crude silk is excluded from the calculations, the textiles' RCRs for China rise to some extent, as indicated in table 1.7.

These findings indicate that, while textiles were an important commodity group in Japanese exports to China, their share of exports to China was generally no higher than their share of total Japanese exports. It should be noted, however, that the RCR for the non-raw-silk textile trade with China was high from 1907 to 1926, the period when the Japanese textile industry began to compete heavily in world markets. In contrast, the RCRs for trade with Taiwan and Korea were very low.

Since Japan's textile industry effectively competed with developed

TABLE 1.4
Composition of Sino–Japanese Trade, by Commodity Groups (percent)

	1887–1896	1897–1906	1907–1916	1917–1926	1927–1936	1930–1939
NOMINAL EXPORTS						
Processed foods	0.9	22.2	8.7	8.2	13.0	11.9
Textiles	11.5	38.7	52.7	55.3	34.5	24.7
Wood products	0.6	1.2	1.8	1.2	0.8	2.0
Chemicals	13.3	7.8	8.7	8.7	10.7	11.6
Ceramics	2.5	1.2	1.6	2.0	1.9	1.9
Metal & metal products	14.1	7.8	6.0	6.9	10.1	13.3
Machinery	0.6	1.6	2.9	4.3	12.0	18.3
Misc. manufactured products	5.9	4.1	6.1	6.0	9.4	8.8
Agricultural products	8.8	1.4	1.2	1.0	1.7	2.0
Marine products	23.5	3.5	3.1	2.3	2.0	2.1
Forest products	2.8	1.5	1.7	0.8	0.9	1.2
Mineral products	15.6	9.0	5.5	3.8	3.0	2.2
NOMINAL IMPORTS						
Processed foods	24.1	5.6	0.3	1.1	2.6	2.8
Textiles	2.3	1.4	1.1	1.4	3.5	3.2
Wood products	0.0	0.2	0.0	0.0	0.0	0.0
Chemicals	8.5	22.2	34.6	33.3	27.1	24.5
Ceramics	0.0	0.1	0.0	0.1	0.4	0.3
Metal & metal products	0.3	1.0	7.2	6.9	6.8	9.6
Machinery	0.2	0.0	0.3	0.3	0.0	0.1
Misc. manufactured products	1.7	1.4	2.1	1.9	1.7	1.7
Agricultural products	62.5	66.8	49.8	46.3	42.9	42.5
Marine products	0.0	0.0	0.0	0.0	0.0	0.0
Forest products	0.4	0.5	0.3	1.1	0.3	0.2
Mineral products	0.0	0.8	4.3	7.6	14.7	15.1

REAL EXPORTS

Processed foods	1.0	25.1	10.4	10.4	13.9	11.7
Textiles	6.1	28.6	44.5	45.7	30.8	24.3
Wood products	0.5	3.1	2.8	1.7	0.7	1.9
Chemicals	15.0	9.9	10.9	9.9	11.8	12.3
Ceramics	1.9	1.4	1.4	1.8	1.7	1.9
Metal & metal products	11.2	5.7	4.3	7.7	11.0	11.8
Machinery	0.5	1.9	3.3	4.8	12.4	19.9
Misc. manufactured products	2.5	2.7	5.9	7.7	9.7	9.0
Agricultural products	10.1	2.0	1.4	1.4	2.0	2.0
Marine products	26.5	5.0	4.7	3.4	2.3	2.1
Forest products	6.0	2.8	2.7	0.8	0.6	1.0
Mineral products	18.7	11.8	7.7	4.7	3.1	2.1

REAL IMPORTS

Processed foods	11.3	3.1	0.2	0.9	2.3	2.5
Textiles	2.6	1.3	1.1	1.2	3.1	2.7
Wood products	0.0	0.2	0.0	0.0	0.0	0.0
Chemicals	5.9	17.0	28.5	31.8	27.2	22.1
Ceramics	0.1	0.1	0.1	0.1	0.4	0.2
Metal & metal products	0.3	0.9	6.7	6.5	7.4	14.7
Machinery	0.2	0.1	0.7	0.6	0.0	0.1
Misc. manufactured products	6.4	3.3	4.5	2.4	1.7	1.5
Agricultural products	73.0	73.1	54.8	49.5	44.7	43.3
Marine products	0.0	0.0	0.0	0.0	0.0	0.0
Forest products	0.2	0.3	0.2	1.0	0.3	0.2
Mineral products	0.0	0.6	3.2	6.0	12.9	12.7

Source: Calculated from data from Japanese Ministry of Finance.

TABLE 1.5
RCRs for Japan's Trade with China, Taiwan, and Korea

	1887–1896	1897–1906	1907–1916	1917–1926	1927–1936	1930–1939
			EXPORTS			
Total China						
Primary goods	1.45	1.02	0.95	1.27	1.19	1.06
Textiles	0.12	0.53	0.83	0.72	0.55	0.61
CMM	3.22	1.94	1.48	1.57	1.79	1.66
Other mfd. goods	0.52	1.99	1.23	1.54	1.48	1.32
Taiwan						
Primary goods	—	0.83	1.34	1.07	2.09	2.07
Textiles	—	0.27	0.31	0.26	0.32	0.33
CMM	—	1.64	2.20	2.65	2.09	1.71
Other mfd. goods	—	3.30	1.97	1.84	2.45	1.32
Korea						
Primary goods	—	—	—	0.60	1.94	1.71
Textiles	—	—	—	0.57	0.49	0.59
CMM	—	—	—	1.83	1.86	1.54
Other mfd. goods	—	—	—	1.92	2.08	1.29

IMPORTS

Total China						
Crude cereals	1.82	1.62	1.72	1.37	1.43	1.94
Raw textile materials	3.39	1.86	0.90	0.65	0.52	0.55
Other raw materials	0.06	0.56	0.97	1.69	1.43	1.15
CMM	0.31	0.71	1.22	1.09	1.35	1.15
Other mfd. goods	0.64	0.33	0.24	0.68	0.36	0.42
Taiwan						
Crude cereals	—	2.33	2.08	1.61	1.78	1.94
Raw textile materials	—	0.01	0.01	0.01	0.01	0.01
Other raw materials	—	0.03	0.28	0.36	0.33	0.36
CMM	—	0.01	0.05	0.05	0.06	0.04
Other mfd. goods	—	2.78	4.79	4.66	4.36	4.80
Korea						
Crude cereals	—	—	—	3.84	3.15	2.81
Raw textile materials	—	—	—	0.37	0.16	0.38
Other raw materials	—	—	—	1.23	0.84	0.49
CMM	—	—	—	0.28	0.56	0.82
Other mfd. goods	—	—	—	0.53	0.70	0.76

Note: CMM products include chemicals, metals, metal products, and machinery.

TABLE 1.6
Regional Textile Shares (percent)

	Total China	Taiwan	Korea	Other Areas
1887–1896	1.1	—	—	98.9
1897–1906	10.7	0.6	—	88.7
1907–1916	18.9	2.3	—	78.8
1917–1926	15.8	1.7	5.2	77.3
1927–1936	10.5	3.0	6.4	80.1
1930–1939	13.4	3.1	8.7	74.5

TABLE 1.7
Regional Textile Shares, Excluding Raw Silk (percent)

	Total China	Taiwan	Korea
1887–1896	0.41	—	—
1897–1906	1.04	0.54	—
1907–1916	1.54	0.60	—
1917–1926	1.30	0.47	1.03
1927–1936	0.85	0.51	0.77

countries in the world market, that industry maintained large shares in markets other than China, Taiwan, and Korea. One reason for that success was that the Chinese market had greatly facilitated the development of Japan's textile industry. Rapidly expanding exports of textiles to China had increased earnings, enabling textile enterprises to reduce unit costs and expand their scale of production. Between 1887 and 1906, textile exports to China substantially increased. Cotton yarn exports, in particular, rapidly rose to exceed Britain's China market share by 1915, and again in 1925. According to estimates of the East Asia Economic Research Bureau (EAERB) of the South Manchuria Railway Company, the shares of China's imports of cotton yarn changed as indicated in table 1.8.

Between 1917 and 1926, textiles still constituted Japan's most important exports to China, with the textiles' RCR increasing to 1 (see table 1.4). Cotton fabrics had begun to replace cotton yarn, and Japan began to outstrip Great Britain in the China textile market, particularly for specialties like Shirting Grey (table 1.9).

Because Britain's competitive position depended on special commodities, one should not conclude from the case of Shirting Grey that Japan dominated the entire Chinese textile market. Britain accounted for a rel-

TABLE 1.8
China's Imports of Cotton Yarn (percent)

	U.K.	Japan	Others
1905	71.5	26.4	2.1
1910	58.9	37.8	3.3
1915	47.1	50.7	2.1
1920	52.3	37.4	10.2
1925	32.0	64.7	3.3

Source: Tōa Keizai Chōsakyōkai, Keizaishiryō (Economic Information) (Dairen: Minami Manshū Tetsudō Kabushiki Kaisha, 1927). Estimates based on figures from Japan's Annual Report of Foreign Trade Statistics.

TABLE 1.9
China's Import of Textiles (percent)

	U.K.	Japan	Others
1905	91.1	0.4	8.5
1910	93.6	1.3	5.1
1915	90.3	9.2	0.5
1920	51.2	48.3	0.5
1924	35.8	64.1	0.1

atively large share of China's high-quality textile imports even into the early 1930s. The figures in table 1.9 merely suggest a general trend of Japanese dominance in China's textile markets.

China's share in Japanese exports dropped sharply in the 1930s, especially for textiles. Not only did the Sino-Japanese War interrupt normal foreign trade, but the development of China's textile industry, promoted by Japanese textile technology, had finally enabled Chinese manufacturers to replace textile imports. Although textiles still remained one of Japan's major export commodities to the world, the China market became less attractive to Japanese textile producers after the mid-1920s.

Japan's capital-intensive manufacturing industries only emerged in the early twentieth century. Their impact upon foreign trade is readily seen in the trade figures for the CMM (chemicals, metals and products, and machinery) industries. According to table 1.5, China's RCR for CMM was high in 1887–1896. This cannot be related to Japan's establishment of heavy industry, however, because in that decade Japan's exports to China were still mainly traditional products like materials for Chinese medicines and copperware. The decline in their RCRs for China in the early twentieth century indicates a drop in China's share of these traditional products.

Only after 1910 did Japan export manufacturing products, and the

TABLE 1.10
Regional Shares of Japan's CCM Exports

	1917–1926	1927–1936	1930–1939
Taiwan	8.3	11.5	10.8
Korea	5.2	11.5	16.4
Kwantung Peninsula and "Manchukuo"	11.4	18.8	25.8
Other China	11.8[a]	11.2	10.5
Others	56.3	47.0	36.5

[a] Includes Manchuria.

CMM's RCR began to exceed 1, indicating that China had become a significant importer of these products. The Kwantung Leased Territory and the territory ceded to the South Manchuria Railway, in particular, accounted for a large part of China's imports of CMM products. Japan's CMM exports to Taiwan and Korea also had significantly increased. The changes in the regional shares of Japan's CMM exports given in table 1.10 support these observations.

Because Japan's new large-scale industries still had high unit costs of production, those enterprises found it difficult to break into world markets. Therefore, they had to turn to the privileged markets in the formal Japanese empire to sell their products. China was a relatively unattractive market for such trade, because some Western countries like the United States still controlled a large share of the Chinese market. Japan's CMM exports to Northeast China only rose rapidly after the establishment of Manchukuo, a market that soon consumed one-fourth of Japan's total CMM exports. The exports of these products to Northeast China greatly facilitated the development of Japan's heavy industry in the 1930s.

Meanwhile, the RCRs of China, Taiwan, and Korea for "other manufactured goods" (mainly the products of various light industries) also remained high. Although these exports did not appear to have any great effect on Japan's economy, small and medium-sized Japanese industries still considered China and the two Japanese colonies their major customers.

What of Japan's foreign investment in China? Japanese textile factories had been established in Central China since the mid-1920s, and more of these firms began investing in Northeast China during the 1930s. Because Japan was a capital-poor economy before World War II, the capital outflows from Japan for these investments were limited. Although investing in the textile industry can generally be explained as a strategy for Japanese firms to keep their China market shares, private investments in Manchuria were encouraged by state policies based solely upon political and military considerations, as chapter 5 makes clear.

Japan's Imports

I have stressed the fact that the China market played a smaller role importing from Japan than exporting to it. China's import share fluctuated at around 15 percent from the 1890s to the 1930s, while the share of Japan's imports from mainland China gradually declined. That decline, as in case of Japanese exports, may have been related to the structural changes in Japanese industry.

But China appears to have become more important for Japan as a supplier of such raw materials as cereals and coal. The impact of cereals' RCRs for China, Taiwan, and Korea is very high (table 1.5). This pattern shows that Japanese industrialization depended upon the import of cereals. China's CMM products being exported to Japan also showed high RCRs. Textile raw materials maintained high RCRs between 1887 and 1906, but those ratios declined thereafter. The RCRs were high for Taiwan's "other manufactured goods," which included refined sugar, again showing Japan's dependence upon this preferred source of supply.

The commercialization of agriculture in China during these decades had been facilitated by expanding world demand, in part from Japanese importers of Chinese fertilizer products and agricultural products like foodgrains and fibers (see table 1.11). Natural fertilizer accounted for a large portion of China's chemical exports, although other chemicals began to take a larger share in the 1920s. The composition of agricultural exports also changed, with semiprocessed cereals replacing textile raw materials as China's main agricultural export to Japan. Since textile raw materials came mainly from Central China, and crude cereals from Northeast China, the changing composition of China's agricultural exports to Japan also signaled a regional shift in trade away from Central China to Manchuria.

This changing source of agricultural supply for Japan can be seen in table 1.12, which gives data for raw textile materials and cereals. The importation of natural fertilizers from China was very important for the development of Japanese agriculture. In the late nineteenth century, natural fertilizer made from fish, especially at Sakhalin and Hokkaido, began to be used to boost agricultural yield. This type of fertilizer was gradually supplanted by the less expensive bean-cake fertilizer from Northeast China, and bean cakes remained essential to Japanese agriculture until the expansion of artificial fertilizer production in the mid-1930s.

Textile raw materials like cotton were imported from China mainly during the early stages of the development of Japan's textile industry. As

TABLE 1.11
Shares of Japan's Nominal Exports from China of Chemicals and
Agricultural Products, by Subcategory (percent)

	1887–1896	1897–1906	1907–1916	1917–1926	1927–1936	1930–1938
Chemicals						
Natural fertilizers	5.7	19.8	31.7	28.3	20.6	15.5
Other chemicals	2.8	2.4	2.9	5.0	6.5	9.0
Agricultural products						
Textile raw materials	49.6	42.1	28.6	18.1	11.6	11.0
Cereals	12.9	22.4	17.8	22.2	27.1	29.1
Other agricultural prod.	0.0	2.3	3.4	6.0	4.2	2.4

Note: Figures for "Textile raw materials" as defined in other tables include nonagricultural products and thus differ from the figures presented here.

TABLE 1.12
Sources of Japan's Agricultural Supply (percent)

	Textile raw materials			Cereals			
	China	Korea	Others	China	Taiwan	Korea	Others
1887–1896	49.1	—	50.5	26.3	—	—	73.7
1897–1906	23.3	—	76.7	20.2	4.9	—	74.2
1907–1916	13.0	—	87.0	24.9	15.4	—	59.7
1917–1926	10.1	3.4	86.5	21.2	10.8	19.3	48.7
1927–1936	7.2	2.2	90.6	20.0	16.6	41.3	22.2
1937–1939	6.3	5.7	88.0	18.8	20.2	41.6	19.4

Note: Dashes indicate figures included in "Others" for these years.

overseas commerce grew, however, Indian and Egyptian cotton took over the Japanese market. This shift may also have been due to technological change: the new "ring" spinning machines required higher-quality raw fiber than the Mule machines had, and Indian cotton was longer-staple than Chinese cotton.[9]

Japanese cereal importers from China also had high RCRs. Japan's colonies supplied Japan with the rice it needed, while China supplied soybeans and a variety of other cereals. It should be mentioned that Korean exports of rice to Japan were only made possible by China supplying Korea with various foodgrains.

In sum, China supplied Japanese industry with various raw materials, including cereals, raw cotton, natural fertilizer, and minerals, and this trade certainly proved crucial for Japan's industrialization. As Japan's industrial structure changed, so too did the composition of Japanese imports from China. The case was quite different for Japan's colonies, whose exports remained limited to a small number of commodities.

JAPAN AS A CHINESE EXPORT MARKET

Any analysis of the economic interdependency of China and Japan requires consideration of Japan as a market for Chinese exports. Because Japan's foreign trade by country was positively correlated by ship registration, tracing the volume of foreign trade carried by ship flag from 1872 onward provides a good coverage of the main trends of Chinese trade.

When one compares Japanese shipping with that of Britain in 1927–1931, a remarkable difference in trade amounts is apparent, but if this is

[9] See Kiyokawa Yukihiko, "Nihon membō sekigyō ni okeru ringu bōki no saiyō o megutte" (On ring spinning machines in Japan's textile industry), *Keizai kenkyū* 36, 3 (1985): 214–227.

combined with trade data for country of the United Kingdom and Hong Kong, the differences become much smaller. Japan's "by ship flag" values are also higher than the "by country" data, but this can be explained by the fact that Japanese ships also transported other countries' commodities to China. The "by ship flag" values probably can serve as dummy variables to show trends in the Japanese share of China's markets, because the pattern of those values is similar to the pattern derived from the data on Japanese foreign trade. For the United States, the "by ship flag" data are about half as large as the corresponding "by country" values. Table 1.13, which gives foreign trade data for Manchukuo in addition to those for China, shows the share distribution of China's import market for the period 1887–1937.[10]

From the late nineteenth to the early twentieth centuries, Britain dominated the China market. Textiles were China's major import from Great Britain, but that country also shipped various other industrial products to China. As mentioned above, more intense Japanese competition in the cotton yarn market forced British exporters out of that market after 1900. Britain's share of Chinese textile imports decreased further as Japan became more competitive in other products as well. The Japanese share of Chinese foreign trade also increased after Germany's withdrawal from China's markets after World War II (note the decline of "Others" in 1917–1926). Because the United States exported nontextile product lines with little Japanese or British competition, the American share shows an upward trend, particularly for heavy-industrial goods like machinery and equipment.

Judging from the "by ship flag" data, Britain also held the dominant share of Chinese exports. This does not necessarily mean, however, that it imported large quantities of Chinese commodities, because a good part of those goods would have been shipped to Britain's colonies. One can conclude, however, that Chinese foreign trade was controlled by British merchants until the end of the nineteenth century. Thereafter, Japan's share of the China trade began to increase, as did that of the United States. As the previous section showed, the composition of Japan's imports changed as Japanese industrialization progressed, but Japan remained one of China's most important export markets.

FINAL REMARKS

The changing composition of trade between China and Japan provides part of the economic context by which to understand the process of Jap-

---

[10] Department of Finance, Government of Manchukuo, *Annual Returns of Foreign Trade of Manchukuo*.

TABLE 1.13
Shares of Foreign Trade with China

	By Ship Flag				By Country				
	Japan	U.K.	U.S.	Others	Japan	U.K.	U.S.	Hong Kong	Others
CHINESE EXPORTS									
1887–1891	5.0	55.6	0.7	38.7	—	—	—	—	—
1892–1896	3.9	55.0	0.9	40.2	—	—	—	—	—
1897–1901	8.1	47.7	1.4	42.8	—	—	—	—	—
1902–1906	7.7	44.6	1.8	45.9	—	—	—	—	—
1907–1911	17.2	36.1	1.1	45.6	—	—	—	—	—
1912–1916	25.3	34.4	1.9	38.4	—	—	—	—	—
1917–1921	41.8	30.9	5.4	21.9	—	—	—	—	—
1922–1926	38.3	30.1	8.1	23.5	25.2[a]	6.4[a]	16.3[a]	16.0[a]	26.1[a]
1927–1931	39.1	27.7	6.7	26.5	24.9	6.8	14.4	17.6	36.3
1932–1937[b]					21.1	8.8	14.2	8.1	47.8
CHINESE IMPORTS									
1887–1891	3.0	67.4	0.4	29.2	—	—	—	—	—
1892–1896	2.4	64.3	0.6	32.7	—	—	—	—	—
1897–1901	8.6	58.5	1.0	31.9	—	—	—	—	—
1902–1906	9.4	55.9	2.6	32.1	—	—	—	—	—
1907–1911	16.7	52.4	0.6	30.3	—	—	—	—	—
1912–1916	28.4	44.0	1.1	26.5	—	—	—	—	—
1917–1921	42.7	32.8	6.6	17.9	—	—	—	—	—
1922–1926	35.1	33.3	8.5	23.1	27.9[a]	10.8[a]	16.7[a]	17.7[a]	26.9[a]
1927–1931	37.2	27.8	7.8	27.2	25.2	8.5	18.2	17.5	30.6
1932–1937[b]					27.1	9.8	17.8	2.0	43.3

Source: By ship flag: Hsiao, *China's Foreign Trade*; by country: author's database.

anese imperialism in China. But considering foreign trade in this way is bound to show greater interdependence of trading partners than Japanese economic exploitation and the use of economic power in China. Nonetheless, China did become an important market for both Japan's exports and imports. Japanese textile exports to China both initiated and fostered this industry's development. But critical as the early phase of the textile trade might have been for Japanese industrialization, China still never took more than 30 percent of Japan's total textile exports. Japan's textile production and sales depended heavily on other markets, especially in the developed countries. Japan also exported industrial products to China, particularly after the establishment of Manchukuo, but the colonies of Taiwan and Korea remained more important markets for these same products. Even so, key segments of Japan's industry appeared to have developed a special dependence upon the China market during certain decades.

Just as Japan's trade with China showed that country's growing dependence upon markets in that huge country, so did China develop important economic dependence upon Japan. Raw cotton from China not only supported the early stages of Japan's textile industry but brought additional cash income to farmers and traders in Central China. The expanding export of fertilizers, fibers, and foodgrains to Japan, particularly from China's Northeast, represented an accelerated commercialization of Chinese agriculture. Regional shifts of foreign trade within China toward the expanding Japanese market naturally meant the reallocation of resources with the Chinese economy. Some regions found their production and trade leveling off, but others experienced a new growth spurt in production and trade.

Thus, the picture of foreign trade between these two countries is mixed and complex. Economic interdependence between Japan and China grew more rapidly in this period than at any previous time in the history of these two countries. Key segments of each country's economy were vitally affected as the composition of trade changed. Foreign trade proved to be a powerful engine of economic growth for different regions and industries within both Japan and China. The pattern of foreign trade described above shows very clearly that by the 1920s, Japan had become China's most important trading partner. Sino-Japanese trade trends clearly reflect the new Japanese dominance in the Chinese economy.

CHAPTER 2

Japan's Big-Three Service Enterprises in China, 1896–1936

William D. Wray

During the decade between the Sino-Japanese and Russo-Japanese wars, Japan's key service firms rapidly built internationally integrated trading networks. By providing commodities that Japan lacked, China played a key, and sometimes decisive, role in the strategies developed by these service firms and in the operations of their international networks. The most important of these firms were Mitsui Bussan (Mitsui Trading Company), Nippon Yūsen Kaisha (NYK, Japan Mail Steamship Company), and the government-controlled Yokohama Shōkin Ginkō (Yokohama Specie Bank). The services they performed for manufacturing industries helped to change Japan's industrial structure by expanding opportunities for manufacturing in Japan. These service firms engaged in numerous transactions that the manufacturers could not perform. They included the provision of foreign exchange facilities (especially important because, although Japan went on the gold standard in 1897, China remained on silver), the carrying of freight at lower rates than Western competitors, gathering of information about markets and sources of supply, handling of international trade negotiations, mediation of technology transfer, and creation of multi-institution trading networks.

These transactions were important in several categories of trade with China: bilateral trade (involving manufactures, resources, or agricultural commodities); third-country trade (that is, trade carried on by Japanese firms between China and countries other than Japan); direct investments (especially after World War I); and numerous loans and credit arrangements (another form of bilateralism, with a more political tinge). This chapter argues that the key service firms relied heavily on third-country trade in building their international networks, and that much Sino-Japanese trade that seemed bilateral was often part of a larger international operation. To date, however, most Western scholars of Japanese business relations with China have studied the bilateral dimension, in part because they have chosen topics like loans or manufacturing. This approach has defined questions in certain preset ways, such as whether Japanese firms found it more profitable to participate in China trade or in trade with the West.

In contrast to this approach, I will suggest that there was no bifurcation, no dichotomy, between China and the West in the business strategy of Japan's largest service firms. Both areas became integrated into an international network. The original impetus to this growth came from the dependence of manufacturing on imported raw materials (raw cotton and iron ore) and advanced machinery. While building networks in support of manufacturing, the service firms developed new interests in third-country trade that transcended the dichotomy between China and the West.

The activity of Japan's shipping firms, trading companies, and banks also had important implications for the regional nature of trade in China. Especially before the Russo-Japanese War, the Yangtze became the principal region within China in the international networks of these firms. Shanghai quickly developed into a kind of hub, linking the Yangtze with international markets and serving as a center for transactions involving the overseas trade of North China.

Besides these three service firms, there were numerous Japanese business enterprises whose functions were also relevant. First, some had similar roles as competitors or subsidiaries of the big three. For example, by World War I private zaibatsu banks began to challenge the international dominance of the Yokohama Specie Bank. In shipping, the Osaka Commercial Shipping Company (OSK), about a decade behind the NYK in opening transoceanic lines, developed its China business even earlier than the NYK. In 1907, these two firms established a subsidiary, Nisshin Kisen (Japan–China Steamship Company), which increased the trade between the Yangtze and overseas markets.

Second, there were some trading enterprises such as Ōkura and Mitsubishi whose ventures were more bilateral. Both were involved in mining in China. This activity forms the basis for some discussion of the Hanyehping Company, the industrial complex south of Hankow that was the subject of well-known takeover attempts by the Japanese in the 1910s.[1] The trading companies imported iron ore from Hanyehping for the Japanese steel industry. This bilateral trade, though, was itself part of a multilateral process, for much of the machinery and equipment for steel manufacturing had to be imported from the West. Thus, the direct im-

---

[1] Ōkura had most of its China investments in Manchuria. Because of space limitations and because Manchuria is dealt with in other parts of this volume, however, I do not discuss direct investments there unless they bear directly on the three firms that are the focus of this chapter. Yokohama Shōkin Ginkō cited hereafter as YSG in titles of frequently cited works.

ports from China and the trade with the West together constituted a vertically integrated network.

Third, colonial banks like the Bank of Taiwan and the Bank of Chōsen obviously performed more of a regional function. However, they too became part of international networks, the Bank of Taiwan primarily through ties with Suzuki Shōten, and the Bank of Chōsen through its financing of trade involving both Korea and Manchuria, which included their overseas trade. In general, I will deal with these other firms mentioned here primarily to provide a broader perspective on the activities of the big three.

There was an important connection, of course, between the China trade and the role of key service firms in changing Japan's industrial structure. During the early period of trade with China, from the 1870s to the late 1890s, service firms were involved primarily in bilateral activity, first establishing transport ties and by the 1890s promoting imports of raw materials and exports of manufactured goods. There developed a mutual dependence between this pattern of trade and the international networks the service firms began constructing in the late 1890s. These networks strengthened Japan's export trade with China, but they were often dependent on profits from third country trade involving China. The World War I decade was characterized by increasing tension in Sino-Japanese relations. The activities of Japan's service firms were one of the sources of this tension through their attempts to take over Hanyehping (a reflection of the rise of heavy industry in Japan) and the China Merchants' Steam Navigation Company.

During the interwar years, the function of Japanese shipping in China began to shift from that of a link in trading networks to support for Japan's diplomatic presence and military actions in China. Shipping acts as a bridge to focus on Japan's changing industrial structure from World War I to the mid-1930s. Two key features of this change were direct investment in China by Japan's light industry, and the development of new products based on more technically sophisticated manufacturing. Service firms supported these changes in several ways. Light industry benefited from their financing and from the links they provided with their third-country trade; while the new manufacturing firms depended, at least initially, on their marketing ability in China. These changes were in the forefront of Japan's evolving comparative advantage and had strategic implications. Yet, by this period there was an increasing bifurcation between these economic goals and Japan's military and diplomatic policies, which began to take on a kind of dysfunctional role with regard to Japan's industrial structure, limiting opportunities for Japan's new business ventures in China.

THE RISE OF INTERNATIONAL BUSINESS, 1875–1919

Early Services and Bilateral Trade

The major features of Japan's early bilateral trade with China were, first, the steamship line between Yokohama and Shanghai, started by Mitsubishi in 1875 and taken over by its successor, the NYK, in 1885; and second, Mitsui Bussan's export of coal from the Miike Mine in Kyushu, which began in the late 1870s. Bilateral trade quickly diversified after the Sino-Japanese War. The peace treaty, with its most-favored-nation clause, for the first time gave Japan the same privileges enjoyed by Westerners, enabling Japanese business to perform a broader range of services. The most important privilege was the right to navigate on China's rivers. That, together with the acquisition of concession areas in central cities like Shanghai and Hankow, helped firms to widen their network of branch offices, thereby lowering their transaction costs. This feature deserves more attention than the right to manufacture in China, which Japan also gained but which was less important in the short run. The first major shipping firm to take advantage of these new rights was the OSK. Beginning in 1898, it opened subsidized lines on the Yangtze and soon increased its share, despite concerted opposition from the pool (the freight conference, or cartel) existing among two British firms and the China Merchants' Steam Navigation Company.

Rapid increase in trade with North China and prospects of linking this with the new routes on the Yangtze induced greater competition between the OSK and the NYK on the direct Kobe-Tientsin line. Also, in 1903 Mitsui Bussan decided to set up a shipping division to facilitate handling of increasingly important commodities such as raw cotton, soybeans, lumber, railroad ties, rice, and sugar. Prior to this, Mitsui's dependence on China had experienced a sudden increase, as its Chinese branches (including Hong Kong) had contributed 20.3 percent of total profits in the 1900–1902 period, compared to only 10.0 percent in 1897–1899. China, in fact, may have been more important to Mitsui in the early years of the century than at any other time. As measured in terms of overall transactions, the contribution of the company's China branches (including Manchuria) fell from 22.9 percent in 1904 to 19.1 percent in 1909.[2]

[2] Ishii Kanji, "Nisshin sengo keiei," *Iwanami kōza, Nihon rekishi*, vol. 16, *kindai* 3 (Tokyo: Iwanami Shoten, 1976), p. 69. Nihon Keieishi Kenkyūjo, ed., "Kōhon Mitsui Bussan Kabusiki Kaisha 100 nenshi," vol. 1 (Tokyo, 1978), pp. 285–286. According to *Mitsui jigyōshi, Honpen*, vol. 3, no. 1 (Tokyo: Mitsui Bunko, 1980), pp. 330–331, by 1920 China accounted for 17.6 percent (including 3.0 percent for Hong Kong) of Mitsui's trade. Trade, however, as measured here by exports and imports, does not seem to be the same category as transactions by branch, as in my text.

Some of the exports to China handled by Mitsui before World War I were really part of wider international business rather than strictly "bilateral" trade. For example, in 1901, 83.2 percent of the coal imported into Shanghai came from Japan, with at least a third of it consumed as bunker fuel by Western or Japanese shipping companies operating on both international and domestic Chinese routes. Mitsui remained by far the largest supplier for this market until well into the interwar years.[3] Cotton, the main commodity in the China trade by the mid-1890s, provides the best-known illustration of the trade's international dimension, embracing the three main service firms. Shifting its main source of raw cotton from China to India, Japan's spinning industry became the heart of what is referred to as "organized entrepreneurship," a cooperative effort involving Mitsui Bussan and specialized cotton traders, who imported raw cotton and exported cotton yarn to China; the Yokohama Specie Bank, which provided financing for foreign exchange; and the NYK, which cut freight rates on both imports and exports by 30 to 50 percent below the Western-controlled rates prevailing in 1893.[4]

Through its involvement in organized entrepreneurship, Mitsui came to be known as an "organizer of the economy," as a *private* force for changing Japan's industrial structure. This broad influence enabled Mitsui to impose particular institutional features on the trade with China. Though beneficial to the manufacturing sector, Mitsui's organizing function often appeared more a mechanism of control than of cooperation. In its contracts with cotton manufacturers, Mitsui often gained sole agency status, that is, "tying" arrangements that usually gave it exclusive marketing rights. Mitsui would also supply raw cotton to a firm, often on condition that it use Mitsui's excellent sales network in China and buy textile machinery imported from Platt Brothers, a British firms for which Mitsui acted as sole agent in East Asia. Under this distribution monopoly, Mitsui received exclusive commitments from manufacturers but retained for itself options that allowed more flexible business dealings. This sometimes led to conflict with the manufacturer, though the latter could

[3] Yamashita Naotō, "Nihon teikokushugi seiritsuki no Higashi Ajia sekitan shijō to Mitsui Bussan: Shanhai shijō o chūshin ni," in Shakai Keizai Shigakkai, ed., *Enerugī to keizai hatten* (Fukuoka: Nishi Nihon Bunka Kyōkai, 1979), pp. 275, 286. Yamashita gives 1903 figures for steamship company purchases (showing 93.0 percent supplied by the Japanese) that omit several firms, including the NYK, which stopped at Shanghai on international routes. The consumption of bunker coal was thus likely even higher than his estimates. The China Merchants' bought only 18.8 percent of the Japanese coal, still five times higher than their purchase from Chinese mines. Cf. Yamamura Rikuo, "Dai ichiji taisengo ni okeru Mitsui Bussan no kaigai shinshutsu," in Fujii Mitsuo et al., eds., *Nihon takokuseki kigyō no shiteki tenkai*, vol. 1 (Tokyo: Ōtsuki Shoten, 1979), pp. 76–80.

[4] For details, see William D. Wray, *Mitsubishi and the N.Y.K., 1870–1914: Business Strategy in the Japanese Shipping Industry* (Cambridge: Harvard University Press, 1984), pp. 293–308.

occasionally win concessions from Mitsui. A case in the cement industry illustrates this. Through its contract with Mitsui, Onoda Cement exported more than a quarter of its production. Taiwan and Korea were the largest markets, but by 1907, 4.5 percent of production went to Shanghai and 2.4 percent to Dairen. The contract, however, gave Mitsui the right to distribute for other cement firms when Onoda could not meet projected demand out of its own production. Sometimes Mitsui went considerably beyond the "spirit" of the contract by signing, for example, an exclusive marketing deal in 1910 with China's Hupei Cement Company, which supplied Shanghai. Following protests from Onoda, Mitsui agreed to restrict its deals with other firms to temporary periods of insufficient output by Onoda and to invest in the firm to build up its capacity.[5]

In 1897, when Japan went on the gold standard, two monetary problems continued to obstruct Sino-Japanese trade. One was the nature of Chinese money. China used silver, though not in the sense of a standard like gold. Since silver was a commodity in China, its fluctuations according to local or international conditions affected the value of the country's currency, sometimes resulting in sudden and drastic shifts in its capacity to conduct trade. The main unit used in international trade was the Shanghai tael. Between 1897 and 1914, the value of one hundred yen fluctuated between about sixty-five and ninety-five taels. A second problem was the strong competitive position of Western banks, especially the British Hongkong and Shanghai Banking Corporation, in the handling of China's foreign exchange. They had two competitive advantages over the Yokohama Specie Bank: they offered lower interest rates and charged about one-quarter tael less for every hundred yen of exchange transaction.[6] The Yokohama Specie Bank, created in 1880 partly to accumulate a supply of specie, originally had a monopoly over government foreign exchange, and this helped to increase its share of the country's foreign exchange business from 3.7 percent in 1882 to 31.0 percent in 1886. The next year it lost its status as the exclusive government agent, and then in 1889 its foreign exchange business was put on a different footing through an agreement under which the Bank of Japan provided it with a ¥10 million permanent loan (doubled in 1899) to finance foreign exchange and began rediscounting the Specie Bank's foreign exchange bills at 2 percent.[7] This was well below the rate at which the Specie Bank dis-

[5] Compare Matsumoto Hiroshi, *Mitsui zaibatsu no kenkyū* (Tokyo: Yoshikawa Kōbunkan, 1979), pp. 476–483; and Nihon Keieishi Kenkyūjo, ed., *Onoda Semento 100 nenshi* (Osaka: Dōsha, 1981), pp. 127–146.

[6] *Kōhon Mitsui*, p. 171; Kojima Hitoshi, *Nihon no kin hon'isei jidai, 1897–1917* (Tokyo: Nihon Keizai Hyōronsha, 1981), pp. 125–127.

[7] Tokyo Ginkō, ed., *YSG zenshi*, vol. 2 (Tokyo: Tōyō Keizai Shimpōsha, 1980), pp. 64–

counted bills of its customers. By 1911, it had come to handle 44.8 percent of Mitsui Bussan's foreign exchange and 52.3 percent for the country as a whole.[8]

Numerous reforms between 1897 and 1906, which contributed to this increasing share, led to changes in the character of the bank. In 1894, it had done 94.9 percent of its business with Europe and the United States and only 5.0 percent with China. Compared to a Western-style, specialized trading and financial organ, it was viewed as a trading bank without a designated area, in contrast to the colonial-style institutions like the Hongkong and Shanghai Banking Corporation and the Deutsch-Asiatische Bank. Exporters, especially in the cotton spinning industry centered in the Kansai, began calling for a special China agency. Supported by chambers of commerce and industry in the major cities, this movement crystallized in a draft bill for a Japan-China Bank (Nisshin Ginkō). Accepted by the cabinet in 1902 (though opposed by Shibusawa Eiichi and Mitsui Bussan's Masuda Takashi on the grounds that it would hurt the Specie Bank's profits), it failed to pass before a Diet dissolution.[9]

While the Nisshin Bank proved abortive, the Yokohama Specie Bank reaped the benefit of the proposals. There were three categories of reform. First, the government granted three million yen in 1897 and ten million yen in 1899 to the bank as a foreign exchange fund to finance cotton exports to China. This raised the share of China branches in the bank's overall operations to 16.3 percent in 1899, initiating a shift away from its exclusively Western orientation. Second, with changes in its documentary export bills in 1899, the Bank lengthened from ten to sixty days the time that a Chinese importer of Japanese textiles would be given to pay after acceptance of bill, the same time British banks had been giving Indian yarn exports to China. Finally, in 1902 the bank began to issue demand drafts as circulating notes, as well as silver yen notes for use as currency. These were issued first through the Tientsin and Shanghai branches in late 1902 and then from Newchwang in early 1903. The number of these notes grew rapidly, especially as the bank had to increase the

---

66; *Yokohama Shōkin Ginkō shi furoku* (Tokyo: Nishida Shoten, 1975), no. 82, pp. 438–444; Hijikata Susumu, *Yokohama Shōkin Ginkō* (Tokyo: Kyōikusha, 1980), p. 78.

[8] Matsumoto, *Mitsui*, p. 550, shows the Hongkong and Shanghai Banking Corporation with 20.3 percent of Mitsui Bussan's business and Mitsui handling 16.7 percent internally. Cf. Ishii Kanji, "Kin'yū kōzō," in Ōishi Kaichirō, ed., *Nihon sangyō kakumei no kenkyū*, vol. 1 (Tokyo: Tokyo Daigaku Shuppankai, 1975), pp. 99–100, esp. table 7; and Kojima, *Nihon no kin hon'isei jidai*, p. 124. For a breakdown by commodity for 1910, see *Yokohama-shi shi*, vol. 4:ge (Dōhen, 1965), p. 740.

[9] Hijikata, *Yokohama Shōkin Ginkō*, p. 122; Ishii, "Nisshin sengo," p. 70; Furusawa Kōzō, "Yokohama Shōkin Ginkō jōrei no seitei to kawase seisaku," in Shibuya Ryūichi, ed., *Nihon tokushu kin'yū rippōshi* (Tokyo: Waseda Daigaku Shuppanbu, 1976), p. 136. On the Nisshin Bank, see Namikata Shōichi, "Nisshin Ginkō hōan no sakusei katei," in ibid., pp. 141–184.

issue to handle army expenditures during the Russo-Japanese War. Yet, the original purpose behind the notes had little to do with military strategy; rather, it was to protect Japanese traders in China against falling silver values after the Boxer Rebellion, which put them at risk in using Chinese currency. Nevertheless, the result of this move into currency extended the bank's functions beyond foreign exchange, giving it a dual character somewhat akin to a colonial financial institution.[10]

The year 1906 saw export promotion measures for Manchuria similar to those taken for China in general between 1897 and 1902. In June, the Yokohama Specie Bank began discounting documentary export bills of no more than four months' maturity at the special rate of 4.5 percent, well below the prevailing 7.0 percent rate.[11] Then, in November it signed a contract with Mitsui Bussan obliging it to accept Specie Bank notes as payment from Manchurian importers of Japanese exports. In return, to stimulate imports from Manchuria it lowered interest charges on import bills from 7 percent to 6.5 percent for companies doing more than three million yen in annual business.[12] This agreement may have been contingent on Mitsui coming to terms with the South Manchuria Railway (SMR). The government directive to the SMR included among its responsibilities "consignment sales of important railway freight." Since selling on consignment was Mitsui's principal business, this wording threatened its advance into the Manchurian market. After applying heavy pressure on the government in August, Mitsui managed to have the offending clause removed. The SMR then agreed to give it special discounts on soybeans shipped to Dairen and named two Mitsui men among its first seven directors.[13] The sequence of events in this case suggests that Mitsui was more adept at exploiting colonial ventures than initiating them.

Third-Country Trade

The perception during the Nisshin Bank debate of the Yokohama Specie Bank as a Western-oriented institution was justified, but the same could have been said of the NYK, and even of Mitsui Bussan, though to a lesser

[10] Furusawa, "Yokohama Shōkin Ginkō," pp. 135–137; Uno Kyūgo, *Nihon kin'yū hattatsushi* (Tokyo: Keizai Jōhōsha, 1925), pp. 180–181.

[11] This meant that a Japanese exporter could receive immediate payment for his Manchuria-bound goods, less the 4.5 percent discounted by the Yokohama Specie Bank. Or, if the exporter waited four months, he could receive the full face value of his bill. For transactions over five million yen, a 4 percent rate applied. *YSG zenshi*, vol. 2, pp. 110–111.

[12] The four months' maturity also applied to these bills. In November 1904, the Specie Bank had been forced to extend the earlier sixty-day period on exchange bills to ninety days in response to a similar move by the Hongkong and Shanghai Banking Corporation. *YSG zenshi*, vol. 2, p. 116; *YSG shi furoku*, no. 152, pp. 814–817; *Kōhon Mitsui*, p. 193.

[13] *Mitsui jigyōshi*, pp. 56–57.

extent. Clearly, all three institutions were primarily international, not regional, firms. Though Mitsui had established its London branch in 1880, with the Yokohama Specie Bank following in 1884, the major impetus to the expansion of international networks came from the opening of the NYK's shipping line to Europe in 1896. After this, third-country trade grew quickly. Unfortunately, differences in statistical categories of profits or business income make comparison between these three institutions very difficult. The most that can be offered are rough estimates. Between 1900 and 1913, the NYK earned approximately half of its income on lines to Europe and America and about one-third in "domestic and near-seas" lines. Between 1899 and 1904, the Yokohama Specie Bank did about three-quarters of its foreign exchange transactions (which by definition excludes the "domestic" category) with the West and less than one-fifth with China. Of the three, Mitsui Bussan seems to have been the least dependent on the West and the most involved in China. Expressed as transactions by branches, its volume of business with Europe and America was roughly the same as with China in the 1907–1909 period. In terms of total imports and exports, its European and American trade was about three times that with China in 1916.[14]

This comparison concerns the functions of the three firms, but the different character of their business makes it difficult to tell the degree of interregional dependence from the statistical breakdown of their business by area. Yet it is clear that third-country trade became increasingly important after the late 1890s. This suggests that China played a more decisive role in the firms' operations than figures showing simply a regional breakdown of business would indicate. Mitsui's third-country trade grew from 0.3 percent of its business in 1897 to 15.5 percent in 1912. And between 1910 and 1919 it increased seventeenfold.[15] Probably most of this depended on China. At first, Mitsui became involved in China more for its role in Asian markets (including India) than for third-country trade, but by World War I it had become virtually impossible to separate these two categories. Third-country trade was the principal reason for NYK interest in China, while the Yokohama Specie Bank often involved the London money market even in bilateral foreign exchange transactions between China and Japan.

NYK dependence on China arose from the unbalanced trade of its European line, which usually contributed 40 percent of the firm's revenue.[16]

[14] Compare Wray, *Mitsubishi and the NYK*, p. 528; Furusawa, "Yokohama Shōkin Ginkō," pp. 136–137; *Kōhon Mitsui*, pp. 285–286; and *Mitsui jigyōshi*, pp. 330–331.

[15] Morikawa Hidemasa, *Nihon zaibatsushi* (Tokyo: Kyōikusha, 1978), pp. 118–120; *Kōhon Mitsui*, p. 298.

[16] For more detailed comments on the connection between the NYK's European and China business, see Wray, *Mitsubishi and the NYK*, pp. 332–355.

Before World War I, there was generally plentiful cargo for the eastbound line from Europe because of imports of machinery and equipment. But in 1900 Japan sent only 21.6 percent of its exports to Europe, which provided Japan with 44.0 percent of its imports. At that time, Europe-bound NYK ships were sometimes loaded to only one-fifth capacity. To sustain its westbound service, the company hoped to carry Chinese exports like soybeans, vegetable oils, grains and cereals, tea, and hides and skins to Europe. The freight conference between Europe and Japan created obstacles to this strategy but, after a fight, in January 1902 the NYK secured conference permission to call at Shanghai en route to Europe.

To maximize its use of Shanghai, the NYK developed a "feeder" strategy of opening lines in China that would connect with its services to Japan and the West. Its first move in this direction was to take a 20 percent interest in the Hunan Steamship Company, a Japanese venture supported by banks and trading companies and set up in 1902 to run between Hankow and Changsha. A second and larger investment was the purchase in 1903 of a small British firm, McBain and Company, which had the best wharfage facilities on the Yangtze, especially at Hankow. However, British firms so frustrated this effort by refusing to let the NYK take over McBain's lease of his Hankow berths that by the time the NYK acquired its own berth in the French concession in 1906, the OSK had substantially improved its Yangtze lines. In response, the NYK ordered three new three-thousand-ton steamers.

The battle among Japanese lines on the Yangtze and vigorous competition from a French firm, the Compagnie Asiatique de Navigation, which aimed to link up with the Peking-Hankow Railway, prompted the Japanese government to intervene and force a merger.[17] A new, subsidized company, Nisshin Kisen, was established in 1907 essentially as a joint venture of the OSK and the NYK. Viewing Nisshin Kisen as a "national policy company," Takamura Naosuke has argued that "by greatly accelerating the expansion of trade between Japan and the central Yangtze region, to a certain extent it performed a function analogous to that of the SMR in Manchuria."[18] When it was formed, Nisshin Kisen already had excess tonnage, which government policy forced it to maintain. With this it succeeded in offering extensive guarantees to shippers, cutting

[17] Kokaze Hidemasa, "Teikokushugi keiseiki ni okeru Nihon kaiungyō," *Shigaku zasshi* 92, 10 (October 1983): 8; *Nisshin Kisen Kabushiki Kaisha 30 nenshi oyobi tsuiho* (Dōshahen, 1941), p. 15.

[18] Takamura Naosuke, *Nihon shihonshugi shiron* (Tokyo: Minerva Shobō, 1980), p. 124. The "to a certain extent" refers to the fact that Nisshin Kisen did not have the territorial administration or other semigovernmental powers of the SMR. See also Kokaze, "Teikokushugi," p. 11, who concludes that Nisshin Kisen "functioned as the main artery of Japan's economic advance into the central Yangtze region."

freight rates and taking substantial business away from the British and the China Merchants' line.

Even before 1907, the impact of Japanese shipping on Hankow had been impressive. As a Chinese port, in 1902 Hankow ranked fourth behind Shanghai, Tientsin, and Canton in importing foreign goods. Over the next three years, its foreign imports rose at an annual rate of 14.5 percent and it moved into second place behind Shanghai. Also, even before the Russo-Japanese War, Japanese cotton yarn accounted for 79 percent of imported yarn in the central Yangtze region, but after the war its share there grew to 91 percent, overwhelming Indian exports.[19] After 1907, Nisshin Kisen continued to facilitate this growing bilateral trade, but, more so than its predecessors, it influenced the westbound transshipment trade at Shanghai. The British had tried to thwart this by offering 40 percent discounts on Europe-bound China freight. But by 1911 the British trading firm Butterfield & Swire concluded that the Nisshin Kisen had a "practical monopoly of the carriage of European cargo from Hankow."[20] This had earlier helped to sustain the NYK's European line during the recession after the Russo-Japanese War, temporarily making the westbound voyage more profitable than the eastbound.

Most scholarship on the third-country trade of Japanese firms has focused on Mitsui Bussan. It became especially active in this field after Yamamoto Jōtarō became its Shanghai branch head in 1901. On the import side, it took advantage of China's railway building by importing railway construction equipment and Oregon pine from the United States. Mitsui's international branch network also gave it the capacity to react to short-term trends. For example, when copper came into greater use as currency in China in 1904–1905, Mitsui supplied most of the copper bullion imported into Shanghai. During World War I, it exploited the suspension of beet sugar shipments from Europe by supplying China with sugar from Java.[21] Generally, exports generated the larger share of third-country trade involving China. Though virtually all Japan's raw silk exports went to America, usually half or more of China's were sold to Europe. Mitsui began to handle Shanghai exports in 1906 and Canton's in 1911. Later, it set up a silk filature in Hankow to export thread to Lyons,

[19] Kokaze, "Teikokushugi," p. 11. How much did Japanese shipping have to do with these increases? One answer is that after 1902 the Germans seem to have cut back on planned investment because of Japanese competition, while the French firm mentioned here did not enter until 1903 and withdrew in 1911.

[20] John Swire & Sons Archive, School of Oriental and African Studies, University of London, JSSI 1/15, January 13, 1911, p. 228; Wray, *Mitsubishi and the NYK*, pp. 384–394; Kokaze, "Teikokushugi," p. 10; Itō Takeo, ed., *Murata Shōzō tsuisōroku* (Osaka: OSK, 1959), p. 306.

[21] *Kōhon Mitsui*, pp. 221–223, 248–250; *Mitsui jigyōshi*, pp. 352–353.

became a supplier of silk reeling equipment, and took a leading role in forming export cartels. During the interwar years, it increased its share of the business, becoming the largest exporter of silk from both Shanghai (a 12.0 percent share) and Canton (29.8 percent) by 1931.[22] Whereas Mitsui handled this as an export shipper, virtually all of the silk bound for Europe was transported by firms belonging to the freight conference between Europe and East Asia.[23] The NYK, the conference's principal Japanese member, carried silk from Shanghai and Hong Kong and tea from Hong Kong.[24]

By far the largest China export in the third-country trade was soybeans. Mitsui began importing them into Japan from the Newchwang area of Manchuria as early as 1889. After the Russo-Japanese War, it began exporting to Europe, and by 1910 its income from this third-country trade in soybeans had reached fifteen million yen. Japan itself remained the largest market until being overtaken by Europe in the interwar years.[25] It was not just the large firms like Mitsui that were involved, however. The small firms provide a useful contrast, particularly in their connection with banks. Kanematsu Shōten, established in Kobe in 1889 primarily to carry on direct trade with Australia, soon developed into a general trading company by diversifying the range of commodities it dealt in, such as wool, cowhides, silk, wheat, and flour. In 1899, with a grand total of thirty-six members, twenty-seven of whom were in the head office, five in Tokyo, four in Sydney, three in Shanghai, and the owner himself in Newchwang, the firm began exporting Chinese soybean oil to Australia. Following the Boxer Rebellion, however, it came upon hard times and could not obtain further bank credit. To the rescue came the Yokohama Specie Bank with emergency financing and some harsh conditions, such as the closure of overseas branches and a staff cutback. Within a few years, Kanematsu had reopened these overseas branches, except for the Sydney office, and by 1918 it had a capital of two million yen.[26]

[22] Lillian M. Li, *China's Silk Trade: Traditional Industry in the Modern World, 1842–1937* (Cambridge: Harvard University Press, 1981), pp. 194–198; *Kōhon Mitsui*, pp. 221–222, 368–369, 458–466.

[23] William D. Wray, "NYK and the Commercial Diplomacy of the Far Eastern Freight Conference, 1896–1956," in Yui Tsunehiko and Nakagawa Keiichiro, eds., *Business History of Shipping: Strategy and Structure* (Tokyo: Tokyo University Press, 1985), pp. 279–305.

[24] Shares appear in P & O Agency and Department Reports, P & O 4/35 to 4/57, P & O Archives, Greenwich Maritime Museum.

[25] *Kōhon Mitsui*, pp. 224, 259–260; Takamura, *Shihonshugi*, p. 133, n. 13; Mitsubishi Shōji Kabushiki Kaisha, ed., *Ritsugyō bōeki roku* (Tokyo: Dōsha, 1958), pp. 422–429. On shipping from South Manchuria to Europe, see Wray, *Mitsubishi and the NYK*, pp. 398, 428–429.

[26] Morikawa Hidemasa, "Sōgō shōsha no seiritsu to ronri," in Miyamoto Mataji et al., eds., *Sōgō shōsha no keieishi* (Tokyo: Tōyō Keizai Shimpōsha, 1976), pp. 73–75.

During the late Meiji and early Taishō periods, Mitsui Bussan consistently handled 20 percent of Japanese foreign trade. This statistic, however, does not include third-country trade and therefore understates Mitsui's influence. Third-country trade was generally not separate from or additional to bilateral trade; rather, it was often linked to it. Without the third-country trade there would have been gaps in the flow of services involving the bilateral dimension. Furthermore, the information gained through the third-country trading networks enabled service firms to act more effectively on behalf of manufacturers. In summary, the three major institutional features that stimulated third-country trade in late Meiji were, first, the establishment of the NYK's European line after the Sino-Japanese War; second, Nisshin Kisen, which strengthened the trade's base area in the Yangtze region; and third, the acquisition of territory in South Manchuria that opened up new opportunities. The structural pattern of this growth in late Meiji put Japanese firms in a favorable position to exploit World War I, when investment in third-country trade paid immense dividends because of the temporary withdrawal of many European firms.

Trade Personnel and Branches

The leaders of the Yangtze business community are well known to us by name. Mitsui's Yamamoto Jōtarō was certainly the doyen of the community. For one thing, he had seniority. He had served off and on in the Shanghai branch since 1887 and had been a pioneer in the third-country trade as vice-head of the branch in the late 1890s. He had also been an initiator of the bean trade, serving in Newchwang in 1891, when by his account he was the only Japanese businessman stationed there.[27] Yamamoto and his henchman, Mori Kaku, are best known in Western historiography as "China hands" acting as a kind of private vanguard in the Japanese advance into Manchuria in the late 1920s and early 1930s. They have not been studied in the West for what they were in 1900—businessmen trying to open opportunities for their companies. Another major figure was Murata Shōzō of the OSK, perhaps the most brilliant young recruit along the Yangtze, known to political historians as a cabinet minister under Konoe in 1940–1941 but to business historians as the most capable shipping executive of the interwar years. Murata, who went to China in 1901 at the age of twenty-four, was a member of OSK's "Shanghai Cabinet," a reference to the talented individuals the company dispatched to China at this time, three of whom later became OSK presidents.

The NYK, the Yokohama Specie Bank, and Mitsui Bussan constituted

[27] *Yamamoto Jōtarō: denki* (Tokyo: Denki Hensankai, 1942), pp. 73–136; *Kōhon Mitsui*, pp. 221–222.

the Big Three in Shanghai. It was said that when a young Japanese businessman arrived in Shanghai, he went first to the NYK, next to the Japanese consulate, and only then to the Chinese Customs office.[28] Mitsui Bussan also enjoyed a kind of elevated status, for its branch head was the only Japanese businessman whose private residence was in the British concession. Both the NYK and Mitsui Bussan had been in Shanghai for several decades. The Yokohama Specie Bank arrived in 1893 and then returned after the war. But Mitsui and the OSK (before the formation of Nisshin Kisen in 1907) probably did the most to penetrate the central Yangtze region. Mitsui's Hankow office, established in 1900 (again temporarily because of the Boxer Rebellion), served an enormous territory embracing Honan, Kiangsi, and Hunan, besides its base in Hupeh.[29] The OSK had set up a branch in Hankow as early as 1898. Several years later, it sent representatives to Chungking as part of an abortive plan to start a steamship service from Ichang. It also had representatives in Foochow (from 1900) and Amoy (1902) to oversee its South China shipping, which connected with its lines to Taiwan.[30] The Japanese concessions in these cities had their own local color. As a shipping center, Shanghai had a "Nagasaki" flavor. Someone dubbed it "Shanghai City of Nagasaki Prefecture." On the other hand, the cotton trading company Nihon Menka and other Osaka firms so influenced Hankow that the Kansai dialect prevailed in its local inns and restaurants. The OSK took things a step further in Hankow by using berths in the "old" (that is, Chinese) city outside the Japanese concession.

Not all the employees in these branches were dispatched from Japan after careful selection by the head office. Some were hired on the spot from a kind of ronin-style labor market. In one case, Hori Shin, later chairman of Kansai Electric Power Company, came to Shanghai in his early twenties to work for a large Japanese retail outfit, where he learned both Chinese and English. Being ambitious, he sought a higher calling with the Big Three. But in his first interview with Mitsui, he developed a dislike for Yamamoto Jōtarō and instead caught on with the OSK.

The experience of these businessmen soon had multilateral as well as bilateral implications. Shortly after Nisshin Kisen was formed, Murata went to the United States to work on the OSK's Hong Kong–Tacoma line. The varied expertise he thus acquired helped him plan the OSK's innovative round-the-world line in 1918. Similarly, Mitsui's Yamamoto spent most of 1900 in America, in between service as vice-head and head of the

[28] *Murata*, pp. 18, 289–307; Nihon Keieishi Kenkyūjo, ed., *Fūtō no hibi: Shōsen Mitsui 100 nenshi* (Tokyo: Mitsui-OSK, 1984), pp. 97–103.

[29] On some of these early branches and offices, see *Osaka Shōsen Kabushiki Kaisha 50 nenshi* (Osaka: Dōsha, 1934), pp. 752–764.

[30] *Yamamoto*, p. 177.

Shanghai branch, preparing, in part, to expand Sino-American trade![31] Institutionally, in some trades Mitsui's branch offices in China became part of fully integrated international operations. For example, in 1920 Mitsui Bussan set up a silk thread division within the company, headquartered in Yokohama and with branches in Shanghai, Canton, New York, London, and Lyons to unify transactions on a multilateral scale.[32] Financially, perhaps the most complex link between China and the West involving Japanese business was the branch organization of the Yokohama Specie Bank. The following is extrapolated from a 1915 explanation by Inoue Junnosuke regarding methods of payment.[33]

JAPANESE EXPORTS TO CHINA

—If the Japanese exports were worth forty thousand yen, the Chinese importer would settle the account at, say, the Yokohama Specie Bank's Shanghai branch by paying thirty thousand taels (depending on the exchange rate) in silver.

[What would the bank then do with the silver?]

—The Specie Bank would then take its silver to the Shanghai money market, where it would buy a Chinese export bill (not necessarily connected with Japanese goods) payable at London. The bank's Shanghai branch then sends the bill to the bank's London branch, which sells it for pounds sterling. (In the meantime, the Shanghai branch has instructed a domestic branch in Japan, most probably Kobe, to pay the Japanese exporter in yen.)

CHINESE EXPORTS TO JAPAN

[Payment must be made in silver. How does the bank obtain this?]

—First, the Specie Bank's Shanghai branch draws a bill on its London branch but sells the bill on the Shanghai money market for silver, with which it buys a Chinese export bill, thereby paying the Chinese exporter. It then sends the export bill to a branch in Japan, which collects payment in yen from the importer.

[This settles the bilateral transaction, but what has happened to the bill drawn on London but sold in the Shanghai market?]

—The Shanghai purchaser (who may have bought it to take advantage of fluctuating exchange rates) sells it to a British bank in Shanghai for silver. The bank then sends the bill to London and has its head office there collect in pounds sterling from the Yokohama Specie Bank's branch.

---

[31] Ibid., pp. 144–145.

[32] *Kōhon Mitsui*, p. 369.

[33] *Yokohama-shi shi*, vol. 4:ge, p. 735. On exchange bills, see Tani Masaki and Ōba Seiichirō, *Gaikoku kawase no chishiki* (Tokyo: Nihon Keizai Shimbunsha, 1981); and William F. Spalding, *Eastern Exchange, Currency, and Finance* (London: I. Pitman, 1918).

Both exports and imports, as Inoue stated, involved transactions in pounds. In the former case, Japan bought; in the latter, it sold. The key point here is that, in Japan's trade with China, if its exports exceeded imports, Japan had a *net gain* in sterling, thereby earning hard currency. This was one major advantage of dealing on the London money market. A second involved interest rates, which were usually more than two percentage points lower in Europe than in Japan. Because of this, the Specie Bank borrowed heavily in Europe, primarily to finance exports to East Asia.[34]

To guard against risk in exchange transactions in China, the Yokohama Specie Bank relied on compradors to serve as mediators with Chinese merchants and guarantee their deals with the bank. There was a brief period after 1917 when it abolished this system at Shanghai and Peking because its compradors or their relatives had absconded with bank funds. Though the comprador community understood these events as irregularities and did not immediately boycott the bank for abolishing its use of compradors, the bank decided to revive the connection in 1924 to stabilize transactions.[35] The Specie Bank's reliance on compradors (if not the irregularities) was typical of Japanese firms. Mitsui Bussan's 1899 dismissal of its compradors in Shanghai (whose services cost about 1 percent of transactions) was not the norm. Because of this, Mitsui went to great lengths to gain the requisite trust from Chinese. It had its employees learn Chinese, dress Chinese-style, wear their hair in pigtails, study the "psychology and national character of the Chinese," try to experience Chinese family life by boarding in Chinese homes, and it even promised a subsidy to employees marrying Chinese women. Reportedly, no one took up the offer.[36] Probably more typical was the experience of shipping firms like Nisshin Kisen, who used compradors, as did the private Japanese banks that began arriving in China during World War I.[37]

Besides the general increase in Japanese trading activity and investment in China during World War I, there were two institutional features that hastened the appearance of private Japanese banks in China. One was the Yokohama Specie Bank's loss of its monopoly (among Japanese institutions) over foreign exchange transactions. The colonial banks, especially

---

[34] Kojima, *Nihon no kin hon'isei jidai*, p, 157.

[35] *YSG shi*, pp. 191–192, 455–458; *YSG zenshi*, vol. 2, pp. 84 and 125; vol. 3, p. 62; Hao Yen-p'ing, *The Comprador in Nineteenth Century China: Bridge Between East and West* (Cambridge: Harvard University Press, 1970), pp. 62, 179.

[36] See comments by Musada Takashi in *Yamamoto*, pp. 117–118. Cf. *Kōhon Mitsui*, pp. 208–209; *Murata*, pp. 291–292. Takamura, *Shihonshugi*, pp. 162, 167, and 172, gives cost of compradors in Mitsui-related cotton spinning firms.

[37] Itō Masanori, "Taigai kin'yū no kōzō," in Andō Yoshio, ed., *Ryōtaisenkan no Nihon shihonshugi* (Tokyo: Tokyo Daigaku Shuppankai, 1979), p. 73.

the Bank of Taiwan, increased their foreign exchange transactions dramatically during World War I. Between 1913 and 1919, the Specie Bank's share of such transactions handled by Japanese banks fell from 85.4 to 42.3 percent, while that of the Bank of Taiwan grew from 12.1 to 37.7 percent.[38] Sumitomo, the first major private bank to enter the foreign exchange business (1903) and the first to establish a branch in Shanghai (1916), received strong support from Osaka businessmen with their traditional ties to the China trade.[39] It was followed into Shanghai in 1917 by the Mitsui and Mitsubishi banks. A second institutional feature was a 12 million yen credit limit the Yokohama Specie Bank placed on Mitsui Bussan in 1910, which forced Mitsui to diversify its sources of funds. This was imposed not because Mitsui's growing demand for credit constituted excessive risk, but because its rapid expansion outstripped the capacity of the Yokohama Specie Bank to provide for its needs.[40] The largest category of its financial needs was for foreign exchange. Besides guaranteeing 7 million yen of the Specie Bank credit to Mitsui Bussan, the Mitsui Bank set up a Foreign Department in 1913 to provide exchange financing and other services. However, as Mitsui Bussan's total credit line increased from 90 to 380 million yen between 1915 and 1919, other institutions gained substantial shares of Bussan's business. The largest increases in Bussan's credit line were extended by the Taiwan and Chōsen banks and European credit houses. Also, by 1919 Bussan's own internal financing covered 23.5 percent of its credit.[41]

With its huge credit Mitsui gained more flexibility in the use of its own capital. In 1913, the firm established guidelines for allocating working capital through its head office. Some branches and divisions recorded surpluses, which they deposited in the head office, while others were extended overdraft privileges totaling over 20 million yen.[42] Shanghai and Hankow alone had access to 30 percent of this. The Yokohama Specie Bank had a somewhat different pattern of allocating capital to its China branches. For example, in 1908 the head office assigned 6.3 million taels at 2.5 percent annual interest to the Shanghai branch to finance exchange transactions. Shanghai retained 2.4 million of this and lent out the rest to other branches, also at 2.5 percent, as follows: 1.4 million to Hong Kong, 1 million to Hankow, and 1.5 million to Newchwang. The bank opened

---

[38] Calculated from Hijikata, *Yokohama Shōkin Ginkō*, p. 163.

[39] *Sumitomo Ginkōshi* (Osaka: Hensan Iin, 1955), pp. 69–70.

[40] *Mitsui jigyōshi*, p. 108; Japan Business History Institute, ed., *The 100 Year History of Mitsui & Co. Ltd., 1876–1976* (Tokyo: The Company, 1977), pp. 55, 109–111; *YSG shi*, pp. 370–372.

[41] *Mitsui Ginkō 80 nenshi* (Tokyo: Hensan Iinkai, 1957), pp. 190–197; *Mitsui jigyōshi*, pp. 38–42, 392–393.

[42] *Mitsui jigyōshi*, pp. 108–109.

its Hankow office only in 1906, in part because the Shanghai branch had till then handled foreign exchange for the whole Yangtze region. At first, the Hankow branch's exchange business covered mainly exports—raw cotton and beancake to Japan, sesame seeds to Germany, and tea to Russia (this last causing great fluctuations in the exchange rate during May and June and necessitating an extended credit period for shippers). On the import side, the foreign exchange business was still small in 1908, mainly because of the continued role of the Shanghai branch. However, because of the increase in direct shipments to Hankow of foreign imports, such as copper for the mint, warships built by Kawasaki Dockyard, weapons, and oil, the branch's transactions in "selling exchange bills" (that is, bills used for remittance) had already begun to grow.[43]

Despite the increasing number of Japanese banks in China, at least among the government-controlled institutions there was still a kind of division of labor by area.[44] According to Itō Masanori, in the export trade the Yokohama Specie Bank dominated in Central China and the Bank of Taiwan was strong in South China, while the Bank of Chōsen's influence was growing in Manchuria and North China. The Specie Bank also maintained a strong hold over the foreign exchange business for imports from Manchuria because of its traditional strength in silver transactions, its close ties with large trading firms that dealt in soybeans, and the fact that it had branches in all major centers in Manchuria and North China. Since the private banks did not establish their branches in Shanghai until World War I, before that it is probably inappropriate to speak of a "zaibatsu presence" in China. There were some exceptions, such as the Mitsui Bank's loans to Chinese enterprises and government institutions in the early 1910s, but most ventures in China were characterized by ties between firms in *different* zaibatsu, or between these firms and nonzaibatsu manufacturers or government institutions. In the period leading up to the Twenty-One Demands of 1915, then, the main actors were trading companies and government banks, not the private banks.

THE EMERGENCE OF CONFLICT

The Hanyehping Episode

Probably the best-known case of Japan's economic imperialism in China was its attempt to control the Hanyehping Company to secure its supply

---

[43] *Yokohama Shōkin Ginkōshi shiryō: Dai ikkai Tōyō shitenchō kaigiroku* (Tokyo: Nihon Keizai Hyōronsha, 1976), pp. 41, 55–56. In 1917, the Hankow branch also began issuing its own banknotes after previously relying on notes from the Shanghai branch. *YSG shi*, p. 462.

[44] Itō, "Taigai," p. 62.

of iron ore. This company had been established in 1908 with three industrial components: the Hanyang arsenal and iron and steel works, across the Yangtze from Hankow; the Tayeh iron ore mines, to the east of Hankow but south of the Yangtze; and the P'inghsiang colliery, farther south in western Kiangsi. Since the diplomatic side of this issue has been studied, I will concentrate here on its connection with business planning and economic change within Japan.[45] Within this framework, there are three major problems: the role of iron ore imports in Japan's movement into heavy industry; the transport contract for both the ore and pig iron; and the series of loans to Hanyehping, its predecessors, and related institutions.

Despite the fact that both of Japan's major zaibatsu, Mitsui and Mitsubishi, had long operated many coal mines with good access to ports, neither had entered the steel industry by the late nineteenth century. Insufficient supply of iron ore was one major reason for zaibatsu reluctance. The government, therefore, took the lead, establishing the Yawata Iron and Steel Works in 1897 in Kyushu with funds from the Chinese indemnity. Yawata then signed a contract with Tayeh mines in 1899 for iron ore supplies. To overcome production problems and secure these supplies, Japan had to provide Tayeh with financing, which it first undertook on a large scale in 1903 with a three-million-yen loan from the Japan Industrial Bank. This began a long-term mutual dependency in which Tayeh and the Hanyehping Company supplied 61 percent of Yawata's iron ore between 1900 and 1914, with about the same percentage of Tayeh's production between 1893 and 1934 going to Yawata.[46] Yet the interruptions were many. Hanyehping's location in the central Yangtze region, where Chinese revolutionaries held sway, prompted further Japanese intervention through an attempted "merger" in 1912 and the Twenty-One Demands of 1915.

Mitsubishi's Business Division (the precursor of its trading company) began carrying Tayeh iron ore to Yawata in 1900. There was, however, substantial competition among the zaibatsu for transport contracts. Mitsui Bussan carried coal to Hankow and wanted the iron ore contract to secure a return cargo. Eventually, the Finance Ministry mediated these disputes, allocating exclusive marketing rights to Mitsui for pig iron and steel from Hanyang and to Ōkura for coal from P'inghsiang.[47] Mitsubi-

[45] Marius B. Jansen, "Yawata, Hanyehping, and the Twenty–One Demands," *Pacific Historical Review* 23 (February 1954): 31–48.

[46] Albert Feuerwerker, "China's Nineteenth Century Industrialization: The Case of the Hanyehping Coal and Iron Company, Limited," in C. D. Cowan, ed., *The Economic Development of China and Japan* (London: Allen & Unwin, 1964), p. 80.

[47] Takamura, *Shihonshugi*, p. 142; Togai Yoshio, *Mitsui Bussan Kaisha no keiei shiteki*

shi, whose interests in Yawata related to the development of trading activity in China (from beer to sesame seeds) and, more importantly, to a whole range of heavy and chemical industries in Japan from shipbuilding to glass manufacturing, renewed the iron ore contract in 1910. In 1923, it passed it on to the Kinkai Yūsen Kaisha, a newly formed NYK subsidiary.[48]

The loans to Tayeh reflect a close working relationship between the government and the trading companies. Since there was competition from Western countries to acquire Tayeh ore, Japan feared hostile reaction from foreign powers and China should the Japanese government or its special financial agencies appear to be taking the initiative on the loans. Instead, the private trading companies, particularly Ōkura and Mitsui, acted as conduits for government funds to the Chinese. Though functioning in a "dummy role," the trading firms acquired the concessions granted by the Chinese, such as Ōkura's marketing rights to P'inghsiang coal. These rights were obtained through a 1907 loan from the Industrial Bank under the terms of which Ōkura received funds at 6.5 percent and lent them to Tayeh at 7.5 percent, the margin being its "commission." Mitsui operated in a similar way, with most of the "private" loans before the war coming from the government.[49]

It is a mistake to see the loans to Hanyehping and other central Yangtze enterprises simply as a means of acquiring resources for Japanese heavy industry. These loans also attest to the export of services through newer technology. Mitsui sought concessions not simply to market resources but also to provide mining supplies, railway materials, electrical equipment, and, of course, weapons. In similar deals, the Mitsui Bank had led other banks in a 2.5-million yen joint loan from 1910 to 1917 to the Hankow Hydroelectric Company, and Mitsui Bussan won the bid in 1916 to expand the Wuhan telephone system, for which it lent funds to the Chinese Ministry of Communications.[50] These projects paved the way for later investments and represented, in general, changes in Japan's in-

---

kenkyū (Tokyo: Tōyō Keizai Shimpōsha, 1974), pp. 282–283; Ōkura Zaibatsu Kenkyūkai, ed., Ōkura zaibatsu no kenkyū (Tokyo: Kondō Shuppansha, 1982), p. 146.

[48] Ritsugyō bōeki, pp. 878–882.

[49] Of the loans to Tayeh, Jansen, "Yawata," p. 35, stated that "most were extended through the Yokohama Specie Bank or the Industrial Bank, but they were financed and arranged by the great zaibatsu firms." The general pattern of lending, however, seems to have been the reverse of this assumption. See Takamura, Shihonshugi, pp. 141–143; Ōkura, Ōkura zaibatsu, pp. 124, 138, 146. For one case that supports Jansen's point, see Wray, Mitsubishi and the NYK, pp. 395 and 604, n. 34. Also, in 1907 the government changed the official lender from the Industrial Bank to the Yokohama Specie Bank. YSG shi, pp. 332–334; Nihon Kōgyō Ginkō 50 nenshi (Tokyo: Rinji Shiryō Shitsu, 1957), pp. 105–110, 229–246.

[50] Mitsui jigyōshi, pp. 290 and 295; Yamamoto, p. 269.

dustrial structure and, in particular, the shift in the nature of Mitsui as a trading company from servicing light industry to a broader role in electrical machinery and heavy industry.

In early 1912, Mitsui, as the lead Japanese negotiator, signed a contract with Hanyehping that would have given it further concessions and Japan joint ownership and management, but in March the Hanyehping stockholders rejected the agreement.[51] However, since Hanyehping was still unable to repay earlier debts, in 1913 the Yokohama Specie Bank worked out a new contract, which probably more than any other ensured the long-term subordination of Hanyehping to its Japanese creditors. The new loan, at 15 million yen far larger than any previous one, assigned 6 million yen to refinance old debt. Its terms mortgaged the whole of the firm's assets and obliged it to repay the loans through its sales to Yawata, the price of which was fixed. The principal negotiator of this loan was Inoue Junnosuke, the most pro-Anglo-American international financier in pre–World War II Japan. In June 1911, Inoue had become vice-president of the Yokohama Specie Bank and "actual director of [its] affairs."[52] Also engaged in this period in lending to China through international consortia, Inoue embodied the integrated policy of Japan's international banks and other service firms toward both China and the West.

Over the next two decades, as is well known, Hanyehping's importance to Japan declined. Demand for its pig iron fell precipitously after World War I, as India became the main foreign supplier during the 1920s. Also, by 1929 shipment of iron ore from Singapore surpassed that from China, while much of the latter was increasingly coming from Japanese-controlled mines in Manchuria. Meanwhile, the Yokohama Specie Bank continued to earn more than just the interest from its loans. It is instructive to compare the bank's loans to Chinese provincial governments, which were obliged to deposit funds from the loans in the Yokohama Specie Bank and to use its foreign exchange services in remitting money overseas. In effect, many of the bank's loans in China followed a cyclical pattern: loans to provincial governments; deposits in the bank; more loans based on these deposits. Something similar developed through the Hanyehping deals. Since the firm was often barely able to meet its annual interest payments, if that, and since it had to repay through earnings from sales to Yawata, in effect Yawata was paying the Specie Bank in yen,

[51] *Yamamoto*, pp. 254–274; Yamaura Takaichi, *Mori Kaku* (Tokyo: Takayama Shoin, 1943), pp. 392–402.

[52] Mitani Taichirō, "Japan's International Financiers and World Politics, 1904–31," *Proceedings of the British Association for Japanese Studies*, vol. 5, pt. 1 (1980), p. 38; *Inoue Junnosuke den* (Tokyo: Ronsō Hensankai, 1935), pp. 83–90; *YSG shi*, pp. 415, 426–428; *YSG zenshi*, vol. 2, pp. 153, 156.

while the Specie Bank kept an equivalent deposit in silver, which it then used as backing for additional loans within China.[53]

Boycotts and Shipping

In contrast to the Japanese "success" in exploiting Hanyehping, Japan was less able to extend its influence over the shipping industry in China during the interwar years. In a case that bore remarkable resemblance to the proposed deal of 1912 with Hanyehping, in the same year the NYK and Nisshin Kisen tried to take over the China Merchants' line.[54] That, too, failed, but the aftermath was very different, for without the kind of contractual relationship between Yawata and Hanyehping, Japanese shipping firms were more vulnerable to Chinese boycotts. The rapid growth of Nisshin Kisen between 1907 and World War I slowed in the 1920s. The Japanese firm confronted not only a renewed British industry in China but also gradually emerging Chinese strength as former junk owners or new capitalists made the transition to steamships. These Chinese gains were uneven, and they occurred mainly in the 1930s after the establishment of some political stability in the Yangtze region under the Nanking Republican government.

According to the Chinese Maritime Customs, Japan's share of ship tonnage entering and departing Chinese ports had risen from 21 to 28 percent between the late Meiji period and the end of World War I. However, by 1932, following the Manchurian and Shanghai incidents, it had fallen to 15 percent (compared with 44 percent for the British and 25 for the Chinese), and it was only able to make a marginal recovery to 17 percent by 1936.[55] These figures show the effect of boycotts, the impact of which varied with the firm. The lines of international firms like the NYK and OSK that touched Chinese ports suffered, but these companies were gradually decreasing their dependence on China. The Dairen Kisen, an SMR subsidiary, operated mainly in Manchuria and North China, with a route to South China after 1928. By conducting most of its business outside the Yangtze area, it avoided the worst of the boycotts, and in 1930 its fleet had 112,000 tons, compared to Nisshin Kisen's 50,000.[56] The lat-

---

[53] *Yokohama-shi shi*, vol. 5, no. 1, pp. 491–493; Feuerwerker, "China's Industrialization," p. 93; Kojima, *Nihon no kin hon'isei jidai*, pp. 140–141.

[54] On this and earlier takeover planning, see Wray, *Mitsubishi and the NYK*, pp. 340, 396–397, 479–480.

[55] *Tōa Kenkyūkai*, ed., *Nihon no tai-Shi tōshi* (Tokyo: Hara Shobō, 1974), pp. 440, 478–480; C. F. Remer, *Foreign Investments in China* (New York: Macmillan, 1933), pp. 423, 469. Data in *Shina kaiun kankei shiryō* (Teishinshō, unpublished file) suggest that these figures should be taken as trend indicators, not as precise statistics.

[56] *Nihon no tai-Shi*, pp. 436–437; Remer, *Foreign Investments* pp. 489–490. Dairen Kisen also benefited from Dairen's status as a free port.

ter firm was the most affected, for its principal operations were on the Yangtze.

Nisshin Kisen's two main British competitors, which were also subject to boycotts, though less frequently, were the Indo-China Steam Navigation Company, a subsidiary of Jardine, Matheson, and China Navigation Company, together with its agent, Butterfield & Swire, subsidiaries of John Swire & Sons. Nisshin Kisen policy differed from these firms' in several ways. Whereas the British had cooperated in a pool with the China Merchants' since the 1870s, Nisshin Kisen was more inclined to operate independently. This policy was determined partly by the government. By its directives, the number of ports at which the firm called and the volume of its tonnage often exceeded levels acceptable to the pool companies. Its subsidies were less in dispute than before 1914, for they had been reduced on most Yangtze routes. Though Nisshin Kisen had joined the pool in 1913, it subsequently withdrew, and during the mid-1920s protracted negotiations occurred over its possible resumption of membership.

These negotiations failed because of Nisshin Kisen's insistence on a 5 percent discount that would ensure it an appropriate market share. The Japanese firm was still inclined, however, toward some cooperation with the pool firms. One reason for this was the threat of entry by other Japanese firms, such as Yamashita Kisen, which, with Mitsui Bussan as its agent, began running from Shanghai to Hankow in 1925. Some British businessmen, especially Butterfield & Swire's H. W. Kent, an advocate of cooperation with Japan, sought to use the Yamashita threat to lure Nisshin Kisen back into the pool. He also argued that, from the British viewpoint, "an alliance with the [Nisshin Kisen] would be a strong protection against further Japanese intrusion," thereby suggesting a kind of buffer role for Nisshin Kisen between the British and Japanese outsiders, which the NYK was already performing on the European line. The pool also offered some potential comfort in the event of a boycott, but during these disruptions the British responded ambivalently to Nisshin Kisen's problems. On the one hand, Kent suggested to the Japanese that "the Pool was a peaceful form of mutual defence" against boycotts, but generally his British colleagues worried that granting Japan concessions during a boycott would be "impolitic" and provoke Chinese antagonism toward their firms.[57]

[57] In a similar case, just after the Manchurian incident in 1931, Mitsui apparently contemplated approaching Butterfield & Swire to look after its interests if it were "forced to leave" Shanghai by Chinese opposition. But the British firm tried to discourage Mitsui from making such an approach, for though they appreciated the "advantage of friendly relations" with Mitsui, they judged the "price too high." Their firm, they said, would be "severely shaken" by the loss of Chinese confidence if it so aided Mitsui during a boycott. JSSIII 2/10 (to China), Oct. 2, 1931. On shipping, see JSSIII 2/3 (1st half, from Shanghai), no. 103, May

A 1923 boycott, during which negotiations with the British occurred, marked the scheduled return of South Manchuria. Other major anti-Japanese actions affecting shipping were the 1925 strikes against foreign industries; the 1927 Hankow incident, which forced suspension of Nisshin Kisen operations except for vessels under naval escort; and the military incidents at Tsinan in 1928 and Shanghai in 1932 (following the invasion of Manchuria), which hurt the NYK because it carried Japanese troops.[58] Generally, though, since the NYK only ran to Chinese coastal ports, it was less vulnerable than Nisshin Kisen. For one thing, it maintained its monopoly over the Yokohama-Shanghai line despite a brief challenge from Yamashita in the late 1920s. Second, it sometimes circumvented boycotts through special arrangements with shippers. Nisshin Kisen's problems, however, hurt the NYK's capacity to load transshipment cargo from the Yangtze area.

The China Merchants' had difficulty exploiting these boycotts for purely Chinese profit, for by the early 1930s the firm had become heavily indebted to British capital, a process that seems to have started in 1912 when the Hongkong and Shanghai Banking Corporation rescued it from the jaws of the Japanese. Nevertheless, although data do not always fit into the perfect series, there seems to have been a substantial improvement in Chinese market share by the mid-1930s. In the 1923–1925 period, the China Merchants' share of pool cargo from Hankow to Shanghai was in the 12 to 15 percent range. Adding three smaller firms (Hung An, Ningshao, and a lumber company) raised the total Chinese share to 20 and sometimes 30 percent.[59] In the August 1935 to July 1936 period, the China Merchants' had a 17 percent share, while the total Chinese share (this time including the Sanpei-Hung An and Ningshao shipping companies) came to 32 percent. These firms did even better on the Shanghai-Hankow route, garnering 36 percent, with 19 percent going to China Merchants' alone. On the other hand, even though Nisshin Kisen's share of the earnings between Shanghai and Hankow seems to have fallen by about 25 percent since the early 1920s, it still held a larger share between Hankow and Ichang than all three Chinese firms together.[60]

Other figures from 1934 to 1936 (see table 2.1) show a dramatic Chinese improvement, this time more at British than Japanese expense. The British attributed their decline to increases in exports by Japanese shippers who supported their national line; intensive rebating by the Chinese; improved through-cargo agreements between the China Mer-

---

18, 1923; 2/4 (2d half, from Shanghai) in no. 104, Sept. 22, 1924; 2/5 (1st half, from Shanghai) in no. 30, Jan. 30, 1925; Wray, "Commercial Diplomacy."

[58] *Nisshin Kisen*, pp. 391–403.

[59] JSSIII 2/3 to 2/5.

[60] JSSIII 2/8 (folder 1332, from Shanghai), March 23, 1937.

TABLE 2.1
Market Share of Cargo (downward Trade from Hankow), 1934–1936 (percent)

	1934	1935	1936
British Lines			
Cargo	57	49	36
Sailings	50	50	45
Japanese Lines			
Cargo	14	17	23
Sailings	12	13	18
Chinese Lines			
Cargo	29	32	38
Sailings	38	35	34

Source: "Memorandum on British Shipping Interests in Yangtze River Trades," JSSIII 2/ 18 (folder 1332, from Shanghai), in no. 19 (March 5, 1937). Companies surveyed are the pool firms, as in note 60.

chants' and government railways; and provincial government involvement in marketing commodities through monopolies that favored Chinese tonnage. These last points clearly indicate the indispensable role of political stability in Chinese commercial success. This was even more evident on the Upper Yangtze trade to Chungking because of the enhanced central government control over Szechwan. There, a rapidly growing new firm, Ming Sung Industry Company, organized by Szechwan capitalists, had by 1937 captured the leading share on the Ichang-Chungking line, and it monopolized the direct trade from Shanghai to Chungking. Its substantial fleet of 20,718 tons represented 11.2 percent of the steamship traffic assigned to Yangtze lines, compared to 18.9 percent for Nisshin Kisen and 34.0 percent for the British.[61] Furthermore, the average age of Ming Sung's ships (11.4 years) was half that of Nisshin Kisen's.

The experience of the Cheng Chi Shipping Company also typifies the "rollback of imperialism" implied in these figures. In 1937, this firm had a respectable 6.6 percent share of the tonnage on Chinese coastal routes (compared to the China Merchants' 8.6 percent).[62] But in 1924, because of war and business setbacks, it had tried unsuccessfully to sell its fleet to Dairen Kisen (the imperialist devil!). From the Japanese side, in 1937 the

[61] Other shares included 16.5 percent for China Merchants' and 13.5 percent for Sanpei-Hung An. See also source for table 2.1. *Shina kaiun*. Despite the British decline on the Yangtze, British firms in 1937 still carried 44 percent of the soybeans from Dairen to Europe, compared to 9.6 percent for Japanese lines.

[62] Dairen Kisen's share was 12.9 percent, Nisshin Kisen's 1.7 percent. *Shina kaiun*.

Oriental Economist responded to the increasing competition of the time by advocating the merger of Nisshin Kisen and the China Merchants'. As a central, pioneering agency of Sino-Japanese collaboration (*gassaku*), the proposed company would integrate Yangtze and coastal routes and overcome the main problems of the two firms: anti-Japanese boycotts and the "oppression" of the China Merchants' by foreign (that is, Western) shipping.[63] One is tempted to say "shades of 1912," but the situation had changed by 1937. The *Oriental Economist*'s position could only be based on military or diplomatic strategy; it was divorced from business priorities. Unlike the years 1900–1914, when firms like the NYK needed China freight to bolster their lines to the West, by the mid-1930s their dependence on China had decreased because of the restructuring of the Japanese economy. This argument is not simply based on the now popular study of industrial structure. It was shared by perceptive observers in the mid-1930s like Butterfield & Swire's agents, who saw that the increase in higher-paying cargo among Japanese exports was beginning to free the NYK's transoceanic lines from dependence on China ports.[64]

CHANGES IN INDUSTRIAL STRUCTURE, 1916–1936

Mitsui Bussan remained by far the largest of Japan's general trading companies in the interwar years, because it followed a risk-avoidance strategy of dealing in basic commodities while at the same time managing the flow of investment, information, and technology for new enterprises. It applied both aspects of this strategy to China. None of Mitsui's competitors came close to matching its influence there. Suzuki Shōten accepted excessive risk and went bankrupt in 1927. The rate of Ōkura's expansion and diversification slowed during the 1920s because of managerial problems. Mitsubishi, the only one of the major zaibatsu whose trading arm failed to make substantial profits during World War I, developed investments that were scattered throughout East Asia from the northern seas to Korea, Manchuria, and Southeast Asia, but its China activities were less at the heart of its overall strategy, which was more oriented to domestic activity, than was the case with Mitsui.

Mitsui's international information network enabled it to respond quickly to changing demand and proved especially effective for its third-country trade. The share of this trade in the firm's total transactions peaked at 33.5 percent in 1919, and although it declined in the 1920s, it never fell below 20 percent. By the early 1930s, Mitsui's three principal cross-trades were rubber (mostly from Southeast Asia to the United

---

[63] *Tōyō Keizai Shimpō*, January 23, 1937, pp. 546–547. In contrast to my above figures, the Japanese writer used 1932 statistics on Chinese debt to justify his case.

[64] Wray, "Commercial Diplomacy," p. 293.

States for the auto industry), soybeans, and wheat. The last two involved China. Soybeans were exported from Manchuria mainly to Germany for use in oil refining, and wheat was imported from the United States for flour milling in China.[65]

The cotton trade, which continued to be of major importance, underwent considerable institutional change in the aftermath of World War I. By 1912, Japanese firms had surpassed Indian exporters in their share of the yarn market in China. But as Chinese yarn production became more competitive, the Japanese increased their exports of cotton cloth. These exceeded the British share of the China market in 1917. Then, the increase in Chinese tariffs in 1919 prompted a new stage in the industry, as Japanese cotton spinners undertook local production in China to protect their yarn markets. Between 1917 and 1925, most leading spinning firms established mills in China. As a result, textiles became the largest area of overseas Japanese investment.[66] Under Yamamoto's leadership, in 1902 Mitsui Bussan had set up the Shanghai Cotton Spinning Company, Japan's first permanent mill in China. It was followed by an even more successful enterprise established by Naigaimen, a specialist cotton trading firm. Mitsui also had financial interests in numerous spinning firms that launched their investments after the war. Moreover, increased production in China opened new opportunities for Mitsui's third-country trade as it began supplying these mills with Indian and, to a lesser extent, American raw cotton, which were used in higher-count yarn production. Mitsui's third-country trade in raw cotton grew so rapidly in the latter stages of World War I that in 1918 it temporarily surpassed its imports into Japan. Roughly half of this cross-trade seems to have been destined for China. By 1920, the cotton trade had grown so large that Mitsui spun it off, establishing a ninety-percent-owned subsidiary, Tōyō Menka.[67]

To remain competitive in China, Japanese mills there had to increase their productivity. This required new automatic machinery and created additional trade for Mitsui. During World War I, Mitsui helped to finance Toyoda Sakichi as he was developing new loom machinery. This was so successful that in 1926 a new company, Toyoda Automatic Loom, was established, but it presented Mitsui with a dilemma, for its sole agency

[65] Yamazaki Hiroaki, "1920 nendai no Mitsui Bussan," in Nakamura Takafusa, ed., *Senkanki no Nihon keizai bunseki* (Tokyo: Yamakawa Shuppansha, 1981), pp. 320–326; *Kōhon Mitsui*, pp. 448–456.

[66] Kuwahara Tetsuya, "The Business Strategy of Japanese Cotton Spinners: Overseas Operations, 1890–1931," in Okochi Akio and Yonekawa Shin'ichi, eds., *The Textile Industry and Its Business Climate* (Tokyo: Tokyo University Press, 1982), pp. 139–166; Kang Chao, *The Development of Cotton Textile Production in China* (Cambridge: Harvard University Press, 1977), pp. 87–134.

[67] *Kōhon Mitsui*, pp. 356–364; Takamura Naosuke, *Kindai Nihon mengyō to Chūgoku* (Tokyo: Tokyo Daigaku Shuppankai, 1982), pp. 75–132; *Yamamoto*, pp. 157–167.

contract for distributing Platt Brothers machinery prohibited it from marketing Toyoda's new loom even in Japan. A 1929 contract, mediated by Mitsui, under which Toyoda sold the patent rights for its new loom to Platt, still did not give Mitsui leeway to sell Toyoda's machine in Chinese and other overseas Asian markets. Coincidentally, however, a 1931 merger between Platt and other British firms rendered the old Mitsui–Platt contract inoperative. The marketing of Toyoda machines then became the heart of negotiations for a revised agreement with the new British firm, prompting diverse proposals within Mitsui itself. The machinery division of the firm's Osaka branch argued that Mitsui should support domestic manufacturers and favored an exclusive marketing deal for Toyoda alone. On the other hand, the Shanghai branch, with its long experience in handling British machinery, strongly urged that the firm preserve its distribution rights for the British in China. Recognizing Toyoda's greater long-term potential in the China market, the head office sympathized with the Osaka branch but sought a "compromise," perhaps opportunistically, that would give it exclusive distribution rights for both Toyoda and the British. Mitsui then turned down British requests (that it ensure against an increase in Toyoda's production capacity and that it include Ōkura in the agreement) and in 1932 secured the sole agency for both. The sales territory designated in the contract was the Japanese Empire, Manchuria, and the Republic of China.[68]

Toyoda thus gained an advantage in the early 1930s as Japanese mills in China began purchasing new spinning and weaving equipment primarily from Japan. This new machinery represents an evolution in Japan's comparative advantage and calls into question the rationale for Japanese economic policy toward China. A 1933 tariff enacted by China protected cotton goods in which China was developing a comparative advantage but was liberal toward raw materials and machinery that the Chinese cotton industry needed. Yet, in 1934 Japanese pressure forced it to raise rates on the latter items and lower them on cotton goods.[69] This pressure can probably be explained by Japan's strategic need to earn hard currency from high-volume exports of cotton textiles, but it did not make good business sense either to Japan's local producers in China or to the exporters of new Japanese machinery. As in the case of shipping, Japan's position on Chinese tariff policy seemed at odds with evolving international patterns of comparative advantage.

Another case of government and military priorities interfering with Japan's markets for more advanced technology occurred in the telephone

[68] Kasuga Yutaka, "1930 nendai ni okeru Mitsui Bussan Kaisha no tenkai katei (2)," *Mitsui bunko ronsō* 17 (December 1983): 90–98.

[69] Takamura, *Kindai Nihon*, pp. 214, 221; Parks M. Coble, Jr., *The Shanghai Capitalists and the Nationalist Government, 1927–1937* (Cambridge: Harvard University Press, 1980), pp. 132–139.

business after World War I. In 1916, when Mitsui Bussan had won the bid for telephone construction from the Chinese Ministry of Communications, it delegated the actual construction to the Nippon Electric Company (NEC), Japan's leading telephone maker. Over the next two years, NEC expanded the Hankow system (previously managed by the German firm Siemens) by installing switching equipment with a capacity of 2,200 circuits. It then opened the Wuchang system and connected the two cities by long distance. These deals led to a 1917 marketing arrangement with Mitsui, which received a 2.5 percent commission on sales of NEC products, promised not to market for firms competing with NEC, and purchased 6.4 percent of NEC's stock. In certain respects, this relationship resembled post–World War II trading company operations in multinational enterprises. Manufacturers have employed trading companies to lay the initial groundwork for their ventures, but once established they often take over the marketing themselves. In this case, NEC was a subsidiary of the American firm Western Electric, which in 1917 owned 50.9 percent of its stock. For several years, Western Electric had been negotiating with the Chinese government to establish a new electrical firm. This led to the formation in October 1917 of a joint venture, the China Electric Company, 50 percent owned by the Chinese government, with Western Electric and NEC each taking up 25 percent of the shares. Now that NEC was a partner with the Chinese government, the contract with Mitsui Bussan was cancelled the next year. Yet, the prospect of expanded sales through the new firm proved illusory. With the 1919 demonstrations against the Japanese retention of former German territory in Shantung, the Chinese began to boycott NEC products. The new firm, then, had to buy more exclusively from Western Electric, leaving NEC in a diminished role.

Nevertheless, boycotts varied by the year and especially with the area. NEC was later able to gain key contracts through joint ventures in Manchuria and even in Shanghai. Another firm active in the Chinese market was Sumitomo Electric Wire. Through a joint venture with Chinese electric light enterprises and other Japanese firms, it took the lead in providing loans to Chinese cities. In 1918, the Sumitomo and Furukawa banks each put up three million yen as part of a ten-million-yen loan package to the Peking Bureau of Communications for telephone expansion. Also participating were the Dai Ichi, Industrial, Taiwan, and Chōsen banks. In later years, the telephone makers had an increasingly protected market in Manchuria, but their initial entry into the China market would have been much more difficult without the aid of the trading companies and the banks.[70]

[70] Nihon Keieishi Kenkyūjo, ed., *Nippon Denki Kabushiki Kaisha 70 nenshi* (Tokyo: Dō Shashi hensan shitsu, 1972), pp. 91–96; Nakase Toshikazu, "Senzen ni okeru Sumitomo

Some Problems of Banking and Currency

Reflecting the increase in overseas manufacturing investment toward the end of World War I, the international operations of Japanese banks grew rapidly in the 1920s. The Mitsui Bank's overall foreign exchange transactions increased sevenfold between 1919 and 1925, while its share of Mitsui Bussan's foreign exchange business rose from 6.7 percent in 1918 to 22.8 percent in 1931. The overseas presence of private banks made it easier for them to finance industrial and trading firms that belonged to the same zaibatsu, but these firms did not become exclusively dependent on the one bank. By 1931, Mitsui Bussan handled 28.7 percent of its own foreign exchange transactions, and it continued to use the services of the Yokohama Specie Bank, the Bank of Taiwan, the Sumitomo Bank, and the Hongkong and Shanghai Banking Corporation, among others. In general, though, the share of the government banks was declining. The Yokohama Specie Bank handled only 17.1 percent of Mitsui Bussan's foreign exchange in 1931, compared to 41.0 percent in 1918, while in 1929 the private banks together for the first time surpassed the Yokohama Specie Bank in total foreign exchange transactions. The means by which the private banks, especially Mitsui, captured such a large share of the business was the huge deposits they held for the related companies in their zaibatsu. They used these deposits not simply to finance trade or to handle exchange transactions for trading purposes, but more so to speculate in foreign currencies.[71] Mitsui's Shanghai branch played an important role in this respect. According to one rough estimate, in 1921 the branch transacted 40 percent of the bank's exchange. This figure fell to 20 percent in 1925 but rose to 60 percent in 1931. Behind this volatility was the fact that the Shanghai branch's principal business was speculation—buying and selling for profit yen, silver, dollars, and pounds.[72]

The Mitsui Bank's vigorous activity in Shanghai grew not just out of the postwar investment in China or the general speculative crisis of 1931 related to the gold standard, but also out of longer-term problems involving China's use of silver. Since the Russo-Japanese War, the Chinese monetary system had been seen as the greatest obstacle to trade relations with Manchuria and to the growth of Japanese investment there. This problem also became acute with regard to investment in China after World War I because of the increased risk to trade caused by the huge

zaibatsu no kaigai shinshutsu," in Fujii, *Nihon takokuseki*, pp. 154–156; Yamamura Rikuo, "Mitsui Bussan," pp. 89–90.

[71] Itō, "Taigai," pp. 57–77; Itō Masanori, "1910–1920 nendai ni okeru Nihon kin'yū kōzō to sono tokushitsu (1)," *Shakai kagaku kenkyū* 30, 4 (February 1979): 26–32; (2), 30, 6 (March 1979): 25; *Mitsui Ginkō*, pp. 436–443.

[72] Itō, "Taigai," p. 71; Itō, "1910–1920 nendai (2)," pp. 26, 34.

fluctuations in the value of silver. During World War I, the Terauchi cabinet set out to "correct" this problem, especially as it affected the triangular trade relations among Japan, Korea, and Manchuria. Terauchi's goal was to integrate the three in a currency bloc that would be implemented by using the Bank of Chōsen to impose a gold standard on Manchuria. In 1917, the Bank of Chōsen took over from the Yokohama Specie Bank the right to issue gold banknotes in Manchuria. Yet, the differing functions of the Bank of Chōsen and the Specie Bank frustrated Terauchi's goal. The Yokohama Specie Bank's silver notes continued to circulate in Manchuria along with the Bank of Chōsen's gold notes. These silver notes played an indispensable role in facilitating the flow of trade and financing between Manchuria and Shanghai, yet their existence was clearly inconsistent with the policy of imposing a gold standard on Manchuria.

To make matters worse, relative to the yen, silver tended to be expensive in Dairen and cheap in Shanghai. This prompted Dairen merchants to speculate by buying silver in Shanghai, creating in the process a credit crisis for the Bank of Chōsen. The situation also made it advantageous for banks to remit money from Shanghai to Japan through Dairen rather than directly to Japan. The great increase in foreign exchange handled by Mitsui's Shanghai branch reflected this condition.[73]

Fluctuations in silver values also affected the cotton trade. Falling values in the late 1920s led to depreciation in China's currency and helped the country's exports. At the same time, it slowed imports, hurting Japanese banks that financed cotton exports to China. The Sumitomo Bank, for example, which had closed its Hankow branch in 1930 because of political disturbances and the decline of imports from Japan, experienced a drastic fall in its volume of foreign exchange transactions during this period. The mid-1930s brought the opposite problem—rising silver values and a mammoth outflow of silver from China. This led to depressed commodity prices and a decline in demand for cotton goods, though Chinese mills may have suffered more than the Japanese.[74]

The eventual solution to this crisis, recommended by a special British commission and expedited by the Hongkong and Shanghai Banking Corporation, took China off silver and introduced inconvertible government banknotes as currency. These monetary issues have been prominent in the study of British economic relations with China, but they have received relatively little attention in the West with regard to Japan's imperialism. One question that might be asked is the extent to which business firms

[73] Namikata Shōichi, "Shokuminchi kin'yū," in Katō Toshihiko, ed., *Nihon kin'yūron no shiteki kenkyū* (Tokyo: Tokyo Daigaku Shuppankai, 1983), pp. 294–297; Itō, "Taigai," p. 74.

[74] *Sumitomo*, pp. 170–173; Coble, *Shanghai Capitalists*, pp. 140–160.

sought government intervention to solve this long-term currency problem even when they may have assumed such intervention would cost them markets in the short run.

Conclusion

The fundamental differences between the currencies of China and Japan suggest that even if Japan had followed a "peaceful" diplomacy toward China, oriented primarily to business interests, there would still have been strong interventionist pressure from business for government action to overcome obstacles to trade. The numerous interventions that did occur—whether territorially in South Manchuria and Shantung, strategically in the case of Hanyehping, or commercially in attempts to tailor Chinese tariff policy to suit Japan's wishes—all had the effect of increasing Chinese opposition to business dealings with Japan. If the main themes here (China's role in Japan's international business and changing industrial structure) were compared to the building of a house, one could conclude that a sturdy foundation was laid but that the pillars above ground were nonetheless bent, and a strong wind threatened the upper stories. Up through World War I, the service firms developed international trading networks in which China served as an indispensable link. There were two trends that undermined the China link in these networks during the interwar years. One was the Chinese opposition that Japan's forceful diplomacy provoked. Another relates to changing patterns of comparative advantage. Before World War I, the economies of the two countries seem to have been mostly complementary; after the war, and increasingly by the 1930s, a more competitive relationship arose in some light industrial sectors. On this last point, a split emerged between some service firms like Mitsui, which, with its flexible strategy, seemed capable of accommodating rather than resisting the increasing range of China's comparative advantage, and the government's economic policy, which was more inclined to freeze China's economic structure in order to preserve Japan's current advantage.

Another ramification of Japan's forceful diplomacy was a regional shuffle in trading patterns. In the 1890s, the Yangtze constituted the Chinese link in the emerging international business of Japan's service firms. Rather than shying away from British superiority there, these firms quickly developed a strong competitive position. The Russo-Japanese War, however, deflected much subsequent investment to the north. It is difficult to compare the relative attractiveness of the north (especially Manchuria) and the Yangtze regions because the main variable was the military presence (and hence protection accorded). Furthermore, the action Japan took in the north greatly damaged its commercial prospects in the Yangtze.

Since the service firms were the first to establish a strong Japanese commercial presence in China, can they be called a "vanguard of imperialism"? Looked at "subjectively"—that is, from the standpoint of their own business strategy—the question is almost irrelevant, for China was usually only auxiliary to their international, multilateral interests. Objectively, however, they clearly led Japan's economic advance into China. Whether this constituted part of an "imperialist advance" is an issue that, for reasons of space, I have not taken up here. Such a question, however, should be prefaced by a distinction among different service functions: the acquisition of resources; the marketing of manufactured goods; and the provision of services, such as transport or foreign exchange transactions. The analysis should then ask where these activities fit in a spectrum that ranges from "normal trade" to "guaranteed access."[75]

A further question that relates to both the character of Japanese imperialism in China and the function of China in Japan's changing industrial structure concerns the comparison between the leading Japanese service firms mentioned here and their foreign, especially British, counterparts. Unfortunately, there is very little useful secondary material on comparable British firms after 1900, though the archives of John Swire & Sons might make such an analysis possible for trading and shipping. The Hongkong and Shanghai Banking Corporation may be the best prospect for comparison, for in many ways it offers the closest parallel, namely, with the Yokohama Specie Bank. Here comparison becomes more than an analytical tool. The Yokohama Specie Bank's attempt to emulate the Hongkong and Shanghai Banking Corporation can be seen as a causative factor in the Specie Bank's policy toward China. The Specie Bank first began issuing currency notes to protect traders from fluctuating silver values, rather than to support broader strategic purposes. Yet, the bank also wanted to use the notes to enhance its reputation, just as the Hongkong and Shanghai Bank had won Chinese confidence through the reliability of its notes. A similar relationship involved the NYK, which modeled itself after Britain's P & O Steam Navigation Company, though more for its transoceanic business than for its colonial role. Japanese firms had ambivalent attitudes toward their British counterparts. On the one hand, they sought to emulate them; on the other, they tried to oust them

---

[75] Guaranteed access could be defined as property rights acquired through force that discriminate against the grantor through their inconsistency with normal international usage. In China they included such foreign rights as navigation on inland rivers, acquisition of concession areas, the issuing of one's own currency, and treaties that erode autonomy—that is, which diminish the property rights of the state, such as the setting of tariffs.

from China, a stance that was a principal motive behind Japan's aggressive economic diplomacy of World War I.

The above comments hold true for the leading banking and shipping firms, but less so for Mitsui Bussan. My impression is that its character as a firm was the least rooted in imitation and its strategy the most independently conceived. Certainly Jardine, Matheson and Butterfield & Swire, both of which emerged as general trading companies, were, through their influence in East Asia, potential models. But neither was able to exploit substantially Japan's changing industrial structure for its own profit. They made a deliberate decision not to invest heavily in Japan's trade (at least not on a scale commensurate with the growth of the economy) because of their perception of Japanese nationalism as an insurmountable obstacle. They chose a specialized strategy of maintaining their principal link with China.[76] Mitsui lacked this specialized dimension. Its business was more general, both by function and by area. This brings us back to banking and shipping, where contrasts as well as parallels can be drawn. The Yokohama Specie Bank, after all, was quite different from the Hongkong and Shanghai Banking Corporation. It was relatively more international in purpose and less specialized in area. And in shipping, despite its emulation of the P & O, the NYK was not the principal bearer of imperial policy after 1905; that role fell to its subsidiaries, Nisshin Kisen in China and Chōsen Yūsen in Korea.

Japan's imperial territory was too close to home, too subject to market fluctuations, and hence risky. Its underdevelopment, as well as the competition from Westerners, imposed too many limits to growth on a strategy of regional specialization. It was less risky to integrate business operations on a multidimensional scale, using China as an initial thrust, as the NYK did, or coming back to it after building an international network, as the Yokohama Specie Bank did. The Nisshin Bank debate is instructive here, in view of China's economic importance to Japan, how few large and autonomous business agencies there were that specialized in China (excluding Manchuria). There were scores of companies set up to promote trade and investment, beginning especially around the time of the 1911 Revolution. But these were almost all joint ventures, representing numerous individual firms. They played important roles as mediators in getting contracts, but they were not the decision makers. That power remained with the service firms themselves or with the export associations of the manufacturers. Perhaps no one would trust the potential monopoly power of a specialized agency. The international firms were thus left to dominate, integrating their Chinese and Western business.

[76] Wray, *Mitsubishi and the NYK*, p. 511. (This paper was completed before the publication of Frank H. H. King, *The History of the Hongkong and Shanghai Banking Corporation*, 4 vols. [Cambridge: Cambridge University Press, 1987]).

CHAPTER 3

Zaikabō: Japanese Cotton Mills in China, 1895–1937

Peter Duus

A passenger on the starboard side of a steamer sailing up the Whangpoo (Huang-pu) River into Shanghai in the mid-1930s could scarcely have failed to notice the serrated roofs, towering smokestacks, and loading docks of the great cotton mills along the opposite riverbank. At the western edge of the International Settlement along the southern side of Soochow Creek there was another equally impressive cluster of mills. The observer might have discovered to his surprise that many of these mills were owned by Japanese companies, not British. The British might dominate the clubs and racetracks in the foreign city, but there was no question about who dominated its spinning and weaving industry. In 1936, Japanese mills accounted for the production of nearly 40 percent of all China's machine-spun yarn and about 57 percent of all its machine-woven cloth. They had long since overtaken British-owned mills. Indeed, the largest cotton manufacturer in Shanghai was Naigai Wata Company, whose nine separate mills all fronted on Soochow Creek. Close by the mill grounds were mess halls and dormitories for workers, company nurseries and infirmaries, spacious residential quarters for Japanese employees, and even a park for the use of employees. Tidiness and order prevailed, and looking down benignly on it all was a bronze statue of Kawamura Rihei, third president of the company.

On the eve of the China War, Japanese-owned cotton mills also accounted for a substantial portion of private Japanese investment in China. According to one contemporary estimate, Japanese investment in China, including loans to Chinese enterprises and loans to the Chinese government, amounted to 1.583 billion yen in 1936. Slightly more than half of this amount (about 840 million yen) consisted of direct investment in Japanese-owned business enterprises—banks, development companies, foreign trading and shipping firms, real estate, and manufacturing concerns. Of these firms, the most important were engaged in foreign trade and cotton manufacturing, each industry representing an investment of about

300 million yen.[1] While Japanese trading firms were active in the rest of the world, the Japanese cotton industry sought overseas investment outside the formal empire only in China. And it was the only Japanese manufacturing industry to do so on a significant scale. Indeed, *zaikabō*, as the Japanese-owned spinning industry came to be called, represents the first case of a multinationalized nonservice industry in Japan.

All this makes zaikabō exceptional, and perhaps not useful as a case study of the relationship between the metropolitan economy and the informal empire in China. On the other hand, its very atypicality raises a series of interesting questions. When did the Japanese cotton manufacturers begin to invest in China and why? Were they attempting to find outlets for "surplus capital" or were they prompted by other motives? And once established in China, how was the industry able to expand so rapidly, bypassing the other foreign firms, and competing successfully with a burgeoning domestic Chinese industry? Did Japanese enterprise succeed because it was backed by Japanese military and political power, or did it capture such a large share of the China market by other means? The answers to these questions perhaps help us gain a better understanding of just what treaty privileges in China meant for the metropolitan Japanese economy—and what they did not.

The Treaty of Shimonoseki

The Treaty of Shimonoseki threw the gates of the China market wide to Japan. It gave Japan most-favored-nation status, opened new treaty ports, secured navigation rights up the Yangtze River, and allowed Japanese to engage in manufacturing in all open cities and ports. Japanese politicians, officials, and businessmen waxed enthusiastic over Japan's economic future there. "Our nation now possesses the same rights and privileges in China as do the various nations of Europe," observed an editorial in the *Tōkyō keizai zasshi*. "Ah, the battle of arms and men has reached its conclusion, and now the battle of commerce begins."[2]

The cotton industry was ready to joust on the battlefield of commerce, but its leaders were not entirely happy about the acquisition of new manufacturing rights. The Japanese government had sought manufacturing rights not in response to domestic pressure but largely to win support from the Western powers.[3] Since the early 1880s, foreign businessmen had been pressing the Chinese government for permission to open textile

[1] Higuchi Hiromu, *Nihon no tai-Shi tōshi kenkyu* (Japanese investment in China) (Tokyo: Seikatsusha, 1939), pp. 234–242.

[2] *Tōkyō keizai zasshi*, no. 774 (May 23, 1895): 635–636.

[3] Cf. the argument in Nakatsuka Akira, *Nisshin sensō no kenkyū* (A study of the Sino-Japanese War) (Tokyo: Aoki Shoten, 1968), pp. 257–287.

mills in the treaty ports. In June 1894, on the eve of the Sino-Japanese War, a shipment of cotton-spinning machinery ordered from Platt Brothers by Jardine, Matheson Company had already arrived at Shanghai as a test of the Chinese prohibition on foreign manufacturing.[4] And not surprisingly, it was Westerners who first took advantage of the new right to establish manufacturing facilities in the treaty ports. A visiting delegation from Lancashire reported optimistically that "spinning mills under foreign management will do well, and those under native management will be driven to the wall."[5]

By 1898, there were four new foreign-owned cotton mills in Shanghai—the Ewo Cotton Spinning and Weaving Company set up by Jardine, Matheson in 1895, the Laou-Kung-Mow Cotton Spinning and Weaving Company set up by another British trading company in 1896, the International Cotton Manufacturing Company established by the American Trading Company in 1896, and the Soy Chee Spinning Company, Ltd., set up by Arnhold Karberg and Company, a German firm. It is worth noting that all of these firms were established by treaty port merchant houses handling imports of foreign yarn and piece goods. It was they, rather than metropolitan cotton manufacturers at home who had pressed for the expansion of foreign manufacturing rights, and it was they who were aware of the opportunities in China and how best to take advantage of them.

Quite naturally, the leaders of the Japanese cotton spinning industry were concerned over the establishment of foreign-owned mills in Shanghai. If Western capital and technology were harnessed to cheap Chinese labor, Japanese yarn exports to China would face serious competition. A mission sent to China by the Greater Japan Cotton Spinning Association (Dai Nihon Bōseki Rengōkai) in October 1895 gloomily concluded that China soon would achieve self-sufficiency in cotton yarn production. But Japanese cotton manufacturers were reluctant to build mills of their own. They were caught in a curious bind. As one member of the mission, Kanazawa Nisaku (Hirano Spinning Company), put it the following June, the Japanese were faced with the choice of "cutting our own throats" by setting up mills in China or letting someone else (i.e., the Westerners) cut them.[6]

In 1895–1896, presumably to protect a share of the market, two groups of Japanese businessmen mounted efforts to establish cotton mills in

---

[4] Kang Chao, *The Development of Cotton Textile Production in China* (Cambridge: Harvard University Press, 1977), pp. 110, 115, 339 n. 17.

[5] *Report of the Mission to China of the Blackburn Chamber of Commerce, 1896–7* (Blackburn: North-East Lancashire Press Company, 1898), p. 11.

[6] Takamura Naosuke, *Kindai Nihon mengyō to Chūgoku* (The modern Japanese cotton industry and China) (Tokyo: Tōkyō Daigaku Shuppankai, 1982), pp. 71–74.

Shanghai. One venture, the Tōyō Spinning and Weaving Company (Tōyō Bōshoku Kabushiki Kaisha), was organized by executives from cotton spinning, weaving and trading companies in Ōsaka under the presidency of Matsumoto Jūtarō (president, Ōsaka Spinning Company) in February 1896. The new company ordered 25,464 spindles from Platt Brothers and Asa Lees in England, purchased a factory site in the International Settlement at Shanghai, and made preparations to bring Chinese workers over for training at mills owned by Ōsaka Spinning Company and Hirano Spinning Company. A second venture, the Shanghai Spinning Company (Shanhai Bōseki Kabushiki Kaisha), was backed by the Mitsui interests in Tokyo, whose chief manager, Nakamigawa Hikojirō, sent his own mission to Shanghai in the summer of 1895. A factory site was bought in the International Settlement, twenty thousand spindles were ordered from Platt Brothers, and an electric light system was ordered from the Shibaura Electric Works.

Unlike the foreign-owned mills, these two Japanese ventures rather quickly collapsed. In March 1896, just a few months after the Shanghai Spinning Company had been formally organized, the management of Mitsui decided to use the spindles ordered for Shanghai to build a mill near the Mitsui-owned Kanegafuchi Spinning Company mill in Kobe, and in February 1897 the Tōyō Spinning and Weaving Company closed down at a loss of 300,000 yen to its investors.

Why did the backers of these two Japanese ventures suddenly change their minds about the wisdom of investing in China? The immediate reason seems fairly clear. Having let the foxes into the henhouse, the Chinese were determined to get them out again. To discourage foreign investment in treaty port manufacturing, the Ch'ing government proposed levying a 10 percent internal tax on all manufactured goods, whether produced by Chinese or by foreign firms. The tax on manufacturing goods was a key issue in negotiations for a Sino-Japanese commercial and shipping treaty that began in the fall of 1895. After a year of hard bargaining, the Japanese government in October 1896 finally agreed to a manufacturing tax if the Chinese agreed to a separate Japanese settlement zone in Shanghai. It was in the midst of these negotiations that the Mitsui interests shifted their plans for a new plant from Shanghai to Kobe, and it was with the announcement of the agreement that the Ōsaka project collapsed.[7]

---

[7] Discussion of these early plans for building cotton mills in Shanghai is based on Takamura, *Kindai Nihon mengyō*, pp. 68–75; Ryūmonsha, ed., *Shibusawa Eiichi denki shiryō* (Materials for the biography of Shibusawa Eiichi), vol. 16 (Tokyo: Shibusawa Eiishi Denki Shiryō Kankokai, 1955–1965), pp. 668–671; Izumi Takeo, "Nihon bōseki shihon no Chūgoku ichiba shinshutsu ni kansuru ichi kosatsu" (A consideration of the advance of Japanese cotton spinning capital into the China market), *Keizai ronshū* 7, 1 (February 1972): 48–57; Kuwabara Tetsuya, "Senzen ni okeru Nihon bōsekikigyō no kaigaikatsudō—Kanegafuchi

DISINCENTIVES TO METROPOLITAN INVESTMENT

Since the manufacturing tax affected Chinese as well as foreign firms, the Shanghai Chamber of Commerce as well as certain top Ch'ing officials opposed it, and the idea eventually was dropped. Even so, the Japanese cotton manufacturers still did not rush to invest in China. Obviously, other considerations than the proposed manufacturing tax affected the business strategy of the Japanese cotton industry in China. One was anxiety over the political situation. The Triple Intervention, the difficulties in negotiating a commercial and shipping treaty, and the generally hostile attitude of Ch'ing officials toward the Japanese created uncertainty over Japan's future in China. It is axiomatic that private capitalists are reluctant to invest in countries where the local government is incapable of guaranteeing stable business conditions, or where their own government is not strong enough to come to their assistance in times of trouble. Political uncertainties diminished after the turn of the century, however, especially after Japan defeated Russia in 1905, so it is necessary to turn to the economic considerations that made metropolitan Japanese cotton manufacturers reluctant to invest in China mills.

First of all, it should be remembered that while the Japanese cotton manufacturers were ambivalent toward the new manufacturing rights established by the Treaty of Shimonoseki, they were enthusiastic about the other economic and commercial privileges acquired. The vastness of the China market may have turned out to be a "myth" for the Westerners, but for the Japanese cotton manufacturers it was a tangible reality. As Mutō Sanji, the aggressive young manager of the Hyogo office of the Kanegafuchi Spinning Company observed in early 1900, "China is a broad and boundless country, whose demand increases day by day, month by month, year by year. . . . One can say simply that the demand for machine-made cotton yarn . . . is practically without limit. . . . I firmly believe the time is coming when Japan will be the England of the Orient."[8] This prediction proved not at all far-fetched.

Japanese cotton manufacturers had been interested in expanding Asian markets since 1890, when the industry had been hit by its first recession. Dumping surplus inventories in external markets was an obvious way to deal with temporary gluts in the domestic market. Sample yarn shipments to China began in the early 1890s. After an extensive lobbying campaign by the Greater Japan Cotton Spinning Association, the Diet

---

bōseiki kaisha no jirei o chūshin to shite" (The overseas activities of Japanese cotton spinning enterprises—Centering on the Kanegafuchi Spinning Company), *Rokkōdai ronshū* 22, 1 (April 1975): 5–9.

[8] Mutō Sanji, *Mutō Sanji zenshū* (The complete works of Mutō Sanji), vol. 1 (Tokyo: Shinjusha, 1963), p. 410.

abolished export duties on cotton yarn, opening the way for a break-through in the China trade.[9] By 1896, about 10 percent of total cotton yarn production was exported, and by 1897 exports of yarn exceeded imports for the first time. The bulk of these exports went to Hong Kong and China (see table 3.1).

This is not to say that exports to China expanded in a unilinear fashion. In 1897, for example, there were fears that exports had reached the saturation point, creating the possibility of overproduction. At meetings of the Great Japan Cotton Spinning Association in 1897 and 1898 there was considerable discussion about ways of encouraging exports, ranging from a complicated system of bounties to firms producing for the export market, through requests to the government for an easing of foreign exchange transactions, to a demand for direct government subsidies for exports. The government was not willing to do much more than help out on foreign exchange problems, and in July 1899 the Yokohama Specie Bank agreed to make three million yen available at low interest rates to help finance cotton yarn exports to Hong Kong and Shanghai.[10] But once this short-lived crisis had been surmounted, exports of cotton manufactures to China continued to grow.

It also became increasingly clear to Japanese manufacturers that neither the new foreign-owned mills in China nor the growing number of Chinese-owned mills posed any significant threat to Japanese exports. For example, after a visit to Shanghai in 1899, Mutō Sanji reported that the mills there were far less productive than the best Japanese mills. While the total number of spindles in the Shanghai plants was impressive, productivity per spindle was about half the Japanese level in Chinese-owned mills and about two-thirds that in Western-owned mills. Mutō also thought the Chinese mills were very badly managed. "One ought to say they have no management methods at all," he noted. The Chinese had no proper accounting systems to show how much raw cotton their mills consumed, how much steam was generated by coal purchased, or what wage outlays were. At the end of the year, they merely subtracted outgo from income to balance the books. The foreign mills were superficially better run, but they still relied on Chinese compradors to buy raw cotton, manage the mills, and market the yarn produced. Mutō concluded that it was unlikely that the Japanese spinning industry would lose out in competition with the Chinese mills. Even the Western-owned mills would not be strong competitors for another two or three years.[11]

[9] See Ijima Manji, *Nihon bōseki shi* (A history of the Japanese cotton spinning industry) (Tokyo: Sogensha, 1929), pp. 115–117.

[10] See Tsusanshō, *Shōkō seisakushi* (A history of commercial and industrial policy), vol. 15 (Tokyo: Tsusansho, 1972), pp. 193–197.

[11] Mutō, *Mutō Sanji zenshū*, vol. 1, pp. 389–406.

Profits in the domestic spinning industry were also at a relatively high level compared to the China mills. The British-owned Ewo Spinning Company did better than the Chinese-owned spinning companies, but average dividends for Japanese spinning firms seem to have run higher than Ewo's dividends down until 1910 (see table 3.2). Given a choice, it made more sense to put capital into expansion at home than into direct investment abroad. The reason that Mutō Sanji had gone to Shanghai in the first place was precisely to determine whether or not Kanegafuchi should build a new mill in Shanghai or use the same funds to take over a bankrupt venture in Japan. His conclusion was that it made no sense to invest in China, where land costs were high and the supply of experienced factory operatives unreliable. A mill built in China would not show a profit during the first year, whereas a similar plant built in Japan would. Furthermore, it would probably take three or four years for a China mill to reach the productivity of a similar plant built in Japan. Hence, he concluded, it made better sense to improve operations at home and increase exports to China than to invest in a Shanghai plant.[12]

On the whole, Japanese cotton manufacturers did well by selling yarn in China instead of spinning it there. By 1914, about 30 percent (by quantity) of all domestically produced yarn was exported. China (including Hong Kong) was the largest and most important customer for these exports, consuming 92 percent of all yarn exports, or about one-quarter of total Japanese production. The China market was only slightly less important to the weaving industry. In 1914, about 70 percent (by value) of cotton piece goods exports, or about 8 percent of total Japanese production, went to China and Hong Kong. The main competitor for the Japanese product was yarn manufactured in British India, but during the decade and a half before 1914 it had gradually lost out to Japanese yarn in Manchuria, North China, and West-Central China.[13] With the future of the China market looking so bright, there were few incentives for direct investment in production facilities there.

For a variety of reasons, then, the domestic Japanese cotton spinning industry showed little interest in taking advantage of the new opportunities for investing in China made possible by the Treaty of Shimonoseki. The Chinese market for domestic yarn and cloth continued to grow, the native industry offered little competition for Japanese goods, and the profit rate on operations in China was not that impressive. Until the out-

[12] Ibid.

[13] The Japanese exported medium yarns (sixteen and twenty counts), whereas the Indian exports tended to be coarser yarns (twelve count or less), and since the Japanese had developed a technique of mixing Indian cotton with Chinese (and later American) raw cotton, the Japanese yarn was a purer white and had a higher lustre. In other words, the Japanese product was of a higher quality than the Indian.

TABLE 3.1
Exports of Cotton Yarn and Cloth, by Country of Destination, 1894–1937 (thousand yen)

	Exports to China	Exports to Hong Kong	Exports to Kwantung Territory	Exports to Korea	Total exports	Total production
1894	384	568	—	—	1,861	24,301
1895	353	458	—	—	2,316	31,869
1896	565	499	—	—	2,224	37,628
1897	627	362	—	—	2,512	49,671
1898	554	589	—	—	2,598	56,669
1899	1,144	872	—	—	3,910	69,800
1900	888	856	—	—	5,724	69,521
1901	1,246	678	—	—	5,462	78,934
1902	2,291	990	—	—	5,998	87,290
1903	2,984	1,113	—	2,409	6,875	88,559
1904	3,068	872	—	3,332	7,743	93,600
1905	4,607	1,087	—	5,235	11,492	129,231
1906	8,161	1,305	—	5,010	15,618	137,780
1907	4,718	1,083	2,731	6,386	16,344	137,619
1908	4,534	424	2,110	5,523	14,611	115,167
1909	6,728	522	3,584	4,509	17,673	152,174
1910	10,078	886	4,980	2,528	20,463	179,470
1911	10,128	562	6,757	9,005	28,685	206,239
1912	12,717	873	9,169	11,192	36,953	237,639
1913	18,965	1,143	9,109	9,410	43,015	280,501
1914	26,139	1,032	3,331	8,563	43,403	255,384
1915	27,332	913	3,178	9,388	47,890	259,880
1916	34,784	1,454	4,025	13,123	73,173	358,162

Year					
1917	84,804	2,648	8,988	20,650	148,108	553,052
1918	88,048	3,621	20,832	30,727	268,600	838,839
1919	143,283	3,208	44,207	70,884	351,195	1,178,745
1920	130,516	9,347	26,593	17,207	352,173	1,090,644
1921	100,988	12,306	15,537	—	203,673	745,040
1922	108,758	10,213	18,494	—	222,052	846,960
1923	100,292	11,625	14,618	—	234,227	921,397
1924	137,921	19,339	15,705	—	326,537	1,066,751
1925	194,013	20,577	19,502	—	432,850	1,213,331
1926	180,077	24,723	16,042	—	416,255	992,667
1927	123,492	29,583	13,119	—	383,837	892,940
1928	158,498	17,464	15,074	—	352,218	964,906
1929	150,116	20,785	15,358	—	412,707	1,071,488
1930	86,914	18,252	9,186	—	272,117	640,558
1931	30,521	9,765	9,717	—	198,732	554,766
1932	37,154	3,755	19,731	—	288,713	620,997
1933	25,605	5,675	40,448	—	383,215	937,752
1934	13,030	7,311	59,470	—	492,351	1,106,407
1935	11,912	9,802	50,955	—	496,097	1,136,043
1936	7,861	15,102	75,553	—	483,591	1,145,968
1937	11,296	9,436	85,174	—	573,065	1,448,814

Source: Kajinishi Mitsuya, ed., *Kindai Nihon sangyō hattatsushi: Sen'i*, vol. 11, statistical appendix, table III-8, pp. 52–53, for export figures, Fujino Shosaburō et al., *Chōki keizai tōkei suikei to bunseki*; vol. 11: *Sen'i kōgyō*, p. 24.

TABLE 3.2
Comparison of Dividend Rates in Chinese and Japanese Spinning Companies, 1903–1920 (percent)

	Ewo spinning	Lao King Mow spinning	Hung Yuan spinning	Jui Chi spinning	Kung I spinning	Yang Shu Poo spinning	Shanghai spinning (Japan)	Naigai Wata (Japan) 1st half/2d half		Japanese domestic spinning companies, average 1st half/2d half	
1903	8	—	—	—	—	—	8	—	—	8.1	8.3
1904	—	8	—	—	—	—	10	—	—	6.5	9.6
1905	16	8	8	5	—	—	20	—	—	17.7	21.9
1906	20	8	8	10	—	—	—	—	—	22.4	24.6
1907	5	—	—	—	—	—	—	—	—	22.9	21.9
1908	10	8	—	—	—	—	—	—	—	11.9	10.2
1909	22	6	10	7	—	—	15	12	12	11.7	11.8
1910	8	—	—	—	—	—	8	12	12	10.9	8.3
1911	14	5	—	—	12	—	8	12	10	9.9	10.5
1912	22	11	8	10	15	—	16	15	20	12.1	14.6
1913	30	12	13.3	12	15	—	20	20	15	15.2	15.3
1914	24	—	6.7	—	12	—	22	15	10	16.4	13.5
1915	32	—	7.5	—	15	—	15	12	12	15.0	15.5
1916	18	—	—	—	9	—	12	15	20	19.8	25.2
1917	40	2.5	16.7	—	20	25	12	25	35	35.0	42.1
1918	24	7	—	8.3	16	5.3	24	45	45	55.6	51.9
1919	36	50	—	50	50	20	36	50	60	51.2	54.2
1920	180	65	—	40	80	100	147	162	60	58.3	27.8

Source: Takamura Naosuke, Kindai Nihon bōsekigyō to Chūgoku, Table 5, p. 81
Note: Dividends shown as percentage of paid-in capital.

break of World War I, the metropolitan manufacturers continued to see China primarily as a market, not as an outlet for investment.

INVESTMENT IN CHINA

All this is not to say that there was no Japanese investment in the Chinese cotton industry. It did not come from the metropolis, however. Just as the initiative for Western investment in treaty port mills had come from Western trading firms already established there, so too the first successful Japanese ventures were organized by businessmen with experience in the China market. All told, there were three cases of Japanese investment in cotton manufacturing facilities in Shanghai before World War I. Each, however, was begun under slightly different circumstances, and each had slightly different results.

The first case involved partial investment by the Mitsui Trading Company (Mitsui Bussan) in the reorganization of a failing Chinese-owned mill in 1902. The decision to do so was made at the initiative of Yamamoto Jōtarō, the Shanghai branch manager. He acted without first consulting his home office, since the mill was available at a bargain price. The home office was not enthusiastic about the move. It took Yamamoto nearly six months to convince Masuda Takashi, the head of Mitsui Bussan, that the investment was a good one. Strictly speaking, the new company, the Shanghai Spinning Company (Shanhai Bōseki Kabushiki Kaisha), was not a Japanese firm but a joint venture whose stockholders included Chinese, American, British, and Indian investors as well as Mitsui Bussan. In 1908, Mitsui expanded the firm by merging it with another floundering Chinese company acquired in 1906, again largely as the result of Yamamoto's efforts.

From Mitsui's standpoint, there were several advantages to this kind of joint venture. Obviously, it did not tie up as much capital as in a wholly owned venture. But it seems probable that Mitsui was less interested in manufacturing cotton yarn than in building its trade in China. The new company was a customer for its raw cotton sales, and its products could also be marketed through Mitsui networks. Furthermore, the organization of the company provided closer ties with the influential Chinese cotton and yarn merchants who coinvested in the firm. In other words, Mitsui seems to have gone into the venture primarily to increase its trading volume.[14]

The second case of Japanese trading company investment was the Chiu Cheng Spinning Company, a joint venture organized in 1907 by a group

[14] Certainly this appears to have been the case according to Mitsui Trading Company records. See Mitsui Bunkō, ed., *Mitsui jigyōshi: Shiryōhen* (History of Mitsui Enterprises: Source materials) (Tokyo: Mitsui Bunkō, 1972), p. 444.

of Chinese merchants and the Nihon Raw Cotton Company (Nihon Menka Kaisha), a trading firm that had been buying raw cotton in China since the 1890s. In 1909, Nihon Menka bought out its Chinese partners and reorganized the company as the Japanese-owned Nisshin Spinning Company, but eventually it sold it to a group of Chinese investors led by one of Jardine, Matheson's compradors. Nihon Menka did not build a completely new mill, but took over old spinning machinery, which it augmented with new machinery from Platt Brothers. Like Mitsui, it used its connections with the Chinese merchant community to raise additional capital and its knowledge of local market conditions to sell its products.

The third and most important case involved Naigai Cotton Company (Naigai Wata Kaisha), a cotton trading firm that had already begun to diversify into manufacturing operations by purchasing two mills in Japan at Denpo (1903) and Nishinomiya (1905). The initiative behind Naigai's investment in China came from its managing director, Kawamura Rihei, an old China hand who had pioneered the development of China as a source of supply for raw cotton for Japanese mills. In contrast to men like Mutō Sanji, who knew China less well, Kawamura was convinced that a Chinese domestic cotton industry eventually would provide stiff competition for Japanese goods. The only way to protect the China market for Japanese cotton manufactures in the long run, he thought, was to build Japanese-owned mills there.

But there were more immediate motives at work, too. In the wake of the Russo-Japanese War, the company's cotton trading operations had begun to suffer for a variety of reasons—a decline in the dependence of spinning companies on trading companies for capital; competition from rivals like Mitsui Bussan and Nihon Menka, which began to buy directly and more aggressively in Indian and American cotton markets; and the emergence of a new competitor, the Gosho Company. The company had been forced to shut down its branch offices in Shanghai and New York, both major cotton trading centers. Given the decline in its competitiveness in the cotton business, it made sense to take advantage of its long experience in the China market by moving into manufacturing operations.[15]

In 1909, Naigai stockholders agreed to establish manufacturing operations in Shanghai, and two years later its mill there began operations. In 1913 and 1914, the company built two larger mills in Shanghai, and in 1917–1918 it built four more. As mentioned, Naigai went on to become the largest single cotton spinning firm in China. At the end of 1937, it owned eighteen mills in China, and in 1936 it accounted for 11 percent of

[15] This discussion of the trading-company-owned mills is based on ibid., pp. 36–52; Takamura, *Kindai Nihon mengyō*, pp. 75–92; Izumi, "Nihon bōseki shihon" pp. 57–79.

all cotton yarn production and 15 percent of all cotton cloth production in the country.[16] What made Naigai's investment in China different from that of Mitsui and Nihon Menka was that Naigai's mills were completely new. The plant built in 1911 was equipped with new Platt Brothers spinning machinery and was powered by electrical machinery bought from Siemens. It was the "model mill" in Shanghai, operating with the most up-to-date equipment on the leading edge of cotton manufacturing technology. The mill, moreover, was wholly owned by Naigai with no backing from Chinese or Western investors. In this sense, the Naigai operation marked the beginning of zaikabō.

Trading company investment in China mills was not impressive in relative quantitative terms. Of the 1,031,297 spindles in China in 1914, only 111,936, or about 9 percent, were owned by Japanese-backed companies. The three Japanese firms controlled less than half the number of spindles owned by Western companies. On the other hand, all three were profitable ventures. Between 1912 and 1915, their dividend rates were equal to or higher than the average dividends of domestic firms. The Shanghai Spinning Company paid dividends of 16 percent in 1912, 20 percent in 1913, 22 percent in 1914, and 15 percent in 1915; Naigai Wata Company paid dividends of 15 percent and 20 percent in 1912, 20 percent and 15 percent in 1913, 15 percent and 10 percent in 1914, and 12 percent in 1915. This record had a powerful demonstration effect at home, creating optimism about the potentialities of investment in China. Indeed, when Wada Tōyōji, president of Fuji Gasu Spinning Company, visited China in 1917 to consider the possibility of investing there, he was impressed by the success of Naigai Wata.[17]

In part as a result of this reassuring visit, Fuji Gasu was soon to invest in China itself—and so were most of the other major metropolitan spinning firms. But it was not simply profitability that drew them there.

THE JAPANESE COTTON INDUSTRY IN CHINA

During the decade and a half following the outbreak of World War I, there were significant shifts in the Japanese cotton industry's strategy toward China. After reaching an all-time peak in 1915, cotton yarn exports to China began a steady decline. This was part of a general decline in Japanese yarn exports, but the rate of decline in China was greater than the overall rate (see table 3.3). By the late 1920s, Japanese cotton spinning mills were producing mainly for the domestic weaving industry, rather

[16] *Naigai wata kabushiki kaisha 50–nen shi* (A fifty-year history of the Naigai Cotton Company) (Osaka, Naigai Wata Kabushiki Kaisha, 1937), appendix, p. 25.

[17] Wada Tōyōji, "Shina bōsekigyō shisatsu" (An investigation of cotton spinning in China), *Nihon bōseki rengōkai geppō*, no. 294 (February 25, 1917): 5–8.

TABLE 3.3
Japanese Export of Cotton Yarn, by Country of Destination, 1913–1937
(pounds)

	China	Manchuria	Hong Kong	Korea	Total
1903	111,709,600	—	7,006,667	3,577,867	122,881,067
1904	86,063,867	—	9,099,867	7,136,133	102,925,334
1905	93,066,400	—	2,953,867	9,946,933	106,953,466
1906	97,287,600	—	2,501,333	6,184,953	106,939,200
1907	76,347,333	—	3,131,733	10,029,200	90,590,133
1908	53,706,800	—	2,604,400	8,722,800	67,137,467
1909	94,440,800	—	1,355,467	5,890,133	103,551,200
1910	120,614,000	—	7,181,067	7,930,133	139,054,000
1911	93,729,733	—	5,167,200	9,131,067	114,003,600
1912	121,679,733	—	11,636,267	8,413,733	149,972,933
1913	155,718,933	—	13,612,400	6,094,667	187,459,467
1914	182,049,467	—	26,449,753	7,608,133	227,996,000
1915	185,568,133	—	26,096,400	10,675,200	230,356,800
1916	176,063,200	—	20,152,533	10,454,667	218,859,200
1917	142,630,267	—	25,362,133	11,038,933	188,341,200
1918	92,675,467	—	25,039,200	5,221,200	168,605,067
1919	62,504,400	—	14,255,533	6,418,933	92,134,800
1920	66,684,267	—	23,339,467	2,213,867	121,970,000
1921	69,833,467	—	22,484,533	—	116,904,400
1922	85,144,667	—	33,357,467	—	157,624,800
1923	48,627,067	—	16,043,334	—	99,329,867
1924	38,614,533	—	24,597,200	—	103,144,267
1925	53,111,200	—	23,515,067	—	124,321,067
1926	29,056,133	—	11,714,534	—	82,220,400
1927	11,504,800	—	5,154,933	—	47,062,400
1928	9,059,667	—	6,368,667	—	28,662,400
1929	7,054,933	—	2,795,467	—	26,960,667
1930	4,600,933	—	5,269,733	—	23,846,400
1931	322,400	537,733	967,733	—	12,690,267
1932	432,933	1,783,067	3,267,200	—	35,842,133
1933	172,400	4,485,067	456,800	—	19,322,133
1934	129,467	4,825,200	141,200	—	25,937,733
1935	167,600	6,776,800	1,407,333	—	38,633,200
1936	226,267	9,981,733	2,713,200	—	44,209,733
1937	796,933	11,030,267	4,167,867	—	51,892,267

Source: Kajinishi Mitsuya, ed., *Gendai Nihon sangyō hattatsu-shi: Sen'i*, vol. 11, appendix, p. 51.

than for the export market. On the other hand, the weaving industry itself had become an export industry. The overseas market for Japanese-made cotton cloth and piece goods was growing by leaps and bounds. In 1914, the cotton weaving industry had exported only about 14 percent of its output, but that figure had risen to 65 percent by 1929 and 72 percent by 1934. The rate of cloth and piece goods exports to China was less spectacular than the overall increase, but China was the largest single foreign market for Japanese-manufactured textiles. From 1918 to 1930, an average of about 41 percent of Japan's cotton piece goods were sold there every year. In other words, after 1914 the Japanese cotton industry shifted from yarn exports to cloth exports in the China market.

More striking than a change in the composition of exports, however, was the enormous expansion in Japanese direct investment in Chinese mills. According to Kang Chao's estimates, there were only 111,936 Japanese-owned spindles in 1914; by 1924 there were 1,218,544; and by 1934 there were 2,242,624 (see tables 3.4 and 3.5). The most dramatic burst of growth came in the years between 1918 and 1922, when most of the major cotton manufacturing firms in Japan had either purchased plants or built new spinning and weaving mills in Shanghai or Tsingtao. By 1930, the Japanese owned 43 mills, or about one-third of the 127 mills then operating in China. In contrast to the pre–World War I years, when the industry had been extremely reluctant to invest in China, it now did so with a vengeance. The question is: Why?

Logically, one might account for this change in the cotton industry's attitude toward direct investment in China in several ways. The first would be to find domestic macroeconomic factors that pushed the cotton manufacturers to invest in China. For example, advocates of the Leninist theory would have one look for falling rates of profit, the accumulation of "surplus capital," and the concentration of enterprises at home to explain the burst of Japanese direct investment in the treaty ports. On the other hand, as several recent writers on imperialism have suggested, what happens on the periphery is often as important in determining the nature of the imperialist relationship at any particular moment as what happens in the metropolis. An alternative explanation, therefore, would be to look at conditions in China that might have pulled the Japanese into investment. Changes in the political or economic situation in China might provide new economic opportunities or threaten old ones. Or finally, to suggest yet a third type of explanation, a complex set of factors, internal and external, might be interacting in such a way that Japanese cotton manufacturers were both pushed and pulled into China investments. The relationship between metropolis and periphery may have been governed by two dynamics, one in China and one in Japan. Evidence suggests that the last explanation is the most persuasive.

TABLE 3.4
Spindles Owned by Chinese, Japanese and Westerners, 1890–1936

	Total spindles	Chinese-owned spindles	Japanese-owned spindles	Western-owned spindles
1890	35,000	35,000	0	0
1891	42,008	42,008	0	0
1892	74,464	74,464	0	0
1893	37,448	37,448	0	0
1894	135,440	135,440	0	0
1895	180,984	180,984	0	0
1896	373,237	228,237	0	145,000
1897	437,477	276,929	0	160,548
1898	509,353	348,805		160,548
1899	539,895	379,347	0	160,548
1900	539,895	379,347	0	160,548
1901	539,895	379,347	0	160,548
1902	539,895	355,435	23,912	160,548
1903	543,763	359,303	23,912	160,648
1904	568,113	383,653	23,912	160,548
1905	582,673	398,213	23,912	160,548
1906	628,257	423,405	44,304	160,548
1907	675,329	459,941	49,016	166,372
1908	703,529	481,861	55,296	166,372
1909	728,057	512,213	55,296	160,548
1910	755,917	540,073	55,296	160,548
1911	778,957	540,073	78,336	160,548
1912	780,857	541,973	78,336	160,548
1913	865,777	520,993	111,936	232,848
1914	1,031,297	673,401	111,936	245,954
1915	1,031,297	619,391	169,952	245,954
1916	1,160,993	758,511	156,528	245,954
1917	1,271,361	857,703	167,704	245,954
1918	1,485,633	998,755	240,904	245,954
1919	1,468,142	889,032	332,922	246,188
1920	2,832,920	1,774,974	801,662	256,284
1921	3,261,060	2,134,854	866,920	259,286
1922	3,610,720	2,272,098	1,080,756	257,866
1923				
1924	3,645,226	2,176,166	1,218,544	250,516
1925	3,572,440	2,034,816	1,332,304	205,320
1926				
1927	3,674,686	2,099,058	1,370,308	205,320
1928	3,850,016	2,181,880	1,514,816	153,320
1929	5,223,956	2,395,792	1,674,844	153,320
1930	4,997,902	2,499,394	1,821,280	177,228

TABLE 3.4 (*cont.*)

	Total spindles	Chinese-owned spindles	Japanese-owned spindles	Western-owned spindles
1931	4,904,788	2,730,790	2,003,388	170,610
1932	5,019,917	2,773,273	2,063,448	183,196
1933	5,171,600	2,885,796	2,098,176	187,628
1934	5,381,688	2,951,436	2,242,624	187,628
1935	5,526,847	3,008,479	2,284,860	233,508
1936	5,635,066	2,919,708	2,485,352	230,006

Source: Kang Chao, *The Development of Cotton Textile Production in China*, pp. 301-304.

The turning point in the cotton industry investment strategy toward China came during the war years 1914–1918, when market conditions in China changed. Imported yarn, Indian as well as Japanese, began to face increased competition from Chinese-owned cotton mills. From the early 1890s, a Chinese import substitute cotton industry developed, partly through government initiative and partly through private investment. New Chinese-owned mills opened nearly every year. Before 1914 the industry was not very stable, and mills often went bankrupt or changed hands for other reasons. But the outbreak of World War I created new opportunities for Chinese investors. Prices and profits leaped to unprecedented heights, and many new investors came into the cotton industry from backgrounds in the cotton trade or other kinds of trade. According to one estimate, Chinese yarn production (by volume) more than doubled between 1913 and 1918, and the number of Chinese-owned spindles grew from 520,993 to 889,032 between 1914 and 1919 (see table 3.4). The Chinese moved into the production of lower count yarns that had been imported from India and Japan. This worried the Japanese manufacturers. Once the Chinese gained in experience, used their profits to improve plants, and sent students abroad to study the latest technology, they would no longer need to buy from Japan.[18]

At the same time the Chinese cotton industry was booming, the Chinese government was also attempting to revise import tariffs upward. In 1902, the import tariff had been fixed at 5 percent ad valorem on the average price of goods between 1897 and 1900. Inflation of prices had subsequently reduced the effective tariff rate to the advantage of foreign imports, such as Japanese yarn, and to the disadvantage of the Chinese. In 1912–1913, the government of Yuan Shih-k'ai had proposed a revision of the tariff schedule to bring the real rate back up to 5 percent ad valorem at current price levels. Owing to opposition from all the foreign powers,

[18] For example, see the comments of Kita Matazō in Ōoka Hazama, *Kita Matazō den* (A biography of Kita Matazō) (N.p.: Nihon Menka Kaisha, 1933), pp. 305–306.

TABLE 3.5
Looms Owned by Chinese, Japanese, and Westerners, 1890–1936

	Total looms	Chinese-owned looms	Japanese-owned looms	Western-owned looms
1890	530	530	0	0
1891	530	530	0	0
1892	1,530	1,530	0	0
1893	1,000	1,000	0	0
1894	1,800	1,800	0	0
1895	2,800	2,800	0	0
1896	3,912	3,016	0	896
1897	3,912	3,016	0	896
1898	3,912	3,016	0	896
1899	3,912	3,016	0	896
1900	3,912	3,016	0	896
1901	3,912	3,016	0	896
1902	3,912	3,016	0	896
1903	3,912	3,016	0	896
1904	3,912	3,016	0	896
1905	3,912	3,016	0	896
1906	3,912	3,016	0	896
1907	3,912	3,016	0	896
1908	3,912	3,016	0	896
1909	3,912	3,016	0	896
1910	3,912	3,016	0	896
1911	4,798	3,016	886	896
1912	4,798	2,707	886	1,210
1913	4,798	2,707	886	1,210
1914	5,488	2,707	886	1,900
1915	5,488	2,707	886	1,900
1916	6,838	4,052	886	1,900
1917	6,920	4,134	886	1,900
1918	7,038	3,502	1,636	1,900
1919	7,959	3,620	1,986	2,353
1920	11,879	7,740	1,486	2,653
1921	16,224	10,645	2,986	2,593
1922	19,228	12,459	3,969	2,800
1923				
1924	22,477	13,689	5,925	2,863
1925	22,924	13,371	7,205	2,348
1926				
1927	29,788	13,459	13,981	2,348
1928	29,579	16,783	10,896	1,900
1929	29,272	16,005	11,367	1,900
1930	33,580	17,018	14,082	2,480

TABLE 3.5 (cont.)

	Total looms	Chinese-owned looms	Japanese-owned looms	Western-owned looms
1931	42,596	20,599	19,306	2,691
1932	39,564	19,081	17,592	2,891
1933	42,834	20,926	19,017	2,891
1934	47,064	22,567	21,606	2,891
1935	52,009	24,861	23,127	4,021
1936	58,439	25,503	28,915	4,021

Source: Kang Chao, The Development of Cotton Textile Production in China, pp. 305–307.

including Japan, this effort was unsuccessful, but the issue revived in 1917 when the Chinese government insisted on a revision of the tariff schedule and a moratorium on Boxer indemnity payments as a condition for entering the war. This diplomatic maneuvering moved the British and Americans to agree to higher tariffs, and the Japanese government followed suit, despite vehement protests from cotton manufacturers that it was a "question of survival" for the industry. The new tariff schedule put into effect in 1919 raised the real tariff rate from 3.5 percent to 5 percent. Although this increase might seem modest, the Japanese Cotton Spinning Association estimated that it would cut the profit margin on Japanese export yarn in half, adding a cost of three yen per picul of delivered yarn that before the war had been sold at six to seven yen.[19]

It also became apparent during the wartime years that production costs were increasing in Japan, and would probably continue to do so. In the 1890s, Japanese labor costs had been low by international standards, lower even than in India, and sufficiently low to deter investment in China. But the wartime boom, which affected Japan as well as China, forced wages upward in Japan even for unskilled female mill operatives, who made up the bulk of the work force in the cotton industry. In 1914, the average daily wage was 0.44 yen for male cotton industry operatives and 0.32 yen for females; by 1919, this had risen to 1.12 yen for males and 0.87 yen for females. In the long term, there also was the passage of the Factory Law of 1915 to be considered. It provided for a reduction in the length of the work day and prohibited night shifts for certain categories of workers. The consequence was certain to be a higher labor cost per unit of output. By contrast, the Chinese population offered a vast reser-

[19] The various petitions and manifestos issued by the Japan Cotton Spinners' Association in protest against the tariff increase may be found in the following issues of Nihon bōseki rengōkai geppō: 255 (November 25, 1913): 3–10; 256 (December 25, 1913): 1–6; 257 (January 25, 1914): 4–8; 258 (February 25, 1914): 1–3; 259 (March 25, 1914): 1–2; 270 (February 25, 1915): 3–4; 295 (March 25, 1917): 1–2 and 12–16; 296 (April 25, 1917): 1–6 and 8–17; 297 (May 25, 1917): 3–34; 301 (September 25, 1917): 3–4; and 308 (April 25, 1918): 1–2.

voir of inexpensive labor, unprotected even by the mildest sort of social legislation. Low labor costs in China, coupled with proximity to sources of raw cotton and a market for cotton manufactures, offered the prospect of lower production costs.

Faced with this array of changing conditions—an increase in Chinese competition, a rising tariff wall in China, and rising production costs at home—the Japanese cotton manufacturers could watch their exports to China drop, withdraw from the market by attrition, and/or seek new markets for lower counts of export yarn elsewhere in the world; or they could avoid direct competition with the new Chinese mills by shifting to export of higher count yarns or cotton textile goods; or for the first time they could take advantage of the manufacturing rights granted to Japan in 1895 to construct factories in the treaty ports for direct sale in the China market, thereby escaping the effects of the new tariff schedule and taking advantage of lower production costs.[20] These alternatives were not mutually exclusive, but the last required capital, and this was abundantly available as a result of the war.

The wartime boom produced enormous profits for the Japanese cotton industry. By the second half of 1918, average profit rates reached 116 percent, and average dividend payments to stockholders ran over 50 percent during the whole year. Since the 1890s, the cotton manufacturers had retained earnings for reinvestment, financing operations, or expansion. The wartime boom enabled Japanese cotton manufacturers to build up internal reserves for new ventures or diversification. This was "surplus capital," but not in the sense of capital unable to find a higher rate of return at home than abroad. It was simply capital available to firms to shift their business strategies. As one visiting American official put it in 1930, the industry's wartime profits were like the hump of a camel which enabled the industry to survive during the 1920s.[21]

Japanese cotton manufacturers used part of these wartime profits to embark on a program of direct investment in China. It should be stressed, however, that this was merely one of several ways in which this "surplus capital" was deployed. Many firms used their wartime profits to absorb smaller firms through purchase or merger, to upgrade technology

---

[20] It is interesting to note that even though production costs were undoubtedly lower in Korea than in Japan, there was no rush to invest there. On the contrary, the cotton manufacturers made strenuous efforts to prevent the Korea Government General from subsidizing a mill financed by private funds. Unlike the China market, the Korean market was secure, free from foreign competition and protected by Japan's own tariff barrier. Had the China market been equally secure, or at least as secure as it had been before 1914, then there might have been no incentive to invest there either.

[21] Charles K. Moser, *The Cotton Textile Industry of Far Eastern Countries* (Boston: Pepperell Manufacturing Company, 1930), p. 5.

through the establishment of integrated spinning-weaving operations or shifting from steam to electrical power, or to diversify into new lines of manufacturing such as wool, silk, or artificial fibers.[22] This underlines the fact that the Japanese manufacturers were not pushed or forced into foreign investment because the domestic market was limited. On the contrary, between 1918 and 1924, when investment in China leapt upward, the expansion of productive capacity at home was equally impressive. The number of spindles rose by 1.6 million, and the number of looms by 24,000. This compared favorably with expansion in China, where the number of Japanese-owned spindles increased by 1 million and the number of Japanese-owned looms only by 4,000 (see table 3.6).

The rush of direct investment in China began in 1918 when Fuji Gasu Spinning Company and two trading companies (Nichimen and Itō Chū) jointly invested in the purchase of Hung Yuan Spinning Company, a failing American-owned enterprise, and reorganized it as a new company, the Nikka Spinning Company, capitalized at ten million yen. Two more mills were added to the existing plant in 1921 and 1923, and in 1924 the company bought two more mills from the Paocheng Spinning Company, a Chinese firm. Anxious not be lost in the competition, other Japanese companies joined the rush. Cotton company directors and managers sailed off on exploratory missions to the mainland, examining possible plant sites and looking at the potential market. By 1924, Dai Nihon, Gōdō, Tōyō, Kanegafuchi, Nisshin, Kurashiki, Fuji, Nagasaki, and Toyota all owned mills. None of the leading Japanese cotton firms wanted the others to get the jump on it. Even Mutō Sanji, the head of Kanegafuchi, who had long argued that building mills in China would cut into Japan's export market and cost jobs at home, and who even in 1917 called the Treaty of Shimonoseki a "great diplomatic mistake," was persuaded that his company could not afford to be left out.[23]

[22] For a discussion of these developments, see Kajinishi Mitsuhaya, ed., *Gendai Nihon sangyō hattatsushi: Sen'i* (A history of the development of modern industry: Textiles), vol. 11(1) (Tokyo, Grendai Nihon Sangyō Hattatsushi Kenkyūkai, 1964), pp. 387–390, 442–444, 451–454.

[23] For Mutō's remark, see Mutō Sanji, "Waga sangyō hatten to Shina kankei mondai" (The development of our industry and the problem of China relations), *Nihon bōseki rengōkai geppō*, no. 295 (March 25, 1917): 13. Details on the burst of Japanese investment in treaty port cotton mills may be found in Takamura, *Kindai Nihon mengyō*, pp. 95–133; Izumi, "Nihon bōseki shihon"; Kuwabara, "Senzen ni okeru Nihon bōsekikigyō"; Nishikawa Hiroshi, " 'Zaikabō' no tenkai to Chūgoku menseihin ichiba no saihensei" (The development of Japanese spinning mills and the reorganization of the cotton goods market in China), *Keizai kenkyū* 27, 1 (March 1977): 351–411; Yang Tien-i, "Chūgoku in okeru Nihon bōsekigyō ('Zaikabō') to minzokubō no sōkoku" (Rivalry between the Japanese spinning industry and Chinese spinning industry in China), in Abe Hiroshi, ed., *Ni-Chū kankei to bunka massatsu* (Tokyo: Gannando Shoten, 1982), pp. 253–275; Tō-A Kenkyūjo, *Nihon no tai-Shi tōshi* (Japanese investment in China) (Tokyo, Tō-A Kenkyūjo, 1942), pp. 215–217.

TABLE 3.6
Comparison of Spinning/Weaving Capacity in Japan and Japanese-Owned Mills in China, 1914–1936 (in thousands)

	Spindles in Japan	Spindles in China	Looms in Japan	Looms in China
1914	2,657	112	25	1
1915	2,808	166	30	1
1916	2,875	157	31	1
1917	3,060	168	36	1
1918	3,228	241	40	1.6
1919	3,488	333	44	2
1920	3,814	802	51	1.5
1921	4,161	867	55	3
1922	4,517	1,081	61	4
1923	4,198	1,081	61	—
1924	4,870	1,219	64	6
1925	5,186	1,332	68	7
1926	5,411	—	72	—
1927	5,751	1,370	72	14
1928	6,281	1,515	71	11
1929	6,609	1,675	73	11
1930	7,045	1,821	76	14
1931	7,375	2,003	74	19
1932	7,848	2,063	76	18
1933	8,525	2,098	83	19
1934	9,326	2,243	87	22
1935	10,330	2,285	90	23
1936	11,976	2,485	96	29
1937	12,297	—	100	—

A bandwagon mentality was clearly at work in the industry. Some companies, however, were more agressive than others in investing in China. In an interesting study, Kuwahara Tetsuya has analyzed the factors influencing the decisions of individual firms. He has concluded, first, that firms most heavily dependent on overseas yarn markets were more likely to invest in China than those who did not; second, that firms with smaller weaving capacities were more likely to invest than those with large capacity, since they were adversely affected by the shift in Chinese demand from yarn to textile goods; and third, that firms producing medium and finer counts of yarn were more likely to invest than those dependent on the production of coarse yarns. These conclusions were based on an analysis of aggregate figures for the whole cotton industry. It is possible that other factors may have been at work as well. In commenting on Kuwahara's conclusions, Miyamoto Matao has suggested that firms with stronger financial positions, that is, larger internal reserves of capital, were probably in the best position to invest in China. Similarly, since wage increases did not rise uniformly across the industry, those firms with labor costs rising at a faster rate had more incentives to set up offshore plants than did those with more rigid labor costs. Obviously, however, a full understanding of the decisions of individual firms will require more extensive research in company archives and reports.[24]

The early 1920s saw rapid growth in the Chinese domestic industry as well, but it is striking to note the growth rate for Japanese-owned capacity was not only higher but steadier. While Chinese spinning companies often changed hands, bought out by other Chinese firms or by Japanese firms, the Japanese firms did not. Similarly, output of Japanese-owned spindles and looms increased at a faster rate than output from Chinese mills (see table 3.7). Most of the Japanese-owned mills were concentrated in Shanghai, the national center of the industry, but there were also several in Tsingtao, which had come under Japanese control during World War I.

The Competitiveness of Zaikabō

Given the Chinese political situation in the 1920s, Japanese investment in the Chinese cotton manufacturing industry could hardly have come at a worse time. When Japanese had first acquired the right to set up manufacturing facilities in China, the Chinese government had been unable to refuse anything to anyone. By the end of World War I, however, foreign economic privileges came under heavy political attack in China, and the Japanese were singled out for special attention. In 1927, Kita Matazo (of Nihon Raw Cotton) grumbled, "Before the Russo-Japanese War, when the Chinese created problems, they paid for it. But since the world war, the Chinese have ignored treaties and everything, and things have changed enormously."[25] Indeed they had. Major boycotts were launched against Japanese goods in 1915, 1919, 1923, 1925, 1927, and 1928. Of the 209 strikes in Shanghai between 1918 and 1929, 119 (or 56.94 percent) occurred in the Japanese-owned mills. In the middle of the 1920s, the new Kuomintang-controlled government attempted to raise tariff rates and recover tariff autonomy. In 1928, a manifesto of the Sino-Japanese Business Association gloomily observed, "The direct and indirect harm suffered

[24] T. Kuwahara, "The Business Strategy of Japanese Cotton Spinners: Overseas Operations, 1890 to 1931," in Akio Okochi and Shinichi Yonezawa, eds., *The Textile Industry and Its Business Climate* (Tokyo: University of Tokyo Press, 1982), pp. 139–166; see also comments on this article in the same volume by Matao Miyamoto, pp. 169–173.

[25] Ōoka, *Kita Matazō den*, pp. 56–68.

TABLE 3.7
Production of Yarn and Cloth of Mills in China, by National Ownership for Selected Years

	Yarn in thousands of bales				Cloth in thousand sq. yards			
	China	Great Britain	Japan	Total	China	Great Britain	Japan	Total
1924	1,183 (62.6)	95 (5.0)	613 (32.4)	1,891	170,655 (48.2)	75,965 (21.4)	107,810 (30.4)	354,160
1930	1,401 (60.3)	96 (3.9)	878 (35.8)	2,456	305,960 (45.1)	69,520 (10.2)	303,520 (44.7)	679,000
1936	1,564 (58.4)	68 (2.5)	1,047 (39.1)	2,680	531,861 (37.0)	80,615 (5.6)	826,633 (57.4)	1,439,109

Source: Takamura Naosuke, Kindai Nihon bōsekigyō to Chūgoku, p. 169.

by all the foreign powers as a result of many years of civil strife have been considerable. Commerce and foreign trade have been hurt and are declining due to the recent radical antiforeign movements, illegal taxes, and the like, and *investments in business enterprises have been under heavy pressure.* If the present situation continues, then both national productive power and market demand in China will continue to decline, and civil strife will exert an unfortunate influence on the economy in general."[26]

Despite these dire prognostications and a deepening rift in Sino-Japanese relations, Japanese-owned cotton mills in China flourished. Their capacity continued to expand, and so did their production. How can one account for this continuing success in the face not only of increased Chinese competition but also of anti-imperialist political pressure?

One might argue that the structure of treaty privilege protected Japanese investments in China. Obviously, the treaty structure guaranteed the political security of the Japanese mills, protecting them against interference by the Chinese government. There was no need for them to purchase manufacturing licenses, nor was there any need to fear arbitrary confiscation. Japanese spinning firms could operate with a degree of autonomy from government interference that Chinese firms could not match, and given the avaricious character of the Chinese government even after the revolution, this was not unimportant. While Chinese mill owners had to pay a melange of levies—local taxes, flood relief taxes, printing taxes—the Japanese had only to pay modest real estate taxes to the International Settlement in Shanghai and fees to the Japanese Residents' Association (Nihon Ryūmindan). And, of course, the treaty structure prevented even strongly nationalist Chinese governments from imposing tariff barriers on goods manufactured in the treaty ports. In other words, the political costs of operating in China were quite low as a result of the extraterritorial status of the Japanese mills—and possibly lower than those of Chinese firms strong-armed by the Nationalist government and other political authorities.[27]

But treaty privileges do not provide a very good explanation for the success of the Japanese mills. Treaty rights were not sufficient to head off boycotts against Japanese goods, whether manufactured at home or in China, nor were they sufficient to prevent intense and often violent labor strife in the treaty ports. And in any case, the British enjoyed the same privileges as the Japanese, but their mills did not do nearly so well. A much simpler explanation for the success of the Japanese cotton industry in China can be found in its ability to compete even as political conditions became more difficult. The Japanese mills were able to produce goods of

[26] Ryūmonsha, *Shibusawa Eiichi*, pp. 494–495. Emphasis added.
[27] Takamura, *Kindai Nihon mengyō*, pp. 190–191.

consistent quality at competitive prices. Otherwise it would have made no sense for Japanese firms to stay in China. To explain the success of zaikabō it is necessary to look at its clout in the marketplace.

In a general way, that clout can be explained by the fact that the Japanese mills were the overseas extension of an industry that had already matured in Japan. The Chinese spinning industry, by contrast, was an infant industry, and its learning curve was much shorter and flatter. The Japanese firms had long experience, a firm financial base, and professional management. While most of the Chinese mill owners and managers were newcomers to manufacturing who came from backgrounds in trade and were often interested only in short-term profit, the Japanese firms were run by corporate managers who looked after their employers' long-term interests. In this respect, the Japanese had an advantage even over the British mills. Their owners often left mill operation to compradors, who bought the raw materials and marketed the finished product. "The compradors have the bad habit of considering their own profit while putting the company profit in second place," a Japanese observer pointed out in 1924. "The reason for good performance in the Japanese-owned mills is that a majority of the managerial staff are Japanese, and the supervision of workers, buying, and selling are all done by Japanese without using Chinese."[28] So while the Chinese cotton industry continued to grow in the 1930s, the better-managed Japanese firms acquired an ever larger share of production.

MANAGEMENT PRACTICES IN JAPANESE AND CHINESE MILLS

Several management practices may have given the Japanese cotton spinning mills advantages over their British and Chinese competitors.

Marketing

Undoubtedly a major advantage the Japanese mills enjoyed was the favorable niche they carved for themselves in the China market.[29] As table 3.8 indicates, the Japanese moved heavily into the production of the finer middle and higher count yarns, suitable for machine weaving, leaving the market for coarser lower count yarns to the British- and Chinese-owned mills, which sold to handloom producers. While the handloom market was large, it was also highly competitive, much more so than the market for higher counts. In effect, this gave the Japanese an automatic advantage. The Japanese firms also created an internal market for their own

[28] Nishikawa Kiichi, *Shina keizai sōran. (3) Mengyō to sen'i manpu* (Survey of the Chinese economy: Cotton and textiles) (Shanghai: Nihondo Shobo, 1924), p. 180.

[29] Takamura, *Kindai Nihon mengyō*, pp. 188–189.

TABLE 3.8
Monthly Production Capacity, Shanghai Mills, by Yarn Count and National
Ownership, 1929 (bales)

Yarn count	Japanese-owned mills		Chinese-owned mills		British-owned mills		Total
8–14	1,262	(6. 8%)	15,340	(82.7)	1,950	(10.5)	18,552
16	7,276	(39. 8%)	10,500	(57.4)	520	(2.8)	18,296
20	15,576	(47. 5%)	12,000	(36.6)	5,200	(15.9)	32,776
21–32	1,554	(50.35%)	1,530	(49.6)	—		3,084
40 +	9,647	(83. 1%)	1,960	(16.9)	—		11,607
Total	36,315	(43. 1%)	41,330	(49)	7,670		84,315

Source: Chin Chen, Chung-Kuo chin-tai kung-yeh-shih tzu-liao, vol. 4, p. 205.

yarn production by building integrated spinning-weaving mills. Depending on the flow of demand, they could produce textiles as well as yarn, or if the market in China stagnated, they could export their production to Southeast Asia, as they began to in the late 1920s.[30]

But the Japanese were also skilled at adapting to the needs of the Chinese market. Even in the late 1890s, before the Japanese had captured a substantial part of the Chinese yarn market or built mills in China, they displayed a sensitivity to local conditions. As a visiting mission from Lancashire noted with some respect, "By almost imperceptible degrees, [the Japanese] are educating and prompting the Chinese taste in matters textile with a tact that is suggestive, and are tempting the Chinese love of dress by a study of requirements, rather than by a speculative intrusiveness, which throws into the market a mass of something which may or may not sell. Versatile and energetic to a degree, not only are they continually introducing new qualities and varieties of goods, but they are closely imitating the older established [foreign makes] . . . with a certain amount of success."[31]

Not only did the Japanese trading companies carry out this kind of "market research," they set up their own marketing networks, deliberately bypassing the compradors on whom the other foreign trading firms relied. By the 1910s, the big cotton trading firms such as Nihon Menka, Tōyō Menka, and Gosho had established branch networks that provided a steady inflow of information about local market conditions. Their agents were well aware of what goods could be sold where and which Chinese dealers were the most reliable. Indeed, it is said that the major trading companies shared information, for example, blacklisting dishon-

[30] Sampei Kōko, Nihon mengyō hattatsushi (A history of the development of the Japanese cotton industry) (Tokyo: Keiō Shobo, 1941) p. 265.
[31] Report of the Blackburn Mission, p. 190.

est Chinese dealers who accepted delivery of goods, then defaulted on payments.[32] When the Japanese began to invest directly in their own mills, it is not at all surprising that they should have carried over these practices from the cotton trade, or that they should have developed vertical integration between cotton trading firms and manufacturing firms. What need was there to pay fees to Chinese compradors and managers to operate their plants when the Japanese could do a better job themselves? According to one estimate, the distribution costs of British textiles in China were about 3.5 times as much as those of Japanese goods.[33]

The Japanese firms were also run by corporate managers who were often willing to take a temporary loss in order to maintain a market share. This was evident from their export marketing practices. As a U.S. Commerce Department report noted in 1916, the Japanese "regulate their prices not always according to the actual cost of goods but according to market conditions. When prices are high and goods are not moving freely they will quote a little under market to get business and keep their machines going."[34] This gave them staying power in the market.

Raw Materials

With respect to raw material costs, the Japanese mills had an automatic advantage because of their product line. In the spinning of cotton yarn, raw cotton accounted for 70–90 percent of production costs, but the higher the count of cotton yarn, the lower the cost of raw cotton. According to the estimate of one mill in Tientsin, raw cotton claimed nearly 88 percent of the cost for ten-count yarn, but only 78 percent for twenty-count. Since the Japanese mills produced higher counts, their raw materials costs were lower.

The Japanese mills were also able to keep their raw materials costs down because they did not have to rely on the purchase of Chinese-grown cotton. Instead, they could use American or Indian cotton, which together accounted for a little less than one-third of the cotton used in the production of manufactured yarn in China during the early 1920s. Most foreign cotton was imported by Japanese trading companies specializing in raw cotton, and much of it was cotton reexported from Japan. In other words, the main company in Japan bought large quantities of raw cotton in the world market to supply both the metropolitan mills and those in

[32] Fong, *Cotton Industry*, pp. 268–271.

[33] Tien-i Yang, "Foreign Business Activities and the Chinese Response, 1842–1937," in Akio Okochi and Tadakatsu Inoue, eds., *Overseas Business Activities* (Tokyo: Tokyo University Press, 1984).

[34] Ralph M. Odell, *Cotton Goods in China* (Washington, D.C.: Government Printing Office, 1916), pp. 107–108.

China. To bring costs down even further, in 1925 an Indian Cotton Importing Association, consisting mainly of four Japanese mills, two Japanese cotton trading companies, one British-owned mill, and four Chinese mills, arranged contracts for reduced shipping rates with NYK, OSK, and P & O lines. The main advantage accrued to the Japanese mills, which consumed most of the Indian raw cotton imports.

The close working relationship between the Japanese-owned mills and Japanese trading companies was also important in economizing on raw materials costs. It is well known that Japanese cotton trading companies enjoyed advantages of scale in both the foreign and the Chinese cotton markets. The "Big-Three" trading firms—Nihon Menka, Gosho, and Tōyō Menka—had far-flung branch office and information networks, and sufficient capital to enable them to buy cotton at the best prices. Even in China, the Japanese firms were strong enough to affect local or regional markets. In Tientsin, for example, raw cotton was traded in Japanese currency, and the Japanese trading companies could manipulate prices by agreeing not to trade in order to force prices down. Japanese cotton trading companies treated the Japanese mills preferentially, providing longer-term credit (often thirty days) on cotton purchases than the Chinese mills enjoyed (usually ten days).[35]

By contrast, the Chinese-owned mills were dependent primarily on domestic supplies of cotton, the price of which fluctuated considerably. Demand often exceeded supply, with the result that prices rose. The Chinese mills, which bought directly in the market without the mediation of large trading firms such as Nihon Raw Cotton, were more at the mercy of the sellers. Since they had few capital reserves and little operating capital, they were less able to control the timing of their purchases. Often they bought speculatively, with disastrous results.[36]

The Cost of Capital

The Japanese mills were also better financed than the Chinese mills. As mentioned, nearly all the Japanese-owned mills were backed by metropolitan Japanese with large internal reserves. Once a metropolitan firm decided to invest in China, it could acquire or ship machinery and build its plant with little need to worry about funds. By contrast, in China, where capital was raised primarily through stock subscription (and where there was no well-developed stock market), spinning firms were often unable to collect the full share of subscribed capital by the time their mills

---

[35] Yang, "Foreign Business Activities," pp. 284–285; Takamura, *Kindai Nihon mengyō*, pp. 186–191; H. D. Fong, *Cotton Industry and Trade in China* (Tientsin: Nankai University, 1932), p. 299.

[36] Kang, *Cotton Textile Production*, pp. 151–152.

were completed. They began operations with a heavy debt burden, and once underway the Chinese mill owners neither set aside reserves nor made sufficient allowance for depreciation of equipment. When a mill showed a profit—as most Chinese mills did during the wartime boom—owners chose to expand rather than retire their debts. As a consequence, the value of their fixed assets often exceeded paid-in capital.[37]

The Chinese mills were also at a disadvantage with respect to operating capital. Whereas the Japanese mills could make favorable credit arrangements with the cotton trading companies for the purchase of raw cotton, or borrow other working capital from the Yokohama Specie Bank, the Industrial Bank, or various private banks operating in China (such as the Mitsui or Mitsubishi banks), the Chinese had to borrow in the domestic credit market, where interest rates were high and terms unfavorable. A 1933–1934 survey indicates that while some mills paid only 6 percent interest rates, others paid as high as 20 percent. To borrow, the Chinese mills often had to mortgage plant or inventories. When hard times hit, they often were unable to repay their debts. The result was sale or foreclosure. Between 1931 and 1934, as a result of direct investment or loans, banks controlled a dominant interest in thirty Chinese mills, of which sixteen were taken over by the bank, four were sold, and five were shut down.[38] By contrast, the Japanese mills could use close ties with Japanese trading firms and banks to tide over the crises, for example, during periods of boycott against Japanese goods.

With limited start-up capital and with little or no reserves built up, and with frequent operating losses, the Chinese mills continued to rely heavily on loans to keep going. According to one estimate, in 1934, 50 percent of the Chinese mills had debt burdens in excess of half of their capital; 40 percent had debts equal to or more than the amount of their capital; and only 10 percent had debts that were less than half their capital.[39] By contrast, very few Japanese mills ran up heavy debt burdens, and certainly none of this magnitude. The upshot was that the Chinese mills were less stable than the Japanese firms, and even those that stayed afloat had higher capital costs.

[37] Ibid., pp. 143–144; Fong, *Cotton Industry*, pp. 220–222 and 317–319; Okabe Masao, "Kaji bōseki no keiei ni okeru mondai" (Problems in the management of the Chinese cotton spinning industry), *Tō-A keizai ronsō* 1, 4 (December 1941): 167–177.

[38] Yang, "Foreign Business Activities," p. 274.

[39] Takamura, *Kindai Nihon mengyō*, p. 186. According to a 1934 survey of sixty Chinese-owned and fifty Japanese-owned spinning companies, the Chinese firms had aggregate reserve funds of 4,792,000 yuan against an aggregate paid-in capital of 187,606,000 yuan, while the Japanese firms had aggregate reserve funds of 38,649,000 yuan against an aggregate paid-in capital of 98,633,000 yuan. In other words, reserve funds constituted only 2.5 percent of paid-in capital for the Chinese firms, but 39 percent for the Japanese firms. Okabe, "Kaji bōseki no keiei," p. 169.

As Kang Chao has pointed out, the financing strategies of the Chinese mill owners had little to do with a general "lack of capital" or "shortage of capital" in China. Rather, they had to do with an investor psychology that focused on short-term profit rather than long-term growth. Payment of dividends took precedence over building up internal capital reserves, depreciating fixed assets, or paying off company debt. The Chinese mill owners aimed at a quick killing in the market rather than efficiency of production or quality of product. There was a speculative bent to the operation of the Chinese mills that was almost entirely absent in the Japanese mills, which were managed by corporate managerial bureaucracies rather than by their owners.[40]

Labor Costs

In comparison with wage rates in the Chinese-owned mills, however, the wage bill in the Japanese-owned mills was rather high. One estimate suggests that if wage rates in British-owned mills were assigned an index of 100, and in Chinese-owned mills an index of 105, then the rate in Japanese mills would have to be set at 127.[41] This suggests that the Japanese enjoyed no advantage in this respect. On the other hand, the Japanese enjoyed a considerable advantage in labor productivity. A variety of surveys suggest that workers in Japanese mills were capable of handling a larger number of spindles or looms, and that energy capacity per worker was also higher, with the result that output per worker was considerably higher (see table 3.9).

The higher labor productivity in the Japanese-owned mills resulted in part from certain technological advantages. For one thing, machinery in Japanese-owned mills tended to be newer and less subject to breakdown. By contrast, machinery in Chinese mills was often secondhand, bought at bargain prices at home or abroad. Nor was there standardization of equipment in the Chinese mills. Often several different types of machines would be used in one mill. According to a survey of forty-one Chinese mills in the early 1930s, 30 percent of the spinning machinery had been manufactured twenty-six to forty-seven years earlier, and 14 percent sixteen to twenty-five years before.[42] Breakdowns in machinery that wasted time and materials, coupled with a casual attitude toward maintenance and repair, considerably reduced the operational efficiency of the Chinese mills, which frequently operated at only partial capacity. Furthermore, while Japanese mills tended to use a uniform supply of cotton and to specialize in the production of a narrow range of yarn counts—perhaps one

[40] Kang, *Cotton Textile Production*, p. 142.
[41] Takamura, *Kindai Nihon mengyō*, p. 179.
[42] Yang, "Foreign Business Activities," p. 275; Kang, *Cotton Textile Production*, p. 161.

TABLE 3.9
Cross-National Comparison of Worker Productivity, 1929

Country	Amount of yarn produced per spindle per hour (momme)	Number of spindles per operative (spindles)	Amount of yarn produced per worker per hour (momme)
U.S. South	4.5	1,120	5,000
U.K. Lancashire	5.0	600	3,000
Japan	5.4	400	2,100
China: Japanese mills	4.5–5.5	200–240	1,000–1,100
China: Chinese mills	3–4	165–240	600–700

Source: Takamura, *Kindai Nihon bōsekigyō to Chūqoku*, p. 81.

or two—the Chinese mills frequently relied on cotton that varied in quality and attempted to produce a wider range of counts. Time was lost as spinning machinery was adjusted to accommodate changing raw material inputs or final product outputs, with a concomitant reduction in labor efficiency.[43] Finally, the Japanese mills tended to be larger in scale than the Chinese mills, and they were often run as integrated spinning and weaving operations. In 1930, for example, while thirty-three out of forty-three Japanese-owned mills were integrated, only twenty-five out of eighty-one Chinese-owned mills were.[44]

Behind these technological differences was a different managerial attitude toward labor. As H. D. Fong observed more generally about Chinese industry, "the Chinese factory substitutes number for efficiency."[45] On the other hand, Japanese managers assumed that it was possible to cut costs by increasing the efficiency of labor. As Japanese managers repeatedly told Arno Pearse on his visit in 1929, "the Chinese make good cotton mill operatives, provided they are properly trained, that they are willing to learn, that they are docile and easily contented."[46] The Japanese managers were able to transform labor recruits who came illiterate, uneducated, and "ignorant of the elements of cleanliness and sanitation"

[43] Kang, *Cotton Textile Production*, pp. 152–153.

[44] Fong, *Cotton Industry*, pp. 218–220.

[45] H. D. Fong, *Industrial Organization in China* (Tientsin: Nankai Institute of Economics, 1937), p. 37.

[46] Arno S. Pearse, *Cotton Industry of Japan and China* (Manchester: Taylor, Garnett, Evans, 1929), p. 149.

into a disciplined work force. Often a cadre of Chinese workers was sent to Japan for a period of training in mill operations there, or Japanese instructors were brought out from the home company. Outside observers inspecting Japanese-owned mills were usually impressed by the order and efficiency on the shop floor. By contrast, in Chinese mills it was not unusual to see workers (especially the younger ones) chatting or playing, taking naps by their machinery, eating lunches during work periods, suckling babies, or even entertaining their children.[47]

Somewhat less clear is the relation of labor productivity to methods of labor management. The British-owned mills in China, and some Chinese-owned mills, relied on a comprador system of labor management: a comprador subcontracted with the company owners to produce yarn at a fixed amount of unit production cost and supervised the whole production process, including the hiring and payment of workers. In other words, the ownership of the mill had no direct relationship with the workers. But most Japanese mills adopted either the "Number One" system or a direct employment system. The former was a kind of labor contracting system, not unlike the *oyabun-kobun* system that prevailed in many early Japanese factories. A general manager was employed by the company with the power to oversee several "Number One" bosses or foremen, none of whom was actually a worker, but who recruited workers, supervised the production line, and paid wages. Under the direct method of labor management, introduced into the Japanese-owned mills, workers were hired and paid directly by the company. On the mill floor, supervisors at the highest level were Japanese, and below them were skilled or experienced Chinese workers, selected for their loyalty to the company, who acted as overseers on the production line.[48]

As one might suppose, the "Number One" system—like the comprador system—was less efficient than direct supervision by company employees. The quality of workers was often poor, incentives for workers to work hard were less, pilfering of materials was common, and the foremen often abused their authority over the workers by demanding kickbacks or using physical coercion. On the other hand, indirect hiring and supervision may also have provided the companies with a buffer against labor discontent. Although there is no clear statistical evidence to indicate which system was more common in the Japanese-owned mills, anecdotal evidence suggests that the Japanese mills, particularly those owned by the larger metropolitan firms, preferred the direct employment system, and many Chinese mills may have followed suit. As Pearse reported, "Several Chinese mill owners had praised to me the superiority of the Japanese

[47] Ibid., p. 164; Takamura, *Kindai Nihon mengyō*, pp. 183–184.
[48] Takamura, *Kindai Nihon mengyō*, pp. 176–177.

system of training a comparatively large number of female overseers and by instituting greater discipline."[49] The reason was simple: it reduced the number of workers required. All this suggests that labor management systems in the Japanese mills may also have given them some advantage with respect to labor productivity.

CONCLUSION

Would the Japanese-owned cotton mills have flourished even had there been no structure of treaty privilege in China? Like all counterfactual questions, this does not admit of a clear answer. On the other hand, attempting to answer it may clarify the economic significance of the treaty system, at least for one Japanese industry.

There can be little doubt that securing manufacturing rights in 1895 was the sine qua non for Japanese investment in China. As Eugene Staley observed long ago, "The permanent investor of bona fide capital wants a long-run promotion of stability, a strong government which can help guarantee tranquility and the security of property."[50] The treaty structure provided a degree of political and legal security that otherwise might not have been obtained. The collective nature of the unequal treaty system brought any Japanese direct investment in China under the implicit protection of the Western powers. To be sure, the collective solidarity of the powers in China eroded in the late 1920s when the British and Americans showed greater willingness than the Japanese to make concessions to Chinese nationalism. But even as Sino-Japanese tension escalated in the early 1930s, the Japanese-owned mills in Shanghai escaped retaliation. Without the treaty structure, it is difficult to imagine this could have happened.

Until the outbreak of the China War, the treaty structure provided a protected enclave in which the Japanese mills could operate safely. Lacking this protected enclave, it seems probable that domestic cotton manufacturers would not have invested in China in the first place. What incentive was there to invest in China if the investment could not be kept secure? The China market was "boundless," as Mutō Sanji had pointed out, but there was no need to build factories there to supply it. Production from metropolitan mills could satisfy Chinese demand for yarn handily, and apparently did so down until World War I. Otherwise, industry leaders would not have waited more than twenty years after the Treaty of Shimonoseki to begin investing in China.

How would the Japanese cotton industry have dealt with rising Chinese

[49] Pearse, *Cotton Industry*, pp. 149, 171–172.
[50] Eugene Staley, *War and the Private Investor* (Garden City, N.Y.: Doubleday, 1935), p. 161.

competition (or increased Chinese tariffs) had there been no treaty structure? Again, no certain answer is possible, but the actions taken by the industry in the 1910s and 1920s suggest that it might have pursued a number of strategies: It might have tried to cut domestic production costs further to make Japanese exports more competitive; it might have engaged in dumping to maintain a market share at all costs; or it might have selected a market niche, such as higher count yarns or finer textiles, where Japan had comparative advantage. And failing that, the industry might simply have sought out new markets in other, less developed countries where it could compete with British and Indian goods, much as it did in the late 1920s and 1930s. In other words, Japanese cotton manufacturers may have decided that, however important China had been, it was by no means indispensable to the survival of the industry.

Although the treaty structure clearly provided a powerful incentive for investment in zaikabō, it cannot fully explain the success of the Japanese mills. As I have argued, that success has to be accounted for the competitiveness of the Japanese mills—their advantages with respect to labor management, capital supplies, access to raw materials, and managerial style. In this respect, the experience of the Japanese mills is very similar to that of other foreign enterprises in China. As Tim Wright has argued in his excellent monograph on the Chinese coal industry, treaty privileges were less important in explaining the success of foreign-owned mines in China in intra-industry competition than considerations such as quality of product, location of the mines, and geological conditions. The claim of many Chinese nationalists, and some historians of China, that the unequal treaty system gave unfair advantages to the Japanese and other foreigners is not convincing, particularly when it is remembered that the modern Chinese spinning and weaving industry continued to grow even after the entry of zaikabō into the China market.[51]

On the other hand, it cannot be denied that factors other than inherent competitiveness were of critical importance in explaining the growth of zaikabō after 1932. The outbreak of the Manchurian incident changed the geographical pattern of Japanese investment. There was little or no expansion of Japanese mill capacity in Shanghai in the 1930s. Most Japanese investment took place north of the Yellow River, especially in Tientsin. During 1935–1936, for example, Japanese firms purchased four out of seven Chinese-owned mills operating in that city. The reasons for this seem clear. Not only had these firms been hit hard by the depression, they were affected by the growing Japanese military and political presence in the north, which cut off their access to the Manchurian market. Moreover,

---

[51] Tim Wright, *Coal Mining in China's Economy and Society, 1895–1937* (Cambridge: Cambridge University Press, 1984), p. 138.

they had to compete with large quantities of Japanese-made cotton goods being smuggled into North China.[52] With their markets shrinking and the Japanese ever more aggressive, Chinese mill owners in the north must have thought it prudent to sell out and cut their losses before the situation deteriorated even further. By the outbreak of the Sino-Japanese War, the Japanese dominated cotton manufacturing in the north, producing 58.7 percent of machine-made yarn and 86.5 percent of machine cotton cloth.[53] Clearly, this sudden upsurge in the Japanese presence in the north was not due simply to the competitive advantages of Japanese management.

Yet there is irony in the fact that zaikabō penetrated North China on the coattails of military and political expansion. On July 29, 1937, three weeks after the Marco Polo Bridge incident, a Chinese force of ten thousand attacked Tientsin; it was forced to withdraw only after heavy air attacks by the Japanese. The Japanese-owned mills in Tientsin escaped heavy damage, but by autumn, as a result of disruption of trade by fighting in North China, they had stopped operation. During the fall of 1937, shelling destroyed parts of many Japanese-owned mills in Shanghai, and the Toyota Spinning and Weaving Company mill on Soochow Creek was completely demolished. And in December 1937, fifteen Japanese-owned mills at Tsingtao were completely destroyed by Chinese forces. Takamura Naosuke estimates that as a result of the war zaikabō had lost 38.5 percent of its spindles, 23 percent of its mules, and 51.1 percent of its looms by the end of 1938.[54] Zaikabō, in short, paid a high price for the transformation of informal empire into direct political control—and found itself much less secure than it had been under the treaty system.

[52] D. K. Lieu (Ta-chun Liu), *The Growth and Industrialization of Shanghai* (Shanghai: China Institute of Pacific Relations, 1936), pp. 421–422.

[53] Sampei Kōkō, *Nihon mengyō hattatsushi* (A history of the development of the Japanese cotton industry) (Tokyo: Keiō Shobo, 1941), pp. 261–262.

[54] Takamura, *Kindai Nihon mengyō*, pp. 227–230.

CHAPTER 4

Japanese Imperialism in Manchuria: The South Manchuria Railway Company, 1906–1933

Ramon H. Myers

At 2:00 P.M. on September 4, 1905, Gotō Shimpei and three companions arrived at the Mukden railway station, having just come from Taipei. Several officers from the Japanese imperial staff headquarters met them and gave Gotō a horse. He quickly mounted and began galloping toward the city's north gate, where the Japanese military headquarters was located. When his companions finally caught up, they found him "engaged in a heated conversation" with General Kodama Gentarō, chief of the military staff in Manchuria.[1] Two days later, Kodama returned to Tokyo to join the Katsura cabinet. Gotō spent the next week touring southern Manchuria and then returned to Taipei. From this brief meeting between two old friends originated the concept of a large railway enterprise to manage Japanese interests just wrested from imperial Russia in a costly, bloody war.

ESTABLISHING A NEW STATE AND PRIVATE ENTERPRISE

What kind of scheme had Kodama and Gotō concocted? They had collaborated in Taiwan for a half decade to lay the foundations for that colony's successful economic development.[2] Now they planned to establish a large-scale railway enterprise in southern Manchuria. This railway scheme probably originated with Gotō, who had been asked by Kodama to draft a plan for how Japan might manage its victory spoils. According to Ueda Kyosuke, who traveled with Gotō in South Manchuria, Gotō

---

[1] Harada Katsumasa, *Mantetsu* (The South Manchuria Railway) (Tokyo: Iwanami Shoten, 1981), p. 38.

[2] Between 1897 and 1903, Gotō and Kodama had combined their talents to transform a backward, economically fragmented, and debt-ridden territory into a modern colony. See Chang Han-yu and Ramon H. Myers, "Japanese Colonial Development Policy in Taiwan, 1895–1906: A Case of Bureaucratic Entrepreneurship," *Journal of Asian Studies* 22, 2 (August 1963): 433–449.

believed that Japan must have a "proper administration of railroads."[3] The railroad track laid by Japanese Army engineers and recently taken from imperial Russia as a reward for persevering in the Russo-Japanese War should be unified under a single system based on a trunk line extending from Dairen to Ch'ang-ch'un and Antung (map 4.1).[4] Gotō also wanted this railway system to be managed separately from any administrative area that Japan might govern, and it ought to have research and development capabilities to exploit the region's rich resources for Japan's strategic interests. Associated with these same efforts, argued Gotō, Japan should encourage its people to settle in Manchuria so that Japanese interests could be further strengthened.

On April 14, 1906, Prime Minster Saionji Kinmochi, accompanied by several top-ranking officials, secretly left Tokyo to tour Manchuria.[5] Upon arriving in Mukden, they conferred with top Chinese officials. Saionji sensed Chinese apprehension about Japanese troops remaining in the region and about Japan's true intentions there. After returning to Tokyo, Saionji convened a meeting of top leaders at his Tokyo office on May 23 to map out a strategy for how Japan should operate in Manchuria. Itō Hirobumi led off by disclosing the contents of a letter he had just received from the English consulate in Mukden, urging Japan to adhere to the "Open Door" policy.[6] Table discussion then turned to how soon Japanese troops should be withdrawn and how Japan should manage the areas formerly held by Russia. Kodama then presented the plan that he and Gotō had privately agreed upon.[7] The meeting adjourned with a general consensus that the Kodama plan should be adopted but modified. Little is known of the deliberations that occurred between May 23 and June 7, when an imperial ordinance announced that a special committee would be designated to establish a special company to manage Japan's economic interests in southern Manchuria. Then, on July 13, the govern-

---

[3] Hara Hiroshi, ed., *Manshū tetsudō kensetsu hiwa* (The Secret Story of the Building of the Manchurian Railway) (Mukden: Minami Manshū Tetsudō Kabushiki Kaisha, 1939), pp. 8–9.

[4] Japan acquired Russia's privileges in Manchuria conferred upon Moscow by previous treaties with Ch'ing China. For these treaties, as well as the twenty-two articles describing the SMR and the forty-three articles for governing the Kwantung Leased Territory, see John V. A. MacMurray, comp. and ed., *Treaties and Agreements With and Concerning China, 1894–1919*, vol. 1 (New York: Oxford University Press, 1921), pp. 555–567.

[5] Harada, *Mantetsu*, p. 43.

[6] Tsunoda Jun, *Manshū mondai to kokubo hōshin* (The Manchurian Problem and National Defense Strategy) (Tokyo: Hara Shobo, 1967), pp. 310–319.

[7] For Gotō's views on the Manchurian railway system that Japan should try to manage and develop, see his *Manshū tetsudō hoan ni kansuru iken* (My comments on the Manchurian railway plan), in *Gotō Shimpei monjo* (The archives of Gotō Shimpei), reel 37.

MAP 4.1   The South Manchuria Railway

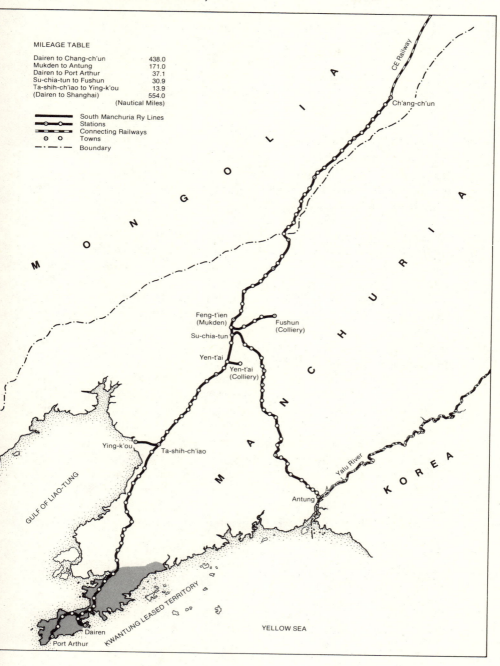

MILEAGE TABLE

Dairen to Chang-ch'un	438.0
Mukden to Antung	171.0
Dairen to Port Arthur	37.1
Su-chia-tun to Fushun	30.9
Ta-shih-ch'iao to Ying-k'ou	13.9
(Dairen to Shanghai)	554.0
	(Nautical Miles)

South Manchuria Ry Lines
Stations
Connecting Railways
Towns
Boundary

ment announced the membership of that committee, with Kodama as chairman.

The organizing committee of seventy-seven members represented a cross-section of government and society: sixteen government officials; five military officers; eight members with high, honorary titles; eight members of the Diet; and forty individuals from business and the professions.[8] On August 11, at the first general meeting called by the SMR organizing committee, the articles governing the management of the company were made public.[9]

The SMR's head office was to be in Tokyo; the authorized amount of capital came to 200 million yen, with the government contributing half that amount; and only Japanese and Chinese could be shareholders. The government's half-million shares, valued at 100 million yen, or half the amount of the authorized capital, represented the company's wealth at that time of rolling stock, coal mines at Fushun and Yen-t'ai, and so forth. The organizing committee estimated that construction costs would come to around 100 million yen for rebuilding the Dairen–Ch'ang-ch'un line, expanding Dairen's harbor, constructing structures, modernizing the two coal mines, rebuilding the Antung-Mukden line, and other tasks.[10] The government also guaranteed a return of 6 percent for fifteen years on the shares subscribed by private investors in this semi-official joint-stock venture.[11] With this new revelation, the public favorably reacted to the new company's offering of 99,000 shares by oversubscribing by a factor of more than a thousand.[12]

Other reactions, however, revealed concern. Newspapers like the *Nippon* expressed amazement at the enormity of capital investment required and the major commitment the government intended to make in southern Manchuria. Others worried about the "small margin for individual enterprises" in the region. The newspaper *Jiji* remarked that the "new railway not only represents the Japanese interests, but as it is the sole line for the use of nations' trade, it ought to be secured against the raids of the mounted bandits who, taking advantage of the impotence of the government of Peking, keep up rampant conduct," an obvious jab at the weak Ch'ing government and a veiled suggestion for more military presence in

[8] For a list of the members assigned to the organizing committee, see *The Japan Times*, July 14, 1906, p. 1. On July 16, Kodama died of a stroke and Terauchi replaced him as chairman of the organizing committee.

[9] Ibid., August 11, 1906, p. 1.

[10] Ibid., August 14, 1906, p. 2.

[11] Steven John Ericson, "State and Private Enterprise: Railroad Development in Meiji Japan," Ph.D. dissertation, Harvard University, 1985, p. 498.

[12] Ibid.

Manchuria to protect the new railroad.[13] The public reacted favorably to the government's decision to establish this huge, officially backed company. Meanwhile, the government informed the foreign community that Japan intended to adhere to the "open door" policy in China.

The company's top command structure quickly took form. On November 8, 1906, the government appointed Gotō Shimpei and Nakamura Zekō as the first president and vice-president, respectively, of the SMR.[14] These two officials then appointed distinguished officials to the company's first board of directors. On November 15, Gotō became the first director of that board, which included Kubota Masachika (governor of Togichi prefecture), Kiyono Chōtarō (governor of Akita prefecture), Kubota Katsuyoshi (director of the Bureau of the National Exchequer), Nonomura Kingarō (an official of the Industrial Bank of Japan), and Kunizawa Shinbei (chief engineer of the SMR).[15] This top team quickly set up a General Affairs Bureau to handle the company's main business and to formulate policies.

Meanwhile, Japanese military labor battalions had already been repairing the railways to be turned over to the SMR. SMR authorities appointed a commission to negotiate with the Russians on procedures to connect the South Manchuria and Chinese Eastern railway lines somewhere outside Ch'ang-ch'un. The company also requested the Formosa Association School in Taihoku (Taipei) to train future classes of students for company service.[16] On January 9, 1907, Vice-President Nakamura negotiated with army officials to transfer the railway system under military control to the SMR by early April, but the military did not relinquish its control over all facilities until the year's end.[17]

Plans were drawn up to widen the line's gauge, and in February the Japanese government purchased fifty thousand tons of steel railway cars from the United States for the SMR. On January 19, the SMR began negotiating with foreign banks for a loan of eighty million yen, of which a portion was to be used for widening the entire line before the end of the year, and another to purchase new rolling stock. By the end of spring 1907, the SMR was mobilizing more capital from abroad, rebuilding the entire line to meet conventional railway standards for using the most advanced rolling stock of the day, building warehouses, docks, and build-

[13] *The Japan Times*, August 15, 1906, p. 5. Other concerns expressed were that the organizing committee for the SMR had too many military officers (see ibid., July 17, 1906, p. 1), but from the figures available their number actually accounted for only 6 percent.

[14] Ibid., November 8, 1906, p. 1. This news report mentioned that Gotō was being perceived as "Kodama the Second."

[15] Ibid., November 15, 1906, p. 1.

[16] Ibid., December 21, 1906, p. 5.

[17] Ibid., January 9, 1907, p. 1.

ings in Dairen, and constructing a spectacular new hotel in that same harbor city for tourists.

As for the company's management style, on April 10, 1907, Baron Gotō informed his staff that he did not intend "to treat South Manchuria as I do Formosa."[18] In other words, from the very outset the SMR leadership never viewed Manchuria as a colony under direct Japanese rule and subject to Japanese law. Japan had privileges and rights in Manchuria that obviously must be respected by the Chinese and other foreigners, but Gotō argued that the Japanese had to coexist peacefully with the Chinese. The SMR staff had to "understand the manners and customs proper to Manchuria and be determined to discharge [their] duty, always bearing in mind the grand objects of the company and [its] own intentions."[19] While Gotō did not reveal those "grand objects," he clearly had in mind the expansion of Japanese interests in the region.

As for the corporate leadership and rank-and-file, Gotō urged everyone to trust him and "be a member of the great family."[20] He also reminded his staff that "their actions reflected upon the company and its prosperity." On May 29, 1907, President Gotō instructed all SMR officials "that the railway passengers should be treated with kindness and cordiality, and special attention should be given to Chinese passengers lest mutual ignorance of speech should cause impoliteness on the part of the officials and consequent bad feelings on the part of the passengers."[21]

Sensitive to the feelings of the Chinese and realizing the necessity to quiet their fears, Gotō visited Kirin province and paid his respects to the Chinese military general in charge. He then visited Peking and had an audience with the emperor and other high Ch'ing officials. Finally, to placate the Russians, he called on Prince Kilkoff in Harbin to express his "profound thanks for the goodwill and kindness showed by him in connection with the negotiations between the two sides."[22] Gotō and other Japanese officials continued to declare in their public speeches that Japan would adhere to the "open door" in Manchuria so that other parties, especially imperial China, could enjoy any economic benefits.

While developing the managerial style within the SMR that would persist for future decades, and going public to express support for the informal empire that foreigners had established in China, Gotō and his staff moved on various fronts to get the company operating in Manchuria. Difficult obstacles had to be overcome. The area under Japanese control still showed the scars of the recent war and was an extremely backward,

[18] Ibid., April 10, 1907, p. 1.
[19] Ibid.
[20] Ibid.
[21] Ibid., May 29, 1907, p. 1.
[22] Ibid., July 24, 1907, p. 1.

poor, and sparsely settled region. In May 1907, a Japanese reporter toured Port Arthur and described the hills as "bare and forbidding." Shell craters "pock-marked" the countryside, and "shattered guns and twisted iron, torn case-mates" were everywhere. Train facilities were exceedingly primitive. After a delay of around five hours, the reporter's train finally left Dairen for Mukden. Leaving the Liaotung, all one could see was "miles of giant millet awaiting the sickle."[23] The line was single-track, and when a train entered the next station a switchman at the other end stood up and waved a green flag. When the train was ready to depart, a switchman at the forward track then waved a white flag. Until that flag appeared, the train could not leave the station.[24] The narrow forty-two-inch track gauge caused considerable bumping and discomfort for passengers. The trains contained neither food nor sleeping accommodations, and the "rolling stock of every description was woefully deficient."[25]

In the spring of 1907, great activity commenced. On April 24, the SMR ordered 180 locomotives and 2,060 railway cars from American manufacturing firms. On May 1, the company purchased a plot of land one mile north of Ch'ang-ch'un's north gate and began constructing a new railway station for its line to link up with the Chinese Eastern Railway.[26] On May 22, Japan ordered another twelve million dollars worth of equipment for the SMR at top prices to ensure rapid delivery. By June, sections of the main trunk line were being double-tracked, and the train time from Dairen to Meng-chia-tun had been cut from two days to one. The Dairen hotel was almost complete, and a hotel for Ch'ang-ch'un was planned. In Dairen, construction began on a new flour mill with the capacity to manufacture seventeen hundred bags of flour each day, a new enterprise the SMR hoped would reap a profit. By the end of June, the SMR employed some ten thousand people at an annual total of five million yen in wages.

In mid-July, President Soyeda of the Industrial Bank of Japan went to London to arrange for the issuing of SMR bonds to raise four million pounds sterling, the equivalent of around forty million yen at the current exchange rate. On July 19, the London *Times* reported that the loans had been "undertaken with great readiness" but that Japan might "regret the issue and think that even an indirect addition to Japan's heavy war debt is to be deprecated."[27] The Japanese, however, never viewed this loan as an extra burden, but merely as a means to upgrade railway efficiency in

[23] "Japan in Manchuria," ibid., May 7, 1907, p. 1.

[24] Harada, *Mantetsu*, p. 52.

[25] *The Japan Times*, May 7, 1907, p. 1.

[26] Ibid., May 11, 1907, p. 1. This new station stood exactly one mile south of the Russian-owned station for the CER. The station would commence business around late August. Ibid., July 24, 1907, p. 1.

[27] Ibid., July 19, 1907, p. 1.

southern Manchuria to generate more profits. On July 23, enough bonds had been purchased to raise half of the loan at terms of 5 percent with repayment in twenty-five years. For the next few days it appeared that the remainder of the bonds would not be purchased, but by August 31 all bonds had been taken, 52 percent purchased by public investors and the balance picked up by financial underwriters.[28] President Soyeda had his loan, and he immediately went to the United States to buy new rolling stock and equipment, much to the chagrin of English manufacturers.

By late summer, the SMR began cutting costs to ensure profits. On August 20, the company closed three transport offices at Dairen, Liao-yang, and Mukden and dismissed "over fifty clerks, some of them of high rank."[29] By the end of August, the company had laid off "over six hundred men in its employ," and about one-third of the staff of the headquarters and other departments were slated for dismissal. In early November, another fifty-four railway employees were discharged, along with a "change of position of more than two hundred officials" the month before. These cost reductions seemed prompted by the need to pay 6 percent dividends to shareholders. During the last six months of 1907 the SMR earned 4.7 million yen, spent 3.9 million, and netted a profit of 800,000 yen.[30] All this with massive rebuilding, purchasing new equipment from overseas, and operating the railway at the same time. Shareholders received their 6 percent dividends, and the company still had a surplus.

For these reasons, then, President Gotō could proudly boast of the SMR's achievements at the general meeting of the board of directors on December 17, 1907.[31] He pointed out that the railroad line between Dairen and Su-chia-tun had been double-tracked and the gauge widened to 56½ inches. New rolling stock from the United States already had arrived and been used on a trial-run basis on the short line connecting Dairen and Port Arthur. Work already had begun at the Fushun colliery to develop new pits and install modern equipment to increase coal output. The company had received numerous new business applications to locate in the Kwantung Leased Territory and in the areas owned by the SMR. The company now generated about five million yen a year, of which four million came from railway operations. Gotō did not express any alarm about the new Peking-Mukden line then being built, simply saying that "though more or less competition may possibly arise, the statistics will assure that the company will secure a fair share of the trade."[32]

Although proud of the SMR's early accomplishments, Gotō was less

---

[28] Ibid., August 31, 1907, p. 2.
[29] Ibid., August 20, 1907, p. 1.
[30] Ibid., December 8, 1907, p. 1.
[31] Ibid., December 17, 1907, p. 1.
[32] Ibid.

happy about certain administrative ambiguities in South Manchuria. The Japanese government never adopted his suggestion that the Kwantung Leased Territory's governor-general also jointly serve as president of the SMR. Therefore, a dual Japanese administrative structure emerged in South Manchuria. The Kwantung governor-general directly reported to the Ministry of Foreign Affairs. On October 13, General Ōshima Yoshimasa, governor-general of the Kwantung Leased Territory, recommended to the ministry that gendarmes to guard the railway be placed under his command.[33] The Kwantung governor-general thereafter would decide how many police should guard the SMR zone and the Japanese consuls in Manchuria. Because there was no unified administration of the Kwantung Leased Territory and the SMR zone, as Gotō had wanted, the existence of two large separate administrative units, often disagreeing about policy, would later make for bureaucratic tension in Japan's administrative control in the region. This was the potential dark cloud that Gotō might have worried about.

DEVELOPMENT OF THE SMR

What did the SMR own and operate? First, it managed the railway lines that extended from Dairen to Ch'ang-ch'un (704.3 km) and from Mukden or Feng-t'ien to Antung (250.2 km); subsidiary lines from Dairen to Ryojun or Port Arthur (50.8 km), from Ta-chih-ch'ai to Ying-k'ou (52.9 km), from Yen-t'ai to the Yen-t'ai colliery (15.6 km), and from Mukden to Fushun (52.9 km); and several spur lines, to make for a grand total of 1,129.1 km, or roughly 700 miles, of railway track. Second, the SMR managed attached areas of land (*fuzokuchi*) along both sides of these railway lines that came to around 233 sq. km in 1931, within which 105 cities of varying sizes were located.[34] Third, the SMR owned and managed numerous properties within these attached areas, including tunnels, bridges,

---

[33] Ibid., October 9, 1907, p. 1.

[34] Mantetsu Chihōbu Zammu Iinkai, comp., *Mantetsu fuzoku shi keiei enkaku zenshi* (Complete history of the management of the South Manchuria Railway Company and its attached properties), vol. 1, sec. 1 (Tokyo: Fudo Zerokusu Kabushiki Kaisha, 1975), chap. 2, pt. 3. The pages are not numbered in this photo-reprint of top-secret reports compiled by the SMR and printed in twenty-eight volumes. References to citations are described by section and volume numbers. Although all Japanese writings and histories about the SMR refer to the "leased zone," the original treaties between imperial China and imperial Russia never stipulated any such "leased zone." Further, the properties acquired near the SMR railway line, such as land, railway stations and other structures, and access routes, were never clarified in any agreed-upon treaties between China and Japan. In fact, there was considerable ambiguity in the various treaty clauses that touched upon this issue. For the best study of the legal rights of the Japanese in South Manchuria from the standpoint of the SMR, see C. Walter Young, *Japanese Jurisdiction in the South Manchuria Railway Areas* (Baltimore: Johns Hopkins Press, 1931), particularly chapters 3 and 5.

TABLE 4.1
Financial Performance of SMR Railways for Selected Years

Period	Net income from railway operations (1,000)	Book value of capital in railways (1,000)[a]	Rate of return (%)
Jan. 1, 1907– Mar. 3, 1908[b]	1,878	6,376	29.4
Apr. 1, 1909– Mar. 31, 1910[b]	4,598	39,549	11.6
Apr. 1, 1911– Mar. 31, 1912[b]	5,302	62,606	8.5
Apr. 1, 1916– Mar. 31, 1917	15,719	74,191	21.1
Apr. 1, 1921– Mar. 31, 1922	45,031	178,847	25.2
Apr. 1, 1924– Mar. 31, 1925	56,008	211,457	26.4
Apr. 1, 1928– Mar. 31, 1929	74,281	249,703	29.7
Apr. 1, 1932– Mar. 31, 1933	65,050	273,663	23.7

Source: Manshū Tetsudō Kabushiki Kaisha, Eigyō hōkokusho, vols. 1–3 (Tokyo: Ryūkei Shobo, 1977). These volumes contain all annual reports of the SMR.

[a] Book value denotes actual paid-in capital.

[b] Data for these years based on averaging values for six-month periods.

schools, parks, administration buildings, public offices, hospitals, libraries, storage areas, mines, and factories.

As a holding company responsible for managing such assets, the SMR earned a high rate of return from its assets until 1933, when the Kwantung Army intervened to reorganize the company.

Consider first the financial performance and operations of the two trunk lines spanning South Manchuria from Dairen to Ch'ang-ch'un and from Mukden to Antung. Until 1910, the Mukden-Antung line operated at a loss (table 4.1). Thereafter, net revenue from the Dairen–Ch'ang-ch'un line exceeded the Mukden-Antung line by a factor of around 15. After 1912, the rate of return persistently remained high. In fact, the SMR's rate of return on railway-invested capital far exceeded that of any other railway in China except for the years 1909–1912.[35] The reason for the

[35] Ralph William Huenemann, *The Dragon and the Iron Horse: The Economics of Railroads*

lower return in these years was the huge initial capitalized value of railway investment relative to the net income then earned.

If the SMR railways earned such a high rate of return on invested capital, they obviously generated a tremendous amount of revenue each year (table 4.2). Using the Dairen price index to deflate the total revenue of SMR railways and then calculating the rate of growth for total revenue during the periods 1907/1909 to 1920/1922 and 1920/1922 to 1921/1933 yields annual growth rates of 8.3 and 7.0 percent, respectively. These annual growth rates indicate that total revenue in real terms more than doubled in each period, with growth slightly lower in the second period because world depression adversely influenced the Manchurian economy at the end of the twenties.

Freight revenue generated over 75 percent of the total revenue except in the first year's operation. A railway earns more revenue if its rolling stock can be used more intensively to carry freight and passengers. By traffic density is meant the quantity of freight and number of passengers carried per kilometer for a given railway route. Comparing the SMR's traffic density with that of other railways in the Chinese national railway system for 1918, one can observe why the SMR railway routes from Dairen and Antung to the heartland of Manchuria had become so profitable (table 4.3).

The index for total traffic density on the main SMR line was more than three times that of the Peking-Mukden and Shanghai-Nanking lines. Even the Antung-Mukden line had a higher index of total traffic than these two Chinese railway lines. Freight traffic density for both SMR lines far exceeded that of any other Chinese railway line, and only four Chinese railway lines had higher passenger traffic density than did the Antung-Mukden line. The SMR generated high railway earnings because it operated very efficient railways that carried a tremendous amount of freight and a large number of passengers per kilometer. Therefore, the earnings per ton and per passenger hauled each day rapidly rose over the period (table 4.2).

If the SMR operated a successful railway enterprise, did its other enterprises do as well financially? The SMR operated many types of enterprises and often ran some of these at a loss (table 4.4).

After the SMR paid all annual obligations to bond holders, accounted for other debt, and covered all losses from current operations, this huge corporation still generated considerable net revenue each year that rapidly expanded over time. The SMR's first-year net earnings of 2.0 million yen

---

in China, 1876–1937 (Cambridge: Council for East Asian Studies, Harvard University, 1984), p. 190. The Canton-Samshui, Hulan-Hailun, and Shenyang-Hailung railways earned nominal rates of return of 14.4, 13.8, and 13.4 percent for selected years that exceeded the rate of return earned by the SMR before the mid-teens.

TABLE 4.2
Performance of SMR Railways, 1907–1933

Period	Total revenue (1,000)	Passenger revenue (1,000)	Freight revenue (1,000)	Freight revenue per day-mile	Passenger revenue per day-mile
1907–08	9,768	3,477	6,291	31	17
1908–09	12,536	3,963	8,573	49	17
1909–10	15,016	3,250	11,766	58	15
1910–11	15,670	3,264	12,406	57	15
1911–12	17,526	4,272	13,254	61	20
1912–13	19,907	5,008	14,899	55	19
1913–14	22,275	5,069	17,206	63	20
1914–15	23,216	4,368	18,848	69	17
1915–16	23,532	4,842	18,690	68	19
1916–17	27,815	6,040	21,775	79	24
1917–18	34,457	8,136	26,321	94	32
1918–19	44,992	10,911	34,081	131	43
1919–20	60,548	14,243	46,305	184	56
1920–21	78,526	14,659	63,867	255	58
1921–22	71,809	12,194	59,615	238	48
1922–23	81,907	12,389	69,518	277	50
1923–24	86,013	13,431	72,582	288	54
1924–25	90,664	13,645	77,019	304	54
1925–26	95,065	14,530	80,535	317	58
1926–27	104,729	15,216	89,513	353	61
1927–28	110,142	16,102	94,040	371	64
1928–29	115,357	17,619	97,738	387	70
1929–30	118,540	17,451	101,089	400	70
1930–31	89,397	11,461	77,936	190	28
1931–32	80,028	9,135	70,893	172	23
1932–33	99,842	14,820	85,022	206	36

Source: Manshū Tetsudō Kabūshiki Kaisha, Eigyō hōkokusho.
[a] For the years 1907–1911, data for freight and passenger revenue per day per mile are based only on the Dairen–Ch'ang-ch'un line and averaged for six-month periods each year. Other railway revenues earned from storage charges, etc, have been excluded.

more than trebled by 1913–1914, doubled again by 1917–1918, and almost doubled again by 1920–1921 in nominal terms. Those net earnings continued to rise during the 1920s until 1931–1932, when they sharply tumbled but then rose the very next year. By all accounts, the SMR generated income from enough activities to cover losses in others. The activities netting the highest losses were administration, the iron-steel enterprise, and hotel services. Railways clearly generated the largest share of the SMR's earnings, with mining net revenue a second. By 1931–1932, the

TABLE 4.3
Traffic Density of SMR Lines and Chinese National Railway, 1918

Railroad	Freight traffic	Passenger traffic	Index of total traffic
Dairen–Ch'ang-ch'un	3,497.7	1,202.5	3,837.9
Antung-Mukden	1,327.2	435.7	1,472.4
Peking-Hankow	833.2	321.0	940.2
Peking-Mukden	931.7	630.2	1,141.8
Tientsin-Pukow	649.7	351.9	767.0
Shanghai-Nanking	772.8	1,272.5	1,197.0
Shanghai-Hangchow-Ningpo	182.8	694.9	414.4
Peking-Suiyuan	271.3	116.8	310.2
Chengting-Taiyuan	369.0	126.9	411.3
Taokow-Chinghua	441.1	69.1	464.1
Kaifeng-Honan	155.0	239.4	234.8
Kirin–Ch'ang-ch'un	337.1	235.2	415.5
Chuchow-P'inghsiang	321.4	62.2	342.1
Canton-Kowloon	45.0	683.9	273.0
Changchow-Amoy	1.8	106.5	37.3

Source: Data for Chinese National Railways, 1918, obtained from Ralph William Huene-mann, *The Dragon and the Iron Horse: The Economics of Railroads in China, 1876–1937* (Cambridge: Council on East Asian Studies, Harvard University, 1984), p. 193. Data for SMR obtained from "28th Report of the SMR," *Eigyō hōkokusho*, vol. 2, pp. 79–82.

Notes: Freight traffic is in thousands of ton-km per route km; passenger traffic is in thousands of passenger-km per route km; index of total traffic is calculated by treating three passenger-kim as one ton-km. Data from SMR 1918 report were in miles and had to be converted to kilometers, and then to the equivalent for freight and passenger traffic.

SMR already had heavily invested in oil shale processing but still earned 289,000 yen net income and 538,000 yen the next year. In other words, the SMR had sufficient wealth to launch new industries that proved to be immensely profitable in spite of their initial high costs.

It should not be surprising, then, that the total revenue produced by the SMR in 1923 came to 185 million yen, compared to the same year's ordinary budget for Korea of 101 million yen and for Formosa of 100 million yen. In that same year, the budget revenues for Siam, Indochina, and the Philippines, when converted to yen, were 62, 60, and 65 million yen, respectively. Only the Netherlands East Indies' budget revenue of 300 million yen exceeded that of the SMR.[36] The SMR also paid top dividends, and its assets greatly increased in value over the period (table 4.5).

The total value of SMR assets (after deducting profits) had doubled in

[36] George Bronson Rea, "The Greatest Civilizing Force in Eastern Asia: The Real Mission of the South Manchuria Railway," *Far Eastern Review* (November 1924): 4.

TABLE 4.4
SMR-Managed Activities: Net Revenue (+) or Loss (−) for Selected Years (thousand yen)

Year	Railways	Shipping	Mining	Harbors	Administration	Ceramics	Hotels	Electricity	Iron & steel industry	Total net revenue[a]
1907–08	+3,657	—	+552	+13	−130	—	−30	−34	—	+2,015
1910–11	+9,198	−254	+1,229	+246	−229	—	−18	−35	—	+3,707
1913–14	+14,360	−126	+1,800	+182	−1,050	+77	−20	+335	—	+7,167
1917–18	+23,599	+1,063	+5,320	+393	−1,608	+162	+36	+635	—	+14,925
1920–21	+48,556	−848	+5,802	−563	−6,159	+170	−167	+473	−6,422	+27,391
1923–24	+56,482	—	+4,078	+74	−8,297	−130	−336	+932	+4,078	+34,795
1926–27	+61,971	—	+5,488	+994	−12,567	—	−336	+271	−3,806	+34,157
1929–30	+74,890	—	12,275	+3,556	−13,598	—	—	—	+542	+45,505
1931–32	+48,185	—	+16	+1,288	−10,877	—	−96	—	−2,980	+12,598
1932–33	+65,050	—	+127	+3,039	−10,687	—	−88	—	−3,900	+48,689

Source: Data from Eigyō hōkokusho, vols. 1–3, and relevant annual reports. Not all SMR activities have been listed.
[a]Total net revenue means net of all costs for all enterprises, plus annual dividend payments, administrative costs for general affairs, and other interest payments or debts. Total net revenue also includes interest earned from SMR assets and all net earnings from enterprise activities.

TABLE 4.5
Financial Performance of the SMR for Selected Years

Year	Total asset value (1,000 yen)	Accounting profit (1,000 yen)	Dividend rate (%)	Total bond interest distributed (1,000 yen)
1907–08	162,708	1,007	6.0	1,023
1910–11	246,143	1,853	6.0	4,563
1913–14	305,338	7,167	6.0	5,564
1916–17	317,694	10,107	6.0	5,564
1919–20	648,843	27,391	6.0	8,814
1922–23	735,598	35,080	7.0	12,423
1925–26	809,209	34,865	7.0	17,095
1927–28	958,674	36,274	6.5	16,631
1929–30	1,041,932	45,505	5.5	15,852
1932–33	1,184,419	61,287	6.0	21,020

Source: Data obtained from annual SMR reports contained in *Eigyō hōkokusho*, vols. 1–3.

nominal terms between 1907–1908 and 1916–1917 and continued to increase rapidly thereafter. By 1930, SMR assets exceeded one billion yen.[37] Company profits rapidly ballooned as well, and the SMR paid stable, high dividends to its bond holders. The company frequently entered the bond market to raise funds for expansion. Between 1910 and 1932, the annual debt paid out each year to these bond holders had increased nearly fivefold. By operating profitable railway and mining enterprises, the SMR easily raised additional capital whenever it wanted to upgrade equipment to keep unit costs low. By using the best technology of the day in its enterprises, the SMR increased its efficiency and profitability so as to be able to repay funds mobilized from financial markets.

Meanwhile, the company's staff increased over the period. In September 1908, the SMR employed 13,621 persons;[38] by the spring of 1915, that number had increased to 18,852, of which the new Central Experiment Institute had 13, soil research another 8, the Industrial Experimental Bureau around 20, and the East Asian Economic Research Bureau about 8.[39] By fall 1924, the company had expanded its workforce to 37,685, with 90

[37] George Bronson Rea claims that in 1919–1920 the total value of SMR property, worth 500 million yen in original cost value, now carried a market value of 1.4 billion yen. See Rea, "Daylight in Manchuria," *Far Eastern Review* (November 1920): 6. Data in table 4.5, column 1, are the total asset values of the SMR for selected years, based on the company's annual report. It is not clear where Rea obtained his estimate.

[38] *Eigyō hōkokusho*, vol. 1, report no. 4, p. 61.

[39] Ibid., report no. 15, pp. 75–76.

in the Central Experiment Institute, 26 working in soil surveys, 88 in experimental agricultural research, and some five hundred in various forms of regional research.[40] Nearly three-quarters of this workforce were local Chinese. By the very early 1930s, around a quarter of a million Japanese lived in Dairen and the SMR-managed properties, and nearly all of them owed their livelihood in some way to the existence of the SMR. The Japanese were everywhere: conducting research, engaging in business, opening up farms, and managing the new wealth.

Foreigners in Manchuria marveled that the SMR operated so efficiently without charging the "wretched likin or any 'squeeze.' " As early as 1914, they pointed out that the SMR "richly deserves all it gets, as it does all its business in such a thorough manner that it attracts trade to itself."[41]

Foreigners also claimed that the SMR's railway services were far superior to those of the three other railway companies in the region. In 1918, a Shanghai journalist complained that the Chinese Eastern Railway was "in a hopeless condition," always late and providing terrible service. The Mukden-Peking Railway, the oldest in the region, was "the most corrupt," and conditions on board were abominable when the weather turned cold. The new Kirin–Ch'ang-ch'un line had been operating only four years and was staffed mainly by Cantonese, but the railway's gradients were too steep and there was "a good deal of vibration and noise in the carriage during motion." As for the SMR, its trains kept excellent time and were clean, warm, and well-lighted. Tracks were well ballasted and the cars did not sway or jolt.[42]

Other foreigners pointed out that the SMR not only had inspired travel and commerce in Manchuria but had spent huge sums for "the well-equipped hospitals in such centers as Mukden, Tieling, Ch'ang-ch'un, and Dairen."[43] Aside from providing medical services and educating Chinese medical students, the SMR also subsidized social and religious activities such as helping Japanese Christians to build a new church in 1921.

By 1913, many observers already noted that Manchuria's bean trade had become the major reason for the region's prosperity.[44] The city of Dairen made this flourishing trade possible. As early as 1910, travelers commented that Dairen was "pre-eminently a new town, full of handsome buildings, from the Sailors' Rest to the Yokohama Specie Bank, situated in wide, well-made roads, and showing plain proof of the nascent prosperity of the place." In fact, Dairen was already referred to as "the only port north of Hong Kong where large steamers can conveniently

---

[40] Ibid., vol. 2, report no. 23, pp. 8–9.

[41] "South Manchuria," *The North-China Herald*, February 14, 1914, p. 443.

[42] "Railways of Manchuria," *The North-China Herald*, February 2, 1918, p. 253.

[43] "Japan's Benefit to Manchuria," *The North-China Herald*, March 4, 1922, p. 582.

[44] "Manchuria Bean Trade," *The North-China Herald*, May 17, 1913, pp. 493–493. [*sic*]

discharge their cargoes," and famous firms like Butterfield & Swire and Samuel Macgregor & Co. already had located there.[45]

By 1920, Dairen's harbor could repair around 100 ships a year and handle over 2,500 ocean-going vessels with a cargo of some 2.8 million tons.[46] It had become China's second largest trading port after Shanghai,[47] and the British journalist Peter Fleming in 1934 described it as "a sort of Japanese Hong Kong, very orderly and hygienic and up to date."[48] In 1929, Dairen's port had 3,884 meters of breakwater enclosing a harbor area of over 3.1 million square meters, with wharfs that could accommodate at one time twenty-nine vessels carrying an aggregate 220,000 tons, as well as a wharf to handle 250 Chinese junks.[49] In that same year, Manchuria produced 220 million tons of soybeans, or nearly two-thirds of the world supply, and most of the region's soybean and derivative exports passed through Dairen to foreign markets.[50] The SMR had diverted virtually all of the trade that had previously passed through Ying-k'ou to Dairen and Antung.

When Newchwang harbor near Ying-k'ou opened to foreign trade after 1860, that center immediately became South Manchuria's main outlet for about two-thirds of the soybean trade. But already in 1907 cotton goods shipped into Manchuria on the SMR line from Dairen were replacing Chinese cotton goods in the Ying-k'ou region. At the same time, the agricultural produce that formerly moved down the Liao River and overland to Ying-k'ou now moved on the SMR lines to Dairen and Antung.[51] In 1911, about 85 percent of South Manchuria's export trade passed through Dairen to Japan, and about 75 percent of that region's imports came from Japan via Dairen and up the SMR line into the hinterland.[52]

By the early twenties, Dairen had "a network of broad, perfect roads, equipped with grand systems of water and drainage works."[53] Electrified

[45] E. G. Kemp, *The Face of Manchuria, Korea and Russian Turkestan* (London: Chatto and Windus, 1910), p. 138.

[46] SMR Shomubu Chōsaka, *Dairenkō haigochi no kenkyū* (A study of Dairen harbor's hinterland) (Dairen: Manshū Nichi-Nichi Shimpōsha, 1923), p. 21.

[47] Ibid., p. 16. Between 1911 and 1920, Dairen's total trade volume had risen 3.4 times, or 18 percent per year.

[48] Peter Fleming, *One's Company: A Journey to China* (New York: Charles Scribner's Sons, 1934), p. 175.

[49] Roy Hidemichi Akagi, *Understanding Manchuria: A Handbook of Facts* (White Plains, N.Y.: N.p., 1931), p. 13.

[50] Ibid., p. 4.

[51] *The Japan Times*, December 27, 1907, p. 1.

[52] Anon., "Saikin nijikkanenkan ni okeru minami Manshū taigai bōeki no sūsei" (The trends for South Manchuria's foreign trade during the past twenty years), *Mantetsu chōsa geppō* 11, 13 (December 15, 1931): 187, 189.

[53] Ueda Kyosuke, "Manchuria in Twenty Years," *The Far Eastern Review* (August 1926): 345.

and with modern banks and shipping companies, this city served as an economic magnet, drawing raw materials from the hinterland to exchange with finished goods and credit. This huge emporium, and all the people who lived and worked there, owed everything to the SMR. As one former SMR employee put it, "The life of all Japanese in the SMR zone, which first began in Dairen, was inextricably bound up, directly and indirectly, and by sight or by ear, with the SMR."[54] Because of the SMR's successful railway and commercial developments, Dairen could attract over half of its merchandise trade from areas south of Mukden and another one-third from the areas north of Mukden. Slightly over half of that merchandise entering Dairen via the SMR consisted of agricultural products, of which the largest component was soybeans and their derivatives, with coal making up another 33 percent, and the remainder an assortment of other products.[55]

What had once been a sparsely settled region around the time of the Russo-Japanese War eventually became a flourishing, highly urbanized zone along the SMR line. By 1929, the SMR linked seventy cities between Dairen and Ch'ang-ch'un and another twenty-six cities between Mukden and Antung. An SMR express train could traverse the 435.8-mile distance between Dairen and Ch'ang-ch'un in twelve hours, and a regular train in eighteen. Similarly, an express train could travel the 161.7-mile line from Mukden to Antung in seven hours, a regular train in ten. The cost of a ticket from Dairen to Ch'ang-ch'un in 1929 came to fifteen dollars for first class, ten dollars for second class, and five dollars for third class.[56] Children under four traveled free, and between four and twelve they paid half fare.

But of even greater importance than providing efficient service and earning profits, the Japanese had overtaken the foreigner in railway enterprise and other activities. In 1930, Japanese imperialism in Manchuria surpassed foreign interests in all of China.

MANAGEMENT OF THE SMR

The Japanese legal scholar Okamatsu Santarō once described the SMR as having the appearance of a commercial company but really functioning as an organization of the state to carry out colonial rule and coloniza-

---

[54] Itō Takeo, *Mantetsu ni ikite* (My life in the SMR) (Tokyo: Keisō Shobo, 1964), p. 34.

[55] SMR Shomubu Chōsaka, *Dairenkō haigochi no kenkyū*, p. 276.

[56] Minami Manshū Tetsudō Kabushiki Kaisha, comp., *Omoidasu no Manshū tetsudō kakueki teisha* (Remembering the Manchurian Railway's railway stations) (Tokyo: Kokusho Kankōkai, 1984), pp. 178–179. Railway class fare data converted from yen to U.S. dollars at the exchange rate of 1 yen = 49 cents.

tion.[57] The SMR regulations followed Japanese commercial law for mobilizing capital, paying earnings, and so forth, but its organization and management complied with public law as any state-run bureaucracy did. The SMR managed railways and other enterprises like any business corporation according to cost accounting methods to earn a profit and disburse earnings to shareholders. But the SMR also performed many tasks that only a state organ could do: operate utilities and manage civil organizations related to law, security, education, public health, and so on. It was a special, hybrid organization unlike any other organization in China under foreign ownership and management.

The Japanese government appointed the president, vice-president, and board of directors after carefully reviewing all candidates. Their term of office usually did not last more than several years. The SMR president reported to the Japanese cabinet, so that the government could direct the SMR activities in accordance with foreign policy and national security aims. The board of directors supervised five major departments, which actually managed the company's business affairs and bureaucratic responsibilities.[58] Figure 4.1 shows the SMR's multifunctional operations.[59]

The responsibilities of the General Affairs Department covered coordination, supervision, and accounting. This department prepared the annual report of all business operations, showing revenue, cost, profit, assets, and liabilities. The Research Department, set up in 1907, carried out a variety of economic and scientific research to determine how the SMR could efficiently develop Manchuria's resources. This department later became the largest foreign research unit in China, larger than any research agency of the Chinese government.[60]

---

[57] Mantetsu Chihōbu Zammu Seiri Iinkai, comp., *Mantetsu fuzoku shi keiei enkaku zenshi*, vol. 1, sec. 1, chap. 3.

[58] The following individuals served as presidents of the SMR between 1906 and 1945: Gotō Shimpei (November 13, 1906, to July 14, 1908); Nakamura Zekō (December 19, 1908, to December 18, 1913); Nomura Ryūtarō (December 19, 1913, to July 15, 1914); Nakamura Yūjirō (July 15, 1914, to July 31, 1917); Kunisawa Shimpei (July 31, 1917, to April 12, 1919); Nomura Ryūtarō (April 12, 1919, to May 31, 1921); Hayakawa Senkichirō (May 31, 1921, to October 14, 1922); Kawamura Takeji (October 24, 1922, to June 22, 1924); Yasuhirō Banichi (July 23, 1924, to July 19, 1927); Yamamoto Jōtarō (July 19, 1927, to August 14, 1929); Sengoku Mitsugu (August 14, 1929, to June 13, 1931); Uchida Yasuya (June 13, 1931, to July 6, 1932); Hayashi Hirōtarō (July 26, 1932, to August 2, 1935); Matsuoka Yōsuke (August 2, 1935, to March 24, 1939); Omura Takuichi (March 24, 1939, to July 14, 1943); Kobiyama Naonari (July 14, 1943, to April 11, 1945); and Yamazaki Motori (May 5, 1945, to September 30, 1945).

[59] Mantetsu Chihōbu Zammu Seiri Iinkai, comp., *Mantetsu fuzoku shi keiei enkaku zenshi*, vol. 1, sec. 2, chap. 3 (pt. 2). Figure 4.1 reflects the SMR structure as of April 1, 1907, but it remained unchanged for decades.

[60] See also Ajiya Keizai Kenkyūjo, *Kyū shokiminchi kankei kikan kankōbutsu sōgō mokuroku: Minami Manshū tetsudō kabushiki kaisha hen* (Bibliography of all related works concerning

FIGURE 4.1 Organization of the South Manchuria Railway Company (April 1907)

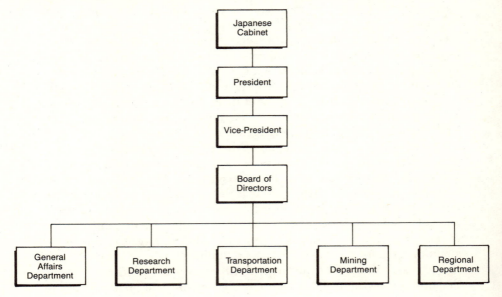

The Transportation Department managed all land and water transport activity for the company. The Mining Department operated all mines and metallurgical industries. Finally, the Regional Department (Chihōbu) managed the SMR's properties. Within this department were two large agencies: One handled general affairs, which included management of land and related properties, education, industry, and city planning; the other took charge of public health, hospitals, and medical institutions as well as public health programs for disease prevention.

How did the SMR manage its properties? The company really operated as a municipal government in the 106 cities under its jurisdiction. Between 1907 and 1911, the population in the leased zone rose from 25,699 to 56,060, more than trebled by 1921, and again more than trebled by 1936 to reach over a half-million, an annual growth rate of around 11 percent.[61] This tremendous growth, fueled by migration from North

---

Japan's former colonial areas: A compilation of works by the South Manchuria Railway Company) (Tokyo: Institute of Developing Economies, 1979), appendix; also Hara Kakuten, *Gendai Ajiya kenkyū seiritsu shiron, Mantetsu chōsabu, Tōa kenkyūjo, IPR no-kenkyū* (Essays on the history of modern Asian research: The SMR Research Institute, the East Asian Research Institute, and research of the IPR) (Tokyo: Keisō Shobo, 1984).

[61] Mantetsu Chihōbu Zammu Seiri Iinkai, comp., *Mantetsu fuzoku shi keiei enkaku zenshi*, vol. 1, sec. 2, chap. 3, pt. 2.

China as well as from Japan, compelled the company to expand its social services.

When the SMR began operating in early 1907, the Board of Directors established the General Affairs Office. Its officials had continuing appointments to manage the large cities of Ta-shih-ch'iao, Liao-yang, Kung-chu-ling, Mukden, and Ch'ang-ch'un. These officials quickly staked out land sites and built their administration offices and other structures. Meanwhile, the SMR also created an agency called the Residents' Association (Kyoryūminkai) in these same cities to assist the General Affairs Office to manage urban affairs and supply services.[62] As chapter 6 shows, Japanese communities elsewhere in China also depended on the Residents' Association to manage Japanese affairs. The Residents' Association managed local construction, public health, and education and reported to the General Affairs Office. Each Residents' Association had a chief, his deputy, and a committee. The local police chief, in fact, directly reported to the association, which functioned as a town council. Anyone living in the SMR zone had to register and, if an adult, could elect committee members of the association.

By the end of 1907, the SMR had abolished the associations and replaced them with a Branch Office (Shutchōjo) in every city of the leased zone.[63] This new office took over city governance. It received operating funds from the company, supplied social services, and maintained law and order. In April 1914, the SMR allowed a new, subsidiary organization to be elected by local people to recommend and assist the Branch Office. This unit, called the Inquiry Committee (Shimon Iinkai), comprised a small group of Japanese and Chinese residents elected by the adult community. Under this administrative structure, then, the SMR managed the cities and people under its jurisdiction.

From the very beginning the SMR promoted an ethos of hard work and efficiency. The staff were loyal to the company, committed to making the company a great colonizing agent in South Manchuria, and proud to be members. More than anyone else, Gotō had set the mood and style of management. He delegated responsibility to subordinates but demanded they produce results. When he quarreled one day with a certain Mr. Shōsei, manager of the SMR's Dairen wharves, complaining that "the job cannot be done that way," Shōsei heatedly replied, "If it cannot be done that way, I am going back to Japan." Rather than sack him for insubordination, Gotō left Shōsei alone to finish the job.[64]

This leadership style was evident everywhere and promoted high-qual-

[62] Ibid., pt. 1.
[63] Ibid., pt. 5.
[64] Tamura Yōsan, "Mantetsu rimen shi" (An insider's account of the SMR), *Mantetsu kaihō*, no. 71 (January 1, 1971): p. 2.

ity, rapid performance. The SMR became staffed with experts of high managerial quality, ready and able to perform at all times on behalf of the company. The company insisted that its manpower talent come from the best universities and have degrees. Company employees (*shain*) were highly paid. They received twice the monthly salary of the temporary Japanese workers hired and six to seven times the monthly salary of Chinese workers.[65] Moreover, they received other benefits such as good housing, medical care, education for their children, and outlets for culture and entertainment. Promotions often brought a short period for study or travel, all paid for by the company. Company incentives encouraged employees to work hard and produce.

Second, the company promoted a teamwork style to tackle problems and find solutions. No task was undertaken without careful investigation, planning, and then a means of implementing policy. For example, in the early years, when the company had to build the Mukden–Antung railway line, Japanese engineering skills and manpower were taxed to the limit because of the large number of gradients, tunnels, and bridges that had to be constructed.[66] But SMR construction crews and engineers tackled this project with zeal and tenacity and finished the job within several years.

Third, the company was sensitive to time and efficiency, whether building railroads, managing railways, constructing mines, producing steel at Anshan, or obtaining petroleum from coal shale at the Fushun colliery. The most advanced technology should be used with the appropriate engineering design. The most advanced capital equipment of the day should be purchased. SMR management always insisted upon buying the best rolling stock, locomotives, and railway tracks from the United States, which had become the leading producer of these items in the world. Between 1907 and 1920, the SMR spent 87.7 million dollars for foreign materials, of which one-third, or about 25.3 million, came from the United States.[67] The great reliance upon U.S. railway capital led one observer to remark, "In its physical aspect the South Manchuria Railway is an American railway, as its rolling stock and other materials are mostly

[65] Andō Hikōtarō, *Mantetsu: Nihon teikokushugi to Chūgoku* (The South Manchuria Railway Company: Japanese imperialism and China) (Tokyo: Ochanomizu Shobo, 1965), p. 114.

[66] Minami Manshū Tetsudō Kabushiki Kaisha, *Manshū tetsudō kensetsu shi* (A record of the construction of the Manchurian Railway System) (Mukden: Shin Tairiku Insatsu Kabushiki Kaisha, 1939), pp. 47–54, for a discussion of the enormous difficulties in building the Antung-Mukden line.

[67] George Bronson Rea, "Daylight in Manchuria," *The Far Eastern Review* (November 1920): 3–18.

of American origin."[68] The total amount spent by the SMR during the years 1907–1920 exceeded the loan-financed investments (67 million dollars) made by the Chinese government for building and maintaining all of its railroads until the year 1918.[69]

In 1924, the SMR purchased the most advanced, state-of-the-art railway rolling stock, five three-cylinder locomotives just manufactured by the American Locomotive Company.[70] Operating on the standard-gauge track of 56½ inches and using bituminous coal for fuel, these engines possessed a regenerative braking system that could hold back trains on a 4 percent grade.

To promote research, the SMR operated the Central Experimental Institute, an eight-division unit that conducted a wide range of experimental work. The company invested huge sums for this institute to research the processing of soybeans and extracting oil from them, manufacturing new chemical products, obtaining oil from coal shale, and so forth.[71] As early as 1910, the institute had developed special earthenware and porcelain for storing soybeans, and then transferred that technical knowledge to private Japanese firms to ferment soybeans.[72] By 1921, the institute's research on oil-shale processing had produced by-products from "dry distillation of oil shale"; in 1928, the institute invented an internal-combustion apparatus for this same process.[73] It also investigated procedures for manufacturing aluminum from aluminum clay and for manufacturing magnesium from magnesite ore.

By maintaining high research and development expenditures, the SMR had introduced a "new haulage plant that was entirely electrically operated" at the Fushun colliery.[74] The new equipment involved mechanical excavators that could penetrate a coal bank to a maximum depth of 750 feet; these excavators then conveyed the coal to vehicle-drawn wagons. Fushun also had a steam power plant to provide its own electrical energy.

[68] K. K. Kawakami, "American Capital for Manchurian Railways," *The Far Eastern Review* (March 1928): 110.

[69] Rea, "Daylight in Manchuria," pp. 3–18.

[70] "Test of the Three-Cylinder Locomotive for the South Manchuria Railway," *The Far Eastern Review* (January 1925): 16–19.

[71] "The Chemical Industry in Manchuria and the SMR Central Laboratory," *The Far Eastern Review* 37, 2 (February 1941): p. 60. For coal mining research and development, see Minami Manshū Tetsudō Kabushiki Kaisha, *Minami Manshū tetsudō kabushiki kaisha dai sanji jūnen shi* (A thirty-year history of the South Manchuria Railway Company), vol. 3 (Dairen: Minami Manshū Tetsudō Kabushiki Kaisha, 1938), pp. 1678–1699.

[72] Henry W. Kinney, "The Subsidiary Enterprises of the South Manchuria Railway," *The The Far Eastern Review* (April 1928), p. 172.

[73] *The Far Eastern Review* 37, 2 (February 1941): 61.

[74] "Skip Haulage Plant at Fushun with Three-Phase Drive," *The Far Eastern Review* (April 1932): 178.

The large investments in both railways and coal mining made it possible for railways and coal mining to generate the largest amount of revenue for the company (table 4.4).

Even though the SMR ran the most modern enterprises in South Manchuria, it still employed large numbers of Chinese to transport cargo from railways and storage buildings to the ships that entered and left Dairen. Former SMR employees always remarked of their amazement, when first landing in Dairen to go to work for the company, that so many Chinese "coolies" worked at the wharves.[75] Instead of using conveyers, electric cranes, and other equipment, there were "swarms of dark-skinned men, clothed in ragged blue cotton trousers and blouses, streaming in procession from the ships, carrying sacks, bales, packages of merchandise on their shoulders."[76] This mixture of modern equipment with a large, unskilled labor force could be found everywhere in the SMR zone and especially at the Fushun and Yen-t'ai coal mines. Complex reasons accounted for why the SMR employed such labor-intensive methods: a reluctance to produce large-scale unemployment; a desire to provide employment for countless Chinese consumers of Japanese goods; and a technology that made possible the use of cheap labor and advanced capital and services.

But without reliable information about Manchuria, SMR officials could not make the company an effective instrument for expanding Japanese interests in the region. For developing the soybean trade, coal mining, and agriculture, for promoting Japanese emigration to Manchuria, and for facilitating the SMR's acquisition of more property, company officials had to understand Chinese laws and customs. Therefore, when Gotō Shimpei assumed the presidency, he quickly established a research department (chōsabu) to make surveys, collect information, publish reports, and manage the company's library. The department was established in November 1906, and by April 1907 a small staff had already adopted the work ethic of Gotō—beginning work at 8:00 A.M. They conducted surveys at the Fushun colliery, set up the East Asian Economic Investigation Bureau in Tokyo, surveyed coal fields at Yentai and Wa-fang-tien, made plans for a library, published a journal, and set about to conduct surveys of the region's economic and traditional customs.[77]

The activities of the research department continued to expand, with branch offices being established in Mukden and eventually in North and

[75] Itō Takeo, *Mantetsu ni ikite*, p. 40.

[76] W. M. Holmes, *An Eye-Witness in Manchuria* (New York: International Publishers, 1933), p. 14.

[77] Kusayanagi Daizō, *Mantetsu chōsabu* (The Research Department of the South Manchuria Railway Company), vol. 1 (Tokyo: Asahi Shimbunsha, 1982), pp. 68–69.

Central China. By 1940, the department had 2,354 research staff.[78] They had helped the Kwantung Army prepare its ambitious industrialization plans in 1937. The research department's survey reports, more than 6,000 published during its lifetime, were of such high quality that Ishiwara Kanji and other officers of the Kwantung Army greatly relied upon them for planning the army's takeover of Manchuria in late 1931. Noted for its great successes in the teens, twenties, and thirties in inventorying the region's resources and providing reports about conditions and people's livelihood, the research bureau expanded its activities to serve Japan's military ventures. In summer 1940, the bureau undertook to produce an authoritative study of China's capacity to wage war with Japan. In that same year, it also studied the inflation already spreading in the new economic bloc of Japan, Manchuria, and China. Overall, the research investigations of the department were of such high quality that its findings have become an indispensable source for scholars in the post–World War II era to achieve a deeper understanding of Chinese society and economy.

By having the Japanese state help fund its start and negotiate treaties with China on its behalf, by pursuing the aggressive management style set forth by Gotō Shimpei, by investing to upgrade capital and acquire the most advanced technology, and by facilitating the collection of relevant information about conditions in Manchuria, the SMR led the way in South Manchuria. Regional development truly flowed from the activities of the SMR. By 1931, the SMR was the dominant force in the region. In that year, total Japanese investment in Manchuria came to 1.7 billion yen (850 million dollars), or about 72 percent of all foreign wealth there.[79] Russian assets valued at 590 million yen came second, to make up 24 percent of total foreign investment there. At least two-thirds of all Japanese investment, and perhaps more, belonged to the SMR. As an imperialist force in the region, what implications did the SMR have for Japanese imperialism in China?

THE SMR AND JAPANESE IMPERIALISM IN MANCHURIA

Gotō Shimpei had conceived of the SMR as an instrument by which Japan could expand its informal empire in China, just as other foreign powers were doing by the Open Door policy of diplomacy with Ch'ing China. Gotō's plan called for finding means other than direct colonial control to

[78] Hara Kakuten, *Gendai Ajiya kenkyū seiritsu shiron*, p. 328.

[79] Amano Motonosuke, "Manshū keizai no hattatsu" (The development of the Manchurian economy), *Mantetsu chōsa geppō* 12, 7 (July 1932): 89. In 1931, one dollar was roughly equivalent to two yen. In 1936, England's direct investment in China, except railways, was $569 million. The SMR's total investment in 1931 probably exceeded $570 million, to make it the largest foreign investor in China.

expand Japan's sphere of influence in China. His strategy called for Japan to use cultural forms for military preparedness (*bunsōteki bubi*) to gain a foothold in southern Manchuria that appeared neither to threaten imperial China nor to alarm the foreign powers, yet gave Japan the capability to strengthen its security in a world it perceived as dominated by predatory foreign powers.[80] The SMR would operate railways and related enterprises, but it would also manage a wide range of cultural and adminstrative activities of a nonthreatening nature. Under the guise of the SMR, then, Japan quietly and gradually expanded its influence in southern Manchuria while developing economic interdependency with the region.

At the time of its inception, the SMR had quickly become integrated with Japan's major colonial enterprises. Some nineteen investors in the SMR who were associated with major Japanese banks and companies also held stock shares in the eight big colonial enterprises of the day. Financial institutions like the Yokohama Specie Bank became heavily involved in SMR business affairs.[81] Companies like Mitsui Bussan conducted considerable business with the SMR. As Dairen harbor prospered through the teens and twenties,[82] numerous Japanese companies increased their business dealings with the SMR, some even locating in South Manchuria.

South Manchuria's total trade from 1911 to 1930 grew at an annual rate of 7.8 percent. Japan's share of that trade averaged around one-third for the entire period. By 1930, around 64 percent of South Manchuria's exports went to Japan, and 62 percent of all imports came from Japan through Dairen alone.[83] As chapter 1 shows, Japan's share of the China trade with South Manchuria rapidly grew after 1907 (fig. 1.1). As Japanese investment increasingly flowed into southern Manchuria, imports from that region into Japan steadily increased, especially cereals and other raw materials. Japan increased its exports of chemicals, metals and products, and machinery to southern Manchuria as well after 1910.

The Japanese government clearly understood the economic importance of Manchuria to Japan's economy and national security at the time the SMR strengthened its hold in that region. And it responded quickly to any external threat that might undermine the SMR's activities. When E. H. Harriman offered Japan a bid to lease and operate the SMR after the Ports-

[80] Gotō discusses this concept in Tsurumi Tūsuke, comp., *Gotō Shimpei den* (Biography of Gotō Shimpei), vol. 2 (Tokyo: Taiheiyō kyōkai Shuppanbu, 1943), p. 10; also see the interpretation of this same concept in Itō Takeo, *Mantetsu ni ikite*, pp. 16–17.

[81] Andō Hikotarō, ed., *Mantetsu: Nihon teikokushugi to Chūgoku* (SMR: Japanese imperialism and China) (Tokyo: Ochanomisu Shobō, 1965), pp. 46–47, 57.

[82] Kitamura Masahika, comp., *Minami Manshū tetsudō kabushiki kaisha dai sanji jūnen shi* (The thirty–year history of the South Manchuria Railway Company) (Tokyo: Ryūkan Shobo, 1976). See appendix volume (maps and tables) and charts B-10 through B-15 for information depicting the rapid growth of traffic through Dairen.

[83] "Saikin nijikkanenkan ni okeru minami Manshū taigai bōeki no sūsei," pp. 187–189.

mouth Treaty, Japan declined.[84] In 1909, the U.S. secretary of state, Philander C. Knox, proposed that an international consortium of lenders grant China a loan to enable it to purchase the Chinese Eastern Railway and the SMR, but Tokyo and Moscow rejected that proposal.[85] The former claimed that the Portsmouth Treaty justified the SMR, and Moscow claimed that its right to free trade in Manchuria already existed.[86] Then in 1910 China obtained a forty-million-dollar loan to build a railway line between Hulutao Port and the Peking-Mukden line and a longer line from Chinchow to Tsitsihar and onward to Aigun. Again, Japan protested that if such lines were to be built, then the SMR should be allowed to extend to Aigun as well.[87]

During World War I, Japan continued to expand its sphere of influence in South Manchuria. In 1915, Tokyo successfully compelled the Republic of China to extend Japan's lease of the Liaotung and the SMR railway to ninety-nine years. Tokyo also obtained an agreement for Japanese financing and control of the new Kirin–Ch'ang-ch'un railway line and the promise that Japan would be consulted if China intended to use foreign capital to construct railways in Manchuria and Mongolia.[88]

But after 1920 events took a different turn, and Japan increasingly found itself on the defensive as Chinese nationalism gained in power and influence. More Chinese during the late teens became alarmed by and infuriated at Japanese expansion into Manchuria. By 1923 and after, the Chinese made greater efforts through strikes, public criticism, and willful destruction of Japanese property to resist that expansion. A commentary in the Manchurian newspaper *Tung-pao* on June 26, 1923, strongly criticized the SMR for not protecting Chinese passengers from being robbed and demanded that "the SMR line should be returned to China and Japanese railway police be withdrawn."[89] On April 26, 1924, Chinese intellectuals convened in the *Tung-pao*'s Mukden office to demand that Japanese-managed educational institutions in the SMR leased zone be returned to China.[90] On August 7, 1925, Chinese students at the SMR's medical college walked out of their classes carrying bannners and demanding that the

[84] Chang Kia-Ngau, *China's Struggle for Railroad Development* (Baltimore: John Day Company, 1943), p. 31.

[85] Chao Wei, "Foreign Railroad Interests in Manchuria: An Irritant in Chinese-Japanese Relations," Ph.D. dissertation, St. John's University, 1980, pp. 156–157.

[86] C. Walter Young, *Japan's Special Position in Manchuria* (Baltimore: Johns Hopkins Press, 1931), pp. 140, 159.

[87] Chang Kia-Ngau, *China's Struggle*, pp. 56–57.

[88] MacMurray, ed., *Treaties and Agreements with and Concerning China, 1894–1919*, pp. 185–186.

[89] Itō Takeo, ed., *Gendaishi shiryō (31): Mantetsu* (Modern historical materials, 31: The South Manchuria Railway), vol. 1 (Tokyo: Misuzu Shobō, 1966), p. 419.

[90] *Gendaishi shiryō (32): Mantetsu*, vol. 1 (Tokyo: Misuzu Shobō, 1966), p. 553.

unequal treaties between China and Japan be terminated; they also drafted a letter to the school authorities complaining of the "slave-like status" of Chinese with respect to the Japanese.[91] On September 4, 1927, some sixty thousand Chinese demonstrated in Mukden to oppose Japanese efforts to establish a new consular office in Lin-kiang county along the Manchurian-Korean border.[92] Countless labor strikes erupted against Japanese firms in places ranging from Dairen to Harbin.[93] The Japanese also found that incidents to disrupt the SMR's line were increasing in these same years.[94]

While Japan could deal with these incidents by using police power and relying upon its leverage with Chinese officials, events came to a boil in 1928 that created a major crisis for Japan in Manchuria. Kuomintang troops had completed their Northern Expedition in 1928, and the new Nationalist government was established in Nanking that same year. In December 1928, the Nationalists signed new treaties regulating tariffs with various foreign powers, thus signaling the end of the informal empire in China by foreign powers. To make matters worse, a group of Kwantung "young officers," led by Colonel Kōmoto Daisaku, blew up a special train carrying the Manchurian warlord Chang Tso-lin, whom Tokyo leaders hoped to win over to support Japanese claims in Manchuria, while returning to Shenyang on June 4, 1928. But just as the foreign powers began relinquishing their special rights and privileges in China, the Japanese realized they were heavily dependent upon Manchuria and could not withdraw as other foreigners were doing. New political groups in South Manchuria and Japan reflected that dependency. They demanded that the government take some kind of action to preserve Japanese interests in the region. At the heart of this crisis was the SMR's connection with so many Japanese interest groups.

Three salient strategies emerged in 1928–1929 to deal with the Manchurian crisis and, paradoxically, all three originated from individuals or groups with some relationship to the SMR. The first strategy, best articulated by Yamamoto Jōtarō, a successful businessman and president of the SMR between July 19, 1927, and August 14, 1929, depended on diplomacy. Japan must persuade China to recognize Japan's "special interest" in Manchuria. Yamamoto argued that China had to comply with Japanese treaties and rights in Manchuria. Moreover, had China not benefited

---

[91] *Gendaishi shiryō (33): Mantetsu*, vol. 3 (Tokyo: Misuzu Shobō, 1966), p. 103.

[92] Dairen Shōgyō Kaigishi, *Hoten ni okeru han-Nichi undō* (The anti-Japanese movement in Mukden) (Dairen: Dairen Shōgyō Kaigishi, 1927), pp. 1–32.

[93] Chong-sik Lee, *Revolutionary Struggle in Manchuria* (Berkeley: University of California Press, 1983), pp. 44–46.

[94] Takeo Itoh, *China's Challenge in Manchuria* (Dairen: South Manchuria Railway Company, 1932), p. 82.

enormously from the sacrifices and hard work borne by the Japanese to develop Manchuria? The Chinese Nationalists should first unify China and put their house in order. But even doing that, countered Yamamoto, would never reduce or remove Japanese rights and privileges in Manchuria. Therefore, the solution to the Manchurian problem was for the Chinese to be reasonable and accept the Open Door policy so that peace and prosperity could exist in the region, and both Chinese and Japanese could prosper. According to Yamamoto, the peace and prosperity in Manchuria depended upon inducing the SMR to develop the region's resources so that Manchuria could be more closely linked with Japan.

> The task of SMR management in the region is to serve as the pivotal agent for the industrial and economic development of Manchuria and Mongolia. By developing the region for the benefit of China and Japan and all of its industries to their fullest measure, the economic ties between both countries will be tightly forged. To that end, the SMR's potential will be brought into full play and be positively focused.

Yamamoto envisioned greater SMR investment in new industries like the production of iron and steel, petroleum, and chemical fertilizers.[95] Fully convinced that the Chinese Nationalists would be persuaded by their derived benefits, Yamamoto and other politicians of the Seiyūkai, along with various Japanese government officials, tried to deal with the new Nanking government in a spirit of preserving the status quo: perpetuating Japan's informal empire in Manchuria.

The Chinese Nationalists of various factions and political persuasions were not interested. Instead, they continued to increase the pressure upon foreigners, especially the Japanese, by fomenting all kinds of incidents and boycotts. With each new incident, whether in Shanghai or Shantung, Japanese business groups immediately appealed to their government to take action and protect their property and lives. The Tanaka Giichi cabinet eventually responded to these demands in 1927–1928 by displaying more Japanese muscle to protect Japanese property and people in China.[96] But for many Japanese, especially in South Manchuria, Tokyo's zig-zag China policy had not really dealt with the new problem.

A second strategy emerged during May 4–6, 1928, when around fifty SMR personnel and officials of the Kwantung Leased Territory met in the SMR auditorium in Dairen to express their deep concern about Manchu-

[95] Hara Yasusaburō, comp., *Yamamoto Jōtarō: Ronsaku* (Yamamoto Jōtarō: Essays on policies), vol. 2 (Tokyo: Yamamoto Jōtarō Denki Hensenkai, 1939), pp. 729, 732, 736, 662, 593, and 673.

[96] William Fitch Morton, *The Tanaka Cabinet's China Policy, 1927–1929* (Ann Arbor: University Microfilms, 1970), p. 356; Ian Nish, *Japanese Foreign Policy, 1869–1942: Kasumigaseki to Miyakezaka* (London: Henley; Boston: Routledge & Kegan Paul, 1977), p. 161.

ria's future. Unhappy with Tokyo's China policy and outraged over the increased Chinese attacks upon Japanese people and property, they proposed to form the Manchurian Youth League (Manshū Seinen Remmei) to resolve the Manchurian problem. By November 1928, around twenty branches of the league had been established in the SMR zone.[97] Kobiyama Naonori, a member of the SMR's Board of Directors, became the head of the league's Board of Directors, which became the brain trust of the league.[98] League members met again during June 1–3, 1929, and on September 21, 1930, to map out a plan of action with these elements.[99] The league urged that the SMR cut back on dividends and use reserves, along with a large subsidy from the Japanese government, to encourage a rapid, large-scale industrialization of Manchuria by Japan. The league also demanded that the Kwantung prefectural model of administration be abandoned, and that Japan administer outright the Liaotung and SMR-managed properties. Japanese consulates should be retained, and the rights of Japanese vigorously protected. Japanese businessmen should invest in Manchuria with the spirit of developing long-term projects in the region. Finally, the league called for a greater effort to promote cooperation between Japanese and Chinese in the region.

The league soon grew in size and influence to send its representatives to areas where it was reported that Chinese officials or police had violated the rights of Japanese citizens.[100] League members favored support of the new regional warlord, Chang Hsueh-liang. They abhorred the terrorist tactics of Kwantung Army officers, but they had no faith in the Tanaka cabinet's doctrine of upholding Japan's rights and benefits in China (ken'eki shugi). They dreamed of establishing a free state of Manchuria where all Chinese and Japanese could peacefully live together and prosper. Their plan for building that free state of Manchuria consisted of three stages.[101] First, league members would distribute pamphlets all over Manchuria to popularize the league's goals. Next, the league would send teams to every city in Manchuria, hold public meetings, and present the league's case, hoping to raise Chinese support for the idea. Finally, the league would send teams to every city to inform the Japanese public about

[97] Manshū Seinen Remmeishi Hensenkai, *Manshū seinen remmeishi* (History of the Manchurian Youth League) (Mukden: Manshū Seinen Remmeishi Kankō Iinkai, 1931), p. 4.

[98] Ibid., p. 90; Takasu Yuzō, comp., *Manshū jihen to Manshū seinen remmei: Manshū kenkoku no urabanashi* (The Manchurian incident and the Manchurian Youth League: the inside story of the establishment of Manchukuo) (Tokyo: Manshū Seinen Remmei Konwakai, 1973), p. 2.

[99] *Manshū seinen remmeishi*, p. 254.

[100] Ibid., p. 195, for the example of a league inquiry into a Japanese talc mine operator near Ta-shih-ch'iao who had reported that thirty armed Chinese police had come to his property, indiscriminately fired their weapons, and ordered his mine to be closed down.

[101] Takasu, comp., *Manshū jihen to Manshū seinen remmei*, pp. 7, 8.

its plans for a new Manchurian state. In this way, the Japanese who lived and worked in Manchuria intended to take their case to the people, elicit public support, and pressure both the Japanese and Chinese governments to create a new state of Manchukuo.

The final strategy to solve the Manchurian problem came from the young officers of the Kwantung Army charged with protecting the South Manchuria Railway and its attached properties. These field-grade officers represented the new, upcoming generation of military leaders about to replace the old Satsuma-Chōshō faction of leaders from the Meiji era.[102] They feared and despised the growing influence of the Soviet Union in Manchuria and the upsurge of Chinese Communist cells there, as well as the spread of communism at home. They had become disillusioned with the Tokyo politicians' attempts to design a China policy and with their failure to solve the problems that engulfed Japan: rising unemployment, the severe poverty differences between cities and villages, and Japan's difficulty in finding markets for its goods. They also detested Chinese nationalism and vowed it must be confined to the south of Manchuria. They were dedicated, in fact, to strengthening Japan's hand in Manchuria to deal with the new crisis there. Rather than seek some working arrangement with the Manchurian warlord Chang Tso-lin, as the Tokyo politicians sought, Kwantung Army officers like Kōmoto Daisaku believed that only by eliminating Chang could their military control in the region be advanced.

When Ishiwara Kanji assumed duty in Manchuria, it was just four months after Kōmoto and other officers had assassinated Chang Tso-lin, and about a month after the formation of the Manchurian Youth League. Ishiwara brought not only a new ideological dimension into the circle of Kwantung Army officers, but also a new sense of urgency to resolve the Manchurian problem with some stunning military tactics. He argued that Japan should form a Pan-Asian League that would be backed up (*engo*) by Japanese military power. Within this league, Japan could be assured of raw materials and markets, and such an economic bloc could bolster Japan's military defenses. This new alliance in Asia was not only to ensure the peace and prosperity of the region, but, more importantly, to prepare Japan for the final war in which it could only triumph if it were well-prepared.[103] Ishiwara and his supporters adopted an extreme solution for the Manchurian problem. Their policy demanded a powerful belief in the

---

[102] See the brief description of the goals, ideas, and temperament of these young officers in Marius B. Jansen, "Introduction," pp. 131–133 in James William Morley, ed., *Japan Erupts: the London Naval Conference and the Manchurian Incident, 1928–1932* (New York: Columbia University Press, 1984).

[103] Ibid., p. 5; see also Mark R. Peattie, *Ishiwara Kanji and Japan's Confrontation with the West* (Princeton: Princeton University Press, 1975), pp. 96–101.

existence of an "oriental spirit" that would provide that sense of unity and purpose that Japan needed to create the Pan-Asian League.

The first step to achieve that goal was to create an independent Manchuria, using force if need be. After Ishiwara and his supporters had successfully engineered the takeover of Manchuria in late 1931, they then installed a Chinese puppet regime to rule that region on their behalf on March 1, 1931.[104] The Kwantung Army then began restructuring the SMR, forcing it to divest itself of the many enterprises it owned and operated, demanding that it only manage all railroads in Manchuria, and insisting that it provide research support for plannng Manchuria's economic development.[105] By 1933, the Kwantung Army had successfully transformed the SMR into an instrument of its bidding.

All three strategies were connected in some ineluctable way to the evolution of the SMR after 1906 and its powerful role in expanding Japanese interests in Manchuria. Ironically, although the SMR had been threatened by Chinese nationalism for more than a decade, it was the complex dynamics within Japan's military establishment and political system that really threatened, and ultimately altered, the status of the company. Japan's informal empire in Northeast China ended with the Manchurian incident on September 18, 1931. A new era of Japanese imperialism in China had begun.

[104] Morley, ed., *Japan Erupts*, sec. 3.
[105] Yasutaka Takahashi, "Minami Manshū tetsudō kabushiki kaisha no kaiso keikaku ni tsuite" (The plan to reorganize the South Manchuria Railway Company), *Shakai kagaku tōkyū* 27, 2 (April 1982): 53–112.

CHAPTER 5

Manchukuo and Economic Development

Nakagane Katsuji

Although Japan's leaders tried to project Manchukuo as an independent state, Manchukuo's leaders and their policies were completely subordinated to Japanese control and interests. Japan's leaders hoped that Manchukuo would serve to counter the Soviet Union and the force of Chinese nationalism. But more important, imperial Japan intended to launch the industrialization of Manchukuo at a pace unprecedented in mainland China's economic history.[1]

After briefly describing the region's development before 1945, this chapter examines policy making in Manchukuo, discusses economic planning and control, traces the financial flows from Japan to Manchukuo, and, finally, evaluates how the Manchukuo government promoted that region's development.

ECONOMIC DEVELOPMENT IN MANCHURIA BEFORE 1945

Manchuria's economic development between 1920 and 1941 can be divided into three phases.[2] The first phase, ending in 1930, represented a pattern of growth based upon staple goods, notably soybeans and derivatives, exported to the world market. About one-third of the region's farming areas supported soybean production, and family farms used tra-

---

[1] See Ramon Myers, *The Japanese Economic Development of Manchuria, 1932 to 1945* (New York: Garland, 1982); Kungtu Sun, *The Economic Development of Manchuria in the First Half of the Twentieth Century*, Harvard East Asian monographs, no. 28 (Cambridge: Council on East Asian Studies, 1973); Ann Rasmussen Kinney, *Japanese Investment in Manchurian Manufacturing, Mining, Transportation and Communications, 1931–1945* (New York: Garland, 1982); Alexander Eckstein, Kang Chao, and John Chang, "The Economic Development of Manchuria: The Rise of a Frontier Economy," *Journal of Economic History* 34, 1 (March 1974); and Kang Chao, *The Economic Development of Manchuria: The Rise of a Frontier Economy*, Michigan Papers in Chinese Studies, no. 43 (Ann Arbor: Center for Chinese Studies, 1982). Also Manshikai, ed., *Manshū kaihatsu 40-nenshi* (Forty-year history of Manchurian development) (Tokyo: Manshū Kaihatsu Kankōkai, 1964).

[2] Kang Chao, "The Sources of Economic Growth in Manchuria, 1920–1941," in Chiming Hou and Tzong-shian Yu, eds., *Modern Chinese Economic History* (Taipei: Academia Sinica, 1979).

TABLE 5.1
Gross Domestic Product by Industrial Origin in China and Manchuria (percent)

| Sector | Manchuria | | | | China Proper |
	1924	1929	1934	1941	1933
A	49.7	50.7	36.2	33.9	65.0
M	14.7	12.9	19.8	20.3	11.5
S	35.6	36.4	44.0	45.8	23.5

Source: Kang Chao, *The Economic Development of Manchuria: The Rise of A Frontier Economy* (Ann Arbor: University of Michigan, 1983), tables 7a, 9.

Note: The "A" sector includes farm production, agricultural processing activities, forestry, and fishing; the "M" sector comprises mining, manufacturing, public utilities, small-scale industry, and construction; the "S" sector comprises all other economic activities.

ditional implements and farming practices. Agricultural production in this frontier region had spread from one area to another after Chinese immigrants had cleared the land and built villages. Soybean production provided the basis for the manufacture of beancakes and bean-oil, the major industry of the region.

In the second phase, 1930–1934, Manchuria's economy experienced the "staple trap," as world demand for agricultural products drastically declined and production became depressed. Between 1934 and 1945, the Manchukuo state began to push industrialization programs to develop new industries in the region.

It was during this third phase that the region's economic structure rapidly changed, with the sectors of agriculture (A), manufacturing (M), and services (S) contributing different shares of the economy's gross domestic product (GDP).

In table 5.1 it is clear that Manchuria had become more industrialized than the rest of China by 1934. Similarly, the sources accounting for the region's economic growth had shifted from land and labor to capital and technology. According to Kang Chao's estimate, the contribution of technical change to the process of economic growth rose from 26 percent in 1924–1929 to 46 percent in 1934–1941 (see table 5.2).[3] Meanwhile, the economy's dependency upon foreign trade as measured by the ratio of foreign trade to gross national product had remained almost constant at around 17 percent.

At the same time, investment as a share of GDP rapidly rose. Eckstein and others have estimated that "fixed capital was 9 percent in Manchuria by 1924, over 17 percent in 1934, and 23 percent in 1939. In contrast, the corresponding rate in China was only around 5 percent in 1933, and the

[3] Ibid.

TABLE 5.2
Sources of Economic Growth in Manchuria, 1924–1929 and 1934–1941

	Output	Capital	Labor	Technical change
1924–1927				
Annual growth rate	5.00	4.80	2.90	1.32
Contribution	5.00	1.97	1.71	1.32
Percent	100	39	35	26
1934–1941				
Annual growth rate	8.50	6.80	3.30	3.78
Contribution	8.50	2.78	1.94	3.78
Percent	100	32	22	46

Source: Kang Chao, "The Sources of Economic Growth in Manchuria, 1920–1941," in Chi-ming Hou and Tzong-shian Yu, eds., *Modern Chinese Economic History* (Taipei: Academia Sinica, 1979).

high Manchurian rates were not attained in the country as a whole until the end of the First Five-Year Plan, around 1956 to 1957."[4]

Just as Manchuria's economic growth deviated greatly from China's economic development, so too did that region's economic system become very different from that of China.

THREE BASIC INSTITUTIONS FOR PROMOTING ECONOMIC DEVELOPMENT

Three institutions are necessary for promoting modern economic development: a formal government, a banking system, and industrial firms. The Manchukuo government was a creature of the Kwantung Army, and state power became far more centralized than when the region was controlled by Chang Tso-lin. After promulgating the "Government Organization Law" on March 9, 1932, Japanese officials established a Board of General Affairs (Sōmuchō) as the control center for the entire administration.

Founded in June 1932, the Central Bank was an amalgamation of three former large Chinese native banks. Central Bank officials immediately standardized the monetary system. They called in fifteen currencies that had formerly circulated and replaced these with new bank notes and coins. By June 1935, 97 percent of all native currencies in circulation before 1932 had been replaced. The notes of the Bank of Korea (Chōsen

---

[4] Eckstein et al., "Economic Development of Manchuria," p. 131. Data sources on gross fixed investment are not given in their article. Kinney, *Japanese Investment*, estimates the investment rate for the industry and transportation sectors as 24 percent in 1937 and 30 percent in 1939. See Kinney, *Japanese Investment*.

Ginkō) were also replaced by the new currency in December 1936. At the same time, the state formed the Industrial Bank (Kōgyō Ginkō) by amalgamating three Japanese banks: the Bank of Korea, the Bank of Manchuria ([Manshū Ginkō) and the Seiryū Bank. Next, the state enacted a new banking law in November 1933 to readjust all native and foreign banking organizations by abolishing many, merging some, and placing others under the Ministry of Finance. Some native banks and savings associations became "modern" banks in this way—"modern" in the sense that they became stock companies.

The state also created new banking organizations to provide low-interest credit to industry. An example is the financial cooperative, which later became agricultural development cooperatives and trade and industrial financial cooperatives. Yet the Industrial Bank was the most important bank among the new banking organizations created by the government and the Central Bank. Its chief role would be to provide long-term credit for the first five-year plan. Finally, the state pegged the Manchurian yuan to the Japanese yen in November 1935. Most Manchurian currencies had been pegged to silver in the Shanghai market, but Japanese officials wanted to abolish the silver standard and insulate the yuan from China's currency system. By linking the yuan with the yen, Japanese officials not only stabilized the yuan but also integrated the economy with the "yen-bloc economy" of the Japanese Empire.

Japanese officials quickly moved to create new industrial organizations as well. Except for the SMR and its subsidiary companies, the region possessed no real modern enterprises before 1932. The first group of such firms, called "special companies," was established by special statutes or treaties between Manchukuo and foreign countries. A second group, "semispecial companies," was also subject to government control and supervision. The state controlled these companies through regulations that covered bonuses and the selection of directors and supervisory personnel. Both types of companies increased to thirty-five by 1937 and to seventy by the end of 1941. Although their number was only about 1 percent of all existing companies, their share of total capital was nearly 54 percent (see table 5.3). Some of these companies were founded only with Manchukuo state capital. Others were created with capital from the SMR, zaibatsu, or the Japanese government.

By the end of 1936, the three basic economic institutions—government agencies, banks, and manufacturing enterprises—had been created by the new Manchukuo state under the strict guidance of the Japanese military. Without this new structure of economic institutions, state policies could never have been carried out. How were these policies, in effect, decided upon and implemented?

TABLE 5.3
Expansion of Special and Semispecial Companies in Manchukuo

	Dec. 1932	Dec. 1934	Dec. 1937	Dec. 1941	June 1945
(1) No of Manchurian companies	1,380	2,188	3,330	6,291	—
(2) Their paid-up capital (million yuan)	788	1,373	1,763	5,675	—
(3) No. of special and semispecial companies	2	1	35	70	—
(4) Their paid-up capital (million yuan)	11	164	651	3,030	3,790
(5) Government share (percent)	—	—	—	29.8	19.0

Source: (1) and (2): Manshūkoku seifu, *Manshū kenkoku jūnenshi* (Tokyo: Hara Shobō, 1969), p. 542. (3), (4), and (5): Sōmuchō Tōkeisho, *Manshū keizai sankō shiryō* (1942?), pp. 158–163; and Chiang Nientung et al., *Wei Man-chou-kuo shih* (Chi-lin: Jen-min Ch'u-pan-she, 1980), p. 271.

THE STATE DECISION-MAKING STRUCTURE

The Manchukuo state was under the complete control of the Japanese army and therefore was merely a puppet regime of Japan. The real ruler of the Manchukuo government was not Emperor Pu-Yi, but the commander of the Kwantung Army, who served concurrently as the Japanese ambassador to Manchukuo. When the government made an important decision, its officials first consulted with the army. The army justified its involvement in all government decisions by the principle of "internal guidance" (*naimen-shidō*). For example, whenever the government appointed high-ranking officials or staff members to special and semispecial companies, the army had to approve. The army's right to approve all personnel management in the Manchukuo government can be found in a Kwantung Army Staff Office document issued in April 1935. When appointing Japanese officials, the commander's authority "must have permanent right of approval." The document further states, "the authority to make any selection of non-Japanese officials is to be made only by the Commander."

The Manchukuo government's top executive official was the Chinese premier, who was always "assisted" by the Board of General Affairs. The board, in reality, managed all affairs of state. The director of the board was always a Japanese official. He chaired the important Wednesday meetings, in which such other high-ranking Japanese officials as vice-ministers and bureau directors participated alongside army staff officials. All state laws and policies were decided in these meetings and then sent

TABLE 5.4
Japanese Officials in the Manchukuo Administration in 1937

	Japanese	Chinese	Total	Japanese share (%)
Central government offices	1,430	1,933	3,363	42.5
Board of General Affairs	132	44	176	75.0
Ministry of Civil Administration	192	127	319	60.2
Ministry of Finance	122	59	181	67.4
Ministry of Industries	123	79	202	60.9
Ministry of Transportation	76	46	122	62.3
Ministry of Justice	64	45	109	58.7
Ministry of Education	34	60	94	36.2
Ministry of Mongolian Affairs	43	47	90	47.8
Courts of Justice and public prosecutors' offices	284	1,269	1,553	22.4
Others	360	157	517	69.6
Other central organizations	2,797	4,205	7,002	39.9
Local government offices	789	1,042	1,831	67.4
Other local organizations	1,267	614	1,881	67.4
Total	6,283	7,794	14,077	44.6

Source: Sōmuchō tōkeisho, Tōkei tekiyō (1937), pp. 181–182.

to the Ministerial Council (Kokumin-kaigi), made up of Chinese ministers and the director of the board, who merely gave formal approval. In essence, the Manchukuo state was entirely managed by Japanese military officials.

In the earliest stages, Japanese military officials only served in the very high positions of the administrative bureaucracy. The army set the total number at 600, of which 120 were Japanese officials. The ratio for Japanese and Chinese officials was fixed for every organ of the government. For example, in the Board of General Affairs and the Capital Construction Bureau (Kokuto Kensetsukyoku), the ratio was 70 percent Japanese officials and 30 percent Chinese. For the ministries of Finance and Industry, it was 60:40, while for less important bodies like the Ministry of Education it was 30:70.[5] But as the state structure expanded, the share of Japanese officials rose. In 1937, their number had increased to 1,430 in central government offices alone, to account for 42 percent of all the staff in those offices. If all state organs, both central and local, are taken into account, the number of Japanese staff at that time totaled 6,283, or nearly 45 percent of all staff (see table 5.4).

[5] Chiang Nien-tung, et al., Wei Man-chou-kuo shih (History of Manchuria) (Chi-lin: Jen-min Ch'u-pan-she, 1980), p. 176.

An organ called the Planning Commission (Kikaku-iinkai) controlled economic affairs. Established in July 1938, the Planning Commission at first only reviewed the allocation of labor, materials, and funds. The commission had a director, and its other members were top officials of ministries, directors of special banks, and specialists. The Kwantung Army's staff officers could attend the Planning Commission's meetings at any time. All commission decisions inevitably influenced industrial firms and related organizations. For example, to allocate producers' goods the Planning Commission drew up a Materials Mobilization Plan. The plan stipulated that a special company, the Nichiman Shōji (Japan-Manchukuo Trading Company), would have the authority to allocate all producer's goods, whether domestically manufactured or imported from Japan. This company, controlled by the Minstry of Economic Affairs (Keizai-bu), was supervised by the Planning Commission. Under the commission, a subcommittee called the Materials Pricing Committee (Busshi Bukka Iinkai) decided the allocation of producers' goods among all sectors and companies (see fig. 5.1). This subcommittee was also staffed by army officers and members of the Japanese Embassy, the Kwantung District Office (Kantōchō), the state, and relevant companies. Army officials always "supervised" the allocation of scarce capital.

Other unofficial organs also managed the Manchukuo staff. Takeda recalls that in 1937 an unofficial committee called the "Three-Man Committee" (the director of the board, the chief officer of the army, and the president of the Central Bank) met and discussed Manchukuo's key issues.[6] Moreover, every Friday the "Manchukuo Summit Meetings" convened at which the commander, the chief officer, the director of the board, and other officials discussed major problems and their solutions.[7]

Japanese official interests controlled Manchukuo's policies through the Army Ministry and the Kwantung Army. Even if Manchukuo state officials had to negotiate with particular Japanese ministries, they could never deal directly with them. All communications first had to be transmitted to the Army Ministry through the Kwantung Army, then to the other Japanese ministries concerned. The General Staff Office of the Japanese army also participated in policy making.

THE DECISION-MAKING PROCESS: THE ECONOMY

Japanese officials strongly favored a controlled economy and drawing up long-term economic plans to promote the region's rapid industrializa-

---

[6] Takeda Hidekatsu, *Manshū dasshutsu ki* (Escape from Manchuria) (Tokyo: Chūō Kōron-sha, 1985), p. 197.

[7] Chiang et al., *Wei Man-chou-kuo shih*, p. 179.

FIGURE 5.1   Decision-making process for allocating producer's goods

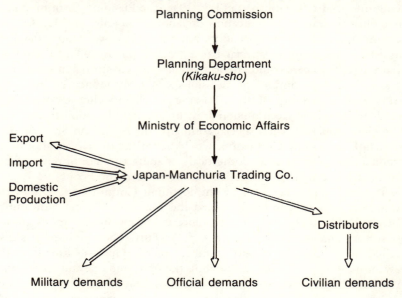

FIGURE 5.1   Adapted from *Manshū teikoku seifu*, p. 652.

tion.[8] A draft called *Manshūkoku keizai kensetsu kōyō* (Outlines for economic construction in Manchukuo) appeared in 1933. That document served as the blueprint for planning economic development. One year before announcing the "Outlines," the Kwantung Army requested the SMR's Economic Research Organization (Keizai Chōsakai) to examine the first phase of Economic Construction Planning. This unit mobilized a staff of three hundred to produce detailed reports on how Manchukuo could be brought under a plan of economic control. The unit and the army's Special Services Organ (Tokumu-bu) held various conferences. As a result, the army officers strongly influenced the final draft of the "Outlines."

The first five-year plan also followed a similar but more complicated

[8] The following description mostly depends on Akira Hara, "1930 nendai no Manshū keizaitōsei seisaku" (Economic control policies in Manchuria in the 1930s), in Manshūshi Kenkyūkai, ed., *Nihon teikokushugika no Manshū* (Manchuria under Japanese imperialism) (Tokyo: Ochanomizu Shobō, 1972).

process. In early 1936, the army again requested the SMR's Economic Research Organization to formulate long-term plans for the second phase of economic construction. This unit produced a draft within several months and presented it to the army in August, and again to the General Staff Office in September. Meanwhile, a special economic research unit under the direction of Colonel Ishiwara drew up a report called *Manshū ni okeru gunjusangyō kensetsu kakujū keikaku* (Plans for construction and expansion of military industries in Manchuria) and submitted it to the General Staff Office, the Army Ministry, the Kwantung Army, and the SMR. In October 1936, a conference of officials from the army, the SMR, and the government integrated these plans into a single comprehensive plan. At a Tokyo meeting in late 1936, which representatives of the above three institutions and the Army Ministry attended, the original draft plans for Manchukuo's industrial development were finally formulated. Those plans were then sent to the Kwantung Army from the Army Ministry after further revision in January 1937, and was officially submitted to the Manchukuo government.

This was the process by which the army and the Army Ministry actually formulated Manchukuo's economic plans, and the Manchukuo government only played a passive role. The Manchukuo state merely served as an agent for the army to draw up plans to achieve its goals.

ECONOMIC CONTROL OF MANCHUKUO

Sharing a common ideology of state planning and control, Japanese officials had agreed from the outset on a strategy of "forced industrialization" to lift the Manchurian economy from its depressed state in the early 1930s. They opted for strict planning and control to initiate rapid industrialization. Japan's army officers had conceived of a state-planned and state-controlled economy even before they created Manchukuo.[9] Their anti-laissez-faire ideology was contained in the famous "Outline for Economic Construction in Manchukuo," announced on March 1, 1932, which clearly stipulated the basic principles for managing Manchukuo's economy. That document contains the following statement to justify state intervention in economic activities: "In view of the evils of an uncontrolled capitalist economy, we will use whatever state power is necessary to control that economy." All important activities associated with national defense or public interests would be run by public enterprises or special state-controlled companies. Although other areas of economic activity would be left to private enterprise, they too would be subject to

[9] See, for example, the army's *Manmō kaihatsu hōsakuan* (A program of measures for Manchurian and Mongolian development) in December 1931.

indirect state controls. For the army, Manchukuo must become an economy without "capitalist oppression."

In the *Nichiman keizai tōsei hōsaku yōkō* (Outlines of economic control measures for Japan and Manchukuo), published in March 1934, the transportation, communications, and other industries closely related to Japan's national defense would be under state control. Moreover, industries producing steel, light metals, petroleum, liquified oil, automobiles, munitions, lead, zinc, asbestos, coal, ammonium sulphate, soda ash, gold, electricity, and lumber would be operated by special companies and would "be directly or indirectly under the protection and supervision of the government of the Japanese Empire." Industries like salt, wood pulp, cotton cloth, wool, flour milling, oil and fat manufacturing, and hemp also were subject to "appropriate administrative or capital control" to "encourage and promote them." Industries like textiles, rice, silk, and fishing were also placed under administrative control to "restrict them in light of the current conditions of similar Japanese industries." Finally, all remaining industries were left to their "natural development."

Such widespread state intervention made Japanese capitalists hesitant to invest in Manchuria. To overcome such apprehension, state authorities announced in June 1934 that Manchukuo welcomed Japanese private investment. They argued that "military-related activities, public enterprises, and industries basic for development, like transportation and communications, steel, light metals, gold, coal, automobiles, petroleum, ammonium sulphate, soda, lumber, etc., required special policies." But they urged all businessmen to invest, even though the state might have to "exercise some administrative control." This conciliatory attitude changed after 1937. In May of that year, state officials drew up the Key Industries Control Law, which made every key industry subject to state approval, control, and supervision by a state ministry. Any industry seeking to expand its productive capacity had to obtain permission from the relevant ministry. At first, twenty-one industries were listed as "key industries," but later their number increased to eighty-six.

Some government officials had been demanding a comprehensive plan for Manchukuo's industrial development ever since 1932. Because the army anticipated war with the Soviet Union, some top military officials perceived that Manchukuo had to defend itself as well as serve as the front line of defense for Japan. That meant building more industry for defense-related needs. Meanwhile, the first Konoe cabinet advocated a comprehensive five-year plan in Japan, insisting that planning in both Japan and Manchukuo be coordinated. Japanese economic policies in the thirties were shaped by conflicting demands by Tokyo and Ch'ang-ch'un over whether the Manchukuo economy should be independent or subordinate to Japan.[10] The economic plans being developed in Manchukuo were aimed at making that economy independent of Japan, and they even called for deployment of resources from Japan to Manchukuo.

The original economic plan called for 55 percent of investment funds to go to the heavy industry sector. The revised plan, formulated after the Sino-Japanese War occurred in July 1937, called for that sector to receive 78 percent. Steel and energy (coal and electricity) alone were supposed to receive 29 percent of all investment funds. But this new plan proved to be a compromise arrangement based upon Manchukuo's continued dependence on the Japanese economy. The war with China had forced Manchukuo's leaders to depend far more on Japan than they had originally intended. In addition, this revised plan called for supplying more raw materials to Japan.

In late 1936, the Nissan concern moved to Manchuria and formed a new special company, the Manshū Heavy Industries Development Company (MHID). This conglomerate had many subsidiaries that were vital for Manchukuo's heavy industrialization (see fig. 5.2).

Did this new plan succeed? One former Manchukuo official surmised that "the plan was a success—even though the actual results did not match the targets of the revised plan. We almost attained the targets of the original plan, and we surmounted many difficulties both at home and abroad."[11] One such difficulty was to acquire sufficient machinery and steel products from Japan. Because Japan had promulgated its Materials Mobilization Plan and imposed state control over all basic materials, few of these vital products could be exported to Manchukuo.

As for evidence of Manchukuo's success in achieving its planned industrial targets, planned and realized output are compared in table 5.5. For pig iron, coal, salt, and thermal power, the new capacity created matched or exceeded the capacity planned in the original plan. But in other areas, the gap was very large.

In 1942, Manchukuo launched a second five-year plan. By now, Manchukuo and Japan were waging total war. The state imposed more controls over materials, labor, financial funds, and prices, and Manchukuo became more subordinated to Japanese interests. For example, Japanese officials even had to approve the procurement prices for Manchukuo coal, steel, and soybeans exported to Japan.[12]

[10] For the two conflicting principles inherent in Manchukuo economic plans, see Shigeru Ishikawa, "Shūsen ni itaru made no Manshū keizai kaihatsu" (Manchurian economic development until the end of the war), in Nihon Gaikōgakkai, ed., *Taiheiyō sensō shūketsuron* (On ending the Pacific War) (Tokyo: Tōkyō Daigaku Shuppankai, 1958), pp. 737–752.

[11] Ōkurashō, *Nihonjin no kaigai keizai katsudō ni kansuru rekishiteki chōsa* (A historical investigation of the overseas empire), vol. 22 (Tokyo, 1950), p. 78. Henceforth, *NKKK*.

[12] See Yutaka Fujiwara, *Manshūkoku tōsei keizairon* (The Manchukuo scheme of economic controls) (Tokyo: Nihon Hyōronsha, 1942), p. 251.

FIGURE 5.2   The Manshū Heavy Industries Development Company (MHID) and subsidiaries—financial flows (million yuan), late February 1942

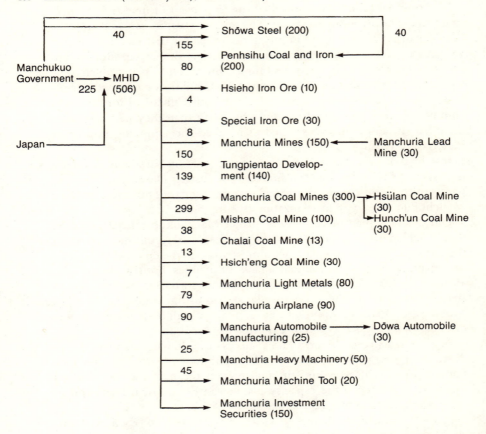

FIGURE 5.2   *Notes*: Figures in parentheses are amounts of paid-in capital. Companies with paid-in capital less than 10 million yuan are omitted.

Source: *Manshū teikoku seifu*, pp. 586–587.

TABLE 5.5

Manchukuo Industrial Development Five–Year Plan for Mining and Manufacturing Sectors: Plan and Performance (thousand tons)

	(1) Capacity, end of 1936	Capacity, end of 1941		Actual performance		4/2 (%)	4/3 (%)
		(2) Original plan	(3) Revised plan	(4) Capacity	(5) Production		
Pig iron	850	2,530	4,500	2,050	1,338	81.0	45.6
Steel ingot	580	2,000	3,160	580	561	29.0	18.4
Steel materials	400	1,500	1,200	675	410	45.0	56.3
Special steel	—	—	100	10	3	—	10.0
Coal	13,558	27,160	34,910	28,300	24,189	104.2	81.1
Liquidified coal	800	800	1,770	10	—	1.3	0.6
Shale oil	145	800	650	282	280	35.3	43.4
Alcohol	15.1	56.7	56.7	15	12	26.5	26.5
Salt	340	973.6	1,402	1,050	—	107.8	74.9
Soda ash	12	72	72	64	61	88.9	88.9
Chemical fertilizer	203	—	454	250	190	—	55.1
Thermal power	458.6	814.6	1,330.6	1,014	—	124.5	76.2
Hydroelectric power	—	590	1,240	100	100	16.9	8.1
Asbestos	0.15	5	5	5	5	100.0	100.0

Financial Plan (million yuan)

	Original plan	Revised plan	Final revised plan
Mining and manufacturing sector	1,391	3,880	4,990
Transportation and communication sector	771	644	640
Agricultural sector	143	135	} 430
Settlement sector	274	303	
Total	2,579	4,962	6,060

Source: Akira Hara, "1930 nendai-no Manshū keizaitōsei seisaku," in Manshūshi Kenkyūkai, ed., *Nihon teikokushugika no Manshū* (Ochanomizu Shobō, 1972), p. 73.

Meanwhile, the Manchukuo state controlled the economy through its special and semispecial companies and the Central Bank. Figure 5.2 shows that both states used the MHID and other companies to control and finance industrial development. MHID capital for its subsidiaries came to 1.1 billion yuan in 1942.[13] The government share in the total MHID paid-in capital amounted to 44.5 percent (225/506). The government controlled 745 million yuan of capital by virtue of its financial leverage in MHID.

But the state relied far more on statutory regulations than on organs to control these enterprises directly. Even private, nonspecial companies had to comply with these strict state regulations. Consequently, many firms complained of inefficiency and "bureaucratism."[14]

Although the state exercised great control over commodity and service markets, factor markets for land, labor, and capital were another matter. The state did not restrict the movement of workers, except between Manchukuo and China proper. The state allowed land to be freely sold. But the state did control most of the capital market. All stock shares in the special and semispecial companies had to be approved and issued under state controls.

PLANNED ECONOMY AND FINANCIAL ECONOMY

Although state officials had created a planned, controlled economy, the state could not provide all of the financial capital required for the ambitious economic plans of the Army. For funding these economic plans, state officials relied upon the SMR, MHID, state organs, Central Bank, Industrial Bank, and Japan. Let us examine each of these sources of financial capital.

South Manchuria Railway Company

Until 1937, the SMR supplied Manchukuo with most of its financial capital for investment. In late 1931, investments in the SMR and its subsidiaries amounted to 85 percent of all Japanese investment in Manchuria. During 1932–1935, Japanese investment increased to 1.181 million yuan, of which 803 million or about 68 percent went to the SMR and its subsidiar-

---

[13] Manshūkoku Seifu, *Manshū kenkoku jūnenshi* (Ten-year history of Manchukuo) (Tokyo: Hara Shobō, 1969), p. 585.

[14] Fujiwara offers three reasons why the management of such companies was very inefficient: (1) "political constraints" from external sources, or lack of autonomy; (2) monopoly, or lack of market competition; and (3) "extensiveness," or scarcity of company managerial personnel. The first two reasons can explain the managerial inefficiency of enterprises in contemporary socialist states.

TABLE 5.6
Investments in Manchuria at the End of June 1945 (million yuan)

	Country	Paid-up Capital	Bonds	Borrowings	Total
SMR subsidiaries and related companies	Japan	1,882	2,863	155	4,900
	Manchukuo	465	564	1,027	2,056
MHID and related companies	Japan	584	863	6	1,453
	Manchukuo	289	2,965	892	4,146
Other special and semispecial companies	Japan	764	658	796	2,218
	Manchukuo	1,041	324	2,280	3,645
Others	Japan	1,929	—	776	2,705
	Manchukuo	216	—	2,809	3,025
Total	Japan	5,159	4,384	1,733	11,276
	Manchukuo	2,011	3,853	7,008	12,872
	Total	7,170	8,237	8,741	24,148

Source: Tung-pei wu-tzu tiao-ch'a wei-yuan-hui, *Tung-pei ching-chi hsiao-ts'ung-shu: tzu-yuan chi ch'ang-yeh* (TCH) (Shenyang, 1948), pp. 29–30.

ies.[15] Although many SMR economic activities yielded a great profit, these retained earnings did not contribute as much to new financial investment as did the issue of new debt: bonds and paid-in capital.[16]

After 1936, the SMR's share in Manchukuo's investment declined. The SMR's financial position worsened in 1934–1935, when it was forced by the state to invest in new railroad construction, just as freight revenues from coal and soybean were declining. Meanwhile, the Japanese capital market had contracted, so that the company could not easily issue bonds in Japan to raise more funds.[17] Leading army officers intended to use the SMR as an instrument to build their new industrial system, and that meant making the SMR manage all railroads.[18] Even though the SMR was not permitted to manage its assets as formerly, it still owned fifty-five subsidiaries at the end of June 1945, and its investments still amounted to about seven billion yuan (see table 5.6). The SMR sold its securities and bonds mostly in Japan and borrowed from the Manchukuo state.

[15] Manshūkoku Seifu, *Manshū kenkoku jūnenshi*, pp. 559–560.

[16] Kinney, *Japanese Investment*, p. 105, table 18.

[17] Manshikai, ed., *Manshu kaihatsu*, vol. 2, pp. 364–365.

[18] The army had already submitted a plan to reorganize the SMR in the spring of 1934, but the plan was aborted because it had been leaked to the SMR at an early stage. Therefore, when the army decided to set up the MHID and at the same time fundamentally reorganize the SMR, the plan was carried out in secret. See Chiang et al., *Wei Man-chou-kuo shih*, p. 276.

The Manshū Heavy Industries Development Company

The MHID replaced the SMR as the motive force for industrialization, especially for the first five-year plan. When the government promulgated the Manshū Heavy Industries Development Company Management Law in December 1937, Nissan became a special company, with 50 percent of its capital held by the government. Some SMR subsidiaries were even transferred to MHID, and by June 1945 MHID controlled forty companies.

MHID funds came primarily from within Manchukuo. Except for paid-in capital provided by the government, the Industrial Bank supplied 29 percent of the total amount. About two-thirds of the total funds raised by MHID came from Manchukuo, largely through the Industrial Bank (table 5.6).

The government, of course, granted the MHID special favors. It guaranteed a minimum return of 7.5 percent for bonds. If MHID's net profit did not reach 6 percent of the total funds it used for domestic undertakings, the government guaranteed to finance the difference for at least ten years. Such state support enabled the MHID to raise considerable funds. But the MHID did not satisfy the government's expectations. Japanese financial investment in the MHID came to less than that made in the SMR even after 1937. Japanese investors still remained apprehensive about the MHID's profitability.

The State

The state directly supplied funds to its special and semispecial companies.[19] It indirectly channeled other funds to various sectors through the Central Bank and the MHID. The central government operated a general and special budget accounting system for these purposes. Special accounts were opened in 1934 to finance enterprises that were under the state's plan (kokusaku). The state's "Investment Special Account," the nucleus of the special account system, received 21 percent of all special account expenditures during the first five-year period. As this account expanded, so too did the number of special and semispecial companies.

State budget revenues consisted largely of taxes and public bonds. The ratio of bonds to the revenue of these two accounts increased from 53 percent in 1934, to 67 percent in 1937, and to 109 percent in 1941 (table 5.7). The ratio of public bonds to net revenues rose from 25 percent in

[19] I have not mentioned so far the role of local government. Since Manchukuo's fiscal system was highly centralized, its role in economic development remained limited. In 1941, the sum of local budget revenues was about one-fifth that of the central government. See Sōmuchō Tōkeishō, *Manshū keizai sankō shiryō* (Manchurian economic reference materials) (Hsinking, 1942), p. 28.

TABLE 5.7
Government Revenues and Expenditures (million yuan)

	1932	1934	1937	1941	1944
General Account					
Expenditures	130	187	268	708	1,315
Revenues	153	215	313	814	1,315
Special Account					
Expenditures	25	132	551	1,941	2,546
Revenues	26	174	677	2,115	2,671
Combined					
Expenditures	119	245	586	1,891	2,741
Revenues	158	320	693	2,050	2,737
Bond Issues					
Domestic bonds	—	4	105	230	472
Borrowings	39	12	21	269	114
Yen bonds	—	10	45	200	15
Total	39	25	171	699	601

Source: TCH appendix tables 6, 7.

1937 to 34 percent in 1941, and then declined to 22 percent in 1944. Until 1941, the Central Bank accepted nearly all bonds issued by the government. After 1942, the state sold bonds mainly to the Savings Department of the Central Bank, which also held all postal savings in Manchukuo.

The Central Bank

Manchukuo's Central Bank issued banknotes, mobilized savings, and made loans. In 1932, the bank loaned 124 million yuan, of which 24 million went to the government. In 1937, the bank loaned 213 million yuan, of which only 37 million, or 17 percent, went to the government. In other words, most bank loans went to nongovernmental organizations, especially nonbanking firms, until 1941, and then to other banks after 1942 (see table 5.8). In 1944, three nongovernmental banks—the Industrial Bank, the Agricultural Development Bank, and the Yokohama Specie Bank—received loans of 4.5 billion yuan, representing 68 percent of the total loans the Central Bank made.

Central Bank loans almost always exceeded its savings (table 5.8). Therefore, the bank issued Central Bank notes to make up for its shortage of savings deposits. Taking 1936 as the base (100), by the end of June 1945 the index had risen to 3,000. Meanwhile, the official index for wholesale

TABLE 5.8
Accounts of the Central Bank (million yuan)

	1932	1934	1937	1941	1944
Currency issued	152	184	330	1,317	5,877
Deposits	50	101	266	676	1,645
Government	30	51	133	210	632
Banks	—	—	26	56	679
Others	—	—	101	320	334
Loans	124	165	213	758	6,586
Government	24	25	37	185	244
Banks	—	—	23	267	5,661
Others	—	—	153	306	682
Securities	12	59	194	1,223	1,620
Public bonds	—	47	117	833	653
Japanese bonds	—	—	65	272	712
Share holdings	12	12	11	118	255

Source: TCH, appendix table 10; Chilinsheng Jinjungyenchiusuo, ed., *Wei Man-chou chung-yang yin-hang shih-liao* (Chilin: Jen-min Ch'u-pan-she, 1984), pp. 505–515.

prices in Ch'ang-ch'un capital was 565, and the black market price was probably more than 4,000.[20]

The Industrial Bank

This bank's funds came from three sources: saving deposits, borrowing, and bond issues. Saving deposits were the main financial source for this bank until the end of the first five-year plan. During the plan period, about 61 percent of the total debits of the bank was covered by saving deposits, but borrowing, particularly from the Central Bank, replaced saving deposits after the second five-year plan started. In 1944, as much as 61 percent of the funds available for the Industrial Bank came from borrowing (table 5.9).

Most of the funds collected in this way flowed into the industrial and mining sectors as loans, which increased from 259 million yuan in 1937 to 1.1 billion in 1941, then to 3.1 billion in 1944. As of the end of March 1944, as much as 1.2 billion yuan, or 38 percent of the bank's loans, was provided to the MHID alone. Moreover, the Industrial Bank's share in the total amount of loans financed by all Manchurian banking organizations tended to rise over time. In 1937, the share was only 36 percent, but it rose to 47 percent in 1940.

[20] Makio Okabe, *Manshūkoku* (Manchukuo) (Tokyo: Sanseidō, 1978), p. 96.

TABLE 5.9

A Financial Profile of the Industrial Bank (million yuan)

	1937	1941	1944
Deposits	244	985	1,895
Borrowings	95	518	3,063
Government	65	194	228
Central bank	0	252	2,781
Others	30	72	65
Bonds issued	0	141	268
Loans	259	1,099	3,076
Securities	85	577	2,260

Source: TCH, appendix table 15.

Japan

Japanese financial sources played a very important role in financing economic development in Manchuria both before and after the Manchurian incident. One estimate shows financial investments totaling 1.8 billion yuan, or 72.3 percent of the total amount of foreign investment in Manchuria before the incident.[21] From 1932 to 1935, Japan invested about 1.1 billion yuan in various securities, to make for a total investment of 2.6 billion yuan, accounting for 97 percent of all foreign investment in this region in 1935.

Japan's investments in Manchukuo can be shown from Manchukuo's balance of payments. Manchukuo always had an unfavorable balance of trade with Japan, except in 1932 (see table 5.10). Its trade deficits reached the high level of 1.0 billion yuan, or 35 percent of total expenditures, in 1941. The country's net capital import from Japan mainly covered these deficits. As Manchukuo's trade deficits rose, so did the net amount of capital imported from Japan (fig. 5.3).

As for Japanese financial investments in Manchukuo, the following developments took place. First, the MHID replaced the SMR and other companies as the primary agent to finance industrialization in the first five-year plan. Second, the share of public bonds in financial investment always remained small. The Manchukuo state did not underwrite the transfer of Japanese financial capital to Manchukuo. Finally, Japanese financial capital increasingly remained invested in Manchukuo. After deducting remitted profits, the share of investment remaining in Manchukuo stood at 56.6 percent in 1932, but rose to 86.6 percent in 1941.[22]

[21] For Japanese investment in Manchukuo, see Ōkurashō, NKKK, vol. 24, pp. 151–158.
[22] Ibid., p. 205.

TABLE 5.10
Manchukuo's Balance of Payments with Japan (million yuan)

	1932	1934	1937	1941	1944
Current balance	89	−196	−359	−636	−876
Visible trade	47	−190	−344	−1,024	−393
Export	232	219	322	485	707
Import	−185	−409	−666	−1,509	−1,100
Invisible trade and transfer	42	−6	−14	389	−482
Capital balance	80	264	341	1,233	−332
New investment	121	233	370	1,461	130
Japanese	160	283	468	1,562	438
Manchukuo's	−35	−50	−98	−101	−308
Recovery of invested funds by:					
Manchukuo	25	37	59	14	52
Japan	−69	−6	−88	−206	−232
Other	—	—	—	−44	−281
Total balance	165	68	−18	597	−1,207

Source: 1932 and 1934: Mantetsu Chōsabu, Manshū gokanen keikaku jūyō shorui (Tokyo: Ryūkei Shosha, 1980), vol. 4, no. 1 (reprint), pp. 182–198; 1937: Ōkurashō, Nihonjin no kaigai keizai katsudō ni kansuru rekishiteki chōsa (Tokyo, 1950), vol. 24, p. 210; 1941 and 1944: TCH, table 23.

As Manchukuo government control over the economy expanded, the amount of Japanese capital that remained in Manchuria steadily increased to contribute to the region's economic development.

The final revised financial plan for 1937–1941 shows that half of the necessary funds projected to finance development had to come from Japan, with Manchukuo providing 28 percent and other countries supplying 22 percent. But as Sino-Japanese relations worsened and then World War II broke out, no countries except Japan supplied funds to Manchukuo. Of all the funds actually earmarked for investment during the five-year plans, Japan provided as much as 60 percent, with the rest coming from the SMR, the MHID, and other sources (see table 5.11).

In addition to the six sources of financial investment discussed above, other organizations also financed Manchukuo's economic development. Regular Japanese banks provided a substantial amount of funds to various sectors in Manchukuo. In 1937, about 23 percent of the loans financed by all banking organizations, including the above two special banks, came from ordinary Japanese banks in Manchukuo and the Kwantung Leased Territory. If the loans extended by those banks in the Kwantung Leased Territory are excluded, the share probably is only 10 percent. Govern-

FIGURE 5.3 Japanese investment in Manchukuo and Manchukuo's trade deficit

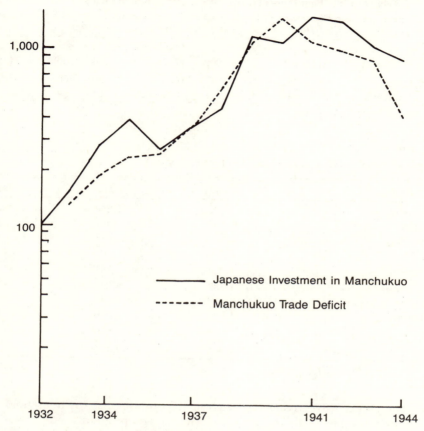

FIGURE 5.3 *Source*: For 1932–1939, *Manshū teikoku seifu*, p. 514; for 1940–1944, *Ōku-rashō*, pp. 156, 200.

ment-supported organizations like the Agricultural Development Cooperatives and the Trade and Industrial Finance Cooperatives also made financial investments in their respective areas.[23]

Finally, the household sector was an important source of savings. No detailed information is available as to how this sector saved and how banks mobilized that sector's savings. From table 5.12 one can deduce that Manchukuo's households, particularly of Japanese citizens, provided about half of the entire savings (as stock) by mid-1944. The government

[23] Other native banking organizations, such as pawnshops, are not considered here because they contributed little to Manchukuo's economic development.

TABLE 5.11
Capital Collected for the First Five-Year Plan, 1937–1941 (million yuan)

	1937		1938		1939		1940		1941	
Planned	419		858		1488		1744		2078	
Actually collected	514	(100)	932	(100)	1757	(100)	1941	(100)	1774	(100)
from Japan	267	(52)	602	(67)	1062	(71)	1266	(66)	1072	(60)
from Manchukuo	247	(48)	330	(33)	692	(29)	675	(34)	702	(40)

Source: Ōkurashō, Nihonjin, p. 136.

TABLE 5.12
Savings and Loans in Manchukuo, mid-1944 (million yuan)

Sector	Savings	Loans	Balance
Households	2,222	1,240	982
Japanese	1,432	366	1,066
Chinese	757	871	− 114
Others	33	3	30
Government	840	241	599
Corporations	1,382	5,025	− 3,643
Banking organizations	342	2,139	− 1,797
Other firms	1,040	2,886	− 1,846
Others	38	610	− 572
Total	4,481	7,113	− 2,632

Source: TCH, appendix table 18.

began an extensive saving campaign in 1939 to mobilize the household sector's "surplus funds" to refinance its investment programs and to control inflation. The enactment of the People's Saving Association Law in June 1942 forced many people to place their savings in banks and post offices.[24]

Financial funds for nonbanking firms came mainly from the Industrial Bank or from Japan after 1937 (see fig. 5.4). These two sources provided direct financial investment in Manchukuo, whereas the government and the Central Bank indirectly invested.[25] The Central Bank indirectly fi-

[24] Okabe, Manshūkoku, pp. 96–97. More detailed information on this campaign is given in Tung-pei Wu-tzu Tiao-ch'a Wei-yuan-hui, Tung-pei ching-chi hsiao-ts'ung-shu: chin-jung (Economic encyclopedia of the Northeast: Finance) (Shenyang, 1948), pp. 176–184.

[25] Kinney drew a slightly different conclusion for 1939. According to her estimates, increases in investment funds for 1939 were 1.8 billion yuan, of which Japan contributed 44 percent, the government 15 percent, and the Industrial Bank 15 percent. See Kinney, Japanese Investment, p. 92, table 15.

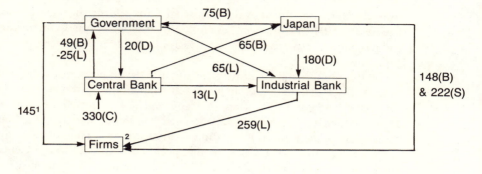

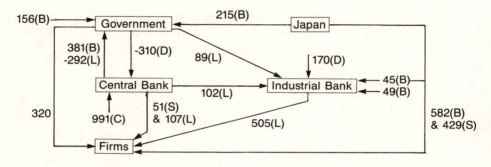

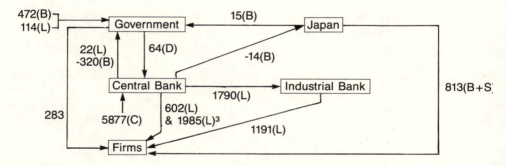

FIGURE 5.4 *Source*: Reconstructed financial statistics for Manchukuo based on scattered data in *Manshū teikoku seifu*; TCH, *Chin-jung*; *Ōkurashō*; *Sōmuchō tōkeisho*; etc.

Note: All figures show annual increases. B, L, S, D, and C indicate bonds, loans, securities, deposits, and currencies issued, respectively.

1 Revenues in the Investment Account of the central government.
2 Includes the SMR, MHID, and other banking organizations except the two special banks.
3 Loans to other banking organizations.

nanced enterprises through the Industrial Bank, while the state induced Japanese capital to come to Manchukuo by establishing new institutions and passing laws to guarantee that investors would receive fixed dividend payments.

Finally, the Central Bank paid for the military expenses of the Kwantung Army.[26] At first, the Japanese and Manchukuo governments paid for those expenses by creating an account called "Allotted Charges for National Defense." When the Japanese fiscal system failed in 1944, Manchukuo alone paid for all Kwantung Army expenses. The Japanese government first ordered the Yokohama Specie Bank to lend to the Central Bank, then backed by the Bank of Japan. The Central Bank directly paid funds to the Japanese army, which in turn transferred those to the Kwantung Army. In 1945, the Central Bank supplied 2.6 billion yuan, or approximately a quarter of the total amount of the bank's loans, to the Shōkin Bank for financing the Kwantung Army.

CONCLUSION

The Japanese army really controlled the state of Manchukuo. Even though the state depended on Japan and the army, its officials still played a formidable role in the region's economic development, but its role was indirect rather than direct. The state created an economic system in which private enterprise and capital were encouraged to operate, and therefore, considerable Japanese private capital was attracted to Manchukuo.

The state mobilized both material and financial resources and directed these to certain industries. In this new economic system, the state raised the investment rate and built much new industry and energy capacity, primarily to satisfy the Japanese military's needs.[27]

But the economy became greatly strained and distorted. As Ann Kinney has argued, Manchukuo's industrialization never advanced by drawing resources from the traditional or agricultural sector into the modern industrial sector.[28] Instead, capital resources came primarily from Japan to promote this "forced industrialization."

Although the state heavily invested in various sectors, particularly in special companies, it was not the biggest investor. Moreover, the state's

[26] See Chi-lin-sheng Chin-jung Yen-chiu-suo, ed., *Wei Man-chou chung-yang yin-hang shih-liao* (Historical notes on the Central Bank of Manchukuo) (Chi-lin: Chi-lin Jen-min Ch'u-pan-she, 1984), p. 12.

[27] Myers says, "What prevented a total collapse of the economy before 1945 when black market activity soared and the price level moved up quickly was the ability of the Japanese to maintain tight administrative control." See Myers, *Economic Development of Manchuria*, p. 260. In view of the number of Japanese officials (see table 5.4), it seems fair to conclude that Manchukuo's administration was quite effective until the collapse of the regime.

[28] Kinney, *Japanese Investment*, p. 146.

share of total invested funds declined over time, as figure 5.4 shows. The state used its powers mainly to enforce its statutes and regulations. To facilitate Japanese investments in Manchuria, the state granted privileges such as tax exemption, which firms like the Manshū Telegraph & Telephone Company, the Manshū Gold Mining Company, and the Manshū Mining Development Company greatly enjoyed.

As for transferring Manchuria's resources to Japan, many have claimed that Japan plundered this region.[29] But Manchukuo almost always had trade deficits with Japan and received a net capital inflow from Japan. Manchukuo certainly supplied large quantities of coal, pig iron, and soybeans to Japan. But these goods never accounted for a large share of domestic production or total demand in the Japanese Empire. In 1941, Japan did not import any of Manchukuo's steel products and only purchased 1 billion tons of coal (4 percent of its domestic production). Japan did purchase 560,000 tons of pig iron (40 percent of domestic output), but far below the planned level of 2 million tons. In 1941, Manchukuo produced 3.4 million tons, but only exported 609,000 tons to Japan.[30]

Japan certainly took far less from Manchukuo than it gave in return. But Japan did not do this out of generosity toward Manchukuo. The Pacific War erupted prematurely before Japan could derive any gain from the enormous investments already made in Manchukuo.

[29] Chiang et al., *Wei Man-chou-kuo shih*.

[30] For figures of steel products, coal, and pig iron, see Ōkurashō, *NKKK*, vol. 24, p. 139; for soybeans, see Sōmuchō Tōkeishō, *Manshū keizai sankō shiryō*, pp. 76, 148.

PART II

Culture and Community

By 1930, not only had Japan begun to emerge as the paramount foreign presence in China, its citizens made up the largest foreign population in the treaty port communities and in the interior. As Mark Peattie's chapter shows, in certain ways the Japanese community in China resembled the rest of the foreign community there. Like the other foreigners, most Japanese lived apart from the indigenous population (except for those Chinese who sought residence in the foreign settlements), governed by their own officials and protected by their own police. Like the other foreigners, the Japanese tried to create islands of the familiar in the vast alien sea that was China. Not only did they enjoy the comforts of home—from pickled radishes to hot baths—they brought with them their own geography and architecture. Just as the foreign community in Peking dubbed peaks in the Western Hills "Mount Bruce" and "Mount Burlingame," so too the Japanese named streets and neighborhoods "Asahi-dori" or "Tachibana-dori." That made it easier to get around, and it held the engulfing reality of China at bay.

The contrasts between the Japanese and the rest of the foreign community, however, are perhaps more interesting than the similarities. If the pattern of Japanese enterprise in China resembled patterns at home, so too the Japanese community in China more closely approximated a cross-section of the metropolitan society than did, say, British residents in China. Distance served as a fine-meshed filter to screen out all but a special breed of Englishmen—the elite and the marginal—whereas all classes of Japanese (except peasant farmers, who had little reason to go) managed to make their way to China. Strictly speaking, the Japanese community in China most closely resembled the Japanese colonial communities in Korea and Taiwan. As Peattie's chapter points out, Kyushu and western Honshu, the regions with the longest historical connections and most voluminous economic relations with the continent, were overrepresented in the community in China, just as they were in Korea and Taiwan.

The class structure of the Japanese community in China was also roughly the same as that in the Japanese colonies. At the top was a transient elite of diplomatic officials or company managers (employees of Mitsui Bussan, OSK, NYK, and other large firms) who worked for large public and private organizations in China; and at the bottom were the more numerous (and possibly more permanent) petty bourgeois settlers (shopkeepers, restaurant owners, construction contractors, and the like) who provided the goods and services the community consumed. Collectively, the Japanese community, made up predominantly of economic small fry, was not as affluent as the Western. Their property and assets were more modest.

The class character of the Japanese community perhaps accounts for other differences. The British residents of the treaty ports, as Peattie suggests, brought with them a grand imperialist style developed after one or two centuries of living in other people's countries—and ruling them. They had their clubs and racetracks, their teas and tiffins, their cricket and polo teams—all the institutions, distractions, and pretensions of upper-class British gentility, intended not only to fend off Chinese culture but also to reaffirm that *taipans* were not inferior socially for being colonials. The British style set the tone, as it did elsewhere in the world, for the rest of the foreign community. By contrast, the Japanese lacked a colonial style in this sense, living in relatively modest fashion, as befitted their station at home. As Peattie points out, the Japanese community was also far less cosmopolitan, mingling less with the other foreign residents, and much more self-contained. Even those few Japanese who adopted the *taipan* style—the representatives of the big shipping, trading, or spinning firms—were not in China long enough to become "old China hands" or to set down deep roots in the foreign community. They looked forward to appointments in New York or London or expected to be called back to home headquarters.

It is possible that the Japanese may have had an easier time adjusting to life in China than the Western residents did. There is evidence, for example, that even British consular officials trained for the China service tended to have substantial adjustment problems. A British inspector-general of consulates reported in 1937 that consuls in China were likely to burn out sooner than those in other countries. In the previous twenty-five years, he wrote, eight had died at their posts, three had committed suicide, four had retired because of ill health, three had been certified insane and committed to asylums, four had been invalided out of the service, ten had been compulsorily retired for reasons ranging from "eccentricity" to marriage with a Chinese, nine had resigned, four had had serious breakdown or illnesses that impaired their efficiency, and one had been killed in a motoring accident.[1] The attrition rate, two per annum, suggests a degree of stress and strain, of psychological and physical impairment, that one would probably not find among the Japanese in China—and possibly it was made worse by the assiduous efforts of the British to avoid "going native" by retreating into a closed world of clubs and gentlemanly sports. Few Westerners bothered to learn the Chinese

[1] Stephen Lyon Endicott, *Diplomacy and Enterprise: British China Policy, 1933–1937* (Manchester: University of Manchester Press, 1975), p. 5.

language, and fewer still to acquaint themselves with China's culture and customs in a serious way.

By contrast, the Japanese from the outset made not only a concerted effort to learn the language but also to gather as much knowledge and information about contemporary China as they could. To be sure, there was a long tradition of Chinese learning in Japan, but classical scholarship provided no clear guide to the present. The perspective of high culture was radically different from the view from the treaty ports. Just as the eighteenth-century French philosophers could turn China into a utopia to criticize their own society while British traders there complained endlessly about its dirt and discomfort, so too those Japanese who went to China during the Meiji period onward had a different impression of its civilization than Tokugawa Confucianists had. They were overwhelmed by the poverty, inefficiency, and disorganization of the country. Even so enlightened a visitor as Yoshino Sakuzo, who arrived in Tientsin in 1906 to serve as tutor to Yuan Shih-k'ai's son, was appalled by what he saw. "Before I came to China, I never imagined that such an irrational and lawless system and organization could exist today in the twentieth century."[2] For Yoshino, this confrontation with a China so near in space but so distant in time and development made him sympathetic to Chinese reform and revolutionary movements. But for others, familiarity with China merely bred contempt, as it did in so many Western visitors and sojourners. For them, China was, as Kishida Ginko called it, "that damned country [baka no kuni]."

Whatever the reaction of individual Japanese to China, the Japanese made a much earlier and more serious effort than any of the other foreigners to learn about conditions in contemporary China in a concerted way. As Douglas Reynolds' chapter shows, even before the Japanese acquired rights under the unequal treaty system, there were many Japanese who realized the need to create a cadre of young Japanese fluent in Chinese and familiar with local conditions who could serve in the vanguard of Japanese trade expansion in China. It was self-evident that one could not penetrate the China market without knowing about it. First the Nisshin Bōeki Kenkyūjo, then the Tōa Dōbun Shoin produced a cadre of informed Japanese who relentlessly gathered information about China. As early as 1906, one alarmed Chinese official complained that the Japanese were beginning to know more about conditions in China than the Chinese themselves did.

The utility of such knowledge was obvious to a variety of interests in Japan. It is significant that the Nisshin Bōeki Kenkyūjo owed its founda-

[2] Yoshino Sakuzo's initial observations on China appear in *Shinjin* 7, 9 (September 1906): 14–18.

tion to the efforts of an army officer (Arao Sei), a businessman (Kishida Ginko), and a local consul (Machida Jitsu'ichi). All three elements—the military, business, and the diplomatic service—later benefited from the work of the Tōa Dōbun Shoin graduates, who not only produced voluminous amounts of raw data about local market and economic conditions, but also funneled political and other intelligence to the Foreign Ministry and the Army General Staff. No wonder that the Foreign Ministry subsidized the activities of the Tōa Dōbun Shoin, supporting its training and intelligence activities in a way that no Western government financed the expansion of knowledge about China.

But if the Japanese were successful in learning about China, they were far less successful in promoting Chinese "understanding" of Japan or in creating a cadre of Chinese sympathetic to Japan. This was ironic, in view of the fact that the idea of *dōbun-dōshu* (common culture, common race) was so central to the Japanese conception of their "special relationship" with China. The Japanese and the Chinese, as the Japanese so often said, possessed a common cultural heritage alien to the other foreign powers in China. By exchanging written notes or carrying on conversations in writing (*hitsudan*), a literate Japanese could make his thoughts generally known to a literate Chinese. Yet this kind of common literacy did not seem to improve cultural communication.

To be sure, as Sophia Lee's chapter reveals, the Japanese began to promote cultural exchanges with China very early on. Moreover, it is significant that government support for such exchange materialized considerably later than government support of the activities of the Tōa Dōbun Shoin and the Nisshin Bōeki Kenkyūjo. The time lag reveals much about the priorities of the Japanese government. The decision to embark on cultural diplomacy was largely a response to the rise of anti-foreign and, more specifically, anti-Japanese sentiment in the wake of World War I. It was a transparent effort to buy Chinese good will at a time when the Chinese seemed convinced of Japan's predatory intentions in China. It also reflected a desire to establish a Japanese cultural presence in China commensurate with its economic presence and to compete with the more aggressive efforts of the Americans and other Westerners to build cultural bridges to China. Echoing earlier calls for Japan to assume a "yellow man's burden," it was argued that Japan had a duty to take up a "civilizing mission" (*kyōka*) in China, just as the other powers had.

As this book makes clear, however, the Chinese were not particularly receptive to Japanese cultural diplomacy. The cultural weight of the Japanese in China was never commensurate with their economic weight. Trade in goods might favor Japan, but trade in knowledge and culture still favored China. The Japanese could communicate with the Chinese, but the Chinese were less willing to listen to them than to the other foreigners.

There were probably three reasons for this. First, the cultural diplomacy of the Japanese, who lacked a tradition of disinterested philanthropy characteristic of the Americans and other foreign nations, seemed to flow from Japan's self-interest rather than any altruistic impulse, and the strings attached to their generosity were sometimes all too obvious. Nowhere were they more obvious than in the pledge required of Chinese students receiving Boxer indemnity stipends to study in Japan: "After graduation, I shall remember this beneficence and strive to reciprocate this favor from His Majesty the Emperor."

Second, the cultural exchange and diplomacy were undermined by the profound distrust of Japan created by the aggressive foreign policy of the Japanese government. Even a simple act of cultural interaction like the flow of Chinese patients into the Japanese-managed Dōjinkai hospitals followed the ups and downs of Sino-Japanese relations at the diplomatic or political level, and so did the flow of Chinese students crossing the ocean to study in Japan.

Finally, the Japanese as well as other foreigners had to cope with a Chinese sense of superiority. Many Chinese regarded Japan as a derivative civilization. *Dōbun-dōshu* implied cultural superiority, not cultural familiarity, to the Chinese. As one Chinese critic of the Wang-Debuchi agreement observed, how could Japan offer anything culturally to China when it had no culture of its own? The Chinese elite simply did not take the Japanese as seriously as they took the other foreigners, and Western ethnocentrism was much easier for the Chinese to tolerate than Japanese ethnocentrism. The Japanese might have excellent gunboats and efficient factories, but, after all, these had been invented in the West, not in Japan, and the material superiority that the Japanese touted as proof of their cultural and moral superiority was simply borrowed from abroad.

It is interesting to speculate what impact Chinese indifference to Japanese cultural diplomacy had on the Japanese. Although it is unlikely that frustration over their inability to promote Chinese "understanding" of Japan was sufficient in itself to make the Japanese more aggressive in China, that frustration undoubtedly helped to create an atmosphere in which a more aggressive policy might appear reasonable. To the extent that the Chinese rejected Japanese efforts at cultural diplomacy, they confirmed a Japanese conviction that they were intransigent in their backwardness and independence. If the Chinese turned away a hand extended in friendship, then it made sense to extend a mailed fist. Such feelings at home, when combined with the frustration of the treaty-port Japanese described in Peattie's chapter, forged a public mood willing to accept a more "positive" China policy.

CHAPTER 6

Japanese Treaty Port Settlements in China, 1895–1937

Mark R. Peattie

With a history of cultural contact with China that spanned more than fifteen centuries, Japan nevertheless came late to China in the nineteenth-century scramble to establish a foreign presence in that grand, decaying empire. By the time that modern Japan first opened diplomatic and trade relations with China in 1871, the West had been inside the gates of that country for three decades: a score of treaty ports had been opened to an aggressive and dynamic new order based on the principles of extraterritoriality and strengthened through nearly two decades of diplomacy, trade, and military force; Western merchants had founded the bases for commercial empires, Western missionaries intruded into Chinese society in the interior as well as in the ports; Western gunboats as well as merchant ships were plying Chinese waters (though Western military garrisons ashore were not as conspicuous as they were to become early in the twentieth century); and, in a number of ports—Shanghai, Tientsin, and Canton, for example—Western nations had secured areas of exclusive European settlement and trade (map 6.1).

Japan renewed its formal relations with China just as China was subjected to the last surge of Western intrusion. Its high tide was marked thirty years later by the Boxer Protocol of 1901. By the early Republican period, the foreign presence had been formidably strengthened throughout China as a whole and had become the dominant fact of life on the China coast and along the Yangtze River Valley—a complex, glittering, arrogant, and ultimately self-destructive network of power and profit. Its outlines have been clearly limned in Albert Feuerwerker's richly detailed chapter that opens the twelfth volume of the *Cambridge History of China*.[1]

---

[1] Albert Feuerwerker, "The Foreign Presence in China," in John K. Fairbank, ed., *The Cambridge History of Modern China*. Vol. 12: *Republican China, Part 1* (New York: Cambridge University Press, 1983), pp. 128–207.

MAP 6.1   Japanese concessions and settlements in China, 1895–1937

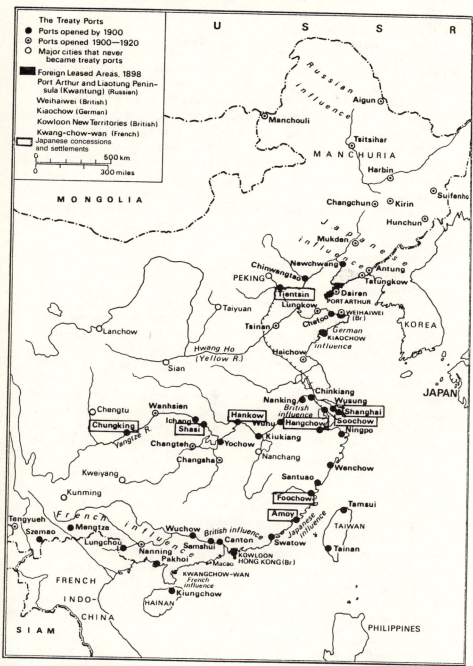

Source: Adapted from map in Feuerwerker, "The Foreign Presence in China," in *Republican China*, 1912–1949, Part 1, Volume 12 of *The Cambridge History of Modern China*, ed. John K. Fairbank (New York: Cambridge University Press, 1983).

The Japanese Settlements as Established by Treaty

As in the development of its formal colonial empire, Japan's tardy participation in the opening and exploitation of China put it at an initial disadvantage in the assertion of its imperial interests. Though the Sino-Japanese Treaty of 1871 provided Japan with extraterritorial privileges, it failed to include a most-favored-nation clause, that great equalizer of rapacious imperialist ambitions in the nineteenth century. Moreover, as Japan had not yet the interest nor the means to do so, it laid no claim to exclusive concessions or settlements. Thus, between 1871 and 1895 the modest Japanese diplomatic, economic, and naval presence rested largely on its somewhat circumscribed treaty rights, on the initiatives of isolated traders and adventurers, and on the cautious intrusion of Japanese warships, sufficiently limited in numbers and purpose to arouse no suspicion from China of the treaty port powers.

Japan's crushing victory over China in 1894–1895, however, brought most of the glittering rewards possessed by the Western nations. The 1871 treaty was succeeded by three new agreements that, along with the Boxer Protocol of 1901, individually and collectively laid the bases for the Japanese presence in China until the 1930s: the Treaty of Shimonoseki in 1895, which accorded Japan most-favored-nation treatment and thus access to all existing treaty ports (plus four new ones) as well as rights of trade, residence, manufacture, and travel enjoyed by other treaty powers; the Treaty of Commerce and Navigation of July 1896, which made a more specific grant of rights to Japan in the open ports and settlements of the sort enjoyed by Western nationals; and the Protocols of October of that year, which provided Japan with a number of exclusive concessions for residence and trade (see below). Finally, through its participation in the international humiliation of China in 1900–1901, Japan was conceded the right, along with Western nations, to station its military forces in North China.[2]

In the two decades after the Shimonoseki treaty, Japan more than made up for its tardy entry into the international competition for profit and influence in China. A mere trickle at first, the flow of Japanese settlers—mostly traders and storekeepers—into the treaty ports soon became a swelling stream. The larger Japanese concessions soon rivaled their European counterparts and became, in the process, small, transplanted Japanese cities in the heart of China. Japanese commerce and industry moved to create and exploit markets for Japanese goods, and the great Japanese

[2] The English texts of these treaties are reproduced in John V. A. MacMurray, *Treaties and Agreements With and Concerning China, 1894–1919*, vol. 1 (New York: Oxford University Press, 1921).

banking houses and shipping firms established offices in all the major ports. Gunboats as well as merchant ships flew the Rising Sun flag far up the Yangtze. Only in the matter of religious proselytization did Japan lag behind the West in China.

The Boxer Protocol of 1901 marked the flood tide of foreign demands intruding on China's sovereignty, and by the second year of World War I, the Japanese presence, now augmented by the military occupation of Tsingtao and the Shantung Peninsula, had not only grown, but in turn fueled further Japanese appetites and ambitions for an intrusion into China on an unprecedented scale. Had Japan been successful in pressing on China the fifth group of the infamous Twenty-One Demands, it would have burst beyond the bounds of the unequal treaty system to make China the semicolonial ward of a single nation. Chinese rejection of the most humiliating of the Demands in 1915 thus kept the Japanese presence within the confines of the imperialist arrangements of the late nineteenth century. In the 1930s, Japanese ambitions in China expanded once again, now unrestrained, however, by caution or consultation with the West. The final series of formal agreements signed between the two countries—the Tangku Truce of 1933, which sealed Chinese recognition of the conquest of Manchuria and Jehol, and the Ho-Umezu and Ch'in-Dohihara agreements of 1935, which surrendered Nationalist control over much of North China and Inner Mongolia—were signed without reference to any Western power, and the advantages they gave Japan were military and political, rather than commercial and diplomatic. The territorial restructuring of those parts of China by these agreements, and the interference in Chinese sovereignty they conceded to Japan in those areas, were so drastic and so sweeping that they mark the transition of Japan's role in China from that of a treaty port power acting in concert with other treaty power nations to that of an unrestrained invader and aggressor in China acting on its own.

JAPANESE IMMIGRATION INTO CHINA

In the early years of Meiji, the Japanese population in China was insignificant—a tiny group of traders and adventurers. But after the signing of the Sino-Japanese Treaty of 1871, the Japanese resident population expanded along with Sino-Japanese trade, slowly at first, then quite rapidly, as Japanese triumphs on the Asian continent appeared to assure a future there for Japanese with ambition and at least a little capital. The successive migrations of Japanese into China were in most cases related to the advantageous results of war. The Sino-Japanese War and the Treaty of Shimonoseki set off a small spurt of Japanese immigration into China several thousand strong; the suppression of the Boxer Rebellion and the subse-

TABLE 6.1
Population Distribution of Japanese Nationals in Selected Cities in Mainland China, 1935

	Men	*Women*	*Total*
China proper	31,854	26,471	58,325
North China	14,797	13,122	27,919
Tientsin	3,383	3,224	6,607
Tsingtao	7,522	7,014	14,536
Central China	16,349	12,707	29,056
Shanghai	14,887	11,573	26,460
Hankow	1,013	857	1,870
Soochow	41	33	74
Hangchow	16	13	29
Shashi	4	3	7
Chungking	27	15	42
South China	708	642	1,350
Foochow	237	150	387
Amoy	270	189	459

Source: Gaimushō Chōsabu, *Shōwa jūnen kaigai hompōjin chōsa hōkoku* (1936), pp. 7–8.

quent signing of the Boxer Protocol set off another. The greatest increase in the rate of Japanese coming to the mainland came in the decade following the Russo-Japanese War, followed by another sizable jump in the decade after World War I, as the growth of Japanese concerns in China lured thousands more Japanese to the mainland.

By 1935, of the nearly 690,000 overseas Japanese, more than 58,000 (or 8.5 percent) were resident on the Chinese mainland (table 6.1). Of these, the overwhelming number settled in cities along or north of the Yangtze: nearly 28,000 in North China, around 29,000 in Central China, but only 1,350 in South China. Given the configuration of land, the indigenous population, and the circumstances of the general imperialist presence as determined by treaty, it was inevitable that the Japanese emigration into China flowed into the cities, four in particular: Shanghai (over 26,000 in 1935), Tientsin (over 10,000), Hankow (1,870), and, after 1914, Tsingtao (over 14,000 in 1935).[3]

The origins, impulses, and composition of these migrations have yet to be studied in detail. But a few generalizations are possible. The major geographic sources of Japanese settlement in China seem to have been the

[3] Gaimushō Chōsabu, *Shōwa jūnen kaigai hompōjin chōsa hōkoku* (Report of investigation concerning Japanese living overseas in 1935) (Tokyo, 1936), pp. 7–8. For more detailed breakdown of figures for distribution of Japanese nationals in China proper, see table 6.1.

TABLE 6.2

Population Distribution of Japanese, Koreans, and Taiwanese within Mainland China, 1930

	Men	Women	Total
North China			
Japanese	13,652	12,086	25,738
Koreans	685	741	1,426
Taiwanese	58	35	93
Central China			
Japanese	14,861	12,213	27,074
Koreans	329	209	538
Taiwanese	338	137	475
South China			
Japanese	870	709	1,579
Koreans	43	10	53
Taiwanese	3,724	3,306	7,030

Source: Gaimushō Tsūshōkyoku, *Zaigai hompōjin kokusei chōsa hōkoku* (1930), pp. 123–35.

western prefectures of Kyushu—most probably because they were simply closer to China than the rest of Japan—and Tokyo, since its enormous population would inevitably make it a significant source of an urban-oriented emigration. In North China, Koreans also formed a significant component of the Japanese settler community; in South China, particularly in Kwangtung province, which faced the Japanese colony of Taiwan, Taiwanese who had become Japanese subjects outnumbered Japanese nationals nearly seven to one (table 6.2).[4]

The composition of these settler communities is not entirely clear. One has the impression that the pioneers of the Japanese political and economic penetration of China were adventurers, opportunists, and even ruffians, and that, judging from the spasmodic outbursts of Japanese civil violence against Chinese in the years after World War I, these elements remained in disturbingly large numbers in the treaty ports. Yet it also appears that in the later decades, the immigrant tide was generally composed of a more stable blend of small traders and shopkeepers and the lesser employees of the great commercial, banking, industrial, and shipping firms that dominated the Japanese economic presence in China (table 6.3). In any event, as Irene Taeuber has written, although they came to

[4] Irene Taueber, *The Population of Japan* (Princeton: Princeton University Press, 1958), p. 198. For figures on distribution of Japanese, Koreans, and Taiwanese in mainland China in 1930, see table 6.2.

TABLE 6.3
Occupational Distribution of Japanese Nationals in China Proper, 1916–1937

Year	Commerce	Industry	Transportation	Government services and professions	Mining	Agriculture
1916	10,398	2,777	1,274	2,611	44	128
1921	12,633	4,924	2,000	8,373	106	75
1926	12,261	1,707	332	2,025	82	63
1929	14,300	1,446	537	3,262	46	44
1931	13,412	2,110	480	3,057	16	45
1933	14,046	2,015	410	3,384	17	31
1934	14,155	1,982	537	3,707	10	36
1935	14,134	1,887	558	4,045	17	36
1937	15,970	1,861	710	4,444	25	30

Source: Ōkurashō Kanrikyoku, *Nihonjin no kaigai katsudō ni kansuru rekishi-teki chōsa*, vol. 27, *Chūoto minami Chūgoku* (Tokyo, 1947), pp. 91–94.

China seeking greater social and economic opportunities than they left in their homeland, most arrived not as despairing tenant farmers, impoverished laborers, or racially suspect immigrants, but as members of an ambitious, profit-seeking, and generally privileged class whose government, by diplomacy and force of arms, had made China accessible, profitable, and comfortable.[5]

ESTABLISHING THE CONCESSIONS

Japan's acquisition of privileged territories in China—the concessions (*senkan kyoryūchi*), literally areas of exclusive settlement—was largely based on two of the three Sino-Japanese agreements of which I have already spoken. The Treaty of Shimonoseki not only guaranteed Japanese access to all existing treaty ports but also added four more: Hangchow, Soochow, Shashi, and Chungking. The Sino-Japanese Protocols of October 1896 expanded on these provisions: Article I awarded Japan exclusive concessions at the four ports mentioned in the 1895 treaty and Article III provided that "upon request of the Japanese Government, the Chinese Government will promptly give their consent to the establishment of settlements possessed exclusively by Japan at Shanghai, Tientsin, Amoy, and Hankow." By the end of 1896, therefore, Japan had obtained from China the right to establish concessions at eight of the sixteen treaty ports

[5] Ibid. For figures on the occupational distribution of Japanese nationals in mainland China in 1916–1937, see table 6.3.

in mainland China where Western powers held similar privileges.[6] Rights to establish a ninth concession at Foochow were conceded to Japan in April 1898.

The actual territorial delineations of the concession area at each of these cities, along with agreement on the specifics of development, rights of residence, and property ownership, had to be worked out in extended negotiations between Japanese consulates at these places and local Chinese authorities. The resulting agreements (*torikime*) had to be approved by both governments. By 1897, such agreements had been worked out for Japanese concessions at Hangchow and Soochow, in 1898 for Tientsin, Hankow, Amoy, Foochow, and Shashi, and in 1901 for Chungking.

Following the precedents set for European concessions in China, the Chinese government purchased or expropriated land at these places, which it then leased in perpetuity to Japan for residence, business, trade, or manufacture. The Japanese consul was the chief official for the local administration of each concession (see below), which was thus in Japanese hands and was financed by local taxes levied by Japanese. Individual Japanese wishing to hold subleases in a concession applied through the consulate, which then collected the rents and turned these over to the Chinese government. Normally, Chinese and foreigners could reside and do business in a Japanese concession but could not own land or property there (and at some concessions could not even sublease).

Like their European counterparts, the Japanese concessions in China were set aside outside the walls of the original Chinese cities, nearly always sited on wasteland stretches of riverbank. Inevitably, in the decade that followed, each prospered or lay fallow in relation to the degree of importance of the particular city in China's foreign trade. Thus, at ports of obvious commercial importance, the Japanese concessions grew rapidly into fully developed urban enclaves, flanked by similarly mature Eu-

---

[6] MacMurray, *Treaties and Agreements*, vol. 1, pp. 20, 68–74, 91–92. In this enumeration of concessions granted to China, I have omitted Tsingtao because of the peculiar circumstances subsequent to Japan's acquisition of rights to establish a concession there. The facts are these: In 1914, Japan, as an Allied belligerent, militarily occupied the German base and colony at Tsingtao; in 1915, Japan forced from China the right to establish an exclusive concession at that port. At the Versailles Peace Conference, however, Japan was pressed to withdraw from Shantung; during the conference, as a compromise, it considered proposing the establishment of a general foreign settlement at Tsingtao (a compromise that aroused a storm of criticism in Japanese press and political circles). Then, at the Washington Conference three years later, Japan agreed to give up the Shantung Peninsula completely and not to press for a concession or settlement of any kind. Thus, although Tsingtao contained the second largest concentration of Japanese in China after World War I, they resided in no specially privileged treaty port area and have therefore not been considered in this survey. W. W. Willoughby, *Foreign Rights and Interests in China*, vol. 1 (Baltimore: Johns Hopkins Press, 1927), pp. 280, 297–298, 316, and 328.

ropean concessions. In those lesser treaty ports where foreign interests were merged into a general area of foreign settlement, the Japanese concessions grew modestly as focal points for Japanese commerce, industry, residence, and consular representation but failed to develop a clearly delineated arrangement of boundaries, streets, or buildings under exclusive Japanese control. At a few places, where Japan alone sought and received the right to exclusive settlement, the concessions failed to develop at all, for reasons, in varying degrees, that had to do with unfortunate location, poor drainage, or the unsettling effects of civil war.[7]

It is important to note at the outset that the Japanese resident population in the formally awarded and internationally recognized concessions formed only part of the Japanese communities in mainland China. They also congregated in cities where Japan held no exclusive rights of settlement, commerce, or industry—by the tens of thousands in Shanghai and Tsingtao, by the hundreds in Nanking and Canton, and by a few score in ports like Ichang, Changsha, and Ningpo. Thus, while it is possible to classify the formal concessions held by Japan according to their administrative structures (see below), it is a good deal more awkward to form a general typology of Japanese communities in China.

The Lesser Japanese Concessions

Soochow, a commercial city at the juncture of the Yangtze and Min rivers, had been opened as a treaty port in 1896 and an international settlement set aside along the south bank of the Grand Canal opposite the south wall of the old city, an area that by 1915 was rapidly being filled by theaters, hotels, and restaurants. A map of the city published in the Japanese Government Railway guide of 1925 shows the Japanese concession just to the east of it, laid out with regular streets, along which were ranged the Japanese consulate, police office, hotels, and restaurants.

The beautiful old provincial capital of Hangchow was also opened in 1896 as a treaty port. An international settlement was marked off at the northwest edge of the city between the Grand Canal and West Lake; next to it, a concession of 120 acres was specifically set aside for Japanese use in 1897. By 1925, the JGR guide tells us, it contained the Japanese consulate and post office and the godowns of the Japan-China Steam Naviga-

---

[7] None of the sources I have used offers any explanation as to why Japan pressed for exclusive concessions at some rather small and inconspicuous ports like Shashi and Chungking but made no effort to do so at the major cities of Nanking or Canton. In my brief descriptions of the lesser Japanese concessions, I have used the following sources: Japan Government Railway [hereafter JGR], *Guide to China* (Tokyo, 1925); Ueda Toshio, *Shina ni okeru sokai no kenkyū* (Study of the concessions in China) (Tokyo: Ganshōdō, 1941); and H. B. Morse, *The Trade and Administration of China* (London: Longmans, Green, 1908).

tion Company, but there were few regular streets within the concession because the engineering work to develop them had been slowed by civil war.

In Fukien province, the port city of Foochow on the Min River, thirty-four miles from its mouth, had been opened to international trade before the creation of foreign residential concessions, and therefore there existed no specifically designated international settlement, though there was a foreign residential quarter in the Nantai district on the south side of the river opposite the city, which possessed a municipal organization of somewhat inchoate form. Although Japan was granted the right to establish its own exclusive concession at Foochow, the Japanese in that place were content to merge their facilities—a consulate, post office, Japanese club, and offices of various firms like Mitsui Bussan, the Osaka Commercial Shipping Company, and the Bank of Taiwan—with the general foreign residential quarter.

At Amoy, the oldest of the treaty ports, the Japanese presence was divided between two islands, Amoy and Kolongsu, though today it is not clear on which of these lay the formally allocated Japanese concession. On the west side of Amoy Island was the crowded native city of the same name. Along the north end of the crowded waterfront of Amoy city were located most of the Japanese businesses, principally the Bank of Taiwan, the Osaka Shōsen Kaisha, and Mitsui Bussan, as well as a few Japanese hotels and restaurants. Across a narrow channel was picturesque Kolongsu Island, reserved largely for the foreign community, whose consulates and residences, including those of the Japanese, set amid luxuriant groves and strangely shaped rocks, were free of the heat and dust of Amoy city.[8]

At Shashi, a rather woebegone treaty port on the Yangtze about nine hundred miles upriver from Shanghai, Japan obtained a concession area about four thousand feet long and about eight hundred feet back from the riverbank. Since the area set aside proved to be too low-lying and thus subject to frequent flooding, the Japanese never established much more than a consulate at the place.

The last-established and most remote of all the Japanese concessions was at Chungking, some fourteen hundred miles up the Yangtze. The city had been designated a treaty port in 1891, but it never developed as

---

[8] In his discussion of the Japanese concession at Amoy, Ueda describes it as a not very choice piece of land on Kolongsu, but in a map of Amoy at the back of his book, he locates it at the southern end of the Amoy City waterfront. The map in the Japanese Government Railway guide shows the Japanese consulate and cemetery on Kolongsu and all the Japanese businesses at the northern end of the Amoy City waterfront but nowhere indicates the location of a Japanese concession on either island. Ueda, *Shina ni okeru sokai no kenkyū*, pp. 375–377; JGR, *Guide to China*, pp. 284–295.

such. Japan, too, had little luck with it, in part because their concession, like that at Shashi, was subject to severe flooding when the Yangtze rose in summer, and in part because it was inconveniently separated from the central Chinese city.

HANKOW

To Hankow, largest of the three Wuhan cities that had developed into one of the great commercial and industrial centers of China, the Japanese Consulate-General at Shanghai had sent a consular clerk to negotiate with the Chinese provincial authorities for an exclusive concession guaranteed by the Protocol of 1896. All the foreign concessions at Hankow extended along a river front of several miles along the west bank of the Yangtze, which in time became the Bund, a handsome Western thoroughfare of great residences and imposing commercial buildings. The Japanese, much to their disgruntlement (it has been asserted), were given a strip of territory approximately twelve hundred feet along the river bank and a thousand feet back from it, at the end of this international city, the most underdeveloped of all the concession areas at the port and the farthest removed from the Chinese city. In 1907, after five years of difficult ne-gotiations with reluctant Chinese authorities, the Japanese consulate fi-nally succeeded in obtaining a three-hundred-foot extension of these concession boundaries. In their enclave of 41.5 acres, the Japanese began to lay out regular streets with Japanese names and to construct buildings in the same ponderous stonework as those in the European concessions. On Kawamachi, the extension of the international Bund that ran along the river front, was located the massive consulate building, as well as the offices and dormitories of the Mitsui Shipping Company.

Between Kawamachi and Heiwamachi, which paralleled it four blocks back from the river, Japanese Hankow developed into an orderly little Japanese city laid out in checkerboard fashion, roughly four blocks deep and five blocks wide. By the 1920s, it included the Hsieh-chang Match Factory, the Nikka Seed Oil Company, the Higashi Hongan Temple, the Hankow Bank, and Taisho Electric Company power plant, a primary school, a Navy Club, a clinic, and numerous inns and restaurants as well as private residences (see map 6.2).[9]

[9] Ueda, *Shina ni okeru sokai no kenkyū*, pp. 343–346; JGR, *Guide to China*, pp. 108–117; and Bōeichō Bōeikenshūjō Senshishitsu [hereafter BBKS], *Senshi sōshō* (War History Series), vol. 72: *Chūgoku hōmen: Kaigun sakusen. (1): Shōwa jūsannen sangatsu made* (Naval operations in the Central China Theater. Part 1: Up to March 1938) (Tokyo: Asagumo Shimbun Sha, 1974), map on p. 157. For some reason, perhaps because the facilities were already available there, the docks and hulks of the major Japanese shipping companies were located outside the Japanese concession farther down the Bund.

MAP 6.2   Japanese concessions at Hankow, central district, ca. 1925

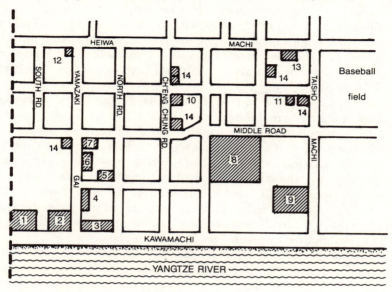

1. Mitsui Bussan Shipping Office
2. Mitsui Bussan housing
3. Japanese Consulate General
4. Consular Police Office
5. Japanese Residents Corporation Office
5. Primary School
7. Navy Club
8. Hsieh-chang Match Factory
9. Nikka Seed Oil Co.
10. Bank of Hankow
11. Hankow *Nichi-nichi Shimbun*
12. Higashi Hongan Temple
13. Taisho Electric Co. power plant
14. Various restaurants, hotels, inns

Source: Adapted from map in Bōeicho Bōei Kenshūjō Senshishitsu, eds., *Chūgoku hōmen: Kaigun sakusen, 1: Shōwa jūsannen sangatsu made* (Asagumo Shimbunsha, 1974).

TIENTSIN

The concession at Tientsin came to be the jewel of Japan's privileged territories in China. In large part, this was due to Tientsin's position as the most important commercial and industrial center in North China and second most important in China as a whole. Though it had certain disadvantages as a port—the Hai River, on which it was situated, tended to silt up in the summer and freeze over in the winter—it was served by excellent rail connections to Peking, Shanghai, and Manchuria. It was, in any event, the chief distribution point for the North China plain and Northwest China, and for this reason it came to be a major arena for the interplay of foreign capital, energy, and power, which all combined to force from China arrangements for exclusive concessions for nine separate nations along the mudflats that flanked both sides of the Hai River south of the city.

Based on the Protocols of 1896, Japanese negotiations for a concession at Tientsin were begun in 1896, but it took two years for the Japanese consulate to conclude an agreement that awarded Japan over 400 acres of land for the purpose. The concession was shaped roughly like an upside-down boot, with its instep on the Hai River, its front side adjoining the old Chinese city, and its calf side sharing a boundary with the French concession (see map 6.3). In 1903, the top of the boot was extended southwestward, giving the concession a total area of 650 acres, the third largest in the city. Farther down the river, below the German concession, docking facilities were provided for Japanese shipping.[10]

Under the general direction of the Japanese government, private enterprise supplied most of the capital and facilities necessary to transform these unpromising 650 acres of mudbank into a thriving Japanese city. It was an effort of major proportions: constructing an embankment and dikes along the river, reclaiming marshy land, digging drainage ditches, laying out regular streets, and putting up the first government and commercial buildings. It had been planned by the Concession Development Office under the consul-general to proceed in two stages, the first involving that portion of the concession area closest to the river, the next third of the concession below to be developed in the second stage; and the final third, the marshiest area to the southwest, to be reclaimed later. Begun in 1900, the work was interrupted that year by the chaos surrounding the Boxer troubles, and in 1901 a good deal of the construction still stood empty, since few Japanese firms or individuals had been tempted to settle in an area that looked so unpromising. When at last work resumed in 1902, it was undertaken by a private construction firm, the Tokyo Tatemono Kaisha (Tokyo Building Company), to which more than half the concession land had been sold. The company completed the first stage of nine wards in 1903, creating in the process a handsome riverfront boulevard, Yamaguchi-gai, and a number of broad parallel streets with suitably auspicious Japanese names—Kotobuki, Asahi, Sakae, and Hanazono—bounded on the east by Akiyama-gai, which formed the boundary with the French concession, and on the west by Fukushima-gai, beyond which lay the Chinese city (see map 6.4).[11]

[10] Ueda, *Shina ni okeru sokai no kenkyū*, pp. 317–320.
[11] Ibid., pp. 320–322.

MAP 6.3 Tientsin, ca. 1915

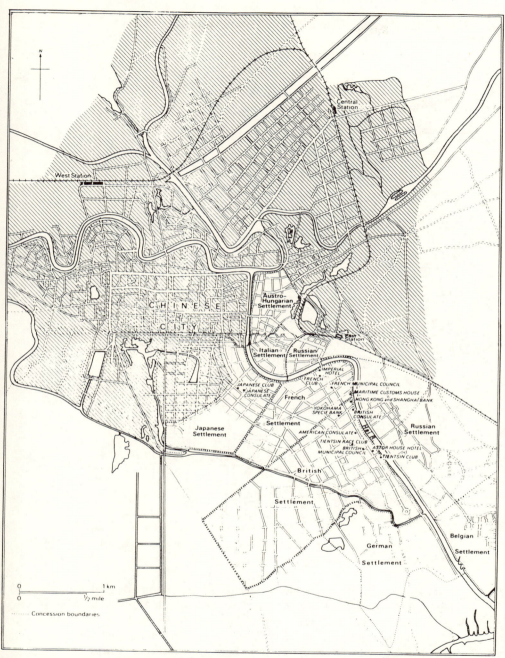

Source: Adapted from map in Feuerwerker, "The Foreign Presence in China."

MAP 6.4 Japanese concession at Tientsin: areas of initial development, 1900–1908

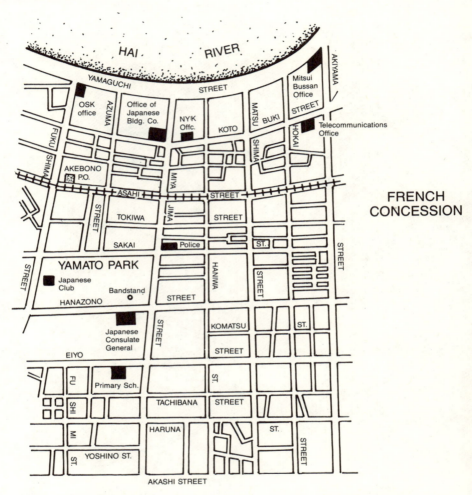

Source: Adapted from map in Tenshin Kyōryū Mindan, comp., *Tenshin Kyōryū Min-dan sanjūshūnen kinenshi* (Tientsin, 1941).

The upper third and the most developed concession area, where only Japanese were allowed to own property, became the business section of Japanese Tientsin. This was composed of city blocks thick with commercial buildings and government offices. Here were the busiest streets, of which Asahi-gai, traversed by a tram line, was most heavily traveled.

The Tokyo Building Company began work on the second construction area in 1903, and by 1908 it had carried the development of the concession southwest to Haruna-gai, after which the company wound up its business. The remaining third of the concession land to the southwest had been sold to individual Japanese and Chinese, to whom its development was entrusted; but being largely marshland, it was neglected for some years. Then, in 1915, a booster group, the Tenshin Umetate Kumiai (Tientsin Land Reclamation Association) was formed among the Japanese residents to push the work forward. By 1920, the concession was essentially laid out, and by 1933 most of its streets were paved.[12]

Long before that, Japanese Tientsin had become a prosperous and bustling city. The trams clanged down Asahi-gai, along which were ranged grocery stores, druggists, restaurants, and inns, and nearer the river were the ponderous stone offices of the great commercial shipping and banking houses. A public park of six acres, Yamato Koen, had been laid out in 1907 in the center of the concession, complete with fountains, a bandstand (named after the pioneering consul-general), a children's playground, and a war memorial to the Japanese heroes of 1900. Toward the lower portion of the concession were the factories and textile mills that sprang up in the 1920s, and in the southwest corner, where Hai-kuang-szu Temple stood, were the barracks of the increasingly strong Japanese garrison (see below).

The growth of the Japanese settler population in Tientsin followed the general chronological pattern already described. There were not more than 50 Japanese in the city before the concession was established; by 1903 there were about 1,300; 5,000 by 1921; and by 1936, spurred by the earlier growth of Japanese industry in the city, there were over 10,000 Japanese residents.[13]

Shanghai

At Shanghai, queen of the treaty ports, the Japanese presence was something of an anomaly. While the city was the earliest and most important focus for the interplay of Japanese power, capital, and settlement in China, these elements did not operate within an exclusive Japanese concession, but within a common zone of treaty-power privilege, the International Settlement (map 6.5).

The first small group of Japanese traders, from Nagasaki, had come to Shanghai in the last years of the Tokugawa Shogunate, seeking commercial information from foreign merchants and consulates there. The first

[12] Tenshin Kyoryūmindan [hereafter TK], ed., *Tenshin kyoryūmindan sanjūshūnen kinenshi* (Commemorative record of thirty years of the Tientsin Residents' Corporation) (Tientsin: published by the Corporation for private distribution, 1941), pp. 213–218, 345–349.

[13] Ibid., p. 483.

MAP 6.5 Shanghai, ca. 1915

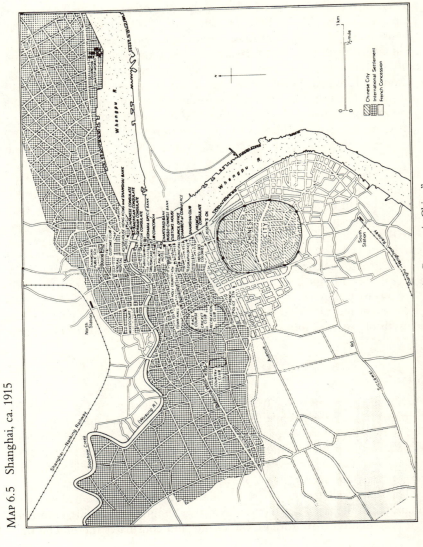

Source: Adapted from map in Feuerwerker, "The Foreign Presence in China."

Japanese firm (a porcelain import-export company) had started business in the city in 1868; a consulate had opened in 1872; Mitsubishi had opened a mail service to Japan in 1875; two years later, Kishida Ginko had established his notorious Rakuzendo—half patent-medicine shop, half army intelligence center—while Mitsui had begun a coal business in 1878. Over the next decade, a range of small businesses dealing in sundries, foodstuffs, art objects, printing, services (inns and restaurants in particular), dry goods, and antiques had established themselves in the port.[14]

The Japanese who managed these small enterprises constituted a small but growing community in Meiji times: no more than fifty persons in 1873; about two hundred in 1877; not quite four hundred in 1890; and about a thousand on the eve of the Sino-Japanese War. Settling mostly in the yet-undeveloped Hongkew district of the International Settlement, north of Soochow Creek, their position before 1895 was ambiguous, since their nation was not a signatory to the joint agreement among the Western powers that had established the Settlement, and thus they could make no legal claims to its privileges.[15]

With the signing of the Treaty of Shimonoseki and the acquisition of most-favored-nation treatment, however, Japan became a full-fledged treaty power. Its consul sat in the Shanghai consular body, and its residents and enterprises now formed a constituent element in the International Settlement, enjoying all the privileges available to the nationals of other treaty powers. The Sino-Japanese accords of October 1896 offered the promise of an even more prominent Japanese position in Shanghai: the right to establish an exclusive concession in the city. Why Japan, in fact, chose not to act upon that opportunity is a matter of conjecture. Some Japanese scholars have asserted that Japan decided not to press its claims to an exclusive concession out of deference to Anglo-American opposition. While plausible (both the British and the Americans had vigorously and futilely opposed the creation of a separate French Settlement in the 1850s), a more likely reason was that the Japanese recognized that it would be more advantageous to operate within the boundaries of the already flourishing International Settlement than to attempt to secure some area outside it, which would inevitably be less conveniently located—much less developed.[16]

[14] Yonezawa Hideo, "Shanhai hōjin hatten shi" (A history of the development of the Japanese in Shanghai), part 2, *Tōa keizai kenkyu* 23, 2 (January–February 1939): 122–125.

[15] Upon the outbreak of the Sino-Japanese War, all but a handful of the nearly one thousand Japanese in Shanghai were evacuated; most returned at the conclusion of the war. Shanhai Kyoryūmindan [hereafter SK], ed., *Shanhai kyoryūmindan sanjūgonen kinenshi* (A commemorative record of thirty-five years of the Shanghai Japanese Residents' Corporation) (Shanghai: published by the Corporation for private distribution, 1942), p. 75.

[16] Uehara Shigeru, *Shanhai kyōdō sokai gai ron* (An introduction to the Shanghai Interna-

In any event, in the decade between the Sino-Japanese and Russo-Japanese wars, the stable and prosperous circumstances in the Settlement lured both kinds of Japanese business—the great banking, shipping, and commercial enterprises as well as small traders and shopkeepers. During these years, the Japanese community grew to several thousand. The next decade saw an even greater increase in the Japanese population, which by 1915 numbered over 7,000, far larger than the British community.[17]

In economic terms, the Japanese did not develop a major stake in Shanghai until World War I. In those years, the diversion of European commercial competition, particularly in cotton textiles, followed in 1918 by higher tariff rates for cotton imports coming into China, were critical turning points for the establishment of the Japanese cotton industry in Shanghai, an enterprise that was to be the cause of much bitterness between the Chinese and Japanese communities. The skyrocket success of the Japanese cotton mills in Shanghai in the immediate postwar years inevitably stimulated further Japanese settlement. By 1920, the Japanese, at ten thousand, were the largest foreign community in the Settlement; by 1930, at thirty thousand, it was more than three times that of the British, a situation that emboldened the Japanese to demand a greater voice in the administration of Shanghai.[18]

Although Japanese enterprises and residents could be found in all parts of the International Settlement, they were increasingly located in the Hongkew district and in what came to be known as the "external roads" area. Broadway in particular, but also North Szechuan, Boone, Chefoo, Woosung, and Woochang roads became crowded with Japanese shops and residences, so that increasingly Shanghai "north of the creek" was not only a densely industrial and commercial region, but one dominated by the Japanese (see map 6.6).[19]

For the Japanese, this demographic domination of the Hongkew district, combined after 1932 with the de facto military control of that sector (see below), came to provide most of the advantages of an exclusive concession with none of the burdens. Although, by the 1930s, Hongkew had become a "Little Tokyo" where Japanese naval troops roamed at will (see below), neither Japanese consular nor naval authorities made any ef-

---

tional Settlement) (Tokyo: Maruzen, 1942), p. 52; and William Johnstone, *The Shanghai Problem* (Stanford: Stanford University Press, 1937), p. 37.

[17] Uehara, *Shanhai kyōdō sokai gai ron*, p. 52; Yonezawa, "Shanhai hōjin hatten shi," part 2, p. 125.

[18] Uehara, *Shanhai kyōdō sokai gai ron*, p. 53.

[19] An interesting collection of photographs depicting the prewar appearance of the Japanese settlement in the Hongkew district is provided in a recently published retrospective volume, Kobori Rintarō, ed., *Natsukashii Shanhai* (Nostalgic Shanghai) (Tokyo: Hokushō Hankōkai, 1984).

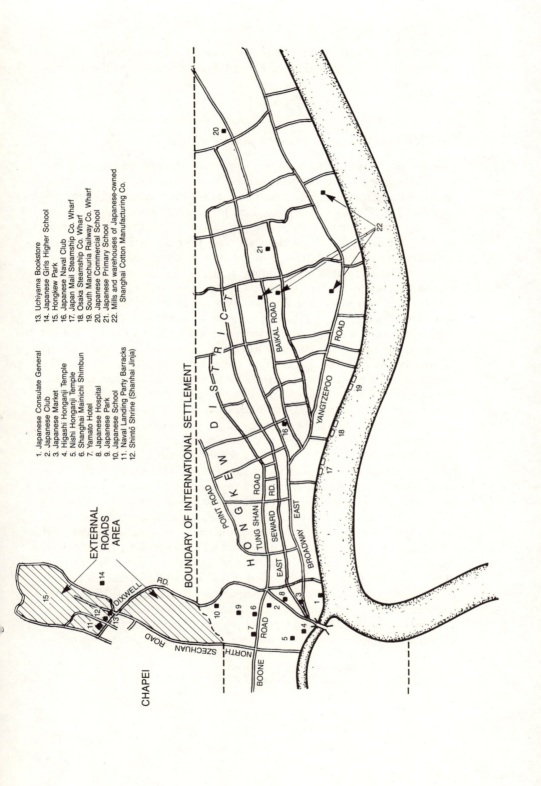

1. Japanese Consulate General
2. Japanese Club
3. Japanese Market
4. Higashi Honganji Temple
5. Nishi Honganji Temple
6. Shanghai Mainichi Shimbun
7. Yamato Hotel
8. Japanese Hospital
9. Japanese Park
10. Japanese School
11. Naval Landing Party Barracks
12. Shintō Shrine (Shanhai Jinja)
13. Uchiyama Bookstore
14. Japanese Girls Higher School
15. Hongkew Park
16. Japanese Naval Club
17. Japan Mail Steamship Co. Wharf
18. Osaka Steamship Co. Wharf
19. South Manchuria Railway Co. Wharf
20. Japanese Commercial School
21. Japanese Primary School
22. Mills and warehouses of Japanese-owned
    Shanghai Cotton Manufacturing Co.

CHAPEI

EXTERNAL
ROADS
AREA

BOUNDARY OF INTERNATIONAL SETTLEMENT

HONGKEW DISTRICT

BAIKAL ROAD

YANGTZEPOO ROAD

POINT ROAD

TUNG SHAN ROAD

SEWARD RD.

BROADWAY EAST

EAST

DIXWELL RD.

SZECHUAN ROAD

NORTH

BOONE ROAD

fort to assume responsibility for public works, fire prevention, health, or education there. Instead, they demanded these services from the municipal government as constituent members of the international community.[20]

SINO-JAPANESE RELATIONS WITHIN THE CONCESSIONS

Chinese populations were always a significant element within the Japanese concessions. This was because none of the concessions was literally an area of exclusive Japanese settlement. From the beginning, it was apparent to Japanese authorities that these privileged areas could not be developed without some participation by Chinese from adjacent neighborhoods, particularly since, at the start, few Japanese arrived to take up residence. Tientsin was a case in point. Under the guiding influence of the pioneering Japanese consul-general, there was a small but steady stream of middle- and upper-class Chinese scholars and officials who came to take up residence in the concession area while it was still largely in the construction stage. From the Chinese point of view, the concession offered not only a reasonably orderly and stable place to reside and do business, but an area of economic growth as Japanese capital poured into it. Amidst the military and political chaos following the October 1911 Revolution, such advantages seem to have been prime considerations for Chinese as well as for Japanese, who began to swell the ranks of the resident population.[21] One gets the impression that, during the period between 1900 and 1915, there were few signs of friction between the two communities. Indeed, there were a number of active efforts at cooperation prior to World War I, including the establishment of several Sino-Japanese friendship and cooperative societies in Tientsin. In all the Japanese concessions, Chinese continued to comprise the large majority of residents, even as relations between the two countries worsened. One can only assume that for those Chinese who thus chose to remain in these territories under Japanese jurisdiction, the advantages of law, order, and relative prosperity must have outweighed whatever national humiliations they may have suffered at Japanese hands. Shanghai was a different case, of course, since Japanese made no formal claims to a separate concession (and therefore could lay down no stipulations), but until 1915 relations between the two communities seem to have been untroubled.

It can hardly be said that relations between Chinese and Japanese in the settlements were ever close or friendly. Given the circumstances of the

---

[20] Johnstone, *The Shanghai Problem*, pp. 290–291.
[21] TK, *Tenshin kyoryūmindan*, pp. 538–539.

1. Mass meeting of the Japanese Residents' Association of Shanghai, Autumn 1931, to denounce Chinese anti-Japanese agitation in China

2. Anti-Japanese rally held by Chinese in the International Settlement, Shanghai, Autumn 1931

3. Japanese textile managers and families in Shanghai

4. Chinese women laborers in a Japanese spinning mill in Shanghai

5. Japanese woman in rickshaw, Shanghai

6. Main street of Hongkew, Japanese quarter, Shanghai

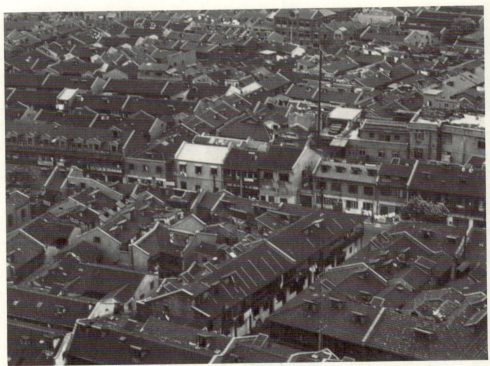

7. View from Ta-hsia overlooking Woosung Road, in the Japanese quarter, Shanghai

8. The Grand Tour: Students of the Tōa Dōbun Shoin set forth on a study trip to various parts of China

9. Imperial Japanese Navy gunboat *Toba*, typical of the many Japanese gunboats that did service on the Yangtze River in the 1920s and 1930s

10. Intense Chinese language class in session at the Tōa Dōbun Shoin

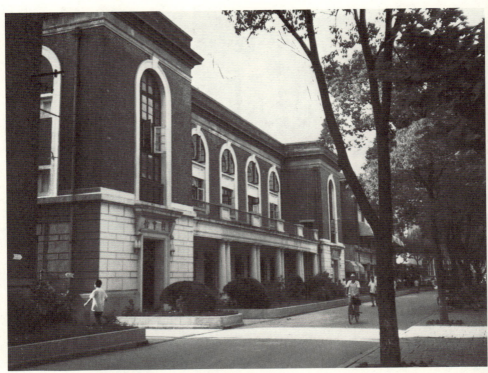

11. Classroom building of the Tōa Dōbun Shoin

12. Acia-lined street in Naniwa-chō, Dairen, Kwantung Leased Territory, Manchuria

13. One of the most prominent imperial structures in Northeast Asia, the Yamato Hotel on the Grand Plaza, Dairen, managed by the South Manchuria Railway Company

14. One of the newly constructed government buildings in Hsinking, capital of Manchukuo, 1934

15. Newly completed buildings in Hsinking, mid-1930s

Japanese presence, it is hard to see how they could have been. For most Japanese in China, like most Westerners, the greatest number of contacts with Chinese appear to have been with tradesmen or domestics—amahs, "boys," and ricksha men—hardly relationships that might foster understanding between the two races (indeed, quantitatively, there were probably even fewer of these contacts than those between Westerners and Chinese). "Up to the present," a Japanese guidebook admitted in 1940, "the feeling of Japanese toward whatever Chinese might be living near them has been to have as little as possible to do with them, and their attitudes of racial superiority [among these Japanese] are quite overbearing."[22] Privileged interlopers, like all imperialists in China, the Japanese all too often let their irritation and disgust at what they saw as the disorder and uncleanliness of the Chinese show through in small manifestations of pettiness and contempt.[23] There were illustrious exceptions to this state of affairs among some Japanese who lived in China, particularly a few scholars, journalists, and literary figures. Among these was Matsumoto Shigeharu, whose astute and sensitive observation of China, as recorded in his autobiographical account of Shanghai in the 1930s, was in large part due to the skein of friendships he formed with educated and informed Chinese during his years in that city.[24] Another sympathetic Japanese resident was Uchiyama Kanzo, a significant broker of Sino-Japanese contacts in the 1920s and 1930s. First coming to China as a Christian missionary, Uchiyama eventually set aside his proselytizing mission and started a bookstore in the Japanese quarter of Shanghai, selling Chinese and Japanese books. In this way, he struck up friendships with a cluster of prominent Chinese literary figures—among them Lu Hsun—and in turn introduced them to his acquaintances on the contemporary Japanese literary scene, such as Satō Haruo and Masuda Wataru.[25]

[22] Gōtō Asatarō, *Shina seikatsu annai* (Guidebook to life in China) (Tokyo: Kōga Shoin, 1940), p. 253.

[23] While stationed with the Japanese garrison at Hankow in 1920, young Major (later General) Ishiwara Kanji noted with indignation that his fellow officers, when alighting from a ricksha, would often simply throw the fare on the ground for the ricksha man to scramble after.

[24] Matsumoto Shigeharu, *Shanhai jidai* (Shanghai years) (Tokyo: Chūo Kōronsha, 1977).

[25] After World War II, Uchiyama was one of the founders of the Sino-Japanese Friendship Association. For this and for his lifetime of sympathetic efforts to promote understanding between the two countries, his name is still revered in China's intellectual circles. See NHK "Dokumento Shōwa" Shūzai Han, ed., *Dokumento Shōwa* (Shōwa documentary), vol. 2: *Shanhai kyūdō sokai* (The Shanghai International Settlement) (Tokyo: Kadokawa Shoten, 1986), pp. 86–110; and Maruyama Noboru, "Lu Xun in Japan," in Leo Ou-fan Lee, ed., *Lu Xun and His Legacy* (Berkeley: University of California Press, 1985), pp. 212, 221–222, and 224, on the role of Uchiyama in promoting literary interchange between Chinese and Japanese writers.

THE CONSULATES

The Japanese consular presence in China was the largest that Japan maintained anywhere in the world. By the 1920s, in addition to its legation at Peking, Japan maintained consulates-general in four cities in mainland China—Shanghai, Tientsin, Hankow, and Canton—and twelve consulates—Nanking, Soochow, Foochow, Hangchow, Tsingtao, Tsinan, Amoy, Changsha, Swatow, Yunnan, Chefoo, and Wuhu. In the great port cities, the Japanese consulates-general grew to the size of small embassies. The Japanese Consulate at Tientsin, established in 1871 with three people, for example, was raised in 1902 to a consulate-general; by 1937, it had a staff of more than fifty and was divided into ten sections.[26] Situated with its Western counterparts along the city waterfront, the Japanese Consulate-General at Shanghai was constructed of stone and brick, three stories high. Its ponderous design was expressive of the scale and permanence of the Japanese commitment in China. The consulates, naturally, were more modest structures with smaller staffs, located within the Japanese concessions or clustered with the consular offices of other treaty port powers.

By and large, Japanese consular staffs in China by the 1920s were thoroughly professional. Equaled only by their British counterparts, Japanese consular officers were the best-informed foreign representatives about the districts in which they were located. While service in China was regarded as less desirable than that in Europe or the United States, there is no evidence that Japanese consular officials in China were less capable than their colleagues in Europe or the United States, though fewer may have been proficient in the language of their host country.

Not surprisingly, it was the consulates that had responsibility for the large Japanese communities in China. Japanese consuls in China generally functioned as did their counterparts everywhere—representing Japanese nationals, furthering Japanese economic interests, and collecting political and economic information of use to their government. Like the consuls of other treaty port powers, they were also responsible for the administration of the various exclusive concessions allotted to their government. It was the individual consuls on the scene who initially negotiated the specific arrangements with local Chinese authorities that worked out the exact boundaries of the concessions. Thereafter, the consul within each concession area was its chief administrator.

It was the responsibility of the consulates for Japanese communities in China that furnished the pretext for Japanese intrusion into Chinese sovereignty in ways that had not been contemplated even by other treaty port

---

[26] TK, *Tenshin kyoryūmindan*, pp. 545–546.

powers. The consular police, justifying their actions by the alleged need to protect and discipline Japanese subjects, and often operating on Chinese soil, was perhaps the most controversial and (to the Chinese) the most offensive aspect of the large Japanese presence (see below).

SELF-GOVERNMENT IN THE CONCESSIONS

At the outset of the Japanese territorial presence in China, the administrative authority of the consulates over the Japanese communities was ill-defined. In the Shanghai International Settlement, the Japanese consulate laid down "Rules and Regulations for Japanese Living in Shanghai" in 1892, but these were generally more concerned with matters of conduct by individual Japanese (regulation of business, travel, and attire) than with guidelines for the administration of the Japanese community as a whole. Within the first few years of the new century, however, as Japanese residents and businesses began to move into the concessions and settlements not only in China, but in Manchuria and Korea as well, the government recognized the need for some overall administrative policy toward Japanese communities in these areas. The result was the "Provisional Regulations for Areas of Exclusive Japanese Settlement" (*Nihon senkan kyoryūchi karikisoku*) promulgated in 1902. By these regulations, each consulate within a Japanese concession was empowered to authorize a committee of three to fifteen Japanese residents (at first selected by the consulate, but after 1904 elected by the resident community itself) to consider various matters of concern to the community. These included public works, sanitation, and collection of taxes. The committee, however, had no standing as a legal or corporate entity, and its resolutions required the specific approval of the consul.[27]

This rather limited ordinance governing concentrations of Japanese subjects in China was superseded three years later by a more inclusive statute, the Residents' Corporation Law, which granted a large degree of autonomy to those Japanese communities in China, Korea, and Manchuria. These communities, by their very size and complexity, needed an autonomous and corporate character. The law provided for the formation of a Residents' Corporation (Kyoryū mindan), a self-governing constituency—not unlike the ratepayers' association of the International Settlement at Shanghai—which would, in turn, elect the members of the legislative and executive organs of the concession administration. Membership in the corporation was limited to adult Japanese males who resided within the concession or settlement and who paid a minimum amount in annual assessments; to incorporated Japanese businesses within

---

[27] SK, *Shanghai kyoryūmindan*, p. 58; Ueda, *Shina ni okeru sokai no kenkyū*, p. 322.

the concession; and to those few Chinese and foreigners who owned property within the concession valued above a certain amount. The Residents' Corporations were to hold all the normal elements of authority in the administration of the concession, save one: police power. That was specifically reserved to the consulate, which also determined the structure of the administrative organs, and which held residual authority over all resolutions, decisions, and acts of these self-governing bodies.[28]

In 1907, acting under the Residents' Corporation Law, the Japanese Foreign Ministry established residents' associations at Tientsin, Hankow, and Shanghai. In Tientsin and Hankow, the Residents' Association, as the basic electorate of the Japanese community, elected several dozen members to represent the Residents' Association (Kyoryū minkai). The association acted as a legislative body, empowered by the consulate-general to initiate legislation, approve budgets, draw up accounts, levy taxes, collect rents and commissions, and provide for and oversee schools, fire protection, sanitation, social welfare, public parks, and amusements. In turn, the Residents' Association in these cities elected six or seven of its members (by secret ballot) to comprise a Municipal Council (Sanjinkai) that, as an executive body, enacted the resolutions of the Residents' Association.[29]

In Shanghai, of course, where the Japanese community was only a constituent element of the International Settlement, the structure of the Residents' Association was considerably truncated. The association was limited in its responsibilities to issues of specific concern to the Japanese community and to expressing the will of that community to the consulate-general. Along with the less influential but even more vociferous Association of Japanese Street Unions, the association assumed ominous proportions as a pressure group in the early 1930s. The overall administration of the International Settlement was in the hands of the Shanghai Municipal Council, to which all foreign ratepayers in the Settlement were entitled to elect members. It was not, however, until World War I and the surge in the size of the Japanese population in Shanghai, which gave it added influence, that the Japanese were able to put a member on the council. In 1915, the head of the Japanese Residents' Association stood for election to the council. He was not elected by the ratepayers as a whole, but the next year the branch chief of Mitsui Bussan did manage to win a seat on the council, an event that marked the emergence of a permanently higher Japanese profile in the international administration of the Settlement. After the German and Russian presence in Shanghai diminished following World War I, Japanese influence in the affairs of the city grew

[28] TK, *Tenshin kyoryūmindan*, pp. 172–174.
[29] Ueda, *Shina ni okeru sokai no kenkyū*, pp. 724–726.

still further, and after 1927, not only did the Japanese increase their representation on the council to two, but they also came to have representation on its various subcommittees. Nevertheless, by the 1930s, the swelling numbers of Japanese in Shanghai and the increasingly strident nationalist sentiment within the Japanese community prompted demands for an even greater share in the administration and control of the foreign municipality at the expense of Western representation, particularly that of the British, who had traditionally dominated, if not monopolized, the Municipal Council. Continuing British intransigence concerning their position in Shanghai, combined with new Japanese belligerence in demanding a greater voice in running the international city, was to provide an acrimonious atmosphere in Shanghai right up to the Pacific War, when, of course, the Japanese took the Settlement over completely.[30]

In the less developed concessions—Soochow, Foochow, Hangchow, Amoy, Chungking, and Shashi—where the Residents' Corporation Law did not apply, the consulates retained more direct and comprehensive authority under the "Regulations for Japanese Residents' Associations" (*Nihon kyoryūminkai kisoku*). In function, composition, and membership, the Residents' Association in each of these place was much like the Residents' Corporations in Tientsin, Hankow, and Shanghai. The association, in turn, elected a small Assembly (*giinkai*) of three or four members that acted, as well as deliberated, on measures—budgets, accounts, and taxes in particular—that were in the common interest of the Japanese community.[31] But its authority was far more restricted than the municipal councils of the larger concessions, and its decisions more automatically subject to the approval of the local consulate. Certainly, the small size of the Japanese communities in these places limited the administrative effectiveness of such residents' organizations, not to mention circumscribing their influence on Japanese policy in the area. (Indeed, at one Japanese concession, Shashi, which contained only seven Japanese residents, it is hard to see how such an organization existed at all.)

It would seem, therefore, that one can create a reasonably simple administrative typology for Japanese resident communities in China between 1895 and 1937. In the first category one could place Tientsin and

---

[30] Uehara, *Shanhai kyōdō sokai gairon*, p. 53; Uchiyama Kiyoshi et al., *Dai Shanhai* (Greater Shanghai) (Shanghai: Dai Shanhai Sha, 1915), p. 199; and F. C. Jones, *Shanghai and Tientsin, with Special Reference to Foreign Interests* (New York: Oxford University Press, 1940), pp. 38–41.

[31] Ueda, *Shina ni okeru sokai no kenkyū*, pp. 729–732. In this regard, the administration of Amoy and Foochow was somewhat different. Because of the proportionately large number of Taiwanese in those cities who had become Japanese subjects, they were represented by a Taiwan Public Assembly (Taiwan Kōkai) elected by adult male Taiwanese who paid a minimum amount in concession dues.

Hankow—exclusively Japanese and fully developed concessions with substantial resident populations, which were to a large extent self-governing. In the second would be the communities at Shanghai, Tsingtao, and Nanking, where there was no exclusive area legally set apart for the Japanese, but where there existed a largely self-governing resident population (organized in the form of a Residents' Corporation). A third type would be those smaller and undeveloped areas in which Japan had legal claims to an exclusive concession (claims that it did not choose to exercise at Foochow), but where the small size of the Japanese community meant that administrative authority was largely consular in nature.

JAPANESE LIFE IN THE TREATY PORTS

Everywhere they congregated in China, the Japanese attempted, not unnaturally, to create those facilities and comforts to which they were accustomed in their homeland. The largest treaty port communities, at Shanghai, Tientsin, and Hankow, provided self-contained and transplanted Japanese worlds. Tientsin and Hankow did so by virtue of their existence as formally set-apart enclaves where all the street names were Japanese and the writ of the Japanese Consulate-General was absolute within the concession; Shanghai by the sheer size of its Japanese community. By the 1930s, much of the Hongkew district in the Shanghai International Settlement was almost as thoroughly Japanized as any of the concessions. Guidebooks of the day stress the ease of the Hongkew area for everyday Japanese living: Japanese goods were sold not only in the several large department stores, but also in the smaller neighborhood shops; Japanese was spoken in most of the Chinese stores of the district; Japanese inns, hotels, and restaurants of varying quality abounded within Hongkew, along with grocery stores, beauty shops, and libraries; Japanese babies were born in Japanese clinics and hospitals in Hongkew, and Japanese ashes were interred in the Japanese cemetery near Hongkew Park.[32]

In all of this, of course, the Japanese and European communities in the treaty ports were similar. Yet there were marked differences between the two. To begin with, the larger Japanese communities were even more self-contained. Where the Western resident was almost entirely dependent upon the Chinese community for daily needs and comforts—from laundry to groceries to haircuts—the Japanese relied to a far greater extent upon the goods and services of their countrymen (though it was certainly not uncommon for more affluent Japanese to have Chinese domestics in

---

[32] Gōtō, *Shina seikatsu annai*, pp. 134–136; and Wakae Tokuo, *Shanhai Seikatsu* (Life in Shanghai) (Tokyo: Dai Nippon Yūben Kao, 1942), pp. 42–43.

their homes). This situation accounts for the sharp difference in the occupational profiles between the Western and Japanese settlements in the
China treaty ports. Where the successful businessman, the prosperous
professional, the civil servant, the engineer, and the educator were all
prominent figures in the European enclaves in China, the Japanese communities were essentially lower middle class. At the top, it is true, there
existed a small circle of those representing the great commercial, shipping, banking, and industrial interests in Japan, but numerically the dominant occupations were those of tradesmen and shopkeepers. In Shanghai,
with the sudden rise in the textile industry after World War I, an increasing number of Japanese in the city were directly employed in the cotton
mills (mostly, one assumes, as foremen, technicians, and clerks), and
many more were indirectly dependent upon them (see below).

The principal occupational patterns of the Japanese concessions go a
long way toward explaining a characteristic of the Japanese concessions
and settlements in China that was common to the formal Japanese colonial empire as well: the absence of a grand colonial lifestyle. The few businessmen and consular officials who formed the small circle of influential
Japanese avoided public displays of any sort. Thus, without a social or
economic elite in the Western treaty port tradition—no great commercial
taipans who maintained themselves in great mansions, no group of bored
but affluent expatriates, not even a corps of glamorous courtesans to
sweep down the Bund in their richly liveried phaetons—the Japanese in
treaty port life lacked the glitter and magnificence of the Western communities in China. In scanning the histories and photographs of Japanese
resident communities there, one notes the absence, for example, of those
luxurious recreational facilities—the Japanese clubs found in Hankow,
Tientsin, and Shanghai seem to have been the exception—with which the
Europeans not only diverted themselves, but sorted out the social status
of their compatriots. Few Japanese in the treaty ports were housed in the
Western-style brick buildings that one saw in the European quarter, and
Japanese-style housing was uncommon. Most Japanese lived in rather
modest Chinese structures, the interiors of which, when they could afford to do so, they made over in Japanese style. Those who were tradesmen or shopkeepers usually lived over or behind their small stores. Prewar photographs of the Japanese quarter along Woosung and Boone
roads in Shanghai show fairly narrow streets along which one- and two-
story buildings are crowded together, though Japanese business and office structures in Tientsin and Shanghai were naturally more imposing.[33]

Moreover, the Japanese resident in China did not generally participate
in the social life of the European. The reasons are probably plain enough:

[33] SK, *Shanghai kyoryūmindan*, pp. 100–101.

the barriers of language, the natural propensity of Japanese to cleave to their own circles, and the overt or tacit racism of treaty port Westerners who were as unlikely to welcome Japanese as Chinese to their bars, clubs, or charity balls.[34] In any event, to Western eyes, the Japanese in treaty ports seemed socially awkward and aloof. Western gunboats anchored on station in the Yangtze, for example, became famous for their rounds of entertaining. Yet despite their common naval mission, Japanese crews seldom joined in their carousing. As Hallett Abend, the noted *New York Times* correspondent, sniffed, "Japan, too, kept gunboats on all the reaches of the Yangtze, but the Japanese were never a social asset there or anywhere else." For their part, the Japanese hardly seemed inclined to bridge the gap. A few prominent Japanese met with their Western opposites on gala occasions such as the annual cherry blossom party in Shanghai given by the Mitsui representative for foreign businessmen at his residence in the French concession, or the emperor's birthday reception for the consular body held on the lawn of the consulate-general, but these were brief and superficial contacts.[35]

Yet the Japanese communities did not lack a social life of their own. The emperor's birthday celebration furnished an occasion for the entire Japanese community in each concession to come together. At Shanghai, the consulate-general would decorate its grounds with hundreds of Japanese lanterns and flags, and if Japanese warships were anchored in the river, they would do the same. Focus of the festivities would be a large garden party on the consular grounds where, after the inevitable speeches and toasts, there would undoubtedly be group photographs of the leading guests, and a buffet of Japanese delicacies, along with *oden* and *sekihan*, all washed down with beer and cold sake.

Social life of a more traditional sort centered around the various associations found in the larger Japanese communities, which catered to the more established and affluent members of the community. Prominent among these was the Japanese Club (Nihonjin kurabu), which provided relaxation for the leading business, consular, and professional figures. The club at Shanghai, founded in 1908, owed its massive and suitably stodgy quarters on Boone Road to its principal patron, the Yokohama Specie Bank. At the Japan Club in Tientsin, one could, for a fairly steep annual fee, stop by for an evening to hoist a beer, read back issues of

---

[34] The general disinclination to mix socially with the Japanese in China was certainly not absolute, however. Matsumoto Shigeharu, for example, became one of the two Japanese members of the Shanghai Club, the preeminent bastion of Anglo-Saxon male privilege in China, when he was a young correspondent in the city in the early 1930s. Japanese guests were also occasionally invited to the club. Matsumoto, *Shanhai jidai*, pp. 104–109.

[35] Hallet Abend, *My Life in China, 1926–1941* (New York: Harcourt Brace, 1946), p. 172; Ernest O. Hauser, *Shanghai: City for Sale* (New York: Harcourt Brace, 1940), pp. 192–194.

Kingu, Kaizō, or *Jitsugyō no Nippon,* or play billiards or mahjong.[36] There were other clubs as well: Shanghai and Hankow sported Navy Clubs for the off-duty recreation of the naval landing parties, and at Tientsin crews of Japanese merchant ships anchored in the Hai River could find relaxation at the Merchant Marine Club near Yamato Park.

Though recreation in the Japanese communities may not have been glamorous, it was certainly varied. In Tientsin, sports were promoted by the Taiiku-kai, which sponsored clubs in archery, baseball, and the martial arts and organized competitions at the local sports stadium. In the summer, the Japanese residents could use the six tennis courts available in the concession, and after 1933 one could take a dip in the public pool on Miyajima Street; in the early fall and spring, horseback enthusiasts could canter about the riding ring down by the garrison barracks, and in the winter, skating was possible on the large rink in front of the consulate-general. For the more reflective, there was a haiku club (founded in 1897); the Tientsin Engeki-kai put on amateur theatricals; and during World War I, the Mandolin Club was popular.[37]

Parks had an important place in Japanese family recreation in the larger Japanese communities. In Shanghai, the favorite spot was the Rokusan Gardens, a landscape garden located at the end of North Szechuan Road in Hongkew. Laid out in 1896 when the district was still undeveloped, the gardens featured an artificial pond, flowering plants, a small Shintō shrine, and a teahouse where Japanese dishes could be ordered. It was a favorite spot for Japanese residents on holiday, though some favored the Tsukinoya Gardens, a smaller park managed by a Japanese restaurant of the same name. Yamato Park in Tientsin was the grandest of all, and featured regular band concerts, pools, fountains, a children's playground, and the inevitable Japanese war monument.[38]

More robust amusement was available at the variety halls, movie theaters, cabarets, and dance halls of Shanghai's Hongkew district. At least one Japanese travel guide to Shanghai intimated that elsewhere in the International Settlement the same sort of entertainment was spicier, yet Japanese in Hongkew did not often go "south of the creek." Certainly, the Japanese concession of Tientsin and the Japanese quarter of Shanghai each contained its share of vice. Prostitution flourished on several levels—

[36] SK, *Shanghai kyoryūmindan,* pp. 1269–1270; TK, *Tenshin kyoryūmindan,* p. 536. Much more than the Western Club in Asia, these institutions were used for public purposes—public meetings and discussions of communitywide issues—and thus performed a central role in the efforts of Japanese communities to protest and organize against Chinese anti-Japanese agitation in the 1920s and 1930s.

[37] TK, *Tenshin kyoryūmindan,* pp. 525–527.

[38] JGR, *Guide to China,* p. 250; SK, *Shanghai kyoryūmindan,* p. 75; TK, *Tenshin kyoryūmindan,* pp. 470–472.

among the barmaids (*shakufu*) in the more rough-and-ready establishments, at a slightly higher level at some of the *ryoriya* and teahouses—most of it undoubtedly licensed according to regulations governing the practice in the empire and home islands.[39]

In the early years of Japan's participation in the treaty port era, health and sanitation were dire problems in the Japanese communities. A Japanese guidebook to Shanghai published in 1915 tells us that fifty-six different diseases accounted for Japanese mortalities in the port between 1906 and 1914, the worst being cholera. Steadily, as water and sewage facilities and hospitals and clinics were established, the problems of communicable disease assumed less frightening proportions. In Shanghai, of course, the Japanese residents benefited from the general health and sanitation facilities of the International Settlement, though the Japanese were quick to contribute services at these institutions that would specifically aid their countrymen. (Two Japanese nurses, for example, were provided to the Shanghai Isolation Hospital to care for Japanese patients.) Even before World War I, a number of Japanese clinics were established in the Settlement, most of them small establishments like the Sasaki Clinic on Whangpoo Road, founded in 1902 by a specialist and staffed by two assistants, four nurses, and a druggist. During the 1920s, as Japanese capital available for hospital construction increased, some of these institutions grew in size and reputation, and by the 1930s, Japanese hospitals in the treaty ports, like the Tientsin Union Hospital, established in 1902 as a small clinic, boasted some of the finest medical facilities in China.[40]

First-rate educational facilities were also a feature of the Japanese communities in China. One has only to skim the photographs of the history of the Japanese community in Shanghai, for example, to realize the value the Japanese residents in China placed on having schools for their children equal to those in the home islands. Some fifteen Japanese schools were located in the Settlement (including a girls' commercial school, two girls' higher schools, a middle school, a vocational school, nine primary schools, and a kindergarten), most of them large facilities of cheerless, factory-like design, but obviously a source of great pride to the Japanese community.[41] Tientsin and Hankow each had a number of secondary and

---

[39] The pages of the official histories of the Japanese settlements in Tientsin and Shanghai are obviously blanched of all indications that vice—prostitution, narcotics traffic, gambling, and such—functioned in those places. An independent source, however, the Chinese newspaper *Ta-kung pao*, indicates that in Tientsin, at least, these activities flourished on a far larger scale in the Japanese concession than in any other. For this information, I am indebted to Sophia Lee's extensive unpublished review of that paper in the 1930s. *Ta-kung pao* apparently regularly reported on vice in the Japanese concession.

[40] Uchiyama, *Dai Shanhai*, pp. 98–99, 114–118.

[41] Until 1935, the expense of maintaining these schools for approximately three thousand students in the Japanese quarter was borne entirely by the Japanese Residents' Corporation

primary schools, and most of the lesser concessions had at least a primary school. Unlike the Western educational effort in China, however, neither the Japanese government nor private organizations attempted to establish universities or colleges (in the general sense of these terms) on the mainland.[42]

The Buddhist temple and the Shintō shrine were ubiquitous features in the physical layout of the Japanese communities in treaty port China. Japanese Buddhism had first come to China with the establishment of a branch temple in the Higashi Honganji chapter of Jōdō Shinshū in 1876. Eventually, each of the concessions had a temple or two—in Tientsin there were seven—but they were of modest size and usually situated in unimposing locations, for their purpose was devotional rather than patriotic. To a degree, they represented a failed mission, since the original hopes of their home sects for massive Chinese conversions had never materialized.

Shintō, or more exactly its nationalistic variant, State Shintō, suffered no such evangelical disappointments, for its purpose was entirely devoted to the glorification of the Japanese nation. Wherever Japanese settled in Asia, the Shintō shrine was a feature of overseas community, bringing to it a sense of stability and security, no less (one supposes) than the way in which the English parish church or the Catholic *eglise* in a hundred exotic imperial sites in Asia brought temporal as well as spiritual assurance to Britons and French in the Orient. But even more than the European church or the Buddhist temple, the Japanese Shintō shrine was the suprareligious manifestation of the power and authority of the Japanese nation. Its setting and arrangement outside Japan were designed to make a statement to Japanese and outsiders alike as to the transplanted majesty of the Japanese state. Along with the massive stone consular offices and bank buildings, the Shintō shrine was often the exception to the generally unimpressive appearance of Japanese architecture in China. Each shrine was positioned in a prominent and easily accessible location in the concession or settlement, its sweeping *torii* gateway leading to relatively spacious grounds that surrounded the shrine buildings. In the Tientsin concession, the Inari Shrine (established in 1906 on Fushimi Street) was modest enough, but the Tientsin Shrine set up in Yamato Park in 1915, dedicated to the Sun Goddess and the Meiji Emperor and staffed by eight priests, was an impressive focus of the frequent ceremonial occasions in

---

and by a small grant from the government in Tokyo, despite the fact that, as ratepayers, the Japanese supported other educational facilities in the Settlement. In that year, after representations by the consulate-general, the Municipal Council set aside funds for the Japanese school system. Jones, *Shanghai and Tientsin*, p. 40.

[42] I leave aside here the highly specialized Tōa Dōbun Shoin, dealt with elsewhere in this volume.

the life of the Japanese community. At Shanghai, a small shrine had been built in the Rokusan Gardens in late Meiji and had been adequate to serve the residents of the Japanese quarter through the Taishō years, but after the involvement of civilians as well as sailors and soldiers in the furious miniwar at Shanghai in the winter of 1932, the community joined the armed forces to lay out a far grander and more chauvinistic shrine adjacent to it to honor the Japanese killed in that conflict. Its intimidating aspect was exemplified by the huge naval cannon that squatted menacingly by the main gate.[43]

JAPAN'S ARMED FIST: GUNBOATS, GARRISONS, AND GENDARMES

Year in, year out, no aspect of the foreign communities in the treaty ports, and of the Japanese settlements in particular, was more galling to Chinese nationalism than the existence of foreign warships in Chinese waters and foreign troops on Chinese soil. Ultimately, it was the Japanese naval and military presence that became most rapacious, but it seems demonstrably true that, initially, Japanese armed forces in the treaty ports were no more provocative than their Western counterparts there.

Like most of the Western treaty powers, Japanese naval and military units in the treaty ports based their existence on one or the other of two claims: arrangements under formal treaty or claim of military necessity, specifically the protection of Japanese nationals and interests in time of trouble. While Japan's one permanent garrison in the treaty ports was based on the former sanction, the Japanese naval presence, like that of the West, could only be justified by the claims of military necessity, since there were no formal treaty arrangements covering foreign naval forces in Chinese waters.

Generally, the navy concentrated its efforts in Central China—particularly the Yangtze River Valley and along the South China coast—while the army regarded North China as its sphere of responsibility. In relation to the Japanese communities in the treaty ports, the most important contingents in China were the Naval Landing Party at Shanghai and the China Garrison Army at Tientsin. Each was originally positioned to defend local Japanese residents and interests, and each was ultimately involved in aggressive operations beyond the limits of the Japanese settlements it was there to protect.

While the Naval Landing Party at Shanghai was only a decade old by the time of the China War of 1937, its antecedents went back four decades before that. The Japanese navy had cautiously entered Chinese waters even before Japan acquired treaty power rights in China, sending two

---

[43] TK, *Tenshin kyoryūmindan*, p. 514; SK, *Shanghai kyoryūmindan*, pp. 1163–1168.

warships to Shanghai in 1884, ostensibly to protect the nation's small interests there, but more probably to show the flag. With the increase in Japanese commerce, consular establishments, and resident population, the number of warships on station was increased to three by the 1880s. Japan's participation in the Boxer Rebellion having shown the importance of having a permanent force upriver on the Yangtze, the navy ordered a small flotilla of gunboats built in 1903–1906 for service on that river. This nucleus of the Japanese naval presence in Central China grew to formidable strength by the 1930s with the addition of destroyers and cruisers.[44]

The Japanese gunboat or destroyer, whether sailing far upriver into the Chinese interior or riding at anchor off the consulate at Shanghai or Hankow, its sunburst naval ensign floating majestically from the taffrail, was a reassurance to Japanese resident populations in the treaty ports, just as, in the Chinese perspective, it represented a truculent assertion of Japanese power in China. Yet by themselves gunboats could not undertake the task of securing buildings and streets and installations ashore in the concessions, or of evacuating Japanese civilians in times of emergency. For these purposes the navy developed the landing party (*rikusentai*) as a skilled and effective unit of men put ashore to secure an area or to evacuate civilians safely. At first, they were scratch contingents from gunboat crews hastily assembled and armed only with rifles. Later, "special landing parties" (*tokubetsu rikusentai*)—larger, more heavily armed contingents, permanently based in Japan or ports in the empire—were transported to the treaty ports at short notice.[45] From 1897, when the first small detachment of twenty men was landed at Shanghai to secure the consulate thereafter a bomb had exploded nearby, the Japanese naval landing parties, often in cooperation with Western counterparts, were put ashore again and again at the Japanese settlements when successive waves of national violence racked China and threatened all foreign interests.

At Shanghai, however, the Special Naval Landing Party became a permanent fixture. Debarking in the International Settlement in 1927, along with Western military contingents, in the face of possible Chinese violence against the Settlement, the Naval Landing Party took up station in the Japanese quarter of Shanghai. Four years later, during a similar crisis in the city, the force was assigned permanent defense of that sector by the Settlement's municipal administration. During that time, the Special Landing Party developed close ties with the Japanese community, including such paramilitary civilian groups as the local chapter of the Imperial

---

[44] BBKS, *Senshi sōshō*, vol. 72, pp. 59–62 and 84–85.

[45] In Western accounts, the *rikusentai* are often described as "marines," but they were, in fact, composed of sailors who were an integral part of the Japanese navy, not amphibious troops of an independent service like the U.S. Marine Corps.

Military Reservists Association, with which it worked closely during the fighting that exploded in Shanghai in January 1932 after the Landing Party moved aggressively against Chinese Nationalist forces stationed outside the Settlement.

When the dust of that conflict settled in May 1932, the atmosphere of the International Settlement and the position of the Japanese armed force within it were changed permanently. Not only had the Special Naval Landing Party set an ominous precedent by violating the traditional neutrality of the Settlement, but it now became the virtual arbiter of the Settlement north of Soochow Creek, as well as of that portion of the Hongkew district around Hongkew Park, immediately north of the Settlement boundary. Permanent barracks of the Special Naval Landing Party were erected near the park. Faced with granite and capable of holding 2,000 men as well as tanks and armored cars, the barracks constituted a fortress covering two city blocks in the heart of the Chinese city. From this bastion Japanese naval troops held maneuvers in the Hongkew district as they pleased, detained and arrested foreign nationals without reference to the municipal police, and generally ran Hongkew as if it were an exclusive Japanese concession.[46]

Sanction for the Japanese military presence in North China was derived from Japan's participation as a signatory to the Boxer Protocol of 1901, which permitted all the signatory powers to establish garrisons to protect the legations at Peking, rail communications from Peking to the sea, and the foreign concessions at Tientsin. Thus was born Japan's protocol force at Tientsin, based in permanent barracks in the southwest corner of the Japanese concession, the remainder divided into small, roving patrols distributed in and around Tientsin. The Tientsin garrison was also authorized to maintain two subgarrisons, one outside Peking to protect Japan's legation there and one at Shanhaikuan at the eastern extremity of the Great Wall, where the Peking-Mukden Railway met the sea.[47]

In 1913, the name of the Tientsin garrison was changed to the China Garrison Army (Shina chuton gun), its size increased to about nine hundred men (hardly the strength of an "army"), and its striking power augmented by the inclusion of an Emergency Expeditionary Force (Rinji hakentai), a mobile unit designed to deal with crisis situations. With each new upheaval in China, the Japanese army undertook to strengthen its protocol force in Tientsin. During the chaos following the 1911 Revolution, extra units were added; during the tensions created by the northward-sweeping Chinese nationalism of the 1920s, its size was doubled to about eighteen hundred men and then increased again during the 1930s.

[46] Jones, *Shanghai and Tientsin*, pp. 46–49; Johnstone, *The Shanghai Problem*, p. 288.
[47] BBKS, *Senshi sōshō*, vol. 72, pp. 45–46; Feuerwerker, "Foreign Presence," pp. 153–154.

By mid-decade, it had grown to four thousand officers and men and was centered on an infantry brigade and an artillery regiment, a formidable force for a supposedly defensive garrison.[48]

Although it could not easily be argued that Japanese military forces in China, like their naval counterparts, ever contributed to the order and security of China, by the 1930s they had become aggressive and rapacious. The one permanent and legally sanctioned garrison on the mainland, the China Garrison Army, was now an agent of military violence and intrigue in North China. In part, this was due to the greatly augmented size and strength of the army, which emboldened its staff to a far greater readiness to take direct action to impose its will on the Chinese authorities in North China. In part, it was due to the newly emerging outlook of Japanese middle-echelon military staffs that were ready to effect, by violent means, one-shot solutions to complex problems, such as those involved in Japan's interests in China and Manchuria. It meant, in any event, that the Tientsin protocol force became far more engaged with offensive preparations and intelligence operations against Chinese nationalism than with mere protection of Japanese life and property in North China. This aggressive stance led to the involvement of the China Garrison Army in the conflict at Tsinan during the second Shantung Expedition and in a violent diversion against Chinese forces during the invasion of Manchuria by the Kwantung Army in 1931, and, of course, to a major role in the invasion of China in 1937. Its subcommands at Shanhaikuan and Peking were even more aggressive: in 1933, the detachment at Shanhaikuan provoked a confrontation with Chinese troops in the city that led to a major conflict involving Kwantung Army units, which were rushed down from Manchuria. Finally, it was a subunit of the Peking Detachment that clashed with Chinese troops on the fatal night of July 7, 1937, at the Marco Polo Bridge, thus igniting the catastrophe of the China War.

Foreign police with powers of arrest over Chinese, as well as foreign, nationals also insulted Chinese sovereignty. To a degree, all treaty powers maintained police establishments in the ports. Under the Land Regulations that set up the International Settlement at Shanghai, moreover, the Shanghai Municipal Council was authorized to establish a police force to maintain law and order in the Settlement, and most of the treaty powers also maintained their own national police forces within their individual concessions. Yet without doubt, the Japanese consular police (*ryōjikan keisatsu*) in the Japanese settlements represented the largest and, to the Chinese, the most outrageously provocative of all the foreign gendarmeries.[49]

---

[48] TK, *Tenshin kyoryūmindan*, p. 556.

[49] Discussion of the evolution of the Japanese consular police may be found in the second

To begin with, Japanese police establishments in China were not restricted within the boundaries of Japan's exclusive concessions but were an arm of Japanese consular offices throughout China, being assigned to each consular district under the direct supervision of each principal consular officer. Moreover, the Japanese consular police established a whole network of personnel and facilities—constables, inspectors, patrolmen, police boxes, barracks, and even detention centers and jails—on Chinese soil, all totally without authorization from Chinese authorities. Finally, Japanese consular police often acted arbitrarily, arresting and detaining Chinese as well as Japanese.

Originally few in number and organized to provide simple security for Japanese consular facilities (in much the same way the U.S. Marines fulfill that function at American embassies today), the Japanese consular police establishments grew in proportion to the multiplicity of functions they were called upon to perform.[50] To the Tientsin consulate, for example, the Foreign Ministry in 1896 had sent a single police inspector, but after the consulate became a consulate-general, with expanded responsibilities for the development of the concession, this number was increased to two inspectors and thirty constables to protect the consular buildings, along with thirty Chinese patrolmen responsible for traffic control within the concession. By 1937, however, the superintendent at the consular police station in Sakae Street directed a force of nearly five hundred policemen: three inspectors, six assistant inspectors, twenty police sergeants, fifty-one policemen, and about four hundred Chinese patrolmen. As the Japanese concession in Tientsin was only 650 acres in area, it is obvious that such a force was far in excess of anything needed to provide simple security for the consular buildings. The functional categories of the consular police establishment were an indication of the degree to which the Japanese government was prepared to interfere with Chinese activities it considered anti-Japanese, as well as the degree to which the concessions themselves now harbored a significant number of Japanese engaged in illegal activities: the higher police (kōtō keisatsu) were responsible for "thought control," by which was meant control of anti-Japanese agita-

---

volume of Gaimushō no Hyakunen Hensan Iinkai, ed., *Gaimushō no hyakunen* (One hundred years of the Japanese Foreign Ministry) (Tokyo: Hara Shobō, 1969), pp. 1370–1408.

[50] The consular police were established in 1880, simultaneous with the appearance of Japanese consular courts in Korea, and were thereafter stationed in Manchuria and China. The first consular police office in China was established in Shanghai in 1884, and by 1886 police offices were attached to the consulates at Tientsin, Chefoo, Soochow, Hangchow, Shashi, Chungking, and Amoy. The Japanese government considered that the legal basis for the consular police in China was confirmed by the 1896 Treaty of Commerce and Navigation, by the 1903 addendum to that treaty, and by enabling legislation in Japan enacted in 1899 and 1919. By 1938, there were 35 consular police offices in China and over 750 Japanese police. Ibid., pp. 1370–1371, 1391–1408.

tion, as well as for censorship within the concession and surveillance of Koreans and foreigners; the judicial police (*shihō keisatsu*) were responsible for dealing with crimes among Japanese (largely black marketeering, corruption and bribery) and Chinese (mostly theft, fraud, embezzlement, violence, arson, and counterfeiting); and the peace preservation police (*hōen keisatsu*) were charged with the enforcement of health and sanitation measures, commerce, construction codes, regulation of prostitution, the enforcement of fire laws and laws on public morals, and control of traffic and transportation.[51]

The position of the Japanese consular police contingent in the Shanghai International Settlement was fundamentally different from that of the consular police elsewhere in China, since it was to a large degree integrated into the municipal police force, which in turn took its orders from the Municipal Council. With the growth of the Japanese community during World War I, a Japanese branch of the Municipal Police was established in 1916 with the assignment of thirty-seven constables from the Tokyo Metropolitan Police. In the 1920s, the Japanese consulate-general demanded the dilution of the traditional British monopoly over the municipal police administration, a demand that resulted in the appointment of a Japanese assistant commissioner. In 1934, in response to the rising tide of anti-Japanese agitation in the Settlement, a Japanese special deputy commissioner was appointed to deal with the problem. By 1937, Japanese police officials were seeded throughout the Shanghai Municipal Police hierarchy, and the Japanese branch included over 180 Japanese constables responsible largely for patrolling the Hongkew district. Yet, subject as they were to the overdirection of an international police body, the Japanese police in Shanghai never provoked the sort of protest the consular police did.[52]

VULNERABILITY OF THE JAPANESE SETTLEMENTS

Forced on an unwilling nation during the last crisis-bound decades of the tottering Manchu dynasty, the Japanese concessions, no less than those of any of the other treaty powers, were an affront and a humiliation to China, but they were accepted with resignation until the upheaval of Chinese nationalism at the end of the First World War. It can be argued, however, that until that time the Japanese concessions, no less than their Western counterparts, provided a certain degree of order and stability amid the political and military chaos following the breakup of Ch'ing China. But after 1918, the successive waves of Chinese nationalism pro-

---

[51] TK, *Tenshin kyoryūmindan*, pp. 396, 546–553.
[52] Uehara, *Shanhai kyōdō sokai gairon*, pp. 114–127; Jones, *Shanghai and Tientsin*, p. 39.

voked within the sizable Japanese resident populations in China such responses as to make the concessions flashpoints of violence rather than oases of stability. In the high noon of international imperialism when Japan acquired these enclaves of special privilege, they were seen by the Japanese as glittering assets, as well as prideful symbols of Japan's attainment of Great Power status. By the 1920s, they had become besieged outposts vulnerable to mounting anti-Japanese agitation from adjacent and hostile Chinese populations, a situation that required either their abandonment or their on-the-spot defense by gunboats and landing parties.

The wave of popular Chinese protest that swept the treaty ports in response to the Twenty-One Demands of 1915 marked the beginning of a darkening era of Sino-Japanese relations just at a time when the Japanese economic stake in China, as well as the resident community dependent upon it, began to assume dimensions that made it particularly vulnerable to Chinese pressure. A complete profile of the Japanese economic commitment in the treaty ports—the web of trading, shipping, banking, industry, and retail interests, all threatened in various degrees by the onset of anti-Japanese nationalism in China—lies beyond the scope of this chapter. One of the more important economic activities among these, however, was the cotton textile industry, the rapid emergence of which during World War I marked the real advance of Japanese industry in the treaty ports.

Japan had exported some coarse cotton yarns and fabrics to the mainland in the early years of Japan's trade with China, but until World War I British imports, aided by a low tariff, had dominated the China market, one of the world's great outlets for finished cotton goods. When wartime needs diverted British cotton manufacturers, Japanese textile companies were quick to exploit this new opportunity. But in 1918, higher rates set for imported cotton yarn extended protection to the struggling Chinese cotton industry. The solution, Japanese cotton manufacturers quickly recognized, was to locate mills in China, where the cost of production was, in any event, cheaper than in Japan. After 1918, when there were some 29,000 Japanese-owned spindles in China, the Japanese cotton industry in China expanded enormously, so that in two years the figure had increased to 867,000 spindles. By the 1930s, the Japanese textile industry in the treaty ports—silks as well as cotton—with its 48 mills, 23,000 spinning machines, well over 2 million spindles, a capital investment of nearly 36 million yen, and a labor force of 69,000 workers, was a major Japanese asset on the Asian continent. It also provided a livelihood for an increasing number of Japanese in treaty ports, particularly in Shanghai and Tientsin. In Shanghai, by 1931, nearly a quarter of the Japanese population of 25,000 was directly connected with the cotton industry, and a large proportion of the remainder did business of one kind or another with the mills. But, dependent as it was on a Chinese market and, to an overwhelming extent, on a Chinese labor force, it was more vulnerable than any other Japanese economic activity in the settlements to two increasingly effective methods of Chinese protest against the advance of Japanese power in China: the strike and the boycott.[53]

Although it is not within the scope of this chapter to chronicle the worsening course of Sino-Japanese relations that grew out of Japanese aggression in China, on the one hand, and anti-Japanese Chinese labor agitation and economic resistance, on the other, a few summary comments are possible.

First, strikes spread with ever-greater prevalence throughout the Japanese textile industry in the treaty ports from 1918 to 1932. British mills were also struck during the 1920s, but those owned by the Japanese were most liable to conflict, partly because of working conditions in the mills, partly because of the deeply rooted sense of outrage among Chinese workers concerning the repeated military aggressions by Japan. During these years, the four Japanese cotton mills in Shanghai were struck 118 times. Inevitably, such labor agitation caused clashes between Chinese strikers and Japanese civilians, prompting an upward cycle of violence. From the mills the strikes spread to the docks of the treaty ports, where Chinese laborers refused to land or unload Japanese cargoes; dispatch of Japanese naval landing parties to break up the Chinese picket lines in turn led to more violence.[54]

Paralleling such labor agitation during this period was a series of increasingly devastating boycotts that not only curtailed the sale of Japanese textiles but also crippled Japanese commerce as a whole in the treaty ports, so that by 1931 Japanese trade at Shanghai, the hub of Japan's commerce in China, was brought almost to a standstill. Moreover, life in the Japanese settlements became ever more difficult. At Shanghai as well as at treaty ports with smaller concentrations of Japanese, such as Foochow, food shortages brought real hardships to Japanese residents. Worst of all, violence against Japanese lives and property at Shanghai, Hankow, Nanking, Tsingtao, Foochow, and Changsha kept the Japanese communities there constantly on edge and necessitated various measures—defensive barriers, naval landing parties, and roving patrols—that maintained them in prolonged states of seige.[55]

---

[53] Jones, *Shanghai and Tientsin*, pp. 144–147; BBKS, *Senshi sōshō*, vol. 72, pp. 56–57; and Richard Rigby, *The May 30 Movement: Events and Themes* (Canberra: Wm. Dawson & Sons, 1980), pp. 6–7.

[54] Rigby, *May 30*, pp. 16, 24, and 28–29.

[55] The best and most detailed study of the evolution and effectiveness of the Chinese

THE JAPANESE COMMUNITIES AS CENTERS OF MILITANCY: THE CASE OF SHANGHAI

In the face of the mounting Chinese threat to their privileges, property, and lives, it is not surprising that the mood of the Japanese resident populations, particularly in the larger settlements, became increasingly unyielding, combative, and vengeful. Indeed, the Japanese resident population of Shanghai, in particular, was far more military and aggressive in its resistance to the Chinese assault on foreign privilege than any of the Western communities in China. Perhaps this was due to the fact that it constituted the largest bloc of foreign residents in the treaty ports. Perhaps this was because, on the one hand, its members felt more directly threatened by Chinese nationalism than the resident communities of any other treaty power, and, on the other, believed that both their numbers and their proximity to the homeland would compel the Japanese government to back up their demands. There is also one other possibility, which, in the absence of any credible study on the subject, can only be a matter of conjecture: the Japanese communities in China, especially the larger ones like that in Shanghai, took a more combative stand, indeed were more prone to violence, because they contained a greater number of the idle and unemployed, including lawless elements, who were more caught up in mob hysteria and who could be mobilized for violent attacks on neighboring Chinese.[56] In any event, it would seem that in mood and outlook the Japanese community in Shanghai in the 1930s bore less resemblance to other foreign communities in the city than it did to the resident population of French *colons* in Algiers in the late 1950s.

During the period 1915–1932, this combative attitude of the Japanese community in Shanghai was heightened by the emergence of various civilian action groups that not only sought to ventilate the views of the community but advocated forceful defense of its interests. Chief among these was the Shanghai Association of Japanese Street Unions (Shanhai Nihon Kakurō Rengōkai), which had its origins in 1915 when a number of block associations in the Japanese quarter, alarmed by anti-Japanese

---

boycotts is still C. F. Remer, *A Study of Chinese Boycotts* (Baltimore: Johns Hopkins University Press, 1933).

[56] As examples of mob violence in the Tientsin concession, one notes two separate incidents, one in 1913 (a fracas between police from the Japanese and French concessions) and one in 1918 (involving Japanese civilians and soldiers of the American protocol force stationed at Tientsin). In each case, the initial incident quickly attracted a formidable mob, variously armed, which had to be confronted by regular forces from the nearby Japanese garrison. In Shanghai in 1918, an altercation between Japanese sailors and Chinese police provoked several days of rampage by Japanese civilians. TK, *Tenshin kyoryūmindan*, pp. 235–238; SK, *Shanhai kyoryūmindan*, p. 347; Francis Pott, *A Short History of Shanghai* (Shanghai: Kelly and Walsh, 1928), p. 225.

agitation subsequent to the Twenty-One Demands and frustrated by the seeming indifference of the Municipal Council, banded together to defend their interests. By the end of the 1920s, the association included virtually the entire Japanese resident population in the city; it had become a vociferous and active pressure group that put Japan's consular representation in Shanghai on the defensive.[57]

Other organizations of a military, patriotic, and militant character were organized in Shanghai during the 1920s. The Shanghai chapter of the Imperial Military Reservists Association (Teikoku Zaigogunjinkai) was formed to promote military and patriotic ideals among Japanese in the Settlement, along with various youth organizations (*seinendan*) instilled with patriotic zeal and maintaining close links to the IMRA. During this time also, civilian vigilante groups, *jikeidan*, began to appear in the Japanese quarter during crisis periods, organized partly by the Association of Japanese Street Unions, with the cooperation most probably of the IMRA. Japanese commercial organizations in the city—the Japan Chamber of Commerce and the Japanese Cotton Spinners Association of China, to name the biggest—also began to pressure the Japanese government to take forceful action as the wave of Chinese boycotts and strikes began to ruin Japanese trade and markets. Lastly, by the autumn of 1931, the Shanghai Japanese Residents' Association itself became an increasingly vociferous element, not only advocating forceful suppression of anti-Japanese agitation in Shanghai, but also organizing Japanese resident communities in China to act as a pressure group upon the Japanese government to carry out such a policy. That autumn, a successively widening circle of Residents' Association meetings were held in Shanghai, culminating in December 1931 with a mammoth meeting of the All-China Assembly of Japanese Residents, which demanded intervention by the Japanese military and a more aggressive attitude on the part of the Japanese government.[58]

By December 1931, as the various pressures generated by countervailing Chinese and Japanese nationalism built up to a crisis, the Japanese community in Shanghai displayed a number of dangerously volatile characteristics: a militant and uncompromising stand on the complete suppression of all forms of anti-Japanese activity, an openly expressed willingness to act in concert with Japanese naval and military forces in a violent solution to the crisis; an almost complete domination and intimidation of Japanese consular representation in the city; and a surprising

[57] SK, *Tenshin kyoryūmindan*, pp. 1072–1074.

[58] Ibid., pp. 18–38; Donald A. Jordan, "The Participation of Overseas Japanese Communities in the Japanese Military Interventions in China, 1931–1932," Symposium on the History of the Republic of China, vol. 4 (Taiwan, 1983). Shanghai Kyoryūmindan, ed., *Shanhai jihen shi* (A history of the Shanghai incident) (Shanghai: 1933), pp. 16–38.

degree of unanimity and cohesiveness among all the Japanese organizations in the city in voicing the views of the Japanese community as a whole and in readiness to take violent action in its behalf. In January 1932, this volatile admixture helped fuel the explosion of open conflict between Japanese and Chinese in Shanghai.

As I pointed out earlier, the end of that conflict left the Japanese in a stronger position, militarily and politically, than ever before. From its fortified barracks in Hongkew, the Shanghai Special Naval Landing Party so thoroughly dominated the Settlement north of Soochow Creek that it became essentially a separate Japanese area over which the Shanghai Municipal Council exercised almost no control; and upon the council itself, the Japanese representatives continued to exert pressure for greater Japanese influence in the management of the Settlement as a whole.[59]

Five years later, Shanghai was once more at the center of Sino-Japanese conflict, which erupted with truly disastrous consequences for both nations. Growing numbers of Chinese troops massing around Shanghai in the weeks following the Marco Polo Bridge incident in July 1937 and the reckless and unauthorized provocation of Chinese authority early the following month by two Japanese naval personnel stationed in Shanghai were the immediate causes of a sudden and explosive crisis between Chinese and Japanese in that city. But unlike the conflict of 1932, the fighting that broke out in Shanghai in early August 1937 originated less in tensions within the city itself than in decisions reached separately in Nanking and Tokyo that expanded a localized conflict into a full-scale war. Yet neither the Japanese communities themselves nor any imagined threat to their safety or economic welfare figured largely in the decision of the Japanese government to thrash the Chinese Nationalists for their supposed intransigence. In Shanghai and Tientsin, the Japanese communities were muted in their response to the crisis, and in Tokyo the government at last concluded that most of the Japanese concessions in China were too great a liability to be maintained. At the urging of the navy, the cabinet decided to withdraw all its nationals from the concessions in South China and the Yangtze River Valley, while it authorized the dispatch of additional forces to defend only the large Japanese communities at Shanghai, Tientsin, and Hankow. By the time that the China War can be said to have begun in mid-August 1937, the evacuation of Japanese civilians from the lesser concession areas had been completed or was un-

---

[59] As Johnstone pointed out in his pioneering study of the causes of international conflict in Shanghai in the 1930s, this period was a three-cornered struggle for control of the Municipal Council between the Chinese and Japanese in which each sought to block any expansion of the other's authority in the city while both endeavored to reduce the long Western (British) domination of the International Settlement. Johnstone, *The Shanghai Problem*, pp. 243–248.

derway. In Shanghai, Tientsin, and Tsingtao, the infusion of large numbers of military and naval forces gave the Japanese a truly intimidating position in those three cities, militarizing the hitherto civilian cast of the Japanese presence there and confirming for all practical purposes the end of Japan's role as a treaty port power and its emergence as would-be conqueror of China.

CHAPTER 7

Training Young China Hands:
Tōa Dōbun Shoin and Its Precursors, 1886–1945

Douglas R. Reynolds

In the forty-five years following the creation of Tōa Dōbun Shoin [East Asia Common Culture Academy] in 1900, China experienced truly monumental changes: the Boxer Uprising and Russia's advance into Manchuria, the Russo-Japanese War and Japan's advance into Manchuria, the demise of the Ch'ing dynasty and the establishment of the Chinese Republic, the warlord struggles and reunification under the Kuomintang, the rise of the Chinese Communist Party and the Kuomintang-Communist struggle, and the fifteen-year war between China and Japan that commenced with the Manchurian incident. Over the course of these years, Dōbun Shoin was burned down twice on account of the fighting and had to move its campus no less than six times. One cannot avoid the feeling that its very survival up to Japan's defeat of 1945 was a miracle. This survival is attributable to the spirit of the school, to the commitment of its different heads, and also to the policy of absolute nonintervention in Sino-Japanese political questions held fast to by Tōa Dōbun Shoin's parent organization, Tōa Dōbunkai. A school like this probably cannot be created a second time.[1]

For China, the years from 1900 to 1945 were the worst of times, some of the most turbulent in its long history. For students at Tōa Dōbun Shoin in Shanghai, judging by their fond memories and recollections, they were the best of times. This chapter looks only incidentally at the good times of the students; its main interest lies in their alma mater—Japan's "largest cultural facility outside of Japan and its colonies," and "by far" its oldest external institution of higher learning.[2] Its particular con-

---

[1] Koyūkai, Daigakushi Hensan Iinkai, comp., *Tōa Dōbun Shoin Daigaku shi—sōritsu hachijū shūnen kinenshi* (History of Tōa Dōbun Shoin University; eightieth anniversary commemorative volume) (Tokyo: Koyūkai, 1982), pp. 73–74. Hereafter, *TDSDS* (1982), to distinguish it from *TDSDS* (1955), a study of the same title also compiled by Koyūkai, the Tokyo-based alumni association of Tōa Dōbun Shoin. See below, note 6.

[2] Ibid., p. 69; and Takeuchi Yoshimi, "Tōa Dōbunkai to Tōa Dōbun Shoin" (Tōa Dōbunki and Tōa Dōbun Shoin), in Takeuchi Yoshimi, *Nippon to Ajia: Takeuchi Yoshimi hyō-*

cern is threefold: the background of Tōa Dōbun Shoin (how it was founded, why it was founded, and by whom); its program and purpose; and its students and their careers. Running through all of these, and serving as a common thematic thread, is the question of the relationship of each to the subject of Japanese imperialism in China. So important is the question of Japanese imperialism to the development of Tōa Dōbun Shoin that this entire chapter is framed around it—before imperialism (to 1894), transition to imperialism (1895–1914), accelerating imperialism (1915–1931), and high imperialism (1932–1945)—each a fifteen- to twenty-year block of time.

To label a country "imperialistic" requires that that country exhibit both intention and capacity to move against another. The will to penetrate and exploit must be accompanied by the capacity to carry out that intention. Without capacity, intention cannot be translated into action. Japan lacked real capacity until relatively late, about the time of the Russo-Japanese War of 1904–1905.[3] An organized plan of action is not required to warrant this label. The acid test lies in results, specifically, a substantial degree of effective control by the outside power over the target country's economy, government, military, or even education and culture. That control, though involving a foreign land and its people, is exercised with primary reference to home-country interests.

Japan penetrating the huge American market in the late 1980s and investing heavily in the U.S. economy is not labeled "imperialistic" both because it is largely welcomed and because its end result is not domination of the U.S. economy and politics from Japan. But a major Japanese (or American or Soviet) presence in a weak economy can quickly lead to a dominating or controlling position in that country's life. My own assessment of Japanese intentions, capacity, and impact with respect to China in 1886–1945 is implicit in my choice of the terms "before imperialism," "transition to imperialism," "accelerating imperialism," and "high imperialism."

---

ronshū daisankan (Japan and Asia: Collected studies of Takeuchi Yoshimi), vol. 3 (Tokyo: Chikuma Shobō, 1966), p. 375, respectively. Takeuchi is comparing Tōa Dōbun Shoin to Japanese institutions of higher learning in Taiwan, Korea, and Manchuria.

[3] Yoda Yoshiie, Senzen no Nihon to Chūgoku (Japan and China before the war) (Tokyo: Sanseidō, 1976), argues convincingly that Japan lacked both the organization and the capital for sustained expansion into China until after 1900. See also Peter Duus, "Economic Aspects of Meiji Imperialism," Social and Economic Research on Modern Japan: Occasional papers no. 7 (Berlin: East Asian Institute, Free University of Berlin, 1980). For an overview of Japanese opinion on the origins, timing, and character of Japanese imperialism and Japan's colonial experience, see Ramon H. Myers, "Post-World War II Japanese Historiography of Japan's Formal Colonial Empire," in Ramon H. Myers and Mark R. Peattie, eds., The Japanese Colonial Empire, 1895–1945 (Princeton: Princeton University Press, 1984), pp. 455–477.

BEFORE IMPERIALISM: PRECURSORS OF TŌA DŌBUN SHOIN

One year before Japan's Meiji Restoration of 1868, Kishida Ginkō (1833–1905), a spiritual founding father of Tōa Dōbun Shoin, returned to Japan from a miserable eight-month business trip to "that damn country" (*baka na kuni*), China. Shanghai, where he had been, was dirty, its government incompetent, and its people devious and deficient in basic human relationships, reports Kishida's diary of the trip.[4] Yet these feelings of repulsion were not allowed to blind Kishida to a good opportunity. Within a year, he was back. He came this time not only to buy, but to sell. He bought a steamship with which he inaugurated Japan's first regular passenger run between Yokohama and Edo (Tokyo). And he sold *seikisui* (spirit-pot waters), a medicated eyewash that later became the cornerstone of a successful drug and bookstore business in Tokyo and China. His sales of *seikisui* in 1868 are said to have been modern Japan's first direct private sales to China.[5]

Back in Yokohama, after March 1868, the hustle and bustle of events surrounding the Meiji transformation inspired him to submit a memorandum on international trade to the new government:

> Lately, everyone has been advocating a policy of *fukoku-kyōhei* [enrich the country, strengthen the military], but most of what they call for goes way overboard, and is impractical. Of ways to enrich the country, agriculture and trade are most important. Of the two, our agriculture was perfected long ago. We have no set methods for trade, however, which Western countries have perfected. Establishing set methods will not be easy, but we can move ahead gradually until our trade is no less inferior to that of Britain, France, and the United States. There is a spot convenient to Japan—China—which is a treasure chest for the Europeans. For Japan to go into trade with Europe and America while neglecting our best money-maker, China, is against all common sense. Our products are, moreover, what the Chinese like best: ginseng, lacquerware, copper, tin, lead, ceramic ware, dried beche-de-mer, sea tangle, dried fish, etc. The Chinese love all these goods; and we produce great quantities of them. Put them on a steamship for Shanghai, and we could make a fortune.[6]

[4] Kishida Ginkō, *Buson nikki* (Woosung diary), in *Shakai oyobi kokka* (Society and state) (Tokyo: Ikkyōsha, n.d.). Excerpts appear in Tōa Dōbunkai, comp., *Tai-Shi kaikoroku* (Memoirs concerning China) vol. 2 (Tokyo: Hara Shobō, 1936, 1968), pp. 9–12.

[5] Etō Shinkichi, "Chūgoku kakumei to Nihonjin, Kishida Ginkō no baai" (Japanese and the Chinese revolution: The case of Kishida Ginkō), in *Nihon no shakai bunkashi* (A social cultural history of Japan), vol. 7 (Tokyo: Kōdansha, 1974), p. 258.

[6] The date of this memorandum was May 1868, according to Tōa Dōbunkai, comp., *Tai-Shi kaikoroku*, vol. 2, p. 4. A later source gives the year as 1873. Koyūkai, comp., *Tōa Dōbun*

How should this trade be organized? Kishida advises, "It would be best to conduct this trade with China by setting up a company. We could then get people to invest in that company, in strict accord with contractual agreements."[7]

Two elements of this memorandum are particularly noteworthy. First is Kishida's operating premise that it is trade that has made Britain, France, and the United States strong, and that trade can likewise make Japan wealthy and strong. Then, having established that China is Japan's best market, he proposes that a company be established, implicitly under government auspices.

That his proposal for a company went to the government rather than to private interests is indicative of the weak position of private enterprise, in terms of capitalization and organization, at this juncture of Meiji history. What is more surprising is that a full two decades later, Kishida's chief "disciple," Arao Sei, formulated a far broader proposal for a Japan-China Trading Company (Nisshin Bōeki Shōkai) with branch offices all over China, which, because of the still-weak position of Japanese capital, also had to fall back upon the government for support.

Nothing came of Kishida's proposal for an umbrella company. In fact, for many years, few Japanese were directly involved in the China trade. Only seven Japanese are known to have resided in Shanghai in 1870.[8] The following year, when Japan signed a treaty of friendship and commerce with China, no Japanese businesses existed in Shanghai. This contrasted with Britain, which, at the end of 1871, had 221 Shanghai businesses with 1,780 employees. The United States at that same point had 42 businesses with 538 employees, Germany 40 with 487 employees, and France 17 with 225 employees. Over the next sixteen years, Japanese started 41 new businesses in Shanghai. By the end of 1887, 25 of these, with 651 employees, were still in operation. Among the survivors were government-favored companies like the shipping company Mitsubishi Kaisha (1875; merged in 1885 with Kyōdō Unyū Kaisha to form Nippon Yūsen Kaisha) and Mitsui Bussan.[9]

Kishida Ginkō was one of the survivors. He had returned to Shanghai

Shoin Daigaku shi (History of Tōa Dōbun Shoin University) (Tokyo: Koyūkai, 1955), p. 3. Hereafter, *TDSDS* (1955).

[7] Quoted in Tōa Dōbunkai, comp., *Tai-Shi kaikoroku*, vol. 2, p. 1. Translated with reference to Ken'ichiro Hirano, "Arao Sei and the Process of the Establishment of the Tōa Dōbun Kai: An Early Advocacy for the Promotion of Sino-Japanese Trade," paper for Seminar in Modern Japanese History, Harvard University, 1964, pp. 23–24. Hirano's superb study has been invaluable for the nineteenth-century aspects of my current research.

[8] *TDSDS* (1982), p. 12.

[9] Machida Jitsu'ichi, "Shōkyō oyobi iken" (Japan's China trade: What is to be done?), detailed report by the Japanese consul at Hankow, December 1889 (115 pp.), in Japan, Gaikō Shiryōkan, 3.2.1.2, n.p.; and *TDSDS* (1982), p. 12.

in 1878 on his third China trip, to open a branch of his successful Ginza drugstore, Rakuzendō.[10] Survival for him was the result of hard work and a keen eye for business. For example, in Shanghai he began to publish "sleeve books" (*hsiu-chen pen*) or pocket editions of the Chinese classics that candidates for the demanding civil service examinations could sneak into their examination halls. These sold like hotcakes, over 150,000 copies a year, and launched Kishida on his publishing and bookstore business, and through that on to friendship with Chinese scholars.[11] Kishida was further sustained by a sense of mission: he saw his China involvements as part of his patriotic duty to open the China market up to Japanese goods.[12] His business success provided him with the means not only to open additional Rakuzendō branches in Foochow (November 1884), Hankow (December 1884), and Changsha (1887), but also to accommodate and feed Japanese students and travelers in Shanghai—as many as fifty to seventy at a time.[13] Among those hosted were adventurers and spies. His encouragement and support of these earned him his reputation as "the father of the *tairiku rōnin* [continental adventurers]" of prewar Japan.[14]

If Kishida can be called "father of the *tairiku rōnin*," then his firstborn— Japan's first *Shina rōnin* (China adventurer)[15]—is incontestably Arao Sei (1858–1896). Arao, younger than Kishida by more than a generation, arrived at views strikingly like his by an entirely different route. While

[10] Tōa Dōbunkai, comp., *Tai-Shi kaikoroku*, vol. 2, p. 4. This trip may only have been exploratory. Machida Jitsu'ichi's generally reliable 1889 report, cited in the previous note, gives the founding date of the Shanghai store as April 1880.

[11] Ibid., pp. 6, 8.

[12] Ibid., pp. 5, 8.

[13] Machida, "Shōkyō oyobi iken," n.p.; and Tōa Dōbunkai, comp., *Zoku tai-Shi kaikoroku* (A record looking back on China, supplement), vol. 2 (Tokyo: Hara Shobō, 1941– 1942, 1973), pp. 428–430.

[14] Etō, "Chūgoku kakumei," p. 216. This essay by Professor Etō is a sensitive, well-crafted portrait of the private Kishida. Kishida's formative influence on Japan's modern relationship with China was so well recognized in the 1930s that it secured him the first twelve pages of the 1,520-page biographical collection, Tōa Dōbunkai, comp., *Tai-Shi kaikoroku*, vol. 2, pp. 1–12. It was the name of Kishida, moreover, that emerged at the head of a list in the early 1940s, in answer to the question, "Who is Japan's outstanding pioneer of modern Sino-Japanese relations?" Those polled were leading Japanese China experts; the results were published in 1943. Cited in Etō, "Chūgoku kakumei," p. 214. See also Douglas R. Reynolds, "Before Imperialism: Kishida Ginkō Pioneers the China Market for Japan," *Proceedings and Papers of the Georgia Association of Historians 1984*, 5 (1985): 114–120.

[15] So identified by the important historian Tōyama Shigeki, in "Jiyū minken undō to tairiku mondai" (The People's Rights Movement and the Continental Question), in *Sekai* 54 (June 1950): p. 30. Cited in Hirano, "Arao Sei," p. 46. One cautionary note: The term *Shina rōnin* implies an unattached adventurer or freelancer. Arao, though independent after 1889, was not unconnected. It could be argued that he therefore does not qualify for this now pejorative label.

Kishida was setting up his Shanghai Rakuzendō in 1878, Arao was just beginning his military education at the Kyōdōdan (School for Noncommissioned Officers). From 1880 to 1882, he was part of the fifth class at Japan's elite Shikan Gakkō or Military Academy. After several years as a second lieutenant with the 13th Infantry Regiment in Kumamoto, he returned to Tokyo in 1885 to join the China Section of the army's General Staff.[16]

Recalling his years with the General Staff in a speech delivered in 1889, Arao stated that, while there, he had carefully calculated the cost of Japan's defense needs over the next ten years. All of Japan's resources, imperial and nonimperial combined, could not begin to cover the minimum thirty million yen annual expenditure needed. "Then it hit me," he said, "that the best way for Japan to build up her strength to deal with foreign powers and to expand her national prestige was to promote the development of commerce and industry, to bring in foreign capital." Japan was too weak, he had felt, to take the profits of her trade with the West out of Western hands; but China was closer to Japan, resembled her in many ways, and therefore seemed a likelier source of profits.[17]

The next year, in 1886, the General Staff sent Arao to China to gather intelligence. One of his first contacts there was Kishida Ginkō. Kishida immediately set him up at his Rakuzendō branch in Hankow. For the next three years, Hankow—"the Osaka of China"—served as Arao's "bandit lair" (*liang-shan po*, from the Ming novel *Shu-hu chuan*), where unattached Japanese gravitated. Arao gave these drifters a place and a purpose. He organized the core group of more than ten into inner and outer units, then ranked these further with accompanying instructions.[18] From Hankow, these associates fanned out in every direction, often disguised as Chinese, wearing queues and Chinese dress, carrying medicines for sale to help finance their expenses.[19] One opened a Rakuzendō branch store in Changsha in 1887, several were sent to the Sino-Russian border to inves-

[16] Hirano, "Arao Sei," pp. 19–20; Inoue Masaji, *Kyojin Arao Sei den* (Biography of a giant, Arao Sei) (Tokyo: Sakuma Shobō), pp. 1–18; Paul Duncan Scott, "Arao Sei and the Formation of Japan's Continental Policy," Ph.D. dissertation, University of Virginia, 1985, pp. 27–35.

[17] Inoue, "Arao Sei," pp. 38–39; Hirano, "Arao Sei," p. 17.

[18] Inoue, "Arao Sei," pp. 40, 13–28; Scott, "Arao Sei," pp. 43–57.

[19] Judging by later reports, spying under the guise of peddling may have become commonplace for the Japanese military in China. U.S. Naval Attaché in Peking Lieutenant Commander I. V. Gillis reported in 1918 that "only the other day I learned that no less than nineteen Japanese officers had been detected by the Chinese authorities travelling throughout the far distant province of Kansu as medicine vendors, pill peddlers, and the like, and how many others were there and not detected is not stated." "Report of Naval Attaché [1918]," in *U.S. Military Intelligence Reports, China 1911–1941* (Frederick, Md.: University Publications of America, n.d.), microfilm, reel 13, pp. 0862–0864.

tigate Russian plans for expanding the Trans-Siberian Railway, and three went into Szechwan province to explore its possibilities as a future military base of operations. Munakata Kotarō (1864–1923), drawn to China from his native Kumamoto by the Sino-French War in 1884, was for more than thirty years (1890–1923) on retainer as a China-based spy for the Japanese navy, during which time he was publisher (in 1896) of the first Japanese-owned Chinese-language newspaper in China, a founding member of Tōa Dōbunkai (in 1898), and was, before his death, founder of Tōhō Tsūshinsha (Oriental News Agency). He was sent by Arao to Peking, where he opened a small shop as a front for "political espionage" on China's four northern provinces.[20]

Just before going to China in 1886, Arao had been queried by a superior officer about his strange but persistent interest in China. (Recall that the road to advancement within the Japanese military, as in other fields during the 1870s and 1880s, was Western-oriented training, not Asian.) "What do you plan to do in China?" this officer had asked. Arao replied, "I will go to China and take it over. Having taken it over, I will give it a decent administration and, through that, try to revive Asia."[21]

We need not put much stock in the youthful bravado of this answer. Contact with the real China, and knowledge of Western reaction to any such efforts, curbed reckless thoughts in this direction. A surer guide to the mature Arao is his lengthy summary report to the General Staff, dated May 10, 1889, tempered by three years in the field. That report concurs with General Staff opinion that Japanese strategic planning requires more intelligence information about China. But it argues that a war with China is not in Japan's interest, and that Japan should seek to revive China and the rest of Asia economically, as a counter to Western penetration.[22]

As a concrete measure, Arao's report proposed the creation of a Japan-China Trading Company centered in Shanghai, with numerous branches throughout China. It advanced three reasons in support of this proposal. First, such a network would avoid arousing Chinese or foreign suspicions as to Japan's intentions and at the same time provide many Japanese merchants with a China trade experience; second, espionage work through

[20] Inoue, "Arao Sei," pp. 29–35; *TDSDS* (1982), pp. 359–362. On Munakata's spying activities for the navy, see Ichiko Chūzō, "Kaisetsu" (Explanatory Note), in Kamiya Masao comp., *Munakata Kotarō bunsho* (The writings of Munakata Kotarō: Secret reports on modern China) (Tokyo: Hara Shobō, 1975), pp. 721–722. For a photograph of Arao and six of his Hankow associates, including Munakata in Chinese queue and dress, see *TDSDS* (1982), p. 17.

[21] Quoted in Kokuryūkai, comp., *Tōa senkaku shishi kiden* (Biographical sketches of pioneer patriots of East Asia), vol. 1 (Tokyo: Hara Shobō, 1933–36, 1966), p. 326; Hirano, "Arao Sei," p. 21.

[22] For the full report, see Tōa Dōbunkai, comp., *Tai-Shi kaikoroku*, vol. 2, pp. 371–396. For an able analysis, see Scott, "Arao Sei," pp. 61–73.

such a network would be largely self-supporting; and third, an organized network would increase Japan's trade with China and thereby assist to "recover our commercial rights [*shōken o kaifuku*]" from Western and Chinese hands. The use of shop fronts as instruments of espionage was further recommended by their successful employment in China by Russia.[23]

After submitting this report, Arao resigned from the military to devote himself completely to planning and promoting his trading company and its auxiliary, Nisshin Bōeki Kenkyūjo (Japan-China Trade Research Institute). His commitment to personnel training derived from the demonstrated incompetence of Japanese merchants in their trading encounters with China. Why do most Japanese who enter the China market go bankrupt? And why do those entering it get warned automatically to brace themselves for failure? Arao's answer to these questions in a speech at Hakata (Fukuoka) in December 1889 was simply that "Japanese merchants lack the knowledge and skills to compete successfully against Chinese merchants in Japan-China trade."[24]

Arao was not alone either in raising these questions or in his prognosis. Machida Jitsu'ichi (1842–1916), Japanese consul at Hankow, had a remarkably similar opinion. A Kagoshima native who served in the Japanese navy from 1872 to 1877, Machida spent several blocks of time in China between 1873 and 1876. In 1875 he visited Hankow. There, "contrary to conventional wisdom," he discovered a vibrant port city with great profit potential for Japanese traders. Ten years later, when Hankow became the site of a new Japanese consulate in 1885, Machida, who had entered the Foreign Ministry in 1882, was appointed its first consul.[25] Thus, it was at Hankow that the destinies of the army man Arao, the entrepreneur Kishida, and the naval, then foreign service, officer Machida intertwined.

Machida had a passionate and even aggressively nationalistic interest in China trade. His reports to the Foreign Ministry are detailed and may well have influenced Arao.[26] His richly documented 115-page report of December 1888, titled "Shōkyō oyobi iken" (Japan's China trade: What is to be done?), examines almost every facet of Japan's China trade since

---

[23] Tōa Dōbunkai, comp., *Tai-Shi kaikoroku*, vol. 2, p. 495.

[24] Quoted in Inoue, "Arao Sei," pp. 39–40, 43.

[25] Tōa Dōbunkai, comp., *Tai-Shi kaikoroku*, vol. 2, pp. 96–97; and Japan, Gaimushō, *Nihon gaikō bunsho* (Documents on Japanese foreign policy), vol. 22 (Tokyo, 1889), p. 594.

[26] After an initial period of warm cooperation, Machida and Arao had a falling out in late 1888 or early 1889. Thereafter, sources that say much about Arao are virtually silent about Machida. Arao's biographer Inoue Masaji, for example, mentions Machida only in connection with obtaining goods from Japan to be sold on consignment through the Hankow Rakuzendō, in Inoue, "Arao Sei," pp. 30–31. Other sources fail to mention Machida at all.

their treaty of friendship and commerce in 1871.[27] It points out that hustling Chinese merchants outmaneuvered Japanese traders in every respect, including the export of new Japanese products and imitation goods. Japanese merchants were severely handicapped by a shortage of capital, combined with the difficulty of obtaining foreign exchange for export purposes, and further by the absence of Japanese shops in China to consign goods for sale.[28] More than that, qualified Japanese to head up and assist in running Japanese shops in China were virtually nonexistent.

"If we were to liken this to war," declared Machida in a metaphor out of his samurai and navy past, "it is not too much to say that it is as if our unsupported troops in enemy territory were stymied for want of supplies and ammunition, whereas enemy troops closing in on our fortified cities [jōka] and well supplied with arms and food were pressing the attack and causing hardships for our people. To turn back the enemy troops we must extend the necessary means to our own people." The "necessary means" was a million-yen fund "to cover the cost of test marketing, studying the actual market situation and training businessmen, and the making of well-trained people." Earlier, in March 1888, Machida had submitted a report that included a five-year plan for a Test Marketing Office (Shibaisho) based at Hankow. That plan was constructed around the million-yen fund. The source of that money was to be "responsible persons, namely, public-minded individuals and persons with surplus capital in amounts ranging from one to two hundred thousand yen [to be loaned to new Japanese enterprises in China] interest-free for a five-year period."[29]

By March 1899, one year later, this test marketing idea, using the same million-yen fund, had been absorbed into Arao Sei's ambitious plan for a Japan-China Trading Company.[30] That is the plan attached to Arao's April 1889 General Staff report, already discussed. As in Machida's earlier proposals, the one million yen were to be raised from among public-spirited businessmen.

So far as is known, Arao obtained no substantial support from business sources. His support came from government leaders. Among those, reportedly, were Prime Minister Kuroda Kiyotaka, Minister of Finance Matsukata Masayoshi, and Minister of Agriculture and Commerce Iwa-

---

[27] Excerpts also appear in Gaimushō, *Nihon gaikō bunsho*, vol. 22 (1889), pp. 598–602.

[28] On this point specifically, in March 1888, Machida had reported in dismay that since his arrival at Hankow in 1885, not one Japanese business had opened there. See Gaimushō, *Nihon gaikō bunsho*, vol. 22, p. 594.

[29] Ibid., pp. 594, 599–601.

[30] Arao is identified as the originator of this plan in the March 1888 report of Acting Consul Itō Yutoku at Hankow to Foreign Minister Ōkuma Shigenobu. Itō praises Arao for his success at military intelligence work, for his management of the Hankow Rakuzendō, and for his thorough knowledge of Chinese trade matters. Ibid., pp. 590–591.

mura Michitoshi. There was talk of an Agriculture and Commerce Ministry grant of 50,000 yen, with a further annual subsidy of 30,000 yen, and procedures were begun to transfer to Arao a large tract of government forest land in Hokkaido, valued at 100,000 yen. With financing secured, Arao set off on a speaking tour to promote China trade and to recruit students for his Nisshin Bōeki Kenkyūjo. More than 300 persons applied for admission, among them former schoolteachers, current high school students (the aspiring elite of Japanese society), and ambitious individuals seeking new avenues for advancement. Applicants were tested in math and English, given physicals, and interviewed, and 150 were accepted for admission.[31]

Then came a crushing blow. The Kuroda cabinet fell, ministry personnel were reshuffled, and the subsidies and promised lands were withdrawn. Alternative sources of funding, private or otherwise, failed to materialize. The General Staff, which had provided the testing and interview sites for institute applicants, came to Arao's rescue. Vice-Chief of Staff Kawakami Sōroku (1848–1899), chief architect of army intelligence operations on the continent—and soon to be hailed "military mastermind of the Sino-Japanese War"[32]—personally approached the government on behalf of his former subordinate and obtained a forty thousand yen subsidy from the Diet. By itself, this amount was insufficient. In the end, it had to be supplemented by personal donations and loans, most regularly from Kawakami himself.[33] With the help of emergency funds, the Nisshin Bōeki Kenkyūjo was inaugurated in Shanghai on September 20, 1890. Its 150 students began their three years of academic training with a curriculum heavily weighted toward language study: twelve hours of Chinese and six hours of English per week, out of forty hours of scheduled classroom instruction. Other classes included commercial geography (shōgyō chiri), Chinese commercial history, accounting, bookkeeping and writing skills, a practicum in Chinese business methods, physical education, and, in the second semester, economics and law.[34] A mandatory fourth year

[31] Hirano, "Arao Sei," pp. 14–16, 29–30; Kokuryūkai, comp., Tōa senkaku shishi, vol. 1, pp. 396–402.

[32] Roger B. Hackett, Yamagata Aritomo in the Rise of Modern Japan, 1838–1922 (Cambridge: Harvard University Press, 1971), p. 162.

[33] Kawakami's biographer, Tokutomi Sohō, suggests that Kawakami's primary motivation in supporting Arao was preparedness for future operations on the continent. Cited in Hirano, "Arao Sei," p. 34. Others who provided direct backing, financial or otherwise, were Vice-Minister of War Katsura Tarō, Chief of General Staff Prince Arisugawa Taruhito, and Tōyama Mitsuru. Ibid., pp. 31–34; and Kokuryūkai, comp., Tōa senkaku shishi, vol. 1, pp. 401–403.

[34] The institute's first-year curriculum chart is reproduced in TDSDS (1982), p. 31. That chart is translated into English and discussed in Douglas R. Reynolds, "Chinese Area Studies in Prewar China: Japan's Tōa Dōbun Shoin in Shanghai, 1900–1945," Journal of Asian

required students to investigate trade conditions and opportunities at major Chinese ports and trading cities. The rationale behind this final year of field work had been articulated by Arao in 1889 at Hakata in a recruiting speech: "Trade is exactly like war," he had declared. "Just as good fighting men cannot be produced by classroom training without field maneuvers, good businessmen require more than textbook learning."[35]

Within two months of the institute's inauguration, however, it was in dire financial straits. Ninety students had suffered heat prostration over the summer, Chinese food had taken its toll, and a student rebellion was brewing. Substantial injections of new funds were needed. In November Arao returned to Japan, where, among other things, he sought out bank presidents, presidents of companies, and business school principals for their support. All showed an interest in eventually hiring a graduate or two, but none offered real assistance with funding. Then, on December 28, came the news that a renewed government subsidy was out of the question. Japan's first Imperial Diet was in session, and the government was under intense pressure from political parties to cut the budget and reduce the land tax. For the time being, new subsidy bills were not being considered.[36] The democratization of Japanese politics thus very nearly cost Nisshin Bōeki Kenkyūjo its life. Only Arao's grim determination prevented it from going the way of Tōyō Gakkan, a Japanese-sponsored Chinese language institute in Shanghai attended by Munakata Kotarō and at least three other Arao associates, which, for financial reasons, closed within one year of its opening in 1884.[37]

For some time, the institute survived by pawning its belongings and by taking advantage of China's three-month system of settling accounts. A steady stream of emergency funding requests flowed from Arao to Japan. Vice-Chief of Staff Kawakami sent money more than once. At one point, he is even said to have pawned his house for four thousand yen for Arao. He further sent Kamio Mitsuomi, an experienced China hand from the General Staff, to bail out and reorganize the institute between April and June 1891. On the other hand, Kawakami, more than any other, urged

---

Studies 45, 5 (November 1986). The most complete history of the institute to date, and the source of most later information such as the curriculum chart, remains the 1908 study of Matsuoka Yukikazu and Yamaguchi Noboru, comps., *Nisshin Bōeki Kenkyūjo, Tōa Dōbun Shoin enkaku shi* (A history of Nisshin Bōeki Kenkyūjo and Tōa Dōbun Shoin) (Shanghai: Tōa Dōbun Shoin, 1908), pp. 1–135. For convenience, when this material from Matsuoka and Yamaguchi is duplicated in *TDSDS* (1982), I cite only the latter source.

[35] Quoted in Inoue, "Arao Sei," p. 44.

[36] Kokuryūkai, comp., *Tōa senkaku shishi*, vol. 1, pp. 403–409; Hirano, "Arao Sei," pp. 31–32.

[37] Ōmori Chikako, "Tōa Dōbunkai to Tōa Dōbun Shoin: Sono seiritsu jijō, seikaku, oyobi katsudō" (Tōa Dōbunkai and Tōa Dōbun Shoin: Their founding circumstances, character, and activities), *Ajia keizai* 19, 6 (June 1978): 84.

Arao to give up his costly trading company ideas and confine himself to his institute.[38] Financial exigencies, in fact, forced Arao's hand. He set aside the company plan and postponed his dream of putting Japan on the road to becoming "the Great Britain of the Orient" by 1897.[39]

In June 1893, after three years of training, eighty-nine students graduated from Nisshin Bōeki Kenkyūjo. This was a major triumph, both for Arao Sei and for Japan—for this was Japan's very first research and training institute on China.[40] It was a personal triumph for Vice-Chief of Staff Kawakami, moreover, because more than seventy of the institute's graduates served as army interpreters and spies during the war with China a year later. And its success is directly relevant to the subject of Tōa Dōbun Shoin, because the institute served as the direct model and inspiration of the latter, Japan's second research and training institution on China. Funds did not allow for extensive student field work, later so central to Tōa Dōbun Shoin. But about forty institute graduates spent a fourth year at the school's Shanghai Trade Exhibition Hall (Nisshin Shōhin Chinretsujo), a shop financed by Okazaki Eijirō (1852–1931), a wealthy Osaka merchant and the sole known example of a major commitment to Arao from a private business source.[41]

TRANSITION TO IMPERIALISM: TŌA DŌBUN SHOIN'S FIRST FIFTEEN YEARS

It was a rare Japanese who raised doubts about Japan's popular war with China in 1894–1895.[42] Arao Sei was one of those rare Japanese, almost unique for a military man. From his wartime retreat at a Zen temple in Kyoto, where he sat out the war, he wrote several thought pieces about the war and its settlement. In his "Tai-Shin iken" (Advice About China), written in October 1894, less than three months after Japan went to war,

[38] Hirano, "Arao Sei," p. 32; and Tōa Dōbunkai, comp., Tai-Shi kaikoroku, vol. 2, pp. 256–257. For more on Kamio and Kawakami toward the end of the decade, see Richard C. Howard, "Japan's Role in the Reform Program of K'ang Yu-wei," in Jung-pang Lo, ed., K'ang Yu-wei: A Biography and a Symposium (Tucson: University of Arizona Press, 1967), pp. 280–312.

[39] Quoted in Inoue, "Arao Sei," p. 46.

[40] Note the full title of Noma Kiyoshi, "Nisshin Bōeki Kenkyūjo no seikaku to sono gyōseki: Waga kuni no soshikiteki no Chūgoku mondai kenkyū no dai ippo" (The character and achievements of the Japan-China Trade Research Institute: Our country's first step in the organized study of the China question), Rekishi hyōron 167 (July 1964): 68–77. For the names of institute graduates, see Matsuoka and Yamaguchi, comps., Nisshin Bōeki Kenkyūjo, appendix, pp. 9–15, 62; also, Scott, "Arao Sei," pp. 124–125.

[41] Hirano, "Arao Sei," pp. 33, 35, 36, and 40.

[42] Marius Jansen, in search of geniune critics of Japan's imperialist course in the 1890s and early 1900s, found only scattered and ineffective voices. See Marius Jansen, "Japanese Imperialism: Late Meiji Perspectives," in Myers and Peattie, eds., Japanese Colonial Empire, pp. 7–15.

Arao proposed that one component for a just and lasting peace be a treaty of trade and commerce more equitable to China than its current treaties with Western powers.[43] One-sided military victories, however, stirred the Japanese public to demand huge indemnities and territorial acquisitions. This alarmed Arao. In his "Tai-Shin benmō" (Refuting Japan's China logic) of March 1895, he warned prophetically,

> If Japan were to demand the cession of a large piece of Chinese territory, the powers would carry out their greedy designs to carve up the rest. . . . Seizing a province or an island at this time is not at all in Japan's interests. . . . Until such time as the Japanese people embrace the Imperial Benevolence and become convinced of the urgent need to help the Chinese in their time of difficulty, occupation of Chinese territory should not be considered.[44]

Japan did acquire Chinese territory. Ironically, one such territory, Taiwan, took the life of Arao Sei. On October 30, 1896, at the age of thirty-eight, Arao died in Taipei of bubonic plague.

By the time of his death, Arao had a well-developed vision of an East Asia united in cooperation and prosperity against the imperialist West. Trade was to be the bonding agent of that solidarity.[45] It was a strange kind of solidarity, however, constructed entirely around the assumption of Japanese leadership and advantage. Where Japan lacked the advantage—as in trade with China—it must obtain it, as we have seen, even at the price of wresting it out of Chinese hands![46] For all his idealism and

[43] The relevant passage is quoted in Inoue, "Arao Sei," pp. 202–203; *TDSDS* (1982), p. 20; and Hirano, "Arao Sei," p. 48.

[44] Quoted in Inoue, "Arao Sei," pp. 206–207; the present translation follows Bunsō Hashikawa, "Japanese Perspectives on Asia: From Disassociation to Coprosperity," in Akira Iriye, ed., *The Chinese and the Japanese: Essays in Political and Cultural Interactions* (Princeton: Princeton University Press, 1980), pp. 333–334. Viscount Tani Kanjō (1837–1911), a retired army lieutenant general and Japan's first minister of agriculture and commerce, 1885–1887, was another outstanding "military" voice against territorial aggrandizement. As the war neared its end, Tani counseled against exorbitant peace terms at the conference table. In a letter to Prime Minister Itō Hirobumi, he took the position "that any demand whatsoever for territorial cessions might obstruct the reestablishment of cordial Sino-Japanese relations in the future." Foreign Minister Mutsu Munemitsu, who called this a "rather extreme position," was quick to add that Tani expressed this view exclusively in private correspondence, so that it had no public impact whatsoever. Mutsu Munemitsu, *Kenkenroku: A Diplomatic Record of the Sino-Japanese War, 1894–95*, ed. and trans. Gordon Mark Berger (Princeton: Princeton University Press, 1983), p. 334.

[45] For a variety of writings around this theme, see Inoue, "Arao Sei," pp. 137–207. For Arao specifically, see Scott's extensive discussion in "Arao Sei," pp. 127–154, 186–203.

[46] Arao was, it is true, an "Asia firster," a term used by Marius Jansen for Konoe Atsumaro in "Konoe Atsumaro," in Iriye, ed., *Chinese and Japanese*, p. 112. This was as distinct from the vast majority of Japanese, who were Europe firsters. But it is impossible to under-

good intentions, then, Arao and his version of Japanese-dominated "co-operation" suffered the same flaws as later versions of a new Asian order under Japanese tutelage: the lack of meaningful restraints on Japanese ambition for leadership and dominance, blindness to the national sensibilities and interests of fellow Asians, and consignment of other Asian nations to the status of junior partners, with Japan in the "controlling position."[47]

At Nisshin Bōeki Kenkyūjo, Arao's right-hand man had been Nezu Hajime (1860–1927), deputy director of the institute and Arao's designated "second self."[48] Nezu, a year younger than Arao, had followed much the same career path as Arao: military training at the school for noncommissioned officers, followed by training at Shikan Gakkō one year ahead of Arao. There, in 1879, the two men had met. A close bond formed around their common China interests—Arao's activist curiosity, which created his desire to go to China and later to promote trade, and Nezu's more ideological bent, which led to his serious study of the Confucian classics and to his personal direction, as headmaster of Tōa Dōbun Shoin from 1900 to 1923, of instruction in Confucian ethics (rinri).[49] Nezu, like Arao, was drawn into service with the Army General Staff after training and field experience. Subsequently, at Arao's request, he was seconded by Vice-Chief of Staff Kawakami to Nisshin Bōeki Kenkyūjo from 1890 to 1893.

Nezu's greatest achievement at Nisshin Bōeki Kenkyūjo was an academic one. For over five months in 1891, he secluded himself night and day to compile Arao's rich data from Hankow into the three-volume *Shinkoku tsūshō sōran: Nisshin bōeki hikkei* (Commercial handbook of China: Essentials of Japan-China trade) (Shanghai, 1892). This landmark compilation, the first of its kind, was a veritable encyclopedia of information on Chinese topography, politics, finance, economy, transport, currency, and trade, filled with insights from the actual observation of Chinese commercial organizations, trade practices, and travel conditions. Its subject, though ostensibly trade, was in fact "living China."[50] Apart

---

stand Arao without keeping in mind that behind his Asia-first stance lay a dedicated Japan firster; his commitment to Asia was strictly in service of his Japan priorities.

[47] For Arao's premise of Japan in the controlling position, see Noma, *Nisshin Bōeki*, p. 73. For Scott's concluding assessment, see "Arao Sei," pp. 204–213.

[48] Arao used the term *isshin-dōtai* ("second self" or "alter ego" or, literally, "one-mind one-body") to impress upon students at his Shanghai Institute that, in Arao's absence, Nezu was in full charge. See *TDSDS* (1982), pp. 21, 28, and 249.

[49] Ibid., pp. 25–26, 28, 71–72, 78, 89–90, and 718–726. It was as a devoted teacher of Confucian ethics that Shoin students best remember this grand patriarch of their school.

[50] Ibid., p. 34; John King Fairbank, Masataka Banno, and Sumiko Yamamoto, *Japanese Studies of Modern China: A Bibliographical Guide to Historical and Social-Science Research on the 19th and 20th Centuries* (Cambridge: Harvard University Press, 1955, 1971), p. 176. For the detailed table of contents of Nezu's rare work, see Tōa Bunka Kenkyūjo, comp., *Tōa Dō-*

from its academic value, it engendered in Nezu a deep personal respect for field work that carried over to his quarter-century administration of Tōa Dōbun Shoin.

The school headed and shaped by Nezu Hajime, molder of the "Shoin spirit," was established in 1900 at the initiative of Prince Konoe Atsumaro (1863–1904), head of the House of Peers and the Peers School. Tōa Dōbun Shoin's sponsoring parent organization, Tōa Dōbunkai (East Asia Common Culture Association), had similarly been founded by Prince Konoe in November 1898 in Tokyo. Tōa Dōbunkai grew out of Dōbunkai (Common Culture Association), established by Konoe five months earlier in June.[51] Dōbunkai is an important connecting thread of this study because its original proponents in 1897 were members of the "Arao group" who had lost Arao only the year before. In 1895, this group had formed the Itsubikai (The 1895 Society) in China, around the person of Arao. They approached Konoe, an acquaintance of Arao, as something of a surrogate for their late leader, inspired perhaps by Konoe's views on a Sino-Japanese alliance (*Nisshin dōmei ron*). Shiraiwa Ryūhei (1867–1942), a graduate of Nisshin Bōeki Kenkyūjo, a minor shipping magnate in China, and from 1922 to 1936 board chairman of Tōa Dōbunkai, spearheaded this effort, taking with him three of Arao's outstanding Hankow associates, Ide Saburō (1862–1931), Nakanishi Masaki (1857–1923), and Munakata Kotarō (1864–1923).[52] The times were propitious. Ever since the Triple Intervention of Russia, France, and Germany in 1895, increasing numbers of Japanese like Konoe were taking alarm at Western encroachments upon China, now perceived as a threat to Japan's vital interests in the region. Konoe agreed to head this new organization, brought in his own associates, and named it Dōbunkai after the sentimental notion of China and Japan united as "one culture, one race" (*dōbun-dōshu*). Its stated purpose was the promotion of Sino-Japanese understanding and trade, and Konoe proved to be an energetic and creative head.[53]

---

bunkai kikan shi, shuyō kankōbutsu sōmokuji (General tables of contents from Tōa Dōbunkai serials and major publications) (Tokyo: Kazankai, 1985), pp. 471–486.

[51] For Dōbunkai's full statement of purpose, including to promote understanding and commerce with China, see Sakeda Masatoshi, *Kindai Nihon ni okeru taigaikō undō no kenkyū* (Studies of movements for a hardline foreign policy in early modern Japan [ca. 1888–1905]) (Tokyo: Tōkyō Daigaku Shuppankai, 1978), p. 118, henceforth *KNTK*; and Ōmori, "Tōa Dōbunkai," p. 80. See also Hirano, "Arao Sei," p. 54.

[52] For convenient biographical sketches on each of these four, see Ōmori, "Tōa Dōbunkai," pp. 78–79. The full extent of Shiraiwa's influence upon Konoe's China thinking is suggested in Katō Yūzō, "Tōa jiron" (East Asian review), in Kojima Reiitsu, ed., *Senzen no Chūgoku jironshi kenkyū* (Studies in prewar Japanese journals of opinion on China) (Tokyo: Ajia Keizai Kenkyūjo, 1978), pp. 10, 17–18.

[53] This is apparent from the many entries relating to Tōa Dōbunkai in Konoe's published diary, Konoe Atsumaro Nikki Kankōkai, comp., *Konoe Atsumaro nikki* (Diary of Konoe

Like contemporaries with good government connections, Konoe turned to the government for funding. For him, but particularly for less well-positioned persons in 1898, access was facilitated by the existence from June to November of Japan's first "party cabinet," organized partly by long-time party rivals Ōkuma Shigenobu and Itagaki Taisuke. Before Konoe's approaches to Prime Minister Ōkuma (who was concurrently foreign minister), the subject of government funding for China projects had already been broached with Ōkuma on behalf of the Tōakai (East Asia Association) by Inukai Tsuyoshi (1855–1932), a party activist and close associate of Ōkuma, and a founding member of the Tōakai. That association, founded in the spring of 1897, brought together some of the great names of mid-Meiji journalism (Kuga Katsunan, Miyake Setsurei, Shiga Shigetaka, and Ikebe Yoshitarō), politicians (Inukai Tsuyoshi and Diet members Hiraoka Kōtarō and Etō Shinsaku), and students of China (most notably Inoue Masaji of Tōkyō Senmon Gakkō, later Waseda University). Its purpose, among other things, was to study China's current affairs and publish the findings, with sympathetic leanings toward reformist efforts like those of K'ang Yu-wei and Liang Ch'i-ch'ao—both of whom were brought into its membership ranks after fleeing to Japan for their lives in October 1898.[54]

Ōkuma had been sympathetic to both Inukai and Konoe in their separate approaches. But his government was in no position to fund multiple China groups with not only similar programs but also "thick personal ties" and overlapping memberships.[55] He advised the merger of the Tōakai and Dōbunkai. This was realized on November 2, 1898, their separate names joined in Tōa Dōbunkai.[56] These various requests to Ōkuma spawned a further important development, the provision by the Diet of secret funds to the Foreign Ministry to subsidize foreign affairs undertakings of nongovernmental agencies. Special impetus for this came also from the influential Diet member Hiraoka Kōtarō (1851–1906), a founding member of the Tōakai and, more significantly, first head of the radical Fukuoka Genyōsha in the early 1880s and a cosponsor of Tōyō Gakkan, the short-lived Chinese language school in Shanghai in 1884. Hiraoka had

---

Atsumaro), 5 vols. (Tokyo: Kajima Kenkyūjo Shuppankai, 1968–1969). The published diary spans the years February 1895 to March 1903.

[54] Sakeda, *KNTK*, pp. 110–111; and Hirano, "Arao Sei," pp. 51–52.

[55] Hirano, "Arao Sei," p. 57.

[56] The merger meeting of November 2, 1898, was a stormy affair featuring a heated debate between Tōakai members who advocated aiding China by supporting the radical reforms of K'ang Yu-wei and Liang Ch'i-ch'ao, and those who stressed the need to protect China from Western aggression by upholding the present Chinese government. Konoe Atsumaro, observing that the common ground of these two positions was the desire to preserve China, proposed that Tōa Dōbunkai adopt "the preservation of China" as its first principle.

been instrumental in the union of political parties that cleared the way for the Ōkuma-Itagaki cabinet, and he was involved in creating that cabinet.[57] He was of the view that

> the slump in our foreign relations is due to the persistent shortage of Foreign Ministry funds, and also to the failure of the government to cooperate with nongovernmental initiatives in foreign affairs [*minkan gaikō*]. An increase in the secret funds of the Foreign Ministry, with a portion to assist the foreign involvements of nongovernment activists, could greatly enhance the administration of our foreign affairs.[58]

The Ōkuma-Itagaki cabinet fell before funding could be arranged; but the following year, the thirteenth Diet voted the Foreign Ministry an eighty-thousand-yen secret fund, of which fully one-half, or forty-thousand yen, went to the amalgamated Tōakai and Dōbunkai. For each of the next fourteen years, from 1899 to 1913, Tōa Dōbunkai received a set forty-thousand yen subsidy from Foreign Ministry funds. (See introductory remarks to table 7.3, below.)

This subsidy, and enlarged Foreign Ministry grants thereafter, gave Tōa Dōbunkai a semigovernmental character. During its first two decades, before the Foreign Ministry had its own full complement of China specialists, Tōa Dōbunkai frequently tailored programs and personnel assignments to ministry needs and requests. In fact, throughout its existence up to 1945, Tōa Dōbunkai reported to the Foreign Ministry.[59] As a result, Marius Jansen is on solid ground in calling Tōa Dōbunkai "in some sense a Foreign Ministry front."[60] Published directives like the fol-

---

[57] Ōmori, "Tōa Dōbunkai," pp. 77–78; Hosono Kōji, "Tōa Dōbunkai no taigai ninshiki to bunka kōsaku no kōzu; Ōbei rekkyō to Shinmatsu Minsho Chūgoku no hazama de" (Foreign consciousness in the planning of Tōa Dōbunkai's cultural work; the Western powers and China in the late Ch'ing and early Republican periods), in Abe Hiroshi, ed., *Nitchū kankei to bunka masatsu* (Cultural conflict in Sino-Japanese relations) (Tokyo: Gannandō shoten, 1982), p. 102, henceforth *NKMB*.

[58] Kokuryūkai, comp., *Tōa senkaku shishi*, vol. 1, p. 608; quoted in Hosono, Tōa Dōbunkai, pp. 102–103; paraphrased in Hirano, "Arao Sei," p. 55.

[59] Tōa Dōbunkai reported to the Foreign Ministry on its programs and needs, consulted about its policies, and submitted full financial statements and reports. These reports and communications are now open for public research use at the Gaiko Shiryōkan in Tokyo. About 75 percent of the archive materials relating to Tōa Dōbunkai and its sponsored projects like Tōa Dōbun Shoin are available on microfilm through the U.S. Library of Congress, *Japan, Ministry of Foreign Affairs, 1868–1945, MT series*, microfilmed for the Library of Congress, 1949–1951. (Consistently omitted from microfilming are Tōa Dōbunkai budgets and accounts, and annual reports. Also omitted are the field research reports of Tōa Dōbun Shoin students.) Their availability is the result of early postwar microfilming by the U.S. Library of Congress of seized Japanese Foreign Ministry and other government records.

[60] Jansen, "Konoe," p. 115.

lowing to field staff in 1901 only substantiate such a view: "Whether in reports or communications, items of a secret nature will in the main be transmitted to the Prime Minister and Minister of Foreign Affairs, the Army General Staff, navy Headquarters, and the Army and Navy ministries; all other things will be published in our association bulletin."[61] But a view overemphasizing the governmental and "intelligence" dimension of Tōa Dōbunkai would miss the complex of other factors responsible for its founding and character.

Most simply, Tōa Dōbunkai was the product of a rising foreign consciousness (*taigai ninshiki*) among Japanese—the acute awareness of Western (including Russian) aggression in and around China and its challenge to Japan and to its emerging Asian interests.[62] From this sprang the desire to understand and cooperate with China against a common threat. Japanese expressions of this desire ranged from utilitarian, sometimes crudely self-serving, projects and programs to selfless devotion to a Chinese cause or person. Some of the more altruistic of these hopes were manifested in the four founding principles of Tōa Dōbunkai: (1) to preserve China *Shina hozen*; (2) to encourage the betterment of China *Shina kaizen*; (3) to study China's current affairs and decide upon appropriate activities; and (4) to arouse public opinion.[63]

Idealism and friendship for China were very much at the heart of Konoe Atsumaro's dream of a school in China for both Chinese and Japanese young people. This dream evolved into Tōa Dōbun Shoin, Tōa Dōbunkai's most ambitious, enduring, and expensive undertaking,[64]

[61] *Tōyō* 4 (May 25, 1901), p. 77; quoted in Ōmori, "Tōa Dōbunkai," p. 81.

[62] "Foreign consciousness" in the initial founding and subsequent projects of Tōa Dōbunkai, such as Tōa Dōbun Shoin in Shanghai, is the central theme of Hosono, "Tōa Dōbunkai," pp. 99–158.

[63] Some confusion surrounds Tōa Dōbunkai's founding principles because, within one year of its founding, "Korea" was incorporated into principles 2 and 3. Korea's inclusion was a requirement for receipt of the Foreign Ministry subsidy—a requirement that vanished with Korea's colonization in 1910. Ōmori, "Tōa Dōbunkai," p. 82. The original four principles of Tōa Dōbunkai, solely concerned with China, appear in the inaugural issue of *Tōa jiron* 1 ([December 13], 1898): 1, 4. These are accurately reproduced in Ōmori, "Tōa Dōbunkai," p. 82, who traces the official inclusion of Korea back to a 1908 publication; in Sakeda, *KNTK*, p. 121; and in Katō, "Tōa jiron," p. 4. Versions incorporating Korea become so standard after 1908 as to even slip into *TDSDS* (1982), p. 48.

Shina hozen refers to the preservation of China from partitioning by the West. Inspired by the same concerns as the American Open Door, the concept lacked the overwhelming commercial overtones of the Open Door. For an informed discussion of the fine points of *Shina hozen* and *Shina kaizen*, see Katō, "Tōa jiron," pp. 19–20.

[64] For the years 1924 to 1929, Tōa Dōbun Shoin absorbed 60 to 70 percent of the Foreign Ministry funds received by Tōa Dōbunkai. This percentage is calculated from charts in *TDSDS* (1982), p. 61, and Ōmori, "Tōa Dōbunkai," p. 89. For its share of Tōa Dōbunkai funds in the initial years up to 1903, see *TDSDS* (1982), p. 710.

which, as mentioned at the opening of this chapter, developed into Japan's largest overseas cultural facility outside of Japan and its colonies. But, from the very outset, problems of realpolitik intervened to rob the dream of its idealism. On the China side of things, in 1898 China was racked by the Hundred Days' Reform of K'ang Yu-wei and Liang Ch'i-ch'ao, in 1899–1900 by the antiforeign Boxer movement of the North, and by violent uprisings like the Kuang-hsu restorationist plot of T'ang Ts'ai-ch'ang of August 1900 in and around Hankow, and the Waichow uprising of Sun Yat-sen in October 1900. Japan, on the other hand, was moving in a direction of tighter statist controls and conservative foreign policies as the fruits and burdens of great power began to accumulate.

On his exploratory mission to China in October 1899, Prince Konoe encountered sharply conflicting attitudes.[65] Leading the list of subjects Konoe wanted to discuss in China was his new organization and its educational and cultural projects,[66] particularly a China school. At Nanking, Konoe met with the influential Governor-General Liu K'un-yi (1830–1902), whose jurisdiction included Shanghai, and at Hankow with the even more powerful Governor-General Chang Chih-tung (1837–1909). Governor-General Chang, who had earlier entrusted the education of a favorite grandson to Konoe, was preoccupied and upset with Japan's harboring the "traitors" K'ang Yu-wei and Liang Ch'i-ch'ao. He took this opportunity to lecture Prince Konoe about the evils of radicals and revolutionaries. The tirade over, Konoe left, "very disappointed."[67] Governor-General Liu, on the other hand, extended Konoe a warm welcome.

[65] While in China, Konoe traveled in the company of Munakata Kotarō, the former colleague of Arao Sei at Hankow, a staff member of his Shanghai Institute, and later a student superintendent at Tōa Dōbun Shoin. From 1896 to 1900, Munakata was based at Hankow as the publisher of the Chinese-language newspaper *Han-pao*, subsidized by Tōa Dōbunkai. *TDSDS* (1982), pp. 361–362; Huang Fu-ch'ing, *Chin-tai Jih-pen tsai Hua wen-hua chi she-hui shih-yeh chih yen-chiu* (Japanese social and cultural enterprises in China, 1898–1945) (Taipei: Chung-yang Yen-chiu-yuan Chin-tai Shih Yen-chiu-so, 1982), p. 257.

[66] These cultural projects included the establishment of Tōa Dōbunkai branches in key cities of China and the founding of subsidized newspapers. Specifics are vividly illustrated in the annual budgets of Tōa Dōbunkai for the years 1899 to 1903, reproduced in *TDSDS* (1982), pp. 50, 710.

[67] Quoted in Jansen, "Konoe," pp. 108, 119–120, from Konoe's diary. Probably unknown to Chang, it was Konoe himself who had raised the money to send K'ang Yu-wei outside of Japan on extended travels, in anticipation of Konoe's trip to China. Ibid., pp. 116–119. Some of Chang's venom at the meeting may have been intended for Munakata Kotarō, whose Chinese-language *Han-pao* took a sympathetic editorial view of the K'ang-Liang reform movement. See Huang, *Chin-tai Jih-pen*, pp. 290–294. Also in the company of Konoe on this trip was Ōuchi Chōzō, principal of Tōa Dōbun Shoin from 1931 to 1940. Ōuchi reports a far more positive and warm reception from Chang Chih-tung, leading to Chang's dispatch of China's first official group of students to Japan. See Ōuchi Chōzō, "Konoe Kazan kō to Tōa Dōbun Shoin" (Prince Konoe and Tōa Dōbun Shoin), *Shina* 25, 2 (February 25, 1934): 144.

He invited Konoe to establish his school in Nanking, where, just seven months later, in May 1900, it was inaugurated under the name Nankin Dōbun Shoin (Nan-ching T'ung-wen Shu-yuan, or Nanking Common Culture Academy).[68]

Back in Japan, Konoe had entrusted the task of drawing up the final plans for Nankin Dōbun Shoin to Tōa Dōbunkai member and secretary-general Major General (ret.) Satō Tadashi (1849–1920), nicknamed "The One-Legged General" on account of an injury from the recent war with China. Satō became so caught up in this enterprise that he asked to be appointed school head. Aspects of his plan alarmed the Japanese military, however. For example, the training of Chinese students had been an assumed part of Konoe's thinking about this school. In a recruiting circular of December 1899, sent to prefectural governors and assembly heads in Japan, Konoe explained,

> The instruction of Chinese students, centered around the Japanese language, will instill scientific thinking in them, and arouse a sense of nationhood [kokkateki kannen]. They will live in dormitories, just like our Japanese students. It is hoped that by bringing Japanese and Chinese students together, close friendships and prolonged mutual help and mutual support will serve greatly to expedite our future dealings.[69]

The problem was that Satō's master plan seemed to be giving away too much. For one thing, it included physical training (taisō) for Chinese students—"to arouse a martial spirit, to nurture a patriotic mettle, and to eradicate effete habits."[70] The Japanese Army General Staff was not pleased. Nor was Army Minister Katsura Tarō, soon to assume the post of prime minister (1901–1906) and a man whose military guarantee was needed.[71] On March 1, 1900, a representative of Konoe sought to reassure Katsura about the nature of the school and its training program. The representative offered assurances that Tōa Dōbunkai had no political ambitions, in Japan or in China; that its sole interest was educational. Katsura,

---

[68] Shu-yuan was a centuries-old Chinese term for "academy." See, for example, Lu Kuang-huan, "The Shu-yuan Institution Developed by Sung-Ming Neo-Confucian Philosophers," Chinese Culture 9, 3 (1968): 102–115. In Japan, however, shu-yuan was never used to mean an educational center. Its adoption is symbolic, therefore, of Tōa Dōbunkai's eagerness to adapt to Chinese ways, as a means of reaffirming its "one culture, one race" sentiment. Ironically, the Chinese government officially abolished the designation shu-yuan in its educational reforms of 1898–1903.

[69] Quoted in TDSDS (1982), p. 68.

[70] Quoted in ibid., p. 78.

[71] Ten years earlier, in 1890, Katsura as army vice-minister had served as personal guarantor of Arao Sei's Shanghai Institute. See Nihon gaikō bunsho 23 (1890): 398. His prime ministership from 1901 to 1906 was the first of three prime ministerships of this powerful elder statesman.

for his part, reiterated that Chinese students must receive no military training; their education must be confined to academic subjects geared to preparing them for admission into regular Japanese schools in Japan. Katsura further insisted that party politicians like Inukai Tsuyoshi be allowed no part in the education of Chinese students. Finally, he demanded that any notion of sending Major General Satō to Nanking be scrapped.[72]

Katsura's intransigence provoked a minor crisis. Fortunately, in the wings was Nezu Hajime, whom Konoe had met in Kyoto in November 1899 on his return from China. Prior to that meeting, Nezu had had no involvement with Konoe or his China organizations. In fact, for a full four and a half years, from October 1895 to March 1900, Nezu had been in retirement, in Zen seclusion at Arao Sei's temple retreat, Jakuōji, in Kyoto. He had withdrawn there immediately after the war with China, in penance and remorse over the deaths of nine Arao associates (the "Nine Martyrs") recruited by Nezu into wartime service as army interpreters and spies, then captured and executed by Chinese authorities.[73] Nezu's acceptance of Konoe's call to head Nankin Dōbun Shoin cleared the way for military approval.

Nankin Dōbun Shoin opened its doors in May 1900, in quarters arranged by Governor-General Liu. A mere twenty-three Japanese students were enrolled, however.[74] The Chinese division, founded in June, had thirty students in separate quarters. The first-year program of the latter consisted solely of language instruction in Japanese, English, and Chinese literature.[75] The Japanese program was hardly any better, with only two qualified Japanese teachers, no real headmaster (Nezu was absent from Nanking for nearly the entire time), and proper instruction only in Chinese and English. It was, as Kumamoto student Naitō Kumaki recalled in his reminiscences, not much of a program.[76]

By early summer, Nanking and the campus were in turmoil. The

[72] Notes from the meeting are reproduced in *TDSDS* (1982), p. 78.

[73] Ibid., pp. 78, 245–247. For biographical sketches of each of the Nine Martyrs, see Kokuryūkai, comp., *Tōa senkaku shishi*, vol. 1, pp. 426–501.

[74] All twenty-three are identified by name and sponsorship in *TDSDS*, p. 80. The small enrollment was the result of a miserable response to Konoe's circular letter of December 1899 to prefectural governors and assembly heads. The letter invited prefectures to sponsor scholarship students, but only Hiroshima, Kumamoto, and Saga prefectures sent students, five public and five self-financed. Konoe's letter is reproduced in ibid., pp. 79–80. The remaining thirteen students were sponsored by other organizations or persons, including seven by Tōa Dōbunkai itself, two by the Ministry of Agriculture and Commerce, and two by Nozaki Bukichirō, one of the highest taxed members of the House of Peers, who ten years earlier had sponsored several students at Arao Sei's Shanghai Institute (one of whom was Shiraiwa Ryūhei), was a close associate of Konoe, and a founding member of Tōa Dōbunkai. Ibid., p. 80; Hirano, "Arao Sei," pp. 36, 44, 53, 61, and 66.

[75] *TDSDS* (1982), p. 80.

[76] Naitō's reminiscences are quoted in ibid., pp. 81–82; also, pp. 372–373.

Boxer movement had reached its climax in North China in May and June 1900. Rumblings and side-effects were being felt all up and down the Yangtze River. Far to the south in Kwangtung province, Sun Yat-sen for some time had been plotting revolt, aided by radical Japanese sympathizers, several of whom (including Miyazaki Tōten and Hirayama Shū) were Tōa Dōbunkai members.[77] Yamada Yoshimasa (1868–1900), one of the two Japanese teachers at Nankin Dōbun Shoin, had met Sun in Tokyo the previous year and promised to support his revolution. At least three older Shoin students were known to be members of the radical Fukuoka Genyōsha.[78]

The "cautious realist"[79] Konoe, sensing trouble, moved to head it off by sending Tōa Dōbunkai director Tanabe Yasunosuke to Nanking in July. What Tanabe found confirmed Konoe's worst fears. Not only was the campus in turmoil, but there was open talk of support for Sun's revolution by both Yamada and acting headmaster Sasaki. Tanabe cabled Konoe for emergency authority to serve as new acting headmaster. He used this authority, then, to ground all activists for one month.[80]

Governor-General Liu, meanwhile, fearful for the safety of Shoin students and staff, personally urged the Japanese to evacuate Nanking for Shanghai until order could be fully restored.[81] Heeding Liu's advice and

[77] Jansen, "Konoe," p. 117. On his trip to China, Konoe had deliberately kept his distance from these radical activists. The most engaging account of Japanese involvement in Sun's movement is that by Miyazaki himself. See Miyazaki Tōten, *My Thirty-Three Years' Dream: The Autobiography of Miyazaki Toten*, trans. Etō Shinkichi and Marius B. Jansen (Princeton: Princeton University Press, 1902, 1982).

[78] *TDSDS* (1982), pp. 81–82, 362–364.

[79] This is Jansen's term, in Jansen, "Konoe," p. 121.

[80] Sometime after August 1900, Yamada Yoshimasa and a student from his home prefecture of Aomori left Shanghai for South China, where Yamada became "the first Japanese martyr of the Chinese revolution" by his death during Sun's October Waichow (Hui-chou) uprising. Yamada's student is reported to have died some dozen years later, serving Sun's Second Revolution of 1913. Kokuryūkai, comp., *Tōa senkaku shishi*, vol. 1, pp. 669–673; *TDSDS* (1982), pp. 82, 362–364.

[81] It is difficult to know what specific influence the post-1898 Yangtze Valley agitation in support of K'ang Yu-wei and Liang Ch'i-ch'ao might have played in Liu's thinking. The agitation culminated in August 1900 around T'ang Ts'ai-ch'ang, a K'ang-Liang follower returned from Japan to organize revolts in support of the restoration of the Kuang-hsu Emperor. In early August 1900, Chang Chih-tung uncovered T'ang's plot for an uprising over a wide area around Hankow. T'ang and twenty to forty others were subsequently arrested, and fifteen to twenty of them, including T'ang, were executed by order of Chang. Chang correctly suspected Japanese sympathy and complicity in the revolt and protested vehemently to the Japanese consul at Hankow and to Konoe in Tokyo. In October, with the agreement of the Japanese Foreign Ministry, Chang bought out *Han-pao*, the Tōa Dōbunkai Chinese-language daily edited by Munakata Kotarō, which like most other Japanese-run papers had expressed sympathy for the K'ang-Liang movement. Chang's purpose was simply to close the paper down, which he did. For a fascinating inside account of Japanese

leaving the Chinese students behind, the Japanese in late August headed downriver to the safety of Shanghai's International Settlement. Temporary quarters were found near P'ao-ma-ch'ang, the celebrated horsetrack of the International Settlement, with the intention of returning to Nanking.

The school never returned. First, a determined Nezu Hajime sought to salvage and revitalize this school by spearheading a carefully organized, nationwide recruitment drive in Japan. During November and December 1900, five knowledgeable Tōa Dōbunkai members, including Tanabe Yasunosuke and Inoue Masaji, later biographer of Arao Sei, blanketed the country on speaking tours. Their efforts produced fifty-one scholarship and four self-financed students from sixteen prefectures and one *fu*.[82] With such numbers, and after consultation with Governor-General Liu, headmaster Nezu (concurrently secretary-general of Tōa Dōbunkai since August 1900) decided to make Shanghai the school's permanent home.[83] Extensive grounds and buildings were found for the renamed "Tōa Dōbun Shoin" south of Shanghai's French concession near the Kiangnan Ar-

---

involvement with T'ang Ts'ai-ch'ang, from the diary of activist Inoue Masaji, see Kondō Kuniyasu, " 'Inoue Masaji Nikki'—T'ang Ts'ai-ch'ang Tsu-li Chün hōki" ("The Inoue Masaji Diaries"—T'ang Ts'ai-ch'ang's Independence Army Uprising), *Kokka Gakkai zasshi* 98, 1/2 (February 1985): 146–178. See also Paula S. Harrell, "The Years of the Young Radicals: The Chinese Students in Japan, 1900–1905," Ph.D. dissertation, Columbia University, 1970, pp. 14–23; William Ayers, *Chang Chih-tung and Educational Reform in China* (Cambridge: Harvard University Press, 1971), pp. 144, 192; and Huang, *Chin-tai Jih-pen*, pp. 20–21, 257–258, 289, and 290–294.

[82] The five recruiters, and their assigned territory, are named in *TDSDS* (1982), p. 86. The early 1901 printed booklet, "Honkai jigyō gairyaku" (Summary of association activities) (Tokyo: Tōa Dōbunkai, 1901), identified forty confirmed and twenty probable scholarship students from two *fu* and eighteen prefectures. These candidates were quite evenly drawn from among Japan's prefectures, from Akita in northernmost Honshu to Kagoshima in southernmost Kyushu. Gaikō Shiryōkan, 3.10.2.13 (U.S. Library of Congress, microfilm reel 773), pp. 127–128. Hereafter Gaikō Shiryōkan, with appropriate reel and page numbers. Nezu receives credit for the idea to expand by a vigorous nationwide recruitment drive, in ibid., p. 125.

[83] *TDSDS* (1982), pp. 85–86. From his two top positions as head (*inchō*) of Tōa Dōbun Shoin for most of the years from April 1900 to 1923, and as secretary-general (*kanjichō*) of Tōa Dōbunkai from August 1900 to 1914, Nezu Hajime was able to influence substantially, if not shape, the direction of Japan's most important agency devoted to China research and education during much of the first quarter of this century. For Nezu's tenure in these two positions, see the comprehensive charts of all *inchō* in ibid., pp. 74–75, and of Tōa Dōbunkai officers in ibid., p. 59.

Lurking in the background of Nezu's decision, but difficult to gauge, is his view of Chinese society as "perverse and old fashioned." His contemptuous view of China, discussed in Noma, "Nisshin Bōeki Kenkyūjo," p. 76, combined with financial exigencies and Nezu's primary commitment to the training of Japanese to serve their country (discussed below), may help account for his dropping the Chinese student program from Tōa Dōbun Shoin in Shanghai.

senal and well away from the Japanese Consulate-General and the main concentration of resident Japanese. There it remained for the next dozen years, until its accidental destruction by fire during Sun's Second Revolution in July 1913.[84]

In less than one year, a vastly different situation had thus developed for this China school: first, a shift in location away from a hinterland setting to the modern city of Shanghai and, second, a shift in ideals and objectives away from educating Chinese and Japanese students together to a policy of educating them separately—Japanese in China, Chinese in Japan. Toward the latter end, Tōa Dōbunkai established a school for Chinese in Japan, the Tōkyō Dōbun Shoin (1901–1922).[85]

At Tōa Dōbun Shoin, each student received training much like that of postwar area studies programs in America: language (spoken, written, and business Chinese, plus English), interdisciplinary coursework with emphasis on the contemporary, training in library and research methods, and extensive travel and field research training providing first-hand knowledge of China's commercial and geographical terrain.[86] Between 1900 and 1945, over 5,000 Japanese passed through Tōa Dōbun Shoin. Of these, 3,652 graduated. In 1945 alone, more than 1,000 were unable to complete their programs due to Japan's loss of the war and surrender. The numbers of graduates, by year and by program, divide naturally at 1939, the year that Tōa Dōbun Shoin was elevated to university *daigaku* status.[87] (See tables 7.1 and 7.7.)

[84] Tōa Dōbun Shoin's inauguration in Shanghai on May 26, 1901, was attended by several hundred people, including representatives of both governors-general Liu K'un-yi and Chang Chih-tung, by Shanghai industrialist Sheng Hsuan-huai, by Japanese Consul-General Odagiri, and by British dignitaries and others. Ibid., p. 87. For a good map of the campus, see Ibid., p. 95. This period is surveyed, by year, in ibid., pp. 85–109.

[85] Between 1901 and its closure in 1922, Tōkyō Dōbun Shoin, whose primary purpose was to prepare Chinese students for entrance into regular Japanese schools, trained 864 Chinese students. For a summary of this school's founding, its program, and a chart of Chinese graduates by year, see Abe Hiroshi, "Tōa Dōbunkai no Chūgokujin kyōiku jigyō: 1920 nendai zenpanki ni okeru Chūgoku nashonarizumu to no taiō o megutte" (Tōa Dōbunkai's educational programs for Chinese and their responses to Chinese nationalism of the early 1920s), in Abe, ed., *NKBM*, pp. 8–10.

[86] For a systematic examination of the language and area training program at Tōa Dōbun Shoin, including curriculum charts, see Reynolds, "Chinese Area Studies in Prewar China."

[87] Until 1921, Tōa Dōbun Shoin was a three-year institution, equivalent to (but not officially) a specialized school or *senmon gakkō* accepting only middle school graduates. To illustrate, the 1914 printed booklet, "Tōa Dōbunkai jigyō teiyō" (Summary of Tōa Dōbunkai Activities), reads, "Tōa Dōbun Shoin (Equivalent to a Higher Commercial School and a Higher School)," in Gaikō Shiryōkan, 3.10.2.13 dainikan (reel 773), p. 585. In July 1921, an Imperial Ordinance formally elevated Tōa Dōbun Shoin to *senmon gakkō* status, with a four-year program. As will be seen below, Tōa Dōbun Shoin was elevated to university or *daigaku* status within a year and a half of the outbreak of full-scale war with China in July 1937.

TABLE 7.1
Graduates of Tōa Dōbun Shoin, by Class—Classes 1–39 (1901–1943)

Class	Political science division	Business division	Agricultural/ind'l. division (1)	Agricultural/ind'l. division (2)	Chinese student division	Total
Three-year program						
1st (1901–1904)	6	54	—	—	—	60
2nd (1902–1905)	12	64	—	—	—	76
3rd (1903–1906)	13	59	—	—	—	72
4th (1904–1907)	12	48	—	—	—	60
5th (1905–1908)	11	76	—	—	—	87
6th (1906–1909)	6	79	—	—	—	85
7th (1907–1910)	6	71	—	—	—	77
8th (1908–1911)	8	54	—	—	—	62
9th (1909–1912)	9	55	—	—	—	64
10th (1910–1913)	5	71	—	—	—	76
11th (1911–1914)	6	69	—	—	—	75
12th (1912–1915)	4	69	—	—	—	73
13th (1913–1916)	2	72	—	—	—	74
14th (1914–1917)	1	77	1	4	—	83
15th (1915–1918)	2	60	7	3	—	72
16th (1916–1919)	6	73	7	11	—	97
17th (1917–1920)	4	68	5	10	—	87
18th (1918–1921)	3	75	5	5	—	88
19th (1919–1922)	phased out	108	phased out	2	—	110
20th (1920–1923)	—	135	—	phased out	—	135
Subtotal						1,613

Four-year program					
21st (1921–1925)	73	—	—	2	75
22nd (1922–1926)	109	—	—	5	114
23rd (1923–1927)	90	—	—	10	100
24th (1924–1928)	80	—	—	10	90
25th (1925–1929)	75	—	—	5	80
26th (1926–1930)	87	—	—	4	91
27th (1927–1931)	91	—	—	6	97
28th (1928–1932)	74	—	—	2	76
29th (1929–1933)	78	—	—	1	79
30th (1930–1934)	91	—	—	3	94
31st (1931–1935)	64	—	—	phased out	64
32nd (1932–1936)	61	—	—	—	61
33rd (1933–1937)	70	—	—	—	70
34th (1934–1938)	88	—	—	—	88
35th (1935–1939)	103	—	—	—	103
36th (1936–1940)	91	—	—	—	91
37th (1937–1941)	103	—	—	—	103
38th (1938–Dec. 1941)	106	—	—	—	106
College program begins; final year of traditional program					
39th (1939–1942)	24				24
Subtotal	24				1,606
Total					3,219

Source: Adapted from TDSDS (1982), pp. 84–85.

RESEARCH OF THE Tōa Dōbun Shoin

Rather than try to exhaust the subject of Tōa Dōbun Shoin in its initial fifteen years up to 1914, the purposes of this volume would be best served by a selective discussion of topical areas most germane to the subject of Japanese imperialism in China. Three areas seem most pertinent: assistance to the Foreign Ministry with information-gathering on political topics; student field investigation reports, as funneled to the Foreign Ministry, Army General Staff, and the Ministry of Agriculture and Commerce; and Tōa Dōbunkai/Tōa Dōbun Shoin on the eve of the Twenty-One Demands.

To facilitate discussion of the topic of assistance to the Foreign Ministry, the following breakdown of foreign ministry commissioned and authorized investigations is helpful.

Research for the Foreign Ministry

1905–1907: Five new graduates of the second Shoin class. Special assignment to major outposts across Sinkiang and Mongolia, to report on Russian activities in the wake of the Russo-Japanese War. Listed below by assigned base, from west to east:[88]
Hayashide Kenjirō (2d class). Based at Ili, Sinkiang, May 1905 to April 1907.
Hatano Yōsaku (2d class). Based at Urumchi (Tihua), August 1905 to June 1907.
Hida Yoshitaka (2d class). Based at Kodbo, Mongolia, May 1905 to July 1906.
Kusa Masakichi (2d class). Based at Uliassutai, Mongolia, May 1905 to July 1906.
Miura Minoru (2d class). Based at Kulun (Urga), Mongolia, May 1905 to July 1906.

1908–1910: Yamaguchi Noboru (5th class). Investigation of general conditions and revolutionary movements in Kwangtung, Kwangsi, French Indochina, Singapore, and Yunnan, from August 1908 to January 1910.[89]

1909–1910: Ide Saburō (Arao Sei associate at Hankow and founding member of Tōa Dōbunkai). Investigation in thirteen provinces of North, Central, and South China, of the workings of China's new

---

[88] For details, see *TDSDS* (1982), pp. 278, 373–375, 404–406. Also Hayashide Kenjirō, "Sanjūnen mae ni okeru 'Ili' yuki no kaiko" (Recollections of travels to 'Ili' thirty years ago), *Shina* 29, 6 (June 1, 1938): 171–188.

[89] The full record of Yamaguchi's assignment, including biographical data and his many very competent, lengthy reports, may be found at Gaikō Shiryōkan, 1.6.1.30.

provincial assemblies, official/nonofficial relations at the local level, provincial educational systems, the campaign to suppress opium smoking, etc., spanning the period from September 1909 to November 1910.[90]

1910–1911: Six Shoin graduates and one nongraduate. Special investigations into local Chinese politics, secret societies, and the activities of the Kuomintang in Central and South China, from September 1910 to March 1911:[91]

Koji Shinpei (2d class). Kiangsi province.

Yoshifuku Okushirō (not a Shoin graduate). Hupeh.

Endō Yasuo (1st class). Hunan.

Yamada Shōji (1st class). Hunan-Hupeh.

Miura Minoru (2d class). Yunnan.

Yamaguchi Noboru (5th class). Kwangtung-Kwangsi.

Nishimoto Shōzō (Nankin Dōbun Shoin). Kiangsu-Anhwei.

1912: Sano Yasushi (2d class). Reports from him and others, from most major cities of China. Seventy-two numbered reports about developments surrounding China's 1911 Revolution, spanning the period from January to July 1912.[92]

1914: Yamaguchi Noboru (5th class). Survey for Tōa Dōbunkai, with Foreign Ministry clearance, to investigate finance and credit in China and the influence of foreigners on same, from June to October 1914.[93]

The Russo-Japanese War of 1904–1905 and China's accelerating movements for reform and revolution formed the background and context of these assignments. The war with Russia and Japan's continental gains from that war both boosted Japanese interest and raised the Japanese stake in China. Suddenly, large numbers of knowledgeable personnel were in demand—and Shoin graduates eager to oblige, "in service to their coun-

---

[90] Ide's detailed itinerary, and his 101 numbered reports, packed with statistical tables and critical observations, are in Gaikō Shiryōkan, 1.6.1.37. Some of his reports and observations are cited in Kawamura Kazuo, "Ide Saburō shi no jiseki ni tsuite: Gaimushō Nitchū kankei shiryō no hakkutsu" (On the exploits of Ide Saburō: Foreign Ministry documents on Sino-Japanese relations unearthed), *Kikan Tōa* 3 (April 1968): 73–93.

[91] Correspondence relating to the planning for these investigations, followed by the reports themselves, is in four separate binders at Gaikō Shiryōkan, from 1.6.1.4-2-1-1 to 1.6.1.4-2-1-1 daisankan. The Shoin class of each investigator was determined by comparing these names to the complete roster of graduates and students, by class, in *TDSDS* (1955), pp. 304–336.

[92] Full reports are contained in Gaikō Shiryōkan, 1.6.1.45–1.

[93] Clearance was obtained at the very top, directly from Foreign Minster Katō Takaaki. See ibid., 1.6.1.31.

try."[94] The five 1905 graduates selected to report about Sinkiang and Mongolia all entered the Foreign Ministry after completing their tours, bringing to seven the number of ministry employees from that class alone.[95] Hayashide Kenjirō of that group went on to become one of a small corps of master interpreters from Tōa Dōbun Shoin, interpreting for the ministry at Japan's most important political and economic negotiations with China.[96] Of the seventy-six graduates of 1905, no fewer than twenty-one joined the army as language officers; many others from the first and second classes had already completed brief tours as wartime army interpreters.[97] Chinese officials, for their part, were so impressed by the Japanese victory over Russia that requests for Japanese instructors and advisors poured in. At least twelve graduates of the second class served for various lengths of time at Chinese military and police academies, normal and commercial schools, and other educational institutions.[98]

Yamaguchi Noboru, whose 1908 Foreign Ministry assignment came at the tender age of twenty-one, filed highly informative reports on local political and revolutionary movements, including reports of Sun Yat-sen's activities in Singapore, supported by maps and statistics, in the best "data-gathering" tradition of his alma mater. Later an editor of *Shina* (The China review), Tōa Dōbunkai's biweekly magazine of China news and analysis, Yamaguchi's crowning publication achievement was the Foreign Ministry–commissioned study *Ō-Beijin no Shina ni okeru bunka jogyō* (Cultural programs of Europeans and Americans in China) (Shanghai, 1921), praised by John Fairbank and Banno Masataka for its "voluminous data . . . not to be found in any one Western work."[99]

Most savvy of this group was Ide Saburō (1861–1931). Like Munakata Kotarō, his fellow Kumamoto samurai and close associate, Ide had gone to China in the 1880s, where he linked up with Arao Sei at Hankow in 1888. Of independent means, Ide then traveled widely until returning to Japan in 1891. After serving as an army interpreter during the Sino-Japa-

---

[94] "Service to one's country" was at the heart of Nezu Hajime's "Principles of Education," written in classical Chinese under the title "Li-chiao kang-ling" and translated into Japanese under the titles "Kyōiku yōkō" and "Rikkyō no kōryō" (Principles of education). This statement was delivered at the Shanghai inaugural ceremonies of Tōa Dōbun Shoin on May 26, 1901. It appears in Japanese translation in *TDSDS* (1982), pp. 717–718; see also pp. 88–89.

[95] Graduates who entered the Foreign Ministry are surveyed in ibid., pp. 277–288; see also pp. 185, 404–406.

[96] Ibid., pp. 373–375; Hirano, "Arao Sei," p. 3.

[97] *TDSDS* (1982), pp. 99, 404.

[98] These twelve, and nine from other early classes, are listed by name and hiring institution in ibid., p. 410.

[99] Fairbank, Banno, and Yamamoto, *Japanese Studies of Modern China*, p. 154. Also, *TDSDS* (1982), p. 417.

nese War, Ide remained in China and in 1897, with colonial Taiwan government assistance and the collaboration of Munakata, purchased the Chinese-language newspaper *Min-pao* (Fukien daily) in Foochow. Two years later, with financial assistance from Tōa Dōbunkai, which Ide had helped to found and which included in its budget the financing of newspapers in China and Korea, Ide purchased and edited the Chinese-language Shanghai paper *T'ung-wen hu-pao* (Shanghai common culture daily).[100]

From Shanghai in 1909, Ide arranged for the Foreign Ministry to supply him a hefty two thousand yen to finance his 1909–1910 investigation of political and educational developments in thirteen Chinese provinces. Judging by several key reports, Ide's interest was more than just reportorial; it was policy-oriented. His "Impressions of Our Country Among Local Chinese" remarks that, ever since Japan's victory over Russia, many Japanese merchants in the interior "look down upon Chinese, earning their dislike."[101] Ide's carefully argued conviction that the alien Ch'ing government's days were numbered inspired him, in his final report to the Foreign Ministry, to recommend among other things that Japan shift its emphasis from ties with a crumbling regime to ties with enduring local elites and the local population:

> Insofar as we attach importance to the people of China, three things are most in need of careful study. One, ways of linking up with the *t'u-hao*, or local power elites, of China's interior. Two, ways of linking up with overseas Chinese. And three, ways of linking up with returned students from Japan. The *t'u-hao* have intimate relations with the local people, and exercise great influence. Overseas Chinese, as the sole importers of foreign capital into China, and through such activities as sponsorship of a major pavilion at the Nanking Exposition and the movement to create a national assembly, are fast coming to be recognized for their influence upon China's people. Returned students from Japan, numbering thirty thousand, are scattered throughout every province, where they are gradually gaining a foothold and their influence taking shape. If these three groupings indeed become major factors in the China of the future, research on them is absolutely essential.[102]

In conclusion, Ide wrote,

> Now, to achieve a shift in our China policy, various kinds of facilities will be required. One urgent need is to win the hearts and minds of the

[100] For an eye-opening chart of Japanese-run newspapers in China, published in Japanese, Chinese, English, and Russian, 1882–1945, see Huang, *Chin-tai Jih-pen*, pp. 262–270. For Ide's biography, see Tōa Dōbunkai, comp., *Tai-Shi kaikoroku*, vol. 2, pp. 529–540.

[101] Gaikō Shiryōkan, 1.6.1.37, p. 31.

[102] Ibid., pp. 98–99; quoted in Kawamura, "Ide Saburō," p. 93. The term *t'u-hao*, in 1910, had apparently not yet acquired its later pejorative meaning of "local bullies and rascals."

Chinese people [*jinshin o shūran suru*] through Japanese and Chinese agencies, starting with the creation of Nanking University [Nan-ching Ta-hsueh] to educate the children of influential *t'u-hao*, simultaneously with the founding of a large and influential Shanghai newspaper. If the feelings of the average Chinese toward Japan can be relatively improved, then, however much the attitude of the Ch'ing government may vacillate from one extreme to the other, there will be trust in our country that will most definitely heighten confidence in matters of trade and guide our relations in all aspects.[103]

The special investigations out of Hankow in 1910–1911 were initiated not from Tokyo but from Peking. In a series of letters in May 1910 to various consuls in China and to Foreign Minister Komura Jutarō, Japan's Minister to China Ijūin Hikokichi emphasized the urgent need for thorough political reporting from consular posts in China, and the need for special funding by the Foreign Ministry. By early June, Tokyo had instructed the Shanghai and Hankow consuls-general to carry out special investigations in their territories. Of the seven investigators operating out of Hankow, all but one were Shoin graduates. Of these, all but Yamaguchi Noboru (fifth class) came out of the first or second Shoin classes. But, like Yamaguchi, all were seasoned China travelers and observers. For Yamaguchi and Miura, this was at least their second assignment for the Foreign Ministry. Two others, Yamada and Endō, as instructors from 1906 and 1907 up until 1910, respectively, at the Wu-ch'ang Military Academy (Wu-ch'ang Lu-chun Hsüeh-t'ang) near Hankow, had the advantage of an inside track into the political and military affairs of Central China.[104] And Nishomito Shōzō was an older Nankin Dōbun Shoin student who, after a brief period as instructor at Tōa Dōbun Shoin, entered journalism in Shanghai. Later, having achieved some prominence, he established the Japanese government-funded weekly *Shanghai* and emerged along with Ōta Toseo (fifth class) as one of the most vocal and influential Japanese promoters of a "Ch'ing restoration" in support of their close mutual friend, Cheng Hsiao-hsu, first prime minister of the puppet state of Manchukuo.[105] The common topics for investigation of all these men were political parties (both open and secret), secret societies, and the military—their interrelations and their attitudes toward foreigners. The 1,500 pages

[103] Gaikō Shiryōkan, 1.6.1.37, pp. 100–101; also, pp. 32–33; quoted in Kawamura, "Ide Saburō," p. 93.

[104] *TDSDS* (1982), p. 410. Endō later served as a director of students at Tōa Dōbun Shoin, which his son also attended. Yamada went on to become editor-in-chief of the influential Japanese-owned, semigovernmental Chinese-language Peking daily, *Shun-t'ien shih-pao*. Ibid., p. 401; Huang, *Chin-tai Jih-pen*, pp. 238, 294–299.

[105] *TDSDS* (1982), pp. 80, 289, 378–379, and 401; Fairbank, Banno, and Yamamoto, *Japanese Studies of Modern China*, p. 95 (entry 4.2.16).

of reports, highlighted by Yamaguchi Noboru's 600-plus pages on secret societies in Kwangtung and Kwangsi provinces and Nishimoto Shōzō's 350 pages on secret societies in Chekiang and Anhwei provinces, are rich in raw data that, to my knowledge, have not been mined.

The seventy-two numbered reports on the Chinese revolution filed by Sano Yasushi and others during the first seven months of 1912 are mimeographed and may be no more than the duplicated reports of China-based correspondents for Tōa Dōbunkai's biweekly *Shina*. If this is correct, these are merely an extension of normal reporting activities. Their duplication, moreover, fulfills Tōa Dōbunkai's 1901 pledge to share sensitive information with appropriate government agencies. More interesting, in terms of "Japanese imperialism in China," are the extensive Japanese army, navy, and Kwantung Leased Territory files for the same period in the Foreign Ministry Archives. Clearly, China's 1911 Revolution had generated great concern, and it triggered a flurry of information gathering and exchange among Japanese agencies in China. The sheer quantity of reports from these agencies suggests that, by 1912, each was well on its way to self-reliance in information-gathering capabilities. This freed them, at least in their own spheres of operation, from dependence upon outside agencies such as Tōa Dōbunkai. Ironically, the realization of Tōa Dōbunkai's founding goals—to promote trade and understanding, and to build up a Japanese presence in China—was beginning to undermine Tōa Dōbunkai's stature. In political importance to the state, it was being eclipsed by the increased direct China involvements of organizations more amply financed and with broader mandates: the Japanese army, navy, and Foreign Ministry, and big business, each served by Shoin graduates to function more fully and effectively in China.

On the eve of the Twenty-One Demands of early 1915, Yamaguchi Noboru undertook a third major investigation of China. Now a member of Tōa Dōbunkai's Research and Publications Division in Tokyo, Yamaguchi received travel authorization from the Foreign Ministry, but not travel funds, estimated at 450 yen. For those funds, Tōa Dōbunkai reported a new source, the colonial Bank of Taiwan.

Student Field Trips

Shifting now to the topic of student investigative field trips, the 1905 Shoin mission for the Foreign Ministry has been called "the spiritual origin" (*seishinteki na genten*)[106] of the Big Trip (*dai ryokō*). The Big Trip—the highlight of every Shoin education—took place during the summer before graduation. Students, in teams of three to nine, traveled expenses-

---

[106] *TDSDS* (1982), p. 185.

paid to the farthest reaches of China and beyond. Their trips generally lasted from forty-five to one hundred days and, over time, blanketed the entire country (see map 7.1). The trips were a great challenge, and fun.[107] But "fun" was incidental to their primary purpose. They were serious exercises in field research. Every team member had responsibility for a particular research topic—geography, transport systems, local produce and manufactures, weights and measures, currency and exchange, local customs, politics, and so forth. Data collection was governed by the rigorous guidelines established in 1904 or 1905 by Field Director Negishi Tadashi (1874–1971), later a well-known China economist at Hitotsubashi University. Negishi's instructions, well worth quoting, were unequivocal: "Record only facts, stay away from [grand] theories, and keep out vague information of doubtful origin."[108]

Back on campus, students wrote up their field notes as research reports (chōsa hōkokusho), which served as graduation theses. These hōkokusho served a further, dual purpose. First, for confidential government reference, copies were forwarded to Tōa Dōbunkai in Tokyo. After recopying each and deleting student names, Tōa Dōbunkai distributed the duplicates to the army's General Staff, the Foreign Ministry, and the Ministry of Agriculture and Commerce, as openly publicized in 1913 and again in 1940.[109]

Second, for public consumption, these reports were edited for publication in a groundbreaking series of encyclopedic studies of China: the twelve-volume Shina keizai zensho (Comprehensive survey of the Chinese economy) (1907–1908); the eighteen-volume, province-by-province Shina shōbetsu zensho (Comprehensive gazetteer of the individual provinces of China) (1917–1920), and the entirely new, eight-volume wartime publication Shinshū Shina shōbetsu zenshi (New and revised comprehensive gazetteer of the individual provinces of China) (1941–1944).[110]

---

[107] The fun aspects of these trips were given expression in the ryokōshi or travel diaries, printed each year as a kind of school annual. Up through 1943, thirty-two volumes of ryokōshi were printed, having missed only the graduation years of 1920 and 1941. The title of each volume, the graduating class, year of travel, and a note on the major Chinese political events of that year are given in ibid., pp. 194–195. For much more about the Big Trip and its origins, in the context of Tōa Dōbun Shoin's overall training and research program, see Reynolds, "Chinese Area Studies in Prewar China."

[108] Quoted in ibid., p. 188. See also Negishi Tadashi, "Gakkai yoteki: Chūgoku jittai chōsa" (Academic notes: Research on actual conditions in China), Hitotsubashi ronsō 23, 5 (May 1950): 88–92.

[109] See Shina 4, 11 (June 1, 1913): 65; Tōa Dōbun Shoin, Sōritsu yonjū shūnen kinenshi (Fortieth anniversary commemorative album) (1940), quoted in TDSDS (1982), p. 194.

[110] Ibid., p. 66; Fairbank, Banno, and Yamamoto, Japanese Studies of Modern China, pp. 177–178. For the introductions and the detailed tables of contents of the twelve- and eighteen-volume encyclopedias, see Tōa Bunka Kenkyūjo, comp., "Tōa Dōbunkai," pp. 487–543 and 545–696, respectively.

MAP 7.1   Routes of student research trips, 1907–1927

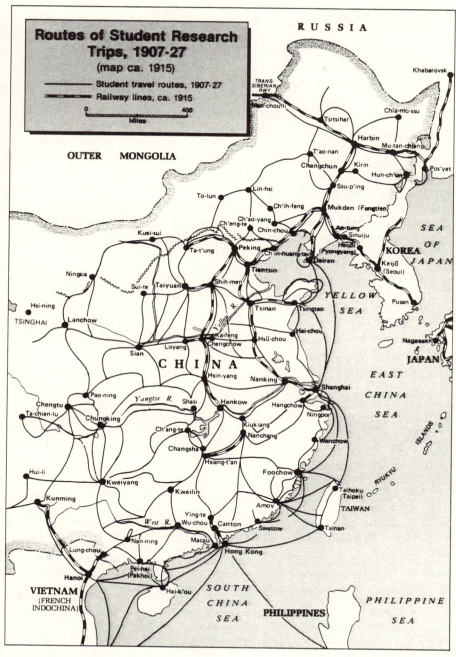

Routes of Student Research Trips, 1907-27
(map ca. 1915)

——————— Student travel routes, 1907-27
▬▬▬▬▬▬▬ Railway lines, ca. 1915

0   400
Miles

RUSSIA

Khabarovsk

TRANS-
SIBERIAN
RWY.
Man-chou-li

Tsitsihar

Chia-mu-ssu

OUTER   MONGOLIA

Harbin
Mu-tan-chiang

T'ao-nan
Changchun   Kirin
Hun-ch'un
Pos'vet

To-lun   Lin-hsi
Ssu-p'ing

Ch'ih-feng
Mukden (Fengtien)

Kuei-sui
Ch'eng-te   Ch'ao-yang
Chin-chou
An-tung
Sinuiju
SEA

Ta-t'ung   Peking
Ch'in-huang-tao
Heijō
(Pyongyang)
OF

KOREA

Ningsia   Sui-te   Taiyuan
Shih-men
Tientsin
Dairen
Keijō
(Seoul)
JAPAN

Hsi-ning
Lanchow
Tsinan
Tsingtao
YELLOW
SEA
Pusan

TSINGHAI

Kaifeng
Hsü-chou
Hai-chou
Nagasaki

Sian   Loyang
Chengchow
CHINA

Hsin-yang
Nanking
Shanghai
JAPAN

Pao-ning
Yangtze R.   Shasi
Hankow
Hangchow
EAST

Chengtu
Ta-chien-lu
Chungking
Ch'ang-te
Kiukiang
Ningpo
CHINA

Nanchang
SEA

Changsha
Hsiang-t'an
Wenchow

Hui-li
Kweiyang
Foochow

Kunming
Kweilin
Taihoku
(Taipei)
RYUKYU ISLANDS

Ying-te
Amoy
TAIWAN

West R.   Wu-chou   Canton
Swatow
Tainan

Lung-chou
Nan-ning
Macau
Hong Kong

Hanoi
Pei-hai
(Pakhoi)

VIETNAM
(FRENCH
INDOCHINA)
Hai-k'ou
SOUTH
CHINA
SEA
PHILIPPINES
PHILIPPINE
SEA

Source: Adapted from TDSDS (1982), p. 192.

The great success of the 1905 mission is said to have loosened the purse-strings of the Foreign Ministry, which in 1907 provided a three-year grant from Boxer Indemnity moneys to finance an annual Big Trip.[111] Ultimate credit for the Big Trip's spiritual origins belongs not to 1905, however, but to the late 1880s and Arao Sei, who insisted upon field training for future China businessmen. Nezu Hajime likewise deserves a full share of the credit. Though not with Arao at Hankow, Nezu in 1891 had edited Arao's Hankow data at Nisshin Bōeki Kenkyūjo, inspiring in him an abiding faith in the practical necessity of field work. He emerged as the biggest booster of investigative field trips (chōsa ryokō) at Tōa Dōbun Shoin, and it was he who had arranged the Foreign Ministry assignments for his five new graduates of 1905.[112]

By 1908, Nezu's Shanghai school was sufficiently established to be dubbed "one of the world's unique schools" by a British Army captain in an article for *The Saturday Review* of Shanghai, following a lengthy visit to the campus. That same article quotes an unnamed Chinese official on the implications for China of such a school.

[The existence of this school in our midst] is reminiscent, for our country, of the French and German situation of the past. In 1870, when France and Germany went to war, the Germans are said to have known more about conditions in France than the French themselves. It's the same for the Japanese in China. But we are powerless to put a halt to it.[113]

"What this bodes for the future, only time will tell," the British captain thought to remark.

[111] The grant was later annually renewed. On Boxer money being the source of funding for the Big Trip, see the twenty-page printed booklet, *Arao Nezu ryōsensei no kyōiku to risō* (The education and thought of masters Arao and Nezu) (Tokyo: Koyūkai, 1961), p. 16.

[112] *TDSDS* (1982), p. 185.

[113] Matsuoka and Yamaguchi, comps., *Nisshin Bōeki Kenkyūjo*, pp. 130–136, reports that this item was published in the April 20 issue of *The Saturday Review*, implying the year 1908. But there is no April 20, 1908, issue—only April 4, 11, 18, and 25. *TDSDS* (1982), pp. 94–97, "retranslates" the former into a prewar Japanese idiom and says that it appeared in an April 1906 issue of *The Saturday Review*. But that weekly began publication only in July 1907! This author, who desperately wanted to see the English original, undertook a nationwide interlibrary loan search in the United States in 1984–1985 without success. Then, in Japan in 1986–1987, I meticulously combed the early holdings (complete from October 5, 1907) at Tōyō Bunko in Tokyo. My conclusion: this lengthy report was never published—except in Japanese translation, in Matsuoka and Yamaguchi. Its author, identified as Captain Kaaton (Curton? Cotton?), must have delivered a copy of his unpublished manuscript to Tōa Dōbun Shoin at the same time as to *The Saturday Review*. But that very "British" magazine, which featured witty and biting news briefs and analyses, original and reprinted articles, entertaining literary pieces, and a "Lady's Page," decided not to use it. (Was it not sufficiently criticial of Japan for its pages?)

Nezu Hajime's hopes for the future, particularly for his school and for his country in China, were no secret. In early 1909, in a fifty-page manuscript titled "The Future of the Ch'ing Economy: Its Relationship to the Business Activities of Western Powers and Japan, and Their Relationship to Tōa Dōbun Shoin in Shanghai," he wrote,

To date, Tōa Dōbun Shoin in Shanghai has graduated 370 students. They are scattered throughout Manchuria and every important part of North, Central, and South China, engaged in every kind of economic activity. To be specific, they have gone into the Chinese interior and its treaty ports to do business directly with China. As an example of direct dealings without the least sense of handicap or trouble, one group in Hankow donned Chinese clothing, went into the cotton-growing districts of Honan province and, using local weights and measures, commercial customs, and currency, purchased directly from the growers. This produced a tremendous profit for them. *Over the past ten years, a period when Europeans and Americans have not come into China to any extent, Japanese have penetrated deep into the Chinese interior and carried on work with the greatest of ease.* In this period, Japanese have gone into sixty-some Chinese localities, rapidly establishing a foundation for business operations [*keizai keiei no kiso*]. This was precisely our larger goal.[114]

The March 1914 printed booklet *Tōa Dōbunkai jigyō teiyō* (Summary of Tōa Dōbunkai activities) picked up where Nezu Hajime had left off in 1909:

Tōa Dōbun Shoin has trained over 850 graduates [*sic*, for 719 graduates], who are now in Manchuria and in virtually every one of China's eighteen provinces. Not a few of the graduates from the first class [an unusually successful group] are branch managers for their companies or heads of independent businesses. *Japan's China affairs at present are run to a considerable extent on the power of Shoin graduates.*[115]

Though exaggerated, this last claim is far from groundless. A printed table in this same booklet (p. 591) substantiates the claim at least in part,

[114] Nezu Hajime, "Shinkoku keizaikai no zento to sore ni taisuru rekkoku oyobi gakoku no keizai keiei narabini Shanhai Tōa Dōbun Shoin no kankei" [1909], carbon copy on Tōa Dōbunkai stationary, in Gaikō Shiryōkan, 3.10.2.13 dainikan (reel 773, pp. 727–789), p. 766. Emphasis added.

[115] In Gaikō Shiryōkan, 3.10.2.13 dainikan (reel 773), p. 586 (emphasis added). This is the 1914 report, mentioned in note 87, which identifies Tōa Dōbun Shoin as "Equivalent to a Higher Commercial School [Kōtō Shōgyō Gakkō] and a Higher School [Kōtō Gakkō]." It was 1921, however, before this school, outside of Japan and under Foreign Ministry supervision, was formally designated a *senmon gakkō* or specialized (higher) school.

TABLE 7.2
Tōa Dōbun Shoin Graduates' Employment, by Place of Work (April 1908)

Site	Number of Graduates
Manchuria	98
North China	29
South China[a]	91
Japan	26
Korea and elsewhere	5
TOTAL:	249

Source: Matsuoka and Yamaguchi, comps. *Nisshin Bōeki Kenkyūjo, TDSDS* (1982), p. 102; and Ōmori, "Toa Dōbunkai," p. 88.
[a] South of Yangtze River.

identifying by name the employers of Shoin graduates, indicating also whether actual work assignments are inside or outside Japan. As early as 1908, Shoin graduates apparently found work mainly in Manchuria and South China (table 7.2).

Surely these are impressive results. But it will be recalled that the original mandate of Tōa Dōbunkai, now twenty-five hundred members strong, had included much more than just training young China hands. The 1914 booklet reminds present members of that mandate: "To enhance friendly intercourse and improve the well-being of both Japan and China through social contact between the two peoples, the education of their youth, the encouragement of trade, and the editing and publication of political and economic investigations."[116] Taking these points in reverse order, publications were a conspicuous success of Tōa Dōbunkai, as revealed by a list of its twenty most important titles.[117] The "encour-

[116] Tōa Dōbunkai, "Tōa Dōbunkai jigyō teiyō" (March 1914), in Gaikō Shiryōkan, 3.10.2.13 dainikan (reel 773, pp. 581–592), p. 582. The membership figure of "over 2,500 members" comes from p. 585.

[117] These titles included the twelve-volume Tōa Dōbun Shoin, *Shina keizai zensho* (1907–1908), in its fifth printing; the five-volume *Shinkoku shōgyō sōran* (General survey of Chinese commerce and industry) (1906–1908), edited by Negishi Tadashi, in its second printing; the first of a two-volume study, *Shina seiji chiri shi* (Political and geographical gazetteer of China) (1913–1915), by Ōmura Ken'ichi of Tōa Dōbun Shoin; reference works on Chinese law, politics, and transportation; *Shina nenkan* (China yearbook); and others. Listed in ibid., pp. 587–589. To organize its research and publications activities, Tōa Dōbunkai in 1907 had established its Research and Publications Division (Chōsa Hensanbu) to supervise its investigative research, editing, and publications activities. That same year, it created its China Economic Research Division (Shina Keizai Chōsabu) to advise and assist local Japanese Chambers of Commerce and Industry with trade and investment opportunities in China. This division and the Research and Publications Division jointly edited the magazine *Shina* for distribution to Tōa Dōbunkai members. To assist in data gathering, the Economic Re-

agement of trade" (meaning trade in Japanese hands) through the publication of basic reference works and the biweekly *Shina*, as well as through the training of young Japanese China experts later employed by government and business and through triennial lecture series throughout Japan, was likewise a notable success. The training of Japanese youth in Shanghai and the training of Chinese youth in Tokyo at Tōkyō Dōbun Shoin were also major achievements.[118] Only in the area of promoting friendly intercourse and social contact were sustained programs lacking, despite expressions of concern such as that by Ide Saburō in 1910. This neglect the Japanese government sought to remedy in the 1920s, using Boxer Indemnity funds. But by then it was too late, because of the well-publicized and repeated clashes between armed Japanese and Chinese workers, students, and soldiers of the turbulent 1920s.

Expanding Dōbun Shoin's Programs in China

No mention is made in this March 1914 report of efforts underway to try to expand Tōa Dōbunkai's China activities. Working plans envisioning a complex of involvements on a grand scale and requiring substantial supplemental funding had, in fact, been under review for at least a year as part of negotiations for a three-year contract with the Foreign Ministry. These plans took for granted the availability of trained personnel from Tōa Dōbun Shoin and asked for an expanded network of Japanese consulates in China.[119] In written form, the hopes of Tōa Dōbunkai are em-

---

search Division dispatched its own investigators to China's most important cities and trade centers. Ibid.

[118] By March 1914, over six hundred Chinese had graduated from Tōkyō Dōbun Shoin since its founding in 1901–1902, preparatory to entering regular Japanese educational institutions. The 1914 printed report further states that more than half of the school's current large enrollment of three hundred were Chinese government scholarship students sent by China's Ministry of War and by Shensi province. A tantalizing appendix names twenty-one graduates and their current positions in the Chinese central government (heading this list was Lu Tsung-yü, China's minister to Japan), twenty-two graduates and their positions in high Chinese provincial government posts, and twelve elected provincial representatives to both houses of China's national assembly. The same chart provides statistics on the number of graduates by year, and on the number of graduates by province of origin (130 from Kwangtung, 107 from Chekiang, 68 from Hupeh, 35 from Szechwan, and so on). "Tōa Dōbunkai jigyō teiyō" (1914), pp. 586–587, 592.

[119] No major expansion of authority or funding could have been accomplished without considerable political support—a subject beyond the scope of this chapter, but demanding a comment here. Going back to Tōa Dōbunkai's origins in 1898, Hirano Ken'ichiro noted that within the ranks of its *hyōgiin* or councillors, "Many of the leading figures of almost all the political parties in both the House of Representatives and the Peers were covered." Hirano, "Arao Sei," p. 59. In its 1914 report, the officers of Tōa Dōbunkai—Marquis Nabeshima Naohiro, president; Viscount (later president of the Privy Council and prime minister of Japan) Kiyoura Keigo, vice-president; Nezu Hajime, secretary general; six directors

bodied most fully in an undated fifteen-point "China Operations Assistance Plan" preserved in the Foreign Ministry Archives and stamped "Received for filing, May 6, 1914" (the day after the Foreign Ministry signed its new three-year contract with Tōa Dōbunkai):

1. Plan to establish a Japanese consulate at every Chinese commercial port
2. Plan to set up China Trade Promotion Centers (Tsūshō Yūdōkan)
3. Plan for tourist promotion between China and Japan
4. Plan for special training of Foreign Ministry secretarial students
5. Plan for adding agriculture and engineering divisions to Tōa Dōbun Shoin
6. Plan for China investigations, compilations, and publications
7. Plan for field research (jitchi chōsa) in the Chinese interior
8. Plan for new Chinese-language newspapers
9. Plan for resident reporters in nationally important cities
10. Plan for resident reporters in provincial cities
11. Plan to train Chinese students in commerce and industry
12. Plan to train Chinese students in Tokyo
13. Plan to offer guidance to Chinese students in Tokyo
14. Plan to establish Japan-China clubs in Japan
15. Plan to set up reception centers for classical Chinese scholars departing China[120]

As part of its campaign for increased funding, Tōa Dōbunkai had likewise prepared a fifteen-page "Outline of Topics for Research and Inves-

---

(kanji); and sixty-two councillors—show great continuity with its founding leaders and members, and read like a Who's Who of the Japanese establishment in government and politics. For some members, too much "politicking" was already going on. An anonymous memorandum received at the Foreign Ministry on July 2, 1914, speaks of membership fears of being dragged into party politics by Tōa Dōbunkai's large contingent of Seiyūkai members and advisors. Gaikō Shiryōkan, 3.10.2.13 dainikan (reel 773), pp. 628–629; see also *Shina* 5, 11 (June 1, 1914): appendix, p. 3. At the end of 1916, someone at the Foreign Ministry used red circles and check-marks to identify current officers who were members of the Japanese Diet and House of Peers. In the House of Peers were Marquis Nabeshima, president; Viscount Katō Takaaki, advisor (sōdan'in) and recent past foreign minister; and twenty-four of eighty-four councillors. In the House of Representatives were Ogawa Heikichi, secretary general; two of seven *kanji* or executive officers; two of nine advisors—Inukai Tsuyoshi and Hara Takashi (Kei), president of Seiyūkai and prime minister from 1918 to 1921; and seventeen of the eighty-four councillors. Gaikō Shiryōkan, 3.10.2.13 daisankan (reel 773), pp. 1006–1011.

[120] "Tai-Shina keiei josei an" (mimeo), in ibid., pp. 495–514. This plan first surfaced in mid-1912, at the May 10 membership meeting of Tōa Dōbunkai, as reported in *Shina* 3, 10 (May 20, 1912): p. 91. The two plans are identical except for the omission of point 12 from the 1912 version.

tigation in the Chinese Interior," also preserved in the Foreign Ministry Archives and stamped "Received for filing, May 6, 1914."[121] This mimeographed item included a range of topics for field research under four headings: geography (including cities, transport networks, and local customs); economics (including capital, labor, land, and industry); commerce (including types of trade and traders, cooperatives, weights and measures, currency, finance, banking, goods, and markets); and politics. Sophisticated and exhaustive, each category and its subcategories evidence the sure hand of experience garnered at Tōa Dōbun Shoin. Only category 4, on politics, seems rough and unrefined. Instead of headings with logical subheadings, everything in this last category is subsumed under nineteen general descriptive phrases such as "The feelings [kanjō] of the average person toward provincial assemblies—especially in the important provincial cities and large market towns." The scope and direction of thinking are conveyed by the introductory passage:

Section Four: Politics
The Investigation of Present Realities

To focus on important conditions within each local area since the emergency [of 1911]: internal troubles among local civilian and military elites; the rampancy of soldiers; the disposition of demobilized troops; the circumstances of students returned home after army service; the performance record of new progressive officials in administration; the good and bad points of fiscal administration; economic changes; people's opinions of the Republican political system; people's feelings about Japanese and other foreigners; the conditions of poor people since the disorder; the conditions of the police; the circumstances of educators; the condition of local assemblies and popular feeling toward them; sentiment toward the present cabinet and its ministers; sentiment toward the former Manchu court; the state of affairs of groups sympathetic to political parties, political factions, and other political matters, etc.[122]

All this detail would be of solely academic interest except for one fact. In the summer of 1914, for the very first time, "politics" served as the primary focus of investigation of Shoin student field research. Seventeen numbered topics for investigation were given to students, and a copy of those topics hand-delivered by its author, Nezu Hajime, to the Foreign Ministry.[123] These seventeen items were closely related to the nineteen in

[121] "Shina naichi kenkyū chōsa yōmoku" (mimeo), in ibid., pp. 515–539, 544–568 (two copies in archives, both on microfilm).

[122] Ibid., pp. 537–538.

[123] This four-page brush-and-ink document, untitled but with Nezu's name on it and

the "Outline of Topics" just discussed. Political matters and political relationships at the local level were the chief concern: people's faith in the new Republican government; the feelings (*kanjō*) of various specified circles toward various specified things, such as the major political parties (Chin-pu-tang, Kuomintang, Tsung-she-tang) and foreign loans; the feelings of officials toward Japanese as opposed to other foreigners; the role of returned students trained in Japan; conditions of agriculture, of economic circles, of educators, and of opium prohibition—all with political implications.

It is impossible to say for certain, but the lengthy report of the Soochow-Hangchow team of students may well typify the reports for all ten teams (seventy-five students) that summer. That report opens with a word-for-word copy of the seventeen questions from Nezu and then proceeds to answer them.[124] The six-man Szechwan team investigating these same sensitive political questions was apprehended by Szechwan authorities. Those authorities filed a vigorous official protest with the Japanese consulate in Chungking, leading to a direct correspondence between the Chungking consulate and Tokyo.[125] The Foreign Ministry must have impressed upon Nezu that his students in the future were not to pursue solely political questions, because in 1915 student reports were back to "normal," their topics dominated by questions of trade and the Chinese economy.[126] Never again did their research come so close to political espionage. But irreversible damage was being done. In Chinese minds, such actions could only reinforce suspicions that Tōa Dōbun Shoin might indeed be a "spy school."[127]

The 1914 negotiations culminated in a three-year, 150,000-yen contract signed on May 5, 1914, with the Ministry of Foreign Affairs. This contract, only a marginal improvement over past annual subsidies of 40,000 yen, contained three articles:[128] (1) investigative activities—20,000 yen per

---

hand-delivered by him on July 12, 1914, is in Gaikō Shiryōkan, 3.10.2.13. For some unfathomable reason, it was not microfilmed.

[124] This is followed by a lengthier section unrelated to Nezu's questions. The 1914 reports were compiled into ten *kan* or "sections" with a detailed index, in Gaikō Shiryōkan, 1.6.1.31 (not microfilmed). The cover letter from Tōa Dōbunkai to the Foreign Ministry is dated September 18, 1916, suggesting the time demands of this reporting procedure.

[125] For the correspondence between the Chungking consulate and Tokyo, see ibid.

[126] For a complete set of 1915 student reports, with table of contents, see ibid., 1.6.1.31–9 bessatsu (not microfilmed).

[127] The phrase "spy school" is attributed to Edgar Snow in a passage from *Red Star Over China*, quoted in *TDSDS* (1982), p. 171. A search of the English original fails to turn up that passage, however. This leads me to speculate that the offending passage may have been inserted into the Japanese translation only. The phrase also appears in Ōmori, "Tōa Dōbunkai," p. 90.

[128] For the draft contract (*keiyakusho sōan*)—identical in all respects to the final "order" (*meireisho*), dated both May 4 and May 6, 1914, which authorized the Finance Ministry to

year for each of three years, to support the field research of 50 to 100 Shoin students traveling for from three to five months to carry out detailed investigations of "political, economic, educational, geographic, and social conditions" in China's eighteen provinces and in Manchuria and Mongolia;[129] and, as needed, resident or short-term investigators dispatched to important centers, their records to be edited for publication. (2) Educational activities: 70,000 yen for fiscal year 1914, solely to expand Tōa Dōbun Shoin's program from its twofold Political Science Division and Commercial Division to a fourfold program including a two-section Agricultural and Industrial Division. (3) China trade promotion activities: 20,000 yen for fiscal year 1914 only, to establish Trade Promotion Centers (Tsūshō Yūdōkan) in China, able to provide lodging, translation, investigation, sales consignment, and other support services to Japanese businessmen.[130]

Though far from achieving the ambitious goals of its working proposals for 1914, Tōa Dōbunkai won a holding action, plus a little. A far more lucrative victory was the earlier 220,000-yen monetary settlement against Yuan Shih-k'ai's government for the accidental destruction by fire of the twelve-year-old Shoin campus during ten days of fighting between pro- and anti-Yuan forces in the vicinity of the Kiangnan Arsenal in late July 1913.[131] Perhaps related to this generous settlement and to the "failure"

release funds at predetermined intervals to Tōa Dōbunkai, and a copy of which was prepared for the signatures of President Nabeshima and Secretary-General Nezu—see Gaikō Shiryōkan, 3.10.2.13 dainikan (reel 773), pp. 606–608. For the two meireisho, see ibid., pp. 613–617 and 622–626, respectively.

[129] In 1915, ten thousand yen was budgeted by Tōa Dōbunkai and "approved" by the Foreign Ministry for eighty-three students to travel about a hundred days in eleven different teams. In 1916, the same amount was approved for eighty-eight students to travel about ninety days in ten teams. See Gaikō Shiryōkan, 1.6.1.31.

[130] To implement this last plan, "in order to develop our commercial power and to expand our trade" in China, Tōa Dōbunkai established its Tai-Shi Bōeki Yūdōbu in late 1914. Only one China center was ever established, in Tsinan, Shantung province, in August 1915. Destroyed by a fire of mysterious origins on May 19, 1919, the Tsinan Dōbun Shōmu Kōsho was operating again by 1921. See Gaikō Shiryōkan, 3.10.2.13 daisankan (reel 773), pp. 669–706, 1080, and relevant portions of printed reports not microfilmed. For the inaugural photo of this center, with smartly dressed Japanese standing in front of a new, two-story building featuring a large sign reading "Commercial Museum" in English, see Shina 6, 17 (September 1, 1915).

[131] Tōa Dōbun Shoin received the full amount of its claim, in a settlement arranged in Peking by Nezu Hajime and Tōa Dōbunkai manager Kashiwabara Buntarō directly with Hsiung Hsi-ling, Yuan Shih-k'ai's premier from July 1913 to February 1914. Kashiwabara Buntarō, "Tōa Dōbunkai sōritsu jidai no Kazan kō" (Prince Konoe at the time of the founding of Tōa Dōbun), Shina 25, 2 (February 25, 1934): 135. See also TDSDS (1982), pp. 106–107, 113. With the indemnity money and the seventy-thousand-yen grant from the Japanese government for the new Agricultural and Industrial Division, Nezu was able to acquire a large plot of land and construct a truly impressive campus just southwest of the French

MAP 7.2 Tōa Dōbun Shoin, Shanghai, 1925

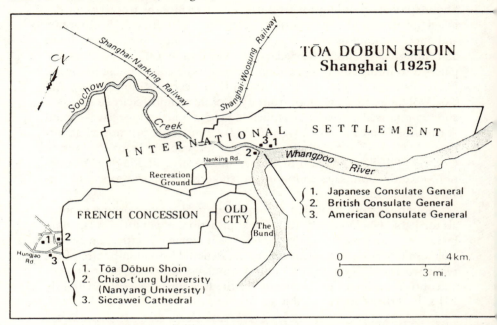

Source: Adapted from Nicholas Clifford, *Shanghai*, p. 3, Yamamoto Takashi, *Japanese Studies of Modern China*, p. 30.

of his Foreign Ministry negotiations, Nezu Hajime, just two weeks after signing Tōa Dōbunkai's May 5 contract with the Foreign Ministry, resigned his post as secretary-general of Tōa Dōbunkai to give full time to Tōa Dōbun Shoin and its grand new 300,000-yen campus (see maps 7.2 and 7.3).

ACCELERATING IMPERIALISM: "TAMING THE WILD SPIRIT" OF TŌA DŌBUN SHOIN

A landmark year for Japanese imperialism in China, 1915 was an uneventful year for Tōa Dōbunkai and Tōa Dōbun Shoin. Having just signed a three-year contract with the Foreign Ministry, and preoccupied with constructing a large new campus for Tōa Dōbun Shoin in Shanghai incorporating its ambitious Agricultural and Industrial Division (1914–1923), Tōa Dōbunkai and Tōa Dōbun Shoin had little direct input into the

concession, in Chinese territory known as "Siccawei" [Hsu-chia-hui], near the large Roman Catholic Siccawei Cathedral. See maps 7.2 and 7.3.

MAP 7.3   Tōa Dōbun Shoin, Hungjao Road campus, 1917–1937 (April 1930)

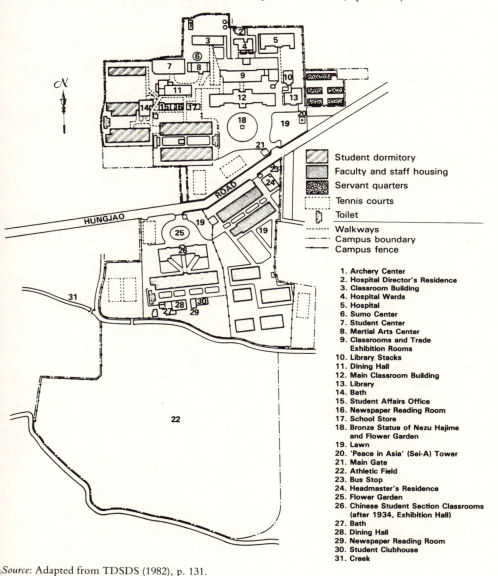

Student dormitory
Faculty and staff housing
Servant quarters
Tennis courts
Toilet
Walkways
Campus boundary
Campus fence

1. Archery Center
2. Hospital Director's Residence
3. Classroom Building
4. Hospital Wards
5. Hospital
6. Sumo Center
7. Student Center
8. Martial Arts Center
9. Classrooms and Trade
   Exhibition Rooms
10. Library Stacks
11. Dining Hall
12. Main Classroom Building
13. Library
14. Bath
15. Student Affairs Office
16. Newspaper Reading Room
17. School Store
18. Bronze Statue of Nezu Hajime
    and Flower Garden
19. Lawn
20. 'Peace in Asia' (Sei-A) Tower
21. Main Gate
22. Athletic Field
23. Bus Stop
24. Headmaster's Residence
25. Flower Garden
26. Chinese Student Section Classrooms
    (after 1934, Exhibition Hall)
27. Bath
28. Dining Hall
29. Newspaper Reading Room
30. Student Clubhouse
31. Creek

Source: Adapted from TDSDS (1982), p. 131.

Twenty-One Demands.[132] Others assumed the initiative. Etō Shinkichi, setting these demands into the context of China's foreign relations, has written,

> With Western attention on Europe, with the general strengthening of Japan's political and military position in East Asia, and with Peking's attitude of appeasement, numerous Japanese officials and agencies, including Minister Hioki in Peking, Governor-General Fukushima Yasumasa of the Kwantung Leased Territory, the Army General Staff, and the Ministry of the Army, urged Foreign Minister Katō to negotiate new demands with China. The Japanese public began to clamor for similar demands.[133]

In other words, all those Japanese agencies that had reported at length about China's 1911 Revolution just three years earlier were now positioned and prepared to act to exploit Western and Chinese weakness.

As if to make up for lost time, Tōa Dōbunkai submitted a three-year "Funding Request for Expansion of Tōa Dōbunkai Activities" on August 2, 1917, asking for 1.215 million yen.[134] That amount was equivalent to nearly ten times Tōa Dōbunkai's three-year allocation of 1914. After, presumably, some hard bargaining with the Foreign Ministry, Tōa Dōbunkai drastically pared its request in December 1917 to 362,000 yen.[135] Interestingly, when the Foreign Ministry gave final approval to this funding request, it authorized a four-year, rather than three-year, subsidy of 582,180 yen.[136] That amount was earmarked almost exclusively for Tōa Dōbun Shoin, suggesting the school's overwhelming importance to the thinking of Tōa Dōbunkai and the Foreign Ministry: (1) 354,510 yen to nearly double the student body of the school by adding seventy students to each of the next four classes, 1918–1921; (2) 183,670 yen for a four-year Chinese Business School (Shinajin Jitsugyō Gakudō) attached to Tōa

---

[132] The Twenty-One Demands consisted of fourteen demands and seven wishes adopted by the Japanese cabinet on November 11, 1914, and presented to President Yuan Shih-k'ai at Peking on January 18, 1915. A useful chart identifying each demand, along with each item's final disposition, is in Shinkichi Etō, "China's International Relations 1911–1931," in John King Fairbank, ed., *The Cambridge History of China*, vol. 13: *Republican China 1912–1949, Part 2* (Cambridge: Cambridge University Press, 1986), pp. 98–99.

[133] This quote is from the prepublication manuscript version of ibid., p. 96. I take the liberty of using Professor Etō's more detailed, preedited wording to underline my particular set of points.

[134] "Tōa Dōbunkai jigyō kakuchō hojo shinseisho," in Gaikō Shiryōkan, 3.10.2.13 dainikan (reel 773), pp. 874–898.

[135] For details, see the mimeographed item of the same title as the above, dated December 1917, in ibid., pp. 1100–1118.

[136] See the Foreign Ministry's "Meireisho" (Official Directive) in ibid., daisankan, pp. 912–918.

TABLE 7.3
Foreign Ministry Subsidy to Tōa Dōbunkai, 1914–1923 (yen)

Fiscal year	Regular operating funds	Special funds	Total
1914	110,000	—	110,110
1915	20,000	—	20,000
1916	20,000	—	20,000
1917	20,000	—	20,000
1918	66,960	284,340	351,300
1919	84,127	407,948	492,075
1920	115,953	—	115,953
1921	171,533	100,000	271,533
1922	179,533	—	179,533
1923	182,726	—	182,726

Source: Huang, "Tung-ya t'ung-wen-hui," pp. 346–347; Huang, Chin-tai Jih-pen, pp. 24–25.

Dōbun Shoin and admitting fifty Chinese per class; and (3) 44,000 yen for research and publications.

During the first fifteen years of Tōa Dōbunkai, from 1899 to 1913, it had received a set annual subsidy of 40,000 yen from the Foreign Ministry. But over the next ten years, from 1914 to 1923, it received the amounts listed in table 7.3.[137] The allocation for fiscal year 1918 of 351,000 yen was by itself more than twice the combined amounts for the four years from 1914 to 1917. Then, in 1919, Tōa Dōbunkai received an additional large supplemental grant to construct the facilities for a new, more ambitious Chinese student program, discussed below.

Most important to the financial story of Tōa Dōbunkai and Tōa Dōbun Shoin was the former's stabilization in 1923. This was the result of the new China Cultural Activities Special Account Law (Tai-Shi Bunka Jigyō Tokubetsu Kaikei Hō), passed by the Diet in March of that year.[138] Inspired by the example of the United States and Great Britain, this law placed Japan's Boxer indemnity funds and credits from the 1922 settlement of former German property claims in Shantung into a special account, administered by the China Cultural Affairs Office of the Foreign Ministry's new Cultural Affairs Division of its Asia Bureau, to fund China-related cultural endeavors like education, medical assistance, research, and scholarly exchange. Between 1924 and 1936, the annual Tōa Dōbunkai subsidy from this one source averaged about 340,000 yen, or

[137] The sole exception to the 40,000-yen annual subsidy involved an extra 2,500 yen in 1910.

[138] For specifics, including excerpts of crucial documents, see Abe, NKBM, pp. 38–40.

some 13 percent of the special account's authorized annual ceiling of 2.5 million yen.[139]

Two years before finances were secured through the special China Account Law, both Tōa Dōbun Shoin and Tōa Dōbunkai had taken giant steps to stabilize their respective structures and finances. Starting in April 1921, as part of its request for elevation in status to a four-year specialized school (*senmon gakkō*), Tōa Dōbun Shoin shifted its school year from the August–June year of Chinese schools to the standard April–March school year of Japan. Then, on July 13, 1921, an Imperial Ordinance elevated Tōa Dōbun Shoin to the status of a *senmon gakkō*, still under Foreign Ministry jurisdiction.[140] Simultaneously, the school began a campaign to build an endowment fund. In just six months, between April and September 1921, it raised the respectable sum of 264,900 yen. Not surprisingly, donors and their contributions show a direct correlation with their utilization of Shoin graduates and services.[141]

In February 1922, Tōa Dōbunkai reorganized itself, with prior approval from both the Education and Foreign Ministries, as the nonprofit Tōa Dōbunkai Foundation (Zaidan Hōjin Tōa Dōbunkai Kifu Kōi).[142] This placed Tōa Dōbunkai on a more solid legal footing, allowed for more professional staffing, and may have helped satisfy the financial and organizational requirements of the Ministry of Education for nongovernmental sponsors of higher schools and colleges.[143]

[139] Huang, *Chin-tai Jih-pen*, pp. 26–27.

[140] *TDSDS* (1982), pp. 60–61, 711–713. For the record of tortured negotiations, especially after the imperial ordinance, between Tōa Dōbunkai and the Foreign Ministry, on the one hand, and the Ministry of Education, on the other, see Gaikō Shiryōkan, 3.10.2.13 daiyonkan (reel 774), pp. 1289–2005. The negotiations were complicated severely by the fact that Tōa Dōbun Shoin was an overseas institution not under direct Education Ministry jurisdiction.

[141] See "Tōa Dōbun Shoin kihonkin" (The Tōa Dōbun Shoin endowment fund), in ibid., pp. 1576–1585. Without providing any background information or introduction, this item simply lists donors by amount and by name. Led by Mitsubishi Gōshi Kaisha and Mitsui Bussan Kaisha, each of which donated twenty thousand yen, this list and effort is a classic example of the Japanese system of bureaucratically orchestrated "giving." For a later example, suggesting a government-industrial-military complex in wartime Japan, see the assessed amounts "as of 1941" for contributions to Tōa Kenkyūjo, 1938–1947, in Fujita Tomosaku et al., "Tōa Kenkyūjo (13): Tōa Kenkyūjo no shūen—sengoban wa doko ni" (Tōa Kenkyūjo, Part 13: The end of Tōa Kenkyūjo—where's its postwar version headed?), panel discussion reported in *Nitchū* 6, 12 (November 16, 1976): p. 57. Significantly, just like the list of contributors to the Shoin endowment fund, the Tōa Kenkyūjo list is headed by the South Manchuria Railway Company, Mitsui, and Mitsubishi.

[142] The occasion for this reorganization was the death of the president and co-founder, Marquis Nabeshima, in June 1921. By this time, many of the aristocratic elder statesmen and peers of the early organization—men, like Nabeshima, of independent means and often independent minds—had been lost to natural deaths and retirement. See *TDSDS* (1982), pp. 60–61, 711–713.

[143] Japan, Ministry of Education, Minister's Secretariat, Research and Statistics Division,

These changes brought institutional stability and greater professional respectability to both Tōa Dōbunkai and Tōa Dōbun Shoin. But, in the words of Ōmori Chikako, such systemization helped "tame the wild spirit" of both[144]—and inhibit any lingering impulses for independent action and thought.

The remaining years of Tōa Dōbunkai and Tōa Dōbun Shoin, up to 1945, were marked by caution and conservatism in support of whatever Japanese group chose to employ their services. This gave them the appearance of passive servants of Japanese imperialism. No example exists of any effort by either to curb or check or even question Japan's growing aggression and militarism in China. In fact, signs point in the opposite direction. To cite some examples of at least ambiguous enterprises, for nine months in 1921–1922, Tōa Dōbunkai realized a plan appearing in its 1917 funding request, to dispatch "border correspondents" (*henkyō tsūshin-in*) to China's border with the Soviet Union and Outer Mongolia. Two correspondents filed copious and detailed reports from Kulun (Urga or Ulan Bator), deep inside troubled Outer Mongolia, and from the Ninghsia-Tsinghai region, while another two filed reports from a variety of other areas, including Ninghsia.[145]

A development of a different character, with chauvinistic possibilities that eventually emerged, was the erection in 1923 of an obelisk on the Shoin campus, the "Peace in Asia Memorial Tower." A lengthy dedicatory inscription written in classical Chinese in 1920 by Nezu Hajime celebrated the great deeds of *chih-shih* (men of will) who risked their lives to found the school and bring peace to Asia.[146] Nearly a dozen years later, in April 1934, the nationalistic school president, Ōuchi Chōzō (1874–1944)—a Fukuoka politician and educator with a Columbia University Master's degree, who for six years had been an intimate associate of Konoe Atsumaro and for twenty-two years, up to 1930, an elected member of the House of Representatives—dedicated the Sei-A Jinjâ or "Peace in Asia Shinto Shrine" on campus. Utilizing the same initial Chinese character (*sei* or *yasu*) as the Yasukuni Jinjâ in Tokyo and in all probability inspired by that national memorial for the repose of the souls of Japan's war dead, this compound enshrined the souls of Konoe Atsumaro, Arao Sei, and Nezu Hajime. Also honored were the souls of 649 other "mar-

---

ed., *Japan's Modern Educational System: A History of the First Hundred Years* (Tokyo: Printing Bureau, Ministry of Finance, 1980), p. 171.

[144] Ōmori, "Tōa Dōbunkai," p. 89. This is the essential meaning, though not the wording, of Takeuchi, *Nippon to Ajia*, p. 391.

[145] For these reports, see Gaikō Shiryōkan, 1.6.1.13 and 1.6.1.80. Besides these reports from Tōa Dōbunkai correspondents, the Foreign Ministry gathered dozens of binders of its own reports on the Russian Revolution and the Siberian Expedition, in ibid., 1.6.3.24.

[146] *TDSDS* (1982), pp. 122–123, 143–144.

tyrs" with Tōa Dōbun Shoin connections.[147] Annual services enabled important school affairs to be reported at the shrine. The next year, in 1935, a Sei-A dormitory was dedicated. At the height of the war with China in November 1941, the student association of Tōa Dōbun Shoin University was renamed the Sei-A Service Society, dedicated to serving the country for peace in Asia.[148]

The Chinese student boom in Japan, reported so glowingly by Tōa Dōbunkai in 1914, collapsed after Japan's Twenty-One Demands of 1915. Chinese graduates of Tōkyō Dōbun Shoin, for example, plunged in number from their high of 146 students in 1913 to 70 in 1914, 40 in 1915, 12 in 1916, 10 in 1917, none reported for 1918, 43 in 1919, 7 in 1920, 10 in 1921, and 5 in 1922, when the school was closed.[149] As numbers declined, official Japanese concern rose. In March 1918, the Diet passed a resolution to establish more and better facilities for educating Chinese, particularly in China.[150] Two months later, the Foreign Ministry provided substantial new funding for Tōa Dōbunkai to create a Chinese Student Division (Chūka Gakuseibu) at Tōa Dōbun Shoin. Fifty Chinese middle school graduates, recruited and publicly funded through provincial officers of education, were to be given a year's language instruction in Japanese and English prior to entering the regular three-year program alongside Japanese students.[151] Altogether, the program was designed to accommodate 200 Chinese students at any one time.

Anti-Japanese feelings around the May Fourth student demonstrations of 1919 caused insuperable difficulties in recruiting Chinese students, however. In June, Foreign Minister Uchida Yasuya advised the Japanese minister in Peking, Obata Torikichi, to recall recruiters if they were unable to meet with appropriate educational authorities.[152] In July, Shoin professor Ujita Naoyoshi found Japanese-trained Chinese warmly receptive in Canton, where he had been sent to open a middle school for Chinese. But, as Consul Ota indicated to him, the "fall from power of Japanese-trained leaders" prevented them from swaying a hostile pub-

---

[147] Ibid., pp. 143–145. In 1954, this shrine was rededicated in Saitama prefecture. For Ōuchi's view of creating a new Eastern Culture by amalgamating the Japanese and the Chinese, then taking only the best from the West, see Ōuchi, "Konoe Kazan," p. 146.

[148] TDSDS (1982), pp. 143, 159, and 161.

[149] Abe, NKBM, p. 9. The grand total of Chinese graduates, 1901–1922, was 864 students.

[150] TDSDS (1982), p. 175.

[151] See "Shina Gakubu to Tōa Dōbun Shoin no kyōtei" (Agreement between the Chinese Student Division and Tōa Dōbun Shoin), mimeo, n.d., in Gaikō Shiryōkan, 3.10.2.13 daisankan (reel 774), pp. 1200–1201.

[152] For this and related correspondence, see Gaikō Shiryōkan, 3.10.2.13 daisankan and daiyonkan (reels 773 and 774), pp. 1030–1145, 1196. See also Abe, NKBM, pp. 16–20, who quotes from some of this correspondence.

lic.[153] As for the Chinese Division at Tōa Dōbun Shoin, recruiting difficulties forced a one-year postponement of its opening.[154] Even after a year, in September 1920, a mere six students could be found to enter the one-year preparatory language course. Those six, and one other, joined Japanese students of the regular twenty-first Shoin class in April 1921.[155]

One wonders just how important the Chinese division was to Tōa Dōbun Shoin. Right at the outset, the school created practical difficulties for its Chinese students. In a classic case of bad timing, 1921 was the year Tōa Dōbun Shoin, for exclusively "Japanese" reasons and without regard to its Chinese students, switched from its twenty-one-year tradition of a Chinese-style (September–June) school year to an alien, Japanese-style (April–March) school year.

The May Fourth era was, moreover, the worst of times to be trying to recruit Chinese students for a Japanese school. Virtually any Chinese student was likely to be offended by one thing or another, including bad grades, and to become a problem if not an outright troublemaker. And trouble there was. On April 7, 1923, in connection with the movement to recover Lushun (Port Arthur) and Dairen from Japan, some "bad elements" (furyō bunshi) issued an anti-Japanese declaration and made threats against the student supervisor. Four ringleaders were expelled for "impertinence" (fukei kōi). That same night, twenty-six Chinese students demanding reversal of the expulsion order took their belongings and those of the four expelled students, plus things belonging to the twenty-nine nonstriking Chinese students, from their dormitory by car. The father of one ringleader from Tientsin, a teacher of Chinese to members of the local Japanese community, was mortified. "I'm so mad I could die [ch'i-fen yü-szu]," he wrote in a public reprimand appearing in the Tenshin ni-chinichi shinbun, possibly under duress. "If you truly desire national salvation, two routes exist. Study hard and learn a practical skill that can meet a national need; or first clean up our own government so it can reform the country and thereby bring about our own self-strengthening."[156]

Other kinds of trouble erupted periodically, usually related to politics. A partial Chinese student strike occurred around the May 25 general

[153] Ujita Naoyoshi, "Kanton gakudō shinsetsu junbi ni taisuru shisatsu hōkoku" (Report on an investigation of plans for the new Canton school) (August 25, 1919), in Gaikō Shiryōkan, pp. 1163–1164. Tōa Dōbunkai had likewise planned to open a middle school in Peking. Both Peking and Canton had to be abandoned, however, for the less politically charged atmospheres of Tientsin and Hankow. For a history of the two middle schools at Tientsin (1921–1945) and Hankow (1922–1945), see Abe, NKBM, pp. 5, 42–75.

[154] Gaikō Shiryōkan, pp. 1131–1133.

[155] For details, see the printed six-month report of Tōa Dōbunkai for April–September 1921, in ibid., pp. 1555–1558.

[156] Ibid., daigokan (reel 774), p. 2047. For related correspondence and reports, see pp. 2030–2046.

strike of 1925, and a full ten-day walkout took place in May 1928 to protest the Tsinan incident.[157] In the wake of the Northern Expedition and the Kuomintang-Communist split of 1926–1927, Chinese students (several with Communist connections) became involved with Japanese students in Marxist study and anti-imperialist activities.[158] So active did these become between 1930 and 1933 that Chalmers Johnson has written, "Tōa Dōbun [Shoin] was a major recruiting ground for Japanese members [of leftist organizations], and by late 1930 what amounted to a Japanese cell of the Chinese Communist Youth League had been established there."[159]

This was not lost on the Japanese consular police at Shanghai. In December 1930, they arrested eight Japanese students for violating Japan's Peace Preservation Act. Though released after interrogation, these eight and six other students were expelled, temporarily suspended, or withdrawn from school; the more radical among them, like Anzai Kuraji (twenty-seventh class), Mizuno Shigeru (twenty-ninth class), and Nakanishi Kō (twenty-ninth class), went on to make their marks as underground workers for the Chinese and Japanese Communist Parties.[160] A second group of twenty Japanese students was arrested in March 1933 and detained for about a month. Their subsequent public renunciation of their radical past, however, effectively broke the back of leftist student activism at Tōa Dōbun Shoin.[161]

Meanwhile, campus political troubles, "the persistent fear of dangerous thoughts [kiken shisō] extending their reach to Japanese students," recruiting difficulties, and poor performance in school resulted in Tōa Dōbunkai's August 13, 1931, decision, with Foreign Ministry approval, to stop recruiting or accepting new Chinese students. Little did anyone think that, just one month later, the school might lose all its Chinese students in their call for a mass exodus to protest Japan's Manchurian inci-

---

[157] *TDSDS* (1982), pp. 178, 180.

[158] Ibid., pp. 141–142, 231.

[159] Chalmers Johnson, *An Instance of Treason: Ozaki Hotsumi and the Sorge Spy Ring* (Tokyo: Charles E. Tuttle, 1964, 1977), p. 55.

[160] Ibid., pp. 54–55; *TDSDS* (1982), pp. 141–142; and Nakanishi Kō, *Chūgoku kakumei no arashi no naka de* (At the eye of China's revolutionary storm) (Tokyo: Aoki Shoten, 1974), p. 16. For general information surrounding the arrest, see pp. 10–22. Nakanishi was one who left Tōa Dōbun Shoin without graduating, moled into the Research Department of the South Manchuria Railway Company through the introduction of Ozaki Hotsumi, where he did some outstanding wartime research, and in the postwar years was elected a Communist member of the House of Representatives. Nishizato Tatsuo (twenty-sixth class), who had graduated in March 1930, before the arrests, joined the Chinese Communist Party in Shanghai in 1933. See his autobiography, *Kakumei no Shanhai de: Aru Nipponjin Chūgoku kyōsantōin no kiroku* (In revolutionary Shanghai: The record of a Japanese member of the Chinese Communist Party) (Tokyo: Nitchū Shuppan, 1977).

[161] *TDSDS* (1982), p. 142.

dent of September 18. Only nine students ultimately withdrew. The forty-five remaining, however, faced a far more pressing crisis just four months later—the Shanghai incident of late January 1932. That prompted twenty more students to withdraw, leaving a mere twenty-five Chinese students in four classes.[162]

The Chinese Student Division came to a formal end with the graduation of its last three Chinese students in 1934. (Students from Taiwan, registered as "Japanese," were not counted among the Chinese students.) What is noteworthy is that a program designed in 1921 to graduate fifty students per class had, after ten classes, graduated a total of forty-eight students—or less than one year's quota (see table 7.1).

More than any other Japanese institution in China, Tōa Dōbun Shoin should have been able to "read" Chinese developments at the grass roots. But the same forces propelling Japanese imperialism at home and in its colonies gained possession of those persons directing Shoin affairs. Moreover, the longing for status and a greater role for their school and its graduates within top educational and employment circles of Japan led school authorities to stress conformity to establishment ways, "Japaneseness," and orthodox thinking—precisely when bold and unconventional approaches and thinking were most needed.

If viewed as a test of cross-cultural understanding and sensitivity, Tōa Dōbun Shoin's performance in the 1920s and thereafter was a miserable failure—a far greater failure than, say, the American Yenching University, a very different kind of institution, but one shaken to its foundations by much the same kind of anti-imperialist, nationalist challenge from China.[163]

Having said this, it is well to remember the limited initial objective of Tōa Dōbun Shoin. The school's fundamental aim was not to produce "scholars" or to train Chinese or to produce great thinkers. Its mission was to train Japanese, or young China hands, with a practical working knowledge of China, to help Japanese interests penetrate China more effectively. How well graduates were contributing to this historic mission as of 1929 is suggested by tables 7.4 and 7.5.

HIGH IMPERIALISM: TŌA DŌBUN SHOIN RISES TO THE OCCASION

The Japanese seizure of Manchuria in 1931–1932 drove Japanese imperialism in China to new heights. Its repercussions, moreover, were felt worldwide, in what is commonly recognized as the opening act of World

[162] Ibid., pp. 181, 182.
[163] For the example of Yenching University, see the excellent study of Philip West, *Yenching University and Sino-Western Relations, 1916–1952* (Cambridge: Harvard University Press, 1976).

TABLE 7.4

Tōa Dōbun Shoin Graduates' Employment, by Type of Work, 1929

Type of employment	Number of graduates
Large industrial and trading companies	924
Banking	121
Education	93
Government employees	110
Chinese government employees	20
Public welfare agencies	32
Journalism	55
Independent business	110
Study abroad	4
Military, by enlistment	20
Other	40
Retired or not employed	320
Incapacitated by illness	8
Total	1,847

Source: Ōmori, "Tōa Dōbunkai," p. 89.

TABLE 7.5

Tōa Dōbun Shoin Graduates' Employment, by Place of Work, 1929

Site	Number of graduates
Manchuria (Northeast China)	415
North China	145
Central China	369
South China	89
Korea	24
Taiwan	22
Japan	730
Europe, U.S., and Southeast Asia	33
Military, by enlistment	217
Total	1,847

Source: Ōmori, "Tōa Dōbunkai," p. 89.

War II. If one were to regard the earlier advance of Japan into Manchuria as heroic—as Japanese once did—then graduates of Tōa Dōbun Shoin are unsung heroes of that advance. Drawing just upon tables in the present study, as early as 1907 (table 7.2), more than one-third of Shoin graduates (98 out of 249) were employed in Manchuria or Northeast China. This was more than in any other region of China, including the vast area of "South China" from the Yangtze River to Canton. As of 1914, the South Manchuria Railway Company alone employed 78 graduates. Fifteen years later, in 1929 (table 7.5), nearly one-quarter of all Shoin graduates (415 out of 1,847) worked in Manchuria.

With the Manchurian incident of September 1931 and formal creation of the puppet state of Manchukuo in February 1932, the stream of Shoin graduates became a flood. As many as 50 percent of the graduates from classes twenty-six to thirty (graduating in the years 1930 to 1934) found employment in Manchukuo, according to alumni records for 1936–1938. Of these, close to half worked for various agencies of the puppet government.[164] By April 1938, a full third, or 884 of 2,684 Shoin graduates, were once again employed in the new Manchukuo (see table 7.6). The numbers seeking employment in Manchukuo after class thirty drop sharply, due— says the official 1982 history of Tōa Dōbun Shoin—to friction with the Japanese military, and to "imperialist" activity that betrayed the high ideals and dreams of a Paradise of the Kingly Way (Ōdō Rakudo) and a harmonious union of the five peoples (*minzoku kyōwa*).[165]

Almost every major administrative or economic organ of post–1932 Japanese penetration into Manchuria or China proper seemed to have a Tōa Dōbun Shoin component or even core. To cite only some outstanding examples, in July 1932 the Manshū Chūō Ginkō (Central Bank of Manchukuo) was created, absorbing all assets and liabilities of former Chinese government provincial banks of China's three northeastern provinces, with sole authority to issue currency. Seventy-five Shoin graduates, many drawn for temporary service from older, established banks, served in this bank's many branches. When the new East Hopeh Autonomous Government was formed in November 1935, Saitō Masami (twentieth class) immediately recruited eleven Shoin graduates with experience in Manchukuo and added more graduates each year thereafter. The Hsin-min Hui (People's Renovation Society), a "mass organization" of Chinese and Japanese established in December 1937 for educational and pacification work in Japanese-occupied territory, had two Shoin graduates in top positions and thirty-one others in lesser posts, including "security" posts. Sixteen of these were "leaders" of their local branch organizations.[166]

[164] The figures for puppet government employees, as of 1936–1938, are twenty from the twenty-sixth class, twenty-seven from the twenty-seventh, twenty-six from the twenty-eighth, twenty-nine from the twenty-ninth, and nineteen from the thirtieth. *TDSDS* (1982), pp. 350–352. For information on Shoin graduates employed in Manchukuo in general, see ibid., pp. 344–352. For those employed by the South Manchuria Railway Company, including some 130 scholarship students sent to Tōa Dōbun Shoin between 1920 and 1945, see ibid., pp. 353–358.

[165] Ibid., p. 344.

[166] Ibid., pp. 331–332, 352–353. For more on the Hsin-min Hui, see Akira Iriye, "Toward a New Cultural Order: The Hsin-min Hui," in Iriye, ed., *The Chinese and the Japanese*, pp. 254–274.

TABLE 7.6
Tōa Dōbun Shoin Graduates' Employment, by Place and Type of Work, 1938
(Classes 1-33)

	China	Manchukuo	Japan	Other	Total
Japanese government employee	93	50	82	3	228
Manchukuo/Mongolia government employee	—	272	—	—	272
Chinese government employee	10	—	—	—	10
Independent business	50	40	156	—	247
Banking	42	92	75	3	212
Large industrial and trading companies	269	361	484	24	1,138
Education	40	18	95	—	153
Journalism	25	24	46	—	95
Public welfare agencies	24	10	37	—	71
Other	50	17	190		258
Total	603	884	1,165	32	2,684

Source: TDSDS (1982), p. 85; Huang, "Tung-ya t'ung-wen-hui," pp. 358–359.

In August 1939, Tōa Kaiun, a "national policy corporation" (kokusaku gaisha), was formed in Tokyo, capitalized at 100 million yen, to bring under Japanese control the transport system up and down the Yangtze River. Thirty Shoin graduates served in this corporation, "making a truly great contribution to the economic development of China." Kachū Kō-gyō, another national policy corporation, was founded that same year to develop mining resources along the Yangtze. The 1982 history of Tōa Dōbun Shoin speaks for itself:

The company set up mining or else administrative offices in each place, according to the nature of the work. In each instance, it first sent out an advance team to make the necessary arrangements. Invariably, the persons sent out at that point were Shoin graduates. This is proof of how important the role of Shoin products was in terms of making contact with the local Chinese population and in dealing with Chinese workers. The most important graduates at the specific mines of the company were [seven names at seven mining sites]; at the regional administrative offices were [three names at Nanking, Hankow, and Suchow].

At least one or two Shoin graduates worked at each of the mine sites. They achieved superior results in dealing with Chinese workers and in having charge of recruitment and policies toward the local residents. Ninety percent of those attending the meeting of labor managers at the main headquarters in Shanghai were Shoin graduates, just as if it were an alumni meeting.[167]

In short, Shoin graduates were in demand even in highly technical firms, for special services as labor managers, negotiators, cultural brokers, and general troubleshooters, to smooth the way for others to carry out their imperialist tasks.

Local Chinese previously engaged in transport and mining, now brought under the umbrella of powerful new Japanese enterprises, may not have been so sanguine about the Japanese "contribution to the economic development of China." M. Searle Bates, an American professor at the University of Nanking since 1920, a man with numerous Chinese contacts and extensive knowledge of the Nanking area, and a scrupulous scholar, conducted extensive investigations in and around Nanking in 1938 and 1939 on behalf of the Nanking International Relief Committee. His findings, as summarized in 1946, raise tough questions about activities like those of Shoin graduates and are pertinent to the subject of Japanese imperialism in China. Bates's statement is cautious, thoughtful, and unique. Never before published or even cited, it is quoted here at length.

During 1938 and the first months of 1939, any Japanese merchant who came to Nanking was offered both a commercial and a residential property, which were taken from Chinese owners by the Special Service Organ of the Army, or by the Gendarmerie. Often no compensation whatever was allowed; but in others a contract was drawn up and filed in Japanese offices, though payments were often withheld and the Chinese owner had no recourse. When a Chinese succeeded in rebuilding some little business, he frequently was required to accept a Japanese partner who provided no capital and who did nothing for the business except to secure needed permits or protection from the Special Service or the Gendarmerie. Moreover, banking, transportation, wholesale dealings in rice, cotton, yarn, building materials, electrical goods, metals, were made monopolies either by direct act or the use of licensing control. Gradually certain Chinese who were co-operating with the army or other Chinese assistants of Japanese organs and firms were

[167] *TDSDS* (1982), pp. 317–318, 324.

allowed fractional participation in these enterprises. But the mass of Chinese business interests were driven into the smallest shops, domestic manufacture, and mere peddling; while thousands of able-bodied men and women were able to live only by accepting the low pay of casual laborers at the Japanese supply dumps or in their transportation enterprises.

The monopolies were used against the interests of Chinese producers and consumers alike. For example, as a member of the Nanking International Relief Committee, with some friendly support from the American Embassy and from Japanese civilian officials, I strove in vain for months at a time to secure the right to buy rice in producing areas. In these efforts I had the same experience of which Chinese merchants constantly complained, that local Chinese officials had no discretionary power, but were required to refer applications to Japanese colonels. The important rice districts between Nanking and Wuhu were held by the Japanese Army to a price of eight and ten dollars per picul when the Nanking price was about twenty dollars; while the Army authorized a Japanese trading concern to move the eight-dollar rice to Tsinan and to Shanghai to sell at forty and forty-five dollars per picul.

Chinese businessmen were throttled by the monopoly of transportation and the discriminatory use of it to control all wholesale trade. I frequently heard them complain bitterly in the course of my investigations that they and their people were reduced to the status of coolies and shopboys for an alien economy. Specifically, they pointed out the discriminatory controls in such varied lines as the following: coal, salt, banking, cotton, metals, cement, lime, electric and water installations.

Furthermore, I learned in the course of my investigations that when a Chinese business was redeveloped after the general experience of burning, looting, and confiscation of commercial sites, it was continually threatened and hampered by the Special Service Section until it accepted a Japanese partner, who then provided the ever-necessary permits and a measure of security in exchange for a first claim on returns and a managerial voice that could summon aid from the military at will.

These facts were notorious. I clearly stated them in writing to the Japanese consul-general, and then published them, without objection or restraint by the Japanese authorities.[168]

Manshū Kōkū and Chūka Kōkū were airline companies under the "heavy-handed direction of the military." Nonetheless, says the 1982 his-

---

[168] M. Searle Bates, "Affidavit of Miner Searle Bates . . . submitted to the International Military Tribunal, Far East, June 25, 1946, concerning the Japanese occupation of Nanking and vicinity . . ." (IMT 432). U.S. Library of Congress, reel WT57, pp. 16–17.

tory of Dōbun Shoin, Shoin graduates followed directives loyally, and "we must not overlook the role of these companies in the economic development of China's interior and in cultural interaction with the Chinese people."[169]

Wars require military intelligence. It was a proud Shoin tradition that its graduates, like those of Nisshin Bōeki Kenkyūjo before them, had served loyally and well in every major Japanese conflict with China since 1894. By 1937, the military demand for Shoin interpreters and intelligence officers was less desperate than earlier, before the army had its own large corps of trained personnel. Nonetheless, Shoin graduates and upperclassmen were called up, and served proudly. As early as August 22, 1937, an agreement was reached between Tōa Dōbun Shoin and Tōa Dōbunkai to release fourth-year students to serve as army interpreters. Then, on September 3, Ōuchi Chōzō, Shoin principal from 1931 to 1940, issued a set of official instructions exhorting students to utilize their knowledge of Chinese language, geography, human relations, and customs "to serve the fatherland with all your hearts" as army interpreters and in other war-related endeavors, for "the eternal peace of East Asia." Starting in November, eighty Shoin seniors signed up on six different occasions in response to army requests for interpreters.[170]

At a higher level of sophistication, in 1938 the Shanghai Consulate-General assigned Foreign Ministry officer Iwai Eiichi (eighteenth class) to organize and head a new and generously funded Special Investigation Unit (Tokubetsu Chōsahan) to gather and analyze wartime data on unoccupied China. Known as the "Iwai Outfit," this unit established a wide network of contacts throughout China and, with a staff of sixty or seventy Japanese, over twenty of whom were new Shoin graduates from classes thirty-five to thirty-nine, carried out some first-rate wartime research and analysis.[171]

To provide sufficient trained personnel for these and anticipated China needs, principal Ōuchi Chōzō launched a campaign to elevate Tōa Dōbun Shoin to university status. By January 1938, an appeal had gone out for alumni support. In that appeal, Ōuchi drew attention to the "great mission" (*dai seimei*) of Tōa Dōbun Shoin in anticipation of Japan's much-expanded role in the "guidance of East Asia" (*Tōa no keirin*)."[172]

---

[169] *TDSDS* (1982), p. 324.

[170] Ibid., pp. 148–150. Ōuchi's official instructions are reproduced in full on p. 149.

[171] Iwai Eiichi, "Shanhai jidai (kōki) no omoide" (Memories of Shanghai, Part 2), *Koyū* 38 (March 1976), pp. 56, 61–62; *TDSDS* (1982), pp. 283, 391–392.

[172] Ibid., p. 155. *Keirin*, a term that appears in the Meiji Emperor's 1868 Charter Oath to mean "the [good] administration of [Japanese] state affairs," was widely used for Japanese aims in Asia in the 1870s and 1880s, as in *Tōa keirin* (implying Japanese "guidance" to improve and strengthen the state administrations of weaker neighbors). Such slogans, re-

Supporting Ōuchi's dreams were elements at the highest levels of government in Japan, most notably Konoe Fumimaro (1891–1945), son of Tōa Dōbunkai founder Prince Konoe Atsumaro, vice-president of Tōa Dōbunkai since reorganization in 1922 and its president since 1936, three-time prime minister of Japan between June 1937 and October 1941, and associated since mid-1938 with the notion that Japan's war with China was a "sacred war" during and after which Tōa Dōbunkai and Tōa Dōbun Shoin would have special missions.[173] Konoe, in his capacity as Tōa Dōbunkai president, submitted the formal request for elevation to Foreign Minister Arita Hachirō on November 8, 1938. The text of that request argued that elevation to university status would not only promote cooperation, friendship, and peace between China and Japan over the long run and "train the leadership to develop Asia [kō-A]," but that in the short run it would contribute in no small way to aiding Japanese imperial troops to bring Japan's conflict with China to an early end.[174] A government bill went to the Diet in January 1939, and on December 26, 1939, an imperial ordinance authorized Tōa Dōbun Shoin to reorganize itself as Tōa Dōbun Shoin Daigaku.[175] It was as a university, therefore, that Tōa Dōbun Shoin ended its days, training the numbers of students and graduates given in table 7.7.

EPILOGUE: DOWN BUT NOT OUT

As a university, Tōa Dōbun Shoin did not have long to prove itself. With the loss of Japan's bid to assume the guidance of East Asia went its own "great mission" to train leaders for that venture. The empire that Shoin graduates had so laboriously helped build up was suddenly reduced virtually to its dimensions of sixty years earlier, when this story began.

Tōa Dōbunkai president and three-time prime minister Konoe Fumimaro was under investigation on charges of being a war criminal. On

---

popularized for the war, thus have a quality of deja vu about them. The crucial difference is that now, unlike the nineteenth century, the full force of a modernized Japanese army is behind their implementation.

[173] On Konoe and the "sacred war," see Kōshaku [Prince] Konoe Fumimaro, "Seisen ichi shūsen (Tōa Dōbunkai no seimei)" (First anniversary of the sacred war [The Tōa Dōbunkai mission]), *Shina* 29, 8 (August 1, 1938): pp. 1–4.

[174] Quoted in *TDSDS*, pp. 155–156. The term kō-A is another wartime term dredged up from the past. Kōakai (Asia Revitalization Association), for example, was an organization founded in 1880 by prominent Japanese statesmen, scholars, and officials, which received an annual imperial grant to support projects like its Chinese language school in Tokyo. Under its subsequent name of Ajia Kyōkai, it was absorbed in 1900 into Tōa Dōbunkai. Ibid., (1982), pp. 41–42. During the Pacific War, the most important use of kō-A was in the all-important Kōain, or Asia Development Board.

[175] For the text of this and related imperial ordinances see ibid., p. 156.

TABLE 7.7

Graduates and Students of Tōa Dōbun Shoin University, by Class—Classes 40–46 (College Classes 1–7), 1939–1945

Class	University graduates; prep. course [yōka] and university [gakubu]	Specialized division students (no graduates)
40th (1939–43) 1st university class	117	—
41st (1940–44) 2d university class	166	—
42d (1941–45) 3d university class	150 (last "graduates")	—
Total	433	—
43rd (1942–) 4th university class	172	—
44th (1943–) 5th university class	192	163 (1st *specialized* class)
45th (1944–) 6th university class	100	131 (2d *specialized* class)
46th (1945–) 7th university class	177	124 (3rd *specialized* class)
Total	641 unable to graduate	418 unable to graduate

Source: TDSDS (1982), p. 154.

December 16, 1945, before he could be brought to trial, Konoe committed suicide. His father's organization, though not accused of war crimes, surrendered the name Tōa Dōbunkai in March 1946 and reconstituted itself under other names, keeping a low profile. Its lesser-known successor organizations, like Kazankai, are presently housed in Tokyo's Kazan Kaikan, an imposing nine-story structure named after Kazan Kō (the Kazan Prince), the honorific title for Prince Konoe Atsumaro. Just down the hill from the Diet building, and literally in the shadow of the Kasumigaseki Building, it sits, appropriately, on Imperial Household land.[176]

Tōa Dōbun Shoin staff and students were repatriated, along with other Shanghai Japanese, on U.S. troopships between January and April 1946. Unable to find sufficient openings at Japanese colleges and universities, they joined with expatriates from Keijō (Seoul) and Taihoku (Taipei) imperial universities to found a new university. This new institution, Aichi

[176] Ibid., pp. 62–63.

University, occupied the grounds and buildings of the Reserve Officer Candidate School of Toyohashi City, not far from Nagoya. It opened its doors in January 1947, and in March it survived inspection by U.S. Occupation officers investigating revival of "the Tōa Dōbun Shoin spy school." Besides fulfilling the promise of a college education for Shoin Daigaku students, Aichi University provided a home for the forty-thousand-volume research library of Tōa Dōbunkai and a home for Tōa Dōbun Shoin student records.[177]

It is the historian's great good fortune that Koyūkai (Shanghai Friends Association), the alumni association for Tōa Dōbun Shoin, has remained vital and active over the years.[178] That association has carefully preserved historical records and alumni reminiscences and is publisher of the superb 775-page history of the school (1982). It puts out *Koyū*, the alumni magazine, as well as updated alumni directories with current addresses.

To my knowledge, no serious thought has been given to reestablishing Tōa Dōbun Shoin in China. The Chinese government would not permit it. It is thus easy to agree with the last sentence of the quotation opening this essay: "A school like this probably cannot be created a second time"—in China or anywhere else in the world.

In closing, what might be said about the role and meaning of Tōa Dōbun Shoin in Japan's modern relationship with China? My own view, simply stated, is that Tōa Dōbun Shoin was an enabling arm of Japanese imperialism in China. Had there been no such institution by the time of the Twenty-One Demands, it—or its collective equivalent—would have been created to produce the trained manpower for Japan's penetration of China.

But there is a more boldly stated view that demands consideration. This is best expressed by Nakanishi Kō, a dropout from the twenty-ninth Shoin class. Tōa Dōbun Shoin was founded, Nakanishi writes, "to train the advance guard of Japanese imperialism in China." Its purpose, he reiterates, was "to train the cadres for Japanese imperialism in China." Even with the best of intentions, Japanese in China invariably became "the tools of Japanese imperialist aggression."[179]

Admirers of Tōa Dōbun Shoin and its precursors expressed views surprisingly similar to Nakanishi's, without mention of "imperialism," of course. In 1912, for example, an advertisement promoting Inoue Masaji's 1910 biography of Arao Sei appeared in *Shina*, the official journal of Tōa Dōbunkai. That advertisement called Arao's Nisshin Bōeki Kenkyūjo

177 Ibid., pp. 166–173. For the quote on "the Dōbun Shoin spy school," see p. 170.
178 For a good summary account of Koyūkai both before and after the war, see ibid., pp. 701–708.
179 Nakanishi, *Chūgoku kakumei*, pp. 7, 8, and 10, respectively. For more on Nakanishi, see note 160, above.

"an officer training school for Japan's trade with China."[180] Twenty-five years later, Kanzaki Kiyoshi, also writing in *Shina*, called Nisshin Bōeki Kenkyūjo and Arao's earlier Hankow Rakuzendō "agencies for China research and political espionage [*seijiteki chōhō*]."[181]

Admirers and critics alike thus employ language that seems to indict. Those indictments raise serious questions, questions that have no simple or final answers. But surely no place is more appropriate to air such questions than a volume on Japanese imperialism in China.

[180] *Shina* 3, 5 (March 5, 1912): *i*.

[181] Kanzaki Kiyoshi, "Hokushi ni okeru Nihongo no bunkateki seiryoku (jō)" (Cultural influences of the Japanese language in North China, part 1), *Shina* 27, 8 (August 1, 1936): 46–47.

CHAPTER 8

The Foreign Ministry's Cultural Agenda for China: The Boxer Indemnity

Sophia Lee

Cultural exchange has become a regular feature of diplomacy in the twentieth century. Officially sponsored opportunities for education and research, and performances in the arts are often touted as one of the more civilized aspects of international relations. However noble the ideal, cultural diplomacy is in reality an alloy of pure self-interest and avowed altruism in variable proportions (some would claim that it is simply a clever ploy to cloak self-interest in the haze of altruism). Whether or not the presence of altruism is verifiable, cultural diplomacy is undeniably fraught with tension between the desire to seek knowledge and express creativity without constraints and the need to conform to domestic and international orthodoxies. Those taking part in cultural activities sponsored by a foreign country risk charges of disloyalty to their own country and impurity in their works. These charges tend to be particularly vitriolic when the country accepting the "favor" is deemed in some way unequal to the one providing it.[1]

When the signers of the Boxer Protocol returned to China their respective shares of the indemnity during the early decades of this century, they stipulated that China use all or part of the remission for cultural purposes. These conditions provided for most of the powers the first opportunity to engage in cultural diplomacy with China. It was cultural diplomacy with an ironic twist: the funds these foreign governments obliged China to spend for the enlightenment of the Chinese people had originally come from China's pinched coffers; moreover, the claims exacted by the powers had been for the most part inflated. Unwilling to grant China autonomous control over the remitted funds, these powers insisted on sharing with China the duties of allocation. Many Chinese found this arrangement a singularly bitter pill to swallow while the world viewed the re-

---

[1] One striking example of this predicament is described in Noriko Kamachi, "Historical Consciousness and Identity: Debate of Japanese China Specialists over American Research Funds," *Journal of Asian Studies*, 34, 4 (August 1975): 981–994.

mission as acts of magnanimity for which China ought to express profound gratitude.

Following the examples set by the Soviet Union, the United States, and Great Britain, the Japanese Diet in 1923 directed the Foreign Ministry to set up a special account, using the remainder of Japan's share of the Boxer indemnity, plus funds from Shantung railroads and other properties, to finance cultural programs for China. Thus, the only non-Western signer of the Boxer Protocol took upon itself the unenviable task of attempting to use cultural diplomacy to win the good will of a neighbor highly conscious of its cultural influence upon Japan in a distant past and deeply wounded by Tokyo's military and diplomatic assaults in recent times.

Unlike the remission policies of most of its Western colleagues, Japan's Boxer legislation did not inaugurate a new phase in its official cultural relations with China, nor did it mark the first time a Japanese government office underwrote cultural activities in China since the two countries assumed modern-style diplomatic relations in 1871.[2] It would indeed be difficult to pinpoint a date in the early Meiji period as the start of modern Sino-Japanese cultural relations because contact between the continent and the archipelago had never been completely suspended in historical times. From the ninth to the mid-nineteenth century, Buddhist monks had been the principal carriers of cultural ideas, and traders, the principal brokers in the exchange of cultural artifacts. When bilateral interaction resumed after the ban on travel abroad for learning and commerce was lifted by the *bakufu* in 1866 (after several *Han* had already ignored the proscription), diplomats and adventurers, journalists and sinologists joined Buddhist missionaries and traders in their journey west to China. These sojourners' activities in China and their impressions of China, though varied, signaled a dramatic reversal of roles in Sino-Japanese cultural relations.[3] Domestic conditions in both countries and international politics channeled the flow of new ideas about government, law, and literature westward from Japan to China.

The pace of cultural interaction accelerated after the Sino-Japanese War (1894–1895) as more Japanese and Chinese traveled to each other's countries. In Japan, several schools were founded to accommodate an increasing number of Chinese students.[4] In China, numerous services and or-

---

[2] Nearly one thousand volumes (*satsu*) of documents detailing all the activities financed by the remitted funds are stored in the Gaimushō Gaikō Shiryōkan under the classification H.

[3] See Marius B. Jansen, "Japanese Views of China During the Meiji Period," in Albert Feuerwerker, Rhoads Murphey, and Mary Wright, eds., *Approaches to Modern Chinese History* (Berkeley: University of California Press, 1967), pp. 163–189.

[4] Sanetō Keishū, *Chūgokujin Nihon ryūgakushi* (Tokyo: Kuroshio shuppan, 1960), pp. 1–87.

ganizations were established to meet the cultural and social needs of growing Japanese communities in the treaty ports. On a smaller scale, an array of Japanese cultural enterprises intended for the Chinese, ranging from Buddhist missionary efforts and Chinese-language newspapers to schools to prepare Chinese for studying in Japan, also began to appear in several major Chinese cities, both within and outside Japanese concessions.[5]

Most of the enterprises for the Chinese relied on financial support from Japanese and Chinese individuals and private organizations. Although the government in Tokyo—the Foreign Ministry in particular—was neither the financial nor the spiritual mainstay of these enterprises, it was far from being uninterested in the cultural activities of its citizens in China.[6] In a negative way, the home government, through its consular system and various police forces stationed in China, was able to monitor and, whenever necessary, to interdict activities it deemed undesirable.[7] In a positive way, the government, no doubt persuaded by notables such as Konoe Atsumaro and Ōkuma Shigenobu, provided encouragement and occasional funding for a handful of Japanese cultural enterprises on the continent, such as the Tōa Dōbunkai (East Asia Common Culture Association) and Dōjinkai (Universal Benevolence Association).[8] Thus, starting from the early 1900s a select group of Japanese cultural organizations in China, some intended primarily for Japanese residents and others for the Chinese, enjoyed semi-official status. Official involvement in these or-

[5] Fujii Masao, *Nihon no zai-Shi bunka jigyō, miteikō* (Tokyo: Tōa kenkyūjo, 1940), enumerates many cultural and social enterprises for both the Japanese and the Chinese in China. Sanetō, *Chūgokujin Nihon ryūgakushi*, pp. 87–99, describes these preparatory schools and their Japanese teachers.

[6] For a brief survey of a few aspects of Japan's official cultural policies in China and the West, plus a selected bibliography, see Robert S. Schwantes, "Japan's Cultural Foreign Policies," in James W. Morley, ed., *Japan's Foreign Policy, 1868–1941: A Research Guide* (New York: Columbia University Press, 1974), pp. 153–183.

[7] The 1896 Treaty of Commerce and Navigation between China and Japan stipulated that Japanese subjects were allowed to reside in the treaty ports without passports, but for travel outside the treaty ports they needed passports issued by the Japanese Consulate and countersigned by Chinese local authorities. See John V. A. MacMurray, ed., *Treaties and Agreements With and Concerning China*, vol. 1 (New York: Oxford University Press, 1921), p. 69.

Although it would be difficult to measure in full the effectiveness of such a surveillance and control system, Japanese consulates certainly did expel from China Japanese who, in official estimation, had become persona non grata. For example, in 1913, shortly after the assassination of Sung Chiao-jen, the Japanese consul in Shanghai ordered Kita Ikki to leave China and to stay away for at least three years. See George M. Wilson, *Radical Nationalist in Japan: Kita Ikki, 1883–1937* (Cambridge: Harvard University Press, 1969), p. 52.

[8] Marius B. Jansen, "Konoe Atsumaro," in Akira Iriye, ed., *The Chinese and the Japanese: Essays in Political and Cultural Interactions* (Princeton: Princeton University Press, 1980), pp. 107–123.

ganizations was the rehearsal for full-fledged engagement in cultural diplomacy when the Boxer funds became available.

Before 1937, neither the Foreign Ministry nor the government as a whole monopolized Japan's cultural relations with China. In fact, it is commonly assumed that cultural relations imply peaceful interaction and that in the Sino-Japanese case during the first half of this century only discord could be found within official purview. Much of our knowledge of Sino-Japanese cultural relations during that time is culled from memoirs and biographies of Japanese and Chinese individuals not directly involved in diplomacy and politics. Friendships among private citizens from the two countries during that period are still celebrated as comforting anomalies in an otherwise traumatic time of aggression and slaughter. Not a famous landmark in modern Sino-Japanese relations,[9] Tokyo's remission of the Boxer indemnity and its accompanying cultural agenda for China are nonetheless also exceptions in an otherwise sordid chapter of diplomatic history. The 1923 legislation and subsequent amendments showed both the limitations and the possibilities of peaceful interaction between two countries so inextricably linked by a shared cultural past and yet so hopelessly entangled in their respective struggles to gain independence and respectability in the modern world.

THE CULTURAL AFFAIRS OFFICE

The Foreign Ministry's cultural agenda for China must be viewed as an integral part of Japan's quest for cultural and moral parity with the West.[10] The most conspicuous refrain in the Diet deliberations concerning the Boxer remission in the early 1920s (and concerning Chinese students in Japan a few years earlier) accentuated Japan's position as the only enlightened country in the East and its duty to advance world civilization. To be regarded as a civilizing leader in the world, some Diet members reasoned, Japan must help China to improve its defective culture, and in turn enhance the image of the East in the eyes of the world. Interestingly, the term used to articulate this "civilizing mission" in China, kyōka, is the Japanese pronunciation of the Chinese term chiao-hua, which the Middle Kingdom had used to rationalize its policies of employing culture and

---

[9] In a standard English-language account of the Boxer indemnity, Japan was excluded from the list of countries that returned the funds to China. See "Late Ch'ing Foreign Relations, 1866–1905," in *The Cambridge History of China*. Vol. 11: *Late Ch'ing, 1800–1911* (Cambridge: Cambridge University Press, 1980), p. 127.

[10] For a discussion of one influential Japanese intellectual's views on this quest, see Peter Duus, "Nagai Ryūtarō and the White Peril, 1905–1944," *Journal of Asian Studies* 31, 1 (November 1971): 41–48.

education to pacify the masses within the empire and the "barbarian neighbors" along its borders.[11]

Though seldom identified explicitly, Japan's security concerns also figured prominently in this civilizing mission. As in many other aspects of its dealings with China, Tokyo kept a wary surveillance over the cultural activities of Westerners in China. It feared that its lackluster performance in the cultural arena on the continent would adversely affect all other aspects of its relationship with China and thus allow the West to maintain the upper hand there. In spite of all their conflicting interests in China, the powers followed the same prescription for cultural diplomacy: relief work and medical services for the masses, and, more important, education, especially higher education, for China's future elites. In part because of the magnitude of China's social and economic problems, and in part because of their faith in the omnipotence of education, the powers believed that to help develop China's education and to train its future leaders at home and abroad would be the best cultural investment to make. They optimistically assumed that Chinese who had benefited from this kind of foreign largesse would without doubt be favorably disposed toward their foreign "patrons" when they assumed leadership positions in China's government, business, and education circles. According to one American educator around the turn of the century, this type of cultural investment in China would yield nothing less than the "intellectual and spiritual domination of its leaders."[12] It was concern over this international competition in China's cultural arena that propelled Japanese officials to reevaluate Tokyo's cultural relations with China in the late 1910s.

Japan's victory over China in 1895 proved its attainment of modern nationhood. The abolition of the civil service examination system by the Ch'ing court a decade later created in China an urgent need for models of and opportunities for modern-style education. These circumstances, aided by geography, provided Japan with an unprecedented opportunity, unrivaled by any other foreign power, to exert considerable influence on China's nascent educational system during the first decade and a half of this century. Thousands of Chinese students enrolled in schools in Japan, and scores of Japanese teachers and educational consultants were invited

[11] Discussions of Japan's "civilizing mission" and the Diet debates concerning the student problem and the Boxer remission are based on Dai-Nihon Teikoku Gikai-shi Kankō Kai, comp., *Dai Nihon teikoku gikai shi* (Record of the Imperial Diet of Japan) (hereafter, *GS*) (Tokyo: Shizuoka, 1926–1930), 40th session (1918), pp. 565–567, 598, 632; 41st session (1919), pp. 1247–1248; 43rd [special] session (1920), pp. 563–564; 44th session (1921), pp. 1462–1463, 1897–1898; 46th session (1923), pp. 313–314, 397–400, 1031–1036; 51st session (1926), pp. 301–304, 340, 763–766, 1081–1082.

[12] Quoted in Michael H. Hunt, "The American Remission of the Boxer Indemnity: A Reappraisal," *Journal of Asian Studies*, 31, 3 (May 1972): 550.

to the continent by China's central and provincial governments. But by the mid-1910s, the numbers of Chinese students in Japan and Japanese teachers in China had both declined. Japan was not able to maintain its preeminent position partly because Japanese discrimination against Chinese students and growing anti-Japanese feelings in China had diminished Japan's prestige. More important, by the early 1910s modern schools were no longer a rarity on Chinese soil, and opportunities to study in other foreign countries became more abundant. The latter development was enhanced by Washington's decision in 1908 to return about two-thirds of its share of the Boxer indemnity to China for the purpose of educating China's youth both in China and in the United States.[13] A dramatic increase in American missionary activities in China's secondary and higher education starting from the first decade of the new century also helped to boost U.S. popularity.[14]

In 1918, during the fortieth session of the Diet the issue of "Chinese students in Japan" appeared on the docket in the lower house. Interest in the student problem was apparently heightened by the impending expiration of an official agreement between Tokyo and Peking to send a predetermined annual quota of Chinese students to Japan. But Diet members were concerned with more than just why fewer Chinese students were coming to Japan and what should be done to reverse the decline. The ramifications of this "student problem" reached far beyond classrooms and dormitories. At stake was not merely the success or failure of Japan's civilizing mission in China; Japan's international prestige was also on trial. Some believed that since World War I had revealed all too clearly the flaws of the West, Japan's duty to contribute to a better world civilization had become more urgent and more justified. Others urged the government to pursue an independent China policy instead of slavishly complying with the wishes of Britain and the United States. Implicit in this call for self-determination was the desire to expel Westerners from Asia. But not everything Western had become unworthy of emulation. Those advocating more funding and better planning for cultural programs for the Chinese recited to fellow Diet members lengthy and awesome descriptions of well-known cultural institutions in China, operated by Western—

[13] Interestingly, some American officials cited the popularity among Chinese students of studying in Japan during the first decade of this century in support of the allocation of America's Boxer remission for educational purposes. See ibid., pp. 539–559; Wang Shu-huai, *Keng-tzu p'ei-k'uan* (Taipei: Academia Sinica, 1974), pp. 269–336.

[14] Between 1900 and 1925, American Protestant workers in China increased fivefold, from about one thousand to five thousand. The year 1925 was a high-water mark for American Protestant educational efforts in China, consisting of "over 300 middle or high schools, with an enrollment of nearly 26,000 students, and sixteen colleges and universities." See James C. Thomson, Jr., Peter W. Stanley, and John Curtis Perry, *Sentimental Imperialists: The American Experience in East Asia* (New York: Harper & Row, 1981), pp. 51–55.

overwhelmingly American—missionary and philanthropic organizations (the Rockefeller-funded Peking Union Medical College, then under construction, received special mention). They also unleashed unsparing criticisms against what they considered to be Japan's feeble cultural efforts. One member grumbled that, unlike the dazzling display of Western culture staged by the powers, Japan's dim cultural presence in China lagged far behind the visibility of its diplomatic and military presence on Chinese soil.[15]

Another "China issue" debated in the Diet in the late 1910s concerned the Boxer remission. In 1917, China had obtained permission from several signers of the Boxer Protocol to delay, for five years, payment of the indemnity as a form of reward for its contributions to the Allied cause. During this hiatus, talks of remission to aid China's education and industry were bandied about in foreign capitals, and China's educational and political leaders lobbied feverishly for remission and for the subsequent funding of their favored projects. Recognizing that remission was to become the consensus among the Western powers, Tokyo began to discuss the possibility of returning its share of the indemnity to China for cultural purposes. Thus the student problem and the indemnity issue, separate but not unrelated, provided the impetus for the 1923 legislation.

The legislation itself was the outcome of several rounds of domestic debates and diplomatic negotiations that also began in the late 1910s. Proposed by Yamamoto Jōtarō,[16] together with several other Diet members, the bill stipulated the establishment of a special account based on the remaining principal and interest of Japan's Boxer indemnity and income from Shantung railroads, public properties, and mining enterprises (acquired from Germany and settled with China at the Washington Conference in 1922).[17] Subject to approval by the Diet, an annual expenditure not to exceed 2.5 million yen (increased to 3 million in 1926) was earmarked for three areas of activities: (1) education, scholarship, public health, and relief work in China; (2) similar activities for Chinese nationals in Japan; and (3) scholarly research on China to be conducted in Japan. A reserve fund was also set up to insure support after the expiration of the Shantung agreement in 1938 and the Boxer agreement in 1945. The

[15] GS, 40th session (1918), pp. 565–567.

[16] Businessman and politician Yamamoto Jōtarō (1867–1936) was an employee of the Shanghai branch of Mitsui Bussan during most of the period from 1888 to 1908, and president of the South Manchuria Railway Company from 1927 to 1929. During the 1911 Revolution, he was one of the Japanese businessmen who helped a group of Chinese students stranded in Japan by paying for their passage home.

[17] Although the special account contained two sources of income, the Boxer and Shantung funds, both primary and secondary sources generally refer to the special account as the Boxer account. This chapter will follow the same practice.

Education Ministry tried to claim a prerogative over the administration of the proposed cultural programs, but prevailing judgment favored the ministry that had negotiated the Boxer indemnity and the Shantung settlement. An office, Tai-Shi Bunka Jimukyoku (China Cultural Affairs Bureau), was created in the Foreign Ministry to supervise and fund various programs in China and Japan.[18]

In the summer of 1923, after the bill was passed, the Foreign Ministry dispatched one of its officials, Okabe Nagakage (1884–1970),[19] and an eminent Tokyo Imperial University professor of medicine, Irisawa Tatsukichi (1865–1938), to China to solicit Chinese opinions and to prepare for negotiations. These two men were greeted by considerable Chinese opposition to the aims and methods outlined in the recently announced cultural agenda. Tokyo's insistence on total control of the funds and Chinese compliance with Japanese regulations invited Chinese animosity. In December 1923, a series of informal negotiations took place in Tokyo between China's minister in Japan, Wang Jung-po (1878–1933), and chief of the new Cultural Affairs Bureau, Debuchi Katsuji (1878–1947).[20] Influenced by the unpopular reception and constructive suggestions Okabe and Irisawa had received in China, these two negotiators decided to shift the focus of the cultural agenda away from educational and medical activities in China, and Chinese students in Japan. Vowing to respect the opinions of Chinese intellectuals, the Wang-Debuchi informal agreement of February 1924 announced that the establishment of research institutes and libraries in China, in particular a humanities institute in Peking and a science institute in Shanghai, would become the core of Japan's cultural efforts.[21] The negotiators reasoned that such a change would bring about

---

[18] The term *bunka* was used by the Foreign Ministry to cover an area broader than what would normally be construed as culture today. In current diplomatic agreements, the term "cultural exchange" often refers only to the humanities and is distinguished from the term "scientific exchange." The institutional history of this office is briefly summarized in Gaimushō Hyakunenshi Hensan Iinkai, ed., *Gaimushō no hyakunen*, vol. 1 (Tokyo: Hara Shobō, 1969), pp. 1039–1048, and described in more detail in Kawamura Kazuo, "Tai-Shi bunka jigyō kankei shi—kansei jō yori mitaru," *Rekishi kyōiku* 15, 8 (August 1967), pp. 80–95. A comprehensive account of the evolution of this Foreign Ministry office and Chinese responses to Japan's efforts in the second half of the 1920s is given in Abe Hiroshi, "Nihon no 'Tai-Shi bunka jigyō' to Chūgoku kyōiku bunkakai—1920 nendai kōhanki o chūshin to shite," *Kan*, 8, 5–6 (1979): 213–278. Also see Wang, *Keng-tzu p'ei-k'uan*, pp. 481–514; and Huang Fu-ch'ing, *Chin-tai Jih-pen tsai-Hua wen-hua chi she-hui shih-yeh chi yen-chiu* (Taipei: Academia Sinica, 1982), pp. 113–126.

[19] Okabe was to head the cultural affairs office from December 1924 to February 1929.

[20] Debuchi was concurrently chief of the Asia Bureau (Ajia Kyoku), a practice sanctioned by the Foreign Ministry's personnel regulations.

[21] Although the Wang-Debuchi agreement was reached in February 1924, it would be useful to investigate whether their decision to found a science institute in Shanghai was in any way influenced by a Chinese decision made public in June 1924 to use the second Amer-

greater Chinese participation on Chinese soil, and hence genuine cooperation between the two countries. The agreement did not, however,
mention that emphasis on these new institutes would not be translated
into munificent appropriations unrivaled by other programs receiving
support from the Boxer account. To insure bilateral cooperation in the
institutes, an advisory committee of twenty—ten Chinese and ten Japanese, plus an additional Chinese serving as chairman—would be formed.
Many Chinese objected to the implication of the term "Tai-Shi," which
they said suggested unilateral action rather than bilateral cooperation.
Others were offended by the use of the name "Shina." As a result, Tokyo
eliminated "Tai-Shi" from the name of the recently created bureau and
changed it to Bunka Jigyōbu (Cultural Affairs Division) at the end of
1924. (The term "Tai-Shi Bunka Jigyō," however, continued to be widely
used by the Japanese until 1945.) In May 1925, Japan's minister in China,
Yoshizawa Kenkichi, presented the terms of the Wang-Debuchi agreement to China's foreign relations chief, Shen Tuan-lin, and obtained formal approval.

Some may consider the changes made in Tokyo commendable gestures
of goodwill toward the Chinese, but many Chinese who had opposed the
original cultural agenda in 1923 remained unconvinced of the possibility
of genuine cooperation. Some argued that the Wang–Debuchi agreement
demanded Chinese submission, not cooperation. Others claimed that Japan was simply engaged in cultural aggression under the guise of Boxer
remission. Ethnocentric critics also questioned Japan's ability to manage
cultural enterprises for China: since Japan had no culture of its own, it
could only benefit from China but had nothing to offer in return.[22]
Chinese opposition was no doubt also inspired by the educational rights
recovery movement of 1924 and the related anti-Christian movement of
1922.[23]

In 1925, a binational committee (officially called the Tōhō Bunka Jigyō
Sōiinkai in Japanese; Tung-fang Wen-hua Shih-yeh Tsung-wei-yuan-hui
in Chinese) was established in Peking, and a subcommittee was formed
in Shanghai to prepare for the opening of the respective institutes. Di-

---

ican remission (authorized by the U.S. Congress in May 1924) for "educational and cultural
purposes, paying especial attention to scientific requirements." See Westel W. Willoughby,
Foreign Rights and Interests in China (Baltimore: Johns Hopkins Press, 1927), pp. 1016–1019.

[22] For summaries of various opposing Chinese views, see Wang, *Keng-tzu p'ei-k'uan*, pp.
497–515; Abe Hiroshi, "Nihon no 'Tai-Shi bunka jigyō,' " pp. 219, 221–222, and 226–229;
and Huang, *Chin-tai Jih-pen*, pp. 199–207.

[23] For a brief discussion of these two movements, see Jessie G. Lutz, *China and the Christian Colleges, 1850–1950* (Ithaca: Cornell University Press, 1971), pp. 215–237. It should be
noted that Chinese ire was not reserved for the Japanese alone. Around 1925, protracted
negotiations and disputes with Great Britain over the management of its Boxer remission
also drew angry protests from Chinese intellectuals.

vided almost evenly according to nationality (with a slight advantage to the Chinese), members of these two committees consisted mainly of Chinese and Japanese scholars, with a handful of officials from both governments.[24] Meetings of the committees in Peking and Shanghai hobbled along while the May 30th (1925) incident and the Northern Expedition added fuel to Chinese nationalism and anti-Japanese sentiments. Intense pressure was placed on Chinese committee members to withdraw; some Chinese members were not at all sure of the efficacy, or even the feasibility, of cooperating with the Japanese. Attempts by the Chinese side to gain more authority were not successful. As if disagreements between the Chinese and Japanese were not enough, the Chinese side was also shaken by internal conflict between older members who had no experience in dealing with the Japanese and younger members who had studied in Japan and spoke Japanese.[25] The coup de grace was delivered in June 1928 when Japanese troops incited hostilities with the Nationalist Northern Expedition forces at Tsinan. All the Chinese members resigned from the committees. The following year the Chinese government terminated official participation in these committees. From 1929 to 1931 the Nanking government, however, did attempt to renegotiate the terms stipulated in the Wang-Debuchi agreement and sought complete control of the funds, but the Manchurian incident destroyed all hopes for a new agreement.

The 1923 legislation was not without detractors back in Tokyo. Hapless ministers and other officials had to endure blunt queries and sharp attacks in the Diet, especially in the lower house. With good reason, some Diet members questioned the wisdom of filling the binational advisory committees with too many political has-beens and old-fashioned scholars on the Chinese side and bureaucratic relics and wizened academics on the Japanese side—all anachronisms in China's new culture. Others were dis-

[24] Many Chinese members of the committee in Peking held degrees from the Ch'ing examination system, and Chinese members of the subcommittee in Shanghai were mostly scientists trained in Japan and the West. The Chinese contingent included Hsiung Hsi-ling (1870–1942), official in the Ch'ing and early Republican governments, and noted philanthropist; Chiang Yung (b. 1878), graduate of Waseda University and chair of the Law Codification Commission of the Peking government in 1913; Cheng Chen-wen (b. 1890), Japanese-trained chemist and member of the T'ung-meng-hui; Chu Chia-hua (1893–1963), German-trained geologist, leader of pro-Kuomintang movement in Peking in the mid-1920s, and president of Academia Sinica from 1940 to 1958; K'o Shao-min (1850–1933), eminent historian and classical scholar who received an honorary doctorate in humanities from Tokyo Imperial University in 1923 for his work *Hsin Yüan-shih*; and Wang Shu-nan (1852–1936), classical scholar and member of the early Republican national assembly. The Japanese contingent included prominent sinologists Hattori Unokichi (1867–1939) and Kanō Naoki (1868–1947), prominent scientists Irisawa Tatsukichi (1865–1938) and Keimatsu Katsuzaemon (1876–1954), and long-time consular official in China Segawa Asanoshin.

[25] Of the twenty-one Chinese members, six were known to have studied in Japan.

pleased with the decision to use portions of this new source of funding to continue Foreign Ministry support of semi-official organizations such as the Tōa Dōbunkai and Dōjinkai. Some pointedly asked whether more Japanese than Chinese were benefiting from the Boxer-funded cultural programs. A few aired their dissatisfaction with Tokyo's overall China policy and chided officials for hiding behind the cultural agenda to avoid more important issues concerning China. After 1923, legislators' familiar complaints of too much funding and no results were also frequently heard on the Diet floor.

Chinese and Japanese opposition notwithstanding, the Pekin Jimbun Kagaku Kenkyūjo (Peking Humanities Institute) was opened in 1927, and the Shanhai Shizen Kagaku Kenkyūjo (Shanghai Science Institute) in 1931. The Japanese continued to observe the regulations established by the joint committees before the Tsinan incident. Therefore, on several occasions when new directors had to be chosen without official Chinese participation, the Japanese side felt obligated to give titles of acting or deputy directors to the newly appointed Japanese directors.

The home office in Tokyo also experienced changes, undertaken in part to mitigate Chinese opposition. In December 1924, the Cultural Affairs Bureau was demoted to a division (*bu*) and placed within the jurisdiction of the Asia Bureau, but the cultural division chief no longer concurrently headed the Asia Bureau. In June 1927, the Cultural Affairs Division was taken out of the Asia Bureau and made into an independent division to minimize political entanglement, real or apparent. Two years later, another change was made to further reduce misunderstanding about the purported apolitical nature of the cultural division: from June 1929 the office of the division chief was no longer held concurrently with other Foreign Ministry duties.[26]

After the Tsinan incident, to offset anticipated decline in Chinese interest in the Foreign Ministry's cultural efforts, Tokyo revived one of the original plans set forth in 1923, namely, sinological research institutes in Japan. The creation of the Tōhō Bunka Gakuin in Tokyo and Kyoto in 1929 realized that plan, thus mitigating Japanese concern over increasing Western involvement in sinological research.[27] Neither the withdrawal of official Chinese participation in the committees nor Nanking's subse-

---

[26] The four officials who held the position of cultural division chief from its founding in May 1923 to the Marco Polo Bridge incident on July 7, 1937, were Debuchi Katsuji (from May 1923 to December 1924), Okabe Nagakage (from December 1924 to February 1929), Tsubogami Teiji (from February 1929 to July 1934), and Okada Kanekazu (from July 1934 to March 1938). All were career diplomats with no apparent academic specialization in Chinese affairs.

[27] These were the predecessors of the present-day Tōyō Bunka Kenkyūjo at Tokyo University and the Jimbun Kagaku Kenkyūjo at Kyoto University.

quent injunction stopped Chinese students in Japan from accepting Boxer scholarships from the cultural affairs office and making use of the dormitories and services provided by the Nikka Gakkai (Japan–China Association), which received Boxer funds. The cultural division also continued to finance trips for Chinese and Japanese intellectuals to lecture and present exhibits in each other's countries. Books were presented to Chinese schools and libraries. Moreover, provisions were made in 1930 to give stipends to Japanese students wishing to study in China. In addition to the Tōa Dōbunkai and Dōjinkai, as mentioned above, the Foreign Ministry also used the remitted funds (principally from the Shantung properties) to support the educational institutions of several Japanese resident associations in China.

Shortly after the founding of Manchukuo in 1932, the cultural division created a Nichi-Man Bunka Kyōkai (Japan-Manchuria Cultural Association) to promote research and preservation work in Manchuria. In response to worldwide disapproval of Japanese action in Manchuria, the division in 1935 added a new section (Kokusai Bunka Jigyō) to oversee and to improve cultural relations with the West. With the onset of the "North China autonomous movement," the cultural division again raised the ceiling of its annual budget and began to broaden the scope of its activities by opening an institute of industrial research in Peking and two libraries for the general public in Peking and Shanghai respectively. But the Marco Polo Bridge incident drastically changed the Foreign Ministry's cultural agenda for China. In 1938, many of the duties of the cultural office were transferred to the newly established Kōain (Asia Development Board), and then in 1942 to the Daitōashō (Greater East Asia Ministry). The Foreign Ministry's Cultural Affairs Division was abolished in 1940. The following year, management of the Boxer account became the responsibility of the Finance Ministry.[28]

[28] Readily available sources only permit a conjectural account of the ways the annual budget was divided among the various recipients. Kawamura Kazuo, "Tai-Shi bunka jigyō," p. 86, offers the following statistics: from 1927 to 1932, the Tōa Dōbunkai received 3.521 million yen; Dōjinkai, 4.415 million; and Nikka Gakkai, 588,000, which may be interpreted as annual expenditures of 590,000 (Tōa Dōbunkai), 736,000 (Dōjinkai), and 98,000 (Nikka Gakkai) yen. According to figures in Abe Hiroshi's study ("Tai-Shi bunka jigyō," p. 225), from 1924 to 1928 the average estimated annual budget for the Peking and Shanghai institutes combined was slightly over 890,000 yen, of which an annual average of approximately 620,000 was spent on construction and renovation of buildings for the two institutes; and from 1929 to 1933, the Tōhō Bunka Gakuin received an annual average of about 160,000 yen (p. 258). From 1923 to 1934, an annual average of about 55,000 yen was appropriated for Japanese scholars to travel to China to present lectures and exhibits; for Chinese scholars to travel to Japan, about 40,000 yen was used each year (Huang, *Chin-tai Jih-pen*, pp. 181–182).

Peking Humanities Institute

To some scholars in both China and Japan, the Peking Humanities Institute and its achievements represented the best in Sino-Japanese cultural cooperation. In 1924, the joint committee in Peking purchased an opulent mansion situated on more than seven acres of land on the city's fashionable Wang-fu-ching Avenue. The mansion had been occupied by Jung-lu, Manchu general and confidant of the empress dowager, and subsequently by Yüan Shih-k'ai and Li Yüan-hung, presidents of the republic. The committee had decided at a meeting in October 1927 that the principal goal of the institute in Peking would be to compile a sequel to the *Ssu-k'u ch'üan-shu t'i-yao* (summaries and annotations of the eighteenth-century compilation, *The Complete Library of the Four Treasuries*), one of several research projects that had received serious consideration in Chinese scholarly circles before Japan returned the Boxer funds. Two months later the institute was officially opened. For about half a decade, ignorance, nepotism, and sinecure seriously hampered progress on the *Ssu-k'u* project. A much-needed housecleaning took place in 1933 when Hashikawa Tokio (1895–1983) was named director of the institute.[29]

To numerous Japanese intellectuals who traveled through and lived in Peking in the 1920s and 1930s, Hashikawa was Japan's unofficial cultural attaché. Accounts by Japanese scholars and students in Peking seldom fail to mention the assistance they received from him. For those studying Republican China, Hashikawa is probably best known as the compiler of *Chūgoku bunkakai jimbutsu sōkan* (a biographical dictionary of modern Chinese cultural figures, published in Peking in 1940). Hashikawa graduated from Fukui Normal School in 1913. In 1917, he went to Peking partly to satisfy a curiosity about China and partly to escape from a dull teaching job at a primary school in Fukui prefecture. During his first decade in China he audited courses at Peking University, learned to speak Chinese, and did research on the poet T'ao Yüan-ming (372–427). He also worked for a Chinese-language newspaper managed by Japanese, *Shun-t'ien shih-pao*, and published a bilingual journal, *Wen-tzu t'ung-meng* (*Moji dōmei*), which was devoted to studies of traditional Chinese culture. He socialized with many Chinese intellectuals and became a close friend of Li Ta-chao, Hu Shih, and Chou Tso-jen, among others. John Leighton Stuart, president of Yenching University, drew this sketch of Hashikawa for Yenching trustees in America: "[He] wore Chinese clothes with per-

---

[29] Unless indicated otherwise, information for this section comes from an interview with Hashikawa conducted by Abe Hiroshi in 1980, published as *Hashikawa Tokio-shi intavyū kiroku* (Tokyo: Tokyo University, Department of International Relations, 1981).

fect taste, talked and looked like a Chinese, is an intimate friend of some of the old scholars on our faculty."[30]

In 1933, when Hashikawa assumed the directorship of the institute, he already enjoyed the friendship and confidence of many eminent Chinese scholars in Peking. His connection with the scholarly community served him well when he reorganized the institute and sought new personnel after dismissing incompetent employees. He attracted to the *Ssu-k'u* project some seventy Chinese researchers, among whom were Hanlin scholars and their disciples with very impressive scholarly credentials. Several researchers had participated in the joint committee negotiations in Peking in the mid-1920s; after official ties were broken, they worked for the institute on an unofficial, piecemeal basis.[31] Very few Japanese were affiliated with the project.[32]

The *Ssu-k'u* project was designed to identify and annotate important works that the original Ch'ing compilers had excluded, such as Buddhist scriptures and Taoist texts, novels and plays, and proscribed works; important works published after the Ch'ien-lung project; and important works of which better editions had been found after the original compilation. Hashikawa received assistance from Chinese scholars and collectors throughout the country. In addition, sources in Japan and Europe were consulted. A specially equipped three-story library was built in the compound to store the books collected for the project.[33]

Some Chinese who supported the project and befriended Hashikawa also took part in anti-Japanese activities. They reasoned that culture and politics were two distinct entities. When Chinese researchers at the Peking institute were accused of treason by their anti-Japanese compatriots, they countered that culture had no national boundary. In 1931, when Hashikawa was visiting Changsha on a research trip, a reception was held in his honor on the campus of Yali College. When he arrived there for the occasion, his Chinese host had to let him in through a back door because an anti-Japanese rally was in progress on campus. Hashikawa recalls that

[30] Stuart made this remark in a letter dated November 22, 1937. In the same letter, he also called the Peking Humanities Institute "the pretentious cultural institute established here long since with Japanese Boxer indemnity funds." This letter is included in the Yenching University files, United Board for Christian Higher Education in Asia.

[31] For example, K'o Shao-min and Wang Shu-nan; see note 24.

[32] For a description of the institute's organization and activities up to 1935, see *Tōhō bunka jigyō sōiinkai narabi ni Pekin jimbun kagaku kenkyūjo no gaikyō* (Peking, 1935). Though not mentioned in print, Hashikawa Tokio was the author.

[33] By 1934, the library had 12,214 *pu* (or about 200,000 *ts'e*) of books. See the catalogues of this library, *Pei-ching jen-wen k'o-hsüeh yen-chiu-so tsang-shu mou-lu*, in eight *chüan*, covering the period up to October 1936, published in Peking in 1938; and a sequel with the same title, in two *ts'e*, covering the period from November 1936 to March 1939, published in 1939. Researchers were able to borrow up to ten titles for a period of two months.

some Chinese guests came to the reception after attending the rally. In fact, a young professor told him that in the name of culture he would honor him, but in the name of politics and diplomacy he would go to an anti-Japanese rally. Of course, the *Ssu-k'u* project, a sinological compilation engaging a group of old-style Chinese scholars, was not a ready-made target for anti-imperialist, anti-Japanese charges. In contrast, when Japanese members of the Shanghai Science Institute conducted field work, they often met with strong Chinese nationalistic opposition. Ironically, it was Japanese apathy, not Chinese antagonism, that nearly put an end to both the project and the institute in Peking.

Since the founding of the institute and the inception of the *Ssu-k'u* project, some Japanese officials and Diet members in Tokyo had argued that the humanities institute was an anachronism, totally irrelevant to contemporary Chinese needs. After the Manchurian incident in 1931 and subsequent events in North China, that view evidently became more persuasive, for in December 1936 the Foreign Ministry authorized the establishment of the North China Industrial Science Research Institute (Kahoku Sangyō Kagaku Kenkyūjo) and the Peking Japanese Modern Science Library (Pekin Nihon Kindai Kagaku Toshokan),[34] to be supported with funds from the indemnity account. These two organizations, together with several other new projects sponsored by the cultural affairs office, competed with the humanities institute for financial support.

After the Marco Polo Bridge incident in July 1937, Peking came under Japanese occupation. In December 1938, the Japanese army succeeded in wresting from the Foreign Ministry jurisdiction over China diplomacy and established the Asia Development Board. Management of the research institutes in Peking and Shanghai, along with many other Foreign Ministry functions in China, became the prerogative of the board.[35] Although records in the Foreign Ministry archives show that funding was earmarked by the Asia Development Board for the Peking institute, Hashikawa reports that he received not a single yen from the board. As a matter of fact, in early 1939 the Foreign Ministry sent him twenty thousand yen with a telegram informing him that it was the final payment. In other words, he was asked to close up shop.

Since 1933, after Hashikawa was put in charge, the *Ssu-k'u* project had been proceeding smoothly. After July 1937, the exodus of scholars from Peking and cessation of communication with scholars working on the project elsewhere in China hampered progress, but enough Chinese researchers remained in Peking to carry on the compilation. It was not surprising that Hashikawa did not follow Tokyo's suggestion to disband.

[34] The name of this library is misleading; the library was actually a general library containing books in Japanese, Chinese, and Western languages on a variety of subjects.
[35] See *Sankō shiryō kankei zakken: Kōain kankei*, in Gaikō Shiryōkan.

But it was no easy task to continue a project when its annual budget was reduced from approximately 100,000 yen to nothing. To raise funds, Hashikawa began to sell everything in the institute that was marketable, save the valuable collection of books the institute had either acquired or been given for the *Ssu-k'u* project. At a time when demand for goods far exceeded supply, items such as bookcases and scrap iron netted high profits. Hashikawa used funds received from these sales to pay researchers. In December 1942, the newly established Greater East Asia Ministry assumed responsibility for the institute as well as several other cultural organizations in China. But, like the Asia Development Board, the new ministry did nothing to help the institute in Peking. Financial restraints and other wartime difficulties notwithstanding, in 1943 a manuscript containing more than fifty thousand entries was completed. The institute had only enough means to print a limited number of mimeographed copies listing about 40 percent of those fifty thousand entries.

During most of his years in Peking, Hashikawa maintained a wary relationship with Japanese officials both in Peking and in Tokyo. He thought they were for the most part ignorant and pompous bureaucrats. Many of them distrusted him. In fact, for a while during the 1920s Japanese intelligence believed that Hu Shih was a top man in the Communist party. And because of his close association with Hu, Hashikawa came under Japanese surveillance. Nevertheless, Japanese officials in Peking shrewdly recognized the value of Hashikawa's connections with Peking's intellectuals, and they were not reluctant to seek his assistance. Hashikawa seems to have cooperated neither graciously nor frequently. But near the end of the war he was willing to let the Japanese ambassador to Nanking, Tani Masayuki, use his *Ssu-k'u* project as a means to initiate reconciliation with Chiang Kai-shek. This rather implausible plot came to naught.

Within a year after Japan's surrender, in compliance with the wishes of the Nanking government, Hashikawa handed over the institute's buildings and library, plus the original manuscript, to a Kuomintang official. Until recently, the original buildings of the humanities institute housed the Institute of Modern History in Peking. In 1977, the Commercial Press in Taiwan published the thirteen-volume *Hsu-hsiu ssu-k'u ch'uan-shu t'i-yao*, based on a copy of the wartime mimeographed edition that Hashikawa had sent to a sinologist at Kyoto University. Although the Commercial Press edition contains only about one-fifth of the summaries compiled by the Peking Humanities Institute, the number of works annotated, 10,070, almost equaled the total number of works copied and titles listed in the original *Ssu-k'u ch'uan-shu* project compiled during the reign of the Ch'ien-lung Emperor.[36]

[36] The editors of the Taiwan publication note similarities in the conditions under which

SHANGHAI SCIENCE INSTITUTE

Together with the Peking Humanities Institute, the Shanghai Science Institute formed the core of the Foreign Ministry's cultural agenda, at least on paper. The institute in Shanghai would appeared to have been an ideal showcase to display Japan's scientific prowess, and its well-equipped laboratories an ideal setting to promote joint research that would benefit both China and Japan. But deteriorating relations between the two countries frustrated the operation of the institute from its inception.

In 1926, the Shanghai subcommittee announced the goals of the science institute: to support purely academic work in the natural sciences and promote scientific research in China; to choose research topics that best meet China's most urgent needs and study scientific features unique to China; and to appoint a Chinese director and select research students only from available Chinese candidates. Seven principal research projects were selected for the seven departments of the institute: (1) Chinese medicine for the pharmacology department, (2) measurement of gravity and terrestrial magnetism for the physics department, (3) fish in the Yangtze for the biology department, (4) physiography of the region south of the Yangtze for the geology department, (5) mineral compounds for the chemistry department, (6) fermented products made in China for the bacteriology department, and (7) epidemic and endemic diseases in China for the pathology department.[37]

In 1928 the subcommittee purchased sixteen acres of land in the French concession, on which Gothic-style buildings, similar to the architecture of Tokyo Imperial University, were constructed for use as offices, laboratories, and residential apartments. When the institute officially opened in April 1931, five months before the Manchurian incident, relations between the two countries were already strained. To avoid unwelcome at-

---

the *Ssu-k'u* sequel, the original *Ssu-k'u* project, and the *Yung-le ta-tien* were compiled: all were accomplished under trying political circumstances and intended to appease Chinese scholars.

[37] Yamane Yukio, "Shanhai shizen kagaku kenkyūjo ni tsuite—tai-Ka bunka jigyō no ikkōsatsu," reprinted in *Chūgoku kankei ronsetsu shiryō*, pp. 320–321. Comparisons might be made with the goals announced in June 1925 by the China foundation, in charge of America's second Boxer remission: the Foundation pledged "to be devoted to the development of scientific knowledge and to the application of such knowledge to the conditions in China through the promotion of technical training of scientific research, experimentation, and demonstration, and training in science teaching," in addition to other cultural enterprises (see Willoughby, *Foreign Rights*, p. 1016). From 1926 to 1936, the China Foundation provided funds for twenty-six endowed chairs in the sciences at established Chinese universities and colleges, annual scientific research grants for Chinese professors and students, and yearly prizes for scientific books and translations. (*Peiping Chronicle*, April 24, 1937, p. 6.)

tention, no public ceremony marked the opening.[38] Perhaps because Chinese members of the subcommittee officially withdrew after the Tsinan incident, a Japanese (Tokyo Imperial University professor of medicine Yokote Chiyonosuke), instead of a Chinese, was named acting director of the institute. The institute failed to attract a respectable number of Chinese scientists. The Manchurian incident and the Shanghai incident further undermined plans proposed by the subcommittee during the preparatory phase. As a result, the difference between the Shanghai institute and the Peking institute is striking: the institute in Peking, certainly after Hashikawa took charge, was principally a Chinese organization headed by a Japanese sinophile; the institute in Shanghai, on the other hand, was strictly speaking a Japanese organization.

The professional staff in each of the seven departments at the Shanghai institute consisted of three to four principal researchers, one or two assistant researchers, one to three assistants, and one or two temporary affiliates. The number of Chinese who became research students was negligible. As of June 1936, twenty-eight Japanese and fourteen Chinese scientists occupied research positions at the institute; Japanese dominance, especially in upper-level positions, was evident in all but the pharmacology department.[39] Graduates of nearby Shanghai Tōa Dōbun Shoin, adept in Chinese and Japanese (plus English in some cases), held most of the administrative positions. In total, the institute employed about one hundred people.

The Shanghai institute was Japan's first comprehensive research institute for the natural sciences. The physical scale of the institute and the scope of its research plans were impressive by contemporary Japanese standards. Its library contained a large collection of foreign scientific journals and books as well as Chinese local gazetteers.[40] Results of research were published in a bilingual (Japanese-Chinese) journal, the *Shanhai shizen kagaku kenkyūjo ihō*.[41] The *Journal of the Shanghai Science Institute*, an English-language publication, disseminated monograph-

[38] Unless indicated otherwise, information about this institute is derived from interviews with former institute members Nishimura Suteya, Kimura Kōichi and close associates of Komiya Yoshitaka, conducted by Abe Hiroshi in 1979–1980 and published as *Intavyū kiroku: Shanhai shizen kagaku kenkyūjo* (Tokyo: Tokyo University, Department of International Relations, 1980), plus two important articles reprinted in Abe's publication: Tsuge Hideomi, "Shanhai shizen kagaku kenkyūjo," originally published in *Kagaku* 7, 13 (November 1937); and "Shanhai shizen kagaku kenkyūjo o kataru—zadankai," originally published in *Kaizō hyōron* (June 1946).

[39] Yamane Yukio, "Shanhai shizen," pp. 322–333.

[40] *Classified Catalogue of Books and Periodicals in the Shanghai Science Institute—Chinese, Japanese, and Western Languages* (Shanghai, 1937).

[41] Titles of the articles from issue no. 1 (1929–1931) to no. 14 (1944) can be found in Yamane, "Shanhai shizen," pp. 328–336.

style reports. An in-house publication, *Shizen*, recorded the activities of the institute and news of its members.[42]

It is generally acknowledged that the institute reached its height in the mid-1930s during the tenure of its second director, Shinjō Shinzō, Kyoto University professor of astronomy and a member of the Shanghai subcommittee. Although many of the Japanese institute members admitted that they were given more freedom in research than had been allowed at their home institutions, the scientists were by no means contented with their working conditions or the results of their research. Their frustration did not spring from dissatisfaction with the laboratory setup. Rather, for those who needed to acquire data outside the laboratories, Chinese indifference and obstruction created serious problems. Not a few experienced temporary imprisonment by Chinese officials when they conducted field work in China's central provinces. Kimura Kōichi, a specialist in Chinese medicine, recalls that on one of his field trips he wore rags to disguise his Japanese identity; this masquerade presumably served its intended purpose. During the war years, the institute was also transferred from the Foreign Ministry to the Asia Development Board and then the Greater East Asia Ministry. Institute members were unable to conduct the kinds of research they had done before the war, and much attention was directed toward various wartime needs, under the order of the military command.

Like the Peking Humanities Institute, the Shanghai Science Institute was not recognized by the Nanking government after 1929. But individual Chinese scientists and several Chinese scientific organizations, including the country's largest and most influential association of scientists, the Shanghai-based Science Society of China (Chung-kuo K'o-hsüeh-she) continued to associate with the institute on a private basis.[43] Common research interests did transcend national animosities. For example, in August 1935 the institute was officially invited to participate in a week-long conference, jointly sponsored by six Chinese science organizations; five from the institute delivered papers there.

Informal contact with Chinese scientists may have been frequent, but Chinese representation in the institute was meager, as mentioned above. Of the fourteen Chinese researchers and assistants identified in available

[42] The institute began to publish a monthly report, *Chūgoku bunka jōhō*, on Chinese academic and cultural affairs beginning shortly before the Marco Polo Bridge incident. This publication included information on the humanities as well as the sciences, and it is an important source for the study of educational and cultural activities in areas controlled by the Japanese and the Kuomintang from mid-1937 to December 1941.

[43] It would be interesting to investigate the institute's unofficial interaction with the Science Society of China, founded in 1914 by American-trained Chinese scientists at Cornell University and moved to Shanghai in 1918.

sources, the educational background of nine is known. Only one among the nine, all born around the turn of the century, was educated at a Chinese university. The other eight were all graduates of Japanese institutions of higher learning; six of them also attended Japanese secondary schools. Several grew up in Japan because their fathers had gone there to study. The haiku and waka written by these Chinese for the in-house publication *Shizen* testify to their familiarity with, and perhaps attachment to, the Japanese lifestyle. T'ao Ching-sun (1897–1952), for example, was the son of a Chinese who had studied in Japan. A resident of Japan from 1907 to 1929, he graduated from the prestigious First Higher School (Dai-ichi Kōtō Gakkō) and specialized in bacteriology at the medical faculty of Kyushu Imperial University. After returning to China in 1929, he taught public health courses at a Shanghai medical school and worked as the director of an experimental model public health station in Wuhsi, Kiangsu, his hometown, before joining the institute in 1931. He married a Japanese, whose sister was Kuo Mo-jo's first wife.[44]

A large number of the Japanese scientists at the institute were young disciples of the Japanese professors who had been members of the Shanghai subcommittee. Many of them after the war assumed leading positions in their respective fields. Among those who became well-known is Toyama Ichirō, who after 1945 was employed in the biology institute of the Imperial Household Agency (Kunaichō), where he conducted ichthyological research with the Shōwa Emperor. A short-term associate of the institute who specializes in neurology, Tsuge Hideomi, is now actively promoting Sino-Japanese friendship.[45] Okada Ietake, a geochemist, is best remembered for his frequent absences from the institute. Unlike most of his Japanese colleagues, he immersed himself in Shanghai's Chinese community. In 1943, he disappeared from the city and reportedly went to the liberated area. After the war he stayed in China, to work, but during the Cultural Revolution he was accused of being a spy and died in prison. In 1956, the Chinese government privately invited Hayami Shōichirō, then physics professor at Kyoto University, to China to help with the construction of the Nanking Yangtze Bridge.

Peking did publicly acknowledge the contribution of another former institute member, Komiya Yoshitaka (1900–1976). Born in Saitama prefecture, Komiya graduated from the First Higher School in 1921 and from the medical faculty of Tokyo Imperial University in 1925. From 1925 to 1930, he worked as an assistant in the hygiene section at his alma mater. As a member of the radical student organization Shinjinkai, he was

[44] A collection of T'ao Ching-sun's writings (in both Chinese and Japanese) has been published in Japanese as *Nihon e no isho* (Tokyo: Futsūsha, 1963).
[45] Tsuge is the author of *Tōa kenkyūjo to watakushi—senchū chishikijin no shōgen*, 1979, and several other works on Sino-Japanese relations.

actively involved in social causes. His own research focused on industrial diseases afflicting laborers. He became a member of the Communist party in 1930 and was jailed for his participation in Communist labor organizations. Released after a three-month imprisonment, he was urged by several professors to go to the Shanghai institute to avoid more trouble with the authorities. In Shanghai he frequently collaborated with T'ao Ching-sun on projects examining parasites. In 1957, through the mediation of the Japanese Socialist Party, Komiya went to China and successfully helped to eradicate the parasitic disease schistosomiasis, which had plagued the Yangtze region.[46] He also received international recognition for his work on this problem.

While awaiting repatriation in 1946, a group of ten Japanese scientists from the institute participated in a symposium to conduct a postmortem on the institute, their years there, and their views on Sino-Japanese relations. Forbidden by the Chinese authorities to carry back to Japan their data and equipment, some of them were trying to reconcile themselves to the forced abandonment of nearly a decade of research. Understandably, this dispirited group regarded themselves as victims of Japanese diplomats and militarists. One botanist summed up the feelings of several of his colleagues when he confessed that before he came to China he had generally regarded scholarship and politics as two distinct entities, but in China he learned that scholarship is invariably affected by politics. He cautioned scholars doing research in a foreign country to take note of its politics; otherwise conflicts will arise even if they consider their research completely apolitical.

The buildings of the Shanghai institute now house botanical and zoological research organizations that belong to the Chinese Academy of Sciences. Further research might uncover the extent to which Chinese scientists have utilized the institute's data and equipment since 1945.

STUDENTS

Although the Wang-Debuchi agreement of 1924 shifted the limelight away from Chinese students in Japan, funding for services and scholarships for these students constituted one of the largest annual Boxer ex-

[46] Schistosomiasis, also known as bilharziasis, is a problem prevalent in the tropics. Schistosomes, commonly known as blood flukes, are the transmitting parasites that are passed from human waste to snails, the intermediate host, and then back to humans through the skin. One variety, *schistosoma japonicum*, is confined to East Asia, particularly the Yangtze Valley. Symptoms of this disease include chronic dysentery, enlargement of the liver and spleen, and anemia. William A. R. Thomson, *Black's Medical Dictionary* (London: Adam & Charles Black, 1981), pp. 781–782.

penditures from 1923 to 1937. Whether by design or by chance, these particular allocations, intended for China's elite-designate (or so the Japanese hoped), were more or less adhering to the dictates of the "civilizing mission."

The cultural affairs office provided yearly support for the Japan-China Association. This association was founded in 1918 when the Chinese government returned the money a group of Japanese businessmen had given to Chinese students stranded in Japan during the 1911 Revolution. In 1921, the association received appropriations from the Education Ministry to construct dormitories for Chinese students; in 1924, the Foreign Ministry's cultural office began to allocate Boxer funds for the association. In addition to providing accommodations, the association offered a variety of services to students, ranging from routine academic counseling to dispensing relief after the 1923 Kanto earthquake. In 1925, the association was given control of the Tōa Kōtō Yobi Gakkō, a preparatory school founded in 1914 for Chinese students, and renamed it the Tōa Gakkō. The association also sponsored lectures, outings, and other social activities.[47] The association's journal, the *Nikka gakuhō* (written mostly in Japanese), provided up-to-date news of colleges and universities back home, current government regulations affecting overseas students, and information about the itineraries of prominent Chinese intellectuals visiting Japan. The journal also published articles ranging from serious discussions of important contemporary issues to jejune accounts of visits to famous Japanese tourist spots.[48]

In 1924, Japanese and Chinese officials agreed to disburse two kinds of Boxer indemnity stipends to Chinese students in Japan. The first category provided a maximum of 320 students with a monthly stipend of seventy yen each, plus medical and travel expenses. The number of scholarships, allotted by province, was based on the provincial share of the Boxer payment and quota in the lower house of the national assembly. Within each province, half of these stipends was, according to regulation, distributed to government-funded students and the other half to self-supporting students. Students attending Japanese government universities were given first priority. It appears that fewer than 320 scholarships were actually awarded each year, and in 1933 only 68 were disbursed. In 1924, the first group of Chinese students awarded this scholarship were asked to sign a statement, which in part declared, "in accordance with the rules concerning scholarships for Chinese students in Japan, as stipulated in the Japanese legislation governing cultural enterprises for China, starting in

---

[47] Sanetō, *Chūgokujin Nihon ryūgakushi*, pp. 117–118.

[48] This journal, begun in February 1927 as a quarterly and changed into a monthly in 1930, is perhaps the single most important source for the study of Chinese students in Japan from 1927 to 1943.

October 1924, I accept with utmost gratitude a monthly stipend of seventy yen. With this financial aid I pledge to devote myself to my studies. After graduation I shall remember this beneficence and strive to reciprocate this favor from His Majesty the Emperor."[49] Needless to say, this requirement piqued many Chinese both in Japan and back home and explains, in part, why the annual quota of 320 was never filled. It is not clear whether students were required to sign this pledge after 1924. Eleven additional scholarships were reserved for teachers from national universities and professional schools to pursue advanced training and research in Japan. The Chinese government and its student supervision office (established in the Chinese Embassy in Tokyo in 1906), together with Japan's Foreign Ministry and perhaps its Education Ministry, jointly administered the selection and disbursement.

A more selective category of scholarships, awarding 150 yen per month, plus research fees, was set up to fund graduate studies for promising Chinese students who had already completed training at either a Japanese university or a professional school. Recommendations for these scholarships were made by Japanese schools, in consultation with Japan's Education Ministry. An average of six or seven scholarships in this category were awarded each year. Several members of the Shanghai Science Institute received this scholarship.

To compensate for unfair selection procedures in the first category, especially for students from provinces with low scholarship quotas, a third category, seventy yen per month for fifty students, was established in 1926. Recipients of this scholarship were recommended by their schools in Japan on the bases of merit and need. In the first year, thirty-five students received this stipend. Because of political instability in China and difficulties in transmitting funds to Japan, in subsequent years the number of recipients was increased by several fold (reaching 283 in 1933), and the amount of stipend slightly reduced. Although it would be difficult to gauge the adequacy of the various monthly stipends for the entire period under discussion here, it should be noted that during the second half of the 1920s entry-level pay at major Japanese companies for graduates of Japanese universities was about sixty yen per month.[50] From 1924 to 1932, these three kinds of stipends, totaling about 3.7 million yen, were given to over 3,500 students.[51]

About 15 to 20 percent of all the Chinese students in Japan between 1924 and 1937 received these Boxer scholarships. It would be useful to

---

[49] Wang, *Keng-tzu p'ei-k'uan*, p. 514. For more information about the three categories of scholarships, see ibid., pp. 526–530, and Huang, *Chin-tai Jih-pen*, pp. 127–140.

[50] Abe Hiroshi, comp., *Intavyū kiroku: Tōhō bunka gakuin, Tōkyō Kyōto kenkyūjo* (Tokyo: Tokyo University, Department of International Relations, 1981), p. 31.

[51] Wang, *Keng-tzu p'ei-k'uan*, p. 530.

know whether these scholarship students differed in any way from the other Chinese students in Japan.[52] But the answer to this question and many more must await a thorough study of Chinese students in Japan in the 1920s and 1930s. At this time only a few general observations can be offered.

One irrefutable statement that can be made about Chinese students in Japan in the 1920s and 1930s is that more Chinese studied in Japan than in any other foreign country.[53] Besides a set of numbers, very little is known about the social and educational background of these students before going to Japan, their experiences in and outside classrooms in Japan, and their professional careers after returning to China. In their studies in Japan, they apparently favored the social and natural sciences over the humanities.[54] It has been suggested that this group was on the whole less prosperous than their compatriots who studied in the United States and Europe.[55] Obviously, the economic advantages of studying in Japan, recognized by Chang Chih-tung in 1898, still held true in the 1920s and 1930s.[56] But Chang's view of Japan as the filter and synthesizer of essential Western knowledge was by this time indubitably held in disrepute. A Japanese education no longer conferred prestige, even though mediocre academic performance was recognized as a problem shared by many Chinese students in Japan as well as in Western countries.[57] The United States and Western Europe were the objects of adulation among many young, educated Chinese. In their estimation, the fact that recipients of Japan's Boxer scholarships did not have to endure the rigors of fiercely competitive selection examinations, required of all aspirants of the American and British Boxer scholarships, simply reinforced the lackluster reputation of education in Japan.[58] Ironically, the quality of education re-

[52] The most comprehensive compilation of the names of Chinese students in Japan is Kōain Seimubu, *Nihon ryūgaku Chūka minkoku jimmei shi* (Tokyo, 1940).

[53] The figures for the students in Japan come from Sanetō, *Chūgokujin Nihon ryūgakushi*; in the United States and Europe, from Y. C. Wang, *Chinese Intellectuals and the West* (Chapel Hill: University of North Carolina Press, 1966), pp. 510–511.

[54] For example, a 1930 survey of 3,064 Chinese who had studied in Japan revealed the following specializations: law, 465; economics, 386; military, 339; engineering, 238; humanities, 232; railways, 143; physical sciences, 138; medicine, 136; agriculture, 81; art, 51; aeronautics, 23; music, 13; others, 819. *Shina jiyō* 13, 5 (November 1930), pp. 85–86.

[55] Y. C. Wang, *Chinese Intellectuals*, p. 155.

[56] In his famous *Exhortation to Learn*, Chang asserted that "Japan is nearby and inexpensive for travel, so that many can go." Quoted in Marius B. Jansen, *Japan and China, from War to Peace: 1894–1972* (Chicago: Rand McNally, 1975), p. 150.

[57] Detailed criticisms were offered in a special issue of *Chung-hua chiao-yü-chieh* 15, 9 (March 1926), devoted to overseas study.

[58] The U.S. Boxer scholarships were first administered by Tsinghua University. After the school became a national institution in 1929, the Nanking government took charge of the selection process; each year, twenty to thirty scholarships were awarded (Wang Shu-huai,

ceived by Chinese students in Japan in the 1920s and 1930s was higher than before. Many students during the early 1900s were interested more in extracurricular activities to promote revolution or quick certificates to parlay into lucrative jobs back home than in serious study. By the 1920s, the Japanese government, with the assistance of the Chinese government, had set up routinized channels to receive Chinese students and to provide the necessary preparatory training, including language study, before matriculation at Japanese institutions.[59]

The low esteem accorded Japanese education, not to mention trenchant expressions of anti-Japanese nationalism, did not inhibit thousands of young Chinese from studying in Japan. In fact, the period from 1934 to the outbreak of the Sino-Japanese War witnessed a tremendous surge in the number of students going to Japan. As would be expected, the contingent from Manchuria was considerably larger than before. But what is remarkable is that the numbers from the rest of China by 1935 surpassed the pre-1931 level.[60] It has been suggested that eagerness to learn about Japan and an exchange rate favorable to Chinese currency generated this "third peak" of Chinese studying in Japan.[61] Employment conditions and intellectual trends in China must also be examined to explain this last surge before the Marco Polo Bridge incident. Perhaps, for those who chose to study in Japan in the mid-1930s, the advantages of *any* kind of an education abroad were attractive enough to outweigh all the unfavorable considerations.[62]

Although it is beyond the scope of this chapter, it should be noted that in 1930 the Foreign Ministry's cultural affairs office also established three categories of scholarships for Japanese students to study in China. The first category was a monthly stipend of 35 yen for graduates of Jap-

---

Keng-tzu p'ei-k'uan, pp. 308–324). In 1937, for instance, over three hundred Chinese students took the nationwide examination competing for the British Boxer scholarships, and twenty-five were awarded the scholarship. (*Peiping Chronicle*, April 27, 1937, p. 12.)

[59] These changes are discussed in Abe Hiroshi, "Chūgoku kindai ni okeru kaigai ryūgaku no tenkai—Nihon ryūgaku to Amerika ryūgaku," *Kokuritsu kyōiku kenkyūjo kiyō, Ajia ni okeru kyōiku kōryū* 94 (March 1978): 5–31; Futami Takeshi, "Senzen Nihon ni okeru Chūgokujin ryūgakusei kyōiku—Tōa kōtō yobi gakkō o chūshin ni shite," in Abe Hiroshi, ed., *Nit-Chū kankei to bunka masatsu* (Tokyo: Gannandō, 1982), pp. 159–208.

[60] *Shina jiyō* 22, 2 (February 1935): 46; 26, 4 (April 1937): 99.

[61] According to Sanetō, *Chūgokujin Nihon ryūgakushi*, p. 129, the other two peaks occurred in 1905–1906 and 1913–1914, respectively.

[62] As would be expected, returned students formed factions, which no doubt affected their employment and social standing. More research is needed to examine the differences and implications of factions formed by returned students. T'ao Hsi-sheng, a journalist and scholar associated with the Kuomintang, recalled that "he was always very awkward and embarrassed when he had to admit that he was not a returned student. Not until the 1930s [when he was in his thirties] could he answer the question with equanimity." James E. Sheridan, *China in Disintegration: The Republican Era in Chinese History, 1912–1949* (New York: Free Press, 1975), p. 138.

anese primary schools to study in Chinese middle schools. The second category, a monthly stipend of 70 yen, was for graduates of Japanese middle schools to study in Chinese junior colleges or universities. The third category, a monthly stipend of 120 yen, was for graduates of Japanese universities or professional schools to receive training in Chinese institutions of higher learning.[63]

Similar to Chinese regard for Japanese education, in the eyes of many Japanese, China was not a desirable place to pursue learning.[64] Although complete figures are not available, one source reports that from the turn of the century to the Marco Polo Bridge incident, about 150 Japanese students in total, funded by various sources, studied at institutions of higher learning in Peking (where together with Shanghai resided the overwhelming majority of Japanese students in China, excluding Manchuria).[65] This small group went to China mostly for sinological training, and from this fraternity emerged several eminent scholars of Chinese studies, such as Kuraishi Takeshiro, Ogawa Tamaki, Yoshikawa Kōjirō, Takeuchi Yoshimi, Imahori Seiji, and Suzue Gen'ichi (the last three received the third category of Boxer scholarships mentioned above).[66]

DŌJINKAI HOSPITALS

The cultural affairs office supplied the Dōjinkai with funding nearly as generous as that for student scholarships and services. With the Boxer funds and its own resources, the Dōjinkai operated four hospitals in China, which benefited more Chinese, from all walks of life, than all the other Boxer-funded programs combined.[67]

---

[63] These Boxer stipends were lower than those provided for Japanese students by their Education Ministry, which had begun to send students to China around 1900. Yoshikawa Kōjirō, a student in Peking from 1928 to 1931, received a monthly stipend of two hundred yen from a privately funded scholarship. He noted that his stipend was more than adequate, but was less than the amount awarded by the Education Ministry. See Yoshikawa Kōjirō, *Yū-Ka kiroku: Waga ryūgakki* (Tokyo: Chikuma Shobō, 1976), pp. 56–57.

[64] The number of Japanese students in China was minuscule compared with the number of Japanese students in the West. Watanabe Minoru discusses Japanese students abroad during the Meiji period in *Kindai Nihon kaigai ryūgakushi* (Tokyo: Kōdansha, 1977–1978). Analyses of Japanese students in the United States in the Taishō and Shōwa periods can be found in John W. Bennett, Herbert Passin, and Robert McKnight, *In Search of Identity: The Japanese Overseas Scholar in America and Japan* (Minneapolis: University of Minnesota Press, 1958).

[65] Li Wen-chi and Takeda Hiroshi, eds., *Pei-ching wen-hua hsüeh-shu chi-kuan tsung-lan* (Peking: Hsin-min Yin-shu-kuan, 1940), appendix.

[66] The overwhelming majority of Japanese students in China resided in Peking and Shanghai. See Kawamura, "Tai-Shi bunka jigyō," p. 98.

[67] The total number of Chinese outpatients treated at the four Dōjinkai hospitals in China was: Peking, 1914–1937, 571,226; Hankow, 1923–1937, 308,526; Tsingtao, 1925–1937,

Founded in 1902, the Dōjinkai was imbued with the same intellectual and political persuasions that had helped to bring into existence the Tōa Dōbunkai, from which, in fact, the Dōjinkai had originally evolved. In 1903, the association became an incorporated foundation with a membership of over two thousand. By 1923, close to forty thousand doctors, industrialists, and government officials were members. As enunciated in its charter, the association intended to establish hospitals in Asian countries, to facilitate the activities of Japanese doctors in these countries, and to encourage Asian students to study medicine in Japan. At first, the organization relied heavily on contributions from members (membership category was determined by the amount of donation). In 1907, an imperial award of five thousand yen lent the Dōjinkai considerable luster, and in 1914 the association was again honored when the Taishō Emperor agreed to assume the title of Dōjinkai president. Four years later, the association began to receive financial assistance from the Japanese government. When the China Cultural Affairs Bureau was formed in 1923, the Dōjinkai became one of the recipients of the Boxer funds.[68]

During its first decade, the Dōjinkai limited its activities to dispatching delegations of doctors and pharmacologists to Korea, China, Southeast Asia, and the South Seas to disseminate medical information and assisting these countries in opening hospitals and medical schools. After 1906, the association began to operate its own hospitals overseas, initially in Korea and Manchuria. After the South Manchuria Railway Company assumed responsibility for Japanese medical activities in that region and the Taiwan colonial administration took charge of supervising medical activities in South China, the Dōjinkai began to concentrate its efforts on North and Central China.

In the 1910s, in conjunction with the construction of the hospital in Peking, the Dōjinkai outlined an ambitious three million yen, ten-year (1918–1927) plan for the construction of Western-style hospitals in important cities throughout Central and North China, with preference to the hinterland. Architects of this ambitious plan, along with many government officials in Tokyo, had hoped that Dōjinkai hospitals in China, especially the one in Peking, would eventually be as famous and respected as the Peking Union Medical College (PUMC). On the eve of the second Sino-Japanese War, however, the association was operating only four

---

385,677; and Tsinan, 1925–1937, 481,562. Figures for Chinese in-patients are smaller but by no means insignificant. Huang, *Chin-tai Jih-pen*, pp. 82–92. Huang has totaled the more detailed statistics given in Ono Tokuichirō, ed., *Dōjinkai sanjūnen shi* (Tokyo: Dōjinkai, 1932) and *Dōjinkai yonjūnen shi* (Tokyo: Dōjinkai, 1943).

[68] The principal sources for this section are *Dōjinkai sanjūnen shi; Dōjinkai yonjūnen shi*; Tōa Dōbunkai, *Tai-Shi kaikoroku*, vol. 1 (Tokyo: Tanshiki Insatsu Kabushiki Kaisha, 1936), pp. 686–693; Fujii, "Nihon," pp. 89–111; and Huang, *Chin-tai Jih-pen*, pp. 69–112.

hospitals in China, none of which, at least in Japanese estimation, could rival the PUMC.

The first hospital, opened in Peking in 1914, consisted of a complex of twenty-two buildings. Because of its reasonable, graduated rates for Chinese patients, the hospital attracted a large Chinese clientele. It also provided free cholera immunization to Chinese residents in Peking. According to one source, in 1917 all the hospitals in Peking treated a total of 81,604 persons.[69] During that year, the Peking Dōjinkai hospital treated a total of 20,871 patients (13,073 Chinese and 3,689 Japanese outpatients; 2,537 Chinese and 1,672 Japanese in-patients).[70] In 1923, construction of the Dōjinkai hospital in Hankow was completed. Two years later, the association took control of two hospitals in Tsingtao and Tsinan, respectively (both were considerably larger than the hospitals in Peking and Hankow). Each of the four hospitals had a Japanese director. The staff at all the hospitals included both Japanese and Chinese doctors, but the former outnumbered the latter by about three to one. Each summer, a handful of Japanese medical students from well-known schools served as interns at the hospital. Comprehensive information on medical services available in these four cities might lead to more reliable assessment of the relevance of these Dōjinkai hospitals to the Chinese population. In addition, the hospitals sponsored occasional visits to the nearby countryside to dispense medicine and provide information on hygiene.

A chart plotting the numbers of Chinese patients using these four hospitals would roughly correspond to the relative intensity of anti-Japanese feelings in China from the 1910s until the Marco Polo Bridge incident. The peaks and the valleys would reveal no surprises. In the Peking hospital, 1919—the year of the May Fourth demonstrations—saw a considerable decline in the number of Chinese patients. The hospital in Tsinan suffered a dramatic drop in that category in 1928, the year of the Tsinan incident. All four hospitals treated fewer Chinese in 1931, the year of the Manchurian incident. In fact, in the fall of 1931, in the wake of the Manchurian incident, Chinese refugees from a Yangtze flood disaster refused relief aid offered by the Hankow Dōjinkai hospital. Each time, after a slump induced by a Sino-Japanese incident, the number of Chinese patients would gradually increase and sometimes even surpass the pre-incident level. All four hospitals were ordered to close shortly after the start of the Sino-Japanese War in July 1937 and then reorganized to meet Japan's wartime needs.

[69] Sydney D. Gamble, *Peking, A Social Survey* (London: Oxford University Press, 1921), p. 118. According to Gamble, Peking had thirty-eight hospitals in 1917 and forty-six in 1919. Out of the sixteen operated by foreigners, nine were Japanese.

[70] Huang, *Chin-tai Jih-pen*, p. 83. I am assuming that Huang's figures referred to individual patients, not hospital visits, which could have been made repeatedly by the same patient.

In addition to the hospitals, the Dōjinkai opened a clinic in Tokyo in 1932 for Chinese sojourners and students. Chinese studying medicine in Japan were treated to professional conferences and sightseeing trips by the association. Two medical schools, one in Japan and one in China, were opened to train Chinese and Japanese, but for a variety of reasons neither stayed in operation for long.

Dōjin, a Japanese-language journal serving general interests, was published, with a brief hiatus, from 1906 to 1938, at first as a monthly and from 1923 as a quarterly. One specialized journal published translations of selected articles from various Japanese medical journals, and another presented findings of research by Dōjinkai members sent to China. The association also published translations of nearly fifty Japanese medical books. One frequent translator was T'ang Erh-ho (1871–1940), who received medical training in Japan and Germany and worked for the Japanese-sponsored government in Peking during the second Sino-Japanese War.

INTERNATIONAL CULTURAL RIVALRY IN CHINA

Some are genuinely surprised to learn that in the 1920s and 1930s, while rushing down the seemingly inalterable path to disaster, Japan's Foreign Ministry was also engaged in peaceful cultural work for China, and that some Chinese actually responded favorably to these efforts. Others condemn these efforts as acts of "cultural aggression," masterminded by rapacious Japanese diplomats and militarists.

The 1923 legislation stipulating Japanese control over the indemnity remission and Chinese compliance with Japanese regulations did not portend harmonious cooperation. The Tsinan incident dispelled any lingering hope for limited official Chinese participation. The Foreign Ministry's cultural office probably overextended itself by funding too many kinds of enterprises; more concentrated support for fewer projects might have yielded better results. Chinese members of the Peking and Shanghai committees who had helped to set the goals of the respective institutes were, on the whole, not leaders of China's burgeoning new culture movement. The *Ssu-k'u* project was a luxury item that could not meet China's pressing cultural and educational needs in the 1920s and 1930s. The Shanghai institute had great potential in promoting joint scientific research and in delivering to China much-needed help in the development of public health and modern medicine. But animosity between the two countries derailed a promising venture, and the institute functioned for all practical purposes as a Japanese research center. In a more tranquil and prosperous time, the research conducted at the Peking and Shanghai institutes might have been better appreciated.

The Dōjinkai hospitals did provide commendable services to the general public. The association's sponsorship of translations of medical textbooks helped to advance medical education in China. The Boxer scholarships enabled a substantial number of young Chinese to study abroad. The influence of Western-trained Chinese, especially those who had studied in the United States, on modern China's education is well known, but the influence from Japan has yet to be examined. One suspects that after extensive research is completed, the results will rest somewhere between Washington's highest hopes and Tokyo's worst fears. On a smaller scale, the Boxer-funded programs also provided salutary career alternatives to a handful of young Japanese college graduates whose employment opportunities at home were becoming more limited.

Competition with the Western powers colored many of Tokyo's cultural policies toward China. Many in the Japanese government regarded the United States as Japan's chief—and in all likelihood unbeatable—rival in China's cultural arena. In 1918, one Diet member declared that the difference between the Dōjinkai hospital in Peking and its neighbor, the Peking Union Medical College (then under construction), was akin to the difference between the houses of common Japanese and the mansions of the Mitsui and Mitsubishi dynasties. He fretted about what the Chinese thought of the obvious disparity.[71] Thirty-some years after they had left China, several Japanese members of the Peking and Shanghai institutes still intimate admiration and envy when they compare their organizations with American-supported institutions such as Tsinghua and Yenching universities, and especially that Rockefeller gem, the PUMC. Such comparisons tend to slight Japanese achievements.

Japanese admirers of these American-funded institutions chose to ignore their negative image in China. Even educated Chinese viewed Tsinghua and Yenching as bastions of elitist privilege. The PUMC may indeed have been the best hospital in the East, but most Chinese regarded it as the hospital for foreigners and rich Chinese. The Dōjinkai hospitals did not project such a forbidding image in Chinese eyes, and in fact they provided a respectable amount of free medical services to needy Chinese. More important, unfavorable comparisons of Japan's cultural efforts with those of the Westerners failed to note that when the Foreign Ministry set out to underwrite a host of cultural activities with the Boxer funds, it was not just competing against the indemnity remission policies of the United States and other Western powers, but was also trying to meet the colossal challenge posed by the estimable coffers and organizational networks of the Christian missionary movement in China.[72] As the Foreign Ministry

[71] GS, 40th session (1918), p. 566.
[72] The Boxer indemnity settlement is an extremely complex issue. The largest claims

publicly acknowledged, by the mid-1920s, Protestant missionary efforts included close to four hundred middle schools, over six thousand kindergartens and primary schools, and more than three hundred hospitals and clinics.[73] By the 1930s, 10 to 15 percent of the total number of Chinese students attending colleges and universities at home were enrolled in sixteen Christian schools (thirteen Protestant and three Roman Catholic).[74]

Since the early Meiji period, Japanese Buddhists had tried to proselytize in China, particularly in its central and southern regions, but this movement attracted considerably fewer preachers and converts than the Western Christians.[75] It may seem odd that Buddhism, albeit Japanese Buddhism, was not able to garner a respectable following in the late Ch'ing and Republican periods. Of all the foreign religions in China in the nineteenth and twentieth centuries, Japanese Buddhism would appear to have been the most familiar to the Chinese. But Japanese stress on sectarianism probably antagonized some potential Chinese converts. Unfamiliar with Japanese Buddhist regulations that had permitted some monks to marry since medieval times and to eat meat since the Meiji Restoration, many Chinese probably were scandalized by the sight of Japanese Buddhist monks flagrantly violating the dietary and marital restrictions assiduously observed by most Chinese monks. News about Japanese monks of dubious integrity and the emergence of Chinese "rice Buddhists" unquestionably maimed the missionary cause. During the

---

settled in the agreement were by Russia (29 percent or some 130 million taels), Germany (20 percent or some 90 million taels), France (15 percent or 70 million taels), Britain (11 percent or 50 million taels), followed by Japan and the United States (each 7 percent with 34 and 32 million taels, respectively), with Italy, Belgium, Austria, and others making up the remainder. See "Foreign Relations, 1866–1905," in *The Cambridge History of China*. Vol. 11: *Late Ch'ing, 1800–1922*, p. 127. Individual remission policies and timetables as well as world monetary fluctuations further complicate one's understanding of the value, real and comparative, of the individual remitted sums. As the figures above indicate, Japan's share of the indemnity was only slightly larger than America's. Though holding a substantially larger claim, the British returned the funds in 1931, later than both the United States and Japan. Moreover, the British remission was invested in various civil engineering projects. Only interest from these investments was spent for cultural purposes. It should also be noted that British missionary activities in Chinese education and social welfare were not as extensive as American efforts.

[73] See Gaimushō Bunka Jigyōbu, *Ōbeijin no Shina ni okeru bunka jigyō* (1925). About a decade later, another survey, similarly based on published works and confidential reports from Japanese consulates in China, appeared as Gaimushō Bunka Jigyōbu, *Manshū oyobi Shina in okeru Ōbeijin no bunka jigyō* (1938).

[74] Lutz, *Christian Colleges*, p. 3.

[75] Fujii Masao's report estimates that on the eve of the second Sino-Japanese War, twelve Buddhist sects in China claimed a total of about 7,000 Chinese adherents (pp. 13–14). In contrast, in the 1930s, the number of Chinese Protestant converts was over 350,000, and the number of Catholic converts even greater. Philip W. West, *Yenching University and Sino-Western Relations, 1916–1952* (Cambridge: Harvard University Press, 1976), p. 12.

Republican period, many Chinese intellectuals regarded Buddhism, in any form, with unyielding disdain. Those who chose to accept Buddhism as a part of their world view usually favored Chinese Buddhism.

Even if the most active Japanese missions had been successful in converting a large number of China's masses, it is doubtful whether they would have been able to wield financial power and provide social services comparable to those of the Western missionaries. The Western missionary efforts in China were the outgrowth of healthy, expanding movements at home; the Nishi and Higashi Honganji missionaries first went to China in the early Meiji period with the hope of reviving a movement persecuted by the authorities at home. The missions were expected to finance their work with little or no help from the home organizations. Despite several diplomatic attempts, Tokyo was never able to obtain for the Japanese missionaries the rights and privileges that enabled their Western counterparts to reside and own property in China's interior.[76]

In the private sector, nothing comparable to the Rockefeller Foundation was established in Japan. Although Japanese captains of industry contributed, for example, to the Dōjinkai and became patrons of the arts, most of their efforts were more modest and self-indulgent than those of their American counterparts. For example, Iwasaki Koyata (1879–1945), a second-generation member of the family that founded Mitsubishi, gave Morohashi Tetsuji, compiler of the *Dai kan-wa jiten*, money to study in Peking from 1919 to 1921, and after his return arranged for him to become director of the famous Seikadō Bunko. This library was based on an eminent Ch'ing bibliophile's collection, which Iwasaki Yanosuke, father of Koyata, had purchased in the Meiji period.[77] A cousin, Iwasaki Hisaya, in 1917 purchased the library of George E. Morrison, advisor to Yüan Shih-k'ai. Morrison's collection of European-language books about China, combined with other acquisitions, became the foundation of the Tōyō Bunko. Many other wealthy Japanese simply amassed large personal collections of Chinese objets d'art and rare Chinese manuscripts.

---

[76] In 1925, the Foreign Ministry's cultural office supplied funding for an East Asian Buddhist conference in Tokyo. It is not clear whether the office sponsored other Buddhist activities. The activities of Japanese Buddhist missionaries in China from the late nineteenth century to 1949 are briefly summarized in Holmes Welch, *The Buddhist Revival in China* (Cambridge: Harvard University Press, 1968), pp. 160–173. Detailed discussions of their activities in the late Ch'ing and early Republican periods can be found in Iriye Akira, "Chūgoku ni okeru Nihon Bukkyō fukyō mondai—Shimmatsu Nit-Chū kankei no ichidammen," and Satō Saburō, "Chūgoku ni okeru Nihon Bukkyō no fukyōken o megutte—kindai Nit-Chū kōshōshi-jō no hitokusahi to shite," reprinted in *Chūgoku kankei ronsetsu shiryō* 3, 1 (January–June 1965): 344–351 and 208–234, respectively. A very small number of Japanese Christian missionaries also went to China, but their activities there were insignificant.

[77] See Morohashi's account in *Watakushi no rirekisho, bunkajin*, vol. 16 (Tokyo: Nihon Keizai Shimbunsha, 1984), pp. 231–285.

The private, secular organizations that did contribute significantly to Japan's cultural efforts in China were, on the whole, not entirely separated from the government. The Tōa Dōbunkai and other groups receiving substantial funding from the Foreign Ministry, such as the Nikka Gakkai and the Dōjinkai, comfortably straddled the public and private spheres. In fact, the extent to which semi-official organizations were engaged in cultural enterprises aimed to benefit the Chinese made the Japanese cultural presence unique among treaty powers in China. This blurred distinction rendered all the more curious and untenable the repeated appeal by Japanese officials to separate politics from Tokyo's cultural agenda.

War ultimately wrecked Japan's "civilizing mission" in China. Catchwords of the Taishō and early Shōwa periods, such as *dōbun-dōshu*, are now regarded as profanities in polite circles. In its literal sense, the concept is, of course, flawed. Japanese and Chinese are not members of the same linguistic family. Japan benefited immensely from Chinese culture, but Japan has a distinct culture, despite disclaimers by Pan-Asianists and Chinese ethnocentrists. In its figurative sense, however, the *dōbun-dōshu* concept, though not always articulated as precisely that term, has always served as a cultural bridge linking Japan and China. This bond may have initially enhanced the progress of the Foreign Ministry's cultural efforts. The decision to prepare a sequel to the Ch'ing *Ssu-k'u* compilation paid homage to traditional Chinese culture and showed Japanese appreciation of sinology. Familiarity with Chinese culture also enabled Japanese scientists at the Shanghai institute to glean data from traditional Chinese local gazetteers and to value Chinese herbal medicine. Linguistic borrowings and knowledge of classical Chinese permitted countless Japanese and Chinese to converse in writing. However imperfect this form of communication, it allowed a degree of intimacy inaccessible to those outside the East Asian cultural sphere. But, to many Chinese, this cultural affinity ultimately made Japan's aggression in China all the more heinous. In rationale and in organization, Japan's "mission in China" was different from the "white man's burden" in China. Sometimes the Chinese treated Japan as just another member of the imperialist pack; sometimes as a singularly virulent predator. This is, however, not to deny that the Chinese carried on a complex love-hate relationship with all foreign powers and everything they represented, and, in addition to showing venomous hatred, the Chinese—and the Japanese—occasionally yearned to be identified with the West, not with each other.

Holmes Welch reports that in a clash between groups of Japanese and Eighth Route Army soldiers during the second Sino-Japanese War, the Chinese were able to seize from the Japanese the sole surviving copy of the Chin dynasty *Tripitaka*. But because the Chinese soldiers stored it in a coal mine, a portion of it was damaged beyond repair. Welch notes, "One cannot help reflecting that this loss would not have occurred if the Japanese had seized and sent them back to Japan; and microfilms would be available abroad today."[78] Some Chinese might share Welch's concern for preservation work and scholarship. More, however, would strongly reprimand him for his insensitivity to Chinese nationalistic feelings. The circumstances surrounding this incident were, to be sure, extraordinary and extreme, but Welch's account in a way encapsulates the fundamental dilemma that plagued all foreign cultural efforts in China. Even when cultural exchange is conducted on the most equitable terms, questions of honor and parity still frequently arise. When a country under the protection of extraterritoriality purports to help another, when the economic disparities between the giver and the receiver are pronounced, and when the needs and the aims perceived by the two sides are incompatible, the line separating cultural assistance from cultural aggression tends to disappear altogether. In the late 1910s and early 1920s, unable to obtain steady support from an instable central government, some Chinese educators lobbied vigorously for the return of the Boxer indemnity for cultural purposes. Their energetic efforts and the entreaties by fellow educators to refrain from "begging" before foreign powers are equally poignant examples of problems inherent in cultural diplomacy between unequals.[79]

Some would argue that the origin as well as the application of the Boxer funds were intolerable insults to Chinese sovereignty. Some would also argue that no matter how sincere and well-intentioned were the motives of individual Japanese participants in the Foreign Ministry cultural efforts, their mere presence in China was a sore reminder of Japanese imperialism. But one must neither dismiss nor denigrate them as the cultural phalanx of an invading army. Men such as Hashikawa Tokio and Komiya Yoshitaka and those Chinese who worked with them deserve to be remembered in a different, kinder light. Neither generosity in funding nor terms favorable to the Chinese in the cultural arena could have assuaged the damage inflicted by military aggression.

From a large corpus of extant archival documents in Japan, one can trace, with considerable accuracy, sketches of all the cultural activities supported by the Boxer indemnity from 1924 until 1937. Sadly lacking is an equally large corpus of accounts of Japanese and Chinese individuals

[78] Holmes Welch, *Buddhism Under Mao* (Cambridge: Harvard University Press, 1972), p. 162.

[79] Perhaps one exception to this was the relationship between Germany and the Nationalist government during the Nanking decade. It was a relationship based on compatible belief in rapid but nonrevolutionary development in the industrial and military sectors. See William Kirby, *Germany and Republican China* (Stanford: Stanford University Press, 1984).

PART III

Experts and Subimperialists

Although Western involvement in the collective informal empire in China contracted during the 1920s and 1930s, the role of the Japanese expanded dramatically with the Manchurian incident. That event marked the beginning of an attempt to abandon the institutions of informal empire for more direct and visible forms of political control in China. What role was played in this process by those Japanese most familiar with and affected by conditions in China?

As a number of scholars of imperialism have argued, the expansion of an imperialist metropole is often not the result of political or economic pressures at home but the work of "men on the spot." D. K. Fieldhouse, for example, has stressed the critical importance of the "subimperialist" in the spread of Western imperialism. By "subimperialist" he means the merchants and settlers who lived and worked in the imperial periphery, and the soldiers and diplomats who represented the metropole there. It was such men who often provided the impetus for the conversion of informal empire into formal. One can think of countless examples in the history of Western imperialism, from French admirals like Rigault de Genouilly in Vietnam to British capitalist adventurers like Cecil Rhodes in South Africa. In the case of British imperialism in China, it was the Jardines and the Mathesons, subimperialists par excellence, who argued in favor of establishing the framework of informal empire, and their successors in the treaty port merchant community (the "old China hands") who sought to push the British Foreign Office into a more aggressive pursuit of British rights and privileges in the latter half of the nineteenth century.

In the case of Japan, the *Shina rōnin* immediately spring to mind as the best example Japanese subimperialism in China. Given the propensity of these romantic adventurers for self-propagandizing, their activities are well known. But it should not be forgotten that there was a legion of more respectable but less visible Japanese subimperialists in China whose activities are described in this and other sections. All of them were no less eager than the rōnin to reshape national policy toward China, and they inundated the metropolis with a flood of information and opinion in the 1910s, 1920s, and 1930s, fuelling the debate on the "China problem." Some, like the China experts in the army and the diplomatic corps, dealt with here in the chapters by Kitaoka and Brooks, were part of the policy-making bureaucracy; others, like the businessmen and traders described by Banno, were members of pressure groups or lobbying groups who tried to work through the political party leadership as well as the bureaucracy. Finally, there was the local garrison army in Kwantung, described by Coox. In terms of social and political status, all these subimperialists were far better positioned to influence government policy than the Genyōsha or Kokuryūkai activists, who were, after all, quintessentially outsiders. Yet it is significant to note that not all of them were equally influential.

On the basis of rationalistic models of bureaucratic decision making, one might be tempted to think that official China experts, either in the military or in the diplomatic corps, would have the most impact on government policy making. The evidence presented in several of the chapters in this section, however, seems to suggest otherwise. Although they provided the home government with information and intelligence on conditions in China far more voluminous than that provided to any Western government, the ability of such experts to affect the shaping of government policy seems to have been minimal.

There appear to have been two reasons for this. First, as both Kitaoka and Brooks point out, the status of the China expert was relatively low in both the military and diplomatic services. Given the overwhelming concern of Japanese political leaders to learn from and to catch up with the West, those in the elite tracks within the military and civilian bureaucracies were those with experience in the Western countries. In most bureaucracies, the highest positions are held by generalists, not specialists, and in Japan to be a generalist was to be familiar with Western practices and institutions on which Japan's modernity was modeled. Those with such knowledge were on the fast track of bureaucratic advancement, while those expert in their knowledge of "backward" countries like Korea and China, no matter how important those countries were to Japan economically and strategically, were rarely able to reach the highest echelons of the official hierarchy. Japanese diplomats recognized the importance of having China expertise to enhance their career prospects and were eager for short-term posting to China, but they also realized that real status and influence within the Foreign Ministry lay with the North American or European desks. And, as Professor Kitaoka points out, even when specialization became important in the army officer corps, non-China specialists still had the edge over China experts in the competition for key decision-making posts.

Second, as both the Kitaoka and Brooks chapters show, official China experts did not always speak with one voice. Army intelligence officers in China reported only on the "China" they saw immediately before them, and that "China" was not always the same. As the Kitaoka chapter points out, their opinions (and intelligence reports) were often influenced by their own bureaucratic interests. They tended to overstate the importance of the Chinese political forces with which they were involved—and sometimes were manipulated by them. Like the blind men describing the elephant, each grasped only one part of the beast, convinced that it represented the whole. Their views were often narrow, self-serving, self-contained, and wrong-headed. But more important, "expert" views within the military and civilian bureaucracies were seldom unified, and a prescient opinion could often be cancelled out by an obtuse one.

The Brooks chapter indicates that there might have been a general consensus that China was in the process of disintegration in the 1910s and 1920s, but very little agreement among officials and politicians on how Japan should respond or which forces Japan should back. A number of Japanese diplomats who served in China correctly predicted that the Kuomintang would emerge as the predominant force in China politics. They urged the government to deal with the new party rather than with the warlords, but their influence was counteracted by contrary views from other parts of the diplomatic service and from the outside as well. The home government received much noise from the official China experts but few signals that were clear or that it wished to hear. In this respect, it should be added, the Japanese bureaucracy was not unique. Consider, for example, how the higher levels of the U.S. State Department and executive branch rejected the advice of their own China experts on how to deal with the Chinese Communist movement in the 1940s.

If the experts do not seem to have played a decisive role in policy formulation, what of the subimperialists outside the government, the business and other interests in the treaty port communities? The Banno chapter gives an interesting glimpse of the political involvement of Japanese merchants and industrialists involved in the China trade. Like the official China experts, they were often divided in their views. Although small traders and merchants involved in the China trade were consistent in protesting against Chinese boycotts in the 1910s and early 1920s, the cotton spinning industry did not become alarmed until the 1923 boycott took aim at yarn produced in Japanese-owned mills in China, just when the industry faced an economic depression at home. Only after 1927 did there develop a consensus between government and business that the main obstacles to protecting Japanese economic interests in China were the new political developments there and in Japan. According to Professor Banno, the more dynamic role of political parties in Japan guaranteed that a party favoring a tougher China policy would eventually come into power. Meanwhile, new threats to Japanese interests in China from Chinese nationalism brought about a convergence of shared government and business interests to impose a tougher policy line toward China. Input from business, therefore, was just one element, and not necessarily the most important one, in shaping China policy.

Yet there is no doubt that subimperialists did play a key role in influencing the shift in China policy during the late 1920s and early 1930s. It was deeds rather than words or opinions, however, that forced the metropolitan government to action. As the Coox chapter shows, the critical event in the shift was the fait accompli presented to Tokyo by the Kwantung Army. It might be possible for the home government to ignore expert opinion or turn a deaf ear to protests from special interest pressure groups, but it had to respond to the independent action taken by its local garrison army in Manchuria. The staff officers in the Kwantung Army had sympathetic backing from some elements in the military high command and from a number of key civilian politicians, but their main advantages were unity in views and commitment to action. They were determined to achieve their ends, no matter what the reaction of the home government. In this respect, they most closely resembled the kind of sub-imperialists who provided momentum for Western imperialist expansion in the nineteenth century. Doihara Kenji liked to think of himself as the "Lawrence of Manchuria," but a better case could be made that Ishiwara Kanji was the "Rhodes of Manchuria." The Kwantung Army, moreover, was not acting on the basis of any very narrow interest, but on the basis of a grand vision of international politics. While the success of the Manchurian incident undoubtedly advanced the careers of men like Ishiwara Kanji and Itagaki Seishiro, they acted on the basis of moral certainties and political convictions, not simple self-promotion, and this perhaps gave their actions a moral authority that the lobbying of, say, treaty port businessmen did not have.

Naturally, the action taken by the Kwantung Army was applauded by many of those pressure groups and experts who advocated a more activist or interventionist policy in China, and its strongest supporters were undoubtedly to be found among the Japanese residents in China. As chapters 4 and 6 showed, the Japanese residents of Dairen and Shanghai were consistently militant and aggressive toward the rise of Chinese nationalist movements, which directly threatened their livelihood and well-being, and occasionally even their life and limb. And after the Manchurian incident, the All-China Assembly of Japanese Residents, acting as a pressure group for the Japanese resident community in China, urged the government to adopt a more forward policy. Indeed, some elements in the Shanghai resident community were directly involved in the provocation of the Shanghai incident in 1932. But, on the whole, the main role of the resident community was to add yet another voice to the chorus urging a policy of expansion and increased political control. Their demands may have increased the tension between China and Japan and further poisoned the atmosphere, but, in the final analysis, the role of the resident community in influencing policy was passive rather than active.

The question remains: why was the fait accompli of the Kwantung

Army able to prevail when the advice of experts and the importunings of pressure groups did not? After all, the home government had not responded to the opportunity created by the assassination of Chang Tso-lin in 1928, so why did it accept the Mukden incident? In part, the answer to that question lies in the audacity of the Kwantung Army's action. It was difficult to repudiate that action without admitting that the civilian authorities had lost control of part of the army, and it was difficult to repudiate an apparently highly successful military operation in Manchuria. Yet that is not the whole answer. The new policy of expansion was influenced as much by what was going on at home—a rural population in distress, shrinking industrial production, strikes and labor unrest, and the outburst of domestic political terrorism—as by what was happening on the continent. In short, it was the timing as much as the audacity of the Kwantung Army that guaranteed its success, and one can well imagine that, had the domestic situation been more stable, the government in Tokyo might well have tried to contain its insubordinate colonial army.

In any event, the Japanese government eventually was less able to resist the importunities and faits accomplis of its subimperialists in China than the British government was, particularly when the treaty port system began to crumble in the late 1920s. During the late nineteenth century, when British power was at its height in China, the British Foreign Office consistently refused the demands of the "old China hands" to turn China into another India. The Foreign Office did not differ with these subimperialists on the importance of protecting British trade, but it did disagree on the future potential of that trade and its relative importance in overall British trade patterns. That official caution, as pointed out elsewhere, persisted into the 1920s and 1930s, making the British more willing to roll with the punches of Chinese nationalism. The Japanese government, of course, was less able to pursue the counsels of caution, because China had become more important for Japan's interests and security after World War I. In the final analysis, the simple facts of geopolitics narrowed Japan's policy choices.

CHAPTER 9

Japanese Industrialists and Merchants and the Anti-Japanese Boycotts in China, 1919–1928

Banno Junji

The economic interests of small Japanese merchants and the large Japanese spinning companies in China were very different in the 1920s. Similarly, Japanese exporters at home and Japanese merchants and industrialists in China had different interests.[1] For these reasons, the activities of these different interest groups exerting pressure on the decision making of the Japanese government may also have differed. Japanese parliamentary democracy was at its height in the 1920s. This new openness made it possible for business associations to exert more power to influence the government and the opposition parties. It is not surprising, then, that these new domestic political developments were associated with a changing policy toward China from noninterventionist to interventionist.[2] Therefore, the attitude of Japanese merchants and industrialists engaged in China must have influenced this change, or have been influenced by it. This chapter aims at analyzing the changing attitudes of, and the differences among, Japanese business groups as well as their impact on decision making for Japan's China policy during this period.

THE ANTI-JAPANESE BOYCOTT OF 1919

Contrary to the optimistic expectations of the Japanese concerned, the anti-Japanese boycott following the May Fourth Movement became more

[1] Peter Duus, "Nihon bōsekikigyō to Chūgoku: keizaiteikokushugi no hitotsu no kēsu sutadī" (Japanese spinning industries and China: A case study of economic imperialism), in Nakamura Takafusa, ed., *Senkanki no Nihon keizai bunseki* (Tokyo: Yamakawa Shuppansha, 1981); Takamura Naosuke, *Kindai Nihon mengyō to Chūgoku* (Modern Japanese cotton industry and China) (Tokyo: Tokyo Daigaku Shuppankai, 1982), henceforth *KNMC*; and Murai Sachie, "Shanhai jihen to Nihonjin shōkōgyōsha" (The Shanghai incident of 1932 and Japanese merchants and industrialists in China), *Nenpō kindai Nihon kenkyū*, no. 6 (Tokyo, 1984).

[2] Akira Iriye, *After Imperialism: The Search for a New Order in the Far East, 1921–1931* (Cambridge, 1965); Banno Junji, *Kindai Nihon no gaikō to seiji* (Foreign policy and domestic politics in modern Japan) (Tokyo: Kenbun Shuppan, 1985), pp. 122–181.

widespread in July and August 1919. In mid-May, Ariyoshi Akira, the consul-general in Shanghai, anticipated that the boycott would cease within a few weeks. Even taking into account the spread of the boycott to Tsingtao and Tientsin, Ariyoshi wrote, it would be over within two months, and there would be no serious damage to the Japanese trade with China.[3] Two months later, however, Ariyoshi reported to Foreign Minister Uchida Yasunari, "To respond to your question about the extent to which the boycott is affecting Japanese trade with China, my answer is that no Japanese goods are being sold here."[4]

In spite of serious damage to Japanese exports to Shanghai, however, the attitude of the Japanese Chamber of Commerce and Industry in Shanghai was astonishingly calm. Even in August 1919, Ariyoshi did not welcome Uchida's suggestion that five hundred dollars be lent to the merchants unable to maintain business because of the boycott. "Long before the boycott, their businesses were not going well," he wrote, "so no one knows whether their difficulties are due to the boycott or not." He even added, "This boycott is rather a good chance for us to weed out small Japanese dealers here (too many in number and too poor in quality). This will enhance our future prosperity." This was not Ariyoshi's personal opinion, but a view shared by all the leading figures in the Japanese Chamber of Commerce and Industry in Shanghai.[5]

The residents in Shanghai whom Ariyoshi expected to be weeded out were "individual dealers who rely solely on trade with Chinese dealers." There were more of these Japanese residents in Tientsin than in Shanghai, so the opinion of the consul-general in Tientsin, Funatsu Shinichirō, was quite different from Ariyoshi's. Funatsu was critical of the detached attitude of Japanese business associations and domestic newspapers toward the small Japanese dealers suffering in China. The Chamber of Commerce in Tientsin shared his opinion.[6]

Despite their differences over policy, Ariyoshi and Funatsu agreed that small dealers were suffering most. Individual dealers in cotton clothing and sundries who had no special connections with big domestic firms had developed business problems. But long before the boycott started, the low-count cotton yarns (except those produced by Japanese cotton mills in China) had not been able to compete with comparable Chinese yarns. In other words, dealers and exporters of cotton yarns had no grounds to complain about the boycott. In 1919, the cotton yarn produced by the Japanese-owned mills in China was still not considered by the Chinese to

[3] Ariyoshi to Uchida, May 16, 1919, in *Nihon gaikō bunsho* (Documents on Japanese foreign policy) (Tokyo: Gaimushō, 1970) (hereafter *NGB*), 1919, vol. 2, pt. 2, p. 1183.
[4] Ariyoshi to Uchida, July 27, 1919, ibid., p. 1373.
[5] Ariyoshi to Uchida, August 6, 1919, ibid., p. 1394.
[6] Funatsu Shinichirō to Uchida, August 5, 1919, ibid., pp. 1390–1393.

be a Japanese product, so "the [boycott] damage to Japanese cotton yarn is rather small." Furthermore, merchants who dealt in goods that enjoyed a monopolistic market share in China could expect quick recovery once the boycott ended. Machine cotton, lace cotton, silk cotton, sugar, coal, and marine products also fell into this category.[7]

In contrast, the dealers in cotton clothing, beer, matches, home-use medicines, soap, and stationery were being severely harmed by the boycott. Recognizing this fact, even the Japanese Trade Association of Cotton Fabrics (Nihon Yushutsu Men'orimono Dōgyōkumiai) in Japan requested that the foreign minister take decisions against the boycott.[8]

From these facts it is clear that only a few Japanese dealers in China and only certain kinds of exporters in Japan requested that the government adopt an interventionist policy toward the Chinese boycott. Other Japanese merchants and industrialists, both in China and in Japan, remained rather hesitant about intervention. Moreover, Japanese cotton yarn production was enjoying an economic boom in Japan at the time. The price of cotton yarn in 1919 was 50 percent higher than in the previous year, and almost twice as high as two years before. The Ministry of Agriculture and Commerce considered this rapid price rise to be the result of excessive exports and issued an ordinance temporarily prohibiting the export of cotton yarn.[9] In other words, cotton yarn producers in Japan could easily find a domestic market to compensate for any losses caused by the boycott. The ministry exempted high-count cotton yarns and cotton clothing from the regulation, but it suggested the possibility of including these products in the near future.

In short, among the various companies engaged in business with China, only a few Japanese dealers suffered from the anti-Japanese boycott in 1919. The political forces representing their demands were also weak. Only the Kenseikai, an opposition party that controlled only about 30 percent of the seats in the Diet, took the same position as these dealers. Katō Takaaki, president of the party, demanded that the Japanese government force the Chinese government to suppress the anti-Japanese boycott. "If the Chinese government is too weak to suppress it," Katō stated, "then the Japanese government should use our military force on behalf of the Chinese government."[10] But we should not conclude that the Kenseikai wanted to represent the interests of the Japanese small dealers in China. The anti-Japanese boycott in 1919 aimed at recovering from Germany the Shantung Peninsula, which Japan had successfully acquired through its Twenty-One Demands in 1915, when Katō had been foreign

[7] Ariyoshi to Uchida, July 28, 1919, ibid., pp. 1366–1379.
[8] Ibid., p. 1423.
[9] *Seiyū*, no. 236 (December 15, 1919): 38–41.
[10] *Kensei* 2, 6 (August 1919): 11.

minister. In other words, the Kenseikai had another reason for advocating a hard-line policy against the boycott—it wished to defend its president's past policy.

No other political party called for a hard-line policy against the Chinese boycott. The government party, the Seiyūkai, criticized Katō. "His speech implies the dispatch of troops to China," said an official party statement. "Our party completely opposes this proposal."[11] Nor was Japanese public opinion aroused against the boycott. In September 1919, Miyazaki Tōten, a well-known sympathizer with the Chinese revolution, wrote: "In these days, when any kind of public speech attracts a large audience, there has been one exception. A meeting held at Kanda the other day by petitioners from Tsingtao attracted an audience of only four hundred. But we should not be surprised by this news. We Japanese are not so biased as to complain about the Tsingtao problem. . . . We are also cool toward the anti-Japanese movement in China."[12]

THE 1923 BOYCOTT

The anti-Japanese boycott of 1923 was a different matter. The attitude of Japanese merchants and industrialists was very different than in 1919. This time, the products made by Japanese cotton mills in China became the object of the boycott. Because the Chinese spinning industries actively supported the boycott, Japanese textile firms in China immediately experienced some negative effects on their business activities.[13] The Japanese Chamber of Commerce and Industry in Shanghai, which had remained indifferent during the previous boycott, became a fierce advocate of an interventionist policy toward China. Moreover, the chambers of commerce and industry in Shanghai, Tientsin, and Hankow worked together to win support from the chambers of commerce in Japan, and they were successful in uniting all Japanese exporters at home. Almost all of the companies engaged in the China trade demanded that the Japanese government take decisive measures against the Chinese boycott.

The most active chamber of commerce was in Tientsin. On May 23, 1923, it adopted a resolution requesting the Japanese government to take "adequate measures of self-defense" to protect Japanese economic interests in China.[14] During July 12–16, the Shanghai, Tientsin, and Hankow chambers of commerce and industry convened in Shanghai a provisional

---

[11] *Seiyū*, no. 232 (August 15, 1919): 16.

[12] Miyazaki Tōten, "Tokyo yori" (From Tokyo), September 2, 1919, in *Miyazaki Tōten zenshū* (Complete works of Miyazaki Tōten), vol. 2 (Tokyo: Heibonsha, 1971), p. 216.

[13] Takamura, *KNMC*, pp. 142–143.

[14] Shanhai Nihon Shōgyō Kaigisho, ed., *Nijū-ikkajo mondai ni kansuru hainichi jōkyō* (The anti-Japanese situation in China over the abolition of the Twenty-One Demands).

general assembly of the Japanese chambers of commerce in China. Several domestic chambers of commerce and industry (including Osaka, Kyoto, Kobe, Nagoya, Hiroshima, Moji, Nagasaki, Fukui, Toyama, and Tokyo), which counted many trading companies among their members, sent delegates to this assembly. Among the resolutions the assembly adopted, the following was the most noteworthy: "All losses caused by the boycott, whether directly or indirectly, should be compensated by either the central or the local government of China." The assembly even added to this resolution a demand that, if the Chinese government did not meet this demand, the Japanese government "should use any necessary direct measures to protect the lives, properties, and trading activities of the Japanese residents in China."[15]

In Japan, the initiative was taken by Osaka exporters, whose share of total exports to China amounted to nearly 70 percent. In late June, the Osaka Chamber of Commerce and Industry sponsored a public meeting on the boycott. One speaker argued, "The boycott is the result of a noninterventionist policy toward China. . . . The time has come to end the noninterventionist policy." Another noted, "Even the Buddha cannot be patient more than three times. . . . The weak diplomacy of the Japanese government should bear the blame for inviting the Chinese boycott."[16] At about the same time, the Tokyo Chamber of Commerce and Industry invited the new Japanese minister to Peking, Yoshizawa Kenkichi, to lunch and urged him to change the China policy. The chamber's vice-president said, "Since the Washington Conference, we have conceded to China as much as possible, . . . but this time we should change this compromising attitude. Please forgive me if I am too harsh, but I believe that now is the time to solve the Chinese problem completely."[17]

A few days before the assembly at Shanghai, five large chambers of commerce and industry in Japan had met with delegates from the National League on the Chinese Problem (Tai-Shi Kokumin Dōmeikai), the Japan-China Trading Association (Nikka Jitsugyō Kyōkai), and the Federation of Tokyo Trading Associations (Tōkyō Jitsugyō Kumiai Rengokai). They agreed to hold a public meeting in Tokyo on July 15, in concert with the assembly in Shanghai.[18] The participation of the Japan-China Trading Association in the antiboycott movement meant that big Japanese spinning companies with factories in China had become advo-

[15] Ibid., pp. 194–202.

[16] Ogawa Heikichi Monjo Kenkyūkai, ed., *Ogawa Heikichi kankei monjo*, vol. 2 (Tokyo: Misuzu Shobō, 1973), p. 192.

[17] *Tokyo shōgyō kaigishohō* (Monthly report of the Tokyo Chamber of Commerce) 6, 8 (August 1923): 19.

[18] Ibid., pp. 14–15.

cates of an interventionist policy.[19] The establishment of a coalition of business associations with a Pan-Asiatic organization like the National League on the Chinese Problem meant that the business world had abandoned its pacifist attitude.

Another reason for this toughening attitude of Japanese merchants and industrialists was the domestic economic situation. As already mentioned, during the previous boycott, the Japanese economy had been booming, and therefore a short-term decline in exports to China had not affected the domestic economy. In contrast, the Japanese economy in 1923 had still not fully recovered from the postwar depression of 1920. The economic difficulties of the export industries had been made worse by the financial policies of the Seiyūkai and the Seiyūkai-supported cabinets of the early 1920s. Because of the Seiyūkai's "positive policy," interest rates remained high, and the depression continued. In August 1923, in a petition to the Ministry of Finance, the Osaka Chamber of Commerce and Industry argued as follows:

Although three years have passed since the depression of 1920, there is still no sign of economic recovery. Instead, the economy is worsening day by day. Prices are still very high and interest rates are higher than in any Western nation. In this situation, it is natural that the money market becomes tight, companies fall into difficulty, and exports decline. If this situation continues, our business world will fall into great difficulty.[20]

This petition indicates that not only the companies involved in the China trade, but other companies as well had suffered business setbacks from the decline in exports to China.

Backed by widespread business support, the major opposition party, the Kenseikai, sent delegates to Foreign Minister Uchida with this demand: "Today, the chambers of commerce and industry throughout Japan, as well as public opinion, are growing angry over your weak diplomacy. In order to correct the past errors, you should take some positive measures to protect the dignity and rights of our nation."[21]

Neither the foreign minister nor the Japanese minister to Peking accepted the claims of the business world and the opposition party that the boycott was so serious. At his luncheon with the Tokyo Chamber of Commerce and Industry, Yoshizawa stated:

Although the anti-Japanese boycott in China is fierce at this moment, I do not think it will continue long. . . . Although the Chinese Na-

[19] Takamura, *KNMC*, pp. 152–153.
[20] *Ōsaka shōgyō kaigisho geppō*, no. 196 (August 1923).
[21] *Ogawa Heikichi kankei monjo*, p. 188.

tional Assembly passed a resolution to rescind the Twenty-One Demands three months ago, it knew that Japan would not agree to it. Among the so-called Twenty-One Demands, the Shantung Peninsula has already been returned to China. Only the Manchurian problem remains. . . . But all the educated Chinese know that Japan will never agree to shorten its leases on Liaotung and Dairen. The very fact that those Chinese who know this so well participated in the movement, along with the students and masses, proves that this boycott is not deeply rooted. Therefore, either with the passage of time or the adoption of proper measures, the boycott will come to an end in the near future.[22]

Foreign Minister Uchida expressed the diplomatic importance of Japan not overreacting to the boycott. In a telegram to Yoshizawa on August 24, he wrote:

Considering the fact that the Chinese domestic situation is very unstable, and that the very existence of the responsible central government is in doubt, we should carefully avoid any action that would cause antagonism among the Chinese people. This is one reason why we have been patient toward the anti-Japanese movement in China. There is another reason, too. Recently, particularly since the Washington Conference, Japanese public opinion on Chinese affairs has become moderate. At present, some businessmen and politicians are advocating extremely tough measures against China, but most of the Japanese people do not support them. . . . Our government wishes to respect this healthy attitude of our people.[23]

When Uchida referred to "most of the Japanese people," he must have had the majority party in mind. The Seiyūkai still maintained its earlier stance toward the Chinese boycott. At both its Tōhoku and Tōkai bloc meetings, Takahashi Korekiyo, the party president, mentioned the Chinese boycott only at the end of his speech. Of course, he showed no overt sympathy with the boycott, but his demands to the government were very moderate. He requested only that the government "take proper measures based on righteousness and preserve the nation's rights and the people's interests."[24] Considering the growing demand for intervention at the time, his speech reflected a noninterventionist stance. In spite of the increasing demands by merchants and industrialists for intervention, the

[22] *Tokyo shōgyō kaigishohō*, p. 21.
[23] Uchida to Yoshizawa, August 24, 1923, *NGB*, 1923, vol. 2, pp. 47–48.
[24] *Seiyū*, no. 275 (November 15, 1923): 1–8.

Seiyūkai-supported government maintained its noninterventionist policy in 1923.

THE DECLINE IN ANTI-JAPANESE BOYCOTTS, 1924–1926

From September 1923 until the end of 1926, anti-Japanese boycotts in China died down. The direct cause of the subsidence of boycotts was the great earthquake in Japan in September 1923. On September 11, Itō Takeo, chief of the Peking branch office of the South Manchuria Railway, observed, "There is no room to doubt the sincerity of the sympathy shown by various societies in Peking for the difficulties the great earthquake has caused the Japanese people."[25] The Chinese were too humane to continue anti-Japanese boycotts in the face of this great disaster in Japan. According to Itō, however, the great earthquake was not the sole reason for the subsidence of boycotts. The Chinese people, he said, had begun to understand Japanese concessions to and repentance toward China. Itō also mentioned the effect of the Lincheng incident of May 1923. After Chinese bandit-guerrillas had attacked the railway, Great Britain had proposed to the other powers that they guard the Chinese national railways themselves. Both the Chinese and Japanese governments disagreed with this proposal, though for different reasons, and as a result, diplomatic relations between the two nations improved somewhat. Itō was correct. About three weeks before Itō's report was written, Foreign Minister Uchida sent a telegram to the Japanese minister in Peking indicating that the British proposal was unacceptable because it would arouse suspicion among the Chinese people.[26]

Sino-Japanese relations also improved as a result of the second Fengtien-Chihli War in 1924. The war ended with the establishment in Peking of a government under Tuan Ch'i-jui and supported by Chang Tso-lin. Now that a pro-Japanese government was in power, even the army's General Staff began to talk about Sino-Japanese friendship and the importance of a noninterventionist policy toward China. In a proposal submitted by the General Staff to a meeting of Japanese intelligence officers in January 1925, some Japanese China watchers urged that Japan not meddle in Chinese affairs:

> We must leave Chinese domestic affairs in Chinese hands. Except for affairs critical to Sino-Japanese relations, we must give the Chinese government a free hand. To defend the Tuan government from other powers, we should stress the importance of the spirit of the Washington

[25] Itō Takeo et al., eds., *Gendaishi shiryō*, vol. 31 (Tokyo: Misuzu Shobō, 1966), p. 547.
[26] Uchida to Yoshizawa, August 24, 1923, *NGB*, 1923, vol. 2, pp. 547–548.

Conference. By doing so, we will be able to help the establishment and maintenance of the Tuan government.[27]

The shift from an anti-Japanese to an anti-British mood in China and the improvement in Sino-Japanese relations under the Tuan government became clearer at the time of the May 30th incident in 1925. As the Japanese minister to Peking admitted, "This incident had its origin in the incident at a Japanese factory, the Naigaimen Factory. In other words, Japan is responsible for today's escalated situation."[28] However, the Japanese government did not take any initiative with the powers.[29] It was afraid of damaging the improved relations with the Chinese government. As a result, Yoshizawa said, the great demonstrations mounted in Shanghai and Hankow on June 25 were "directed solely against the British residents."[30]

The improvement in Sino-Japanese relations brought on a split among the Japanese merchants and industrialists. A few days before the demonstration in Shanghai, the Shanghai Chamber of Commerce and Industry sent a petition to Foreign Minister Shidehara requesting suppression, in concert with Britain, of "the movement led by the communists."[31] But the view of delegates from the twelve chambers of commerce and industry in Japan who spent a month in China during late August and early September was quite different in tone. According to their report, "in the beginning" the attitude of the Chinese people was "70 percent anti-Japanese and 30 percent anti-British"; then it had shifted to "50-50"; and by mid-August, when the delegates visited Shanghai, "anti-Japanese voices have disappeared completely, and anti-British voices have replaced them totally."[32]

The report of these delegates proved correct. In March 1929, the *Monthly Report* of the Osaka Chamber of Commerce and Industry summarized developments from the May 30th incident until the Tsinan incident of May 1928:

Our trade with China, particularly with the cities along the Yangtze River, has developed successfully during the past seven or eight years. This success is due to the good relationship between Japanese merchants in China and Japanese companies at home. This has been particularly true of our trade in cotton fabrics. This tendency was accelerated by the feverish anti-British atmosphere that originated in Hong Kong

[27] Japanese Military Archives, T.597 (microfilm).
[28] Yoshizawa to Shidehara, June 2, 1925, *NGB*, 1925, vol. 2, pt. 1, p. 61.
[29] Yada Hichitarō to Shidehara, June 1, 1925, ibid., p. 58.
[30] Yoshizawa to Shidehara, June 16, 1925, ibid., p. 94.
[31] June 20, 1925, ibid., pp. 108–109.
[32] *Shōkō geppō* (Monthly report of the Tokyo Chamber of Commerce and Industry) 1, 1 (April 1926): 1–2.

and Canton. The anti-British fever throughout China brought about a decline in British trade and an increase in Japanese trade. Since then, almost all British goods have disappeared from Hankow, and Japanese goods have replaced them. In Hankow, Japanese merchants supply twenty million taels' worth of cotton piece goods, ten million taels' worth of sugar, seven million taels' worth of coal, and ten million taels' worth of sundries. Although the Japanese residents of Hankow were forced to return home for a few months following the April 12 incident instigated by the Chinese Communist Party in 1927, trade there soon recovered. As is well known, this expectation was betrayed by the Tsinan incident of 1928.[33]

This overview account clearly indicates that Japanese business in China had quickly improved after the brief 1923 boycott.

BUSINESSMEN AND BOYCOTTS AFTER THE TSINAN INCIDENT

The Japanese chambers of commerce and industry in China held consistent attitudes toward the Chinese boycott movement during the three major boycotts in the first half of the 1920s. They had always demanded that the Japanese government alter its noninterventionist policy. But their protests failed to influence the government's China policy. Except for the 1923 boycott, even the Japanese export companies at home had maintained a noninterventionist attitude. After the Tanaka Giichi cabinet formed in April 1927, however, the tougher policy toward China demanded by Japanese business associations in China began to be reflected in the government as well. After the Tsinan incident of 1928, in particular, the Japanese merchants and industrialists in China began to receive strong support from both the Japanese government and domestic exporters for a tougher China policy.

This radical shift occurred not simply because of the expansion of anti-Japanese boycotts in China, but also because of significant political changes in both countries. In Japan, the most important change was the new perception shared by the ruling elite of the South Manchuria crisis, a crisis created by the collision of Chinese nationalism with the deeply entrenched Japanese interests in that region, as reflected by the interests of the South Manchuria Railway Company. During its short term of office in 1924, the Kiyoura cabinet had drafted "A General Plan for China Policy," which recommended: "We should maintain and expand our sphere of influence in South Manchuria, particularly in the northern part,

---

[33] *Ōsaka shōkō kaigisho geppō*, no. 262 (March 1929): 20–21.

where our settlement and special interests have been very weak."[34] This attitude toward Manchuria was very different from that of previous governments. Although these governments had never given up the idea of maintaining Japan's special interests in Manchuria, neither had they tried to expand them. As long as the Japanese government had been satisfied with the status quo in Manchuria, it could maintain a noninterventionist policy toward China.

At the time of the Kuo Sung-ling incident in December 1925, Prime Minister Katō Takaaki said that it "does not matter for us Japanese at all whether Chang Tso-lin or Kuo Sung-ling wins."[35] Given this stance, not even the Kuomintang's Northern Expedition was looked upon as a serious threat. But when the Japanese government decided to expand its special interests in the northern part of South Manchuria, the local government elite and their networks under Chang Tso-lin became indispensable. The Kiyoura cabinet alone could not promote this policy, because it was overthrown by the second "movement for constitutional government" in mid-1924. But from 1927 to 1928, the Tanaka cabinet succeeded in doing so. The new policy of defending Chang's government in Manchuria to safeguard Japanese interests there already threatened by Chinese nationalism, combined with a tougher China policy by Japanese merchants and industrialists in China, resulted in the dispatch of Japanese troops to Shantung in 1927 and 1928.

Another important change in Japanese domestic policies was the development of the two-party system. A split in the majority party, the Seiyūkai, over universal suffrage and an increase in the Kenseikai's Diet representation owing to its initiative in promoting universal suffrage brought about a de facto two-party system in Japan. As has already been seen, support by the opposition party for Japanese merchants and industrialists in China had no concrete effect on government decision making. But once a two-party system was in place, the opposition party could expect to come to power within a few years and carry out its policies.

At the end of 1925, the Seiyūkai, now the opposition party, changed its previous policy of nonintervention in China. At first, the party advocated the use of military power only to defend Japan's interests in South Manchuria.[36] But once the Northern Expedition began, it also called for a policy of protecting Japanese residents in those areas of mainland China where they were engaged in business activities. Since the Kenseikai government had advised Japanese residents in China to return home during the confusion created by the Northern Expedition, the Seiyūkai's posi-

[34] *Nihon gaikō nenpō narabini shuyō bunsho* (Chronology and main documents of Japanese foreign policy), vol. 2 (Tokyo: Nihon Kokusai Rengō Kyōkai, 1955), pp. 62–63.

[35] *Seiyū*, no. 298 (January 1, 1926): 46.

[36] Banno, *Kindai Nihon*, pp. 168–170.

tion marked a clear policy difference between the government and opposition parties. Since the Seiyūkai expected to come to office when the incumbent cabinet resigned, it pursued more concrete activities than the opposition parties had in the past. In February 1927, the party sent two well-known China specialists, Yamamoto Jōtarō and Mori Kaku, on a visit to Shanghai, Nanking, and Hankow. That was one month before the Nanking incident, and two months before the party came to power.

Yamamoto, the former senior executive of Mitsui Bussan, had important talks with the senior staff member of the Japan-China Spinning Company (Nikka Bōseki), Tōyō Spinning Company (Tōyō Menka), and the Association of Japanese Spinning Companies.[37] On his return to Japan in early April, Yamamoto gave a speech about his impressions of China. After explaining that Chinese leaders really believed they could bring down the Japanese economy by blocking Chinese trade with Japan, and that the Chinese people were shifting again from an anti-British to an anti-Japanese mood, he said: "If we leave the situation as it is now, we will be forced to call the Japanese residents home; to concede the recovery of tariff autonomy by China; to recognize the abolition of extraterritoriality in China; and finally, to give up all our special interests in China, including those in South Manchuria."[38]

It should be noted that Yamamoto paid more attention to the problems of the Japanese residents in mainland China and to Sino-Japanese trade than to the Manchurian problem. He obviously worried about the end of the treaty port system and how Japan's privileges in China could still be guaranteed. Therefore, the Seiyūkai defended the dispatch of the first Shantung Expedition by the Tanaka cabinet in May 1927 as necessary to protect Japanese residents and trading activities.[39] For the first time since 1919, Japanese dealers and industrialists in China and exporters at home found their government ready to send troops to protect their economic interests against anti-Japanese boycotts in China.

In spite of the Tanaka cabinet's military intervention in 1927, the anti-Japanese boycott did not become as serious as anticipated. Chiang Kai-shek did not want to have a serious confrontation with the Japanese government before his power had been sufficiently consolidated to deal with Chang Tso-lin, and Chinese dealers knew that. They had bought Japanese goods before the boycott started, and they were ready to start selling them as soon as it ended.[40]

The attitude of the Kuomintang in 1928, however, was quite different

[37] Hara Yasusaburō, ed., *Yamamoto Jotarō denki* (Biography of Yamamoto Jotarō) (Tokyo: Yamamoto Jōtarō Ō Denki Hensankai, 1942), pp. 500–502.

[38] *Seiyū*, no. 315 (May 1, 1927), pp. 9–16.

[39] *Seiyū*, no. 320 (August 1, 1927), p. 28.

[40] Murai, "Shanhai jihen," pp. 207–208.

from the previous year. The spirit of nationalism had intensified within the Kuomintang, and this new force became focused on the conspicuous Japanese presence in China. After the clash between Chinese and Japanese military forces at Tsinan in April–May 1928, the Kuomintang government organized a nationwide anti-Japanese boycott. Japanese dealers and factories in China and Japanese exporters at home faced the longest and most serious boycott of the 1920s.

It is worth noting that no Japanese business association opposed the government's hard-line policy. Instead, these associations called for an even tougher policy. In Shanghai, the entire Japanese business community, from large spinning companies to small sugar dealers, united in an association called "The Friday Association," which persisted in requesting that the Japanese government increase the number of troops.[41] Japanese dealers in Hankow took the same attitude. From the end of 1928 to the beginning of 1929, there were "no exports to Japan, not to speak of imports from Japan" in Hankow, and Japanese dealers there asked the government "not to be satisfied with temporizing measures, but to adopt a determined attitude in order to root out anti-Japanese movements in China."[42] The Japan-China Trading Association, one of the major pressure groups representing spinning industry interests, also welcomed the Shantung Expedition and called for the long-term stationing of Japanese troops there. Association member Shiraiwa Ryūhei made the following comment at a roundtable talk on June 21:

> At the recent general meeting of the Japanese chambers of commerce and industry, all the delegates from the chambers in China gathered with firm resolution. The continued instability in China made their attitude tougher. The chambers of commerce at home supported their attitude at the meeting. Before the Tanaka cabinet came to office, the Osaka Chamber of Commerce and Industry requested that the government adopt tough measures toward the Chinese boycott, and the Tanaka cabinet began to put their wishes into effect. . . . Thus, the general meeting of the chambers was united in its demand to send troops to China.[43]

Of course, each business association supported this resolution for different reasons. The merchants most hurt by the boycott were the cotton textile dealers in China. The Trade Association of Japanese Cotton Dealers in China asked Osaka exporters to stop sending goods to Shanghai,

[41] Ibid., p. 212.
[42] *Ōsaka shōkō kaigisho geppō*, no. 262 (March 1929): 21.
[43] *Minsei* 2, 7 (July 1, 1928): 35–36.

because there were no bids.[44] In contrast, Osaka exporters were optimistic about the effect of the boycott. According to Shiraiwa, they "did research on the effects of the Chinese boycott on their trade since 1923, and reached the conclusion that it had been rather small."[45] But Osaka exporters had another reason for requesting tough measures. They were afraid of an increase in customs duties if the Chinese government recovered tariff autonomy. To prevent this, they joined in the protests of the Japanese dealers in China. The standing director of the Osaka Chamber of Commerce and Industry stated at its general meeting on September 28, 1929:

> We Osaka merchants are greatly concerned about Chinese moves toward increasing customs, since our export to China is more than 70 percent of Japan's total exports. Some Western nations may concede recovery of tariff autonomy by China because there is no solid collaboration among the powers as before. But since Japanese exports to China amount to more than 30 percent of total world exports to China, we are not able to concede it. If the Chinese government increases the rate of customs considerably, the damage to us will be serious.[46]

Increases in customs duties, however, would not have any effect on Japanese-owned spinning and weaving mills in China.[47] The Shanghai Japanese Chamber of Commerce and Industry, which included the big spinning companies among its members, wanted to use the tariff problem as a bargaining chip. At its committee meeting on October 13, the chamber suggested that the foreign minister concede an increase in customs rates on condition that the Chinese government dissolve anti-Japanese organizations.[48] Despite these differences in motivations, all the Japanese merchants and industrialists agreed on supporting and encouraging the government's tough new policy toward China.

CONCLUSION

During the ten years from 1919 to 1928, there were four major anti-Japanese boycotts in China. The responses of Japanese merchants and industrialists in both China and Japan to these boycotts were not the same. In 1919, only the small dealers in China asked the government to take decisive measures. This was the basis for the oft-repeated remark: "Around

[44] "Daikyūkai kinyōkai hōkokusho" (Report of the ninth Friday meeting), August 24, 1928.

[45] *Minsei* 2, 7 (July 1, 1928): 35–36.

[46] *Ōsaka shōkō kaigisho geppō*, no. 257 (October 1928): 8–9.

[47] Takamura, *KNMC*, p. 155.

[48] Murai, "Shanhai jihen," pp. 213–214.

the time of the Washington Conference, Japanese merchants and industrialists had been peace-loving."[49] At the time of the 1923 boycott, however, merchants and industrialists demanded almost unanimously that the government take decisive measures against it. Even domestic exporters, who later discovered that the boycott's effect on their trade was not substantial, displayed the same attitude as the Japanese dealers in China. Big Japanese spinning companies in China, which had not been targets of the 1919 boycott, were among the fiercest supporters of a tough policy against China in 1923. If there had been no dominant party system at the time, the Japanese government might have been forced to change its noninterventionist policy toward China. After the general election of 1920, the majority party, the Seiyūkai, had occupied more than 60 percent of the seats in the Diet, while the opposition party, the Kenseikai, which had advocated a hard-line policy toward China, had only 20 percent.

Luckily for the Kenseikai cabinet that came to office in 1924, the situation in China changed greatly after the massive earthquake in Japan. If there had been no change, the government party would have demanded the same policy that it had advocated during its period of opposition. If that had been the case, the Kenseikai would have faced a dilemma between liberal domestic policies and an imperialistic foreign policy. This good fortune continued even after the May 30th incident. Although Japanese dealers and industrialists in China requested that the government change its policy of nonintervention in China, export companies at home maintained a noninterventionist stance in the expectation of a shift in China from an anti-Japanese to an anti-British mood. The domestic political situation was also advantageous for the Kenseikai cabinet. The Kenseikai had already changed its China policy with the appointment of Shidehara as foreign minister, but the Seiyūkai, now in opposition, hesitated to change so quickly the China policy it had held since the Hara cabinet. The establishment of a pro-Japanese government in Peking supported by Chang Tso-lin also helped Shidehara to maintain a noninterventionist policy.

With the Kuomintang engaged in its Northern Expedition in 1926 and a resurgence in Chinese nationalism, especially in Manchuria, the situation in both Japan and China changed drastically. From the end of 1925, the opposition party, the Seiyūkai, began to worry about Japan's special interests in South Manchuria and to take measures to preserve them. Under the new two-party system, it could expect to put its policies into effect when it came to power. The Northern Expedition and rising Chinese nationalism threatened this new Seiyūkai policy, and it also threatened the interests of Japanese merchants and industrialists. Thus, the Tanaka

---

[49] *Minsei* 2, 7 (July 1, 1928): 37.

cabinet could use Japanese merchants' and industrialists' demands for protection in China as an excuse to send troops that were, in fact, intended to defend the Chang Tso-lin government.

After the assassination of Chang Tso-lin by Kwantung Army officers in 1928, the government had to consider both the interests of the Kwantung Army and the private Japanese economic and political interests in China analyzed above. Once a link between Japanese interests in mainland China and Japanese policy toward South Manchuria had been established, they never diverged from one another. Nor did the relationship between the political parties and Japanese merchants and industrialists diverge. When the Seiyūkai came to office, Japanese merchants and industrialists could expect tough new measures against Chinese boycotts. Although Japanese and Chinese government differences after the Tsinan incident in 1928 increased, the differences in the views of various economic groups in China and the Japanese government greatly decreased.

CHAPTER 10

China Experts in the Army

Kitaoka Shin'ichi

Prior to any analysis of China experts within the Imperial Army of Japan, such as that of their policies, ideas, roles, and backgrounds, it is necessary to find out who they were. This is not easy at all. The army was a much bigger organization than the Foreign Ministry, for example, and was concerned much more deeply with China problems than most other political institutions. Many officers had worked in China and continued to have a keen interest in Chinese affairs. To be regarded as a China expert, one had to have spent much time there. However, it was not uncommon for those with such long experience to be regarded as having outdated ideas on China. The Japanese word *Shinatsū* sometimes implied that the person so designated was out of touch.

If one tries to find out who the real China experts were, or to shape a proper definition of what a China expert is, the task might never end. On the other hand, if one uses an objective measure such as the length of service in China to define China expert, it would be impossible to track down all of them. To avoid such difficulties, I will simply regard experience in or with China as expertise on China and will call officers with such experience China experts. Second, I will focus on officers in posts that were expected to determine the army's China policy, rather than on the China experts themselves. Third, I will examine how China experts cooperated with each other in a few cases. In this way I hope to show the role of China experts as a whole in the formation of the army's China policy.

In the first half of this chapter I will focus on four key posts to examine how much expertise on China their occupants possessed. These posts are: chief of the Second Bureau of the General Staff, who was responsible for the collection and analysis of foreign intelligence; chief of the China Section, who was responsible for China intelligence within the Second Bureau; military attaché at the Japanese legation (embassy after 1935); and chief of the Kwantung Army Staff. In the last half of the chapter, I will examine the anti–Yuan Shih-k'ai policy in 1915–1916, and three intervention plans to assist Chang Tso-lin in 1922–1925, to see how China experts worked together in the foundation of China policy.

ARMY HEADQUARTERS

In May 1896, a major reorganization of the General Staff (GS) was completed. The formerly small GS was expanded into a big, modern organization with six bureaus: the First Bureau for operations; the Second for mobilization and formation; the Third for foreign intelligence; the Fourth for transportation and communication; and so forth. This reorganization was, needless to say, to prepare for an anticipated war with Russia. Much importance was attached to intelligence, and the first independent department for foreign intelligence was thus created.

Within two years, another change was introduced. The former First, Second, and Third bureaus were integrated and divided geographically. Namely, the First Bureau was made responsible for operations, mobilization and formation, and intelligence regarding the eastern part of Japan, Korea, and Manchuria; the new Second Bureau was responsible for matters related to the western part of Japan, Taiwan, and China, except Manchuria. The reason for this change is not clear yet, but probably the army wanted to concentrate its effort on matters directly related to the coming war with Russia.

The Intelligence Bureau

After the war with Russia began, it became evident that the intelligence on Russia had been quite inadequate: The revolutionary situation in Russia was overestimated, and the carrying capacity of the Siberian Railway was underestimated.[1] In short, intelligence had been distorted by wishful thinking when it was handled by those involved in operational planning. That is the reason the First Bureau (Operations Bureau) and the Second Bureau (Intelligence Bureau) were separated once again in December 1908. At the same time, a section system was introduced into the GS. The Second Bureau consisted of two sections: the China Section and the Europe-America Section.[2]

[1] Ariga Tsuta, "Sanbō-honbu, gunrei-bu jōhō bumon no hensen," paper presented to the annual convention of the Senshi Kenkyū Happyō Kai, 1984.

[2] Later in 1936, the Russia Section was separated from the Europe-America Section. The Stratagem Section was created in 1937 but reduced to a desk in 1943 and abolished in 1945. See Takeyama Morio, "Rikukaigun chūō kikan no seido hensen," in Nihon Kindai Shiryō Kenkyū Kai, ed., *Nihon rikukaigun no seido soshiki jinji* (Tokyo: Tokyo University Press, 1971), pp. 411–435. In the same study see "Sanbō honbu no ka han oyobi shuyō hanchō," pp. 382–385; and Ariga, "Sanbō-honbu."

In table 10.1 are shown the Second Bureau chiefs from its creation in 1908 until the end of 1937.[3] I begin my analysis with 1908 because it was only after the Russo-Japanese War that real efforts to recruit and organize China experts were begun. I end with 1937 because when the war with China deepened, the role of China experts changed considerably.

All seventeen bureau chiefs were graduates of the War College. Attendance at the War College was a real career advantage for officers. According to one estimate, seven out of ten graduates were promoted to major general or even higher, but only one out of one hundred nongraduates could expect the same. The same estimate shows that five out of seven major generals were promoted to lieutenant general, and one out of these five lieutenant generals advanced to full general.[4] Among the seventeen chiefs of the Intelligence Bureau, six were promoted to general, eleven to lieutenant general, and none retired as major general. Because the post was usually filled by a major general near promotion, it is not surprising that all seventeen advanced to lieutenant general or higher. Still, that six of them became generals was a remarkable achievement.

One factor that accounts for their success is their record in the War College. Nine graduated with honors. This was a remarkable ratio, because only about six were honor graduates among about sixty graduates each year.[5] Moreover, many of them had strong personal backing. Among the eight men who served as bureau chief during the Meiji-Taishō period, three were from Satsuma and three were from other parts of Kyushu. They all were active members of what I call the Uehara faction, which centered around General Uehara Yūsaku (field marshal after 1921), who was chief of the General Staff from 1915 to 1928.[6] One of the other two (Nakajima) was also close to Uehara and married one of his daughters. During the Shōwa period, such strong factional connections did not exist, but four out of nine bureau chiefs were married to the daughter of an influential general. In sum, the chiefs of the GS Intelligence Bureau were successful major generals with strong academic credentials and strong political support who could expect further success in their careers.

The Intelligence Bureau chiefs may be compared with the chiefs in two other bureaus: the First or Operations Bureau of the GS, the rival of the

[3] The data for tables 10.1–10.4 are taken mainly from *Seido soshiki jinji* and Toyama Misao, ed., *Rikukaigun shōkan jinji sōran* (Tokyo: Fuyō Shobō, 1981), and are supplemented by all the biographical materials that appear in the notes.

[4] Toyama, *Rikukaigun shōkan jinji sōran*, pp. 39–40.

[5] *Seido soshiki jinji*, pp. 271–328.

[6] See Kitaoka Shin'ichi, *Nihon rikugun to tairiku seisaku, 1906–1918* (Tokyo: Tokyo University Press, 1978), pp. 74–83, for the rise of the Uehara faction.

TABLE 10.1
Chiefs of the General Staff Intelligence Bureau

1908–1909	Matsuishi Yasuharu (1859–1915, Fukuoka)
	1. MA; 1883; WC; 1890; lieutenant general
	2. India (1893–1894), Taiwan (1895–1900), Germany (1900–1903); chief of First Bureau (1906–1908)
	3. Bureau chief of operations (1909–1911)
1909–1914	Utsunomiya Tarō (1861–1922, Saga)
	1. MA; 1885; WC; 1890; general
	2. India (1893–1894), England (1901–1906); bureau chief of operations (1908–1909)
	3. Commander of Korea Army (1918–1920), supreme military councilor (1920–1922)
1914–1916	Fukuda Masatarō (1866–1932, Nagasaki)
	1. MA; 1887; WC; 1893; general
	2. Germany (1897–1900), Austria (1903–1904, 1907–1909); chief of Kwantung Army Staff (1912–1914)
	3. Vice-chief of GS (1918–1921), commander of Taiwan Army (1921–1923), privy councillor (1930–1932)
1916–1917	Machida Keiu (1865–1939, Kagoshima)
	1. MA; 1887; WC; 1893; general
	2. Russia (1900–1904), France (1906–1909); military attaché (1914–1916)
	3. Supreme war councillor (1923–1925)
1917–1918	Nakajima Masatake (1870–1931, Kochi)
	1. MA; 1890; WC; 1899; lieutenant general
	2. Russia (1910–1912, 1915–1916); GS section chief of Europe and America (1912–1915)
	3. None
1918–1919	Takayanagi Yasutarō (1869–1951, Ishikawa)
	1. MA; 1892; WC; 1899; lieutenant general
	2. Russia (1906–1908, 1917–1918); GS section chief of operations (1910–1914)
	3. None
1919	Nakajima Masatake (see above)
1919–1922	Tanaka Kunishige (1869–1941, Kagoshima)
	1. MA; 1893; WC, 1900; general
	2. United States (1906-1910), Great Britain (1917–1919), Paris Peace Conference (1919), Washington Conference (1921–1922)
	3. Commander of Taiwan Army (1926–28), supreme war councillor (1928–1929)

TABLE 10.1 (*cont.*)

1922–1925	Itami Matsuo (1875–1958, Kagoshima) 1. MA; 1896; WC; 1902; lieutenant general 2. Brazil (1906–1909), United States (1910–1911, 1913–1916), South America (1913), Great Britain (1919–1922) 3. Head of War College
1925–1928	Matsui Iwane (1878–1948, Aichi) 1. MA; 1897; WC; 1906; general 2. Peking and Shanghai (1907–1911), Indochina (1913), Shanghai (1915–1919), Europe and America (1914–1915, 1928–1929), Harbin (1922–1924), Geneva Conference for Arms Limitation (1931–1932) 3. Supreme war councillor (1933, 1934–1935), commander of Taiwan Army (1933–1934), commander of Middle China Area Army (1937), cabinet councillor (1933–1940)
1928–1929	Ninomiya Harushige (1879–1945, Okayama) 1. MA; 1900; WC; 1910; lieutenant general 2. Great Britain (1912–1915, 1925–1927) 3. GS bureau chief of general affairs (1929–1930), vice-chief of GS (1930–1932), minister of education (1944–1945)
1929–1931	Tatekawa Yoshitsugu (1880–1945, Niigata) 1. MA; 1901; WC; 1909; lieutenant general 2. Great Britain (1911–13, 1916–1918), India (1913–1916), League of Nations (1920–1923); GS section chief of Europe and America (1924–1928), military attaché to China (1928–1929), Geneva Conference for Arms Limitation (1931–1932) 3. GS bureau chief of operations (1931–1932), ambassador to USSR (1940–1942)
1931–1932	Hashimoto Toranosuke (1883–1952, Aichi) 1. MA; 1902; WC; 1910; lieutenant general 2. Russia (1913–1919, 1922–1924); GS section chief of Europe and America (1928–1929) 3. Chief of Kwantung Army Staff (1932), GS bureau chief of general affairs (1933–1934), vice-minister of war (1934–1935)
1932–1933	Nagata Tetsuzan (1884–1935, Nagano) 1. MA; 1904; WC; 1911; lieutenant general 2. Germany (1913–1914), Denmark and Sweden (1915–1917), Austria (1920–1921), Switzerland (1921–1923) 3. Bureau chief of military affairs (1934–1935)
1933–1935	Isogai Rensuke (1886–1867, Hyogo) 1. MA; 1904; WC; 1915; lieutenant general 2. China (1917–1918), Kwangtung (1920–1922, 1925–1928), Europe (1932–1933); military attaché (1935–1936)

TABLE 10.1 (cont.)

	3. Bureau chief of military affairs (1935–1937), chief of Kwantung Army Staff (1938–1939)
1935–1936	Okamura Yasuji (1884–1965, Tokyo) 1. MA; 1904; WC, 1913; general 2. Tsingtao (1915–1917), Peking (1917–1919), Europe (1921–1922), Shanghai (1923–25, 1932) 3. Commander of North China Area Army (1941–1944), supreme commander in China (1944–1945)
1936–1937	Watari Hisao (1885–1939, Tokyo) 1. MA; 1905; WC; 1913; lieutenant general 2. Great Britain (1916–1917), United States (1917–1919, 1928–1930), Philippines (1922) 3. None
1937–1938	Honma Masaharu (1887–1946, Niigata) 1. MA; 1907; WC; 1915; lieutenant general 2. Great Britain (1918–1921, 1930–1932), India (1922–1925) 3. Commander of Taiwan Army (1940–1941)

Notes: Category (1) is years of graduation from the Military Academy (MA) and War College (WC) and rank at retirement. Category (2) is service in China or other foreign countries, and important posts before becoming chief. Category (3) is selected notable posts thereafter.

Second Bureau, and the Military Affairs Bureau in the War Ministry, the most powerful department of the whole army. The Operations Bureau had eighteen chiefs during the same period. Ten were promoted to general (including two field marshals), six were promoted to lieutenant general, and two others retired without promotion. The Military Affairs Bureau had seventeen chiefs. Eight of them advanced to general and nine to lieutenant general, with no major generals. The apparently remarkable achievement of the Intelligence Bureau was somewhat overshadowed by its rivals.

The gap widens further if one looks at later career development. There were three war ministers, one GS chief, and three inspectors-general of military education who had served as chief of the Operations Bureau. There were three prime ministers, four war ministers, one GS chief, one inspector-general, and four governors-general of Korea who had served as Military Affairs Bureau chief. However, no former Intelligence Bureau chief advanced beyond vice-chief of the GS or vice-minister of the War Ministry. Intelligence Bureau chiefs failed to reach the real center of power.

What helped the Operations Bureau chiefs was their War College records. Seventeen out of eighteen chiefs had graduated with honors. On the other hand, the existence of patronage was less clear. By contrast, only six out of seventeen chiefs of the Military Affairs Bureau graduated from the War College with honors. However, many of them had strong patrons. Of the eight bureau chiefs who served during the Meiji and Taishō periods, five came from Chōshu, and two of the other three were on very good terms with the Chōshu faction. During the Shōwa period, chiefs in the Military Affairs Bureau had close relations with the most powerful faction leaders in the army at the time, such as Ugaki Kazushige or the Kōdō faction generals. A close relationship with a strong patron—stronger than, say, Uehara—was necessary for an officer to become chief of the Military Affairs Bureau, and so it was little wonder that such a patron often pushed his protégé upward even higher.

In comparison to the GS Bureau of Operations and the War Ministry's Military Affairs Bureau, the GS Intelligence Bureau was probably a place for the near-best. What kind of officers, then, served as chiefs of the Intelligence Bureau? It seems to me that there were three career types: generalists, European or American experts, and China experts.

The first four chiefs were all generalists. Each had spent several years in Europe. All had some notable bureaucratic experience as section chief or bureau chief, and all had some experience in or on China. Matsuishi Yasuharu had been chief of the old GS Second Bureau, where matters related to China were handled. It is said that the intelligence system on China was first organized under his leadership.[7] Utsunomiya Tarō was sent to China in 1899 by Kawakami Sōroku, the GS chief, to persuade Chinese leaders to cooperate with Japan in coping with the Western encroachment. It is said that after his trip many Chinese officers were sent to the Military Academy in Japan.[8] His service in England also had much to do with the Chinese situation. After the Russo-Japanese War, Utsunomiya was one of the two officers most highly awarded because of contributions to the war in foreign countries.[9] Just before becoming bureau chief, Machida Keiū was the military attaché at the legation in Peking, where he carefully watched over such negotiations as the Twenty-One Demands, and Fukuda Masatarō became the chief after serving as chief of the Kwantung Army staff in Manchuria, where he witnessed Japan's diplomatic dealings with China and other powers to establish special rights and interests there. In sum, these four men were semispecialists in Chinese affairs, with much experience in other areas, including service in

[7] Tai-shi Kōrō-sha Denki Hensan Kai, ed., *Tai-Shi kaikō-roku*, vol. 2 (Tokyo, 1936), pp. 1248–1250.

[8] Ibid., pp. 797–798.

[9] Tani Hisao, *Kimitsu Nichi-Ro senshi* (Tokyo: Hara Shobō, 1966), p. 275; *Tai-Shi kaiko-roku*, vol. 2, p. 798.

foreign countries. They were also politically active officers who had close relations with Uehara Yūsaku and later with Tanaka Giichi.

Of the later bureau chiefs, only Tatekawa Yoshitsugu belonged to the generalist type. He had much experience in England, had served as military attaché at Peking before becoming the Second Bureau chief, and later served as the First Bureau chief. Like the other generalist chiefs, he was politically active and was close to a strong patron, Ugaki Kazushige.

The second type was the European or American expert. The four chiefs who served from 1917 to 1925 all belonged to this category. Nakajima Masatake and Takayanagi Yasutarō were Russian experts with little experience in other fields. Tanaka Kunishige and Itami Matsuo were Anglo-American experts with very limited experience in other matters. In the 1930s, Hashimoto Toranosuke, Watari Hisao, and Honma Masaharu were specialists on Russia, the United States, and Great Britain, respectively.

The third type was the China expert. Matsui Iwane was the first real expert to emerge as bureau chief in any part of the army. He began his involvement with China immediately after his graduation from the War College. It was a custom that top students at the War College be given a chance to study abroad after graduation. Most chose to go to Germany, France, England, Russia, or the United States. Before Matsui, who was at the top of the class of 1906, only one had chosen China; no other top student in the history of the War College before or after him had done so.[10] Aside from Matsui, only Isogai Rensuke and Okamura Yasuji were China experts. Like him, they worked mostly in or on China and had little experience in other fields.

Under what circumstances were these men appointed as chiefs of the Second Bureau? For the generalist chiefs who served down to 1917, not much explanation is needed. In this office, able and ambitious officers could influence Japan's expansion on the Chinese continent during this period, and by so doing use the post as a power base. Actually, the Second Bureau was one of the most important sources of Japan's China policy.[11]

Appointments from 1917 through 1931 seem to have been made mainly to cope with the international situation. Nakajima and Takayanagi were appointed to lead the Siberian intervention. The appointments of Tanaka and Itami were related to Anglo-American dominance. It is likely that Ugaki chose Matsui to handle the complicated Chinese situation.[12] The appointments of Ninomiya and Tatekawa, who were both

[10] *Seido soshiki jinji.*
[11] See Kitaoka, *Nihon rikugun*, especially pp. 95–99.
[12] It is said that Matsui had close relations with Hata Eitarō, Ugaki's right-hand man, and

close to Ugaki, were natural, too, because Anglo-Japanese cooperation was becoming very important in the effort to cope with Chinese nationalism, particularly under Ugaki's China policy.[13] Hashimoto's appointment was probaby made by War Minister Minami Jirō, who was worried about Russia with regard to Manchuria, a concern shared as well by Ugaki, the man behind Minami.[14]

The appointments after Hashimoto, however, are difficult to explain in the same way. Why was Nagata appointed Second Bureau chief instead of First Bureau chief, a post that better fitted him? Why was Okamura, a China expert, replaced by Watari, an American expert, when the situation in North China was serious? Why was Watari succeeded by Honma, a British expert, in the initial stages of the war with China? One important element was the factional conflict within the army. In Nagata's case, the Kōdō faction wanted to have the First Bureau in their hands.[15] That is why Nagata became Second Bureau chief. Appointments of China experts were related to the factional conflict, too. Isogai was made chief because a neutral officer was needed to stand between Nagata and Obata Toshishirō, central figures of the Tōsei and Kōdō factions, respectively.[16] Okamura, one of the few officers close both to Nagata and Obata, was expected to help solve the conflict between them, but after the February 26 incident in 1936 he was replaced, in part because he was close to the Kōdō faction.[17]

Several rough generalizations might be made about appointment to the post of chief of the Second Bureau. First, generalists could become chief by their own ability and exert strong influence on the army's China policy. There was a tendency, however, toward specialization in the post which paralleled the bureaucratization of the whole army. After 1917, only Tatekawa was a generalist. Introduction of China expertise through generalist chiefs became more difficult after World War I. Second, European and American experts could become chief much more easily than China experts. However, they were surprisingly lacking in China experience. Third, China experts could become chief when supported by strong leaders within the army. Such leaders, however, were in charge of

---

therefore belonged to the Ugaki group. See Takamiya Tahei, *Jungyaku no Shōwa shi* (Tokyo: Hara Shobō, 1971); originally published as *Gunkoku taihei ki* in 1951.

[13] Ibid., p. 64.

[14] On the relationship between Ugaki and Minami, and on Minami's perception of the Manchurian problem, see Kitaoka Shin'ichi, "Rikugun habatsu tairitsu no sai kentō," in Kindai Nihon Kenkyū, ed., *Shōwa ki no gun bu* (Tokyo: Yamakawa Shuppansha, 1979).

[15] Kitaoka, "Rikugun habatsu," pp. 60–61.

[16] Takamiya, *Jungyaku no Shōwa shi*, p. 150; Itō Kinjirō, *Riku kai gun jin koku ki* (Tokyo: Fuyō Shobō, 1980); originally published as *Gunjin washi ga kuni sa* in 1939.

[17] Funaki Shigeru, *Okamura Yasuji taishō* (Tokyo: Kawade Shobō Shinsha, 1984), pp. 258, 288–289, and 315.

China policy themselves, leaving little room for expert chiefs. Moreover, as is well known, no solid, undisputed leader was established after Ugaki. It is ironic that two China experts became chief under such circumstances. Because they were often absent from Tokyo, they were less involved in factional conflicts, but precisely for that reason they were welcomed to the post. Needless to say, they could never guide the army's China's policy very effectively when the army was torn by conflict.

In sum, it was very difficult for a China expert to be chief of the Intelligence Bureau. It was even more difficult for a China expert to put his plan into practice even if he were appointed to the post, because he lacked his own independent power base.

The China Section

There were sixteen chiefs of the China Section from 1908 to 1937 (see table 10.2). All sixteen graduated from the War College, but there was only one graduate with honors among them. In the Europe-America Section of the Second Bureau, eight of eighteen chiefs were honor graduates. The Operations Section of the First Bureau, the most elite section of the GS, had fourteen honors graduates among the eighteen who served. Another prestigious section, the Military Administration Section of the War Ministry's Military Affairs Bureau, had twelve honors graduates out of twenty. The top students in the War College often became chiefs of one of the elite sections (such as the Operations Section, Military Administration Section, and Europe-America Section) but rarely became chief of the China Section.

Among the sixteen former China Section chiefs, two became generals, twelve became lieutenant generals, and two became major generals (no field marshals). The record of Europe-America Section chiefs was two generals, fourteen lieutenant generals, and two major generals (one field marshal). Among the former Military Administration Section chiefs, the record was an unbelievable ten, nine, and one (one field marshal), which was even higher than the record of the Military Affairs Bureau chiefs and the Operations Bureau chiefs. If one ignores the record of the Military Administration Section, the China Section's record was not very good, but not very bad.

However, with regard to promotion to important posts in the ministry or the GS, the achievement of the China Section chiefs was poor. To make the comparison easier, I would like to consider only the three key positions in the Army High Command (namely, the war minister, GS chief, and inspector-general of Military Education), their three vice-chiefs, and the bureau chiefs of the ministry and the GS. Surprisingly, no former China Section chief was ever appointed to any one of these positions. On

TABLE 10.2
Chiefs of the General Staff China Section

1908–1909	Furukawa Iwatarō (Hyogo) 1. MA; 1891; WC; 1900; major general 2. Unknown
1909–1913	Onodera Jūtarō (1870–1939, Tokyo) 1. MA; 1891; WC; 1900; lieutenant general 2. China (1901–1902)
1913–1915	Ishimitsu Maomi (1870–1937, Kumamoto) 1. MA; 1890; WC; 1900; lieutenant general 2. Commander of Stationary Troops at Tientsin (1916–1918) 3. Provost marshal (1918–1919)
1915–1917	Hamaomote Matasuke (1873–1944, Wakayama) 1. MA; 1893; WC; 1900; lieutenant general 2. Manchuria (1903?–1904?), Russia (1906–??), chief of Kwangtung Army Staff (1918–1921), Harbin (1921–1922)
1917–1918	Vacant
1918–1919	Honjō Shigeru (1876–1945, Hyogo) 1. MA; 1897; WC; 1907; general 2. Peking and Shanghai (1908–1913), chief of China Desk (1913–1918), Europe (1915–1916), Advisor to Chang Tso-lin (1921–1924), military attaché (1925–1928) 3. Commander of Kwantung Army (1931–1932), supreme war councillor (1932–1933), chief military attaché aide-de-camp to the emperor (1933–1936), privy councillor (1945), baron (1935)
1919–1921	Takada Toyoki (1875–1964, Ishikawa) 1. MA; 1896; WC; 1903; lieutenant General 2. China Section (1909–1913), Tientsin (1913–1915), Tsingtao (1918–1919, 1921–1922), commander of Stationary Troops at Tientsin (1926–27)
1921–1923	Kusaka Misao (18??–19??, Fukushima) 1. MA; 1899; WC; 1909; major general 2. Tsinan (1919–1921), Mukden (1926–1927)
1923	Vacant
1923–1926	Satō Saburō (1881–1964, Yamagata) 1. MA; 1902; WC; 1912; lieutenant general 2. Peking (1916), chief of China Desk (1918–1919, 1921–1923), Shanghai (1919–1921), Tsinan (1928–1929), military attaché (1929–1931)
1926–1930	Tashiro Kan'ichirō (1881–1937, Saga) 1. MA; 1903; WC; 1913; lieutenant general 2. China Section (1915–1916, 1918–1922, desk chief, 1919– 1921), Peking (1916–1918), Hankow (1923–1924), military

TABLE 10.2 (cont.)

	attaché (1931–1932, 1932–1933), commander of Stationary Troops at Tientsin (1936–1937)

1930–1932   Shigetō Chiaki (1885–1942, Fukuoka)
1. MA; 1905; WC; 1918; lieutenant general
2. Peking (1923–1924), Kwangtung (1924–1925), Shanghai (1927–1929), chief of China Desk (1926–1927, 1929–1930)

1932   Iwamatsu Yoshio (1886–1958, Aichi)
1. MA; 1905; WC; 1918; lieutenant general
2. China (1919–1922), Shanghai (1925–1927), chief of China Desk (1927–1928), Nanking (1932–1933)
3. Commander of First Army (1941–1942), supreme war councillor (1942–1943)

1932–1934   Sakai Takashi (1887–1946, Hiroshima)
1. MA; 1908; WC; 1916; lieutenant general
2. China (1919–1921), China Section (1921–1923), Shanghai (1923–1924), Hankow (1924–1925), Tientsin (1929–1932, 1934–1935)

1934–1936   Kita Seiichi (1886–1947, Shiga)
1. MA; 1907; WC; 1919; general
2. Tientsin (1911–1916), China (1921–1923), chief of China Desk (1925–1926, 1928–1929), Great Britain (1927–1928), Nanking (1929–1931), Shanghai (1932), Kwangtung Army Staff (1932–1934), military attaché (1936–1937)
3. Commander of First Area Army (1944–1945)

1936–1937   Nagatsu Sahishige (1889–19??, Aichi)
1. MA; 1911; WC; 1920; lieutenant general
2. Tientsin (1922–1923), United States (1925–1927), Peking (1931–1933), Kwantung Army Staff (1933–1934, 1934–1936)

1937   Kagesa Sadaaki (1893–1948, Hiroshima)
1. MA; 1914; WC; 1923; lieutenant general
2. North China (1929–1931), China Section (1931–1932, 1933–1934; desk chief, 1933–1934), Tientsin (1932), Shanghai (1934–1935), GS section chief of stratagem (1937–1938), section chief of military affairs of the War Ministry (1938–1939)

1937–1939   Watari Sakon (acting chief, 1937–1938; chief, 1938–1939) (1893–1951, Tokyo)
1. MA; 1915; WC; 1926; lieutenant general
2. China Section (1929, 1936–1938); desk chief of strategic geography, 1936–1938, Hankow (1934–1936)

Notes: Category (1) is years of graduation from the Military Academy (MA) and War College (WC) and rank at retirement. Category (2) is service in China or other foreign countries. Category (3) is selected notable posts thereafter, if any.

the other hand, nine out of eighteen former Europe-America Section chiefs were promoted to at least one of them. The record for the Operations Bureau chiefs was seventeen out of nineteen; and twelve out of twenty for the Bureau of Military Administration chiefs. Actually, other than Honjō Shigeru, no one became famous after being the chief of the China Section. Even Honjō's fame was acquired by coincidence. When the Manchurian incident took place, he was commander of the Kwantung Army, but he was not a strong leader.[18]

Honjō, however, occupies an important place in the history of the China Section. Unlike his predecessors, who did not have much experience in China, Honjō began his involvement with China immediately after graduation from the War College in 1907. Only Banzai Rihachirō, class of 1900, and Matsui Iwane, class of 1906, did the same. After Honjō, no one did the same until Doihara Kenji and Satō Saburō, both class of 1912. After that, an average of four students a year were sent to China upon graduation until 1933. The recruitment of these officers to learn about China corresponded with the Chinese situation. Banzai was chosen to go in the midst of the Boxer Rebellion; Matsui and Honjō were chosen to cope with the new situation after the Russo-Japanese War; and the system of regular recruitment was introduced as a result of the Chinese revolution. Matsui and Honjō, who had been in the same class at the Military Academy, were between Banzai, the last old China expert, and the new generation. It is interesting that both of them were appointed to important positions by Ugaki: Matsui as chief of the Intellegence Bureau, and Honjō as commander of the Kwantung Army.[19]

After about five years in China, Honjō became chief of the China Desk. It is not clear when this two-desk system (China Desk and Strategic Geography Desk) was established, but probably Honjō was the first chief of the China Desk. He was the leader of the desk and section for seven years altogether, except for a trip to Europe and America. Many future China experts came to work under him, and the China Section became better organized as the center for China experts in the mid-Taishō period.

The development of the China Section was probably completed by 1923, when Satō Saburō became the first new-generation China expert to serve as its chief. In April of that year, for example, the section chief was Colonel Kusaka Misao, and the desk chief was Satō (lieutenant colonel,

---

[18] Even Itō Kinjirō, who on the whole praised Honjō very highly, admitted that Honjō would never have become famous had he not been involved in the incident as commander of the Kwantung Army, and he said that Honjō was a kind of robot. See Itō, *Riku kai gun*, p. 270.

[19] Ugaki wrote in his diary that he had selected Honjō because of Honjō's experience in China. Tsunoda Jun, ed., *Ugaki Kazushige nikki*, vol. 2 (Tokyo: Misuzu Shobō, 1970), p. 994.

promoted to section chief in August). Working under Satō were majors Okamura Yasuji, Itagaki Seishirō, Doihara Kenji, Iwamatsu Yoshio, and Sasaki Tōichi, and captains Kita Seiichi, Sakai Takashi, and Nagami Toshinori, all of whom later became famous China experts.[20]

As the China Section developed bureaucratically, another tendency began to appear: lack of mutual circulation of its personnel among other departments. As shown in table 10.2, after Satō, China Section chiefs all had more or less similar careers. Once in a while they served as commander or staff member of a field unit, but for the rest of their careers they just went back and forth between China and the China Section. They were likely to end up as military attaché or commander of the garrison troops in Tientsin. They rarely went to foreign countries other than China and rarely worked in any other department of the army in Tokyo, or even in the Kwantung Army. Among the twelve chiefs after Hamaomote Matasuke, no one but Nagatsu Sahishige had more than a year's experience in Europe or America. Kita Seiichi had been in the Bureau of Military Affairs, and Kagesa in the same bureau and in the Operations Bureau before becoming section chief, but none of the other ten had. No chiefs but Kita and Nagatsu had worked in the Kwantung Army either. On the other hand, very few officers of other departments had experience in the China Section, except for the Kwantung Army Staff officers, as will be shown later. In short, the better the China Section was organized as a center for China experts, the more isolated it became. It is said that officers in other departments came to regard the China Section officers as somewhat strange.[21] It seems that this isolation resulted, first, in a lack of breadth in the views of the China Section officers and, second, in difficulty securing the cooperation of other departments.

It is hard to tell whether or not the China Section did a good job. Some thought that Japan's intelligence system on China, which was headed by the China Section, was excellent.[22] At the outbreak of the Sino-Japanese War in 1937, however, one of the most critical moments in modern Japanese history, China Section officers unanimously advocated the so-called "Slash China" policy, which made its local solution impossible.[23] When the war dragged on, it became clear that maps of Hong Kong and places

[20] Funaki, *Okamura Yasuji*, p. 37.

[21] Okada Yoshimasa, "Shina ka," in *Rekishi to jinbutsu*, vol. 170 (Tokyo: Chūō Kōronsha, August 1985), p. 67.

[22] "Mitsu dai nikki" (Bōeichō sensi bu) 1926, cited in Terunuma Yasutaka's introduction to Itō Takashi et al., eds., *Honjō Shigeru nikki* (Tokyo: Yamakawa Shuppansha, 1982), p. 16.

[23] Takahashi Hisashi, "Nikka jihen shoki ni okeru rikugun chūsū bu," in Kindai Nihon Kenkyū Kai, ed., *Nihon gaikō no kiki ninshiki* (Tokyo: Yamakawa Shuppansha, 1985), p. 190.

other than coastal areas were either lacking or very inaccurate, and that no study had been made of historical battles in important places—how Hankow, for example, had been captured or defended in the past.[24] Probably both assessments were true: The China Section might have done a great job in information gathering but did poorly in making judgments and in making basic studies about China. The latter failure was caused at least in part by the lack of broader views and experiences there. The chief of the Second Bureau, who should have made up for these shortcomings, usually did not have much knowledge about China, as has already been seen.

When Okamura Yasuji met with Idogawa Tatsuzō, one of the well-known early China experts, the latter advised the future chief of the Second Bureau that anyone who wanted to work on China should achieve a good record in the War College and go to Europe first so that he could get an influential position in the GS or in ministry.[25] Banzai Rihachiro wanted to educate a young officer who had already seen Europe and America to become a future China expert.[26] But the ideal of the China expert as an officer with wider background, as envisaged by Idogawa and Banzai, was never achieved in the Second Bureau or in the China Section.

EXPERTS IN THE FIELD

If the army's China policy originated from the Second Bureau of the GS, including the China Section, in Tokyo, two major sources of the army's China policy on the continent were the military attaché at the legation (embassy after 1935) and the Kwantung Army staff.

Military Attaché

Among the four posts under examination, that of military attaché had the longest history. The first military attaché to China was appointed in 1880. To make comparison easier, however, table 10.3 covers only the same period as tables 10.1 and 10.2.

The post was filled by fewer officers, and their average tenure was consequently longer. Aoki Norizumi, for example, served four times, for more than twelve years altogether. Before 1905, Kajiyama Teisuke had served only once, but for almost six years, and Kamio Mitsuomi served

---

[24] Inada Masazumi's comment on the education in the War College, in Jōhō Yoshio, ed., *Rikugun Daigakkō* (Tokyo: Fuyō Shobō, 1973), pp. 320–321.

[25] Funaki, *Okamura Yasuji*, pp. 20–21.

[26] Banzai to Hamaomote, December 10, 1919, in Yamaguchi Toshiaki, ed., "Hamaomote Matasuke monjo," Kindai Nihon Kenkyū Kai, ed., *Kindai Nihon to higashi Ajia* (Tokyo: Yamakawa Shuppansha, 1980), pp. 212–214. Cited hereafter as HMM.

TABLE 10.3
Military Attachés at the Legation (Embassy after 1935) in China

1905–1913	Aoki Norizumi (also in 1897–1900, 1901–1902, 1903–1904) (1859–1924, Miyazaki) 1. MA; 1879; lieutenant general 2. China (1884–1888), Belgium (1891–1893); advisor to Yuan Shih-k'ai (1900), advisor to Li Yuan-hung (1917–1923)
1913–1914	Saitō Suejirō (also in 1916–1918) (1867–1921, Osaka) 1. MA; 1889; WC; 1897; lieutenant general 2. Hangchow (1899–1904), Europe (1910), commander of Stationary Troops at Tientsin (1915–1916), Peking (1918–1919)
1914–1916	Machida Keiu (see table 10.1)
1916–1918	Saitō Suejirō (see above)
1918–1922	Higashi Otohiko (Yamaguchi) 1. MA; 1893; WC; 1900; lieutenant general 2. Great Britain (1908–1910)
1922–1925	Hayashi Yasakichi (1876–1948, Ishikawa) 1. MA; 1896; WC; 1903; lieutenant general 2. Germany (1909–1913), GS section chief of Europe and America (1917–1919), section chief of military affairs (1921–1922)
1925–1928	Honjō Shigeru (see table 10.2)
1928–1929	Tatekawa Yoshitsugu (see table 10.1)
1929–1931	Satō Saburō (see table 10.2)
1931–1933	Tashiro Kan'ichirō (see table 10.2)
1933–1935	Suzuki Yoshiyuki (1882–1956, Yamagata) 1. MA; 1902; WC; 1911; lieutenant general 2. Manchuria (1919–1924), Mukden (1929–1931)
1935–1936	Isogai Rensuke (see table 10.1)
1936–1937	Kita Seiichi (see table 10.2)
1937–1938	Harada Kumakichi (1888–1947, Tokyo) 1. MA; 1910; WC; 1916; lieutenant general 2. China Section (1920), China (1920–1923), Peking (1927–1929), chief of China Desk of Military Affairs Bureau (1929–1930), Europe (1930–1931), Nanking (1931–1932), Shanghai (1932), Kwantung Army (1932–1935)

Notes: Category (1) is years of graduation from the Military Academy (MA) and War College (WC) and rank at retirement. Category (2) is service in China or other foreign countries, and important posts before becoming attaché. Category (3) is other notable posts thereafter, if any.

twice, for more than four and a half years. Among those in table 10.3, Saitō Suejirō served twice, for more than three and a half years. It is difficult to evaluate the role of these attachés, because from 1911 to 1927 Banzai Rihachirō, probably the most famous China expert in the whole history of Japan's army, served as a kind of semi-official attaché or sometimes as the real attaché.

The history of the military attachés can be divided into three periods. The first lasted until 1918. During this period, with one exception (Machida), the post was occupied by China specialists who all worked in close relationship with Banzai, whose influence was strong. As will be seen later, China policy was discussed by the attaché, Banzai, chief of the General Staff, vice-chief of the General Staff, and chief of the Second Bureau.

The second period was from 1918 to 1925, when the two attachés had no real experience in or on China. Higashi Otohiko was from Chōshū and formerly a military attaché in England. The next attaché, Hayashi Yasakichi, had worked mainly in the Bureau of Military Affairs, close to Ugaki. Banzai's influence had seen its peak under the Terauchi cabinet, but it was particularly diminished by the defeat of the War Participation Army in 1920, which Banzai had expected to make the central power of China.[27]

Instead, a new center of influence was emerging in Tokyo. The China Section of the GS began to have some influence in Peking through the post of assistant attaché, established in 1916. Between 1921 and 1927, for example, this post was filled by such important officers as Kōmoto Daisaku, Shigetō Chiaki, Itagaki Seishirō, and Sasaki Tōichi.

These talented and ambitious young officers, however, must have been frustrated in Peking. First, the central government's China policy was not activist in this period. There was a big gap between the Tokyo government and the officers in Peking, and it was impossible for junior officers to have much influence on the government while serving under nonspecialist attachés. Second, there was an important gap between senior officers and junior officers in Peking on the question of China's political future. For example, Sasaki was one of the first officers to predict the eventual victory of the Chinese Nationalist party, but his superior officers did not accept his opinion.[28] Many of these young China Section officers

---

[27] Banzai to Uehara Yūsaku, August 22, 1920, in Uehara Yūsaku Kankei Monjo Kenkyū Kai, ed., *Uehara Yūsaku kankei monjo* (Tokyo: Tokyo University Press, 1976), p. 380.

[28] Sasaki Tōichi began his study of the Chinese Nationalist party in 1922 in Kwangtung. His sympathy for it was not listened to, however, but ridiculed when he returned to Tokyo in 1924. The attitude of his superiors was no different in Peking, where he was the assistant attaché from 1926 to 1927. Sasaki, *Aru gunjin no jiden* (Tokyo: Keisō Shobō, 1967), pp. 87, 111–123, and 134.

had served in the south, often corresponded with each other, and came to attach more importance to the south than did their superiors in Peking.[29]

The third period began with the appointment of Honjō in 1925. The gap between junior and senior officers did not disappear, however, because Honjō still followed Tanaka's policy and put much importance on Chang Tso-lin.[30] But the center of Chinese politics was beginning to move toward the south. It was symbolic that Banzai left Peking in 1927. After Honjō and Tatekawa, Sato Saburō became the attaché in 1929, the real China Section officer in charge of this post. It was symbolic again that the attaché left Peking for Shanghai in 1930, in the middle of his tenure. However, it was probably too late. There was very little room for the attaché to maneuver for or against Chiang Kai-shek from Shanghai by then. Japan could neither assist him nor assist his greatest opposition, the Chinese Communist party, against Chiang. In short, the attaché's traditional approach to the Peking government—manipulation of the conflicts among warlords—was no longer effective toward the Nationalist party.[31] As a result, the attaché could not provide leadership for Japan's China policy any more effectively in the third period than in the second.

Chief of Staff of the Kwantung Army

The careers of fifteen chiefs of staff of the Kwantung Army are listed in table 10.4.

The history of the Kwantung Army from its creation in 1906 until the outbreak of the Sino-Japanese War in 1937 can be divided into three periods. Before 1919, the commander of the army was concurrently governor of the Kwantung Territories, and the post of chief of staff was filled by such activist officers as Fukuda, Shiba, Nishikawa, and Takayama.

[29] Kōmoto had served in Hankow and Yunnan, made contacts with Ts'ai O, and helped the Yunnan Army from 1915 to 1916. Itagaki also served in Yunnan during 1918–1919. Okamura in Shanghai during 1923–1926 and Isogai in Kwantung during 1920–1922 are other examples. See Sagara Shunsuke, *Akai yūhi no masunoga hara ni* (Tokyo: Kōjin Sha, 1978), pp. 35–40; Itagaki Seishirō Kankō Kai, ed., *Hiroku Itagaki Seishirō* (Tokyo: Fuyō Shobō, 1972), p. 90. As for communications between them, the diary of Okamura Yasuji has much information (Funaki, *Okamura Yasuji*).

[30] It is not that Honjō did not place much importance on the South, but he had been so close to Chang in his years as advisor to him that he lacked detachment in his attaché years. Nihon Kindai Shiryō Kenkyū Kai, *Suzuki Teiichi shi danwa sokki*, vol. 1 (Tokyo, 1971), pp. 255–256; Sasaki, *Aru gunjin no jiden*, p. 130.

[31] When Sasaki was selected to serve in Nanking in 1927, Matsui Iwane, chief of the Second Bureau, told him that Banzai's mission was over, that Suzuki should become the Banzai of the South, and that becoming an advisor to Chiang Kai-shek would be the shortest way. Sasaki responded that he would never go to Nanking if he had to become advisor, as he had been disgusted so much by the incompetence of Chang Tso-lin's advisors. Sasaki, *Aru gunjin no jiden*, p. 147.

TABLE 10.4
Chiefs of the Kwantung Army Staff

1906–1907	Kamio Mitsuomi (1855–1927, Nagano) 1. MA; 1876; general 2. China (1882–1886), military attaché at the legation in China (1892–1894, 1895–1897), Europe (1899–1900); commander of Stationary Troops at Tientsin (1905–1906) 3. Commander of Expeditionary Force to Tsingtao (1914–1915), baron (1916)
1907–1912	Hoshino Kingo (Niigata) 1. MA; 1882; WC; 1890; lieutenant general 2. Unknown
1912	Shiba Katsusaburō (1863–1938, Ibaraki) 1. MA; 1885; WC; 1890; lieutenant general 2. Europe (1908) 3. Chief of Military Affairs Bureau (1912–1915)
1911–1914	Fukuda Masatarō (see table 10.1)
1914–1916	Nishikawa Torajirō (1867–1944, Fukuoka) 1. MA; 1889; WC; 1897; lieutenant general 2. China (1900), Great Britain (1902–1904) 3. GS chief of Fourth Bureau (1916–1917), commander of First Division (1921–1922)
1916–1918	Takayama Kimimichi (1867–1940, Kagoshima) 1. MA; 1889; WC; 1899; lieutenant general 2. Kweichow (1902–1904), Kwantung Army (1906), Mukden (1912)
1918–1921	Hamaomote Matasuke (see table 10.2)
1921–1923	Fukuhara Yoshiya (1874–1952, Yamaguchi) 1. MA; 1894; WC; 1903; lieutenant general 2. France (1907–1911)
1923–1925	Kawada Meiji (Kōchi) 1. MA; 1898; WC; 1908; lieutenant general 2. Unknown
1925–1928	Saitō Hisashi (1877–1953, Ishikawa) 1. MA; 1898; WC; 1907, lieutenant general 2. Peking (1911–1912), Shanghai (1912–1916), Kirin (1918–1921); GS section chief of transportation (1922–1923)
1928–1932	Miyake Mitsuharu (1881–1945, Mie) 1. MA; 1901; WC; 1910; lieutenant general 2. Austria-Hungary (1919–1922)
1932	Hashimoto Toranosuke (see table 10.1)

TABLE 10.4 (*cont.*)

1932–1934	Koiso Kuniaki (1880–1950, Yamagata) 1. MA; 1900; WC; 1910; general 2. Kwantung Army (1912–1915), China Section (1915–1917), Europe (1922); bureau chief of military affairs (1930–1932), vice-minister of war (1932) 3. Commander of Korea Army (1935–1938), minister of colonization (1939, 1940), governor of Korea (1942–1944), prime minister (1944–1945)
1934–1936	Nishio Toshizō (1881–1960, Tottori) 1. MA; 1902; WC; 1910; general 2. Germany (1914–1915) 3. Vice-chief of GS (1936–1937), inspector-general of military education (1938–1939), supreme commander in China (1939–1941), supreme war councillor (1941–43)
1936–1937	Itagaki Seishirō (1885–1948, Iwate) 1. MA; 1905; WC; 1916; general 2. Kunming (1917–1919), Hankow (1919–1921), China Section (1922–1924, 1926–1927), Peking (1924–1926), China (1927–1928), Kwantung Army (1929–1933, 1934–1936) 3. Minister of war (1938–1939), commander of Korea Army (1941-1945)
1937–1938	Tōjō Hideki (1884–1948, Tokyo) 1. MA; 1905; WC; 1915; general 2. Switzerland (1919–1921), Germany (1921–1922), GS section chief of organization and mobilization (1931–1933); Manchuria (1935–1937) 3. Vice-minister of war (1938), minister of war (1940–1941), prime minister (1941–1944), chief of GS (1943–1944)

Notes: Category (1) is years of graduation from the Military Academy (MA) and War College (WC) and rank at retirement. Category (2) is service in China or other foreign countries, and important posts before becoming chief. Category (3) is other notable posts thereafter, if any.

They were one of the sources of the army's China policy during the Chinese revolution in 1911–1912 as well as during World War I. Still, they were basically under the control of the senior generals like Yamagata Aritomo and Terauchi Masatake, or under the control of the GS.[32]

An important change was introduced in 1919. The governor-generalship was to be filled by either a civilian or an officer, and the commander

[32] The army did not give serious cosideration to the so-called First Manchuria-Mongolia Independence plan, and the second was part of a larger plan by the GS. See Kitaoka, *Nihon rikugun*, pp. 92–96.

of the Kwantung Army was placed under the orders of the GS and no longer answered to the governor-general. That meant a decline in the influence and prestige of the Kwantung Army, a change reflected in the appointments to the post of chief of staff. Fukuhara Yoshiya was a lesser-known Chōshū general who had worked mainly on and in France. Kawada Meiji was a rather obscure general, too. As will be shown later, the Kwantung Army was not able to realize its plan of assisting Chang Tso-lin effectively on three occasions in 1922–1925. Moreover, the army's manpower strength was at its lowest in the mid- and late 1920s.[33]

After the Manchurian incident, everything changed drastically. After 1932, the Kwantung Army commander served simultaneously as governor-general of Kwantung and as ambassador to Manchoukuo. The positions of commander and chief of staff became more important and more coveted posts: The former was occupied by such important generals as former Inspector-General Mutō Nobuyoshi, former Supreme War Counsellor Hishikari Takashi, former War Minister Minami Jirō, and former GS Vice-Chief Ueda Kenkichi; the latter post was filled by lieutenant generals who hoped to be vice-minister of war or at least the GS vice-chief. At the same time, the post of vice-chief of staff of the Kwantung Army was filled by major generals. In many ways, the post of chief of staff was about as important as it had been under the old system. During the 1930s it was filled by Okamura Yasuji (1932–1934), Itagaki Seishirō (1934–1936), Imamura Hitoshi (1936–1937), and Ishiwara Kanji (1937–1938). The list of names of commanders, chiefs of staff, and vice-chiefs of staff is astounding. None of them could be omitted easily from even a short history of Shōwa Japan. The Kwantung Army was staffed by important officers and played a decisive role in the formulation of Japan's foreign policy from the Manchurian incident to the outbreak of the Sino-Japanese War.

No explanation may be necessary about the change from the first period from the second. Simply stated, it was prompted by the rise of democracy in Japan and all over the world after World War I. The change from the second to the third period, however, was more complicated. What interests me is the fact that China experts of the new generation were coming to work in Lushun in the late 1920s. For example, Saitō became the chief of staff in 1925 after the Kuo Sung-ling incident; Kōmoto became senior staff member in 1926 and was succeeded by Itagaki. This change was at least partly caused by the development of the China Section, which had produced too many officers to be absorbed within the

---

[33] In 1922 and 1923, an arms reduction plan was enforced by Army Minister Yamanashi Hanzō. As a result, each infantry regiment lost one of its four battalions. The Kwantung Army was no exception. Therefore, it was about three-fourths its original size. Moreover, it desperately lacked modern equipment. See Itagaki Seishiro Kankō Kai, ed., *Hiroku Itagaki*, p. 32.

section.[34] Until this period, the introduction of expertise on mainland China had been rather uncommon in the Kwantung Army. Moreover, as will be shown later, these new-generation China experts had opposed previous policies of the Kwantung Army, so it was natural for them to try to change those policies. The murder of Chang Tso-lin, by which Kōmoto hoped to solve the Manchurian problems "fundamentally," was a clear departure from the Kwantung Army's traditional policy of indirect control over Manchuria through Chang. The China experts finally took control of the army's China policy not in Tokyo or in mainland China but in Manchuria in 1928–1931.

The role of China expert was not rewarding. Such an expert had to spend much of his career in China or just going back and forth between Japan and China. Because he had a mediocre record in the War College, and because he was usually busily engaged in China affairs, he rarely had the chance to study in Europe or to serve in the real centers of army power such as the Military Affairs Bureau of the War Ministry or the First Bureau of the GS. It is little wonder that he lacked broader views on international relations and domestic politics. When he was in Tokyo, he worked mainly in the China Section of the Second Bureau. He could be promoted to Section Chief, but probably no further. The Second Bureau chief was usually an officer who had experience in Europe and who had a patron. The China expert lacked both. He stayed out of Japan too long to make such political connections, particularly after World War I, when career specialization developed, and his chance of becoming chief of another bureau was even less. His final post, at best, would probably be military attaché in Peking or commander of the garrison troops in Tientsin.

China experts were not able to occupy higher posts in the central bureaucracy of the army and thereby dominate its China policy. That does not necessarily mean, however, that they did not have much influence on army policy. It was still possible for a China expert to exert influence from the periphery or from lower posts. To discern the ways in which they could influence the army's China policy, I will examine a few cases in which many China experts worked together.

THE LIMITS OF COLLABORATION

On March 7, 1916, the Ōkuma cabinet adopted a new China policy which stated that, to promote Japan's influence in China, Yuan Shih-k'ai

---

[34] Because China experts particularly needed experience, they usually stayed in the same post longer than the officials in other departments, and they often served in the same place in China more than once. Each class of the War College usually produced two or three well-known China experts. Thus, the bureaucratic promotion system and the recruitment of experts were often contradictory.

had to be removed from power. This anti-Yuan policy was the most aggressive policy adopted toward China before the Manchurian incident, though it has not drawn much interest from historians. It is, in my opinion, worth noting not only because of its naked aggressiveness, but also because of the leadership behind it. It was probably the only China policy in which the Army General Staff clearly took the lead.[35]

Ousting Yuan Shih-k'ai

There were two important preconditions for the adoption of this policy. One was the change in the cabinet. In August 1915, Katō Takaaki, president of the Dōshikai, the major government party, resigned from the cabinet as foreign minister. Two of his fellow ministers followed. Although Katō lacked the shrewdness of Hara Kei, his rival, he was a strong leader, particularly in his control of foreign policy. After Katō's resignation, Prime Minister Ōkuma served concurrently as foreign minister until October, when Ishii Kikujirō, ambassador to France, came back to succeed him. As Ōkuma lacked command of complicated matters, and Ishii had little experience in China, cabinet leadership in China policy had weakened by the fall of 1915, even though its political base had expanded as the result of its rather unexpected victory in the general election in March. Since the vacated cabinet posts were assumed by former Kokumintō politicians who had developed close ties with the roving China hands (*tairiku rōnin*) in their years in opposition during the 1900s, the cabinet had become susceptible to their influence.[36]

The other precondition was a change within the army, and the GS in particular. There had emerged a younger generation who wanted a more active policy on China than that of senior Chōshū generals like Yamagata and Terauchi. They were led by Uehara Yūsaku and Tanaka Giichi. Though defeated in the Taishō political crisis of 1912–1913, they had succeeded in regaining power. Tanaka was appointed GS vice-chief in October 1915, and Uehara chief in December 1916. Compared to this strengthened GS, the War Ministry was weak because of War Minister Oka's illness. Terauchi, a senior Chōshū general who later bitterly opposed the anti-Yuan policy, could not intervene in the GS because he was serving as governor-general in Korea, and Yamagata, whose attitude to-

---

[35] See my more detailed coverage of this policy, particularly in the context of domestic politics, in Kitaoka, *Nihon rikugun*, chap. 3, sec. 1.

[36] For more analysis of the Ōkuma cabinet and Dōshikai, see Kitaoka, "Seitō seiji kakuritsu katei ni okeru rikken dōshikai-kenseikai," in *Rikkyō hōgaku* (January 1983; September 1985).

ward this policy was not clear, was mostly ill in bed. The GS thus had the best chance to exercise the lead in shaping China policy.[37]

When it became clear in the summer of 1915 that Yuan was planning to restore the monarchy with himself as emperor, those Japanese who favored greater expansion into China responded in two ways. One position was represented by Machida Keiu, military attaché at Peking, in a letter to Uehara in September. He predicted that Yuan would have to ask for Japan's support at almost any cost in order to suppress domestic political opposition because he could not expect much help from the European powers. However shrewd Yuan might be as a politician, he would have to listen to Japan. Machida proposed that Japan make a bargain with Yuan, offering him support in return for some right or interest.[38]

Quite a different policy was proposed by Uchida Ryōhei, one of the most influential *tairiku rōnin*. According to him, Yuan was most skillful in taking advantage of foreign threats. Whenever Japan came up with any demand or request, Yuan would portray it as a serious crisis for China, appeal to the whole nation to unite around him, and consolidate his position without conceding anything to Japan. Uchida proposed, therefore, that Japan should do nothing officially, but help the anti-Yuan movement secretly until Yuan fell from power.[39]

Uchida's policy was put before the cabinet by former Kokumintō ministers, while Machida's policy, with support and advice from Tanaka, was argued by War Minister Oka in the cabinet meeting on October 14.[40] As a result, a compromise was reached. The cabinet decided to send a note indicating that Japan regarded it as desirable to postpone the monarchy plan in order to maintain peace and order in the Far East, since it might provoke uprisings. The same kind of compromise was again made on November 18, and a similar note of warning was sent on December 15.

This compromise did not disappoint the GS, since taking a tough policy at the outset could be a part of a strategy to make a bargain with Yuan on better terms. In Peking, Banzai Rihachirō, who had a long and close relationship with Yuan, was working hard, with the support of Tanaka through confidential telegrams, to persuade Yuan's government to take a "pro-Japanese" course. According to Banzai himself, his idea was to consolidate peaceful relations between China and Japan to block the advance of the Western powers. His plan included the dispatch of a special mission

---

[37] Kitaoka, *Nihon rikugun*, pp. 281–290.

[38] Machida to Uehara, September 19, *Uehara monjo*, p. 482.

[39] Ōtsu Jun'ichirō, *Dai Nihon kensei shi*, vol. 7 (Tokyo: Hōbun Kan, 1928), pp. 680–684.

[40] On Uchida's persuasion of former Kokumintō ministers, see Kokuryūkai, ed., *Tōa senkaku shishi ki den*, vol. 2 (Tokyo, 1935; reprinted by Hara Shobō in 1966), pp. 591–597. On Tanaka's role, see Tanaka to Terauchi, October 13, 1915, "Terauchi Masatake kankei monjo" (Kokuritsu kokkai toshokan kensei shiryō shitsu).

to Japan from China to show respect for Japan's leadership in Asian matters, the provision of Japanese financial assistance to China, and the granting of mining concessions by China. As the miserable failure of an uprising by Chen Chi-mei in Shanghai on December 5 demonstrated, Yuan's power looked fairly stable in Peking. When China began to show submissiveness to Japan, Banzai thought it time for Japan to move toward recognition of the monarchy. Minister Hioki and chargé d'affaires Obata were of the same opinion about the recognition. China decided to send the special mission to Japan, and Japan accepted this proposal informally. It appeared, at least to the Japanese authorities in Peking, that Japanese recognition of Yuan's monarchy plan, and hence the bargain with him, was near.[41]

Japanese policy changed quickly, however, when T'ang Chi-yao, Ts'ai O, and Li Lieh-chun declared the independence of Yunnan and announced that military action would be taken against Yuan. When the Chinese minister told Foreign Minster Ishii on January 5 that China would establish the monarchy in early February 1916, Ishii reserved his answer. On January 15, Ishii told the Chinese minister to suspend the plan to dispatch a special mission. On January 19, the cabinet decided that Japan would not recognize the monarchy even if China established it, ignoring the situation in the south. Two days later, China announced the postponement of the monarchy plan.[42]

Behind this was a change in the GS policy. Tanaka's change of mind is indicated in his letter to Banzai on December 28. On January 17, Tanaka drafted a telegram to Banzai explaining the suspension of the special mission plan and telling him that Japan could not recognize the monarchy before the uprising in Yunnan had been suppressed. Tanaka urged Minister Oka to get the cabinet to agree on the policy of ousting Yuan as early as February 1.[43] By the end of January, a regular meeting on China policy was organized by the chief of the Foreign Ministry's Political Affairs Bureau, the chief of the War Ministry's Military Affairs Bureau, the chiefs of the GS First and Second bureaus, and their counterparts in the navy.[44] Second Bureau Chief Fukuda, who had been scheduled to move to a higher position in Korea, remained in his office to lead the meeting.[45]

[41] Banzai to Tanaka, December 28, 1915; January 3, 1916; January 14, 1916, "Tanaka Giichi kankei monjo" (Yamaguchi ken kōbunsho kan); Chargé d'Affairs Obata to Foreign Minister Ishii, October 16, 20; Minister Hioko to Ishii, December 15, 1915, in Gaimushō, ed., *Nihon gaikō bunsho, taishō 4 nen, dai 2 kan* (Tokyo: Gaimushō, 1967) [hereafter cited as *NGB*, 1915, vol. 2], pp. 79, 81–83, and 174–175.

[42] Cabinet decision, January 19, 1916; Ishii to Hioki, January 21, 1916, *NGB*, 1916, vol. 2, pp. 13, 16.

[43] Tanaka to Banzai (draft), January 17, 1916, HMM, p. 221; Tanaka to Oka, February 1, March 9, 1916, "Oka Ichinosuke kankei monjo" (Kokkai toshokan kensei shiryō shitsu).

[44] Yasumi Saburō, *Omoi izuru koto domo* (1957), p. 112.

[45] Teranishi Masatake to Fukuda Masatarō, January 13, 1916, HMM, p. 220.

From mid-January, therefore, the GS not only changed its policy but also began to lead the movement toward an even clearer anti-Yuan policy.

What was the reason for the sudden change in the GS position? The GS as a whole had been prorevolutionary and anti-Yuan since the Revolution of 1911, when Utsunomiya Tarō, the Second Bureau chief, had tried to help the south but was reined in by the government.[46] With a few exceptions like Banzai, who had a special relationship with Yuan, younger GS officers, particularly China experts under the influence of Utsunomiya, were overwhelmingly anti-Yuan.[47] As will be seen later, the GS dispatched those China experts to various places in China to watch the situation carefully. Their intelligence and judgment were very much anti-Yuan. Japanese newspapers and magazines also opposed Yuan overwhelmingly.[48] Tanaka, Fukuda, and Machida, who had favored a bargain with Yuan, were generalists without much first-hand experience in China. In the face of mounting opinion against Yuan, they could not but be tempted to take a policy that looked more popular and more advantageous than a bargain. That was probably the reason for their sudden change of heart.

Though previous studies have tended to stress the success of the revolutionary National Protection Army, its progress was rather slow and difficult in the first two months. Kweichow, regarded as an ally of Yunnan from the beginning, did not make its declaration of independence until January 27. No other province joined in before Yuan declared abandonment of the monarchy plan on March 22. For the revolutionaries to succeed, it was necessary at least to get support from Szechwan to reach the Yangtze or from Kwangtung to reach the sea in order to import munitions, but neither of these goals had been achieved by then.[49] The military front was still at the Szechwan-Kweichow line. Though Yunnan was too far away for Yuan to suppress the revolution quickly, the situation was delicate. Therefore, Japan's policy had important implications.

In Hankow, an old China hand, Teranishi Hidetake, had become an advisor to Li Yuan-hung in 1913. He voluntarily left active service in 1914 in order to be able to act more freely. He believed that the war in Europe would disrupt Chinese politics once again and that the Wuhan area would become one of the most important political centers, as it had been in the Revolution of 1911.[50] When the Yunnan uprising began, it was believed that Yuan's ability to suppress it would depend on the attitudes of the warlords along the Yangtze, and that a military expedition to Szechwan

---

[46] See Kitaoka, *Nihon rikugun*, pp. 94–96.

[47] Teranishi to Uehara, February 19, 1916, HMM, p. 237.

[48] Banzai to Tanaka, January 14, 1916, "Tanaka monjo."

[49] Yoshino Sakuzō, *Dai san kakumei go no chūgoku* (1921), in Yoshino, *Yoshino Sakuzō hakushi minshushugi ronshū*, vol. 7 (Tokyo: Shin Kigensha, 1948), pp. 170–178.

[50] Tai Shi Kōrō Sha Denki Hensan Iinkai, ed., *Zoku Tai-Shi kaiko roku*, vol. 2 (Tokyo: Dai Nihon Kyōka Tosho Shuppan, 1941), p. 806.

would be sent through Hankow.[51] As Teranishi had predicted, Hankow acquired great political and military importance in 1916.

As early as January 13, Teranishi wrote to Fukuda that sympathy for Yuan was waning so quickly that Japan should decide to defeat Yuan as soon as possible. On January 30, he also wrote to Saitō Hisashi of the China Desk of the China Section, responding negatively to Saitō's inquiry about whether the warlords along the Yangtze might be persuaded to rise against Yuan. On February 1, he again wrote to Fukuda about the weakness of the Yunnan army: They did not have machine guns; Yuan's expedition to Szechwan was led by a competent man; and loans to Yuan from the Yokohama Specie Bank, Ōkura, and Mitsui were being planned. Unless the government suppressed such loans and helped the revolutionaries, he predicted, Yuan might win and succeed in his enthronement plan. On February 19, he wrote to GS Chief of Staff Uehara, repeated his points, and referred to a rumor that the ambiguous attitude of high-ranking officers was preventing the army from taking a definite anti-Yuan policy, despite unanimous support for such a policy by the younger officers. Teranishi urged a clear-cut anti-Yuan policy.[52]

Captain Ono Kōki was sent to Kwangtung. In his letter to Section Chief Hamaomote, he referred to a rumor that Japan was planning to make a bargain with Yuan and criticized it bitterly. Japan should not pursue minor rights or interests, he argued—it should aim at the overthrow of Yuan itself. Because of the strategic importance of Kwangtung, his greatest concern was how to persuade the military governor, Lung Chi-kuang, to join the Yunnan side. Lung was then regarded as a subordinate of Yuan, but formerly he had been a follower of Ts'en Ch'un-hsuan, an old rival of Yuan. According to Ono, Lung was an opportunist and therefore would not rise for any cause but would side with the stronger. The best policy, he argued, was to persuade Ts'en with the financial assistance of a few million yen, then Lung would follow. Technically, Ono was not authorized to help the revolutionaries at the beginning of February, but he was already so committed to them that he was given a warning by the GS.[53]

Major Yamagata Hatsuo had been dispatched to Yunnan. His letter to Fukuda dated January 19 reveals that he was chosen by Fukuda to proceed to somewhere near Kwangchow and was ordered to advance further to Yunnan, and that Fukuda had told Yamagata before his departure that he did not care who became the emperor of China. In this letter, Yamagata did not conceal his dislike of Yuan, and he expressed an earnest desire to

---

[51] Even Banzai, who believed in Yuan's eventual victory, thought the same way. Banzai to Tanaka, January 14, 1916, "Tanaka monjo."

[52] HMM, pp. 220, 227, 230, and 237.

[53] Ono to Hamaomote, January 18, February 18, 1916, ibid., pp. 222–223, 234–235.

help the revolutionaries succeed. He, too, was thus exceeding the scope of his assignment.[54]

Aoki Norizumi, one of the best-known China experts, had been the commander of the fortress in Lushun since August 1913. He was already a lieutenant general, a rank too high for him to engage in active service as a China expert on the spot. On December 27, however, he was assigned to work for the GS and was ordered to Shanghai, the place of asylum for many formerly influential politicians. If the north and south came to a deadlock—which was very likely—it was predicted that they would strike a compromise through arbitration by the senior politicians in Shanghai.[55] Aoki's mission was to contact them and ensure that such a compromise would be advantageous to Japan. When Yuan announced the abandonment of the monarchy plan on March 22, it was thought a compromise was near. A ceasefire agreement was reached on March 31. The problem was the terms of compromise: restoration of the republican system, or Yuan's retirement as president or from any power. On March 28 or 29, Chief of Staff Uehara sent a telegram drafted by Tanaka, ordering Aoki to persuade anti-Yuan leaders to unite and pursue the overthrow of Yuan.[56]

After the cabinet decision of March 7, various policies were initiated. Ts'en Ch'un-hsuan was invited to Tokyo; loans were negotiated in March to help the Yunnan Army with his support; and Ts'en returned to China in April.[57] In April, Sun Yat-sen was also given assistance and directions, and he returned to Shanghai in early May.[58] Soon after his arrival there, the revolutionaries attempted an unsuccessful uprising.[59] In Shantung, another revolutionary uprising was planned, and it began in May.[60] The GS was behind all these activities. It would be a long story to relate all the details, but the basic idea was simple: The revolutionaries in many places were assisted by loans and munitions; neutral warlords were persuaded to rise against Yuan; and an attempt was made to achieve unity among the anti-Yuan leaders. The GS coordinated these efforts, but "republicanism" or opposition to Yuan's despotism was behind the Chinese involvement.

The situation was different in Manchuria, however, where there was no influential revolutionary movement to be used. Instead, there were two types of opposition to Yuan: the Manchu restorationists and the Mongols. The first plan of the GS in Manchuria was to combine these

[54] Ibid., pp. 223–224.
[55] Yoshino, *Dai san kakumei no chūgoku*, pp. 255–256.
[56] HMM, p. 242.
[57] Drafts of telegrams in March 1916, no. 1, no. 4, ibid., pp. 240–240 [*sic*].
[58] Tanaka to Aoki (draft), n.d., 1916, no. 3, no. 4, ibid., pp. 246–247.
[59] Kokuryūkai, ed., *Tōa senkaku shishi ki den*, vol. 2, pp. 598–611.
[60] Ibid., pp. 612–615; Tanaka to Aoki (draft), n.d., 1916, no. 4, HMM, p. 247.

two. The idea originated with such *tairiku rōnin* as Kawashima Naniwa, but the GS intervened in the name of assistance and assumed leadership. For that purpose, Doi Ichinoshin and Koiso Kuniaki were sent to Manchuria.[61] Doi was an old China hand whose career included study and service in Foochow, espionage in Manchuria before the Russo-Japanese War, and service in Peking.[62] Former Consul Morita Kanzō was sent to Manchuria to explain the government policy to the Japanese authorities there and told them not to suppress uprisings too strictly if these were intended to oppose Yuan.[63]

There was a second plan, however, and that was to persuade Chang Tso-lin to rise against Yuan or at least declare independence. The Foreign Ministry and the consuls in Manchuria preferred a declaration of independence by Chang because it would be much less disruptive. Within the GS, Tanaka came to support this idea by the end of March when it was reported that Tuan Chi-jui, a military governor close to Yuan, was planning to leave for Manchuria, and that Chang, who would take over the governorship there might favor independence. On March 31, Tanaka sent a telegram to Doi telling him to postpone his plan until the GS completed coordination with the southern movements. On April 10, Tanaka ordered Kwantung Army Chief of Staff Nishikawa Torajirō, who was behind Doi, to pursue Chang to declare independence.[64]

Nishikawa responded immediately in letters to Tanaka on April 12 and to Fukuda on April 16. He did not oppose Chang's independence but argued that an uprising by the restorationists should precede it. First, he thought that Japan should not rely solely upon the south: Even if order were restored in China by someone Japan favored, such as Ts'en or Ts'ai, he would be reluctant to make any concessions to Japan, inasmuch as he had become the leader of China. Therefore, Japan had to achieve some kind of fait accompli in Manchuria before China was reintegrated, so that Manchuria would be given a special position in China. For that purpose, Chang was not reliable: He might declare independence, but the declaration might be delayed or nominal because there was not much for him to gain by it. Hence, Nishikawa favored an uprising by the restorationists, whose base was in Lushun under his control.[65]

Foreign Ministry officials shared those concerns about Chang, and so did Tanaka, who to some extent preferred approaching Chang. Because

[61] Kokuryūkai, ed., *Tōa senkaku shishi ki den*, vol. 2, pp. 636–637, 640; Kurihara Ken, "Dai ichi-ji, dai ni-ji manmō dokuritsu undō to Koike seimu kyokuchō no jinin," in Kurihara, ed., *Tai manmō seisaku shi no ichimen* (Tokyo: Hara Shobō, 1966), p. 148.

[62] *Zoku Tai-Shi kaiko roku*, vol. 2, pp. 907–914.

[63] Ishii to Hioki, March 19, 1916, *NGB*, 1916, vol. 2, pp. 854–855.

[64] Tanaka to Nishikawa, March 31, April 10, 1916, ibid., pp. 856, 860.

[65] Nishikawa to Tanaka, April 12, 1916; to Fukuda, April 16, 1916, HMM, pp. 243–245.

Chang had been close to Yuan, Tanaka speculated that Yuan might use Japan's approach to Chang to advertise Japan's ambition to unite the nation again around him. Hence, Japan could not undertake frank negotiations with Chang. For example, when Chang offered some rights and interests informally to get Japan's assistance, Japan could make no clear answer, out of fear that it might be communicated to Yuan. By about May 20, it had become clear that Chang had no sympathy for the movement in the south, and thus, Japan's approach to Chang could not but be lukewarm.[66]

The GS, however, could not get the uprising scheme underway either. There was opposition from the south. Major Idogawa Tatsuzō, an old China hand, wrote to Uehara from Kwangtung on May 2, telling the chief of staff that Japan's assistance to the restorationists would have a bad effect in the south. Moreover, there was fear that, should the uprising take place and be suppressed, Japan's prestige and influence would be badly hurt. The GS had to choose the best timing for it. In Tanaka's view, the best time for an uprising by the Mongols and the restorationists would be at the final military showdown between the north and south.[67] It was doubtful, however, that such a time would come. In short, although the plan for an uprising by the restorationists and Mongols was not abandoned, it was not pursued wholeheartedly. Like the plan for Chang Tsolin, it was in a kind of limbo. That was probably why the uprising in Shangtung in May was started before either Manchurian plan could be carried out.

The anti-Yuan policy ended when Yuan died suddenly on June 6, so we cannot tell exactly how the GS would have integrated all its various plots: revolutionary movements in the south, the restorationists' uprising in Manchuria, the Mongol uprising, and the approach to Chang. It is also difficult to make a full evaluation of this anti-Yuan policy. It is possible, however, to draw some tentative conclusions regarding the role of China specialists.

First of all, although the army's China policy is usually characterized as involving arbitrary decisions and actions by the army, this was not the case. There was close policy coordination among the army, navy, and Foreign Ministry. While the GS had strong leaders like Uehara and Tanaka, the Foreign Ministry and the cabinet lacked them. In this situation, the GS could take the lead within the government, using the intelligence on China gathered by its many experts there.

Second, contrary to the common assumption that decision-making

[66] Tanaka to Nishikawa (draft), n.d., ibid., p. 245; Ishii to Yada, June 5, 1916, *NGB*, 1916, vol. 2, pp. 884–885.

[67] Idogawa to Uehara, May 2, 1916; Tanaka to Morioka, n.d. [mid-May], HMM, pp. 248–249, 253.

took place from the bottom up, the formulation of the anti-Yuan policy was directed by Uehara, Tanaka, and the Second Bureau chief, Fukuda. Tanaka's role was particularly notable. He drafted many important telegrams concerning not only basic policies but also detailed instructions. Using the intelligence sent from Japanese officers in various parts of China, he made judgments and gave directions. In sum, Tanaka apparently was in control of almost everything. Because of, and not in spite of, his direct control over the matter, however, he was often influenced by intelligence from the China experts. Reports from Banzai in Peking, from the officers in the south, and from Nishikawa in Lushun very much influenced him. Thus, the decision making in this case was top-down in appearance, but bottom-up in substance.

Third, the policies or arguments put forth by the China experts were split in many directions. The one thing they all had in common was a tendency to place much importance on the activities the experts were engaged in. Banzai in Peking, Yamagata Hatsuo in Yunnan, and Nishikawa in Lushun, for example, all had succeeded in establishing good relations with Yuan, the Yunnan Army, and the restorationists, respectively, and they competed with each other to get GS support for their plans. Although they were attached to Chinese leaders in order to manipulate them to promote Japanese interests, they in fact sometimes served the interests of these Chinese leaders.

The activities of the China experts as a whole posed another difficulty for the central leadership in the GS. Namely, China policy became more difficult to integrate because of the variety of policies they proposed, and it became more changeable and inconsistent because of competition among them. When one policy appeared to have reached a deadlock, the GS was tempted to take another. This difficulty might have been negligible in the early stages, when the policy goal was to defeat Yuan, but it became much greater later, when a plan for what was to come after Yuan had to be prepared, or where, in a place like Manchuria, contradictions between different plans could harm Japan's interests considerably. Even a leader as competent as Tanaka could not handle this problem effectively.

The anti-Yuan policy was one of the few China policies in which the GS took the lead. China experts were given an opportunity to influence the GS and consequently national China policy, and in fact they had much influence. However, the very fact that all China experts were successful in their respective bailiwicks led the anti-Yuan policy into a deadlock. As a result, all the China experts remained frustrated.

Assistance to Chang Tso-lin

Next I would like to examine the role of China experts in three cases where the army wanted to intervene in Chinese politics to assist Chang

Tso-lin in 1922–1925. As these have been studied much more than the anti-Yuan policy of 1916, my analysis will be much less detailed.[68]

When the conflict between Chang Tso-lin and Wu P'ei-fu became serious, Chang asked Japan for arms aid in January 1922. To promote Japan's interest, the Kwantung Army proposed that Japan assist Chang against Wu, who was regarded as being under Anglo-American influence. Foreign Minister Uchida Yasuya rejected the proposal, and during the First Fengtien-Chihli War in April–June 1922, Japan remained loyal to the principle of nonintervention. In the Second Fengtien-Chihli War in September–October 1924, Foreign Minister Shidehara prevented the Katō Takaaki cabinet from deciding to intervene, even though not only the Kwantung Army but also most members of the cabinet favored it. As is well known, however, intervention was made secretly. With the consent of War Minister Ugaki and GS Chief Uehara, some army officers persuaded Feng Yü-hsiang, who had been on Wu's side, to rise against Wu. Chang won the war because of Feng's coup d'etat, but Shidehara remained uninformed about these secret activities of the army officers. In the Kuo Sung-lin incident in November–December 1925, the Kwantung Army insisted on intervening to defend Chang once again, and it finally did so. On the pretext of preserving order in Manchuria, it stretched the directions of the cabinet by issuing warnings to both Chang and Kuo, which was more beneficial to Chang in substance, and it provided some secret assistance to Chang. Chang would never have won the war without this intervention by the Kwantung Army.

Previous studies have interpreted these three cases as illustrating the growth of the army's influence over Japan's China policy and the widening of the gap between the policies of the Foreign Ministry and the army. My observation is much different.[69]

First, it is necessary to examine more carefully what was at stake. In the First Fengtien-Chihli War, Chang's power in Manchuria was not threatened, and Japan's special rights and interests were secure there. The goal of intervention was to establish a pro-Japanese government in Peking through the victory of Chang. It was not certain, however, that Japan could have gotten a "better" government in Peking even if Chang had replaced Wu successfully. To the extent that it represented the Chinese people, no government in Peking would listen to Japan easily, and neither could any government be utterly anti-Japanese. Wu was not always anti-Japanese, and there was no guarantee that in the future Chang would be a reliable friend of Japan if he came to power. In short, insofar as Japanese

[68] Ikei Masaru, "Dai ichiji Hō-choku sensō to Nihon," "Dai niji Hō-choku sensō to Nihon," in Kurihara, "Dai ichi-ji"; Usui Katsumi, *Nihon to Chūgoku* (Tokyo: Hara Shobō, 1972), pp. 255–269; Banno Junji, "Dai ichiji Shidehara gaikō no hōkai to Nihon rikugun," in Banno, *Kindai Nihon no gaikō to seiji* (Tokyo: Kenbun Shuppan, 1985).

[69] Ikei, "Dai ichiji," p. 224.

influence in Peking was at stake, the policy of intervening to assist Chang was not convincing.

In the Second Fengtien-Chihli War, Wu and Chang opposed each other near Shanhaikuan, and Wu would have invaded Manchuria if he had won there. Moreover, during the Kuo Sung-lin incident, Wu was about to cross the Liao River to reach the South Manchuria Railway zone. Chang's defeat was quite probable in the former case, and almost certain in the latter. It was natural that many Japanese feared that Japan's rights and interests in Manchuria would be hurt. Thus, it was not so much that the influence of the interventionists became stronger in Japan as that the situations for Japan's China policy had so worsened that many more Japanese agreed on intervention. If only influence in Peking had been at stake in 1925, Japan would never have intervened; and if Wu had been about to cross the Liao River in 1922, Japan would have intervened. The issue in 1924–1925 was, in short, not Japan's advance, but its retreat.

Second, the so-called dual diplomacy is not convincing either. In 1922, Akatsuka Masasuke, consul-general at Mukden, thought that Chang should be assisted. In 1924, Akatsuka's successor, Funatsu Shin'ichirō, argued that Japan should remain neutral for the moment but should intervene by force, if necessary, should Chang be defeated. Funatsu's successor, Yoshida Shigeru, was basically of the same opinion in 1925. Rivalry between diplomats and army officers was not at all clear in Manchuria in these three cases.[70]

What about Japanese authorities in Peking, then? Both Minister Obata and Banzai were of the opinion in 1922 that Wu had not always been anti-Japanese, and that Japan should keep in close touch with him, too. Only Military Attaché Higashi agreed with the Kwantung Army. In 1924, Minister Yoshizawa Kenkichi and Attaché Hayashi argued that Japan should manipulate Wu and Chang by giving assistance to both. In 1925, Yoshizawa criticized the warning about the preservation of order in Manchuria issued by the Kwantung Army based on the directions on Shidehara, because it aroused strong anti-Japanese sentiments in Peking. Since the military front was far from Peking, the activities of the military attaché were not clear, but Suzuki Teiichi, who was working under Attaché Honjō, was sympathetic to Kuo. In short, with only one exception, Japanese authorities in Peking 1925 were opposed to overcommitment to Chang. Dual diplomacy was not evident in this case, either. More remarkable was the conflict between the Japanese authorities in Peking and Manchuria.[71]

[70] Akatsuka to Uchida, January 14, 1922, *NGB*, 1922, vol. 2, pp. 268–269; Funatsu to Shidehara, September 4, 1924, *NGB*, 1924, vol. 2, pp. 340–342; Yoshida to Shidehara, November 27, 1925 (nos. 203 and 206), *NGB*, 1925, vol. 2-2, pp. 805–807.

[71] Obata to Uchida, January 14, 1922, *NGB*, 1922, vol. 2, pp. 269–275; Banzai to Uehara,

The difference between them is easy to understand. In Peking, Japanese authorities had to be sensitive about the public opinion of the Chinese and of other powers; they had to maintain good relations with the Peking leaders to carry out their business, no matter who was in power. Wu and Kuo gave assurances that they would respect Japan's rights and interests in Manchuria more than Chang did. On the other hand, Japanese authorities in Manchuria did not have to be sensitive about public opinion; they had already established close relations with Chang, and Chang argued that Wu was under Anglo-American influence and Kuo was under Russian and Nationalist influence. In both Peking and Manchuria, Japanese officers and officials attached more importance to the warlords whom they had been close to than to their rivals. In other words, although they intended to exploit the warlords to promote Japan's interests, in fact they were exploited to serve the warlords' interests.[72]

It appears that in Tokyo Ugaki was in charge of the army's China policy in 1924 and 1925. He proudly wrote in his diary—actually a memoir—that he had defended Manchuria from the invasion of the anti-Japanese warlords Wu and Kuo. However, his policy was not all that consistent or clear-cut. He did not favor a complete defeat or a complete victory for Chang in the early stages of the Second Fengtien-Chihli War, but he subsequently changed his policy. He was sympathetic to Kuo before the Kuo Sung-lin incident, but on this he also changed later. Ugaki was caught between the policies proposed by Peking and by Manchuria. He shifted his support from the former to the latter and was criticized by both as a result.[73] The same could be said of Foreign Minister Shidehara, who remained loyal to the principle of nonintervention and was criticized by the interventionists in Manchuria for doing so. The warnings he sanctioned in 1925 and 1926, though technically neutral, were very beneficial to Chang, as Minister Yoshizawa criticized them from Peking.[74] In that sense, the difference between Shidehara and Ugaki was not as great as that between the Japanese authorities in Peking and Manchuria.

From the discussions above, we can make the same points with regard to the China experts within the army as we did in examining the anti-Yuan policy in 1915–1916. First, contrary to the widely accepted "dual diplomacy" thesis, diplomats and military officers cooperated fairly well

January 10, 1922, ibid., pp. 266–267; Higashi to Ono, January 17, 1922, ibid., p. 276; Yoshizawa to Shidehara, October 4, 1924, *NGB*, 1924, vol. 2, pp. 382–386; Ikei, "Dai niji," p. 220; Yoshizawa to Shidehara, December 19, 1925, *NGB*, 1925, vol. 2-2, pp. 921–922; *Suzuki Teiichi shi danwa sokki*, vol. 2, pp. 269–270; Banno, *Kindai Nihon*, pp. 139–140.

[72] Typical persuasion of Wu to Japanese authorities is seen, for example, in Yoshida to Shidehara, October 12, 1924, *NGB*, 1924, vol. 2, pp. 395–397.

[73] Banno, *Kindo Nihon*, pp. 136–137.

[74] Yoshizawa to Shidehara, December 19, 1925, *NGB*, 1925, vol. 2-2, pp. 921–922.

in Tokyo, Peking, and Manchuria. Second, though Ugaki was a strong leader and appeared to be in command of the army's China policy, the role of China experts was far from negligible. They could exert much influence on the central bureaucracy through their activities in Peking or Manchuria. Third, China experts did not cooperate well with one another. Rather, they competed to get the backing of the army's central bureaucracy. As a result, the army's China policy was changeable and inconsistent. The role of China experts within the army, including the mode of their influence, was more or less similar in 1922–1925 to what it had been in 1915–1916.

It should be noted, however, that the context of the army's China policy was much worse in 1922–1925. Japan had just agreed to the principle of nonintervention at the Washington Conference in 1921–1922. Older imperialist powers such as Germany, Russia, and France had collapsed or had lost influence in the Far East, and Anglo-American dominance had been established all over the world. Nationalism was also awakening among the Chinese people. Backed by the rise of democracy in Japan and all over the world, Foreign Minister Shidehara had relatively tight control of foreign policy. It was quite natural that the army's policy was much less ambitious in 1922–1925 than it had been in 1915–1916. Because many China experts active in 1922–1925 had been involved in the anti-Yuan policy, they must have felt this retreat keenly.[75]

One notable development during the struggle in China in 1922–1925 was the emergence of the young China experts who had worked in the China Section: Kōmoto Daisaku (class of 1903 at the Military Academy), Okamura Yasuji (class of 1904), Isogai Rensuke (same), Sasaki Tōichi (class of 1905), and Suzuki Teiichi (class of 1910). Kōmoto was assistant attaché in Peking in 1921–1922; Okamura served in Shanghai in 1923–1925; Isogai in Kwangtung in 1920–1922 and 1925–1927; Sasaki in the same place in 1922–1924 (and as assistant attaché in Peking in 1926–1927); and Suzuki in Peking in 1923–1925. These men communicated with each other often and shared various ideas. One of these was their focus on the Nationalists' influence in the south. Sasaki and Isogai were probably the best informed about the Nationalist party. Sasaki, in particular, was the first to predict the eventual victory of the Nationalist party, but very few outside this group listened to him.[76]

Consequently, these young China experts opposed the Kwantung Army's policy of assistance to China. In the Kuo Sung-lin incident, Sasaki and Suzuki were sympathetic toward Kuo, who was close to the Nation-

[75] For example, see Sagara, *Akai Yūhi*, pp. 35–40, for Kōmoto's experience in Yunnan, one of the centers of anti-Yuan activity.

[76] Funaki, *Okamura Yasuji*, p. 118. See also note 28.

alist party. They opposed the policy of manipulating warlords, tradition-ally favored by Peking officers like Banzai and Hayashi, because it did not take the Nationalist party into account.[77] Sasaki and Okamura, more-over, were opposed to attaching "advisors" to warlords, the army's tra-ditional approach to them, because they thought the advisors could not make judgments free and independent of the warlords.[78] Their opposition to the army's China policy was, thus, fundamental. Their conclusion was: The Nationalist party would win eventually; Japan would not be able to cope with the Nationalists through policies like the manipulation of the warlords in Peking or the indirect control of Manchuria through Chang; Japan would have to deal with the Nationalists either by striking a bargain with them or by confronting them; neither of these policies would be possible unless Japan had direct control of Manchuria.[79]

This policy did not have much support within the army in 1922–1925. As was pointed out earlier, however, some of these China experts began to work in the Kwantung Army. It was natural for them to try to change its policy. Seen in this context, the murder of Chang in 1928 and the Manchurian incident in 1931 followed this new line. Kōmoto planned and carried out Chang's assassination while corresponding with Isogai in To-kyo and Sasaki in Nanking.[80] And, as is well known, Itagaki, a former assistant attaché in Peking and successor to Kōmoto in the Kwantung Army, played a major role in the Manchurian incident.[81]

In Manchuria, these young China experts were free from the con-straints that had frustrated them in mainland China. It was much easier to win the support of public opinion on Manchurian problems. In Man-churia, the China experts could rely on their own military force, while south of the Great Wall, they had to rely upon the warlords', and they

[77] Suzuki's and Sasaki's dislike for Hayashi and Honjō are seen in *Suzuki Teiichi shi danwa sokki*, vol. 2, pp. 267–268; and Sasaki, *Aru gunjin no jiden*, p. 130.

[78] See note 31 for Sasaki's opposition; and Funaki, *Okamura Yasuji*, pp. 140–141, for Oka-mura's.

[79] Sasaki, *Aru gunjin no jiden*, p. 134. Among the former China Section officers mentioned here, only Suzuki was of the opinion that Chang should be used in Manchuria, and Suzuki harshly criticized Chang's murder in his memoirs. However, he disliked the traditional pol-icies of both the Kwantung Army and the "old China hands" in Peking like Banzai, thinking they all lacked broader views to cover the south. He proposed that Japan solve the Manchu-rian problem by negotiating with the Nationalists while, on the one hand, assisting their efforts to integrate China and, on the other, establishing a firmer Japanese influence in Man-churia. Thus, his plan of exploiting Chang was, it seems to me, of secondary importance in his whole policy. *Suzuki Teiichi shi denwa sokki*, vol. 1, pp. 16, 58, 68, 179, 215–216, 286, and 293.

[80] An interesting letter from Kōmoto to Isogai is cited in Sagara, *Akai Yūhi*, pp. 148–150. See also *Suzuki Teiichi shi denwa sokki*, pp. 192–193.

[81] Ishiwara Kanji, another hero of the Manchurian incident, also had experience in Han-kow in 1920–1921, though he was not a China expert.

could expect additional force from Korea. Their new China policy was easy to carry out in Manchuria when the old army China policies of assisting Chang or manipulating warlords had come to a deadlock. The drastic change in Japan's China policy after 1928 took place in this way. The new generation of army China experts finally succeeded in exerting decisive influence over Japan's China policy and turned it in a new direction, not knowing, unfortunately, that it was the way to disaster.

CONCLUSION

It is said that the China experts within the army first emerged during preparations for the war with Russia, when officers were sent to China to secure friendly relations with that country.[82] In fact, China cooperated with Japan during the Russo-Japanese War. Even a kind of joint espionage was undertaken against Russia.[83] Officers such as Aoki Norizumi established their careers as China experts in such activities. The memory of this Sino-Japanese cooperation in coping with the Western threat remained as an ideal in the army.[84] Many promising officers would not have entered the unrewarding field of China affairs unless motivated by this ideal.

Needless to say, China cooperated with Japan during the Russo-Japanese War because Russia was the greatest threat to China. After Japan replaced Russia as the most threatening nation, China had much reason to resist Japan, and very little reason to cooperate with it. Japanese-Chinese cooperation became even more difficult when warlords began to compete with each other after the fall of Yuan Shih-k'ai in 1916, and when anti-imperialism became the most appealing common cause to unite China, particularly after World War I. These were the difficulties the army's China experts had to confront in dealing with Chinese politics.

Another difficulty was posed by the army bureaucracy itself. Important posts were usually given to officers with excellent records at the War College, expertise in operations, or experience in foreign countries other than China. China experts, therefore, could not occupy posts that would allow them to command the army's China policy from Tokyo, while high-ranking officials in the GS and the War Ministry had to deal with the intelligence reports and activities of these China experts without the benefit of much experience in China. The situation was not too bad in the 1910s,

---

[82] *Tai-Shi kaiko roku*, vol. 2, pp. 271–278.

[83] Tani, *Kimitsu Nichi-Ro senshi*, pp. 280–281.

[84] A former China Section officer recalls that the tradition of the China Section was, briefly, *Nisshi shinzen* (Sino-Japanese friendship or cooperation). See Okada, "Shina ka," p. 66.

when many top leaders had at least some experience in China. When specialization developed within the army, however, and the number of generalist-type officers dwindled, even such important posts as the GS Second Bureau chief, which were of critical importance in shaping the army's China policy, came to be occupied by non-China specialists more frequently.

It is not the case that the China experts were not influential after World War I. They could, in fact, exert much influence over the army's China policy through their activities there. Their policies often differed, however, because their warlord contacts differed. When China experts on the scene competed with each other for Tokyo's approval of differing policies, it became very difficult for the GS and the War Ministry to integrate policy. As a result, the army's China policy became changeable and inconsistent.

The flow of influence between Tokyo and the China experts and warlords in China worked both ways, however. Since Tokyo's policy was changeable, China experts in the field insisted on their policies, expecting Tokyo to change, and Chinese warlords went on fighting, encouraged by these China experts. It might be said, therefore, that on the whole the activities of the China experts naturally tended to check the unification of China, whether they liked it or not. Their efforts to bring about the unification of China were much more likely to fail than their efforts against it. In 1915–1916, they succeeded in overthrowing a government, but establishing a new one was much more difficult. In 1922–1925, it was not that the army did not want to reunite China at all, but rather that it tried to form a coalition among Chang Tso-lin, Tuan Ch'i-jui, and Sun Yatsen, which, considering the diverse backgrounds of these leaders, was a fantasy, not a policy.

In any case, the army's China policy reached a deadlock in the first half of the 1920s. International relations and domestic politics constrained the army. The direction of army China policy was in the hands of officers who were not specialists on China. China experts within the army served actively in China, but this made the conflicts among Chinese warlords even sharper, and all became more anti-imperialistic as a result of these conflicts. The policy deadlock was felt most keenly by the growing number of young China experts in the China Section. They foresaw the Nationalist party's eventual victory and realized Japan's inability to handle the Nationalists by the army's traditional methods. The greatest opposition to the Nationalists was the Communists, but it was impossible for Japan to assist them; and the warlords in the north were too divided to unite against the south. For these reasons, the China experts cut the Gordian knot and changed Japan's China policy fundamentally.

In so doing, they destroyed the army's central authority as well. After

1931, freed from this authority, China experts played more important roles more often in shaping the army's China policy. Their successes in the field, however, were often harmful to the army's China policy and to the China policy of Japan as a whole. Doihara Kenji, a famous China expert, played a key role in the so-called North China Autonomous Movement in 1935, but this movement made the resolution of the Manchukuo problem between Japan and China impossible.[85] In July 1937, the China Section proposed a "Slash China" policy and made an early resolution of the Sino-Japanese War impossible as well. This might have been avoided if the authority of the army's central bureaucracy had remained intact. The First Bureau, led by its chief, Ishiwara Kanji, opposed the "Slash China" policy.

Of course, there were all kinds of China experts, many of them capable and well-intentioned. What was really more important, however, was the system that organized and used these China experts within the army. Unless the system changed, the army's China policy, it seems, was doomed to fail, regardless of the intentions and capabilities of individual China experts.

[85] Doihara Kenji Kankō Kai, ed., *Hiroku Doihara Kenji* (Tokyo: Fuyō Shobō, 1973), p. 24.

CHAPTER 11

China Experts in the Gaimushō, 1895–1937

Barbara J. Brooks

Japan's remarkable and rapid progress from closed country in the 1860s to aggressive and autonomous expansionism in the 1930s is an historic phenomenon not yet adequately researched or understood, especially in terms of the more subtle, informal facets of the story. The explanation for the rise of this small non–Western nation must take into account the key role of its diplomacy and, within that, its Gaimushō (Foreign Ministry). The rapid development of this institution, following its inception in 1869, was keyed both to Japan's initial priority of raising its diplomatic status vis-à-vis the Western powers[1] and to the overall Meiji accomplishment in setting up political institutions.

While the fledgling Gaimushō was struggling to meet the challenge of modern diplomacy in the early years of Meiji, it was also undergoing administrative and bureaucratic reforms that transformed it by 1895 into a professional diplomatic service comparable to any in the Western world.[2] On the eve of the period under consideration, in 1894, the system of diplomatic examinations for entrance into the Gaimushō was established, creating a recruitment procedure for ministry personnel generally acknowledged to be meritocratic.[3]

In the same year, with the British repudiation of unequal treaty advantages like extraterritoriality, the Meiji oligarchs seemed to have finally

---

[1] About the diplomatic motives of the Meiji drive to modernize, see Marius Jansen, "Modernization and Foreign Policy in Meiji Japan," in Robert E. Ward, ed., *Political Development in Modern Japan* (Princeton: Princeton University Press, 1968), pp. 149–188.

[2] An overview of Gaimushō development from 1869 to the 1920s is in Takeuchi Tatsuji, *War and Diplomacy in the Japanese Empire* (New York: Doubleday, Doran, 1935), pp. 67–87. For the most complete treatment, see Gaimushō Hyakunenshi Hensan Iinkai, ed., *Gaimushō no hyakunen* (One hundred years of the Foreign Ministry) (hereafter *GNH*), vols. 1 and 2 (Tokyo: Hara Shobō, 1969).

[3] For the examination system, see Robert M. Spaulding, Jr., *Imperial Japan's Higher Civil Service Examinations* (Princeton: Princeton University Press, 1967), pp. 100–110; *GNH*, vol. 1, pp. 217–252. Hata Ikuhiko, *Kanryō no kenkyū* (Studies on the bureaucracy) (Tokyo: Kōdansha, 1983), p. 75, notes that in the Meiji teens the Foreign Ministry recruited many aristocratic youths returned from foreign study, but this changed with the initiation of the examination system.

achieved the major diplomatic goal of parity in relations with the great powers of the West.[4] Subsequent history, however, would prove this illusory and fuel Japan's gradual but steady progress toward the outbreak of explicit hostility with the Anglo-American powers. During this time, the initial testing ground for the world war to come would be on the Asian continent neighboring Japan.

In this historical context, it is necessary to examine the Gaimushō's personnel system and patterns of careers and interest groups with focus on China. China's importance to the Gaimushō not only arose from the fact that Japan's relations with other powers in the period prior to 1937 primarily centered on issues arising from its China policy, but was also due to the stationing in China of the ministry's largest proportions of personnel, among whom were arguably Japan's most systematically trained and most accurate China experts. Unfortunately, as this chapter will argue, close examination of the institution reveals that much of this expertise was stymied in the lower ranks and lacked power to influence major decisions made by the Japanese leadership above.

Throughout the period, the Gaimushō drew numbers of the personnel posted to China from graduates of various lower-ranking Japanese institutions that provided training in Chinese studies and language. Some of these men did make it up into the ranks of the career track by dint of hard study to pass the highest-level examinations, but virtually none of them could gain promotion to the highest decision-making levels in the ministry. Throughout, the elitist control of positions such as minister, vice-minister, chief of the Bureau of Political Affairs, and others remained with the mainstream elite university graduates. Even among the elite graduates, these positions fell mostly to those who had held high-level posts in Europe and the United States, not to speak of connections they may have had that reached outside the Gaimushō.

This is not to say that some of these mainstream diplomats did not also devote time, sometimes a great deal of it, to China affairs and to posts held in China. In the early period, some of them are notable for their at least initial commitment to Chinese affairs, due to memberships in Asianist societies in student days. Later, particularly after 1920, many younger men made a reputation in China matters that helped their careers, often by gaining the patronage of higher-level officials who benefited from their China-watching knowledge. They, in turn, also relied on the lower-level "China hands" in the field to keep informed.

The first section attempts to delineate the types of personnel in the Ministry who had training in and knowledge of China affairs and describes the structural and sometimes psychological aspects of the Gaimushō personnel system, which inhibited the fullest use of these men's

---

[4] Jansen, "Modernization," p. 178.

expertise. The second part illustrates the limitations of the institution dynamically, by examining specific career cases in relation to events within the period covered by this book.

The Professional Bureaucracy

While many leading Meiji diplomats, including Yanagihara Sakimitsu (1850–1894), who as first Japanese ambassador to China presented diplomatic credentials on November 30, 1874, were broadly active statesmen, by the turn of the century, foreign minister appointees such as Katō Takaaki and Komura Jūtarō, whose entire careers were clearly identified with the Gaimushō, made their appearance. In the prewar period, the post of foreign minister and other upper-level positions in the Gaimushō never escaped being subject to change with the shuffling of cabinets and the flow of political currents. The trend in general throughout the 1920s and 1930s, however, was for the position of foreign minister to be held by an experienced, professional diplomat, and virtually all ambassadors and consuls-general were career men.[5] Thus, the ministry firmly established its bureaucratic and political independence with the appointment of Shidehara Kijūro as foreign minister in 1924, considering that he was the first professional diplomat to achieve this position after both passing the competitive entrance examinations and serving as vice-minister for three years, from 1916 to 1919.[6]

The Japanese Foreign Ministry also emerges as a genuinely precocious example of modern diplomatic bureaucracy when it is contrasted with other contemporary diplomatic corps. A relevant example is the diplomatic service of Great Britain, the nation often viewed as Japan's major contender for power and privilege in China during this period. The Foreign Office also possessed China experts within its renowned China Service. However, assessment of the overall professionalism of the Foreign Office must take into account its lingering upper-class traditions and its caste-riddled structure. For example, it was only after World War I that recruits to the Foreign Office or the Diplomatic Service (distinct services with almost no movement of personnel between them) received any salary during their first two years. Even then, only the wealthiest could afford to enter the diplomatic service, due to the ongoing burden of private expenses they might incur in postings abroad.

The British diplomatic service retained the separation of its different bureaucratic arms down to 1943, when Foreign Secretary Anthony Eden

---

[5] Takeuchi, *War and Diplomacy*, pp. 70–72.

[6] For a view of the ministry as a modernized bureaucracy even prior to recruitment by exam, see Fujimoto Hirō's essay in *Kyoto daigaku jinbun kagaku kenkyūjo shokyōdō hōkoku—Goshi undō no kenkyū 1–3, Nihonteikokushugi to goshi undō* (Japanese imperialism and the May Fourth Movement) (Kyoto: Dōyōsha, 1982), pp. 13–27.

introduced long-overdue and extensive reforms amalgamating consular and diplomatic services.[7] This meant that only after 1943 could a member of the consular staff, previously considered "an inferior type of diplomat,"[8] theoretically entertain the ambition of rising to serve as minister, a figure also said to be, "to the British traders of Shanghai, a remote and unusually inaccessible being."[9] In fact, however, because of the special circumstances of the China field, at least one British minister in Peking, Sir John Newall Jordan, minister from 1913 to 1920, had made the remarkable jump from consular to diplomatic services[10] and thus was perhaps a less remote figure to British residents. By definition, however, the China Service diplomat was stationed in China for life and could not get promotion beyond the consular level. In contrast, the majority of Japan's top diplomats in China had both extensive prior consular posting in China and experience in the home office at Kasumigaseki that distinguished their record, and presumably their authority, from their British counterparts.

Thus, when considering Japanese career diplomats in China, their identity as elitist bureaucrats within the context of both Japanese society and their home ministry cannot be overlooked, in contrast to members of the British China Service, who were likely to have relatively little influence in the Foreign Office at home. The generally accepted and widely assumed characteristics of civil servants in Japan's government ministry today may be said to hold true for prewar career diplomats as well. Thus, as indicated in table 11.1, between 1893 and 1941, 69.8 percent of the successful candidates passing the diplomatic examinations were graduates of Tokyo Imperial University, and of those, 93.8 percent were from the Law Faculty.[11] Without doubt, the majority of career diplomats were imbued with the particular consciousness and loyalties to former schoolmates that give meaning to the concept of *gakubatsu* (school cliques) in the Japanese bureaucracy.[12]

[7] The pre–World War I Foreign Office is described in Zara Steiner, *The Foreign Office and Foreign Policy, 1898–1914* (Cambridge: Cambridge University Press, 1969), pp. 10–21. Later reforms are discussed in Harold Nicholson, *Diplomacy* (Oxford: Oxford University Press, 1939; rev. ed., 1950), pp. 206–214.

[8] Lord Strang, *The Foreign Office* (London: George Allen and Unwin, 1955), p. 124.

[9] Ibid., p. 132.

[10] For a summary of Jordan's career and the diplomatic community in Peking, see Albert Feuerwerker, "The Foreign Presence in China," *The Cambridge History of China*, vol. 12 (Cambridge: Cambridge University Press, 1983), pp. 147–165.

[11] Hata Ikuhiko, "Nihon no gaikōkan, 1868–1982 (Japanese Diplomats, 1868–1982)," in Nihon Kokusai Seiji Gakkai, *1982 nendo shūki kenkyūkai* (Annual convention for 1982), October 23–24, 1982, p. 9.

[12] For Tokyo University's law graduates and their careers, see Hata, *Kanryō no kenkyū*, chap. 7, pp. 172–191.

TABLE 11.1

Educational Breakdown of Successful Candidates of the Higher Diplomatic Examinations, 1894–1941[a]

School rank	School name	Successful candidates
1	Tokyo University (Law Faculty)	471 (442)
2	Tokyo Commercial School (later Hitotsubashi)	93
3	Tokyo Foreign Languages School	18
4	Kyoto University	10
5	Waseda University	10
6	Kyushu University	6
7	Tohoku University	5
8	Keio University	5
9	Tōa Dōbun Shoin	4
	[school history lacking]	6
	[school history unclear]	3
Total		675

Source: Compiled from Hata Ikuhiko, *Senzenki Nihon kanryōsei no seido, soshiki, jinji* (Tokyo: Tokyo Shuppankai, 1981).

[a] In addition, from 1942 to 1948, ninety-nine men were recruited directly to the Gaimushō from those who passed the regular civil administrative test, and twenty-nine men to the Far Eastern Ministry.

If anything, elitism was reinforced by the Gaimushō's elite position among other ministries in the Japanese bureaucracy. As Table 2 indicates, from 1894 to 1948, 62.7 percent of career diplomats attained *shinnin* rank (the highest rank of Japan's civil service, "personally appointed" by the emperor), compared with a mere 22.4 percent in other ministries.[13] Recruits to the Foreign Ministry who were graduates of institutions other than Teidai, who sometimes had labored for years in preparation for the diplomatic examinations, had to adjust to the "aristocracy" they found in the Gaimushō.[14] Just as significantly, the diplomatic service often bred in its members a pride in and elite consciousness of knowledge of Western etiquette and languages, acquired from life in diplomatic posts abroad.

The internal reinforcement of the ministry's elitism and esprit de corps, however, also derived from the hierarchy of the different tracks found in the Gaimushō. From the inception of the upper-level diplomatic exami-

[13] Takeuchi, *War and Diplomacy*, p. 77. For discussion of *shinnin* officials, see Spaulding, *Civil Service Examinations*, p. 328.

[14] Ishii narrates his period of adjustment to the aristocratic ways of diplomats in Ishii Itarō, *Gaikōkan no isshō* (My life as a diplomat) (Tokyo: Taihei Shuppansha, 1974), p. 19. He discusses his audience with the emperor on achieving *shinnin* rank, pp. 397–400.

TABLE 11.2

Comparisons of Personnel Achieving Highest Civil Service Rank: Diplomats versus Other Ministries' Personnel

	Period					
	1	2	3	4	5	Total
Regular Entrants (A)	594	1,458	1,730	2,920	2,756	9,458
No. achieving shinnin (B)	235	469	427	400	585	2,116
(B)/(A) %	39.6	32.2	24.7	13.7	21.2	22.4
Diplomats Entrants (C)	76	101	188	120	297	782
No. achieving shinnin (D)	36	62	112	83	198	491
(D)/(C)%	47.4	61.4	57.6	69.1	66.7	62.7

Source: Compiled from Hata Ikuhito, "Nihon no gaikōkan, 1868–1982," in Nihon Kokusai Seiji Gakkai, *1982 nendo shūki kenkyūkai* (October 23–24, 1982), p. 9.

Notes: Period 1 = 1894–1906; Period 2 = 1907–1917; Period 3 = 1918–1925; Period 4 = 1926–1935; Period 5 = 1936–1948.

Diplomatic entrants who passed both sets of examinations have been eliminated from the figures for (A).

After 1942, under the unified system in which all entrants, both diplomatic and regular, passed the combined examination, those who became diplomats are included under (C).

In the diplomatic service, *shinnin* official rank included ambassadors, ministers, and bureau chiefs.

nations in 1893, lower-level examinations for the so-called noncareer track (at that time divided into students [*ryūgakusei*] and chancellors [*shokisei*]) were established.[15] This latter category of minor diplomats will be discussed further below, for their special importance to the China field. To be sure, the working relations between career and noncareer diplomats called for the clear subordination of the latter, in terms of both levels of politeness and terms of address in speech, and in work assignments as well.[16]

These factors—elite school consciousness, uniform career paths and goals, an atmosphere of special cultural knowledge, and the presence of subordinates who clearly respected institutional rank—which brought

[15] *GNH*, vol. 1, pp. 221–227.

[16] Interview with Oka Muneyoshi, who entered the noncareer track in 1930. For the relationship between a consul-general and a *shokisei*, see also Oda Takebu, "Shanhai Sōryōji Yada Shichitarō" (Yada Shichitarō, Consul-General of Shanghai) in *Rekishi to jimbutsu*, October 1973, pp. 204–211.

elite cohesiveness to career diplomats, must be set against various accounts of factionalism in the Gaimushō.[17] Such groupings, usually centered in the home ministry and around central personalities, materialized
and faded through the 1920s, although after the Manchurian incident, a
sharper division between Axis- and army-oriented diplomats and "liberal" or Anglo-American sympathizers may be said to have existed.
Throughout both decades, however, the Gaimushō's general practice of
breaking up interest groups by means of the transfer of involved personnel abroad (or from one country to another) was effective in blunting the
effects of factionalism in internal ministry politics.[18] Nevertheless, the
formation of interest groups in general within the Japanese Foreign Ministry is an important element to bring to the discussion that follows of the
possibility of China interest groups or a collective opinion found in so-
called China service (*Chaina sabisu*)[19] diplomats.

As outlined above, with the inauguration of diplomatic service exams
in 1894 and the regularization of most administrative and bureaucratic
rules, the Gaimushō as institution became firmly established. Shidehara
entered with the fourth class; his peers and seniors who entered by examination numbered no more than fifteen men.[20] By the Paris Peace Conference of 1919, the number of recruits by examination into the career
track had increased to about two hundred. The early entering classes usually numbered under five men, and only in 1905 did entering class size
first exceed ten. Although the initially small numbers of younger person-

---

[17] In particular, Usui Katsumi has outlined several different groups in "The Role of the
Foreign Ministry," in Dorothy Borg and Shumpei Okamoto, eds., *Pearl Harbor as History*
(New York: Columbia University Press, 1973), pp. 127–148. For another view of the for-
mation of the pro-Axis group after the Manchurian incident, and its link to the earlier re-
form group of the 1920s, see Tobe Ryōichi, "Gaimushō no kakushinha to gunbu" (The
Gaimushō Reform Clique and the army), in Miyake Masaki, ed., *Tairiku senkō to senji taisei*
(Continental expansion and the wartime order) (Tokyo: Daiichi Hōki Press, 1983), pp. 89–
123. Also *GNH*, vol. 2, pp. 180–205.

[18] An example is the case of Arita Hachirō, who as a leader of the "reform group" in the
early 1920s found himself transferred to the least desirable post of all, Siam. Arita, *Bakahachi
to hito wa iu* (Some call me "Stupid Hachi") (Tokyo: Kōwadō, 1959), pp. 29–31; also Kase
Shunichi, *Nihon gaikō no shuyakutachi* (The main actors in Japanese diplomacy) (Tokyo:
Bungei Shunjū, 1974), pp. 80–81. In the early thirties, the tables were turned when Arita,
now vice-minister, himself attempted to transfer the new "young officers," in particular
Shiratori Toshio, to positions abroad. Arita, *Bakahachi*, p. 62; Shigemitsu Mamoru, *Gaikō
kaisō* (Diplomatic memoirs) (Tokyo: Mainichi Shimbunsha, 1953), p. 168. Outspoken diplomats in China service received the same fate: Hayashi Kyūjirō was transferred from Mukden to Brazil following the Manchurian incident, and Ishii Itarō was exiled to Bangkok from
Shanghai in 1936.

[19] The term dates from the interwar period, as in Yoshioka Fumiroku, "Waga chūshi no
kenkyū—chaina sabisu no teishō" (A Study of our Envoys to China—A Proposal for the
China Service), *Gaikō jihō* (Diplomatic review) 74, 732 (June 1, 1935): 163–173.

[20] For career information, see Hata Ikuhiko, *Senzen Nihon kanryōsei*, pp. 427–446.

nel may have inhibited the formation of perceptible interest groups prior to Versailles, events at the conference and the larger numbers of junior diplomats working there combined to create the first group movement. For the purposes of this essay, two aspects of this early interest group should be noted. First, among other reforms, it achieved a system of study abroad for young recruits into the career track; and second, as a movement started and then contained completely within the Foreign Ministry, in many respects it served to strengthen the insularity of the Foreign Ministry, and particularly of the Gaimushō's mainstream "Kasumigaseki" or Anglo-American-oriented diplomats.[21] The strong institutional identity of Japan's top diplomats, in both the twenties and thirties, may have limited their larger concerns to preserving their bureaucratic jurisdiction or reputation rather than to issues of national or international consequence.

Nurturing China Expertise

From the beginning, the Gaimushō had its China experts, and many of the most knowledgeable of them were not career-track professionals. A Nagasaki-born Chinese, Tei Ei-nei (Cheng Yung-ning), played a significant role as interpreter and tactician in negotiations for the first Sino-Japanese treaty, concluded in 1873. Tei later served as acting ambassador in Peking from 1874 to 1875 and again during 1878–1879.[22] While not much is known about the Tei family, more than one of them found employment in the Foreign Ministry. As late as 1904, one of them, Tei Ei-chō (Cheng Yung-ch'ang), retired from the post of consul at Newchwang.[23] Undoubtedly, many men in diplomatic service rendered invaluable service on the scene in China through their language and cultural familiarity, but many remain unknown, probably because they had far fewer opportunities to rise in the hierarchy.

There is apparently a tradition, still alive today, among career diplomats that an assignment to or association with China was a less desirable career path than a similar assignment pattern in Western countries.[24] In-

---

[21] *GNH*, vol. 1, pp. 734–757.

[22] Chow, Jen Hua, *China and Japan: The History of Chinese Diplomatic Missions in Japan, 1877–1911* (Singapore: Chopmen Enterprises, 1975), pp. 33 and 42–43. For appointments abroad (ambassadors, ministers, consuls-general) see Gaimushō Gaikō Shiryōkan, Nihon Gaikōshi Jiten Henshu Iinkai, ed., *Nihon gaikōshi jiten* (Encyclopedia of Japanese Diplomacy) (Tokyo: Ministry of Finance, 1979), pp. 351–386.

[23] Yoshizawa Kenkichi, *Gaikō rokujūnen* (Sixty years of diplomacy) (Tokyo: Jiyū Ajiasha, 1958), p. 27.

[24] Interview with Ogawa Heishirō, a career diplomat who entered in 1938 and was sent to study in Peking, and whose career culminated in his ambassadorship to China, 1973–1977.

deed, a fair level of criticism was aimed at the Gaimushō during the 1910s and early 1920s on this point. In the Diet, for example, in 1913 and 1921, various representatives complained about the frequency of personnel change in China, alleging that diplomats used China posts only as stepping-stones to more attractive appointments in Europe or the United States, and requesting that consular appointments be made longer. As a result of the attention given to this China situation, the Diet and the ministry combined efforts to enhance appointments to China, particularly by raising the salary of the minister appointed to the legation to that of ambassadorial rank.[25]

Despite these allegations, the importance of China in the diplomatic service cannot be overlooked.[26] The number of personnel in China, for example, fluctuated from 269 in 1911 to 193 in 1918, to rise to 403 in 1931 and to 761 in 1937.[27] By 1938, consulates and consulates-general (including branch offices) numbered 40 in China and 42 in Manchuria.[28] Perhaps from as early as the end of the Sino-Japanese War, China had become a field where there was action, and ambitious young career diplomats, while they may have seen service in China as a stepping stone, nevertheless realized the value of a record of experience there.[29]

The seeming contradiction between these two images of China service is easier to understand if the structural or institutional relationship of the Gaimushō to knowledge of China is examined. Although a clear association with posts in Europe and the United States remained of primary importance, with the increasing importance of China as Japan's major diplomatic arena, expertise in Chinese affairs became a close second as a requirement for top-level personnel. In the 1920s and 1930s, therefore, while many foreign ministers had predominantly European and American experience, they always had subordinates close by who could be relied upon for China expertise.

[25] Takeuchi, *War and Diplomacy*, p. 86.

[26] The Gaimushō Shiryōkan (Archives of the Japanese Foreign Ministry) series M 2.2.0, 1-3, on appointments abroad, reveals the importance of the China field; it contains five volumes for Europe, five for the United States, four for Asia and Nanyō, and a total of eight for China and Manchuria.

[27] These figures, which include both China and Manchuria, are taken from *Gaimushō nenkan* (Annual reports of the Foreign Ministry), vol. 1, 1918; and from *GNH*, vol. 2, pp. 1520–1610.

[28] *Nihon gaikō nenpyō narabi ni shuyō bunsho, 1840–1945* (Tokyo: Hara Shobō, 1965), pp. 97–98.

[29] Chow, *China and Japan*, p. 230. According to Ian Nish, concerning the period of the Anglo-Japanese alliance, 1908–1923, "Things changed gradually as the highpoint of service abroad came to be China, the place where ambitious young men were likely to score a success; but this change did not take place until the 1920s." *Alliance in Decline: A Study in Anglo-Japanese Relations, 1908–23* (London: Athlone Press, 1972), p. 3.

Shidehara, for example, formed a relationship with his younger colleague, Saburi Sadao, from the time the latter was on his staff at the embassy in Washington, from 1919 to 1922.[30] Saburi subsequently became Shidehara's closest representative in China affairs, and in particular contributed much toward recognition and correction of discriminatory tariffs imposed on China at the Peking tariff conferences held in 1925 and 1926.[31] Shidehara appointed Saburi as legation minister in 1929, but the latter's sudden death intervened.[32] The appointment was eventually assumed by Shigemitsu Mamoru, who also was an advisor to Shidehara on China affairs.

While younger diplomats like Saburi and Shigemitsu (and Yoshida Shigeru, who became close to Tanaka Giichi) furthered their careers on the top-level path in the Gaimushō by developing some reputation for China experience and knowledge of China affairs, they in turn undoubtedly relied heavily on lower-level figures in the Gaimushō who might more accurately be called "China experts." Such men spoke Chinese and, sometimes to their frustration, spent long periods posted in China. Saburi, for example, probably depended on Horiuchi Tateki's language and economic skills at the Peking tariff talks, and Shigemitsu maintained into postwar years his cordial relationship with men like Ota Ichirō and Shimizu Tōzō.[33]

How did the Foreign Ministry acquire these men in the field? As previously mentioned, from 1894 the Gaimushō had a program of foreign study, which financed students to study the critical languages of the day in the countries in which they were spoken.[34] The first class numbered seventeen students, of whom five were sent for study of Chinese, six for Russian, two for Korean, and four for Spanish. Later, many other languages, such as Thai (1900), German (1909), Mongolian (1920), Persian (1926), and Arabic (1927), were added. Of 325 students sent abroad by 1937, only 67 were sent to China.[35] This relatively modest proportion,

---

[30] Kase, who calls Saburi Shidehara's "pet," clearly describes the latter's reliance on Saburi in China matters, *Nihon gaikō*, pp. 14–16.

[31] For the conference proceedings, see Horiuchi Tateki, *Chugoku no arashi no naka de* (Amidst the China storm) (Tokyo: Kangensha, 1950), pp. 49–65. The conference and Saburi's role as "contact man" for Shidehara are also described by John van Antwerp MacMurray in his Memorandum of November 1, 1935, to the Department of State, Division of Far Eastern Affairs, pp. 12–14, from the papers of John van Antwerp MacMurray, Princeton University Library.

[32] *GNH*, vol. 1, pp. 894–900. Also Shidehara Kijūrō, *Gaikō gojūnen* (Fifty years of diplomacy) (Tokyo: Yomiuri Shimbunsha, 1951), p. 97.

[33] Interview with Mrs. Kobayashi Keijirō (daughter of Shigemitsu Mamoru).

[34] Gaimushō Shiryōkan, file M 2.4.2, 1.

[35] Lists of the *ryūgakusei* and their destinations are given in *Gaimushō nenkan*, 1961, pp. 30–36.

relative to China's importance, most likely reflects the fact that there were many other Chinese-language students, educated by other methods, available for recruitment into the lower ranks of the Gaimushō.

These Gaimushō scholarship students were often recruited into employment in China's Japanese consulate as interpreters (*tsūyakukan*) and in other posts, systematically receiving promotion and salary raises, and might even by special appointment become consuls, but only in their country of language expertise. *Tsūyakukan*, in turn, might be promoted to the status of *shokisei* after two years of service, with the stipulation that they stay in their country of language expertise for over a year.[36]

In addition, the students and lower-level employees of the Gaimushō could all take examinations for the higher-level tracks, and there are several cases of individuals who went rapidly from student to diplomat. Honda Kumatarō, sent to study Chinese in the first class in 1894, succeeded in passing the *shokisei* exam the following year and the career examination in 1898. Honda's career included several years in China as well as London, Switzerland, and Austria, before his early retirement in 1931. After his retirement, he made a reputation as a foreign policy critic and particularly attacked Shidehara's "weak diplomacy." In 1940, he was appointed ambassador to the Nanking government under Wang Ching-wei.[37]

Another case of a diplomat who first entered as a student is that of Uchiyama Iwatarō, who upon completing his course of Spanish-language study at the Tokyo School of Foreign Languages (today's University of Foreign Studies in Sugamo, Tokyo), in 1909 went to study in Madrid as a *ryūgakusei*. His subsequent career offers an interesting contrast to similar Chinese-language students who rose in the ranks in China service. In 1912, he was appointed a *shokisei* in the legation in Madrid, thereby doubling his income. His duties then were mostly reading Spanish newspapers and attending sessions of Spain's parliament to keep abreast of political currents. At the beginning of World War I, when for various reasons the Foreign Ministry's original staff of six in the legation in Madrid was reduced, with the departure of the acting minister due to poor health, Uchiyama became for a time the sole Japanese diplomat on the Iberian Peninsula.[38] Such a situation would have been unimaginable

[36] Ibid., 1918, pp. 112–113.

[37] Honda, however, was a graduate of Tokyo Imperial University. Even so, he writes of his pride in his new status after passing the diplomatic examinations and being sent to China again in *Jimbutsu to mondai* (Personalities and problems) (Tokyo: Senkura Shobō, 1939), p. 75.

[38] Uchiyama, who became governor of Kanagawa prefecture in the postwar period, narrated these facts to his biographers in Kanagawa Shimbun, *Hankotsu nanajūnana nen: Uchi-*

in the well-staffed China territory, although *shokisei* in several instances became acting consuls and heads of branch offices.

Finally, in 1916 Uchiyama returned to Japan and passed the career examinations, only to be disappointed in his subsequent assignments, which he attributed to the fact that he did not graduate from Teidai. He clearly felt that the mainstream elite of the Gaimushō were assigned to China, Europe, and the United States, while he found himself in Eastern Europe, South America, and the Middle East, with only a year in the home ministry in Tokyo. Upon passing the examination, he looked forward to his immediate assignment in China as a chance to improve his career, only to have the order changed to a post in Chile before he left Tokyo.[39]

Uchiyama's positive perception of the "China track" is significant in that it gives an idea of the hierarchy of values involved in judging what stigma attached to career association with China. On the one hand, particularly by the 1920s, a record of assignment that included both China and the West was desirable, and China experience was certainly preferable to experience in other, more obscure, and often underdeveloped countries. On the other hand, however, perhaps due to the growing number of employees in China, exclusive or predominant assignment in China ensured a diplomat of a career that remained in the middle ranks.

In addition to the recruitment of students, *shokisei*, or chancellors, entered the Gaimushō by examination from 1894.[40] By 1937, the numbers of these men reached 481,[41] and it may be assumed that a fair proportion of that number were in China service. Some of these men were graduates of the Foreign Language schools in Tokyo and Osaka, but far and away the major training school for *shokisei* in China was the Tōa Dōbun Shoin, established in Shanghai in 1900.[42]

---

yama Iwatarō no jinsei (Seventy years of stubbornness: The life of Uchiyama Iwataro) (Yokohama: Kanagawa Shimbun Sha, 1967), pp. 27–32.

[39] Ibid., pp. 36–38. He was rescued from Chile when assigned to the Paris Peace Conference, where his skills at arranging accommodations and managing the delegation's activities were appreciated, and where he enjoyed drinking and playing bridge with younger diplomats like Yoshida Shigeru and Ashida Hitoshi.

[40] It is difficult to find much information about the backgrounds and career patterns of *shokisei*, although Gaimushō Shiryōkan, M 2.4.2, 3-1, contains twelve volumes of progress reports on assorted new *shokisei* recruits.

[41] Lists of the names of entering *shokisei* may be found in *Gaimushō nenkan*, 1961, pp. 17–23. The class size is greatest during 1918–1922 and then declines (from around twenty-five to around ten), to rise again suddenly in 1932 with twenty-six recruits, after the Manchurian incident.

[42] Interviews with Ogawa Heishirō and Oka Muneyoshi (a graduate of Tokyo Foreign Language School). See also *Tōa Dōbun shoin daigakushi* (History of Tōa Dōbun Shoin) (Tokyo: Iyukai, 1982), pp. 277–288. Oka himself says he found employment difficult to find upon graduation in Chinese language, and he passed the *shokisei* exam in 1930. About one

As the cases of Honda and Uchiyama illustrate, *shokisei* and others employed in various capacities by the Gaimushō sometimes passed the diplomatic examinations and entered the ranks of career diplomats, but they were the exception. Those in this category who can be clearly identified with China service are listed in table 11.3. These nine men's careers are indicative of the negative association of the "China track," because none of them rose very high in the diplomatic service, and many of them remained in China until the end of their careers. In a sense, they represent the tip of the iceberg; below their ranks were numerous personnel who had experience and training in Chinese affairs.

Two prewar career diplomats went fairly directly from the Dōbun Shoin to the Gaimushō. Ishii Itarō was the first, entering in 1915. He had graduated in 1908 and worked for about four years for the South Manchuria Railway before quitting to return to Tokyo, where he embarked on a long period of self-study at the public library in Ueno to prepare for the diplomatic examinations. He passed them on his second attempt in 1915.[43] Horiuchi Tateki passed the examinations on his fourth try, in 1918, after a period of study of law at Kyoto University.[44]

The Dōbun Shoin produced other China hands who advised the Gaimushō in many different temporary capacities on China affairs. The most outstanding of them seems to have been Shimizu Tōzō, a man greatly admired for his depth of knowledge of Chinese culture and language and for his calligraphic talent.[45] Shimizu graduated from the Dōbun Shoin in 1915 and remained in Shanghai, where he worked in a joint venture company and served briefly in the army before becoming a teacher at his alma mater in 1918. In 1929, he left Shanghai to become a commercial advisor (*shokutaku*)[46] to the ministry's First Section in the Bureau of Commercial Affairs. From 1932, he was back in China as a first secretary–interpreter

---

hundred fifty examinees competed for eleven places. See Oka, *Sōseki sanbō zakki* (Miscellaneous notes in Sōseki Mountain Cottage) (Tokyo: privately printed at Dōgakusha, 1983), p. 26.

[43] Ishii, *Gaikōkan no isshō*, pp. 14–16. Yoshizawa Kenkichi, while a graduate of Teidai, had been a student of English literature rather than law, and he also gives an account of his great efforts to prepare for the exams as an extracurricular project while a university student. Yoshizawa, *Gaikō rokujūnen*, pp. 12–15. Those who passed despite their unorthodox backgrounds must have studied long and intensively.

[44] Horiuchi, *Chūgoku no arashi*, p. 39.

[45] Shimizu is well remembered by Kobayashi, Oka, and Ogawa for his fluency in Chinese culture (interviews). He was particularly learned in Chinese calligraphy and painting and wrote two books on these subjects: *Chūgoku shohō ryakushi* (A short history of Chinese calligraphy) and *Chūgoku shoka ichiran* (Introduction to Chinese calligraphers). Despite his amazing fluency in Chinese, his strong Ibaragi accent in Japanee is remembered. See *Tōa dōbun shoin daigakushi*, pp. 382–384.

[46] Gaimushō Shiryōkan, M 2.1.0, 5, contain five volumes on *shokutaku* or "part-time" employment in foreign posts, and M 2.1.0, 4–5 has another three on this type of employ-

TABLE 11.3
Men Who Rose from the Lower Ranks in China Service

Name	School	Shokisei or other	Higher exam	Highest post
Honda Kumatarō	Teidai	1895	1898	Minister, Berlin
Kishida Eiji	Tokyo Foreign Languages	1908	1916	Consul, Newchwang
Wakasugi Kaname	Dōbun Shoin	1908	1917	Minister, United States
Uchida Gorō	Postal service	1915	1920	Consul-general, Amoy
Shimizu Kyō	Dōbun Shoin	1917	1921	Vice-consul, Shanghai
Yonegaki Kōgyō	Tokyo Foreign Languages	1919	1924	Consul-general, Canton
Iwata Reitetsu	Dōbun Shoin	1922	1929	Head of 2d Sec., 3d Div., Bureau of Information
Yoshioka Takeryō	High school, Chin-chou	1918	1931	Consul, Tsingtao
Toshikawa Jūzō	Osaka Foreign Languages	1932	1937	Ambassador, Israel

Source: Hata, Senzenki Nihon kanryō, pp. 427–443.

(*ittō tsūyakukan*), working for the Gaimushō in various places until the end of the war. After the war, he was a lecturer in the research institute then established within the ministry and also served as legation minister in Taiwan. Shimizu also published books of essays on China during his time in Shanghai from Uchiyama Shoten, now a well-known store for Chinese books in Tokyo's Kanda, which were distributed by the Dōbun Shoin.[47]

Shimizu's astute appreciation of contemporary Chinese affairs and the need for Japanese policy makers to understand the changing scene in China is indicated by two articles he published in the Gaimushō-affiliated periodical *Gaikō jihō* in 1929. The first one, in the January issue, is titled "Changes in the Modern Chinese World of Thought" and outlines twentieth-century Chinese political thought and parties, with special attention to contemporary cliques within the Kuomintang.[48] Perhaps of more interest, in his December article titled "On the Permanence of China's Anti-Japanese Movement," he argued that anti-Japanese boycotts and demonstrations in China had entered a new phase, changing from the emotional, student-led uprisings begun in the May Fourth era to calculated, ΚΜΤ-planned programs that were not going to subside. Japan, he argued, had to wake up to this reality and reevaluate its priorities.[49] Although it is hard to assess the impact of a figure like Shimizu on the Gaimushō and its China information or policy, his existence as a "China expert," primarily advising and interpreting for China service diplomats, cannot be overlooked. Nonetheless, although men like Shimizu might have a reputation as "China watchers," they remained peripheral to the mainstream hierarchy of Gaimushō careers. Their advice and knowledge, when effectively used, were first absorbed and legitimized by an "orthodox" diplomat, such as Shigemitsu Mamoru in the case of Shimizu.

Finally, returning attention to the upper-level career paths in the ministry, it is important to note that some career diplomats were also sent to China expressly to study its language and culture, just after passing the entrance examinations. As mentioned above, this was a result of the reform movement that began at the Versailles Peace Conference. Thus, after 1921, some recruits, usually the highest-ranked examinees, were sent to study in foreign countries, where they were given almost total

---

ment between ministries in Tokyo. Translated as legal (or economic or political or technical) advisor to the Ministry of Foreign Affairs, *Gaimushō nenkan*, 1937, appendix 1.

[47] One is Shimizu Tōzō, *Shin Shina no dammen* (Fragments of the new China) (Shanghai: Uchiyama Shoten, 1929).

[48] Shimizu Tōzō, "Gendai Shina shisōkai no hensen," *Gaikō jihō* 49, 578 (January 1, 1929).

[49] "Shina hai-Nichi no eizokusei ni tsuite," *Gaikō jihō* 52, 601 (December 15, 1929).

freedom for two or three years in one university or perhaps several in the region.[50]

Very few men were sent to China, perhaps reflecting both the undesirable assignment it might have been and the fact that China expertise was sufficiently available elsewhere. The first new recruit, Ota Ichirō, was sent in 1924, but it was not until 1935 that Kojima Tasaku was next sent. The third case was Ogawa Heishirō, sent in 1938 for a period of three years to Fu Jen University in Peking, where his study was cut short by wartime complications. Ogawa's experience was also relatively free of direct association with the Gaimushō, although he took occasional tests to check his language progress at the embassy and later did some work interpreting.[51] Not much is known about Kojima, but both Ota and Ogawa definitely became recognized within the Gaimushō as China hands.

The discussion above has described the whole range of diplomatic employees in the Gaimushō who had expertise and experience in Chinese affairs and has tried to resolve why conflicting images of such people or career patterns may have existed within the ministry. The sections below profile four diplomats most active in the years following 1919, which coincide with the appearance of a critical mass of younger career-track personnel in the Gaimushō, with the period after the clear formation of one interest group among personnel in the first reform movement, and also with the force of "Kasumigaseki," or Shidehara diplomacy, in its strongest period.

These diplomats substantiate the discussion above by representing career types that logically emerge from the circumstances of the Gaimushō's pattern of employment of China expertise. Yoshizawa Kenkichi was a mainstream, high-level, predominantly Western-oriented diplomat who derived prestige and status from various sources, including experience in both China and Europe, Teidai credentials, and powerful marriage connections. Yada Shichitarō came into the Gaimushō with a Teidai background and a strong commitment to Asian affairs over Western. Both he and Ariyoshi Akira, a graduate of Hitotsubashi, were career-track diplomats who found their professional careers defined by and limited to their China experience, which never put them into the limelight or high-level posts within the Gaimushō offices in Tokyo. The career of Ishii Itarō, a Tōa Dōbun Shoin graduate, offers some variation on this pattern, perhaps because of his greater patronage by superiors who relied

---

[50] One account of this type of experience in England may be found in Tajiri Akiyoshi, *Tajiri Akiyoshi kaisōroku* (Memoirs of Tajiri Akiyoshi) (Tokyo: Hara Shobō, 1977), pp. 1–8. Tajiri was free to study at four universities in England for three years after entering in 1921. Afterwards, however, his career was almost completely in China.

[51] Hata, *Senzen kanryō*, pp. 227–243; and Ogawa (interview).

on both his clearly recognized China expertise and his well-known opposition to Japanese army intervention in China's affairs.

THE 1920s: YADA SHICHITARŌ AND YOSHIZAWA KENKICHI

Following World War I, the Treaty of Versailles, and the Washington Conference, for Japan the 1920s were a period of relative international cooperation and increasing economic and trade relations with China, disturbed, however, by Chinese boycotts in 1923 and 1928.[52] Domestically, liberal trends toward reform and political party democracy set the background for the Foreign Ministry's own reform movement. The second half of the twenties witnessed the unification of China through the KMT's Northern Expedition and the rise of Chiang Kai-shek as a national leader, but many Japanese viewed this dramatic change for China as yet more chaos on the continent that threatened Japanese interests and lives. The Seiyūkai and the Tanaka cabinet helped fan Japanese anti-Chiang fervor, culminating in the Tsinan Expedition of 1928 and the creation of an atmosphere in the army that brought about the assassination of Chang Tso-lin in the same year.

As a young man, Yada Shichitarō (1879–1957) became caught up in the Asianism of the mid- to late-Meiji period. He was a student of the Meiji intellectual, writer, and newspaper editor Shiga Shigetaka, one of the major figures in the movement against Westernization that gained momentum in the 1880s and 1890s. Shiga, among other activities, emphasized commerce as a basis for a New Japan, coined the term *kokusui hozon* (preservation of the national essence), and encouraged Japanese settlements in Brazil.[53] Yada's connection with Shiga is further demonstrated by the fact that, after choosing a career in diplomacy, a means to further Japan's relations with non-Western countries, he also married Shiga's daughter.

Yada graduated from the Law Faculty of Tokyo Imperial University in 1906 and passed the diplomatic examinations in 1907. His subsequent career was almost entirely in China, where he served in lower posts in Canton, Hankow, Tientsin, and Mukden, with a few years in London and San Francisco from 1919 to 1923. During 1923–1927, as consul-general in Shanghai, he represented Shidehara diplomacy during the troubled Northern Expedition, when Chiang Kai-shek's troops caused damage to property and some loss of life in the foreign community, particularly dur-

[52] See Banno Junji's chapter in this volume (chapter 9).

[53] For Shiga and his place in the intellectual atmosphere of his time, see Kenneth B. Pyle, *The New Generation in Meiji Japan* (Stanford: Stanford University Press, 1969), pp. 56ff.

ing the Nanking incident of March 24, 1927.[54] Yada, acting on Shideha-ra's instructions and also on his own initiative, helped to maintain a rela-tively calm and militarily restrained Japanese reaction to the events, despite the pressure of public opinion at home and the temptation to en-dorse the gunboat diplomacy seemingly advocated by particularly the American and British communities in China. He met with Chiang Kai-shek following the Nanking incident (during which the Japanese Consu-late had been invaded by unruly troops) and earned the latter's respect for his adroit handling of the situation.[55]

In August 1928, Yada was called to Tokyo to discuss Chinese affairs with Prime Minister Tanaka and other government leaders. His arrival was featured in the major newspapers, which also relayed his message that Japan should develop a new attitude toward China, starting with trade issues like the tariff treaty problems, to help ease the growing anti-Japanese sentiment in China. At the same time, he reassured Japanese readers that Chiang Kai-shek was in good health and was bound to stay on the scene. Despite thoroughgoing criticism from the Seiyūkai, Yada remained in Shanghai as consul-general after this stir of publicity over his call for moderation toward China.[56]

Yada retired from the foreign service in 1934 and worked for a short time as an advisor in Manchukuo, where one of his jobs was lecturing Pu-Yi on current events. Later, in 1937, he was appointed by Konoe Fu-mimaro as the head of the Dōbun Shoin, but he remained only one year— perhaps, as suggested by a biographer, because, as a liberal and moderate, he found the students of the time far too imperialistic and nationalistic.[57]

Yada's career reflects several facets of the China service diplomat. First, his clear record of posts primarily in China likely ensured him a secure but not powerful position in the middle echelon of the ministry. Second, his major role in the turbulence of Sino-Japanese politics in the 1920s was as the mouthpiece of Shidehara, a higher-level diplomat relying greatly on his expertise but still controlling the decisions. Third, even in his postcareer assignment as head of the Dōbun Shoin, this China service diplomat, now engaged in reproducing his own kind, found his value and employment circumscribed to the Chinese scene.

In the 1920s, another diplomat, Yoshizawa Kenkichi, was posted to Peking, first as acting minister and then as minister from 1923. Yoshi-zawa, later chosen by Prime Minister Inukai (also closely related to him

---

[54] See Usui Katsumi, *Nitchū gaikō: hokubatsu no jidai* (Sino-Japanese diplomacy: The Northern Expedition) (Tokyo: Hanawa Shinso, 1971), pp. 18–60.

[55] A personal account of Yada's meeting with Chiang is in Oda Takebu, "Shanhai Sōryōji Yada Shichitarō," *Rekishi to jimbutsu* (October 1973), pp. 207–208.

[56] See, for example, *Asahi shimbun*, August 20, 1928, and August 22, 1928.

[57] Oda, "Yada Shichitarō," p. 211; and *Tōa Dōbun Shoin daigakushi*, pp. 257–258.

by marriage) as foreign minister in 1932, is an example of a mainstream, top-level career diplomat who benefited in his advancement within the ministry from China experience, but who also relied on his wider connections with Japanese elites inside and outside the Gaimushō. Yoshizawa, a graduate of Tokyo Imperial University, entered the diplomatic service in 1899 and first served in China, where he was at Amoy when the Boxer Rebellion broke out. Later, he served in the consulate-general in Shanghai, where he met Yuan Shih-k'ai on official business. During the Russo-Japanese War, he traveled to take up a new assignment at Newchwang, during which he witnessed the aftermath of the fighting. Thus, as a young diplomat, Yoshizawa had wide experience in China itself.

The later Yoshizawa, even as representative in Peking, carried out important negotiations with Western powers, such as the establishment of a Japan-USSR treaty in 1923.[58] He was also active during the tariff meetings in 1925–1926, in which Saburi Sadao and Horiuchi Tateki played minor roles as China advisors, as mentioned above. Like Yada, Yoshizawa worked calmly through the crises caused by the Northern Expedition and was critical of Japan's military designs in China.[59] In 1928, he published an article in *Gaikō jihō* that stressed the return of political stability to China and the importance of Sino-Japanese trade relations.[60]

Both Yada and Yoshizawa represent the beginning of a trend that continued down to 1937, for many diplomats in the China field to argue that the Nanking government offered a real chance for the unification and peaceful governing of the country, an opinion not generally accepted at home. As Chinese nationalism and KMT stability and legitimacy increased in the late 1920s and 1930s, far too few Japanese at home realized it was becoming impossible to advocate increasing Japanese control in China on the basis of domestic chaos there. If there was a position maintained by an interest group of China service diplomats in the late twenties and thirties, it was in opposition to this prevalent attitude in Japan, evident in the press, in army statements, and in political discourse. Diplomats on the scene (but not all of them) recognized the strength of Chinese nationalism and tried to give Chiang Kai-shek better recognition in Japan as acknowledged leader in China. In this effort, they were following the trend not only of Western powers and their representatives in China, but also of mainstream Kasumigaseki or orthodox diplomats.

---

[58] Arita Hachirō, then first secretary at the Peking Legation, describes Yoshizawa and Soviet Minister Lev Karakhan and Yoshizawa, in *Bakahachi*, pp. 32–34.

[59] Yoshizawa, quoted in the *Asahi shimbun*, August 22, 1928, urged moderation in China policy.

[60] Yoshizawa, "Yo no tai-Shi hōshin" (My strategy toward China), *Gaikō jihō* 78, 575 (November 1, 1928).

Yoshizawa, however, later found himself in the difficult position of rationalizing Japan's actions in the Manchurian incident of 1931. As leading representative at the League of Nations on September 18, 1931, his responsibility was to keep the League informed as it debated its course of action. Tokyo, however, chose to keep Yoshizawa in the dark, directing only a set response to questions: that the incident would be contained. This was especially damaging because the Chinese delegation had so many reports contradicting this representation of the state of affairs. Yoshizawa later wrote of his astonishment when details of negotiations in Tokyo that had been withheld from him found publication in Tokyo newspapers.[61] Later, as foreign minister, he followed Inukai in working to maintain the status quo for Japan in world affairs by containing the army's actions in Manchuria.[62] In undertaking these assignments, Yoshizawa, unlike the lower-level China service diplomats, compromised the delivery of a clear message that China could work out its problems autonomously.

Yoshizawa and others, such as Shigemitsu Mamoru and perhaps Arita Hachirō, identified themselves as diplomats experienced in China, but at the same time, they had careers culminating in responsibility for negotiations with greater, Western powers. The next section will concentrate further on men who, like Yada, had their careers primarily focused on China, and who were in a more tangible sense China hands.

THE 1930s: ARIYOSHI AKIRA AND ISHII ITARŌ

The 1930s began with great tension for Japan domestically and internationally over China affairs. With the Manchurian incident of September 1931, the way to full-scale Sino-Japanese War in 1937 may have been decisively paved. Many Japanese leaders, however, perhaps particularly within the Gaimushō, worked steadily to prevent growing hostilities and refused to share the perception that Japan's military role in China should be expanded. Examination of diplomats and events in Shanghai after 1931 helps reveal how a certain climate of optimism regarding the resolution of Sino-Japanese conflict developed among men working in negotiations with the KMT in the period from 1932 to 1936.

In 1915, Ishii Itarō was the first graduate of the Tōa Dōbun Shoin to enter the Gaimushō by examination. While his first post was back in

[61] Yoshizawa, *Gaikō rokujūnen*, p. 123. Kase notes Yoshizawa's poor performance at the league, also due to his inadequate English, in *Nihon gaikō*, p. 14.

[62] This, however, meant early de facto recognition of the army's plans for Manchukuo. See the record of Yoshizawa's conversations with army leaders in Mukden in January 1932, in "Manshū jihen" (Manchurian incident), *Gendaishi shiryō (7)* (Tokyo: Misuzu shobō, 1964), p. 340; and Yoshizawa, *Gaikō rokujūnen*, p. 132.

China, he was also in the Japanese Embassy in Washington during the Washington Conference years and worked in the Bureau of Commercial Affairs in Kasumigaseki from 1925 to 1928, when he was sent to England for a year as a first secretary. These experiences gave Ishii a breadth of experience and contacts within the bureaucracy that made his later career of greater potential impact in actual decision making in Japan itself than any other Dōbun Shoin graduate.

In 1929, he became consul-general in Chihlin, Manchuria, and thus had first-hand experience of the Kwantung Army's actions during the Manchurian incident. Afterward, he was posted as consul-general in Shanghai, where he was active in Japanese dialogues with the Nanking government, working under Minister Ariyoshi Akira.

Ishii's own memoirs are studded with his confrontations with military men. As early as 1923, for example, he records a heated argument at a party with a military attaché who was convinced that Ishii's suggestion that Japan stop awarding honors and titles was an affront to the status of the emperor.[63] In Chihlin, he was angered by the brutal treatment the Kwantung officers used to force the local Chinese authorities to declare their independence—at gunpoint. From this time on, he later wrote, he "resolved to maintain a steadfast attitude of passive resistance toward the army."[64] In 1932, the army scored his uncooperative attitude and requested his recall to Japan.[65] He was ordered back, only to be reassigned to Shanghai soon afterward.

Ishii's conflicts with military men are not isolated examples. In the years prior to the Manchurian incident and also afterwards, there were innumerable instances of such clashes. Cases of consuls being slapped in public by military men, or of military men criticizing, for example, the inadequacy of the annual New Year's ceremony at the consulate honoring the emperor, do not seem out of place in the general atmosphere.[66] The polarized army versus Gaimushō climate of Manchuria at this time certainly confirmed in Ishii a lasting contempt for military solutions.

After the Manchurian incident and the Shanghai violence of 1932, progress in the negotiation of problems between the Chinese and Japanese governments was achieved, notably through the efforts of Minister Ariyoshi Akira, who first assumed his appointment as minister with spe-

---

[63] Ishii Itarō, *Gaikōkan no isshō*, p. 106.

[64] Ibid., p. 173.

[65] Ibid., p. 174.

[66] These two examples from Oka (interview); they happened in Kairyū (Hai-lung), the small branch office where he worked in 1930. See also Morishima Morito, *Inbō, ansatsu, guntō: gaikōkan no kaisō* (Conspiracies, Assassinations, and Sabres: Memoirs of a Diplomat) (Tokyo: Iwanami Shoten, 1984; reprint), p. 55, for a description of army officers brandishing swords and threatening uncooperative Gaimushō personnel.

cial *shinnin* status in July 1932 and later in 1935 the higher status of Japan's first ambassador to China.

Ariyoshi's career places him firmly within the China service category: a graduate of Tokyo Commercial School (later Hitotsubashi), he was a diplomat with fifteen or more years of prior consular experience in China as well as service in the Great Power diplomatic arena during his ministership to Switzerland, where he also held a post in the League of Nations. From his experience as consul-general in Shanghai from 1909 to 1919, he derived an understanding of the 1911 Revolution and contacts with Sun Yat-sen and other revolutionaries that were the basis for later appreciation of Chinese nationalism in the 1930s.[67]

As minister in Shanghai, Ariyoshi set his own style of openness and association with Chinese leaders, receiving criticism from the Japanese community and the army for his initial statement, on his arrival in Shanghai, that Japanese action in Manchuria was "going too far" (*ikisugi*) and for his meeting with Chang Hsueh-liang on an early trip to Peking. His accomplishments in negotiations included his adroit defusing of the impact of Japan's Amau Statement, asserting Japan's role in "maintaining peace" in East Asia, in April 1934, and the resolution of postal and transport problems arising from China's nonrecognition of Manchukuo.

In early 1935, the climate of diplomatic optimism was further raised when Foreign Minister Hirota Kōki, in a speech before the Diet, emphasized greater future understanding between the two countries and promised there would be no outbreak of war during his tenure. Following this, Ariyoshi had discussions with KMT Foreign Minister Wang Ching-wei and Chiang Kai-shek himself that seemed to promise some resolution of further Sino-Japanese problems, including control of anti-Japanese activities.

In May 1935, on a return trip to Japan, Ariyoshi gave a speech to the Japanese Diplomatic Association (Nihon Gaikō Kyokai) that reflected his hopes for the future. He stressed that the appointment of Wang Ching-wei as foreign minister in 1934 had marked a change for the better, and he noted a speech by Wang that indicated this. A meeting of Japanese consuls had indicated that anti-Japanese incidents in their areas of jurisdiction were lessening, while Japanese shipping was flourishing. The problem posed by the creation of Manchukuo was also diminishing as the Chinese recovered from the "operation" that had removed the "cancer" of Manchuria. He concluded with a strong plea for greater Japanese recognition of and economic aid to Chiang Kai-shek and the Nationalist regime, reminding his audience that many Nanking officials had studied in

[67] Ariyoshi's career is best outlined in Matsumoto Shigeharu, *Shanhai jidai* (Shanghai years) (Tokyo: Chūō Kōronsha, 1977), pp. 176–208.

Japan and spoke good Japanese, and that the KMT regime was, after all, increasingly recognized by the Great Powers.[68]

The optimism expressed by Ariyoshi in May did not last long, as through the summer of 1935 Japanese ultranationalism at home was fanned by the assassination of General Nagata and the resulting trial, and Chinese activism did not prove to subside significantly. By early 1936 and especially following the February 26 incident, Japan's China policy seemed to lie outside mainstream Gaimushō influence and in the hands of the army and its sympathizers.

A brief examination of one of the many incidents in Shanghai during this period may aid in understanding the divisions that arose among Japanese personnel, both Foreign Ministry and others, serving in China at the time, and further demonstrate the manner in which some of these like-minded China service diplomats operated together. Also in May 1935, the leftist Chinese periodical *Hsin sheng* published an article titled "Hsien-hua huang-ti (Idle talk of emperors)" under a pseudonym, which went unnoticed by Japanese residents until the article was run, over a month later, in a Tientsin newspaper published from the French settlement.[69]

The content of the article concerned emperors all over the world, describing them as puppets and not actual rulers. The Japanese emperor, it went on sarcastically, was also a puppet, the real rulers being the military and propertied classes. As the emperor was said to have made contributions in biological science, his duties as emperor could be considered as meaning a loss to science.

Once exposed, this article caused a furor among residents in Shanghai, particularly among the military, who regarded it as disrespectful of the emperor. Ishii and Ariyoshi set to work, first making a formal protest to the Shanghai municipal government and then seeking apologies and proper punishment of the offenders. The Chinese side was cooperative, and thus the issue seemed to have reached a settlement.

However, according to Iwai Eiichi, a *shokisei* working in the embassy (also a Dōbun Shoin graduate and a China expert who later set up an

---

[68] Ariyoshi Akira, "Saikin no Ni Shi kankei" (Recent Sino-Japanese Relations), Nihon gaikō kyokai kōen tōsha (Reproductions of speeches of the Japanese Diplomatic Association), May 1935, mss.

[69] Tu Chung-yuan, ed., *Hsin sheng chou-k'an* (New life weekly), May 4, 1935, pp. 312–313. This incident is dealt with in a discussion of the Shanghai press in Parks Coble, Jr., "Chiang Kai-shek and the Anti-Japanese Movement in China: Zou Tao-fen and the National Salvation Association, 1931–1937," *Journal of Asian Studies* 44, 2 (February 1985): 299–300. The most complete account is in Nihon Kokusai Seiji Gakkai, Taiheiyōsensō Genin Kenkyūbu, *Taiheiyō sensō e no michi* (The Road to the Pacific War), vol. 3 (Tokyo: Asahi Shimbunsha, 1962), pp. 94–97. See also Ishii, *Gaikōkan no isshō*, pp. 193–197; and Matsumoto, *Shanhai jidai*, pp. 252–257.

effective information-gathering network in Shanghai), at this point he was informed by Chinese journalist friends that the real responsibility for the censorship of such articles lay not with the municipal government but with the KMT itself. Iwai, realizing that Ariyoshi and Ishii might prefer not to act on this information and further inflame the incident, went with this information to Lieutenant Colonel Kagesa Sadaaki instead.[70]

As Iwai anticipated, the problems of settling this incident were greatly exacerbated when this new development was brought out, particularly as it was found fairly impossible to put the magazine's editor on trial or discover the real author. Some of the military in Shanghai even went so far as to demand the dissolution of the KMT itself over this incident.[71] Ariyoshi next negotiated a settlement of the affair with Foreign Minister T'ang Yu-jen, but he received great censure from the military and Japanese residents in Shanghai for his weakness in the matter. Both Ariyoshi and Ishii received great numbers of poison-pen letters throughout the incident.[72]

The groupings of men in this incident are suggestive of the later divisions in the Foreign Ministry that developed over the issue of whether to maintain (or revive, after Konoe's *aite ni sezu* statement) relations with Chiang Kai-shek as a negotiating partner in China, or to seek a new leader—that is, Wang Ching-wei. Later, both Kagesa and Iwai worked to bring about the Wang government in Nanking. Ishii at this time achieved a surprising promotion to chief of the Bureau of Asiatic Affairs, which may have been part of a peace effort undertaken initially with the appointment of Satō Naotake as foreign minister. In this configuration, the reliance of a high-level diplomat, Satō, on the lower-ranking China expert, Ishii, again emerges.[73] Ishii, surviving Satō's tenure as foreign minister into that of Ugaki Kazushige, worked heroically as bureau chief to convince the Japanese government to continue to negotiate with Chiang Kai-shek, even after Konoe's *aite ni sezu* statement denying this possibility.[74]

---

[70] Iwai Eiichi, *Kaisō no Shanhai* (Memoirs of Shanghai) (Tokyo: Izumi Insatsu, "Kaisō no Shanhai" Shuppan Iinkai, 1983), pp. 51–56.

[71] Matsumoto reports military men making this demand were just seeking full-scale war with China, p. 255.

[72] Ishii, *Gaikōkan no isshō*, p. 195.

[73] A very positive evaluation of Satō's program as foreign minister is given in Usui Katsumi, "Satō gaikō to nitchū kankei" (Satō's Diplomacy and Sino-Japanese Relations), in Aruga Tadashi and Iriye Akira, eds., *Senzenki no Nihon gaikō* (Tokyo: University of Tokyo Press, 1984). Ishii himself expressed surprise at being returned from the *ubasuteyama* (graveyard) of a post in Siam to this position, *Gaikōkan no isshō*, p. 233.

[74] About Ishii's policy recommendations in 1938 regarding the KMT, see John Hunter Boyle, "Peace Advocacy During the Sino-Japanese Incident," in Hilary Conroy and Alvin Coox, eds., *China and Japan: Search for Balance Since World War I* (Santa Barbara: ABC-Clio, 1978), pp. 255–263.

Although it is difficult to say whether a consensus existed among a majority of China service diplomats in the 1930s, in this and other incidents in Shanghai there emerged a grouping of men such as Ariyoshi, Ishii, and Horiuchi Tateki who generally agreed in their views of how Japan should proceed in China. They were generally anti-expansionist, but, more importantly, they recognized that Chinese nationalism had finally arrived and that Japan was mistaken in choosing a course of military force in China. While they tried in various ways to influence the future direction of Japan's policy in the direction of peace, they were more often caught up in the everyday tasks of managing increasingly difficult jurisdictions in their jobs as consuls or secretaries. By and large, their rank as bureaucrats never rose high enough to get them into positions where they could seriously think of bringing about change.

Conclusion

Most China experts in the Foreign Ministry spent their careers in the lower realms of the institution. The reasons for this stemmed both from problems concerning the educational credentials of China expertise recruits into the ministry, and especially into its career track, and from perceptions of the prestige of posts held in China. Diplomatic experience in China did have a place in top-level career patterns, but too much of it relegated a career to mid- or lower-level ministry levels.

China experts made their way up through the ministry hierarchy mainly by means of patronage relationships with higher-level diplomats. To fully answer the question of why the fairly consistent advice from the lower China service officials who advocated recognizing Chiang Kai-shek's government could not restrain Japanese aggression in China, one must understand the dynamics of decision making in the upper echelons of the Gaimushō. I have not tried to explain this complex issue except to suggest that the insularity and eliteness of the Gaimushō itself were major factors. Further areas to explore include a study of interinstitutional conflicts, both in Tokyo and in the China field, which perhaps served to fix the diplomatic focus on bureaucratic jurisdiction, rather than on the larger foreign policy objectives.

The Foreign Ministry, along with other institutions in Japan, had been created to make Japan equivalent to the major Western powers. Perhaps for this reason, Japan's most Anglo-American-oriented statesmen dominated amongst the ministry's top level personnel. Ironically, however, with the passing of time, the Gaimushō's major arena of activity came to be China, not the West. The institution's response to this new develop-

CHAPTER 12

The Kwantung Army Dimension

Alvin D. Coox

Any discussion of the Japanese military garrison in Manchuria after 1905 must address the question of nomenclature and function. Until the 1930s, the force that came to be known as the Kwantung Army possessed a rather misleading geographical identification deriving from its historical antecedents and, more importantly, constituted an army in name alone. In Western usage, an army usually consists of at least two corps, each built around two divisions or more, in addition to organic and supporting troops and trains. Not until after the Manchurian incident of 1931–1932 did the Kwantung Army ever attain such strength.[1]

Although confusing to those who were not in the Japanese military (and even to those within that army), these matters of terminology are not irrelevant accidents of history. They reflect fundamental Japanese imperial policy toward the Asian continent in general and toward the former Northeast provinces of the Chinese Empire in particular. In the case of the Kwantung Army, its genesis dated back to the era of the Russo-Japanese War of 1904–1905, and its function was inextricably entwined with the defense of rail lines and zones of influence, exercised exclusively within the boundaries of South Manchuria.

ORIGINS AND EARLY HISTORY, 1905–1914

During the Russo-Japanese War, the Japanese army had advanced as far north as Ch'ang-ch'un and had conquered all of South Manchuria—the area that had been occupied by Russian troops in force at the time of the Boxer Uprising of 1900 and that had not been relinquished by them afterward. The Japanese Field Forces in Manchuria had served under the commander in chief of the Manchuria Army (Manshūgun Sōshireikan).

By the terms of the Portsmouth Treaty in September 1905, the victorious Japanese not only ousted the Russians from South Manchuria but also took from them the balance of the twenty-five-year lease of the Liao-

[1] See Alvin D. Coox, *Nomonhan: Japan Against Russia, 1939*, vol. 2 (Stanford: Stanford University Press, 1985), p. 1075.

tung region, which the Chinese had first yielded in 1898. Renamed the Kwantung Leased Territory, this Japanese-occupied strategic zone at the southern tip of the peninsula contained the great port of Dairen (Dalny or Talien) and the major fortress and ice-free naval base at Port Arthur (Lushun or Ryojun). In addition, the Japanese acquired the right to the Ch'ang-ch'un–Port Arthur main segment of the rail network that the Russians had constructed to the south of the Chinese Eastern Railway, their shortcut across Manchuria to Manchouli in the west and Vladivostok in the east. The Chinese government gave its nominal consent to these arrangements by the Treaty of Peking in December 1905.[2]

The new Japanese sphere of influence in South Manchuria needed to be consolidated and protected, especially since according to the peace terms the combat forces of both the Japanese and the Russians were to be withdrawn from Manchuria within eighteen months, by the spring of 1907. Japanese strategy demanded a sizable military presence in South Manchuria, even in peacetime—the origin of the force known later as the Kwantung Army.

In October 1905, shortly after the Portsmouth settlement, a Kwantung Military Government (Kantō Sōtokufu), headed by General Ōshima Yoshimasa, was established at Liaoyang under the Manchuria Army. Since there was soon no requirement for a combat staff organization, the Manchuria Army headquarters was returned to Japan. Thereupon, in November 1905, national responsibility for the security of South Manchuria was assumed by Imperial General Headquarters (IGHQ) in Tokyo, to which General Ōshima and his command were subordinated. The mission of the Kwantung Military Government was to administer the leasehold, handle army affairs, and defend the region. The number of regular soldiers that Japan might station in the Kwantung Territory was not stipulated by treaty, but the initial strength of the Kwantung Garrison amounted to two regular army divisions and fortress units stationed at Port Arthur and Dairen.[3]

To defend the tracks and concessions in the South Manchuria Railway zone, the Japanese side had insisted at Portsmouth on the right and indeed the duty to station railway guard soldiers along the right-of-way. Subject

[2] Tsunoda Jun, ed., *Manshū mondai to kokubō hōshin: Meiji kōki ni okeru kokubō kankyō no hendō* (Tokyo: Hara Shobō, 1967), pp. 267–271; Bōei kenkyūsho senshi shitsu, *Senshi sōsho* (hereafter BKSS, SS), vol. 27: *Kantōgun (1)* (Tokyo: Asagumo Shimbunsha, 1969), p. 13; Kurihara Ken, *Tai-Man-Mō seikakushi no ichimen* (Tokyo: Hara Shobō, 1966), pp. 9–10; Shimada Toshihiko, *Kantōgun* (Tokyo: Chūō Kōronsha, 1965), pp. 5–11; *Gendai shi shiryō* (hereafter GSS), vol. 11: *Manshū jihen (2)* (Tokyo: Misuzu Shobō, 1965), p. 276.

[3] Ōyama Azusa, *Nichi-Ro sensō no gunsei shiroku* (Tokyo: Fuyō Shobō, 1973), pp. 201–212; BKSS, SS, vol. 27, p. 13; Tsunoda, ed., *Manshū mondai*, pp. 282–283, 298–332; Kurihara, *Tai-Mao-Mō*, pp. 38–39.

to Chinese ratification, the Russian and Japanese negotiators agreed that no more than fifteen such guards might be detailed per kilometer of track. In practice, the number of men was to be held to a minimum, "having in view the actual requirements." During the subsequent discussions at Peking, the Chinese authorities particularly resisted the idea of allowing foreign guards and other evidence of foreign authority on Chinese territory permanently. If, for example, the Japanese demanded the right to deploy the maximum number of railway guards, the working distance between Ch'ang-ch'un, Dairen, and Port Arthur (755 km) would alone justify eleven thousand men.

From the arguments of Foreign Minister Komura Jūtarō, chief delegate at Portsmouth and Peking, it is apparent that the Japanese government viewed the defense of Manchuria from two angles. First, Komura predicted another war between Japan and Russia. Second, he insisted that a Japanese guard force was imperative until such time as "tranquillity" was restored to Manchuria and China itself became fully capable of protecting the lives and property of foreigners. By an additional accord appended to the treaty of December 1905, the Chinese government reluctantly agreed to the stationing of the Japanese railway guards in the hope that this provision might prove to be temporary.[4]

In 1906, over the objections of the Japanese army, the cabinet in Tokyo agreed to replace the Kwantung Military Government (which had been relocated to Port Arthur) with a peacetime Kwantung Government-General (Kantō Totokufu). The most significant feature of the reorganization was the transfer of the Japanese administration in Manchuria from the control of IGHQ to the Foreign Ministry, insofar as civil affairs were concerned. Nevertheless, the government-general was by no means freed from a strong military coloration. By imperial ordinance, the Kwantung Governor-General—a lieutenant general or full general on active duty—was to "take charge of the defense of the territory within the limits of his jurisdiction" and, whenever he found that an emergency existed, was authorized to employ military force. Apart from the regular units in the leasehold, that force included the railway guards, since the Government-General was also responsible for the protection and operation of the South Manchuria Railway. General Ōshima, the former military governor, was retained as governor-general from September 1906 until April 1912.

To handle military matters in Manchuria, an Army Bureau was set up under the governor-general. His military superiors in Tokyo were the

---

[4] Nakamura Kikuo, Manshū jihen (Tokyo: Nihon Kyōbunsha, 1965), pp. 64–65; BKSS, SS, vol. 27, passim; GSS, vol. 11, pp. 159, 289–290; Tsunoda, ed., Manshū mondai, pp. 284–296.

chief of the army's General Staff (GS) for the categories of operations and mobilization; the war minister for personnel; and the inspector-general for training and education. By the time the Japanese army of occupation was removed and the South Manchuria Railway Company became operational in 1907, the governor-general could call upon the following military forces: "six new independent garrison battalions, made up of regular soldiers serving as railway guards and deployed at important train stations such as Kaiyuan and Mukden [Shenyang or Fengtien], with central headquarters in Kungchuling; a regular army garrison of one division stationed in the Kwantung Leased Territory; a heavy siege artillery battalion assigned to the fortress at Port Arthur."[5]

THE WORLD WAR I PERIOD AND ITS AFTERMATH

The outbreak of the First World War in the summer of 1914 gave Japan a great opportunity to strengthen its control over Manchuria and to acquire other parts of China, such as Shantung, the site of a German leasehold. The overthrow of the Manchu dynasty in 1912 had left China racked by civil unrest and the rivalry of cliques, warlords, and opportunists. No support for China could be expected now from the European powers, and the Japanese cemented their existing diplomatic links with the British and the French by entering the war on the Allied side in late August.

After crushing German resistance in Shantung by early November, Japan turned immediately against China and sought to impose the harsh and self-serving Twenty-One Demands upon the weak regime in Peking. Under tremendous Japanese pressure, which extended to the threat of force in the event of noncompliance, President Yuan Shih-k'ai was finally compelled in May 1915 to accept most of Japan's terms. Insofar as Manchuria was concerned, the most important feature was the extension of the Kwantung lease and of the South Manchuria Railway and Antung–Mukden railroad accords to a term of ninety-nine years; that is, from the approaching expiration date of 1923 to a far-off 1997.[6]

With their grip on Manchuria tightened as a result of the Chinese concessions of 1915, Kwantung Governor-General Fukushima Yasumasa and the South Manchuria Railway Company pressed the Japanese government to untangle the snarled lines of authority and competitive relationships that had evolved between the civilians and the military, and especially to strengthen the hand of the governor-general vis-à-vis the

---

[5] BKSS, SS, vol. 27, pp. 13–15; Tsunoda, ed., *Manshū mondai*, pp. 333–341; *Taiheiyō sensō e no michi* (hereafter *TSM*), vol. 1 (Tokyo: Asahi Shimbunsha, 1962–1963), p. 190; Kurihara, *Tai-Man-Mō*, pp. 18–43, 240–284; Ōyama, *Nichi-Ro*, pp. 213–230.

[6] BKSS, SS, *Daihon'ei rikugunbu (1–10)* (1967–1975), vol. 8, pp. 202–207; Kurihara, *Tai-Man-Mō*, pp. 115–125, 146, 341–359.

consuls dispatched to Manchuria by the Foreign Ministry. General Terauchi Masataka, who as war minister had headed the organizing committee of the South Manchuria Railway, became prime minister in October 1916 and soon endorsed the recommendations of those who agreed
with his own harsh policy of continental expansion.

As a result, in 1917 the Kwantung governor-general was made responsible to the prime minister instead of the foreign minister and was, in
addition, assigned to oversee the managing director of the SMR. Under
this arrangement, Lieutenant General Nakamura Yūjirō (the railway
president since 1914) was appointed governor-general in July 1917. From
Tokyo, a Department of Colonial Affairs was to coordinate matters
(other than diplomacy) affecting the leasehold and the South Manchuria
Railway Company, to which the management of the Chōsen [Korea]
Railway Company was added. Within the Government-General, a Military Police Command was created to handle not only the army police
forces in the leasehold but also the consular police.

The authority of the Kwantung governor-general thus reached its peak
during World War I, a period when the Japanese military and their associates were in the ascendancy. It is no coincidence that Gotō Shimpei, the
first president of the South Manchuria Railway, served in General Terauchi's cabinet as home minister from 1916 until April 1918 and then as
foreign minister until the resignation of the government in September of
that year.[7]

Terauchi's replacement, Hara Takashi, and the Gaimushō were determined to reform Japan's entire colonial administration in favor of civilian
leadership as a rule. In South Manchuria, the centralized structure of the
Kwantung Government-General was terminated in April 1919, and the
military and political spheres were separated for the first time. Replacing
the military governor-general of the Kwantung Leased Territory was a
civilian governor (chōkan) appointed by the throne. Guidance on external
affairs would be provided by the Foreign Ministry, and advice on transportation matters by the president of the South Manchuria Railway Company. The initial governor under the new system was Hayashi Gonsuke,
a senior diplomat with extensive experience concerning China.[8]

The old Army Bureau at Port Arthur was removed from the governor's direction and reorganized as Kwantung Army Headquarters. The
first commander of the Kwantung Army was Lieutenant General Tachibana Koichirō, age fifty-eight, whose record included membership in the
Portsmouth delegation in 1905. Tachibana was responsible not to the civil

[7] Kurihara, *Tai-Man-Mō*, pp. 43–57, 239–274.
[8] Ōyama, *Nichi-Ro*, pp. 231–255; *Manshū mondai*, pp. 333–341; Kurihara, *Tai-Man-Mō*,
p. 58.

governor but directly to the war minister and the GS chief in Tokyo. Though the civil governor might ask the Kwantung Army commanding general for military assistance to preserve peace and order, he could not assume control of either the regular forces or the railway guards.

It is important to note that since the Kwantung Army commander (always a lieutenant general or full general) was appointed by the high command in Tokyo and was responsible only to it, he could operate in the name of the supreme command prerogative (*tōsuiken dokuritsu*) and take independent action if desired, without interference in practice. Even before the Manchurian incident, an American expert on South Manchuria discerned that the Japanese railway guards had become "an instrument of a military clique in Tokyo, acting through" the commander of the Kwantung Army.[9]

At the time of its creation in 1919, the Kwantung Army was more an administrative than a tactical grouping. Although it retained the previous mission of defending the Kwantung leasehold and the rail lines in South Manchuria, it still disposed of only one ground division (rotated from the homeland every two years) and the six independent garrison battalions of railway guards. As for the latter, War Minister Yamanashi Hanzō considered abolishing them unilaterally during the era of international disarmament plans in 1922. Their strength remained at six battalions, however, until War Minister Ugaki Kazushige (Kazunari or Issei) "streamlined" the Japanese army in 1925 in a budget-cutting move and lopped off two of the guard battalions in the process. With the resurgence of Russian strength in Siberia and the return of Japanese military men as prime ministers (e.g., General Tanaka Giichi, 1927–1929), the two railway guard battalions were restored in 1929.[10]

THE BEGINNINGS OF EXTRACURRICULAR ZEALOTRY

Meddling in Chinese affairs by the Japanese authorities in South Manchuria was apparent even in the era of the *totokufu* or Kwantung Government-General, especially after the outbreak of revolutionary disturbances in China late in 1911. Only about a week before the child emperor Pu-Yi abdicated in February 1912, a bridge was blown up north of Shanhaikuan, on the Manchurian side of the Great Wall, causing a train from Peking to overturn, with heavy casualties. Because Japanese troops were on guard along the rail lines, it is probable that the Japanese army was secretly involved in a plot to sever Manchuria and Mongolia from China during the

[9] C. Walter Young, *Japan's Jurisdiction and International Legal Position in Manchuria*, vol. 3: *Japanese Jurisdiction in the South Manchuria Railway Areas* (Baltimore: Johns Hopkins Press, 1931), p. 291; BKSS, *SS*, vol. 27, pp. 13, 15; Kurihara, *Tai-Man-Mō*, p. 59.

[10] BKSS, *SS*, vol. 27, p. 14.

chaotic winter of 1911–1912. Japanese army activists, including Kwantung Governor-General Ōshima, wanted two divisions to be rushed to Manchuria, but Premier Saionji Kinmochi and his foreign minister, Uchida Yasuya, were able to prevent escalation of the crisis.[11]

There were sporadic collisions between Japanese troops and local Chinese forces after the overthrow of the Manchu dynasty, amid the interplay of regional separatism, rebellion, and banditry involving eastern Inner Mongolia, North China, Jehol province, and North Manchuria. After one shooting affray known as the Chengchiatun [Tenkaton] incident, which involved Japanese troops and Chinese police in August 1914, Kwantung Governor-General Fukushima Yasumasa made a number of recommendations to the Foreign Ministry calling for stern action against China. Although they were not accepted immediately, some of Fukushima's ideas can be discerned in the Twenty-One Demands.

At the same time that those demands were forced on China in May 1915, the new Kwantung governor-general, Nakamura Satoru, advised the War Ministry that *totokufu* administration and the garrison division headquarters should be moved north from remote Port Arthur to Mukden, a far better strategic location vis-à-vis the Russians in the context of South Manchuria and eastern Mongolia, both of which were touted as the lifeline of Japan. Lieutenant General Nakamura had various other practical suggestions, including realignment of the fuzzy boundaries between South and North Manchuria to include in the Japanese sphere all of Fengtien and Kirin provinces, and deployment of the troops at Kungchuling northward to Ch'ang-ch'un. Having so recently extorted major concessions from China, however, the Japanese Foreign Ministry was not particularly sympathetic to Nakamura's proposals.[12]

A new and more ambitious Japanese plan to separate Manchuria and Mongolia from China by force materialized in early 1916 during the last stage of Yuan Shih-k'ai's stormy career. The driving force behind the plan was the deputy chief of the army General Staff, Tanaka Giichi, abetted by Kwantung Governor-General Nakamura. In this instance, however, the commander of the 17th Division garrisoned in Manchuria, Lieutenant General Hongō Fusatarō, and the commander of the Independent Garrison Unit battalions, Major General Fujii, did not concur.

Two Japanese consuls were particularly critical of the Tanaka-Nakamura scheme: Yada Shichitarō at Mukden and Yoshida Shigeru at Antung. A more practical approach, the consuls urged Foreign Minister Ishii Kikujirō, would be to support the pretensions of a certain Chinese division commander, Chang Tso-lin, a former bandit chieftain who was

[11] Shimada, *Kantōgun*, pp. 15–16.
[12] Ibid., pp. 17–30.

known to crave the post of governor of Mukden. Ishii agreed with Yada and Yoshida, as did General Tanaka, surprisingly. Tanaka, in fact, ordered the Kwantung governor-general to confer with Chang and encourage him to rise. However, the death of Yuan Shih-k'ai in June 1916 caused the Japanese to reverse their China policy, accept the new national president, Li Yuan-hung, and abandon the separatist movement for the time being.[13]

The decade following the death of Yuan Shih-k'ai was a period of internecine warlordism and factionalism in China generally regarded as the bleakest years in the history of the tormented republic. Chang Tso-lin's Fengtien Army helped the Chihli Clique to overcome the Anhwei Clique, but by 1922 the forces of Fengtien and Chihli were at each other's throats. The Kwantung Army's encouragement of Chang Tso-lin did not save him from defeat, although the Japanese military presence in South Manchuria assisted him in holding onto the Northeast provinces, independent of the government in Peking. Foreign Minister Uchida's policy of nonintervention in the Chinese civil war overcame any adventurist intentions on the part of the Kwantung Army.[14]

In the autumn of 1924, Chang Tso-lin's Fengtien Army waged a war of revenge against the Chihli forces. This time, the Japanese consuls in Manchuria were seconded by the Kwantung Army staff and certain members of the Katō Takaaki cabinet in arguing that cooperation with Chang Tso-lin would favor Japan's best interests. Nevertheless, as Uchida had done in 1922, Foreign Minister Shidehara Kijūrō vigorously opposed intervention. Shidehara's policy of restraint seemed to bear fruit when the Chihli Army's defense of Peking collapsed as the result of a mutiny by Feng Yü-hsiang, known as "the Christian general."

What Shidehara did not realize was that the Kwantung Army under General Shirakawa Yoshinori had been extremely active behind the scenes, apparently with the connivance of high-ranking military officials in Tokyo like War Minister Ugaki. Japanese army officers serving as advisors to Chinese warlords—the shadowy "China hands"—played an important role in the outcome of the Second Fengtien-Chihli War. Working with Chang Tso-lin were Teranishi Hidetake, a retired colonel, and Matsui Shichio, a colonel on active duty. A famous intelligence officer, Lt. Col. Doihara Kenji, was operating in the camp of Feng Yü-hsiang, together with Major Matsumuro Takayoshi, Feng's military advisor. According to reliable sources, one million yen passed from Chang to Feng through the Japanese officers.[15] By engineering the defeat of the Chihli

---

[13] *Manshū mondai*, pp. 752–775; Kurihara, *Tai-Man-Mō*, pp. 94, 103, 139–159.

[14] BKSS, *SS*, vol. 8, p. 262; Kurihara, *Tai-Man-Mō*, pp. 163–189.

[15] Sagara Shunsuke, *Akai yūhi masunogahara ni: kisai Kōmoto Daisaku no shōgai* (Tokyo: Kōjinsha, 1978), p. 97; Kurihara, *Tai-Man-Mō*, pp. 193–224; BKSS, *SS*, vol. 8, p. 263.

Clique, without the sanction or knowledge of the civilian government in Tokyo, the Kwantung Army was gaining confidence in its ability to do as it pleased in fragmented China.

In October 1925, a coalition of warlords renewed the civil war against Fengtien. At this juncture, it was Chang Tso-lin who was betrayed by a subordinate, Kuo Sung-ling, who proceeded to march on Mukden itself. Once again, the leading Japanese officials in Manchuria, including Chang's advisor, Matsui, recommended that Chang Tso-lin be saved. The Kwantung Army commander, General Shirakawa, sought authority to block Kuo's advance by inserting Japanese troops at the Liao River line.

This time, War Minister Ugaki concurred with Foreign Minister Shidehara that Japan should not "pull Chang's chestnuts from the fire."[16] For the moment, the Kwantung Army was to limit itself to safeguarding public order by concentrating elements of the 10th Division at Mukden. From this episode the Kwantung Army had learned a lesson that would be put to dangerous use on many a future occasion: Act first whenever possible, lest docility elicit prohibition from higher headquarters.

Meanwhile, by late November 1925, the Fengtien Army had been beaten and Chang Tso-lin was near elimination. The high command in Tokyo had instructed the Kwantung Army merely to warn both sides to respect Japan's interests; but when about two thousand of Kuo's men tried to cross the Liao River and head toward the town of Yingkow at the northwestern base of the Liaotung Peninsula, General Shirakawa decided to act first. On his own initiative, Shirakawa ordered the local unit commander on the rail line to block Kuo; drawing on the pretext of maintaining law and order, Japanese forces would not allow Kuo to advance to Yingkow. Indeed, Shirakawa proceeded to trace an arbitrary 30-km buffer strip on each side of the South Manchuria Railway, which Kuo's troops in particular were not to enter. Apprised of this action after the fact, War Minister Uchida reduced the extent of Shirakawa's buffer zone by more than half; and Foreign Minister Shidehara sent Consul Yoshida instructions that in effect lifted the prohibition on Kuo's entry into Yingkow if public safety was not thereby endangered.

General Shirakawa still felt that sterner action was imperative, and he was determined to disarm Kuo's men if they were bent on occupying Yingkow. Therefore, Shirakawa sent a token company to the town and even attached a dozen Japanese artillerymen to the Fengtien Army to help operate the Chinese heavy cannon. More resources were needed, however, and Shirakawa would have to obtain them from outside the Kwantung Army. When strictly military matters were involved, obstacles were not insuperable. The seriousness of Shirakawa's intentions is discernible

[16] BKSS, *SS*, vol. 8, pp. 262–264.

from the fact that he borrowed (with the high command's permission) two infantry battalions and two field artillery battalions from the Japanese Korea Army and was even able to wheedle a composite brigade from the homeland for deployment at Mukden.

Thanks to the Kwantung Army's favor, the fortunes of Chang Tso-lin were restored by the end of December 1925. Kuo Sung-ling tried to flee but was caught by Chang's men and executed. Feng Yü-hsiang (who had backed Kuo this time) escaped to Russia. Chang Tso-lin entered Peking in triumph in April 1926. The following year, he assumed the grandiose rank of marshal.[17]

Japanese Army advisors had again played a significant part in the warlords' machinations and rivalries: Matsui Shichio with Chang Tso-lin, Matsumuro with Feng Yü-hsiang, and Sasaki Tōichi with the unfortunate Kuo Sung-ling. More importantly, in 1924 and particularly in 1925, by acting so zealously General Shirakawa had set an ominous example for the Kwantung Army of "going off on its own hook [dokusō]" in Manchuria. That Shirakawa's reputation was not at all damaged in military circles in Tokyo, however, is demonstrated by his appointment soon afterward as war minister in the cabinet formed in 1927 by General Tanaka Giichi, three years his senior.

EXPERIMENTING WITH DIRECT ACTION

While the strife of the warlords was ravaging the north of China, the chance to unify the country progressed in the south. After the establishment of a Nationalist (Kuomintang or KMT) government in Canton in July 1925 and the elimination of regional opposition by the summer of 1926, the commandant of the Whampoa Military Academy, Chiang Kai-shek, led the National Revolutionary Army in the Northern Expedition, which, despite many vicissitudes, was ultimately successful in breaking the power of the warlords. Although deflected by Japanese army units protecting Tsinan in Shantung, Chiang was able to maintain his momentum and advance on Peking in the spring of 1928.[18]

[17] Itō Musojirō, *Manshū mondai no rekishi*, vol. 2 (Tokyo: Hara Shobō, 1983), pp. 777–778; Sagara, *Akai yūhi*, pp. 100–108.

[18] BKSS, SS, vol. 8, pp. 274–278; *TSM*, vol. 1, pp. 305–309; Shinmyō Takeo, *Shōwa seiji hishi* (Kyoto: San'ichi Shobō, 1961), pp. 326–328; and *Shōwa shi tsuiseki: ankoku jidai no kiroku* (Tokyo: Shin Jinbutsu Ōraisha, 1970), pp. 33–44; Nakamura, *Manshū*, pp. 57–63, 79–93; Takamiya Tahei, *Gunkoku taiheiki* (Tokyo: Kantōsha, 1951), pp. 36–43; Usui Katsumi, ed., *Shō Kaiseki hiroku*, vol. 8 (Tokyo: Sankei Shimbunsha, 1975–1977), pp. 12–46; *Dokyumento Shōwa shi*, vol. 1 (Tokyo: Heibonsha, 1975), pp. 226–252, 254–256; *Nihon no rekishi*, vol. 24 (Tokyo: Chūō Kōronsha, 1965–1967), pp. 148–156; Shigemitsu Mamoru, *Gaikō kaisōroku* (Tokyo: Mainichi Shimbunsha, 1953), pp. 57–71; Sagara, *Akai yūhi*, pp. 109–138.

Clinging to Peking, Chang Tso-lin found himself caught between Nationalist Chinese and Japanese military and political pressures. If, as expected, Chang's forces were defeated by the Nationalists and retreated to Manchuria, the Kwantung Army, pleading neutrality, intended to disarm them—and any KMT troops that came in pursuit—near Shanhaikuan. Even more significantly, the Kwantung Army, which would have moved from Port Arthur to Mukden, planned to take forceful action to maintain security in Manchuria by radiating from the Mukden area to Chinchow, with the support of the South Manchuria Railway. At the last moment, however, the Tanaka Giichi government, vacillating in its attitude toward Chang Tso-lin, recoiled from endorsing the military plan, to the astonishment of the jingoists at Kwantung Army Headquarters. Instead, a reluctant Chang was prevailed upon by his Japanese military advisors to leave Peking "voluntarily" and proceed to his domain in Manchuria, there to rebuild his forces under Japanese protection.

Since Tokyo had not authorized decisive military action, and since Chang Tso-lin might take other steps, the senior Kwantung Army staff officer, Colonel Kōmoto Daisaku, now took matters into his own hands. Apparently he had had the idea for some six months of eliminating the bothersome Chang Tso-lin once and for all. To test the feasibility of fomenting an unsuspected train "accident," Kōmoto had arranged to blow up two Chinese Eastern Railway bridges a month apart in early 1928.

From the success of his trial efforts, as measured by press reaction (which never sniffed out the Japanese), Kōmoto became convinced that he could inculpate Chinese warlord rivals of Chang. A Japanese army demolitions expert, brought from Seoul, drew about 150 kg of explosive charges from Kwantung Army ordnance supplies. Cohorts of Kōmoto received very specific assignments. On the morning of June 4, on the outskirts of Mukden, the destruction of Chang Tso-lin's railway car was accomplished with murderous perfection. Although the Chinese authorities did not immediately reveal the death of the marshal. Kōmoto's scenario for a perfect crime had included the killing of three Chinese vagrants dressed as guerrillas, the finding of bombs made in Russia, and the discovery of secret papers on one corpse.[19]

Premier Tanaka, it is said, wept when news of Chang Tso-lin's death reached him. "What fools! They [the Kwantung Army] behave like children," he lamented to General Ugaki. "They have no idea what the parent has to go through." Kwantung Army Headquarters had denied complicity even in classified messages sent to the vice-minister of war, and Kō-

[19] Usui Katsumi, "Chō Sakurin bakushi no shinsō," *Chisei*, suppl. 5 (December 1956), pp. 26–33; Togawa Isamu, "Chō Sakurin ansatsu jiken," *Shūkan gendai*, July 2, 1961, pp. 53–62; BKSS, *SS* vol. 8, pp. 58–65; Kojima Noboru, *Manshū teikoku*, vol. 1 (Tokyo: Bungei Shunjūsha, 1974), p. 257.

moto himself brazened it out when he was called to Tokyo. Unfortunately for the plotters, however, one of the Chinese vagrants got away from his would-be murderers, and there were also payoff problems. Thus, details of the assassination began to leak out, although censorship prevented the Japanese press from alluding to more than "a certain serious incident in Manchuria."

In the end, Premier Tanaka, who served concurrently as foreign minister, incurred the emperor's displeasure and resigned, to die several months later in despair. Kōmoto was retired from the army for having "committed a mistake in guarding the railway," but the suspicion could never be laid to rest that at least the Kwantung Army commander, Muraoka Chōtarō, and perhaps his chief of staff, Saitō Hisashi, were indirectly involved, and that Kōmoto was acting at the behest of his superiors. After all, the Japanese consul-general in Mukden, Hayashi Kyūjirō, had got wind of the plot before its execution and had protested to the army commander beforehand.

The Kwantung Army heads had certainly wanted Chang Tso-lin out of the way. Did this go so far as to mean the marshal's murder, something not advocated by either the government or the army General Staff? According to a postwar Japanese revelation, Kōmoto admitted privately to a political leader in 1930 that General Muraoka had put him up to the idea of the assassination, to which he was at first opposed.[20] Sasaki Tōitsu, however, a lieutenant colonel when reassigned to Chiang Kai-shek in 1928, has said that it was he who first suggested the assassination scheme to Kōmoto.

Kōmoto had evidently hoped that the murder would lead to major disturbances, the immediate seizure of Mukden and the eventual control of all of Manchuria, and the installation of a puppet leader in the detached provinces. The local Chinese authorities kept calm, however; Chinese troops backed away; and the Kwantung Army chief of staff had second thoughts about allowing the alerted Japanese units to sortie from their barracks into Mukden prematurely.

General Shirakawa, who was Kwantung Army commander in 1925 and was now war minister, proposed (for reasons of "security") to give the Kwantung Army, poised at Mukden, two additional missions: to move out along the rail lines and disarm "confused" Chinese troops; and to concentrate and protect Japanese residents even at such places as Harbin and Kirin. Shirakawa called for reinforcements to be authorized in support of what might amount to a preventive takeover of Manchuria; in

---

[20] Shinmyō, *Shōwa seiji*, pp. 44, 101; Ugaki Kazunari, *Shōrai seidan*, as told to Kamata Sawa'ichirō (Tokyo: Bungei Shunjūsha, 1951), p. 317; Sagara, *Akai yūhi*, chaps. 6–7; Hayashi Kyūjirō, *Manshū jihen to Hōten sōryōji* (Tokyo: Hara Shobō, 1978), pp. 18–27; BKSS, *SS*, vol. 8, pp. 65–66.

other words, a realization of the Manchurian incident that did not take place for another three years. The cabinet rejected Shirakawa's proposal; and the Kwantung Army, which was standing by to exploit the situation, was disappointed for the second time in two weeks. It would profit from the latest "bitter lesson" of the fruits of subordination.

Although Chang Tso-lin was dead, Manchuria had been neither occupied by the Nationalists nor detached from China by the Kwantung Army. The accession of the old warlord's unexpectedly independent-thinking son, Chang Hsueh-liang (called "the Young Marshal"), did not sit well with all Japanese. Still, in one respect the Japanese were in agreement, regardless of complicated individual preferences for a successor: Kuomintang influence—and Chinese unity—must be thwarted in the Northeast provinces. Such hopes were undone fairly soon, for the Young Marshal, though beset by Japanese pressure, announced adherence to the Nationalist government by the end of 1928 and got Jehol added to the three Northeast provinces. At home in Japan, Shidehara Kijūrō, who replaced Tanaka as foreign minister in the new Hamaguchi Osachi cabinet of July 1929, pursued a milder policy stressing economic rather than military approaches to diplomacy.

To the Manchurian Incident

By 1931, the officers at Kwantung Army Headquarters, like many of their colleagues in the homeland, had become exasperated by the social, political, and economic reverses afflicting Japan domestically and internationally. They felt that Japanese interests in Manchuria were being slighted, despite Japan's investments there since 1904. (It was often stressed that Japan had lost 100,000 men and expended two billion yen during the Russo-Japanese War.) Too often, it was alleged, high-level Japanese diplomats and military officers avoided postings to China or Manchuria, the abode of "carpetbaggers." Far greater prestige derived from assignment to European posts, especially to Germany or France.

To the Kwantung Army, however, the expansion of Communist influence from China proper and from the Soviet Union via the latter's Chinese Eastern Railway rights was very real. Retention of Japanese interests in Manchuria was regarded as a matter of national security, for the Northeast constituted a buffer against threats from Russia or China and a springboard for possible operations against those countries or Mongolia. The only choice, it began to be thought, was between disengaging totally from Manchuria or compelling China to abandon the so-called recapture of national rights. Kwantung Army Headquarters, in particular, clamored for the latter course.[21] Force, not diplomacy, seemed to be the only real alternative.

Nevertheless, as mentioned at the outset of the present chapter, the instrument for the conquest of Manchuria in 1931 was an army in name only. In all, the military manpower under the control of the Kwantung Army did not exceed 10,400. There was no spare matériel, and trucks and engineers were in especially short supply. Logistical backup was lacking for a force designed merely to garrison the Leased Territory and the railway zone.[22]

After the Manchurian incident, when responsibility for the client state of Manchukuo would lead to reinforcement that for the first time made technical sense of the term "army" (gun), the same expansion of its role would render the designation "Kwantung" anachronistic. Three reasons may be adduced for the survival, from 1905 to 1945, of the nomenclature for the Kwantung Army:

First, during the period after Japan's initial successful overseas war, against China in 1894–1895, each of the original colonial garrisons was officially separated from the jurisdiction of the civil governors in due course and, regardless of the number of troops assigned to it, was called an army, as in the case of the Taiwan Army (whose strength did not amount to even one division), the Korea Army (never more than two divisions in peacetime), and the Kwantung Army.

Second, a sense of historical continuity and a desire to sanctify the treaty basis for Japan's presence in Manchuria caused retention of the wording for Kwantung, drawn, of course, from the leasehold of the Kwantung Territory—"the most civilized area of Manchuria," as one Japanese publicist put it.

Third, independence was not envisaged for Taiwan or Korea, whereas the so-called empire of Manchukuo would be endowed with its own forces. Thus, the term "Manshūgun" was reserved for the Manchukuo Army, and the old, distinctive wording "Kantōgun" was retained for the Japanese garrison, the Kwantung Army.[23]

Accounts of the instigation and course of the Manchurian incident of 1931–1932, and particularly of the roles of such plotters as Kwantung

[21] *TSM*, vol. 1, pp. 353–358, 422; Kokusai Zenrin Kyōkai, ed., *Manshū kenkoku no yume to genjitsu* (Tokyo: Kenkōsha, 1975), pp. 240–242; Nakamura, *Manshū*, pp. 32–34; Kojima, *Manshū teikoku*, vol. 1, pp. 87–96, 107–122.

[22] Coox, *Nomonhan*, vol. 1, pp. 26–27; author's interview with Katakura Tadashi. Also see *GSS*, vol. 11, pp. 289–295, 903–904; bkss, *SS*, vol. 27, pp. 14–15; ibid., vol. 53: *Manshū hōmen rikugun kōkū sakusen* (1972), pp. 6–7; Kojima, *Manshū teikoku*, vol. 1, pp. 102–106, 156; Nakamura, *Manshū*, pp. 121–122; Imai Takei, *Shōwa no bōryaku* (Tokyo: Hara Shobō, 1967), p. 30.

[23] Author's interviews with Imaoka Yutaka, Katakura Tadashi, Nishihara Yukio, Hata Ikuhiko.

Army staff officers Itagaki Seishirō and Ishiwara Kanji, abound to a degree that renders a retelling redundant.[24] For the purposes of the present chapter, therefore, I shall address my attention to the era of Manchukuo, the ward of the Kwantung Army.

The Kwantung Army and the Greening of Manchukuo

The history of the Kwantung Army after 1931 encompasses the history of Manchukuo and the policies of the Japanese toward the puppet regime. Kwantung Army staff officers saw themselves as the best kind of civilizers and empire-builders, with a Heaven-sent opportunity to demonstrate "ability in the handling of men of diverse breeds and the development of virgin territory that in history has been the privilege of the new and the best."[25] As a contemporary Japanese writer observed, for the first time "a nonwhite race has undertaken to carry the white man's burden, and the white man, long accustomed to think the burden exclusively his own, is reluctant to commit it to the young shoulders of Japan, yellow and an upstart at that."[26] To the journalist John Gunther, the Kwantung Army was making of Manchukuo a type of "proving ground, a testing station for social and economic theory . . . the great guinea pig of Asia."[27]

Lieutenant General Koiso Kuniaki in 1933 described Japan's policy as the unification and rationalization of the economic systems of Japan and Manchukuo, and the utilization of the resources of the two countries in order to improve their economic positions in the world. Though paying lip service to the encouragement of foreign investment and the principles of the Open Door, Koiso publicly called for the consolidation of Japan's economic position in Manchukuo before any of the world powers started economic activities there. The authoritarian military thrust of the economic policy fostered by the Kwantung Army is reflected in the stipulation that national considerations must take precedence over those of individuals, and that the economic structures of Japan and Manchukuo must be so meshed as to meet wartime necessity. The public interest in the two countries must govern the establishment of industries in Manchukuo.[28]

Old zaibatsu conglomerates had long pursued a vigorous role in Man-

---

[24] See Coox, *Nomonhan*, chaps. 2–3.

[25] John N. Penlington, *The Mukden Mandate: Acts and Aims in Manchuria* (Tokyo: Maruzen, 1932), p. 264.

[26] K. K. Kawakami, *Manchoukuo: Child of Conflict* (New York: Macmillan, 1933), p. vi.

[27] John Gunther, *Inside Asia* (New York: Harper, 1939), p. 123.

[28] *The Japan-Manchoukuo Year Book, 1940: Cyclopedia of General Information and Statistics on the Empires of Japan and Manchoukuo* (Tokyo, 1939), pp. 620–621; Tsunoda Jun, ed., *Ishiwara Kanji shiryō*, vol. 1 (Tokyo: Hara Shobō, 1967–1968), p. 343 (1939).

churia. Mitsui Bussan, first into the region in 1908, made enormous profits from the soybean trade, and Ōkura had gained a powerful foothold in the coal and iron sectors. After Russian firms withdrew from North Manchuria during the Bolshevik Revolution, the semigovernmental South Manchuria Railway more than doubled its capitalization. By the early 1920s, it also doubled its passenger and freight loads. Using the profits of its transportation monopoly, and working closely with Japanese banks like the Yokohama Specie Bank and later the Bank of Chōsen, the South Manchuria Railway invested deeply in Manchurian heavy industry, which it accorded preferential freight rates. SMR geologists were active in discovering mineral deposits.

Although the South Manchuria Railway possessed immense military value, the Kwantung Army sought "reforms" where the private capital sector was concerned. One of the reformist measures was to organize the Japan-Manchuria Trading Company to replace SMR sales and supplies activities. South Manchuria Railway subsidiaries—chemical, steel, and electric power—were reorganized.[29]

The Kwantung Army, it has often been said, warned that capitalists would not be allowed into Manchukuo. Katakura Tadashi, a staff officer at the time of the Manchurian incident, calls the charge exaggerated. What the Kwantung Army really meant, he argues, was that they did not want greedy capitalistic tycoons to exploit the outcome of the Manchurian incident for unfair profits. A more precise rendering of the Kwantung Army's original economic reservations would be opposition to the expansion of old-line monopolies in Manchuria. Though commerce, industry, and finances were important to Japanese interests, the main investments had continued to emphasize railroads, harbors, mining, forestry, and agriculture. In other words, the Japanese investors in Manchuria had been furthering the underdevelopment of the traditional economy while engendering the modern economy.[30]

In addition to castigating traditional big business and special interests, the Kwantung Army wanted to exclude "degenerate and grasping" Japanese political parties from Manchukuo. Formation of a single, authoritarian-style Concordia Association (Kyōwa Kai) was the Kwantung Army's preference in the matter of creating grass-roots politics in the new state. Drawing on the ideologues of *minzoku kyōwa* (racial harmony), Ishiwara and Katakura—who were instrumental in the establishment of the association in July 1932 as a substitute for traditional parties—spoke of warding off communism, constructing a moral nation through ethnic

[29] *Nihon no rekishi*, vol. 22, pp. 385–386; vol. 23, p. 212; *Japan-Manchoukuo Year Book, 1937* (Tokyo, 1936), p. 667.

[30] Satō Kenryō, *Daitōa sensō kaikoroku* (Tokyo: Tokuma Shoten, 1966), p. 108; *Manshū kenkoku*, pp. 134–146. Also author's interview with Katakura Tadashi.

harmony, and preventing the growth of an overweening bureaucracy. Although Pu-Yi was named honorary president of the association and Kwantung Army commander Honjō Shigeru its honorary advisor, and although the Manchukuo premier was president, the key officials were three Japanese directors: Colonel Itagaki, Komai Tokuzō (Pu-Yi's "consultant"), and Major General Hashimoto Toranosuke, who had replaced Miyake as Kwantung Army chief of staff.

Behind the scenes, the 4th Section (Civil Affairs) of Kwantung Army Headquarters influenced Concordia Association policy, which was designed to achieve domestic pacification and to suggest a program of unity rather than Japanese domination. By the organization's own admission, the spur to success was the Kwantung Army, its "inner supreme guiding force." By 1934, the association numbered 300,000 members enrolled in 900 local branches.[31]

The ambitious enterprise known as Manchukuo required new sophistication in government. Idealists on the Kwantung Army staff wanted an administration based on merit, "absolutely free from the irregularities, corruption, and peculation that had characterized the old regime under the warlords, and that marked all government in China proper."[32] By all accounts, the most difficult period for Manchukuo in administrative terms occurred between the time the embryonic government was formed in Hsinking (old Ch'ang-ch'un) in February–March 1932 and the time when Kwantung Army Headquarters followed from Mukden in June of the same year.

Without constant military guidance at the outset, the Manchukuo bureaucrats wasted time with Japanese officials at restaurants until all hours and slept until noon. Concerned over the unstable situation, the chief of the army General Staff hastened from Tokyo to Hsinking to discipline as well as encourage the Japanese and Manchukuo officials.[33] Trained and efficient Chinese administrators were certainly unavailable in sufficient numbers, so that "Japanese organizational ability and executive efficiency seem to have been availed of wherever necessary." Still, some observers noted that the quality of the Japanese bureaucrats was not consistently good.

In numbers, the Japanese component in Manchukuo's governmental structure was certainly dominant. Of twenty-seven bureau chiefs, seventeen were Japanese. Two Japanese served on the Privy Council. The Board of General Affairs, all-important in the formative year of 1932, was headed by Komai Tokuzō. Of 135 central officials, 100 were Japanese,

---

[31] *GSS*, vol. 11, pp. 828–829, 843–850. Also author's interview with Katakura Tadashi.
[32] Kawakami, *Manchoukuo*, p. 149.
[33] Privileged Kwantung Army source.

especially numerous in the areas of finance and supply. In all, over 200 Japanese served as officials of the new state in 1932, exclusive of local authorities, government enterprises, and the armed forces. Japanese officials exerted greater influence than even these statistics suggest, because they occupied the preponderance of vital posts involving the most responsible and important duties. Vice-ministers, for example—the key men—were regularly Japanese.[34]

Even enemies of Manchukuo, however, had to admit that the Japanese were able to recruit a sizable number of generals and high officials of the former Chang Hsueh-liang regime. Although some critics called the higher Manchukuo officials "leftover old literati" and figureheads, other observers remarked that Manchu emphasis on a Confucian basis for government and education served the needs of the Japanese, who could now use it to counter Kuomintang and Communist activities on behalf of nationalism.[35] As a British commentator noted, if the Chinese had opposed the new state with passive resistance the way the Germans had sabotaged the French in the Ruhr crisis of 1923, "the Japanese would have had either to abandon the attempt [to create a puppet state] altogether or else annex Manchuria outright."[36]

PROBLEMS OF DOMESTIC SECURITY

In the view of the Kwantung Army staff, nation building would be impossible unless Manchukuo's security were assured. Actual or potential threats to that security emanated from Nationalist China and Soviet Russia, externally; and from what the Japanese termed "bandits," internally. The latter were a motley and dispersed force of professional brigands, opium smugglers, patriotic or ideological adherents of the Kuomintang and the Communists, warlords' followers, unemployed ex-soldiers, vagrants, displaced railway workers, and distressed farmers (called "bandits of despair"). As one foreigner saw it, "In a repressive society demoralized by foreign imperialism and warlord-inflicted misery, banditry remained one of the few roads open for human beings to assert themselves."[37] Arnold Toynbee, who traveled in South Manchuria shortly before the Mukden incident of 1931, discerned conditions peculiar to a frontier territory

[34] League of Nations, *Manchuria: Report of the Commission of Enquiry Appointed by the League of Nations* (Washington, D.C.: U.S. Government Printing Office, 1932), p. 99; Kawakami, *Manchoukuo*, pp. 146–152; *Japan-Manchoukuo Year Book, 1937*, pp. 637, 692.

[35] Warren W. Smith, Jr., *Confucianism in Modern Japan: A Study of Conservatism in Japanese Intellectual History* (Tokyo: Hokuseidō, 1973), pp. 190–194.

[36] Arnold J. Toynbee, *Survey of International Affairs, 1932* (London: Oxford University Press, 1933), p. 456, n. 4.

[37] Herbert P. Bix, "Japanese Imperialism and the Manchurian Economy, 1900–1931," *The China Quarterly*, no. 51 (July–September 1972): 434, n. 25.

undergoing rapid settlement and development, comparable to the situation in the Australian hinterland and the American West in the nineteenth century. Since a greater degree of insecurity was observable in Manchuria close to the fringes of settlement, Toynbee questioned the Kwantung Army's claim of a recrudescence of brigandage in the built-up areas.[38]

The Japanese explanation was that bandit forces, which had approximated a total of 130,000 men in early 1932, had swollen to 200,000 in summer and a peak of 360,000 by autumn as the result of major accretions from the remnants of the army of Chang Hsueh-liang.[39] The "bandit menace" led the Kwantung Army to clear away kaoliang fields for hundreds of meters along both sides of railroad rights-of-way, to spread apart double-tracked rail lines across rivers, and to store ammunition near military camp guardrooms, unlike the practice in Japan.[40]

To buttress its own pacification capability, the Kwantung Army in March 1932 sponsored the creation of a Manchukuo Army, whose expenses were footed entirely by the Japanese War Ministry until fiscal year 1934–1935. Typical of Japanese propagandists' hyperbole on behalf of the puppet army is the following passage: "Just as Manchukuo is a State made up of diverse races, so is the Manchukuo Army composed of men recruited from various races—the Japanese, who are the motivating force behind the nation, Manchurians, Hans, Mongols, and even Russians."[41]

Although the Kwantung Army admitted few of its own casualties during bandit-suppression operations, it is significant that the Japanese losses were mainly in officers. The high ratio of officer casualties is undoubtedly attributable to the Japanese need to fight in the forefront of the Manchukuo Army, to which many Kwantung Army officers were attached in key positions. Even open sources revealed that Japanese army generals commanded a number of the pacification campaigns: Major General Hino Takeo (Chientao, July–September 1934) and Major General Fujii Jūzaburō (Chientao, January 1935).[42]

Drawn at first mainly from elements of Chang Hsueh-liang's forces and ex-brigands, Manchukuo Army soldiers were of dubious reliability; they often deserted or rebelled, and they suffered many a reverse in combat. Indeed, the Kwantung Army was chary about providing heavy

[38] Toynbee, *Survey 1932*, pp. 446–447.

[39] *Japan-Manchoukuo Year Book, 1937*, pp. 727–728; *1940*, p. 696; BKSS, *SS*, vol. 8, pp. 128–129.

[40] Author's interviews with Nishiura Susumu, Imaoka Yutaka.

[41] *Oriental Year Book, 1942* (Tokyo: Asia Statistics Company, 1942), p. 542.

[42] *Japan-Manchoukuo Year Book, 1937*, pp. 725, 729; *1940*, p. 637; Tsuji Masanobu, *Nomonhan* (Tokyo: Atō Shobō, 1950), p. 23; BKSS, *SS*, vol. 8, p. 118; GSS, vol. 7, pp. 590–592; vol. 11, p. 947.

weapons and ammunition to its protégés, who, as the real bandits exulted, were their best source of supply for military stores.

Still, under Kwantung Army tutelage, the Manchukuo Army troops, especially when rotated from desolate garrisons, began to give a creditable account of themselves.[43] Undoubtedly, the puppet forces, by their numbers alone, helped to ease the combat burden of the Kwantung Army. For the conquest of Jehol province in early 1933, for example, a large portion of the Manchukuo Army—forty-two thousand men—operated in support of the Kwantung Army.

Better quality was infused into the Manchukuo Army by the introduction of native conscripts untainted by a questionable past. According to Kwantung Army advisors, the Manchukuo forces performed particularly well against guerrilla elements in eastern Manchuria and, in fact, endured hardships better than the Japanese. Plotting data on banditry like a fever chart, the Kwantung Army claimed that, despite many ups and downs, dissident forces had been steadily reduced over time, leaving vestiges mainly in the northeast. Whereas in 1932 some bandit forces had numbered as many as thirty thousand armed men, the groups in 1938 were said to average fewer than thirty horsemen.[44]

PENETRATION BEYOND MANCHUKUO

Of larger moment for the Kwantung Army than the domestic pacification of Manchukuo was the relationship of the new protectorate to China. To consolidate the approaches from Inner Mongolia, Kwantung Army forces in the first months of 1933 penetrated "disaffected" Jehol province and seized their main objectives against an estimated 235–245,000 Chinese troops. By March 4, all of Jehol was cleared; the Great Wall was reached by March 10. In April, in the face of Chinese "provocation," the Kwantung Army extended its operations across the wall into North China. By the terms of the T'angku Truce, signed by the local commanders at the end of May 1933, eastern Hopeh province—some 13,000 sq. km between Manchuria and Peking—was demilitarized. Chinese troops were to be withdrawn from this zone, subject to verification by the Kwantung Army, which would then fall back north to the Great Wall. A police force friendly to Japan would be responsible for security in the buffer region.

The net result of the Kwantung Army's actions of 1933, from the Chinese standpoint, was the loss by default of the defenses of Peking and

---

[43] BKSS, *SS*, vol. 8, pp. 118–130.

[44] Ibid., p. 341; Gunther, *Inside Asia*, pp. 131–133; *Japan-Manchoukuo Year Book, 1937*, pp. 727–737; *1940*, pp. 636–637; Tsuji, *Nomonhan*, pp. 27–28, 31.

Tientsin. From the Japanese standpoint, the Manchurian incident was officially over.[45]

Intensified efforts to solidify and enlarge the Japanese position were undertaken by the Japanese army in 1935, especially after the Okada Keisuke government implemented a conciliatory policy of exchanging ambassadors with China in May. Kwantung Army staff officers had already met in January at Dairen to devise strategy for the penetration of North China. Major General Doihara Kenji, the old China hand attached to the Office of Strategic Services (Tokumu Kikan or OSS), traveled at various times to the Peking region from his headquarters at Mukden to explore the possibilities of creating a nominally autonomous regional administration in North China.

Chahar province was the Kwantung Army's first objective, but ultimately Shantung, Hopeh, Shansi, and Suiyuan provinces were to be severed from Nationalist China politically and economically. Once such a new regional regime was established, the Kwantung Army hoped to force or cajole it (preferably without recourse to invasion) into giving Japanese interests the untrammeled chance of exploiting the markets and resources of all North China.[46]

In June 1935, Lieutenant General Umezu Yoshijirō, the commander of the Tientsin Garrison in North China, extracted major concessions from General Ho Ying-chin, the Nationalist minister of war and head of the Peking branch of the National Military Council.[47] According to the terms of the Ho-Umezu agreement of June 10, Chinese government troops and Kuomintang organs were to be withdrawn immediately from Hopeh and officials unacceptable to the Japanese dismissed, and anti-Japanese agitation was to be discontinued.[48]

Doihara next worked strenuously in the autumn of 1935 to bring about the Kwantung Army's larger scheme of regional autonomy, dealing only with the opportunistic local Chinese leaders and bypassing both the Kuomintang government at Nanking and the Japanese Foreign Ministry. Behind him stood fifteen thousand Kwantung Army troops massed at Shanhaikuan with air support. Learning of these unauthorized developments, the central authorities in Tokyo advised against arbitrary action.

Unexpectedly foiled in his grandiose ambitions, Doihara instead ar-

---

[45] *GSS*, vol. 7, pp. 511–584; Hata Ikuhiko, *Nitchū sensō shi* (Tokyo: Kawade Shobō Shinsha, 1961), pp. 6–7; *TSM*, vol. 3, pp. 16–50.

[46] BKSS, *SS*, vol. 8, p. 423.

[47] *Kindai no sensō*, vol. 5 (Tokyo: Jinbutsu Ōraisha, 1966), pp. 49–53; Hata, *Nitchū sensō*, pp. 32–36; *TSM*, vol. 3, pp. 112–120; *GSS*, vol. 8, pp. 73–76.

[48] Hata, *Nitchū sensō*, pp. 13–31; Jōhō Yoshio, *Saigo no sanbō sōchō Umezu Yoshijirō* (Tokyo: Fuyō Shobō, 1976), pp. 179–189; *TSM*, vol. 3, pp. 98–112; *GSS*, vol. 8, pp. 68–72, 77–101.

ranged the formation in Tientsin, in late November, of the East Hopeh Anti-Communist Autonomous Council, under Japanese military control.[49] Since this act contravened the terms of the T'angku Truce of May 1933, Chinese reaction was vehement. The Nanking regime struggled to limit such Japanese political schemes while not overtly provoking Kwantung Army military retaliation.

In December, at Peking, Doihara orchestrated the formation of the Hopeh–Chahar Political Council. The body, however, was subordinate to the Executive Yuan, the Nationalist government's highest administrative organ, contrary to Doihara's original intention to merge the Hopeh–Chahar and East Hopeh councils and to ensure their control by the Japanese army.

Transferred to Japan in March 1936 after about six months of activity in North China, Doihara told Japanese reporters in Peking, "Japan does not aim at making North China a second 'Manchukuo,' completely separated from Nanking, but is seeking to make the region an experimental ground for actual Sino-Japanese rapprochement by means of economic and military cooperation."[50] When Tōjō Hideki was war minister in 1941, however, he confided to a subordinate that the whole North China separatist movement had been conducted in amateurish fashion, and that the establishment of the buffer zone between Manchukuo and China led to abuse by smugglers—"a horrible kind of filth attached to the military"— which only served to provoke anti-Japanese feelings on the part of the Chinese.[51]

The Nanking government, engaged in unification efforts and a long series of campaigns against the Chinese Communists, was still unprepared to challenge the Japanese military. Chiang Kai-shek had long been pursuing the policy that "unless the critical moment for sacrifice has arrived, we do not speak lightly of sacrifice, in order to avoid the premature outbreak of war." In addition, pro-Japanese elements remained fairly influential in Kuomintang foreign policy circles.

As for the Japanese themselves, although only partially successful in their stratagems in North China, until mid-1936 they were distracted by various problems in the homeland, such as the serious 2–26 Mutiny in Tokyo. Calm prevailed in Manchukuo, where Itagaki, now Kwantung Army chief of staff, and Tōjō, commander of the Military Police, swiftly arrested military and civilian suspects before they could foment distur-

---

[49] *Kindai no sensō*, vol. 5, pp. 49–51; Hata, *Nitchū sensō*, pp. 32–36; *TSM*, vol. 3, pp. 111–120; *GSS*, vol. 8, pp. 73–76.

[50] B. Winston Kahn, *Doihara Kenji and the "North China Autonomy Movement," 1935–1936* (Tempe: Arizona State University, 1973), pp. 44–45.

[51] Satō, *Daitōa*, pp. 107–108.

bances, and strongly urged the high command to suppress the Imperial Way insurgents mercilessly.[52]

FIASCO IN INNER MONGOLIA

Tanaka Ryūkichi, who had touched off the 1932 Shanghai incident to distract attention from Manchuria, was a lieutenant colonel by 1936 and attached to the intelligence staff at Kwantung Army Headquarters. As a Mongolia expert of long standing, he had been concentrating on building up Inner Mongolian forces friendly to the Japanese. The Kwantung Army viewed Inner Mongolia as a buffer against Communist inroads from the Mongolian People's Republic (Outer Mongolia) and as a base of operations against the Chinese Nationalists. Playing upon the dream of the Mongol Prince Teh for a Greater Mongolia, Tanaka diverted sizable funds amassed from "special trade" (a euphemism for smuggling and narcotics activity) to support the prince's "autonomous" regime. The Kwantung Army also disbursed very large sums of money to what was labeled the Mongol independence movement.

By the fall of 1936, Lieutenant Colonel Tanaka was more or less ready for another military adventure, as dangerous as the Shanghai incident: a campaign, using Mongol puppet forces, against Suiyuan in Inner Mongolia. Some of the Japanese intelligence officers who worked most closely with the Inner Mongols strongly opposed the projected offensive at such an early stage of the buildup; one such officer was ousted for his troubles.

Tanaka later blamed Prince Teh for pressing for premature action, but Colonel Mutō Akira, the Kwantung Army's director of intelligence, supported aggressive policies and overruled all objections. Tanaka had privately contacted the Chinese chieftain in Suiyuan, Fu Tso-i, and others. Yet, because Prince Teh was advocating independence for all of Inner Mongolia and Tanaka had called for the overthrow of Chiang Kai-shek, no progress could be made in collateral discussions.

An ultimatum was finally sent to Fu, who rejected the anti-KMT conditions and concentrated his forces to meet the incursion in the middle of November. The invading vanguard was small—a mere two thousand soldiers; but the Kwantung Army arranged for support by eighty aviation volunteers headed by a retired Japanese Air Force major in charge of perhaps two dozen planes, few of the combat variety. The Manchukuo Telephone and Telegraph Services, the Manchukuo Airways Company, and the South Manchuria Railway assisted in various ways.

The Inner Mongolian soldiers were still poor in quality and lacking in fighting spirit. At the first real Chinese counterattack on November 18,

[52] Alvin D. Coox, *Tojo* (New York: Ballantine Books, 1975), p. 29.

they fell back quickly, some without firing. Although the Inner Mongolian losses were not severe, the Chinese side made great propaganda capital out of the so-called victory. According to the Chinese, the invaders were Kwantung Army regulars wearing Mongol insignia. Fu Tso-i became a hero overnight.[53] Many Japanese sources agree that the setback to the Inner Mongolians provided an important psychological reinforcement to sagging Kuomintang morale.

When Foreign Minister Hirota Kōki denied on November 21 that the Japanese government had any connection with the Suiyuan affair, he was telling the truth. Not only were the Foreign Ministry and the navy in the dark, but even the Kwantung Army was out of touch with Tanaka's close-to-the-vest handling of the venture, to the extent that the staff in Hsinking originally believed that there had been a victory for the Inner Mongolian/Japanese side.

Chiang Kai-shek moved large forces, estimated at more than 200,000 men, toward the north, threatening the whole Japanese position in North China. Nationalist troops seized vital Pailingmiao on November 24; an Inner Mongolian "division" fled precipitously when armored vehicles were sighted. There was some controversy between the Inner Mongolian command and the OSS advisors (the latter having scarcely escaped from Pailingmiao) concerning the feasibility of recapturing the town. At an emergency conference, a flustered Tanaka is said to have encouraged or goaded Prince Teh into mounting a counteroffensive.

Some four thousand Inner Mongolians under a Japanese major launched the foolhardy attack in the snow on the night of December 2–3, were smashed the next day, and fell back once more, tormented by frostbite and by pursuers. A revolt now occurred among elements of the Inner Mongolian forces; the insurgents murdered their Japanese military advisor, a retired colonel, and others, before defecting to the Nationalist side. The Kwantung Army, fearing that annihilation of their outnumbered Mongolian allies was near, sent the deputy chief of staff, Major General Imamura Hitoshi, to Tokyo around December 10. He was to obtain authorization for Kwantung Army forces to be committed in an emergency, and to secure more funds to support the Inner Mongolian activities.

In Tokyo, the central authorities were in a bad mood. Even before Major General Imamura's arrival, the Japanese government had decided to prevent enlargement of the Suiyuan incident, and the army General Staff was to issue the necessary orders. Thus, when Imamura appeared in Tokyo, not only was his request turned down, but he was also sternly reprimanded by Lieutenant General Umezu Yoshijirō, now vice-minister of

[53] *Far Eastern Economic Review*, May 30, 1975, p. 30.

war. The Kwantung Army, growled Umezu, had been conducting actions "off the track of the high command's intentions on every occasion" and had rendered an "impolite reception" to the new GS War Guidance section chief, Colonel Ishiwara, when that old principal from Mukden incident days had gone to Hsinking in late November to try to convince the staff to suspend the "premature and excessive" Suiyuan operation. Umezu pointedly reminded Imamura that he had been sent to Manchukuo in the first place to prevent this very type of subversion. Imamura said nothing.

Lack of cooperation and coordination between the Kwantung Army and sister forces in the field now became apparent. The Japanese garrison army in North China had resented the Kwantung Army's intrusion into what they considered their bailiwick ever since the days of Doihara's "meddling" in matters affecting northern Chinese autonomy. As a result, the Kwantung Army had encountered difficulty even in getting ammunition to Jehol via Tientsin and Peking. How to end the Suiyuan operation was the latest subject of mutual unhappiness between the Japanese field commands. Fortunately for the Japanese, Chang Hsueh-liang seized Chiang Kai-shek at Sian on December 12. Though Kwantung Army Headquarters may originally have toyed with the idea of renewing the Suiyuan offensive, it was decided eventually to pursue a wait-and-see policy, because of Tokyo's displeasure and the dim prospects for military success.

An armistice soon became inevitable, and Prince Teh made the best of a difficult situation by announcing on December 15 that he would not take mean advantage of China's current misfortune by prolonging the struggle. By the end of January 1937, the Inner Mongolian forces had generally fallen back to their starting locations. Tanaka returned to Hsinking in a state of uncharacteristic depression.

Thus did the Kwantung Army bungle the Suiyuan campaign. Not only had the progress of the Inner Mongolian independence movement suffered, but the Japanese also lost ground against China. Even Tanaka had to confess that the Suiyuan episode would have to be called a failure. Recent Japanese scholarship confirms this candid view. The Suiyuan affair aroused suspicion abroad regarding Japan's motives and enhanced Chinese nationalism and confidence, leading to an unexpectedly fierce reaction after the Sino-Japanese clash at the Marco Polo Bridge in July 1937. Some go so far as to suggest that the so-called China incident might have started at the time of Tanaka's invasion of Suiyuan if there had been no Sian affair. Tsuji Masanobu, an exemplar of insubordination in his own right, provides a particularly acerbic commentary on the fiasco at Suiyuan: "Staff Officer Tanaka Ryūkichi had wanted to equal the achievements of Generals Itagaki and Ishiwara by establishing a second

Manchukuo through an attempt to bestow independence on Inner Mongolia. . . . While he was consoling himself with the news that Chiang Kai-shek had been incarcerated at Sian, the Nationalists and the Communists worked to build a combined anti-Japanese Popular Front."[54]

DABBLING IN THE CHINA INCIDENT

Sino-Japanese relations, which had been deteriorating at the same time that the Popular Front was emerging in China, collapsed in the summer of 1937. Lieutenant General Tōjō Hideki, the Kwantung Army chief of staff since March, had for some time been extremely hawkish toward China. On June 9, for example, he advised the army General Staff that the Nationalist regime should be eliminated before attending to the Russian problem, to remove any threat to Japan's rear. To those who were nervous, he retorted that there was nothing to fear from the Soviet Union, the only great power that could, realistically, intervene. On the Asian continent, hostilities would end in a quick Japanese victory, for the Chinese armed forces were inconsequential except in number.

As soon as the Marco Polo Bridge affray occurred on July 7, the Kwantung Army rushed a message to the chief of the army's General Staff, in the name of Commanding General Ueda Kenkichi, to the effect that infantry and air force units were being readied for action against North China. The next day, Kwantung Army Headquarters issued an unusual statement, strictly on its own initiative, since affairs outside of Manchukuo lay beyond its official purview. Chinese actions had been outrageous, said the statement, and the authorities in Hsinking were watching events very closely.

At the same time, Tōjō's deputy chief, Major General Imamura, and a number of staff officers were sent to Tokyo to urge decisive action against China by the high command. In these activities, the Kwantung Army was fully supported by the Korea Army, whose commander, Lieutenant General Koiso Kuniaki, was a former Kwantung Army chief of staff. The Imamura team encountered opposition from the GS Operations Bureau chief, Major General Ishiwara Kanji, and from War Guidance Colonel Kawabe Torashirō, in particular. Kawabe argued that the Kwantung Army was underestimating China, was intruding into high command affairs, and was behaving imprudently. The jingoists prevailed, however. On July 11, the high command approved sending to North China the

---

[54] Tanaka Ryūkichi, "Shanhai jihen wa kōshite okosareta," *Chisei*, suppl. 5 (December 1956), pp. 183–186; Tsuji, *Nomonhan*, p. 35; Imamura Hitoshi, *Imamura taishō kaisōroku*, vol. 3 (Tokyo: Jiyō Ajiyasha, 1960), pp. 75–76; Hata, *Nitchū sensō*, pp. 105–125; *Kindai no sensō*, vol. 5, pp. 56–59; *TSM*, vol. 3, pp. 232–236, 370; Imai, *Shōwa*, pp. 88–100.

forces recommended by the Kwantung and Korea armies, plus three divisions from the homeland.[55]

Although Ishiwara believed that the Kwantung Army should not be distracted from its main operational problem—the Soviet Union—Tōjō (Ishiwara's nemesis) wanted to clean up Chahar province, not only to team up with the hard-pressed Japanese forces in the Tientsin area and thus eliminate Chinese resistance in North China, but also to carry out the Kwantung Army's old scheme of controlling adjacent Inner Mongolia through a separatist regime confronting Outer Mongolia and the USSR. To the surprise of many, in mid-August 1937, a mere month after the Marco Polo Bridge clash, Tōjō created a combat headquarters, flew out of Hsinking, and personally conducted a blitzkrieg by three brigades against a huge force supposedly numbering 100,000 Chinese soldiers. The Tōjō Corps achieved extensive military successes in Chahar and Inner Mongolia within two weeks, overrunning both Kalgan (Changchiakow) and Tatung. As Tōjō had hoped and expected, Tokyo approved his actions after the fact.[56] In thinking that the main hostilities against China would be mercifully short, however, Tōjō and the other hawks miscalculated grievously. Indeed, the command of the ever-widening war in China required the activation of Imperial General Headquarters in November.

THE NORTHERN PROBLEM

To this point, I have alluded to the Northern or Russian Problem only in passing. My emphasis has been on Manchuria because that was always the preoccupation of the Kwantung Army, culminating in the creation of Manchukuo and leading to an interest in expanding that foothold on the Asian continent. After all, the Kwantung Army was the honored offspring of a major Japanese war on the Asian mainland and had been created to guard the Manchurian fruits of victory.

From the outset, Yamagata Aritomo and other Japanese leaders had advocated a concurrent China policy that primarily represented only a means, not an end. That end was the protection and development of Japanese "special interests" in Manchuria. Especially after the Korean protectorate was established in 1910, the main Japanese strategic concern on

[55] BKSS, SS, vol. 8, pp. 429–430, 437–440; GSS, vol. 9, pp. 3–4; Satō, Daitōa, pp. 72–76; Hata, Nitchū sensō, pp. 144–146; Ishiwara shiryō, vol. 1, pp. 438–439; TSM, vol. 4, pp. 11–16.

[56] BKSS, SS, vol. 8, pp. 463–464; GSS, vol. 9, pp. 107–115; GSS, vol. 12, pp. 465–473, 545–546; Umemoto Sutezō, Riku-kai meishō hyakusen (Tokyo: Akita Shoten, 1971), p. 186; TSM, vol. 4, pp. 27–28; Kindai no sensō, vol. 5, pp. 88–89.

the continent was Manchuria, specifically, the Northeast provinces, not China south of the Great Wall.[57]

After some false starts aimed at the seizure of all of Manchuria, the remarkable success of the Mukden incident in 1931 changed and enlarged the Kwantung Army's orientation phenomenally. The Chinese portal needed to be safeguarded, to be sure, but now the so-called Northern Problem became overpowering. There were thousands of miles of self-selected border to defend against the Soviet Union and the Mongolian People's Republic. The Kwantung Army's famous anti-Communist stance was as much geostrategic as ideological, eyeing Russia, China, and the Korean Peninsula from a perceived notion of national self-defense. To this, a legal basis was afforded by the Japan-Manchukuo mutual defense protocol of 1932.

Actually, Japanese response to a realistic Northern Problem had been minimal for a decade after the fall of the tsarist regime in 1917 and the establishment of the Soviet Union. Militarily, the turning point can be said to have occurred in 1929 when Russian forces defeated Chang Hsueh-liang's armies with astonishing ease. The creation of new Russian power in Siberia, under the aegis of Marshal Bliukher, and the walling of the frontiers abutting Manchuria naturally stimulated countermeasures and nervousness on the part of the Japanese.[58] Whereas in 1930–1931 the Kwantung Army disposed of little more than 10,000 men, the numbers and the structure increased very sizably in the years after the Manchurian incident. By the end of 1931, there were already 64,900 troops in the Kwantung Army. The subsequent buildup is shown in table 12.1.

From the survey of military developments after 1905, it is evident that the Kwantung Army was not a real army, in the accepted sense of the word, with balanced or truly offensive capabilities, until after the Manchurian incident. The Kwantung Army's strength was distributed along the rail lines, and its headquarters and core forces were located off the beaten path, at Port Arthur. It should not be confused with the powerful field force that came to be known as the "million-man Kwantung Army" created after the Kantōkuen Special Maneuvers of 1941, or even with the big paper tiger that could do little more than snarl at the Russians in 1945.

During the period emphasized in this study, the Kwantung Army fought the Russians only once in force: in 1939 at Nomonhan/Khalkhin

---

[57] Author's interview with George Akita (Tokyo, 1984) on Yamagata Aritomo and his "theory of racial conflict." Also see James B. Crowley, *Japan's Quest for Autonomy: National Security and Foreign Policy, 1930–1938* (Princeton: Princeton University Press, 1966).

[58] Saburo Hayashi in collaboration with Alvin D. Coox, *Kōgun: The Japanese Army in the Pacific War* (Quantico, Va.: Marine Corps Association Press, 1959), p. 3. Also the author's interviews with Nishihara Yukio, Imaoka Yutaka, Hayashi Saburō.

TABLE 12.1
Buildup of Kwantung Army Forces, 1932–1939

Year	Manpower	Infantry divisions	Aircraft	Tanks
1932	94,100	4	100	50
1933	114,100	3	130	100
1934	144,100	3	130	120
1935	164,100	3	220	150
1936	194,100	3	230	150
1937	200,000	5	250	150
1938	220,000	7	340	170
1939	270,000	9	560	200

Source: Coox, Nomonhan, vol. 1, p. 84, table 7.1.

Gol.[59] Other trials of arms were skirmishes only.[60] Nevertheless, the prime hypothetical enemy of the Kwantung Army was always the Soviet Union, and contingency plans, training, and intelligence activities reflected that fact throughout the dozen years of the life of the state of Manchukuo. In keeping with the offensive orientation of the Japanese army, the planners in Hsinking devised plans to invade the USSR and to conquer Siberia from the Maritime province westward to Chita and Irkutsk. Only after Japan's own fate was sealed in the last years of the Pacific War were the now-unrealistic offensive war plans revised to recognize the imbalance.[61]

The plains of Manchuria afforded the Kwantung Army terrain for exercises and maneuvers that was not available in the constricted, craggy Japanese homeland. It was, therefore, in Manchuria that Japanese armored divisions were created and tested, originally with a view to war against the Soviet Union. No Japanese field army had higher morale or motivation than did the Kwantung Army, for it was constantly on the verge of hostilities against the Russians, and it bent every effort to be ready for a decisive offensive. In turn, this orientation fostered an aggressive, indeed defiant, outlook among the staff officers assigned to Hsinking. Unfortunately for the Japanese, the dysfunction between capabilities and practicalities was exposed, at great cost, during combat operations against the Soviet army at Nomonhan in 1939.[62]

[59] See Coox, Nomonhan.
[60] For details, see ibid., vol. 1, chaps. 7–11.
[61] Operational plans are detailed in ibid., pp. 8–91, and vol. 2, pp. 1055–1061.
[62] See ibid., vol. 2, chap. 42.

CONCLUSION

The most that could be said for the Kwantung Army until the late 1930s is that it was indubitably the most compact and best-trained military forces on the Asian continent, a potential piranha in a sea of flabby Chinese fish. Until Manchukuo was carved from the flesh of China in 1931–1932, the Kwantung Army—available for nearby activities like the Tsinan operation in 1928—did not dabble or interfere significantly in Chinese mainland affairs. It could not have abstained entirely from the civil strife that raged among the Kuomintang, Communist, and warlord factions, even if it had wanted to. Nevertheless, the Kwantung Army's interloping actions before the Manchurian incident were essentially of an extracurricular and peripheral quality. After all, there was a North China Garrison Army whose birth dated back to 1902, even before that of the Kwantung Army, and which was highly jealous of its own turf.

After the creation of Manchukuo, Japanese publicists described the strategic relationship between Manchukuo and the rest of the Asian mainland, as they saw it, in the following terms:

> The penetration of the Bolshevist influence into North China, through Sinkiang and Outer Mongolia, has come to constitute a grave menace to the security of the Japanese Empire. In view of her important rights and interests in that region and of its territorial contiguity to Manchukuo, her ally, the question of the maintenance of peace and order in North China is of special concern to Japan. In North China, the interests of Japan, Manchukuo, and China are directly and closely bound up, and the readjustment of [their] relations is a prerequisite to the stabilization of East Asia. England has for centuries past maintained that she cannot permit the Low Countries to be dominated by any hostile Power on the [European] Continent. Similarly, under no circumstances can Japan tolerate the filtration of Bolshevist activities into this part of the world. Japan looks upon North China as the vital line of her defense, constituting herself as the stronghold against the onslaught of the Communist aggression in China.[63]

There was also plenty for the Kwantung Army to do inside Manchuria: to nurture the client state of Manchukuo; to ensure security through the suppression of guerrillas, bandits, and dissidents; and to develop autarkic assets centering on the mighty South Manchuria Railway conglomerate in the tradition of the East India Company. Indeed, the Japanese literature

---

[63] *Japan in East Asia* (Bristol, England: printed for private distribution, March 1939), pp. 23–24.

abounds with comparisons of Japan's aspirations to those of the British in Egypt and India, and of the Americans in the Philippines and Panama.

The negative aspects of imperialism in general, and of Japanese imperialism in particular, have long been featured in the writings on the topic. "The arrogance of the empire, its greed and its brutality," wrote James Morris, "was energy gone to waste."[64] Morris was describing the world's greatest empire, the British, but his words apply equally to the Japanese. Still, in the case of Japan—so late on the scene of empire-building—the army in Manchuria could at last try to put into practice the broad theories of men like Ishiwara Kanji, especially as they pertained to racial harmony between Japan, Korea, and China, and coexistence for a greater good.

Cynics might charge that "greater good" should be read as "Japanese good," but, as was true of the great European empire builders, the Kwantung Army did evince a peculiar elan, ethos, and esprit. Nor were human qualities absent: courage, adventure, devotion, and a brand of idealism or sense of the *mission civilisatrice* espoused by French overseas elitists. Even during World War II, an Allied observer, Sir Frederick Whyte, could dare to note that there was more to Japanese military motives and purposes than fire and rape, more than "ruthless and efficient exploitation of opportunity." Whyte detected in the Japanese imperialists "a missionary spirit which was neither selfish nor brutal."[65] This was, of course, a minority view among Allied publicists, but our examination of the Kwantung Army of the 1930s tends to support Sir Frederick's hypothesis.

To the Kwantung Army, the establishment of Manchukuo was "not the end of a successful adventure, but the first step along a new road to national greatness."[66] Tōjō Hideki, as war minister, mobilized all the verbiage of the nationalist and apologized for cathartic imperialism and mystical destiny:

The Manchurian incident was a Heaven-sent tocsin signaling at home and abroad the epoch-making dawn of East Asia. Before the . . . Incident, our public opinion was divided, suffering from domestic trouble and foreign evil. And the successful armament limitation conferences, under the beautiful name of so-called liberalism and national self-determination, merely increased foreign contempt for Japan. But with the extension of the incident, the Japanese people rose to the occasion in the loyal and courageous Yamato spirit and, becoming unified under

[64] James Morris, *Farewell the Trumpets: An Imperial Retreat* (New York: Harcourt Brace Jovanovich, 1979).

[65] Sir Frederick Whyte, *The Rise and Fall of Japan* (London: RIIA, 1945), pp. 32–33.

[66] Hugh Byas, *The Japanese Enemy: His Power and His Vulnerability* (London: Hodder & Stoughton, 1942), p. 71.

the August Virtue of His Majesty, marched forward toward the disposal of the incident on the basis of justice.[67]

The best of the Kwantung Army ideologues had a large vision of Manchuria as a paradise and a treasure house—a source of raw materials, a safety valve for Japan's surplus population and unemployed, and a base for the development of heavy industry, from which the "old capitalist houses" would be barred. "Is it too extravagant to say," a Japanese apologist asked in 1932, "that these half-dozen different races of Orientals now gathering in Manchukuo may be mixed and fused in due course and develop a freshly vigorous type of nation, as has been done on the North American continent?"[68]

In due course, the presumable success of Manchukuo would exert an irresistible appeal on neighboring regions of China, kept safe by the Kwantung Army until they could protect themselves one day. On Manchukuo's model, a wall would be built, "wider than any constructed by the ancient Chinese, against Communism, bandits, and the lords of squeeze." Only violent envy could explain external opposition to these vistas of prosperity built with magnanimous Japanese assistance.[69]

Despite the high hopes and the idealism, the Japanese scenario crumbled. Ishiwara castigated Tōjō and his shortsighted, grasping, and petty cronies who dominated policy in Manchukuo. The protégé state, claimed Ishiwara when he was sent to the Kwantung Army as Tōjō's deputy chief of staff in the autumn of 1937, had lost the character of unselfishness and idealism that he and his associates had fostered; it was now the nest of opportunists and vested interests. From plush, kingly headquarters in Hsinking, the Kwantung Army and its bloated Manchurian Affairs Section were "bossy thieves" despoiling a betrayed populace.[70]

Ishiwara's comments may be colored excessively by his dislike of Tōjō, but there can be no doubt that when jingoists, opportunists, carpetbaggers, and shady characters flocked to Manchukuo, much of the early idealism and patriotism floundered in greed, indifference, and arrogance. Thus, gentle old Lieutenant General Hishikari Takashi, in command of the Kwantung Army between 1933 and 1934, provoked the resentment

---

[67] Remarks delivered on the tenth anniversary of the Manchurian incident. Otto D. Tolischus, *Tokyo Record* (New York: Reynal & Hitchcock, 1943), p. 252.

[68] Akimoto Shunkichi, *The Manchuria Scene* (Tokyo: Taisho Eibunsha, 1933), p. 331.

[69] Percy Noel, *When Japan Fights* (Tokyo: Hokuseido, 1937), p. 245.

[70] Yatsugi Kazuo, *Shōwa dōran shishi*, vol. 1 (Tokyo: Keizai Ōraisha, 1971–1973), p. 128: Ōtani Keijirō, *Shōwa kenpei shi* (Tokyo: Misuzu Shobō, 1966), pp. 426–433; Aritake Shūji, *Shōwa no saishō* (Tokyo: Asahi Shimbunsha, 1967), pp. 174–175; Mori Shōzō, *Senpū nijūnen* (Tokyo: Kōjinsha, 1968), p. 75; Mark Gayn, *Japan Diary* (New York: W. Sloane Associates, 1948), pp. 189–190.

and contempt of his petty staff by showing kindness even to the lowliest Manchurian natives. Hishikari was reputedly hounded out of office.[71]

As for the South Manchuria Railway system, which had worked hand in glove with the Kwantung Army at the outset, it burgeoned into a conglomerate of vast economic and strategic dimensions. According to its critics, it ended up deploying a "stupendous bureaucracy of parasites" whose main function was said to consist of "spending money recklessly, especially on nonproductive enterprises connected with domestic politics."[72] According to an official pronouncement that rippled with venom, the South Manchuria Railway Company was "an anachronism, intent on maintaining its kingdom and not understanding the post-[Manchurian] Incident outlook."[73]

As for the Kwantung Army itself, in the 1930s it acquired a reputation, at worst, for insubordination in terms of central control; or, at best, for being a free-wheeling entity. Its place in the Japanese political and military structure centered on the unique fact that the commanding general of the Kwantung Army wore two hats: as nominal ambassador to the client state of Manchukuo, and as field force commander under the aegis of the high command in Tokyo. Since he was always a very senior general in the Japanese army, the commander of the Kwantung Army possessed great dominion, being located in the direct chain of command to the imperial throne. Thus, he could wield enormous authority unavailable to other field force commanders. This was never more true than in the case of moving troops under his own command; on the basis of military mission—to defend Manchukuo against aggression and to maintain internal security—the Kwantung Army commander claimed the right to shift formations, large and small, as he saw fit, without prior central sanction.

The preceding facts generated another special characteristic ingrained in the Kwantung Army: the customary hawkishness of its staff. In the heyday of staff politics (*bakuryō seiji*), headquarters officers like Ishiwara, Itagaki Seishirō, Tsuji Masanobu, and Hattori Takushirō exerted an influence out of proportion to their relatively modest ranks. Personnel assignments, regardless of suspicions that have been voiced, were not handled by the military authorities in Tokyo in collusive fashion.[74] Nevertheless, staff officers serving in Japan craved dispatch to a field army in the knowledge that career advancement (especially the attainment of general officer rank) depended on important line duty. The Kwantung Army was especially favored and pampered because of its crit-

[71] Nakamura Bin in *Hiroku Daitōa senshi*, vol. 2 (Tokyo: Fuji Shoten, 1953–1954), p. 162.
[72] Akimoto, *Manchuria Scene*, pp. 35–38.
[73] Gunther, *Inside Asia*, p. 125, citing the official Manchukuo news agency.
[74] Author's interviews with Hata Shunroku, Matsumura Tomokatsu, Inada Masazumi, Nishihara Yukio, Nishiura Susumu.

ical, frontline, anti-Soviet role. "You were not considered to be a 'real officer,' " remarks one Japanese authority, "if you did not serve in the Kwantung Army."[75]

After achieving a peak of esprit and quality in 1941–1942, the Kwantung Army underwent eclipse and dilution as Japan's own fortunes waned. When the bayonets of the enfeebled Kwantung Army were withdrawn in August 1945 and Soviet forces overran the region with ease, the whole shaky edifice of Manchukuo toppled, leaving scarcely a ripple of empire. Apart from failing to defend the client state and allowing the puppet emperor Pu-Yi to fall into Soviet hands without a struggle, the Kwantung Army has never been forgiven by Japanese for commandeering transportation for its exclusive use and for abandoning hundreds of thousands of Japanese colonists—men, women, and children—to cruel deprivation, disease, and death.[76] The old image of Kwantung Army soldiers bravely charging across the borders into the teeth of Soviet defenses was supplanted by the sight of the Kwantung Army taking to its heels and shrieking the equivalent of "*Sauve qui peut!*" In short, what has been termed the "blatant fiction" of Manchukuo never took healthy root under the Japanese raj and its Kwantung Army prop.

[75] Nakamura Bin in *Hiroku Daitōa*, vol. 2, p. 162.
[76] Coox, *Nomonhan*, vol. 2, pp. 1069, 1073–1074. Also see Louis Allen, *The End of the War in Asia* (London: Hart-Davis, MacGibbon, 1976), pp. 193–218.

PART IV

Commentary

CHAPTER 13

Japanese Imperialism in China:
A Commentary

Albert Feuerwerker

The chapters in this volume intentionally restrict their focus to the origins and operations of the principal China-based institutions established by Japanese imperialism, and to the impact of Japan's China "empire" upon forces and conditions within Japan itself. These are, of course, central matters to any consideration of Japanese imperialism in China. But they do not, by far, exhaust the subject or the possible viewpoints and questions from which it might be approached.

If the essays had been undertaken by Chinese scholars or by a group of experts on China, rather than by scholars of modern Japan, for instance, their *problematik* would surely have been centered on an analysis of the effects upon twentieth-century China of the large and aggressive Japanese presence on the continent. They would have been certain to condemn the enormous crimes committed by Japan in China by attaching the adjectives "obscene" and "destructive" to the phrase "large and aggressive" above. Good scholarship in this instance, I suggest, would in no way be harmed if it were prefaced by an appropriate moral statement—indeed, its weight would be enhanced by such a demonstration that it was deliberately lifting only one corner of the rug on this occasion. Japanese trading companies, railroad lines, military units, and educational institutions in China were not just supporting actors in a melodrama about somebody else's Japanese "imperialism" impinging upon a supine China.

Japan's involvement with China since the Sino-Japanese War of 1894–1895 was both quantitatively and qualitatively more portentous than that of the European powers who "opened" China via the southeast coast and the Opium Wars or via the contemporaneous Russian descent along the Amur River into imperial China's Northeast. It must be remembered, first, that the extent of physical harm suffered by China and the Chinese from Japanese armed aggression probably substantially exceeded that resulting from the Opium Wars (Britain and France), the Sino-French War of 1884–1885, and the Boxer Expedition (many powers, but especially the Russians in Manchuria). The Chinese officially claim that between

1931 and 1945 Japan was responsible for the death of 3.8 million soldiers, the killing or wounding of 18 million civilians, and the destruction of $120 billion of property.[1] Second, Japan ruled a large amount of Chinese territory in Manchuria for four decades; and its army occupied much of northern and eastern China for nearly ten years. The absolute number of individual Japanese who experienced direct and sustained contact with China and the Chinese, and the range and variety of these interactions (in Japan as well as in China, if one recalls the migration of Chinese students and political refugees to Japan in the early twentieth century), have no real equivalent in their impact on China—except perhaps for the case of the Christian missionary presence. Paralleling the resulting (fictive?) phenomenon of special Japanese "expertise" with respect to matters Chinese, there was, of course, the real fact that many Chinese modern minds were "made in Japan."[2]

The authors, again by design, do not probe the various "theories" of the origin and nature of the phenomena that they severally refer to as "imperialism." That, perhaps, is just as well, given the difficulty of arriving at a definition unburdened with ideology that deadens wit. In particular, it may be at times a vain exercise to suggest that neither economic causes (a "falling rate of profit" for capital, for example) nor economic consequences (such as "exploitation" of labor, or unfavorable terms of trade) are necessarily or even frequently the most significant or the most interesting matters to investigate. Still, we need some working definition under which to group the disparate events and institutions under consideration here. I suggest that by "imperialism" we should mean the employment of force or the threat of force by a stronger nation to control or influence, and to extract privileges from, a weaker nation.[3] To use somewhat abstract language, in the sphere of economic relations between the imperialist power and its weaker object, this definition implies the common occurrence of economic transactions outside of a fully free market, that is, in circumstances where one partner has special privileges. Although this is not inevitably a zero-sum game, the likelihood is that the stronger power's gains will be relatively larger than those of its weaker partner, and its losses correspondingly smaller. Thus, the South Manchu-

---

[1] Lloyd E. Eastman, *Seeds of Destruction: Nationalist China in War and Revolution, 1937–1949* (Stanford: Stanford University Press, 1984), and Hsi-sheng Ch'i, *Nationalist China at War: Military Defeats and Political Collapse, 1937–1945* (Ann Arbor: University of Michigan Press, 1982), detail the military and political destructiveness of the Sino-Japanese War.

[2] See especially Akira Iriye, ed., *The Chinese and the Japanese: Essays in Political and Cultural Interactions* (Princeton: Princeton University Press, 1980).

[3] Albert Feuerwerker, *The Foreign Establishment in China in the Early Twentieth Century* (Ann Arbor: Center for Chinese Studies, University of Michigan, 1976), describes and analyzes the multiple guises in which imperialism appeared to the Chinese in the first years of the Republican era.

ria Railway Company prospered, when it did, in some part because it was blessed with territorial rights, privileged status, and the backing of the Kwantung Army if necessary. It was not just a matter of its trains usually running on time, the efficient management of its rolling stock, or the quality of the machinery installed in its mines and factories in Manchuria.

But the critical loci of gains and losses between an imperialist power and its object are as likely to be in the realms of politics, culture, and individual psychology—where true zero-sum conditions almost always prevail—as in the form of unequal economic transactions. What made Japanese economic penetration truly "imperialistic" was what it shared with the totality of the Japanese presence in China: an invasion of China's sovereignty that derogated not only the autonomy of an abstract polity, but also, more critically, the autonomy of particular and individual Chinese who apprehended and reacted to the intruding foreign presence. Superimposed on the immediate, measurable consequences of Japan's trade and investment in China; of its territorial enclaves; of the China experts in its army and the China hands in the Diet; of its teachers, advisors, journalists, and adventurers was a common propensity to self-inflation, a derision in some cases of Chinese culture and capabilities, an egregious certainty that what the Japanese did was best for China as well as for themselves.

In the case of the Europeans in China, who shared in these ubiquitous foreign attitudes, it is easy to describe them as racist. But is that characterization also fitting for the Japanese, who were not only "orientals" but also participants in a "Sinic culture" that had originated in China? Is it a matter of "You always hate the one you love"—that the ambiguity of Japan's historical cultural relations with China contributed to the intensity and special nature of Japan's self-justification for aggression on the mainland? Perhaps so, but that ambiguity, of course, also extended to the modern West, whose encroachments Japan of the Meiji era hoped to withstand precisely by adopting much of its material culture. This dual cultural ambiguity, the continuing power of the myth of the enormous "sacrifice" that had been expended in wars with China and Russia in order to gain a strategic foothold in Manchuria, as well as the geographical "facts" of realpolitik with which Japan's leaders (in the fashion of their contemporaries in other nations) justified themselves—all of these help us to understand why the Kwantung Army remained untouchable.

If the strand of "pan-Asianism" in Japan's posture toward China and Southeast Asia was a counterpart to the European "white man's burden" in Africa and Asia, it was also something else again. Western imperialism—as I have defined it above—encompassed all of Asia, and the Asian response was nowhere merely one of passive acceptance. But the European and the American were perhaps too powerful—and too attractive—

to be successfully resisted. So much the more so if each Western colony or dependency went it alone. Prior to the coming of the Europeans in the sixteenth century, the western Pacific Ocean had already been the locus of a highly developed international network of Asian commerce in which Japanese ships and merchants played a substantial role.[4] The concept of a pan-Asian resistance to Western imperialism was thus not wholly an artificial one. In the early twentieth century, some Japanese aided the revolutionaries who sought to replace the Ch'ing dynasty with a republic that might better resist Western encroachments. Some Chinese, especially among those who had studied in Japan, were strongly impressed by Japan's ability to recover its losses quickly and to join the Great Powers as nearly an equal.[5] If there had been greater Japanese self-restraint, less aggressive egoism, the avoidance of the ignominious treatment to which Japan in fact subjected China and the Chinese (and the Southeast Asian nations occupied by Japan during World War II)—what big "ifs"!—was it perhaps possible that a genuine Asian alliance in opposition to the importunate West could have emerged under Japan's leadership?

Given both the scale of the Japanese impact upon China and the element—ambiguous, to be sure—of cultural sharing, it is remarkable how little, in fact, of the Meiji Japanese model of "modernization" was put into effect in China (at least before the most recent post-Mao changes). In another place one could perhaps make a strong argument in support of the view that it was precisely Japan's experience with nation building and economic development in the Meiji period and later that held the most useful lessons for a China that was searching for its own viable road to wealth and power. I do not have any numbers to cite, but I would guess that before 1937, overall, there were fewer Japanese in regular contact with Chinese intellectuals in China's universities and other cultural institutions than there were Europeans and Americans. Thus, one critical source of direction and intellectual stimulus was limited. Why? Was it not in large part because academic institutions were the natural centers of a burgeoning Chinese nationalism that increasingly came to see Japanese

[4] Some examples of the literature on premodern Asian international trade are K. N. Chaudhuri, *The Trading World of Asia and the English East India Company, 1660–1760* (Cambridge: Cambridge University Press, 1978); Louis Dermigny, *La Chine et l'Occident: Le Commerce à Canton au XVIIIe Siècle, 1719–1833*, 4 vols. (Paris: SEVPEN, 1964); Sarasin Viraphol, *Tribute and Profit: Sino-Siamese Trade, 1652–1853* (Cambridge: Harvard University Press, 1977); Iwao Sei'ichi, *Shuinsen bōekishi no kenkyū* (A study of the red-seal ship trade) (Tokyo: Kōbundō 1958); Iwao Sei'ichi, *Shuinsen to Nihon-machi* (Red-seal ships and Japanese overseas trading settlements) (Tokyo, 1978); and William S. Atwell, "International Bullion Flows and the Chinese Economy *circa* 1530–1650," *Past & Present* 95 (May 1982), pp. 68–90.

[5] See Marius B. Jansen, *The Japanese and Sun Yat-sen* (Cambridge: Harvard University Press, 1954); Susan H. Marsh, "Chou Fo-hai: The Making of a Collaborator," in Iriye, ed., *The Chinese and the Japanese*, pp. 304–327.

imperialism as a greater threat to national and personal autonomy and interests than its European and American counterparts? Chinese nationalism perhaps could find a larger space for the more flexible and certainly more distant West than it could for a Japan decked out with *kokutai*, the warrior spirit, and a severely patronizing patron-client sentiment.

For twentieth-century China, the consequences of its confrontation with Japan in all its aspects were surely portentous. If nothing else, the Japanese armies destroyed the Kuomintang's best troops, helped undermine its morale, and thereby eased the way for the Chinese Communist party to challenge effectively its archrival for the leadership of China.[6] Stated more broadly, Japanese imperialism, and that of the West, were the midwives of modern Chinese nationalism, one of the three indispensable banners under which every claimant to legitimate and effective power in twentieth-century China was required to march. Combined with a popularly supported program for socioeconomic reform, and protected by convincing armed force, the nationalist banner held highest was a powerful symbol indeed in the struggle for political power. Even if the several guises of Japanese imperialism had been relatively benign—which they were not—Chinese nationalism could not apprehend them apart from the condescension and arrogance that permeated every act—from importing cotton textiles, to shipping on the Yangtze River, to railroad operations in Manchuria, to petty struggles over diplomatic protocol and the minutiae of extraterritorial privilege. Thus, it was not just the actual institutions and actions of Japanese imperialism in China, as these are described in the chapters in this volume, but also the heightened Chinese apprehension of them as larger than the documented record, that gave a powerful impetus to political mobilization in twentieth-century China and greatly reshaped its history.

One powerful reason for the greater harshness of Japanese imperialism—in reality quite as much as in Chinese perceptions of it—was surely the fact that, compared to its European and American Great Power rivals, Japan was a latecomer. Japan's modern state building and industrialization are, of course, phenomena of the late nineteenth century and after. If Japan was the only Asian nation to make this transition before the late twentieth century, it is still the case that the European powers had already

---

[6] Chalmers A. Johnson, *Peasant Nationalism and Communist Power: The Emergence of Revolutionary China, 1937–1945* (Stanford: Stanford University Press, 1966); Tetsuya Kataoka, *Resistance and Revolution in China: The Communists and the Second United Front* (Berkeley: University of California Press, 1974); Lyman P. Van Slyke, "The Chinese Communist Movement During the Sino-Japanese War, 1937–1945," in John K. Fairbank and Albert Feuerwerker, eds., *The Cambridge History of China*. Vol. 13: *Republican China, 1912–1949. Part 2* (Cambridge: Cambridge University Press, 1986), pp. 609–722; and the items cited in note 1, above, analyze the Japanese "contribution" to the Chinese Communist victory.

successfully trodden that road. And only after the 1894–1895 war does Japan's economic role in China truly begin to compete with (and later to rival) the British, who had been Number One since the Opium Wars. Professor Gerschenkron has astutely argued that, for the latecomers in the process of industrialization, the role of the state was necessarily larger than in the case of the pioneers—and thus, the quotient of authoritarianism was greater.[7] If this reasoning is applicable to the economic and political changes in Japan from the Meiji era onward, does it not also apply in the matter of Japan's late arrival on the China scene? To break into a context dominated by an Anglo-French-American-Russian-German oligopoly and to gain a political and economic share commensurate with Japan's self-perception of its geographically and culturally determined special interests, was not a greater coarseness, a larger involvement by the Japanese state (and, therefore, the activation of its intense sovereign *amour propre*) almost an inevitability? The degree of attention, discussion, influence, and control over all Japanese activities in China by agencies of the Japanese government seems to have exceeded that of the other powers, except possible tsarist Russia. The discrepancy between the dreams of wealth and glory and the arrogant impatience of the treaty port British, on the one hand, and the greater realism of the Foreign Office in London, on the other, does not appear to have been so large in the case of Japan.[8]

As it happened, few Japanese challenged the Kwantung Army. Although there does seem to have been a complex range of opposition to at least the worst excesses of Japanese imperialism in China, it was never really very effective. Why not? Was it possibly because the Christian socialists were so few in number and so foreign ("un-Japanese") in outlook? Even those Japanese who professionally were assumed to know the most about the reality of China were, overall, characterized by a conspicuously ambiguous response to the contemporary Japanese role on the mainland of Asia—and in not a few cases, by full support for Japan's militaristic adventures in China. Naitō Konan, for example, can be seen both as a supporter of Japanese aggression when he contended that China's salvation lay in close cooperation with Japan and as genuinely seeking to promote a blending of Confucian tradition with modern political change in China—a road that, in Naitō's view, Japan itself had successfully followed.[9]

[7] Alexander Gerschenkron, *Economic Backwardness in Historical Perspective* (Cambridge: Harvard University Press, 1962).

[8] See Nathan A. Pelcovits, *Old China Hands and the Foreign Office* (New York: Institute of Pacific Relations, 1948).

[9] Joshua A. Fogel, *Politics and Sinology: The Case of Naitō Konan (1866–1934)* (Cambridge: Harvard University Press, 1984), is in part an effort to consider this most eminent Japanese

But is it actually the case that the Japanese were, as they claimed to be, more knowledgeable about China than the Caucasian foreigners from Europe and America? There is nothing in any language really comparable in scope and detail to the research publications of such Japanese organizations as the Tōa Dōbun Shoin and, especially, the research offices of the South Manchuria Railway Company.[10] Even the quite enormous English-language output of the Maritime Customs pales by comparison. The Japanese diplomatic archives until, say, 1930 often rival those of the British in the detail and apparent verisimilitude of their local consular reporting on Chinese affairs. Japanese diplomatic personnel frequently were reasonably well-trained in the Chinese language. Many, many Japanese resided or traveled in China. Thousands of Chinese students and politicians and traders passed years in Japan. How much of this "knowledge," however, penetrated very deeply into the Japanese psyche? Did not the psychological antibodies of bullying and insensitivity powerfully counteract most cases of possible infection? Knowledge—in the form of scholarly books and reports and learned specialists—thus coexisted in tension with dark ignorance.

China's modern history, I have asserted and it is generally believed, was significantly shaped by its interaction with Japan. Beyond the consequences suggested above, I have referred only in passing to modern Japan as a transmitter—and, in fact, sometimes as the most important immediate source—of European-Western technology, ideas, values, culture, and language in supplement to the dosages that China received directly from the West. While the origins might have been European, there inevitably occurred subtle transformations as these elements of cultural transfusion were filtered through the Japanese experience and the Japanese language into Chinese forms and the Chinese language. My competence here is small, but this would seem to be a most fruitful area for research by scholars interested in political and religious values, literature and the arts, and comparative psychology. Even when we restrict our inquiry to terminology, the consequences of the words (Chinese "characters") the Meiji Japanese chose to translate—such critical foreign terms as "liberty," "democracy," "nation," "proletariat"—and which were then imported into Chinese were possibly most profound. Can we understand what Lu Hsun thought, or Liang Ch'i-ch'ao, Ch'en Tu-hsiu, Kuo Mo-jo, Sun Ya-tsen, and Chiang Kai-shek, without a due appreciation of how the whole outside world at one critical time was funneled through the Japanese

---

sinologist in the larger context of Japanese intellectuals' views of Japan's role in the modern world.

[10] See John Young, *The Research Activities of the South Manchurian Railway Company, 1907–1945: A History and Bibliography* (New York: East Asian Institute, Columbia University, 1966).

books and periodicals they read and the Japanese teachers, soldiers, writers, and politicians with whom they talked?

Finally, I wish to turn very briefly from this rambling commentary on the consequences for China of its twentieth-century encounter with Japan to the Japanese focus that is the subject of most of the papers in this volume. A mirror image of the assertion that one result of the 1937–1945 war with China was to weaken the Kuomintang sufficiently to give the Chinese Communists an unexpected opportunity to contend for power would, I suppose, be an assertion that Japan's defeat in that unjustifiable war made possible the genuine refounding of a democratic and open society in Japan—a process aborted after its seemingly promising Meiji beginnings. This is, no doubt, a matter about which scholars of Japan have written, and I shall not here pursue it further in such large terms. On a much smaller scale, it would be of considerable interest to know more precisely what the items of cost were (and their size) of Japan's multifaceted adventures in China, and what were the gains for the Japanese economy and society as a whole and for individuals and firms. Did the Chinese market, for instance, make it easier for Japanese firms at home to operate at the optimal technical scale? How essential were Chinese raw materials for what sectors of Japan's industry? Were the "profits" of the China venture plowed back into economic expansion in Japan? It is difficult enough to try to answer these questions in the instance of economic relations—trade, investment, international finance—but probably even more demanding in the cases of politics, culture, and the like. Did Japan's early twentieth-century parliamentary experience founder in some part because the political parties were corrupted into supporting militaristic adventures on the continent? Perhaps "corrupted" is the wrong word—could it be that the essence of popular support for political movements included inescapably a jingoism that uncritically backed Japanese imperialist actions in China? How were the form and quality—if not the essential substance itself—of Shōwa culture affected by Japan's experience of China in the 1930s and 1940s?

One should properly conclude by querying whether these confrontations of the first half of the twentieth century, seeming so potent and consequential, continue to affect Sino-Japanese relations in the last quarter of that century. Their memory, at least, certainly does—as I would judge from a 3:00 A.M. anti-Japanese demonstration by university students in the streets of the capital of Szechwan province witnessed by this observer as recently as late 1985. But the political, military, economic, and ideological-cultural circumstances in both nations were so much altered in the third quarter of this century that the inauspicious past probably provides little guidance—other than a caution—for the events of the immediate present.

Contributors

Banno Junji is Professor of Modern Japanese History, Institute of Social Science, University of Tokyo. He has published four books in Japanese on Japanese foreign and domestic policies in the prewar period. The English version of his first book was translated by Professor J. A. A. Stockwin of Oxford University and will be published under the title of *The Establishment of Constitutional Government in Japan* (Routledge and Kegan Paul).

Barbara J. Brooks is Assistant Professor at the Centre for East Asian Studies, McGill University, where she teaches Japanese economic and social history. She received graduate training in Chinese and Japanese history at Princeton University. Her current projects include a book-length study of the Japanese Foreign Ministry's activities in China, and a biography of the Manchu adventuress and spy, Kawashima Yoshiko.

Alvin D. Coox is Professor of History and Director of the Japan Studies Institute at San Diego State University. The holder of a doctorate from Harvard University, he is the author of seven books or monographs, the most recent being the two-volume *Nomonhan: Japan Against Russia, 1939.* He has published numerous articles on Japanese modern military, and diplomatic history in journals in the United States, Japan, and Britain; co-authored or co-edited three books; and contributed chapters to twenty-four collections and encyclopedias. The American Military Institute recently awarded him the Samuel Eliot Morison Prize for distinguished professional contributions to the field of military history.

Peter Duus is William H. Bonsall Professor of History at Stanford University. He has taught at several other institutions, including Washington University, Harvard University, and Claremont Graduate School. He is the author of *Party Rivalry and Political Change in Taishō Japan, Feudalism in Japan*, and *The Rise of Modern Japan*, and the editor of volume 6 of the *Cambridge History of Japan.* He is currently at work on a book about the Japanese takeover of Korea during the Meiji period.

Albert Feuerwerker is A. M. and H. P. Bentley Professor of History at the University of Michigan, Ann Arbor. He has written extensively about modern Chinese history, especially nineteenth- and twentieth-century economic history.

Nakagane Katsuji is Professor of Economics at Hitotsubashi University. He is the author of *An Analysis of Socioeconomic Structure in Rural Manchuria* and co-author of *Studies on People's Commune System.*

Kitaoka Shin'ichi is Professor of Modern Japanese Politics and Diplomacy at Rikkyo University, author of *Nihon rikugun to tairiku seisaku, 1906–18* (Army and continental expansionism in modern Japan, 1906–18) (1978), *Kiyosawa Kiyoshi, Nichi-Bei kankei e no dōsatsu* (Kiyosawa Kiyoshi, insight into US-Japanese relations) (1987), and *Gotō Shimpei, gaikō to vijon* (Gotō Shimpei, diplomacy and vision) (1988).

Sophia Lee is an Assistant Professor of History at the University of Tulsa. Currently she is completing a book on Beijing during the Japanese occupation (1937–1945).

Ramon H. Myers is Senior Fellow and Curator-Scholar of the East Asian Collection of the Hoover Institution on War, Revolution and Peace at Stanford, California. He is also the author of *The Chinese Peasant Economy* (1970) and *The Chinese Economy Past and Present.* He was formerly Associate Editor of *The Journal of Asian Studies* and Editor of *Ch'ing-shih wen-t'i.* With Mark R. Peattie he co-edited *The Japanese Colonial Empire, 1895–1945.*

Mark R. Peattie served for nine years with the United States Information Agency in Japan before obtaining a doctorate from Princeton University in modern Japanese history. Prior to joining the faculty of the University of Massachusetts, Boston, where he is currently professor of history and director of the program in East Asian Studies, Peattie taught at the Pennsylvania State University and the University of California at Los Angeles. He is the author of *Ishiwara Kanji and Japan's Confrontation with the West* and *Nan'yō: The Rise and Fall of the Japanese in Micronesia, 1885–1945*, and co-editor, with Ramon H. Myers, of *The Japanese Colonial Empire, 1895–1945.*

Douglas R. Reynolds is Associate Professor at Georgia State University in Atlanta, is author most recently of the revisionist study, "A Golden Decade Forgotten: Japan-China Relations, 1898–1907," in *The Transactions of the Asiatic Society of Japan* (1987). From 1986 to 1988, he was a Visiting Research Scholar at The University of Tokyo where he continued his study of Tōa Dōbunkai and Tōa Dōbun Shoin. Under a 1987–1988 grant from The History of Christianity in China Project, he began his systematic look at Japanese Buddhist Missionary activities in China, 1873 to 1945, seeking a comparative understanding of the Chinese response to Japanese Buddhism versus modern Christianity.

Mizoguchi Toshiyuki is Professor of Economics at the Institute of Economic Research, Hitotsubashi University, and author of *Personal Savings and Consumption in Postwar Japan* and *Long-Term Economic Statistics of Former Japanese Colonies.*

William D. Wray is an associate professor of history at the University of British Columbia. Before joining its faculty he taught at Harvard University. He is the author of *Mitsubishi and the N.Y.K., 1870–1914: Business Strategy in the Japanese Shipping Industry* and articles on freight conferences and is the editor of *Managing Industrial Enterprise: Cases from Japan's Prewar Experience* (1989). He is currently researching the Japanese electrical industry, preparing another volumn on the NYK, and acting as a consultant to the *Japanese Yearbook on Business History.*

Index

agricultural commodities in Sino-Japanese trade: cereals, 12, 14, 25, 27, 30, 40; raw cotton, 25, 27, 30, 32, 35, 92–93; soybeans, 40, 42, 48, 57, 116–117, 124, 134, 143

agricultural development cooperatives, Japanese, 153

agriculture, Chinese, 25

Aichi University, 269–270

Ajia Kyōkai, 268n

Akatsuka Masasuke, 362

Alcock, Rutherford, xvi

Amoy, xxii, xv, 44; Japanese concession in, 172–175, 188, 191

anti-Japanese boycotts. See boycotts

Anzai Kuraji, 260

Aoki Norizumi, 344–345, 357

Arao Sei, 164, 213–224, 238, 244, 257, 270

Arita Hachirō, 357n

Ariyoshi Akira, 315, 389–391

banking and banks
—individual Japanese banks: Agricultural Development Bank, 149; Bank of Japan, 36, 156; Bank of Korea (Chōsen Ginkō), 6, 33, 47–48, 59, 135–136, 410; Bank of Manchuria, 136; Bank of Taiwan, 6, 33, 46–48, 59–60, 175, 241; Central Bank (of Manchukuo), 135–136; 146–149, 154–156, 263; Dai-ichi Bank, 59; Furukawa Bank, 59; Industrial Bank of Manchukuo, 136, 146, 148–150, 156; Japan-China Bank (Nisshin Ginkō), 37–38, 64; Japan Industrial Bank, 49–50, 59, 94, 107; Mitsubishi Bank, 47, 50, 60, 94; Seiryū Bank, 136; Sumitomo Bank, 47, 59–61. See also Yokohama Specie Bank
—Japanese banking in China, 33, 36–38, 60–62
—other foreign banks in China: Deutsche-Asiatche Bank, 37; Hong Kong and Shanghai Banking Corporation, 36–38, 54, 60–64

Banzai Richachirō, 342–347, 353–354, 360, 365

Boxer indemnity and remission by the Powers, xxv, 165, 244, 247, 255, 272–273, 278. See also cultural programs and exchanges; Japanese Foreign Ministry programs

Boxer Rebellion, 169, 199, 231

Boxer scholarships, 295

boycotts: anti-British, 322–323; anti-Japanese, 52–56, 59, 87–89, 205–207, 314–329, 383

Buddhism: Japanese proseletyzing efforts in, 302–303; Japanese temples in China, 176, 181, 197, 303

business, Japanese, in China. See banking and banks; boycotts; chambers of commerce and industry, Japanese; cotton spinning industry, Japanese; industry, Japanese, in China; investment, Japanese; service enterprises, Japanese, in China; shipping and shipping companies in China; South Manchuria Railway Company; textiles, Japanese; trade and trading companies, Japanese, in China

Canton: Japanese residents in, 174, 188; and Japanese trade, 41–42, 45

cereals. See under agricultural commodities in Sino-Japanese trade

Chahar Province, 415, 421

chambers of commerce and industry, Japanese: in China, xxvii, 207, 317–318, 323; in Japan, 318–319, 322, 326–327

Ch'ang-ch'un, 102–110, 116–118, 121, 142, 397, 401, 411

Changsha, 174, 188, 205, 214–215

Chang Hsueh-liang, 130, 407, 419

Chang Tso-lin, 128, 135, 321, 324–325, 328–329, 401–404; Kwantung Army's as-

Chang Tso-lin (*cont.*)
sassination of, 405–407; Kwantung
Army's manipulation of, 358–367
Chefoo, 188
Chen Chi-mei, 354
Cheng Chen-wen, 281n
Chengchiatun Incident, 401
Chiang Kai-Shek, 386–387, 390–393
Chiang Yung, 281n
China
—anti-Japanese nationalism, xxv, 98, 328–
329; directed against Japanese cultural activities in China, 304–306; directed
against Japanese interests in Manchuria,
127–132; directed against Japanese settlements and concessions, 203–209, 312–
313; directed against Toa Dobun Shoin,
258–261; response to Japanese imperial-
ism assessed, 431–438. *See also* boycotts
—government of: Ching, xvi–xviii, xxiv,
102, 104, 106, 125, 240; Nationalist
(Kuomintang, Republican), xxiv–xxv,
127–128, 169, 325–328, 365–367, 383,
387, 390
—Japanese views of. *See under* Japanese imperialism in China
China adventurers. *See tairiku rōnin*
China Cultural Activities Special Account
Law, 255–256
"China experts." *See under* Japanese army;
Japanese Foreign Ministry
China Garrison Army. *See under* Japanese
army, field commands and field agencies
Chinese Maritime Customs Service, 52
Chu Chia-hua, 281n
Chungking, Japanese concession in, 172–
176, 191
coal, 34–35, 51
Concordia Association, 410–411
consular police. *See* Japanese police in
China
continental adventurers. *See tairiku rōnin*
cotton spinning industry, British, 65, 67,
71, 76, 83, 97–98
cotton spinning industry, Chinese, 81, 87,
90–98
cotton spinning industry, Japanese
—cost of capital of, 93–95
—dominance of in China, 65–66, 184, 204
—impact of anti-Japanese nationalism and

boycotts on, 87, 89, 205, 315–318, 325–
327
—impact of Japanese military and political
expansion on, 100
—incentives and disincentives for Japanese
investment in, 69–87
—individual firms and associations: Fuji
Gas Spinning Company, 77, 85; Greater
Japan Cotton Spinning Association, 67,
69–70, 83; Hirano Spinning Company,
67–68; Indian Cotton Association, 93; Japan-China Spinning Company (Nikka
Bōseki), 85, 325; Japanese Cotton Spinners Association, 207; Japanese Trade
Association of Cotton Fabrics, 316; Kanegafuchi Spinning Company, 68–69,
71, 85; Nihon Menka Kaisha (Japan Raw
Cotton Company), 44, 76, 87, 91, 93;
Naigai Cotton Company (Naigai Wata
Kaisha), 65, 76, 77; Naigaimen, 57, 322;
Nisshin Spinning Company, 76, 85;
Osaka Spinning Company, 68; Shanghai
Spinning Company, 57, 68, 75, 77; Toyoda Automatic Loom, 57–58; Tōyō
Menka, 57, 91, 93, 325; Tōyō Spinning
and Weaving Company, 68, 85; Toyota
Spinning and Weaving Company, 85,
100; Trade Association of Japanese Cotton Dealers in China, 326
—inherent competitiveness of, 87–90, 99
—initial growth of under Treaty of Shimonoseki, 66–68
—labor costs involved in, 83–84, 95–98
—management practices compared with
those of Chinese cotton spinning industry, 90–98
—marketing practices of, 90–92
—question of treaty privileges related to,
66, 89–90
—raw materials involved in, 92–93
—taxation and tariffs related to, 69, 83–84,
89. *See also* cotton trade, Japanese; textiles, Japanese
cotton trade, Japanese: in cotton yarn, 22,
28, 41; in raw cotton, 25, 27, 30, 32, 35,
92–93. *See also* cotton spinning industry,
Japanese; textiles, Japanese
cultural programs and exchange, Japanese
—Foreign Ministry programs of: general
overview, 272–275; "civilizing mission"
behind, 275–278; Dojinkai and Japanese

medical facilities in China, 297–300; faced with competition from Western institutions, 301–302; failure of assessed, 164–165; institutional initiatives under Wang-Debuchi agreement, 279–284; linked to Boxer indemnity legislation, 278–279; Peking Humanities Institute, 284–287; Shanghai Science Institute, 288–292, 300; undermined by Sino-Japanese animosity, 300, 304–306
—efforts of Japanese Buddhists, 302–303
—limited participation in by the private sector, 303–304
—See also Tōa Dōbun Shoin: efforts toward Chinese students

Dairen, 36–38, 396–397; and South Manchuria Railway, 102, 104, 107–111, 121, 126–129; superiority of as an entrepôt, 116–117
Daitoasho. See under Japanese government
Debuchi Katsuji, 279, 282n
dōbun dōshu (common culture, common race), xxvi, 164–165, 224, 304
Dōbunkai, 224, 226
Doihara (Dohihara) Kenji, 342–343, 368
Doi Ichinoshin, 358
Dōjinkai, 274, 282, 303–304. See also cultural programs and exchange, Japanese: Foreign Ministry programs of

East Hopeh Anti-Communist Autonomous Council, 416
Endō Yasuo, 237, 240
Eto Shinsaku, 225
"external roads area," Shanghai, 184
extraterritoriality, xxv, xxix

Factory Law of 1915, 83
Fengt'ien. See Mukden
Fengt'ien and Chihli wars, 361–363, 402–403
Feng Yu-hsiang, 361, 402, 404
fertilizers, 14, 25, 27, 30
Foochow, 214, 239; Japanese concession in, 173, 175, 188, 191, 205
Formosa Association School, 105
France, economic interests of in China, 178, 183, 206n
"Friday Association, The," 326
Fujii Jūzaburō, 413

Fukuda Masatarō, 333, 336, 347–348, 350, 355, 360
Fukuhara Yoshiya, 348, 350
Fukuoka Genyosha, 225, 231
Fukushima Yasumasa, 254, 398
Funatsu Shin'ichirō, 315, 362
Furukawa Iwataro, 340
Fushun colliery, 104, 108–109, 122–124

Gallagher, John, xi, xiv–xv
Germany, economic interests of in China, 173, 178, 190
gold standard, Japanese conversion to, 31, 36, 61
Gotō Shimpei, 101–109, 121, 125, 399
Great Britain
—British residents and community in China, 161–163, 184, 191
—economic interests of in China, 3–4, 6; acquired through unequal treaty system, xiv–xix; cotton spinning, 65, 67, 71, 83, 97–98; shipping and trade, 22, 27–28, 35–37, 41, 53–58, 61–63; threatened by Chinese boycotts, 322–323
—Foreign Office, xxv, 6, 313, 371–372
—and informal imperialism, xiv–xix, xxiv–xxvi, 5

Hamaomote Matasuke, 340, 343, 348
Hangchow, Japanese concession in, 172–175, 188, 191
Hankow, 223, 228, 240, 245; Japanese concession and community in, 170–173, 176–177, 187–188, 190–196, 208; Japanese economic enterprises in, 32–34, 41, 44, 47–49, 53–54, 59–61
Hankow Incident of 1927, 54
Hanyang arsenal and steel works, 49
Hanyehping Company, 32–33, 48–52, 62
Hara Takashi (Kei), 399
Harada Kumakichi, 345
Harriman, E. H., 126
Hashikawa Tokio, 284–287, 305
Hashimoto Toranosuke, 334, 337–338, 348, 411
Hata Eitarō, 337n
Hattori Unokichi, 281n
Hayami Shōichirō, 291
Hayashi Gonsuke, 399
Hayashi Yasakichi, 345–346, 362, 365
Hida Yoshitaka, 236

Higashi Otohiko, 345–346
Hino Takeo, 413
Hiraoka Kotarō, 225
Hirayama Shu, 231
Hirota Kōki, 390
Hishikari, 350
Ho Ying-chin, 415
Honda Kumatarō, 379, 381–382
Hongkew district, Shanghai, 184, 192, 195, 200, 203, 208
Hongō Fusatarō, 401
Honjō Shigeru, 340, 345, 362, 411
Honma Masaharu, 335, 337–338
Hori Shin, 44
Horiuchi Tateki, 378, 381, 387, 393
Hoshino Kingo, 348
Hsinking. See Ch'ang-ch'un
Hsin-min Hui, 263
Hsiung Hsi-ling, 281n
Hupei Cement Company, 36

Ichang, 54–55, 174
Ide Saburō, 224, 236, 238–239, 247
Idogawa Tatsuzō, 344, 359
Ikebe Yoshitarō, 225
Imahori Seiji, 297
Imamura Hitoshi, 350, 418–419
immigration. See Japanese immigration into China
imperialism in China. See informal imperialism; Japanese imperialism in China; unequal treaty system in China
Imperial Military Reservists Association, 199–200, 207
India, 51, 71, 81, 83
industry, Japanese, in China
—changes in related to Japanese economic activity in China, 33, 56–60
—cotton spinning. See cotton spinning industry, Japanese informal imperialism: described and analyzed, xi–xiv; related to unequal treaty system in China, xiv–xix. See also Japanese imperialism in China; unequal treaty system in China
—manufacturing, 11–12, 23, 31–33
—textile (general). See textiles, Japanese
Inner Mongolia, abortive Japanese adventure in. See under Kwantung Army
Inoue Junnosuke, 45–46, 51
Inoue Masaji, 225, 232, 270
"internal guidance," 137

Inukai Tsuyoshi, 225, 230, 248n
investment, Japanese
—in China, 24, 31; initial disincentives to Japanese investment, 69–75; investment in cotton spinning industry, 75–77
—in Manchuria, 32n, 60, 146–147, 151–152
Irisawa Tatsukichi, 279, 281n
iron ore, 49, 51
Ishii Itarō, 381, 388–389
Ishii Kikujirō, xxvi, 352, 354, 401
Ishimitsu Maomi, 340
Ishiwara Kanji, 125, 131, 141, 187n, 312, 350, 368, 410
Isogai Rensuke, 334, 337, 345, 364–365
Itagaki Seishirō, 343, 346, 348, 350, 365, 411, 416
Itami Matsuo, 334, 337
Itō Hirobumi, xxiii, 5, 102, 222n
Itō Kinjirō, 342n
Itō Takeo, 321
Itsubikai, 224
Iwaii Eiichi, 267, 391–392
Iwamatsu Yoshio, 341, 343
Iwasaki Koyata, 303

Japan Mail Steamship Company. See Nippon Yusen Kaisha
Japan-China Association, 293
Japanese army
—assistance of Chang Tso-lin, 360–366
—"China experts": introduced, 330–331; in Intelligence Bureau, 337–339; in China Section, 343–344; career limitations of, 351; role of assessed, 366–368
—China Section, GS, 339–344
—efforts to oust Yuan Shih-kai, 351–360
—field commands and field agencies: China Garrison Army, 198, 200–201; Special Service Organ, 140, 265–266. See also Kwantung Army
—General Staff (GS), 139, 141, 164, 215–216, 236, 242, 321, 331. See also Japanese army: Intelligence Bureau, GS; Japanese army: China Section, GS
—Intelligence Bureau, GS, 331–339
—intelligence efforts in China related to tairiku rōnin, 214–221, 233
—Kwantung Army chiefs of staff, 347–351. See also Kwantung Army
—manipulation of Chinese warlords, 352–366

—military attaches in China, 344–347
—Operations Bureau, GS, 331–338, 342
—organizational units of other than GS: War College, 332, 335–336; Military Affairs Bureau, 335–336, 339; Military Administrative Section, 336
Japanese clubs in China, 176, 194–195
Japanese colonial empire, xi–xii, 4–5, 14–17
Japanese consular offices in China, 188–189, 192, 202, 217–218, 231n, 233, 240, 250, 267, 274n; in Chungking, 250; in Hankow, 217–218, 231n, 240; in Shanghai, 176, 188, 197, 233, 240, 267; in Tientsin, 202. See also Japanese police in China; Japanese Foreign Ministry
Japanese Diet, xxii, 5, 69, 104, 226, 273, 277, 281, 377
Japanese Foreign Ministry, 109, 190, 202, 399
—"China experts": career prospects assessed, 370–371; contrasted with British China service, 371–372; recruitment of, 376–378; collaboration among, 391–393; specific cases: Yada Shichitaro, 385–386; Yoshizawa Kenkichi, 387–388; Ishii Itaro, 388–389; Ariyoshi Akira, 389–391; role of assessed, 393–394
—and Chinese warlords, 358, 362–364
—confrontations with Kwantung Army, 389
—Cultural Affairs Division, 255, 279–283. See also cultural programs and exchange, Japanese: Foreign Ministry programs of
—cultural programs in China. See under cultural programs and exchange, Japanese
—development of, 369–370
—elitist position of, 372–376
—examination tracks in: ryugakusei, 374, 379; shokisei, 374, 379–381
—and Toa Dobunkai, 226–227, 236–244, 247, 250–256
—See also Japanese consular offices in China
Japanese government
—Greater East Asia Ministry (Daitoasho), 283, 287, 290
—Ministry of Agriculture and Commerce, 230n, 236, 242, 316
—Ministry of Education, 256, 279, 294
—Ministry of Finance, 49

—See also Japanese Foreign Ministry
Japanese immigration into China, xxii–xiv; into China proper, 169–172; into Manchuria, 116. See also Japanese settlements, concessions and communities in China
Japanese imperialism in China: as informal imperialism, xi–xxiv; Japanese economic presence in China assessed, 3–9; Japanese views of China, xii–xiv, 71, 75, 309; "sub-imperialists" in China defined and assessed, 309–313. See also banking and banks; cultural programs and exchange, Japanese; Japanese army; Japanese Foreign Ministry; Japanese settlements, concessions and communities in China; Kwantung Army; Manchukuo; service enterprises, Japanese, in China; shipping and shipping companies in China; South Manchuria Railway Company; Tōa Dōbun Shoin; trade and trading companies, Japanese, in China; unequal treaty system in China
Japanese navy in China, 198–200, 205
Japanese police in China, 201–203
Japanese settlements, concessions and communities in China, 44, 161–164, 315, 324
—anti-Chinese agitation by Japanese community in Shanghai, 206–208, 312
—daily life in, 192–198
—initial establishment of, 172–174
—Japanese immigration and, 169–172
—laws and regulations covering Japanese residents, 189–191
—organizations of Japanese residents in, 121, 189–190, 197, 206–207
—and outbreak of China War, 208–209
—role of Japanese army in, 200–201
—role of Japanese navy in, 198–200
—role of Japanese police in, 201–203, 260
—self-government in, 189–192
—Sino-Japanese relations within, 186–189
—specific settlements and concessions: the lesser concessions, 174; concession in Hankow, 176–177; concession in Tientsin, 177–181; settlement in Shanghai, 68, 181–186
—as a target of anti-Japanese nationalism, 203–205
—treaty origins of, 168–169
jikeidan, 207

Kachū Kogyō, 264
Kagesa Sadaaki, 341, 343, 392
Kajiyama Teisuke, 344
Kamio Mitsuomi, 220, 344
Kaneko Fumio, 4
Kano Naoki, 281n
Kansai Electric Power Company, 44
"Kasumigaseki diplomats," 376, 384, 387
Katakura Tadashi, 410
Katō Takaaki, xxiii, xxix, 248n, 254, 316,
    324, 352, 371
Katsura Tarō, xxii, 219n, 229–230
Kawada Meiji, 348, 350
Kawakami Sōroku, 219–223, 336
Kawamura Rihei, 65, 76
Kawashima Naniwa, 358
Kazankai, 269
Keimatsu Katsuzaemon, 281n
Kenseikai, 316–317, 319, 324, 328
Kent, H. W., 53
Kimura Koichi, 290
Kishida Ginkō, 163–164, 183, 212–217
Kita Ikki, 274n
Kita Seiichi, 341, 343, 345
Kiyono Chōtarō, 105
Knox, Philander C., 127
Kōain, 268n, 283, 286–287
Kōakai, 268n
Kobiyama Naonori, 130
Kodama Gentarō, 101–104
Kōdō faction, 336, 338
Koiso Kuniaki, 349, 358, 409
Kojima Tasaku, 384
Koji Shimpei, 237
Kokumintō, 353
Kolongsu Island, 175
Komai Tokuzō, 411
Komiya Yoshitaka, 291–292, 305
Kōmoto Daisaku, xxviii, 128, 131, 346,
    351, 364–365
Kōmura Jutarō, xxi, 240, 371, 397
Konoe Atsumarō, 224–230, 257, 268–269,
    274
Konoe Fumimarō, 43, 268–269, 392
Korea Army, 404
Korea as a Japanese market, 11, 17, 22–25,
    27, 30, 33, 61, 84
K'o Shao-min, 281n
Koyūkai, 270
Kubota Katsuyoshi, 105
Kubota Masachika, 105

Kuga Katsunan, 225
Kunchuling, 398, 401
Kunizawa Shinbei, 105
Kuomintang. See under China, government
    of
Kuo Sung-lin Incident, 361–364, 403–404
Kuraishi Takeshirō, 279
Kuroda Kiyotaka, 218
Kusaka Misao, 340, 342
Kuwahara Tetsuya, 86–87
Kwangtung Province, 171
Kwantung Army, xxvii–xxviii, 125, 130–
    132, 201; abortive adventure in Inner
    Mongolia, 417–420; assassination of
    Chang Tso-lin, 404–407; character of at
    time of conquest of Manchuria, 407–409;
    chiefs of staff of, 347–351; confrontations
    with Foreign Ministry, 389; confronts
    Russian power in late 1930s, 421–423;
    and development of Manchuria, 139–
    141, 156; and domestic security of Man-
    churia, 412–414; early political machina-
    tions in Manchuria, 400–404; as guiding
    force behind establishment and control
    of Manchukuo, 135, 139, 409–412; inter-
    vention in outbreak of war with China,
    420–421; origins and early history of,
    395–400; penetration of Jehol and North
    China, 414–417; and reorganization of
    South Manchuria Railway, 110; its role
    in China assessed, 424–428; success of in
    early 1930s, 312–313
Kwantung Government General, 397
Kwantung Leased Territory, xiii, xxiii, 7,
    11, 14, 16n, 24, 108–109, 129, 152, 396–
    399
Kwantung Military Government, 396–399

labor, 83–84, 95–98, 124
Liang Chi'ch'ao, 225, 228, 231n
Liaotung Peninsula, xii, xxii–xxiii, xvii,
    130
Li Hung-chang, xxii
Li Lieh-chun, 354
Li Yuan-hung, 402
Liu K'un-yi, 228, 230–231, 233n
Lu Hsun, 187
Lung Chikuang, 356
Lushun. See Port Arthur

Machida Jitsuichi, 217–218

Machida Keiu, 333, 336, 353, 355
Manchukuo, 14, 24, 27, 30, 131–132, 263;
  administrative agencies of, 137–142; eco-
  nomic development of, 135–156; Japa-
  nese establishment of, xviii; Kwantung
  Army's control of decision-making
  structure, 135–139, 409–412. *See also*
  Manchuria
Manchukuo Airways Company, 417
Manchukuo Telephone and Telegraph
  Company, 157, 417
Manchuria
—Japanese acquisition of rights in, xxiii
—Japanese economic interests in, 9, 12, 25,
  32–34, 40, 48, 51, 57, 59–64
—Kwantung Army's machinations in, to
  1931, 357–358, 360–368
—Kwantung Army's seizure of, 1931–
  1932, 261–263, 365, 368, 407–408
—and South Manchuria Railway. *See* South
  Manchuria Railway Company
—*See also* Manchukuo
Manchuria Army, 395–396, 408, 413–414
Manchurian currencies, 136
Manchurian Incident of 1931. *See* Manchu-
  ria: Kwantung Army's seizure of
Manchurian Youth League, xxvii, 130–131
Manshū Gold Mining Company, 157
Manshū Heavy Industries Development
  Company, 143–144, 146, 148
Marco Polo Bridge Incident of 1937, 201,
  208
Masuda Takashi, 37, 75
Masuda Wataru, 187
Matsui Iwane, 334, 337, 342
Matsui Shichio, 402–404
Matsuichi Yasuharu, 336
Matsukata Masayoshi, 218
Matsumoto Jūtarō, 68
Matsumoto Shigeharu, 187, 194
Matsumura Takayoshi, 402, 404
May Fourth Movement, 258
May Thirtieth Incident of 1925, xxv, 281
Minami Jirō, 338, 350
Ming Sung Industry Company, 55
Miura Minoru, 236–237, 240
Mitsubishi zaibatsu, 49–50, 56, 183
Mitsui Bussan (Mitsui Trading Company),
  7–8, 68, 75, 126, 161, 175, 183, 190, 410;
  as a major Japanese service enterprise in
  China, 31–64

Mitsui zaibatsu, 68
Miyake Mitsuhara, 348
Miyamoto Matao, 87
Miyazaki Tōten, 231, 317
Mizuno Shigeru, 260
Mori Kaku, 43, 325
Morita Kanso, 358
Morohashi Tetsuji, 303
Mukden, 102, 104, 107–111, 116, 118, 121,
  127
Munakata Kotaro, 216, 220, 224, 228n,
  231n, 238–239
municipal councils. *See* Japanese settle-
  ments, concessions and communities in
  China: self-government in
Muraoka Chotarō, 406
Murata Shōzō, 43–44
Muto Nobuyoshi, 350
Mutō Sanji, 69–71, 76, 85, 98
Mutsu Munemitsu, 222n

Nagami Toshinori, 343
Nagata Tetsuzan, 334, 338
Nagatsu Sahishige, 343
Nakajima Masatake, 332–333, 337
Nakamigawa Hikojirō, 68
Nakamura Satoru, 401
Nakamura Yūjirō, 399
Nakamura Zekō, 105
Nakanishi Kō, 260, 270
Nakanishi Masaki, 224
Nankin Dōbun Shoin, 229–231. *See also*
  Tōa Dōbun Shoin
Nanking, 174, 188, 192, 205, 228, 231, 265
Nanking Incident of 1927, 386
Nationalist Government. *See under* China,
  government of
National League on the Chinese Problem,
  318–319
National Protection Army, 355
naval landing parties. *See* Japanese navy in
  China
Negishi Tadashi, 342
Newchang, 117
Nezu Hajime, 223–224, 230–232, 244–245,
  247n, 250–252, 257
Nichi-Man Bunka Kyōkai, 283
Nikka Gakkai, 203–204
Ningpo, 174
Ninomiya Harushige, 334, 337
Nippon Electric Company, 59

Nippon Yūsen Kaisha (NYK, Japan Mail Steamship Company), 7, 63, 93, 161; as a major Japanese service enterprise in China, 31–35, 38, 40–44, 52–56
Nishikawa Torajirō, 348, 358, 360
Nishimoto Shōzō, 237, 240–241
Nishio Toshizō, 349
Nishizato Tatsuo, 260n
Nisshin Boeki Kenkyūjō (Japan-China Trade Research Institute), 163–164, 217–224, 244, 267, 270–271. See also Tōa Dōbun Shoin
Nonomura Kingarō, 105
North China, 7, 34, 169–171n, 178, 200
North China Industrial Research Institute, 286
Northern Expedition of 1928, 128, 260, 281, 328
Nozaki Bukichirō, 230n

Obata Torikichi, 258, 354
Obata Toshishirō, 338
Ogawa Heishirō, 384
Oka Ichinosuke, 353
Okabe Nagakage, 279, 282n
Okada Ietake, 291
Okada Kanekazu, 282n
Okamura Yasuji, 335–338, 343–344, 350, 364–365
Okazaki Eijirō, 221
"Ōkuma doctrine," xxvi
Ono Kōki, 356
Onoda Cement Company, 36
Onodera Jutarō, 340
"Open Door," xiii, 102, 105–106, 125, 129, 227
Oriental Development Company, 6
Oriental Economist, 56
Ōsaka & Sino-Japanese trade, 46–47, 58, 68
Ōshima Yoshimasa, 109, 396–397, 401
Osterhammel, Jurgen, xvn
Ōta Ichirō, 378, 384
Ōta Toseo, 240
Ouchi Chozo, 257, 267
Ozaki Hotsumi, 260n

peddling, 215n
Peking Humanities Institute. See cultural programs and exchange, Japanese: Foreign Ministry programs of

Peking Japanese Modern Science Library, 286
Peking Union Medical College, 278, 298–301
P'inghsiang colliery, 49
Platt Brothers, 35, 58, 67–68, 76–77
Port Arthur (Ryojun; Lushun), 107–109, 396–398, 401
prostitution, 195–196
Pu-Yi, Henry, 411

Railways: Chinchow-Tsitsihar railway, 127; Chinese Eastern Railway, 105, 107, 116, 127; Chosen Railway Company, 399; Kirin-Ch'ang-ch'un railway, 127; Peking-Hankow Railway, 40; Peking-Mukden railway, 108, 111, 127, 200; Shanghai-Nanking railway, 111. See also South Manchuria Railway Company
Rakuzendo, 183, 214–215, 218n, 271
regional concentration ratio, 17, 22–25, 27
Revolution of 1911, xii, xiv, xvii, 237, 241, 254
Revolution of 1913, 232n, 233
Robinson, Ronald, xi, xiv–xvii
Rokusan Gardens, Shanghai, 195, 198
Russia, imperial, 102, 105–106, 125, 127, 190
Russo-Japanese War, 237
Ryojun, 109. See Port Arthur

Saburi Sadao, 378, 387
Saionji Kimmochi, 40, 102
Saitō Hisashi, 348, 350, 355, 406
Saitō Masami, 263
Saito Suejirō, 345, 346
Sakai Takashi, 341, 343
Sano Yasushi, 237, 241
Sasaki Toichi, 343, 346, 365, 404
Satō Haruo, 187
Satō Naotake, 392
Sato Saburō, 340, 342–343, 347
Sato Tadashi, 229–230
Science Society of China, 290
Segawa Asanoshin, 281
Seiyūkai, 319, 324–325, 328–329
service enterprises, Japanese, in China: and anti-Japanese boycotts, 52–56, 59; early services and bilateral trade in China, 31–38; general analysis of, 62–64; Japan's changing industrial structure and, 56–59; problems of banking and currency relat-

ing to, 60–62; and third country trade, 38–43; trade personnel and branches, 43–48. *See also* banking and banks; shipping and shipping companies in China; trade and trading companies, Japanese, in China

Shanghai, 210, 213, 219, 225, 228, 231–233; Japanese economic activity in, 32–61, 65–98; Japanese settlement and community in, 44, 170, 172, 181–198, 204–209

Shanghai Incident of 1932, 54, 200, 208, 261

Shanghai Institute, 228–230

Shanghai International Settlement, 181, 189, 195–196, 200–203, 208

Shanghai Isolation Hospital, 196

Shangai Municipal Council, 190–191, 197, 201, 208n

Shanghai Science Institute. *See* cultural programs and exchange, Japanese: Foreign Ministry programs of

Shanhaikuan, 200–201, 400

Shantung Peninsula, 169, 173

Shiba Katsusaburō, 348

Shibaura Electric Works, 68

Shidehara Kijūrō, xxvii–xxix, 363–364, 371, 378

Shiga Shigetaka, 225

Shigemitsu Mamoru, 378, 383, 388

Shigeto Chiaki, 341, 346

Shimizu Tōzō, 378, 381, 383

Shina (China Review), 238, 241, 247

Shina rōnin. See tairiku rōnin

Shinjō Shinzō, 290

Shinkoku tsūsho sōran: Nisshin bōeki hikei (China trade handbook: essentials of Japan-China trade), 223

Shintō shrines, 197–198

shipping and shipping companies in China
—Chinese shipping companies: Cheng Chi Shipping Company, 55; China Merchants Steam Navigation Company, 33–35, 40, 52–56; Ningshao Shipping Company, 54; Sanpei-Hung An Shipping Company, 54
—freight conference concerning, 40, 42
—individual Japanese shipping companies: Chōsen Yūsen Kaisha, 64; Dairen Kisen, 52, 55; Hunan Steamship Company, 40; Kinkai Yūsen Kaisha, 50; Mitsubishi

Shipping Company, 213; Nisshin Kisen Kaisha (Japan-China Steam Navigation Company), 7, 32, 40–44, 46, 52–55, 64, 174–175; Ōsaka Shōsen Kaisha (OSK, Ōsaka Commercial Shipping Company), 7, 32, 34, 40, 43–44, 52, 93, 161, 175; Yamashita Kisen, 53, 54. *See also* Nippon Yūsen Kaisha (separate entry)
—Japanese shipping, 27–28, 33–34, 39–41, 52–56
—other foreign shipping companies in China, 27–28; Indo-China Steam Navigation Company, 53; Compagnie Asiatique de Navigation, 40; McBain and Company, 40

Shiraiwa Ryūhei, 224, 230, 326–327

Sino-Japanese Business Association, 87

South China, 170–171; and Japanese shipping and trade, 44, 48

Shashi (Shasi), Japanese concession in, 172–175, 191

Shibusawa Eiichi, 37

Shimonoseki, Treaty of. *See under* treaties, protocols, conventions, truces, and agreements relating to imperialist presence in China

silver, 36, 60–61

"slash China" policy, 343, 368

Soochow, Japanese concession in, 172–174, 188, 191

South Manchuria Railway Company, xxvii, xxviii, 4–8, 17, 22, 24, 38, 40, 52, 256n, 260n, 262, 323; as an agent of Japanese imperialism in Manchuria, 125–132; contribution to economic development of Manchuria, 116–118, 126–127, 136, 140–141, 146–147, 152; efficiency and superior service, 116, 121–123; initial organization of, 101–109; "leased zone" in South Manchuria, 109n; main trunk line, 107–109; management structure, 118–121; management style, 106, 121–123; organization of, 119–120; other properties and activities, 107–112; research and development activities, 17, 115–116, 119, 123–124, 140–141; revenues of, 109–115, 124; rolling stock of, 105, 107, 123; staff, 116; subsidiary rail lines, 104, 109–111, 116–118

soybeans. *See under* agricultural commodities in Sino-Japanese trade

Special Naval Landing Party. *See* Japanese navy in China
Ssu-k'u chuan-shu t'i-yao compilation project, 284–287, 300
steel industry, Japanese, 32
Stuart, John Leighton, 284
"sub-imperialists" in China discussed in general, 309–313. *See also* Japanese army; Kwantung Army, *tairiku rōnin*
Sun Yat-sen, 228, 231, 357, 360, 390
Suzue Gen'ichi, 297
Suzuki Teiichi, 362, 364–365
Suzuki Yoshiyuki, 345
Swatow, 188

Tachibana Koichiro, 399
tairiku rōnin (continental adventurers) and *shina ronin* (China adventurers), 214, 309, 352–353, 358
Taiwan, Japan's trade with, 11, 14, 17, 22, 24, 27, 30, 44
Taiwan Public Assembly, 191
Taiwanese, 171, 191n
Takada Toyoki, 340
Takahashi Korekiyo, 320
Takayama Kimimochi, 348
Takayanagi Yasutarō, 333, 337
Takeuchi Yoshimi, 297
Tanabe Tasunosuke, 231–232
Tanaka Giichi, 352–354, 359–360
Tanaka Kunishige, 333, 337
T'ang Chi-yao, 354
T'ang Erh-ho, 300
T'ang Yu-jen, 392
Tani Kanjō, 322n
Tani Masayuki, 287
T'ao Ching-sun, 291
tariff policy, Chinese, 58, 62
Tashiro Kan'ichirō, 340, 345
Tataekawa Yoshitsugu, 334, 336–337, 345, 347
Tayeh iron mines, 49–50
Tei Ei-cho, 376
Tei Ei-mei, 376
telecommunications in China, 59, 157, 417
Teranishi Hidetake, 355, 360, 402
Terauchi Masatake, xxvii, 61, 349, 352, 399
textiles, Japanese: domestic Japanese textile industry, 11, 25; Japanese exports of to China, 17, 22–24; Japanese textile indus-

try in China, 57–58; silk, 11–12, 14, 41–42, 45. *See also* cotton spinning industry, Japanese; cotton trade, Japanese
Tientsin: Japanese concession and community in, 170–173, 177–181, 186–188, 190–197, 202, 206n, 208–209; Japanese economic activities in, 37, 41, 92–93, 99–100
Tientsin Land Reclamation Association, 181
Tientsin Union Hospital, 195
Tōa Dōbunkai, 8, 210, 216, 224, 230–232, 236, 239–247, 251–260, 267–269, 274, 282, 304. *See also* Tōa Dōbun Shoin
Tōa Dōbun Shoin, 163–164, 289, 380–381, 383–386
—as agent of Japanese imperialism, 261–268, 270–271
—background to founding of, 212–232
—Chinese nationalism directed against, 258–261
—development of, 1900–1914, 233–235
—efforts toward Chinese students, 229–230, 233, 247, 258–261
—established at Shanghai, 232
—graduates of, 234–235
—growing importance of in Japan's China policy, 244–247
—Japanese imperialism as a background to, 210–211
—reorganized, disbanded, and reconstituted under other names, 268–270
—research activities for Foreign Ministry of, 236–241; student research trips, 241–244; expansion of, 247–252
Tōa Gakkō, 293
Tōa Kaiun, 264
Tōakai, 225–226
Tōhō Bunka Gakuin, 282–283
Tōhō Bunka Jigyo Soinkai, 280
Tōjō Hideki, xxix, 349, 416
Tokyo Dōbun Shoin, 233, 247. *See also* Tōa Dōbun Shoin
Tōkyō Tatemono Kaisha, 178–179
Tōyama Mitsuru, 219n
Tōyō Bunko, 303
Tōyō Gakkan, 220, 225
Toyoda Sakichi, 57
trade and trading companies, Chinese, 27–28
trade and trading companies, Japanese, in China

—China's place in overall Japanese foreign trade, 10–13
—China trade central to Japan's informal empire in China, 29–30
—compared with Japan's trade with areas other than China, 14–17
—early Japanese trade in China, 34–35
—exports to China, 17, 22–25, 77–79
—financial transactions involved in, 45–48
—imports, 25, 27
—individual trading companies and associations: Dai Nihon Company, 85; Federation of Tokyo Trading Associations, 318; Gōdō Company, 85; Gosho Company, 76, 91, 93; Itō Chaū Trading Company, 85, 326; Japan-China Trading Association, 326; Kanematsu Shoten, 42; Mitsubishi Trading Company, 32, 49; Nagasaki Company, 85; Nichi-Man Shōji Kaisha (Japan-Manchuria Trading Company), 139–140; Nichimen Trading Company, 85; Ōkura Trading Company, 7, 32, 49, 50, 56, 410; Suzuki Shōten, 33, 56. See also Mitsui Bussan
—related to Japan's third country trade, 38–43
—trading companies, personnel and branches of, 43–48
—trend of trade within China, 13–14
trade and trading companies, Western, in China, 6, 22
—individual trading companies: American Trading Company, 67; Butterfield and Swire, 41, 53, 56, 64, 117; John Swire and Sons, 53; Jardine, Matheson, and Company, 6, 64, 67, 76
treaties, protocols, conventions, truces, and agreements relating to imperialist presence in China: Boxer Protocol of 1901, 166, 169–170, 200, 272–273; Chefoo Convention, xv; Ch'in-Dohihara Agreement of 1935, 169; Ho-Umezu Agreement of 1935, 169, 415; Tangku Truce of 1933, 169, 414, 416; Treaty of Commerce of 1873, xx; Treaty of Commerce and Navigation, 168, 176, 274n; Treaty of Friendship and Commerce of 1871, 169, 218; Treaty of Peking, 396; Treaty of Shimonoseki, xxi–xxii, xxvi, 66–71, 85, 168–169, 172, 183; Treaty of Tientsin, xv

Triple Intervention, xxii, 69
Ts'ai-O, 354
Ts'en Ch'un-hsuan, 356–357
Tsinan Incident, 54, 201, 260, 323, 326
Tsingtao, 169, 173n, 188, 192, 205; Japanese rights to establish concession in, 173n
Tsubogami Teiji, 282
Tsuge Hideomi, 291
Tsukinoya Gardens, Shanghai, 195
Tuan Chi-jui, 358, 367
Twenty-One Demands of 1915, 48–49, 169, 204, 207, 236, 241, 254, 258, 270, 316, 320, 336–337, 352, 398

Uchida Ryōhei, 353
Uchida Yasunari, 315, 319–321
Uchida Yasuya, 258, 361, 401–402
Uchiyama Iwatarō, 38, 379–380
Uchiyama Kanzō, 187
Ueda Kenkichi, 350
Uehara Yūsaku, 332, 336–337, 352, 357–360
Ugaki Kazushige, 336–339, 346, 364, 400, 403
unequal treaty system in China: as informal imperialism, xiv–xix; Japan and collapse of, xxiv–xxix; Japan's privileges under related to Japanese cotton spinning industry in China, 66–75, 89, 98–100; Japan's role in, xix–xxiv; as a target of Chinese nationalism, 127. See also informal imperialism; Japanese imperialism in China
United States and Japanese trade, 56–57
Utsonomiya Tarō, 333–336, 355

Wada Toyoji, 77
Wang Ching-wei, 390, 392
Wang-Debuchi agreement, 165, 279. See also cultural programs and exchange, Japanese, Foreign Ministry programs
Wang Jung-po, 279
warlords, Chinese: and Japanese army in China, 352–366; and Japanese Foreign Ministry in China, 358, 362–364
Watari Hisao, 335, 337–338
Watari Sakon, 341
Wuchang, 59
Wuhu, 188
Wu P'ei-fu, 361, 362

Yada Shichitarō, 385–386, 401–402
Yamada Shoji, 237, 240
Yamada Yoshimasa, 231
Yamagata Aritomo, xii, xxvi, 349, 352
Yamagata Hatsuo, 356, 360
Yamaguchi Noboru, 236–241
Yamamoto Jōtarō, 41–44, 57, 74, 128–129, 278, 325
Yamanashi Hanzō, 350n, 400
Yamato Park, Tientsin, 181, 195, 197
Yanagihara Sakimitsu, 371
Yangtze River, Japanese shipping and trade on, 40, 44, 53–56, 66, 264, 322
Yangtze River Valley as an important economic area, 32–34, 40–44, 48–52, 62, 166, 174, 208
Yawata iron and steel works, 49–52
Yen-t'ai colliery, 104, 109, 124

Yokohama and Japan's China trade, 34, 45
Yokohama Specie Bank (Yokohama Shōkin Ginkō), 5, 7–8, 70, 94, 116, 126, 149, 156, 356, 410; as a major Japanese service enterprise in China, 31–51, 60–64
Yokote Chiyonosuke, 289
Yoshida Shigeru, 362, 378, 401–402
Yoshino Sakuzō, 163
Yoshizawa Kenkichi, 318–319, 322, 362–363, 384, 387–388
Yuan Shih-kai, 81, 163, 251, 254n, 387, 398; Japanese army machinations against, 352–360
Yunnan, 188
Yunnan uprising, 355

zaikabō. See cotton spinning industry, Japanese